Frommer's®

Puerto Rico

10th Edition

by John Marino

Wiley Publishing, Inc.

ABOUT THE AUTHOR

John Marino has written extensively about Puerto Rico and the Caribbean for Reuters, *The Washington Post, The New York Times, Gourmet,* and other publications. He lives in San Juan with his wife, Jova, and son, Juan Antonio, who both provided valuable research and insight for this book.

Published by:

WILEY PUBLISHING, INC.

111 River St.
Hoboken, NJ 07030-5774

ISBN 978-0-470-64014-2 (paper); 978-0-470-91100-6 (ebk)

Editor: Erica Rex with Stephen Bassman
Production Editor: Michael Brumitt
Cartographer: Anton Crane
Photo Editor: Richard Fox
Production by Wiley Indianapolis Composition Services

Front cover photo: Fort San Cristóbal in San Juan. © David Sanger Photography/Alamy Images
Back cover photo: La Mina Falls in El Yunque rainforest.© Gabriel Jaime Jimenez/eStock Photo

For information on our other products and services or to obtain technical support, please contact our Customer Care Department within the U.S. at 877/762-2974, outside the U.S. at 317/572-3993 or fax 317/572-4002.

Wiley also publishes its books in a variety of electronic formats. Some content that appears in print may not be available in electronic formats.

Manufactured in the United States of America

5 4 3 2 1

CONTENTS

5 WHERE TO STAY & DINE IN SAN JUAN 95

6 WHAT TO SEE & DO IN SAN JUAN 154

7 NEAR SAN JUAN 195

8 PONCE & THE SOUTHWEST 214

9 MAYAGÜEZ & THE NORTHWEST 238

10 EASTERN PUERTO RICO 262

11 VIEQUES & CULEBRA 277

12 FAST FACTS 298

Index 304

LIST OF MAPS

HOW TO CONTACT US

In researching this book, we discovered many wonderful places—hotels, restaurants, shops, and more. We're sure you'll find others. Please tell us about them, so we can share the information with your fellow travelers in upcoming editions. If you were disappointed with a recommendation, we'd love to know that, too. Please write to:

Frommer's Puerto Rico, 10th Edition
Wiley Publishing, Inc. • 111 River St. • Hoboken, NJ 07030-5774
frommersfeedback@wiley.com

AN ADDITIONAL NOTE

Please be advised that travel information is subject to change at any time—and this is especially true of prices. We therefore suggest that you write or call ahead for confirmation when making your travel plans. The authors, editors, and publisher cannot be held responsible for the experiences of readers while traveling. Your safety is important to us, however, so we encourage you to stay alert and be aware of your surroundings. Keep a close eye on cameras, purses, and wallets, all favorite targets of thieves and pickpockets.

FROMMER'S STAR RATINGS, ICONS & ABBREVIATIONS

Every hotel, restaurant, and attraction listing in this guide has been ranked for quality, value, service, amenities, and special features using a **star-rating system.** In country, state, and regional guides, we also rate towns and regions to help you narrow down your choices and budget your time accordingly. Hotels and restaurants are rated on a scale of zero (recommended) to three stars (exceptional). Attractions, shopping, nightlife, towns, and regions are rated according to the following scale: zero stars (recommended), one star (highly recommended), two stars (very highly recommended), and three stars (must-see).

In addition to the star-rating system, we also use **seven feature icons** that point you to the great deals, in-the-know advice, and unique experiences that separate travelers from tourists. Throughout the book, look for:

special finds—those places only insiders know about

fun facts—details that make travelers more informed and their trips more fun

kids—best bets for kids and advice for the whole family

special moments—those experiences that memories are made of

overrated—places or experiences not worth your time or money

insider tips—great ways to save time and money

great values—where to get the best deals

The following **abbreviations** are used for credit cards:

AE American Express
DC Diners Club
DISC Discover
MC MasterCard
V Visa

TRAVEL RESOURCES AT FROMMERS.COM

Frommer's travel resources don't end with this guide. Frommer's website, **www.frommers.com**, has travel information on more than 4,000 destinations. We update features regularly, giving you access to the most current trip-planning information and the best airfare, lodging, and car-rental bargains. You can also listen to podcasts, connect with other Frommers.com members through our active-reader forums, share your travel photos, read blogs from guidebook editors and fellow travelers, and much more.

THE BEST OF PUERTO RICO

1

It's only the size of Connecticut, but Puerto Rico pulsates with more life than any other island in the Caribbean. Whether it's the beat of *bomba y plena,* salsa, or reggaeton, there's a party going on here 24/7.

The four million people who live here have perfected the art of having fun on their dazzling island, and visitors are free to join right in. Puerto Ricans love their island and take pride in showing off its charms, which makes them among the world's great hosts. Especially on weekends, there seems to be something going on just about everywhere—whether it's an art fair in Old San Juan, a pig roast in the rural mountain area outside town, or a volleyball competition or free concert on the beach in Isla Verde. More so than on any other island, visitors are more likely to rub elbows with locals in Puerto Rico because so many of them are out enjoying themselves. For island hotels and restaurants, local residents are an important and loyal part of their clientele.

Puerto Rico is blessed with towering mountains, rainforests, white sandy beaches along Caribbean shores, and a vibrant culture forged from a mix of Caribbean, Hispanic, African, and U.S. influences. Culture vultures will find a wealth of historic buildings and monuments, many of them dating back some 500 years to the Spanish conquistadors. There are three world-class museums and a thriving gallery scene in San Juan. The city is more intimate but just as exciting as Miami or Las Vegas, and the sophisticated fashion sense of the city and its inhabitants will genuinely impress visitors. San Juan's nightlife, dining scene, casinos and live performance calendar are just as noteworthy. Add some of the best golf and tennis in the West Indies, posh beach resorts, tranquil and offbeat inns and guesthouses, and you've got a formidable attraction.

Good service, once notoriously lacking in Puerto Rico, has been improving for several years now. You'll still find both not so benign neglect and outright gruff service, but the majority of hotel and restaurant employees are absolutely delightful these days.

Puerto Rico is a crowded island, which makes for some traffic congestion, especially during the morning and afternoon rush hours, but visitors won't really notice except during holiday weekends. There are country and coastal retreats where visitors can escape the masses, but you are never too far away from anybody in Puerto Rico.

Tourists are generally safe, and a crime in a tourist district is rare. But homeless drug addicts and mentally ill beggars are a common sight in San Juan. There are also unfortunate problems with littering and treatment of animals—but great strides in these areas are being made. Most of Puerto Rico's crime and social problems remain largely invisible to tourists.

A clue to the Puerto Rican soul is reflected in the national anthem, "La Borinqueña," which describes the island as a "flowering garden of exquisite magic . . . the daughter of the sea and the sun." Get to know this garden and the people who call it home.

THE best BEACHES

White sandy beaches and idyllic offshore islands are what put Puerto Rico on tourist maps in the first place. The best beaches are labeled on the "Puerto Rico" map on p. 76.

- **Best for Singles (Straight & Gay):** Sandwiched between the Condado and Isla Verde along San Juan's coast, **Ocean Park** beach attracts more adults and less of the family trade. The wide beach, lined with palm and sea grape trees, fronts a residential neighborhood of beautiful homes, free of the high-rise condos that line other San Juan beaches. A favorite for swimming, paddle tennis, and kite surfing, the beach is also a favorite spot for young and beautiful *sanjuaneros* to congregate, especially on weekends. Knowledgeable tourists also seek out Ocean Park, which has several guesthouses catering to young urban professionals from the East Coast, both gay and straight. There definitely is a South Beach–Río vibe here, with more than a fair share of well-stuffed bikinis, but it's decidedly more low-key and Caribbean. It's a good spot for tourists and locals to mix. There are a few beachfront bar/restaurants housed in the guesthouses, good for a snack or lunch or cold drink. See "Diving, Fishing, Tennis & Other Outdoor Pursuits," in chapter 6.
- **Best Beach for Families: Luquillo Beach,** 30 miles (48km) east of San Juan, has better sands and clearer waters than most in San Juan. The vast sandy beach opens onto a crescent-shaped bay edged by a coconut grove. Coral reefs protect the crystal-clear lagoon from the often rough Atlantic waters that can buffet the northern coast, making Luquillo a good place for young children to swim. Much photographed because of its white sands, Luquillo also has tent sites as well as picnic areas with changing rooms, lockers, and showers. See "Luquillo Beach" in chapter 7.
- **Best for Swimming: Pine Grove Beach,** which stretches between the Ritz-Carlton and the Marriott Courtyard at the end of Isla Verde near the airport, is a crescent, white-sand beach, whose tranquil, blue waters are protected by an offshore reef from the often rough Atlantic current. By the Ritz-Carlton and the Casa Cuba social club to the west, the water is completely sheltered, and a long sandbar means shallow water stretches a long way offshore. There's more of a surf to the east, which is a popular spot for surfing, boogie boarding, and body surfing. The waves are well formed but never too big, which makes it a perfect spot to learn to surf. Local surfers give lessons and rent boards from this beach, which is also a favorite for small sail boats and catamarans. There are no public facilities here, but it's a short walk to restaurants in the Isla Verde district. Both hotels on

the beach have restaurants, bars and restroom facilities. The beach also connects to the **Carolina Public Beach,** which has lockers, outdoor showers and restrooms, and is immediately adjacent to the east. If you are driving here, parking at the public beach may be your best bet. It's right off Rte. 187 on the road to Piñones. Otherwise, enter the beach near the Ritz-Carlton or Marriott Courtyard hotel. Outside San Juan, the best beaches for swimming are probably Guánica's **Playa Santa** and **Caña Gorda** beaches in southwest Puerto Rico. The water is extremely warm and absolutely calm year round, and both spots boast wide, white-sand beaches with vistas of nothing but Caribbean Sea and hilly coastline.

- **Best for Scenery:** In the southwestern corner of Puerto Rico, **Boquerón Beach** and its neighboring area brings to mind a tropical Cape Cod. The beach town of Boquerón itself, filled with colorful scenery, stands along the coast just beside the beach running along a 3-mile (4.8km) bay, with palm-fringed white sand curving away on both sides. The water is always tranquil, making it perfect for families and swimming. There's fine snorkeling, sailing and fishing as well. The beach here is also one of the Puerto Rico's state-run public beaches, with lifeguards, lockers, bathrooms, showers, a cafeteria and sundries shop, and picnic tables and barbecue pits. The village is a ramshackle collection of open-air establishments along the coast selling seafood and drinks. Fresh oysters are shucked on the spot and doused with Tabasco. Try the fried fritters filled with freshly caught fish or Caribbean lobster. There are plenty of interesting photo ops at this beach and its adjacent town. See "The Southwest Coast," in chapter 8.
- **Best for Surfing:** The winter surf along Puerto Rico's northwest coast is the best in the region. Generally regarded as one of the best surf spots across the globe, it draws surfers from around the world. **Rincón** is the center of the island surf scene, but it extends to neighboring **Isabela** and **Aguadilla.** Dubbed the "Caribbean Pipeline," winter waves here can approach 20 feet (6.1m) in height, equaling the force of the surf on Oahu's north shore. Rincón became a renowned surfing destination when it hosted the 1968 world surfing championships. Famed surfing beaches in town include **Puntas, Domes, Tres Palmas,** and **Steps.** In Aguadilla, surfers head to **Gas Chambers, Crash Boat,** or **Wilderness;** in **Isabela,** preferred spots include **Jobos** and **Middles.** The best time to surf is from November through April, but summer storms can also kick up the surf. In the summer season, however, when the waves diminish, these northwest beaches double as perfect spots for windsurfing and snorkeling, with calm waters filled with coral reefs and marine life. See "Rincón," in chapter 9.
- **Best for Windsurfing:** Puerto Rico is filled with places for windsurfing and, increasingly, kite surfing. San Juan itself is a windsurfer's haven, and you'll see them off the coast from **Pine Grove** beach near the airport all the way west to where **Ocean Park** runs into **Condado** at **Parque del Indio. Punta Las Marías,** between Ocean Park and **Isla Verde,** is a center of activity. The **Condado Lagoon,** just behind the oceanfront strip of hotels, is also popular for windsurfing. (It's increasingly popular with kayakers too.) The northwest, from **Rincón** to **Isabela,** is another center for windsurfing, with strong winds throughout the year.
- **Best Beaches for Being Alone:** Puerto Rico is filled with isolated sandy coves and virgin white beaches accessible only by dirt roads that only the locals seem to

know about. The best, all guaranteed to delight the escapist in you, stretch between Cabo Rojo (the southwesterly tip of Puerto Rico) all the way east to Ponce. **Guánica** has several, including **Las Paldas** and **La Jungla,** which are empty except during holiday weekends. In Fajardo, a 2-mile (3.2km) hike from the **Seven Seas Public Beach** will reward you with the breathtaking **El Convento Beach,** along the miles-long undeveloped coastline stretching between Fajardo and Luquillo. Besides the governor's official beach house, a rustic wooden cottage, there is nothing but white-sand beach and pristine aquamarine waters. The area is a nesting site for endangered sea turtles, and there is excellent snorkeling just offshore, where the water is rife with unspoiled coral reefs and marine life. Environmentalists hope to turn the area into a nature reserve, but two hotel projects are also planned for the area. The government has indicated it wants to develop small-scale, low impact tourism for the area. **Vieques** and **Culebra,** the **Spanish Virgin Islands,** also have their fair share of deserted, out of the way beaches. Because access to many of these is limited due to poor roads, it is necessary to bring supplies, including fresh drinking water. See the box, "Puerto Rico's Secret Beaches," in chapter 8.

- **Best for Snorkeling:** On the main island, the best spot for snorkeling is probably Fajardo's **El Convento Beach** (mentioned above). The southwest, from **Guánica** through **Boquerón,** also has excellent snorkeling with plenty of reefs and marine life right offshore. In the summer, once the big surf quiets down, several beaches in the northwest, from **Rincón** to **Isabela,** also boast good snorkeling. **Steps** is one of the best spots. The islands of **Vieques** and **Culebra** also have great snorkeling. On Vieques, try **Media Luna, Navio, Red,** and **Blue** beaches on the eastern side, and in the west, **Green Beach.** Culebra's most popular beach, **Flamenco** is picture perfect and has very good snorkeling, but a 20-minute hike from its parking leads to the **Playa Tamarindo** and **Playa Carlos Rosario,** beaches enveloped by a barrier reef. A quarter-mile (.4km) to the south is a place called **"The Wall,"** which has 40-foot (12m) drop-offs, rainbow-hued fish, and other delights.

THE best HOTEL BEACHES

- **El San Juan Hotel & Casino** (San Juan; ✆ **787/791-1000**): This posh resort occupies the choicest beachfront real estate in San Juan at the heart of Isla Verde, a fat golden beach lined by luxury hotels and condominiums on one side and aquamarine waters on the other, evoking South Miami. The lush, multilevel pool area and outdoor restaurants form an oasis right off the beach, which pulsates with beautiful crowds and activity every day of the week. You can do it all, from parasailing to taking a catamaran trip, but sunbathing and splashing in the surf are the main attractions here. The hotel has a full array of watersports and other activities and is home to some of the city's best restaurants and nightclubs. See p. 155.
- **Copamarina Beach Resort** (Caña Gorda; ✆ **787/821-0505**) lies west of Ponce, Puerto Rico's second-largest city, in the coastal town of Guánica. A laid-back retreat, the resort is located off a breathtaking country road that winds over a mountainside and back down toward the mangrove-lined coast. It sits on one of

the prettiest and least crowded beaches in southwestern Puerto Rico, beside the Gúanica Dry Forest nature reserve and bird sanctuary. See p. 226.

- **The Ritz-Carlton San Juan Spa & Casino** (Isla Verde; ✆ **787/253-1700**): This elegant sandstone and azure blue resort blends effortlessly into its setting on one of San Juan's most pristine beaches at the secluded eastern end of Isla Verde. Majestic stone-lion fountains and towering rows of royal palm trees run through its pool area. A large gate opens to the white-sand beach, whose tranquil aquamarine waters are sheltered by a large coral reef offshore. See p. 124.

THE best SCUBA DIVING

With the continental shelf surrounding it on three sides, Puerto Rico has an abundance of coral reefs, caves, sea walls, and trenches for divers of all experience levels to explore. See "The Active Vacation Planner," in chapter 3.

- **Metropolitan San Juan:** This easy beach dive off the Condado district in San Juan is not as spectacular as other dives mentioned here, but it's certainly more convenient. Lava reefs sculptured with caverns, tunnels, and overhangs provide hiding areas for schools of snapper, grunts, and copper sweepers. In the active breeding grounds of the inner and outer reefs, divers of all levels can mingle with an impressive array of small tropical fish—French angels, jacks, bluehead wrasse, butterfly fish, sergeant majors, and more—along with sea horses, arrow crabs, coral shrimp, octopuses, batfish, and flying gurnards. Visibility is about 10 to 20 feet (3–6m). The Condado reef is also ideal for resort courses, certification courses, and night dives. See "Diving, Fishing, Tennis & Other Outdoor Pursuits," in chapter 6.
- **Mona Island:** Mona Island, 40 miles (64km) west of the city of Mayagüez in western Puerto Rico, is the Caribbean version of the Galápagos Islands. Renowned for its pirate tales, cave-pocked cliffs, 3-foot-long (.9m) iguanas, and other natural wonders, its waters are among the cleanest in Puerto Rico, with horizontal visibility at times exceeding 200 feet (61m). More than 270 species of fish have been found in Mona waters, including more than 60 reef-dwelling species. Larger marine animals, such as sea turtles, whales, dolphins, and marlins, visit the region during migrations. Various types of coral reefs, underwater caverns, drop-offs, and deep vertical walls ring the island. The most accessible reef dives are along the southern and western shores. There are a number of outfits operating trips from the west coast of Puerto Rico. The boat ride now takes about 3 hours through the often rough Mona Passage. See the box, "Mona Island: The Galápagos of Puerto Rico," in chapter 9.
- **Southern Puerto Rico:** The continental shelf drops off precipitously several miles off the southern coast, producing a dramatic wall 20 miles (32km) long and teeming with marine life. Compared favorably to the wall in the Cayman Islands, this Puerto Rican version has become the Caribbean's newest world-class dive destination. Paralleling the coast from the seaside village of La Parguera to the city of Ponce, the wall descends in slopes and sheer drops from 60 to 120 feet (18–37m) before disappearing into 1,500 feet (457m) of sea. Scored with valleys and deep trenches, it is cloaked in immense gardens of staghorn and elkhorn coral, deep-water gorgonians, and other exquisite coral formations. Visibility can exceed 100 feet (30m). There

are more than 50 dive sites around Parguera alone. See "The Southwest Coast," in chapter 8.

- **Fajardo:** This coastal town in eastern Puerto Rico offers divers the opportunity to explore reefs, caverns, miniwalls, and channels near a string of palm-tufted islets. The reefs are decked in an array of corals ranging from delicate gorgonians to immense coral heads. Visibility usually exceeds 50 feet (15m). Divers can hand-feed many of the reef fish that inhabit the corals. Sand channels and a unique double-barrier reef surround Palomino Island, where bandtailed puffers and parrotfish harems are frequently sighted. Cayo Diablo, farther to the east, provides a treasure box of corals and marine animals, from green moray eels and barracudas to octopuses and occasional manatees. See "Fajardo," in chapter 10.
- **Humacao Region:** South of Fajardo are some 24 dive sites in a 5-mile (8km) radius off the shore. Overhangs, caves, and tunnels perch in 60 feet (18m) of water along mile-long (1.6km) Basslet Reef, where dolphins visit in spring. The Cracks, a jigsaw of caves, alleyways, and boulders, hosts an abundance of goby-cleaning stations and a number of lobsters. With visibility often exceeding 100 feet (30m), the Reserve offers a clear look at corals. At the Drift, divers float along with nurse sharks and angelfish into a valley of swim-throughs and ledges. For the experienced diver, Red Hog is the newest site in the area, with a panoramic wall that drops from 80 to 1,160 feet (24m to 354m). See "Palmas del Mar" in chapter 10.

THE best SNORKELING

Puerto Rico offers top-notch snorkeling even though freshwater run-offs from tropical outbursts feeding into the sea can momentarily cloud the ocean's waters. In most places, when conditions are right, visibility extends from 50 to 75 feet (15–23m).

One of the best ways to experience this wonderful sport, even if you are staying in San Juan, is to take one of the day trips on one of the several luxury catamarans plying the waters off the coast of Fajardo, which make for some of the finest snorkeling in the Caribbean. They usually anchor on the beach of a small cay for lunch and some sunbathing and swimming. Transportation from San Juan area hotels is often provided. It's worth the trip even if you don't want to snorkel. There are a number of reputable operators (see "Watersports" in chapter 10).

- **Mona Island:** This remote island off the west coast of Puerto Rico (see "The Best Scuba Diving," above) also offers the best snorkeling possibilities. The reefs here, the most pristine in Puerto Rico, are home to a wide variety of rainbow-hued fish, turtles, octopuses, moray eels, rays, puffers, and clownfish: the single largest concentration of reef fish life in Puerto Rico. You must bring your snorkeling equipment to the island, however, as there are no rentals available once you are here. See the box, "Mona Island: The Galápagos of Puerto Rico," in chapter 9.
- **Caja de Muertos:** The best snorkeling off the coast of Ponce is on the uninhabited coast island of Caja de Muertos (Coffin Island). This island got its name from an 18th-century French writer who noted that the island's shape resembled a cadaver in a coffin. Over the years there have been fanciful legends about the island, including tales of necrophilia, star-crossed lovers, and, of course, piracy. Several outfits will take you to this remote spot for a full day's outing, with plenty of snorkeling. See "Ponce," in chapter 8.

- **La Parguera:** The reefs surrounding the offshore cays just off La Paguera in southwest Puerto Rico are another fine spot for snorkeling. Several boat operators right in town will either rent you a boat with a guide or drop you off on one of the islands and return at a prearranged timed. See p. 67.
- **Fajardo:** On the eastern coast of Puerto Rico, the clear waters along the beachfront are the best on mainland Puerto Rico for snorkeling. The best beaches here for snorkeling are walking distance from the Seven Seas public beach: **Playa Escondido** and **Playa Convento.** The snorkeling at Las Cabezas de San Juan nature refuge is also spectacular. See "The Best Beaches," earlier in this chapter, and "Fajardo," in chapter 10.
- **Vieques & Culebra:** For a quick preview of the underwater possibilities, refer to "The Best Beaches," earlier in this chapter. For more information, see chapter 11.

THE best GOLF & TENNIS

- **Río Mar Beach Resort & Spa: A Wyndham Grand Resort** (Río Grande; ✆ **787/888-6000**), two world-class golf courses are located here in the shadow of El Yunque rainforest along a dazzling stretch of coast. The entire 6,782 yards (6,201m) of Tom and George Fazio's Ocean Course has seaside panoramas and breezes, and fat iguanas scampering through the lush grounds. The other course, a 6,945-yard (6,351m) design by golf pro Greg Norman, follows the flow of the Mameyes River through mountain and coastal vistas. The resort is a 30-minute drive from San Juan on the northeast coast. Wind is often a challenge here. See p. 202.
- **Dorado Beach Resort & Club** (Dorado; ✆ **787/796-8961** or 787/626-1006): With 72 holes, Dorado has the highest concentration of golf on the island. The legendary Dorado Beach and Cerromar hotels run by Hyatt are now gone, but the four courses and other facilities—spectacular tennis courts, pools, and beaches—live on. There are two luxury hotels on the site now under development. Of the courses, Dorado East is the favorite. Designed by Robert Trent Jones, Sr., it was the site of the Senior PGA Tournament of Champions throughout the 1990s. True tennis buffs head here, too. The Dorado courts are the best on the island.
- **El Conquistador Resort & Golden Door Spa** (Fajardo; ✆ **787/863-1000**): This sprawling resort on Puerto Rico's northeast corner is one of the island's finest tennis retreats, with seven Har-Tru courts and a pro on hand to offer guidance and advice. If you don't have a partner, the hotel will find one for you. There are also outstanding golf facilities as well. See p. 267.
- **Palmas del Mar Country Club** (Humacao; ✆ **787/285-2221**): Lying on the east coast on the grounds of a former coconut plantation, the Palmas del Mar resort boasts the second-leading course in Puerto Rico—a par-72, 6,803-yard (6,221m) layout designed by Gary Player. Some crack golfers consider holes 11 through 15 the toughest five successive holes in the Caribbean. There's also an 18-hole championship-caliber course designed by Rees Jones. The Palmas del Mar Tennis Club meanwhile boasts the largest facilities in the Caribbean, and it has recently begun to host large-prize pro tournaments. See p. 271.
- **Trump International Golf Club** (Río Grande; ✆ **787/657-2000**): Located on 1,200 acres (486 hectares) of glistening waterfront, there are two recently

improved 18-hole golf courses designed by Tom Kite that allow you to play in the mountains, along the ocean, among the palms, and in between the lakes. Its bunkers are carved from white silica sand. Real estate magnate Donald Trump, in conjunction with local developer Empresas Díaz, Inc., is in the initial stages of developing some 500 luxury residences here. See p. 200.

THE best HIKES

Take a hike. Puerto Rico's mountainous interior offers ample opportunity for hiking and climbing, with many trails presenting spectacular panoramas at the least-expected moments. There are also awesome beachfront and coastal trails around the island. See "The Active Vacation Planner," in chapter 3, for detailed information.

- **El Yunque** (✆ **787/888-1880** for information): Containing the only rainforest on U.S. soil, the El Yunque National Forest east of San Juan offers a number of walking and hiking trails. The rugged El Toro trail passes through four different forest systems en route to the 3,523-foot (1,074m) Pico El Toro, the highest peak in the forest. The El Yunque trail leads to three of the recreation area's most panoramic lookouts, and the Big Tree Trail is an easy walk to gorgeous, refreshing La Mina Falls, the perfect picnic stop. Just off the main road is La Coca Falls, a sheet of water cascading down mossy cliffs. See "El Yunque," in chapter 7.
- **Guánica State Forest** (✆ **787/724-3724** for information): At the opposite extreme of El Yunque's lush and wet rainforest, Guánica State Forest's climate is dry and arid, the Arizona-like landscape riddled with cacti. The area, cut off from the Cordillera Central mountain range, gets little rainfall. Yet it's home to some 50% of all the island's terrestrial bird species, including the rare Puerto Rican nightjar, once thought to be extinct. The forest has 36 miles (58km) of trails winding through four forest types: Tabonuco Forest, Palo Colorado Forest, Sierra Palm Forest, and Dwarf Forest, which create a magnificent tangle of vegetation, ranging from tall-treed-canopy, to low-lying upland swamp trees, to palms, to a sweep of dwarf evergreens that look like bonsais. See p. 225.
- **Mona Island:** Off the western coast of Puerto Rico, this fascinating island noted for its scuba-diving sites provides hiking opportunities found nowhere else in the Caribbean. Called the "Galápagos of Puerto Rico" because of its unique wildlife, Mona is home to giant iguanas and three species of endangered sea turtles. Some 20 endangered animals also have been spotted here. Eco-tourists like to hike among Mona's mangrove forests, cliffs, and complex honeycomb of caves, ever on the alert for the diversity of both plant and animal life. There are 417 plant and tree species, some of which are unique and 78 of which are rare or endangered. More than 100 bird species (two unique) have been documented. Hikers can camp at Mona for a modest fee, but they will also have to hire transportation to and from the island. See the box, "Mona Island: The Galápagos of Puerto Rico," in chapter 9.

THE best NATURAL WONDERS

- **El Yunque** (✆ **787/888-1880**): Thirty minutes by road east of San Juan in the Luquillo Mountains and protected by the U.S. Forest Service, El Yunque is Puerto Rico's greatest natural attraction, the only tropical rainforest in the United

States National Forest System. It sprawls across 28,000 acres (1,133 hectares) of the rugged Sierra de Luquillo mountain range, covering areas of Canóvanas, Las Piedras, Luquillo, Fajardo, Ceiba, Naguabo, and Río Grande. The area is named after the Indian spirit Yuquiye, which means "Forest of Clouds," who local Taínos thought protected the island from disaster in times of storms. Originally established in 1876 by the Spanish Crown, it's one of the oldest reserves in the region. There are some 240 species (26 endemic) of trees and plants found here and 50 bird species, including the rare Puerto Rican Parrot (scientific name: *Amazona vitatta*), which is one of the ten most endangered species of birds in the world. The foot-long parrot is bright green, with red forehead, blue primary wing feathers, and flesh-colored bill and feet. Some 100 billion gallons of rain fall here annually. Visitors and families can walk one of the dozens of trails that wind past waterfalls, dwarf vegetation, and miniature flowers, while the island's colorful parrots fly overhead. You can hear the song of Puerto Rico's *coquí,* a small tree frog, in many places. See "El Yunque," in chapter 7.

- **Río Camuy Caves** (© **787/898-3100**): Some 2½ hours west of San Juan, visitors board a tram to descend into this forest-filled sinkhole at the mouth of the Clara Cave. They walk the footpaths of a 170-foot-high (52m) cave to a deeper sinkhole. Once they're inside, a 45-minute tour helps everyone, including kids, learn to differentiate stalactites from stalagmites. At the Pueblos sinkhole, a platform overlooks the Camuy River, passing through a network of cave tunnels. See "Arecibo & Camuy," in chapter 7.
- **Las Cabezas de San Juan Nature Reserve** (© **787/722-5882**): This 316-acre (128-hectare) nature reserve about 45 minutes from San Juan encompasses seven different ecological systems, including forestland, mangroves, lagoons, beaches, cliffs, and offshore coral reefs. Reservations are necessary to enter, and the park is open 5 days a week (Wed–Sun). The park staff conducts tours in Spanish and English from 9am through 2pm. Each tour lasts 2½ hours and includes rides on trolleys and a walk along boardwalks through oceanfront mangrove forest. Tours end with a climb to the top of the still-working 19th-century lighthouse for views over Puerto Rico's eastern coast and nearby Caribbean islands. Call to reserve space before going, as bookings are based on stringent restrictions as to the number of persons who can tour the park without damage to its landscape or ecology. One of the finest phosphorescent bays in the world is located here, and local tour operators take you in a kayak or electronic boat to experience the animals' glow firsthand during nighttime tours. See the box, "To the Lighthouse: Exploring Las Cabezas de San Juan Nature Reserve," in chapter 10.

THE best FAMILY RESORTS

Puerto Rico has a bounty of attractions, natural wonders, and resorts that welcome families who choose to play together. Here are some of the best.

- **Caribe Hilton** (San Juan; © **877/GO-HILTON** [464-4586], or 787/721-0303): The Kidz Paradise center has games, toys, beach items and sports stuff for children free of charge available 9am to 5pm through a lending desk. There's a full recreational program with indoor and outdoor activities and a free welcome gift for children 12 and under. There are a video arcade, bicycle rentals, gym, tennis courts, and watersports equipment rentals. The hotel's family policy grants free stays to children 17 and under when staying in their parents' room, one free babysitting service, free meals to children under 5, and free breakfast and discounts on other meals for children 5 to 12. See p. 113.

- **Marriott Courtyard Aguadilla** (Aguadilla; © **787/658-8000**): The whole family will love this hotel with pool, aquatics playground, and spacious guest rooms. It's near some of the prettiest beaches on the island, and right around attractions such as the Camuy Caves, Arecibo Observatory, local water park, and ice skating rink. Beautiful beaches ring the coast here from Isabela to the east and Rincón to the west. See p. 258.
- **El Conquistador Resort & Golden Door Spa** (Las Croabas; © **800/468-5228** or 787/863-1000): Located 31 miles (50km) east of San Juan, this resort offers Camp Coquí on Palomino Island for children 3 to 12 years of age. The hotel's free water taxi takes kids to the island for a half- or full day of watersports and nature hikes. The Coquí Waterpark also adds to the family appeal. Boasting several pools (including its main 8,500-sq.-ft. main pool, several slides, a rope bridge and a winding river attraction), this resort has some of the best facilities and restaurants in eastern Puerto Rico and all of the Caribbean. See p. 267.

THE best HONEYMOON RESORTS

- **El San Juan Hotel & Casino** (Isla Verde; © **787/791-1000**): Newlyweds will find themselves at the heart of San Juan's vibrant nightlife scene, yet they will be ensconced in luxury along a beautiful stretch of beachfront. In fact, the hotel boasts probably the best nightlife and entertainment, as well as fine dining, of any property in San Juan—and the competition is fierce. There's live music at the casino or adjacent nightclubs. Its elegant lobby, with wooden paneling and a sprawling, opulent chandelier, is a magnet for the young, beautiful, and moneyed visitors. Set on 12 lush acres (4.9 hectares) of prime beachfront, the rooms are as light and airy as the setting. Honeymooners might want to try an Ocean Front Lanai room or one of the resort's villas. See p. 122.
- **Hotel El Convento** (Old San Juan; © **800/468-2779** or 787/723-9020): Newlyweds can sleep in and spend their afternoons wandering the Old City or lolling around the rooftop splash pool, with its sweeping vistas of San Juan Bay and the bluff overlooking the Atlantic Ocean. There are bougainvillea and tropical flowers hanging from seemingly every window and terrace, as well as colorful, restored Spanish colonial architecture everywhere you turn. You'll feel spoiled by your room's marble bathroom and elegant bed. Explore Old San Juan; it's chock-full of galleries and historic fortresses and churches, wonderful cafes and funky shops. The Romantic Memories of San Juan package will get you fresh flowers, champagne, and chocolates in your room, but all guests get a world-class wine and cheese tasting every evening on one of the hotel's many spectacular terraces. There are also pre- and post-cruise packages. See p. 108.
- **Horned Dorset Primavera Hotel** (Rincón; © **800/633-1857** or 787/823-4030): The most romantic place for a honeymoon on the island (unless you stay in a private villa somewhere), this small, tranquil estate lies on the Mona Passage in western Puerto Rico, a pocket of posh where privacy is almost guaranteed.

Accommodations are luxurious in the Spanish neocolonial style. The property opens onto a long, secluded beach of white sand. There are no phones, TVs, or radios in the rooms to interfere with the soft sounds of pillow talk. This is a retreat for adults only, with no facilities for children. Seven-night packages, with all meals included and round-trip transfers from the airport, are featured. See p. 248.

- **Inn on the Blue Horizon** (Vieques; ✆ **787/741-3318**): Celebrate your honeymoon in tropical splendor at this property on an oceanfront bluff overlooking the idyllic south coast of Vieques and the neighboring village of Esperanza. Relax with the sea breeze in the sumptuous furnishings of the main building's open-air atrium, or watch the sunset at the circular Blue Moon Bar, which overlooks the striking coastline. The pool sprawls across the horizon with the beach and ocean beyond it, but the private rooms feel like home (somebody's extremely well-appointed home), with beautiful cotton linens, antique furniture, and art. Romantic packages suitable for honeymooners are available. Make sure to rent a jeep to explore secluded beaches or the hilly, forested interior of the island. See p. 285.

THE best BIG RESORT HOTELS

- **Ritz-Carlton San Juan Spa & Casino** (San Juan; ✆ **800/241-3333** or 787/253-1700): At last Puerto Rico has a Ritz-Carlton, and this truly deluxe, oceanfront property is one of the island's most spectacular resorts. Guests are pampered in a setting of elegance and beautifully furnished guest rooms. Hotel dining is second only to that at El San Juan, and a European-style spa features 11 treatments "for body and beauty." See p. 124.
- **Gran Melía Puerto Rico Golf Resort and Villas** (Río Grande; ✆ **866/436-3542** or 787/809-1770): Twenty two-story villas are spread across a gorgeously landscaped property hugging the northeast coast in the shadow of the mountainous rainforest, El Yunque. The facilities are first rate; the stately lobby is a traditional mix of Puerto Rican and Spanish influences, flanked by an African-inspired meditation pond out front and Asian-inspired lagoons behind, where most of the resort's top-notch restaurants are located. The rooms are spacious and have great views of the lushly landscaped walkways or the broad beachfront that runs the length of the property. The two adjacent Trump golf courses are world class, and the pool and beach area offer all major watersport activities. There's a full range of children's activities and organized fun for adults as well, from yoga lessons to beach volleyball games. The resort spa has first-class facilities and a wide range of treatments. See p. 201.
- **Rio Mar Beach Resort & Spa: A Wyndham Grand Resort** (Rio Grande; ✆ **800/4RIOMAR** [474-6627] or 787/888-6000): This $180-million, 481-acre (195-hectare) resort, 19 miles (31km) east of the San Juan airport, is one of the largest hotels in Puerto Rico, but personal service and style are hallmarks of the property. Eleven restaurants and multiple lounges boast an array of cuisines. It has two championship golf courses, two pools, a beach and watersports, horseback riding, fine tennis facilities, a full range of children's activities, entertainment and nightlife activity, and anything else you might need for your perfect Caribbean getaway. The resort is blissfully situated between the El Yunque rainforest and a beautiful stretch of north coast beach. See p. 202.

- **El Conquistador Resort & Golden Door Spa** (Las Croabas; ✆ **800/468-5228** or 787/863-1000): The finest resort in Puerto Rico, this is a world-class destination—a sybaritic haven for golfers, honeymooners, families, and anyone else. Three intimate "villages" combine with one grand hotel, draped along 300-foot (91m) bluffs overlooking both the Atlantic and the Caribbean at Puerto Rico's northeastern tip. The 500 landscaped acres (202 hectares) include tennis courts, an 18-hole Arthur Hills–designed championship golf course, and a marina filled with yachts and charter boats. There's a water park and an island beach just offshore for guests. See p. 267.

THE best MODERATELY PRICED HOTELS

- **Gallery Inn at Galería San Juan** (San Juan; ✆ **787/722-1808**): The most whimsically bohemian hotel in the Caribbean sits on a coastal bluff at the edge of the historic city. Once the home of an aristocratic Spanish family, it is today filled with verdant courtyards and adorned with sculptures, silk screens, and original paintings of artist Jan D'esopo, who, along with husband Manuco Gandía, owns the inn. Many of the rooms have dramatic views of the coast, with two historic Spanish forts framing the view. Staying in one of the comfortable rooms here is like living in an art gallery. See p. 110.
- **At Wind Chimes Inn** (San Juan; ✆ **800/946-3244** or 787/727-4153): This renovated and restored Spanish manor house, a favorite with families, is one of the best guesthouses in the Condado district. The inn, which offers spacious rooms with kitchens, lies only a short block from one of San Juan's best beaches. There's also a pool and a nice restaurant/bar catering exclusively to guests. The nearby sister property **Acacia Sea Side Inn** is another good option, and guests at the Acacia can use the Wind Chimes' pool and get access to its bar/restaurant. See p. 118.
- **Copamarina Beach Resort** (Caña Gorda; ✆ **787/821-0505**): In an undeveloped coastal area of Guánica, at the edge of the Guánica Dry Forest, this resort was once the private vacation retreat of local cement barons—the de Castro family. Today it's been converted into one of the best beach hotels along Puerto Rico's southern shore. In fact, its beach is one of the best in the area. Set in a palm grove, the resort is handsomely decorated and comfortably furnished, with a swimming pool and two tennis courts. See p. 226.
- **Casa Isleña Inn** (Rincón; ✆ **787/823-1525**): Located on a beautiful beach in the Puntas sector of this west-coast surf capital, this casually elegant inn is a great value of surprising quality. A contemporary Ibero-Caribbean theme runs throughout its rooftop, beachfront and garden terraces, and inspires its colorfully painted architecture and the furnishing of its spacious, comfortable guest rooms. The only drawback is you might find it difficult to ever leave here, since it has one of the best pools in town in front of some of the nicest beach. But with a new tapas bar now open, you might not have to. The last time we visited was in the off season, in early summer, when the place was left blissfully to ourselves and a handful of other guests. See p. 250.

- **Crow's Nest** (Vieques; © **787/741-0033** or 741-0993): Sixteen suites with kitchenettes and lounging/reading areas are spread out across this sprawling property in the lush Vieques countryside. The pool and its beautifully tiled terrace are surrounded by tropical plants and the green hillsides of this island paradise. The staff is extremely helpful, and the restaurant, Island Steakhouse, is top notch (with enough seafood and other nonsteak fare to please everyone). Its country-home setting off the beach is in fact a unique and charming part of the typical Vieques vacation experience. See p. 286.

THE best ATTRACTIONS

- **The Historic District of Old San Juan:** There's nothing like it in the Caribbean. Partially enclosed by old walls dating from the 17th century, Old San Juan was designated a U.S. National Historic Zone in 1950. Some 400 massively restored buildings fill this district, which is chockablock with tree-shaded squares, monuments, and open-air cafes as well as shops, restaurants, and bars. If you're interested in history, there is no better stroll in the Caribbean. It continues to be a vibrant cultural center and enclave of the arts and entertainment, as well as one of the region's culinary capitals. See "Seeing the Sights," in chapter 6.
- **Castillo de San Felipe del Morro** (Old San Juan): In Old San Juan and nicknamed El Morro, this fort was originally built in 1540. It guards the bay from a rocky promontory on the northwestern tip of the old city. Rich in history and legend, the site covers enough territory to accommodate a 9-hole golf course. See p. 154.
- **The Historic District of Ponce:** Second only to Old San Juan in terms of historical significance, the central district of Ponce is a blend of Ponce Creole and Art Deco building styles, dating mainly from the 1890s to the 1930s. One street, Calle Isabel, offers an array of Ponceño architectural styles, which often incorporate neoclassical details. The city underwent a massive restoration preceding the celebration of its 300th anniversary in 1996. See "Ponce," in chapter 8.
- **Museo de Arte de Ponce** (Ponce): This museum has the finest collection of European and Latin American art in the Caribbean. Edward Durell Stone, the architect of the Museum of Modern Art in New York City, designed the building. Contemporary works by Puerto Ricans are displayed, as well as works by an array of old masters, including Renaissance and baroque pieces from Italy. It is slated to reopen in late 2010 following a renovation and expansion. See p. 218.
- **Tropical Agriculture Research Station:** These tropical gardens contain one of the largest collections of tropical species intended for practical use. These include cacao, fruit trees, spices, timbers, and ornamentals. Adjacent to the Mayagüez campus of the University of Puerto Rico, the site attracts botanists from around the world. See "Mayagüez," in chapter 9.
- **The City of San Germán:** Founded in 1512, this small town in the southwestern corner of Puerto Rico is Puerto Rico's second-oldest city. Thanks to a breadth of architectural styles, San Germán is also the second Puerto Rican city (after San Juan) to be included in the National Register of Historic Places. Buildings, monuments, and plazas fill a 36-acre (15-hectare) historic zone. Today's residents descend from the smugglers, poets, priests, and politicians who once lived here

in "the city of hills," so-called because of the mountainous location. See "San Germán," in chapter 8.

- **Iglesia Porta Coeli (San Germán):** The main attraction of this ancient town is the oldest church in the New World. It was originally built by Dominican friars in 1606. The church resembles a working chapel, although mass is held here only three times a year. Along the sides of the church are treasures gathered from all over the world. See "San Germán," in chapter 8.
- **Puerto Rico Museum of Art (San Juan)** features interesting traveling shows and a growing permanent collection emphasizing local artists in impressive surroundings—a restored 1920s classic in Santurce. There are beautiful botanical gardens outside, and a theater exhibits cutting-edge films and performances of all types. There are day workshops open to the public and children's activities held here nearly every weekend, and the museum is home to one of the island's top few restaurants, Pikayo, which takes Puerto Rican cuisine to artful new heights. See p. 159.

THE best RESTAURANTS

- **Aquaviva** (San Juan; ✆ **787/722-0665**): This ultramodern, sleekly tropical restaurant looks as cutting edge as its "seaside Latino cuisine." Its buzzing, blue interior lightly evokes the shoreline and an aquarium all at once. Ceviche rules at the raw bar, and hot and cold seafood "towers" group several of the inventive appetizers into a large portion for guests to share. The menu is expansive and full of wonders—grilled mahimahi with smoky shrimp salsa or seared halibut with crab and spinach fondue. The catch of the day is cooked with consummate skill. See p. 131.
- **Barú** (San Juan; ✆ **787/977-7107**): Fashionable and popular, this Old World–styled restaurant is actually a creative culinary showcase for fusion Caribbean-Mediterranean cuisine and a popular nightspot. Craftsmanship marks the menu, which specializes in inventive risottos and carpaccios. See p. 131.
- **Parrot Club** (San Juan; ✆ **787/725-7370**): This place still sets the standard in style and service, and its Nuevo Latino cuisine beats any of the hotshot restaurants of its genre in New York and Miami that we've tried. The menu here is a thoughtful restyling of Puerto Rican and regional classics, drawing on the island's Spanish, African, Taíno, and American influences. There's a *criolla*-styled flank steak and a pan-seared tuna served with a dark rum-orange sauce. See p. 132.
- **Bistro de Paris** (Santurce; ✆ **787/998-8929**): This Parisian-style bistro serves up French classics with technical grace and passion, and pampers diners with beautiful and comfortable surroundings. It's the stomping grounds of the island's moneyed class, and business leaders, senators, celebrities, and former governors can be seen on any given day. It is right across from the beautiful Puerto Rico Art Museum, a short walk or bus ride from Condado.
- **Budatai** (Condado; ✆ **787/725-6919**): Roberto Trevino's Asian-Latino cuisine has found its rightful home in this luxurious and stylish restaurant with an ocean-front view at the heart of Condado. With an emphasis on Puerto Rican herbs and seafood, the dishes rely on herbs and inspiration from the Far East without ever feeling too far away from home. There's a full sushi bar and lots of ceviche. Start with pork dumplings with shaved truffle and the fried calamari and sweet onion,

and then try a main course of steamed halibut and seasoned potatoes or a Spanish sausage and filet mignon with duck-fat potatoes and Asian mushrooms.

- **El Picoteo** (at El Convento Hotel Old San Juan; ✆ **787/723-9202**): Housed in a courtyard and terrace of this beautiful hotel, this spot may be the best tapas restaurant in all of Puerto Rico, and is definitely the choicest spot to soak up the spirit of Old San Juan. Classic Spanish tapas, from spicy potatoes to garbanzo salad to octopus ceviche, are served amidst the blooming bougainvillea. Enjoy the sangria while you overlook either the hotel's interior courtyard or the parade of partygoers along Calle Cristo.
- **Pikayo** (at the Condado Plaza Hotel & Casino, Condado; ✆ **787/721-6194**): Recently relocated to this new location, Pikayo is as dramatically beautiful as its previous incarnations and remains a fitting restaurant setting for the upscale *criolla* cuisine of island celebrity chef Wilo Benet. It has a menu as artful as its setting. The menu, with dishes such as Caribbean lobster tail with chorizo sausage and gaunabana beurre blanc, or veal scaloppini with prosciutto and sweet pea risotto, fuses Caribbean, European, and Californian influences. For Benet, however, it's all about making high art out of his hometown cuisine. See p. 142.
- **Perla** (Condado; ✆ **787/721-7500**): Diners eat within a shimmering, seashell shaped room on the beach, a fitting setting for the "urbane" menu dreamed up by well known chef Dayne Smith. The menu skitters from American roasted lamb loin to baby striped bass and oysters, and the room itself seems to float atop the sea it fronts. The food lives up to the awesome setting. See p. 128.

THE best OFFBEAT TRAVEL EXPERIENCES

- **Attending a Cockfight:** Although a brutal sport that many find distasteful, cockfighting is legal in Puerto Rico and has its devotees. The most authentic cockfights are held in small central mountain towns, and it's popular along the south coast, such as in the town of Salinas. But it's not necessary to go that far to witness one of these bouts. Three fights a week are held at the **Coliseo Gallistico,** Isla Verde Avenue 6600 (✆ **787/791-6005**), in San Juan. Betting is heavy when these roosters take to the ring. See "San Juan After Dark," in chapter 6.
- **Diving off Mona Island** (Mayagüez): Surrounded by some of the most beautiful coral reefs in the Caribbean, Mona Island has the most pristine, extensive, and well-developed reefs in Puerto Rican waters. In fact, they have been nominated as a U.S. National Marine Sanctuary. The tropical marine ecosystem around Mona includes patch reefs, black coral, spore and groove systems, underwater caverns, deepwater sponges, fringing reefs, and algal reefs. The lush environment attracts octopuses, lobster, queen conch, rays, barracuda, snapper, jack, grunt, angelfish, trunkfish, filefish, butterfly fish, dolphin, parrotfish, tuna, flying fish, and more. The crystal waters afford exceptional horizontal vision from 150 to 200 feet (46–61m), as well as good views down to the shipwrecks that mark the site—including some Spanish galleons. Five species of whales visit the island's offshore waters. See the box, "Mona Island: The Galápagos of Puerto Rico," in chapter 9.
- **Visiting Vieques & Culebra:** Puerto Rico's offshore islands—still relatively undiscovered by the modern world—remain an offbeat adventure, and they've got great

beaches, too. The most developed is Vieques, which attracts visitors with its gorgeous stretches of sand with picnic facilities and shade trees. It is an ideal retreat for snorkelers and tranquillity seekers. The beaches are nearly always deserted, even though they are among the Caribbean's loveliest. Nearly three-quarters of the island is owned by the Fish & Wildlife Service. The even-less-developed Culebra has a wildlife refuge, coral reefs, and Playa Flamenco, another of the Caribbean's finest beaches. And is it ever sleepy here! Culebra, without a doubt, is your best choice of location if what you really want is to do nothing more complicated than luxuriate on the beach and swim or snorkel. See chapter 11.

- **Spending the Evening at Mosquito (Phosphorescent) Bay** (Vieques Island): At any time, except when there's a full moon, you can swim in glowing waters lit by dinoflagellates called *pyrodiniums* (whirling fire). These creatures light up the waters like fireflies, and swimming among them is one of the most unusual things to do anywhere—truly a magical, almost psychedelic experience. It's estimated that a gallon of bay water might contain about three-quarters of a million of these little glowing creatures. See chapter 11.
- **Puerto Rican Road Food:** No other place offers as many road-side treats as Puerto Rico. There's something good to eat around virtually every turn in the road. My family's favorites include barbecued chicken stands along Rte. 116 in Guánica, the pizzerias lining the northwest coast from Arecibo to Mayagüez, and the simple seafood restaurants fronting the quaint and picturesque harbor of Naguabo on the east coast. And you can't really forget Puerta de Tierra's oceanfront **El Hamburger,** or the taco joints along the old Caguas highway. Also try **Piñones,** east of Isla Verde (which has probably the largest concentration of *frituras,* fried beach snacks, near San Juan). Farther east, the cluster of food stands near the **Luquillo** public beach and Hwy. 3 are legendary for their seafood, as well as barbecued chicken. Make sure to try an *arepa,* a light flour pastry often filled with ceviche but also made with coconut flavor and eaten plain with coffee for breakfast. For succulent roast pork, chicken, and turkey, head to a string of open-air restaurants specializing in *criolla* barbecue in the mountain town of **Guavate,** about a half-hour south of San Juan. In all the years my family and I have been eating in Puerto Rico, we've never eaten at a bad restaurant. There simply isn't any bad food to be had here.

PUERTO RICO IN DEPTH

2

Puerto Ricans are intensely proud of their culture, a rich brew of Taíno Indian, Spanish, African, and American influence, and most relish showing off the best of it. Yet visitors will be just as struck at the worldliness of most Puerto Ricans as they are by the beat of salsa music, the symphony of flavor in a seafood stuffed *mofongo,* or the long line of master island painters, print makers, and song writers. That too results from its historic forging from several distinct world cultures.

For more than a century, Puerto Rico's political life has been dominated by its century-old ties to the United States. Those ties have been largely beneficial, and most Puerto Ricans cherish their U.S. citizenship and want to maintain the current political relationship, either through continued commonwealth status or statehood. A smaller percentage favor outright separation from the United States to make Puerto Rico a sovereign nation (the pro-independence party gubernatorial candidate usually gets 5% of the vote). Yet, the relationship with the United States is also the source of island society's central anxiety, which centers on the need for a "permanent" political status.

Millions of Puerto Ricans have flocked stateside over the last 6 decades in search of economic and educational opportunities and an improved quality of life, and they continue to do so. In fact, Puerto Ricans living stateside now just about equal the number living on the island: roughly four million. But for most stateside *boricuas,* their allegiance still belongs to their island homeland, which means frequent trips during vacations and holidays. A sizeable number of Puerto Rican passengers are on most planes from the states arriving at Luis Muñoz Marín International Airport in San Juan. They will burst into applause upon touchdown on Puerto Rican soil. Many others return to Puerto Rico after retiring.

The first wave of island migrants during the 1940s and 1950s largely settled in and around New York, and came seeking blue-collar jobs and the hope for a better future for their families. Today, the typical migrant is more likely a highly educated professional moving to south or central

Florida pursuing greater career advancement opportunities and an improved quality of life.

Puerto Rican writer René Marqués, who came of age in the 1940s and 1950s when Puerto Rico was modernizing into an industrial economy and getting a big dose of U.S. influence, spoke of the dual nature of his island, which nevertheless contributed to its uniqueness. "Puerto Rico has two languages," he claimed, "and two citizenships, two basic philosophies of life, two flags, two anthems, two loyalties."

PUERTO RICO TODAY

Puerto Rico often makes headlines in U.S. news media, and daughters and sons of the island, from pop star Ricky Martin to actor Benicio Del Toro, have given U.S. and world audiences a taste of the enormous talent of this small island, which is also evident in the storied ledger of island baseball sluggers and boxing champs, from Roberto Clemente to Felix Trinidad. Of course, the news is not always good, and recent struggles with both crime and economic issues have also drawn headlines.

Puerto Rico, however, also draws attention because it is among the most developed destinations in the Caribbean and a true regional hub for transportation and telecommunications, with a modern infrastructure and a diversified economy.

A Changing Economy

Puerto Rico is the easternmost of the Greater Antilles (18 15 N, 66 30 W), and the fourth largest island in the Caribbean after Cuba, Hispaniola (which comprises the Dominican Republic and Haiti), and Jamaica. The island is located at the crossroads between North and South America, at just 3½ hours airtime from New York, 60 minutes from Caracas, and at only 4 days sailing from Atlantic ports in the U.S. and ports in the Gulf of Mexico. The Puerto Rican territory includes three other small islands, Vieques, Culebra and Mona, as well as numerous islets.

Some 3,900,000 people live in Puerto Rico, approximately one-third of them within the San Juan metropolitan area. The island, with an area of 3,435 square miles (9,000 sq. km)—110 miles long by 39 miles wide—has a mountainous interior and is surrounded by a wide coastal plain where the majority of the population lives. Rainfall averages 69 inches (175 cm) per year and year-round temperatures range from 74°F (23°C) in the winter to 81°F (27°C) in the summer.

Relationship with the United States

Puerto Rico came under the European sphere of influence in 1493, when Christopher Columbus landed here. Shortly thereafter the island was conquered and settled by the Spaniards. It remained a Spanish possession for 4 centuries.

The territory of Puerto Rico was ceded to the United States upon signature of the Treaty of Paris, on December 10, 1898, a pact which ended the Spanish-American War. Puerto Ricans have been citizens of the United States since 1917. In 1950, after a long evolution toward greater self-government for Puerto Rico, the Congress of the United States enacted Public Law 600, which is "in the nature of a compact" and which became effective upon its acceptance by the electorate of Puerto Rico. It provides that those sections of existing law which defined the political, economic, and fiscal relationship between Puerto Rico and the United States would remain in full force. It also authorized the people of Puerto Rico to draft and adopt their own

Constitution. The Constitution was drafted by a popularly elected constitutional convention, overwhelmingly approved in a special referendum by the people of Puerto Rico and approved by the United States Congress and the president of the United States, becoming effective upon proclamation of the governor of Puerto Rico on July 25, 1952. Puerto Rico's relationship with the United States is referred to herein as commonwealth status.

The United States and the Commonwealth of Puerto Rico (the "Commonwealth") share a common defense, market, and currency. The Commonwealth exercises virtually the same control over its internal affairs as do the 50 states. It differs from the states, however, in its relationship with the federal government. The people of Puerto Rico are citizens of the United States but do not vote in national elections. They are represented in Congress by a Resident Commissioner who has a voice in the House of Representatives but no vote. Most federal taxes, except those such as Social Security taxes, which are imposed by mutual consent, are not levied in Puerto Rico. No federal income tax is collected from Puerto Rico residents on income earned in Puerto Rico, except for certain federal employees who are subject to taxes on their salaries. The official languages of Puerto Rico are Spanish and English.

Governmental Structure

The Constitution of the Commonwealth provides for the separation of powers of the executive, legislative, and judicial branches of government. The governor is elected every 4 years. The Legislative Assembly consists of a Senate and a House of Representatives, the members of which are elected for 4-year terms. The highest court within the local jurisdiction is the Supreme Court of Puerto Rico.

Puerto Rico constitutes a District in the Federal Judiciary and has its own United States District Court. Decisions of this court may be appealed to the United States Court of Appeals for the First Circuit and from there to the Supreme Court of the United States.

Its progress and relative economic strength compared to Caribbean nations has stemmed from its economic diversity. The $93.3-billion economy comprises manufacturing 41.5%, finance, insurance and real estate 17.7%, trade 12.7%, government 9.6%, transportation and public utilities 6.5%, construction and mining 2.1%, and agriculture 0.5%.

Puerto Ricans' annual income is the highest in Latin America, and their average life expectancy has risen to 73.8 years. The island's economy began evolving from its agricultural base in the 1950s when the Operation Bootstrap industrialization program began attracting stateside manufacturing plants. The sector, powered by Puerto Rico's unique political status that allows firms to escape federal taxation, grew to represent nearly half of the island. The demand for an educated workforce has resulted in at least 12 years of schooling for ordinary workers. More importantly, the solid manufacturing industry sparked the growth of a whole host of professional services on the island, including legal, financial, engineering, and accounting, so that today Puerto Rico remains a regional center for most professional services. The island has a number of universities, including the highly regarded University of Puerto Rico, with specialized programs in engineering, medicine, law, and increasingly research and development in a number of fields, including the life sciences.

Manufacturing, for so many years the workhorse of the island economy, has been hit by competition from low-cost destinations, as well as high local utility, shipping, and other fixed costs.

The sector's decline began in 1996, when a 10-year phase-out of U.S. industrial tax breaks began. This marked the end of 75 years of federal incentives that attracted stateside industries and helped make Puerto Rico the Caribbean's industrial powerhouse. Puerto Rico continues to produce about half the prescription drugs sold in the United States, nevertheless.

In response to the industrial exodus, the government is trying to entice existing high-tech industry to stay through an increased focus on research and development. Another target is an island life-sciences research and manufacturing sector through joint private-industry and university ventures.

A big strategy will also compensate for the loss in manufacturing by increasing other economic drivers, from agriculture to shipping to increased professional services, which could be anything from healthcare to finance.

The Tourism Industry

Tourism, which represents about 6% of the gross national product, is a small but important economic segment, and a good source of employment, especially for the island's well-educated, worldly, bilingual youths. The current administration, as with past administrations, wants to double the size of tourism to 12% of the economy.

At once both labor-intensive and environmentally friendly, tourism is seen as a partial answer to the slowdown in the manufacturing sector. Still, there are challenges: A Cuban reopening to the American tourism market could steal business from Puerto Rico, which saw its tourism industry's growth fueled enormously by the embargo imposed on Castro's communist government. Before Fidel Castro took over Cuba in 1959, Americans by the thousands flocked to Havana, and Puerto Rico was a mere dot on the tourist map.

Others say the island could still prosper with an open Cuba because the local tourism product is top of the line, aimed at the most wealthy and discriminating of travelers. They also predict Puerto Rico tourism industry players will have a role in an open Cuba.

Regardless, the tourism industry has been a perennially important part of the island's economic success, and it is poised to take on an even more significant role in the future. The industry will redirect its focus, providing more opportunity for those interested in ecotourism, and smaller scale projects, diverging from the oceanfront resort tourism of Condado and Isla Verde, which still define the Puerto Rico experience for most visitors. The effort to diversify will result in more boutique properties, secluded beach getaways and mountain eco-lodges, which is good news for travelers here.

Crime & Unemployment

Even with its advanced economy, Puerto Rico struggles with an unemployment rate surpassing 14% in recent years and a per capita income about half the level of the poorest U.S. state, Mississippi. Its bloated government bureaucracy is an increasing problem, responsible for deficit spending and high local taxation.

Mirroring the U.S. mainland, rising crime, drugs, AIDS, and other social problems plague Puerto Rico. Its association with the United States has made it a favorite transshipment point for drug smugglers entering the U.S. market (because once on the island, travelers don't have to pass through Customs inspectors again when traveling to the United States).

The drug problem is behind much of local violent crime, including killings that have pushed the local murder rate to among the highest in the United States.

Other violence and social ills associated with drugs have also beset the island.

Although the drug issue is of epidemic proportions, you can visit Puerto Rico and be completely unaware of any criminal activity. Tourist areas in San Juan (including Old San Juan, Condado, and Isla Verde) are generally free of violent crime and theft, and efforts in the past 20 years to resolve the drug and crime problem have helped make safer streets.

The 51st State?

The New Progressive Party wants to make Puerto Rico the 51st state, but the opposition is strong, both on the island and in Congress. A nonbinding referendum in 1998 stayed the New Progressive's bid for statehood.

The other major party, the Popular Democratic Party, backs the continued commonwealth status, while the Puerto Rican Independence Party typically achieves about 5% of popular support in gubernatorial elections. These three parties have dominated island politics of the last 4 decades.

See "Give Me Liberty or Give Me Statehood," on p. 32 for more.

HISTORY 101

In the Beginning

Although the Spanish occupation was the decisive factor defining Puerto Rico's current culture, the island was settled many thousands of years ago by Amerindians. The oldest archaeological remains yet discovered were unearthed in 1948. Found in a limestone cave a few miles east of San Juan, in Loíza Aldea, the artifacts consisted of conch shells, stone implements, and crude hatchets deposited by tribal peoples during the first century of the Christian era. These people belonged to an archaic, semi-nomadic, cave-dwelling culture that had not developed either agriculture or pottery. Some ethnologists suggest that these early inhabitants originated in Florida, immigrated to Cuba, and from there began a steady migration along the West Indian archipelago.

Around A.D. 300, a different group of Amerindians, the Arawaks, migrated to Puerto Rico from the Orinoco Basin in what is now Venezuela. Known by ethnologists as the Saladoids, they were the first of Puerto Rico's inhabitants to make and use pottery, which they decorated with exotic geometric designs in red and white. Subsisting on fish, crab, and whatever else they could catch, they populated the big island as well as the offshore island of Vieques.

By about A.D. 600, this culture had disappeared, bringing to an end the island's historical era of pottery making. Ethnologists' opinions differ as to whether the tribes were eradicated by new invasions from South America, succumbed to starvation or plague, or simply evolved into the next culture that dominated Puerto Rico—the Ostionoids.

Much less skilled at making pottery than their predecessors but more accomplished at polishing and grinding stones for jewelry and tools, the Ostionoids were the ethnic predecessors of the tribe that became the Taínos. The Taínos inhabited Puerto Rico when it was explored and invaded by the Spanish, beginning in 1493. The Taínos were spread throughout the West Indies but reached their greatest development in Puerto Rico and neighboring Hispaniola (the island shared by Haiti and the Dominican Republic).

PONCE DE LEÓN: MAN OF myth & legend

For an explorer of such myth and legend, Juan Ponce de León still remains an enigma to many historians, his exploits subject to as much myth as fact.

It is known that he was born around 1460 in San Tervas de Campos, a province of Valladolid in Spain, to a noble Castilian family. The red-haired youth grew into an active, aggressive, and perhaps impulsive young man, similar in some respects to Sir Francis Drake in England. After taking part in Spain's Moorish wars, Ponce de León sailed to America with Columbus on his second voyage, in 1493.

In the New World, Ponce de León served as a soldier in the Spanish settlement of Hispaniola, now the island home of Haiti and the Dominican Republic. From 1502 to 1504, he led Spanish forces against Indians in the eastern part of the island, finally defeating them.

In 1508, he explored Puerto Rico, discovering gold on the island and conquering the native tribes within a year. A year later, he was named governor of Puerto Rico and soon rose to become one of the most powerful Europeans in the Americas. From most accounts, Ponce de León was a good governor of Puerto Rico before his political rivals forced him from office in 1512.

At that time he received permission from King Ferdinand to colonize the island of Bimini in the Bahamas. In searching for Bimini, he came upon the northeast coast of Florida, which he at first thought was an island, in the spring of 1513. He named it La Florida because he discovered it at the time of Pascua Florida or "Flowery Easter." He was the first explorer to claim some of the North American mainland for Spain.

The following year he sailed back to Spain, carrying with him 5,000 gold pesos. King Ferdinand ordered him back to Puerto Rico with instructions to colonize both Bimini and Florida. Back in Puerto Rico, Ponce de León ordered the building of the city of San Juan. In 1521, he sailed to Florida with 200 men and supplies to start a colony. This was to be his downfall. Wounded by a poison arrow in his thigh, he was taken back to Cuba in June 1521 and died there from his wound.

Legend says Ponce de León searched in vain for the so-called Fountain of Youth, first in Bimini and later in Florida. He never once mentioned it in any of his private or official writings—at least those writings that still exist—and historians believe his goal was gold and other treasures (and perhaps to convert the natives to Catholicism).

His legacy lives on at the Casa Blanca in Old San Juan (p. 161). Casa Blanca is the oldest continuously occupied residence in the Western Hemisphere and the oldest of about 800 Spanish colonial buildings in Old San Juan's National Historic Zone. In 1968, it became a historic national monument. Today the building is the site of the Juan Ponce de León Museum. The conquistador's carved coat of arms greets visitors at the entrance.

Taíno culture impressed the colonial Spanish, and it continues to impress modern sociologists. This people's achievements included construction of ceremonial ballparks whose boundaries were marked by upright stone dolmens, development of a universal language, and creation of a complicated religious cosmology. They believed in a hierarchy of deities who inhabited the sky. The god Yocahu was the supreme creator. Another god, Juracán, was perpetually angry and ruled the power of the hurricane. Myths and traditions were perpetuated through ceremonial dances *(areytos)*, drumbeats, oral traditions, and a ceremonial ballgame played between opposing teams (10–30 players per team) with a rubber ball; winning this game was thought to bring a good harvest and strong, healthy children. Skilled at agriculture and hunting, the Taínos were also good sailors, canoe makers, and navigators.

About 100 years before the Spanish invasion, the Taínos were challenged by an invading South American tribe—the Caribs. Fierce, warlike, sadistic, and adept at using poison-tipped arrows, the Caribs raided Taíno settlements for slaves (especially female) and bodies for the completion of their rites of cannibalism. Some ethnologists argue that the preeminence of the Taínos, shaken by the attacks of the Caribs, was already jeopardized by the time of the Spanish occupation. In fact, it was the Caribs who fought most effectively against the Europeans; their behavior led the Europeans to unfairly attribute warlike tendencies to all of the island's tribes. A dynamic tension between the Taínos and the Caribs certainly existed when Christopher Columbus landed on Puerto Rico.

To understand Puerto Rico's prehistoric era, it is important to know that the Taínos, far more than the Caribs, contributed greatly to the everyday life and language that evolved during the Spanish occupation. Taíno place names are still used for such towns as Utuado, Mayagüez, Caguas, and Humacao. Many Taíno implements and techniques were copied directly by the Europeans, including the *bohío* (straw hut), the *hamaca* (hammock), the musical instrument known as the maracas, and the method of making bread from the starchy cassava root. Also, many Taíno superstitions and legends were adopted and adapted by the Spanish and still influence the Puerto Rican imagination.

Spain, Syphilis & Slavery

Christopher Columbus became the first European to land on the shores of Puerto Rico, on November 19, 1493, near what would become the town of Aguadilla, during his second voyage to the New World. Giving the island the name San Juan Bautista, he sailed on in search of shores with more obvious riches for the taking. A European foothold on the island was established in 1508, when Juan Ponce de León, the first governor of Puerto Rico, imported colonists from the nearby island of Hispaniola. They founded the town of Caparra, which lay close to the site of present-day San Juan. The town was almost immediately wracked with internal power struggles among the Spanish settlers, who pressed the native peoples into servitude, evangelized them, and frantically sought for gold, thus quickly changing the face of the island.

Meanwhile, the Amerindians began dying at an alarming rate, victims of imported diseases such as smallpox and whooping cough, against which they had no biological immunity. The natives paid the Spanish back, giving them diseases such as syphilis against which they had little immunity. Both communities reeled, disoriented from their contact with one another. In 1511, the Amerindians rebelled against Spanish attempts to enslave them. The rebellion was brutally suppressed by the Spanish forces of Ponce de León, whose muskets and firearms were vastly superior to the hatchets and arrows of the native peoples. In desperation, the Taínos joined forces with their traditional enemies, the Caribs, but even that union did little to check the growth of European power.

Because the Indians languished in slavery, sometimes preferring mass suicide to imprisonment, their work in the fields and mines of Puerto Rico was soon taken over by Africans who were imported by Spanish, Danish, Portuguese, and British slavers.

By 1521, the island had been renamed Puerto Rico (Rich Port) and was one of the most strategic islands in the Caribbean, which was increasingly viewed as a Spanish sea. Officials of the Spanish Crown dubbed the island "the strongest foothold of Spain in America" and hastened to strengthen the already impressive bulwarks surrounding the city of San Juan.

Pirates & Pillaging Englishmen

Within a century, Puerto Rico's position at the easternmost edge of what would become Spanish America helped it play a major part in the Spanish expansion toward Florida, the South American coast, and Mexico. It was usually the first port of call for Spanish ships arriving in the Americas; recognizing that the island was a strategic keystone, the Spanish decided to strengthen its defenses. By 1540, La Fortaleza, the first of three massive fortresses built in San Juan, was completed. By 1600, San Juan was completely enclosed by some of the most formidable ramparts in the Caribbean, whereas, ironically, the remainder of Puerto Rico was almost defenseless. In 1565 the king of Spain ordered the governor of Puerto Rico to provide men and materials to strengthen the city of St. Augustine, Florida.

By this time, the English (and to a lesser extent, the French) were seriously harassing Spanish shipping in the Caribbean and north Atlantic. At least part of the French and English aggression was in retaliation for the 1493 Papal Bull dividing the New World between Portugal and Spain—an arrangement that eliminated all other nations from the spoils and colonization of the New World.

Queen Elizabeth I's most effective weapon against Spanish expansion in the Caribbean wasn't the Royal Navy; rather, it was buccaneers such as John Hawkins and Sir Francis Drake. Their victories included the destruction of St. Augustine in Florida, Cartagena in Colombia, and Santo Domingo in what is now the Dominican Republic, and the general harassment and pillaging of many Spanish ships and treasure convoys sailing from the New World to Europe with gold and silver from the Aztec and Inca empires. The Royal Navy did play an important role, however, as its 1588 defeat of the Spanish Armada marked the rise of the English as a major maritime power. The Spanish then began to aggressively fortify such islands as Puerto Rico.

In 1595, Drake and Hawkins persuaded Queen Elizabeth to embark on a bold and daring plan to invade and conquer Puerto Rico. An English general, the Earl of Cumberland, urged his men to bravery by "assuring your selves you have the maydenhead of Puerto Rico and so possesse the keyes of all the Indies."

Confident that the island was "the very key of the West Indies which locketh and shutteth all the gold and silver in the continent of America and Brasilia," he brought into battle an English force of 4,500 soldiers and eventually captured La Fortaleza.

Although the occupation lasted a full 65 days, the English eventually abandoned Puerto Rico when their armies were decimated by tropical diseases and the local population, which began to engage in guerrilla warfare against the invading army. After pillaging and destroying much of the Puerto Rican countryside, the English left. Their short but abortive victory compelled the Spanish king, Philip III, to continue construction of the island's defenses. Despite these efforts, Puerto Rico retained a less-than-invincible aspect as Spanish soldiers in the forts often deserted or succumbed to tropical diseases.

A Dutch Threat

In 1625, Puerto Rico was covetously eyed by Holland, whose traders and merchants desperately wanted a foothold in the West Indies. Spearheaded by the Dutch West India Company, which had received trading concessions from the Dutch Crown covering most of the West Indies, the Dutch armies besieged El Morro Fortress in San Juan in one of the bloodiest assaults the fortress ever sustained. When the commanding officer of El Morro refused to surrender, the Dutch burned San Juan to the ground, including all church and civil archives and the bishop's library, by then the most famous and complete collection of books in America. Fueled by rage, the Spanish rallied and soon defeated the Dutch.

In response to the destruction of the strongest link in the chain of Spanish defenses, Spain threw itself wholeheartedly into improving and reinforcing the defenses around San Juan. King Philip IV justified his expenditures by declaring Puerto Rico the "front and vanguard of the Western Indies and, consequently, the most important of them and most coveted by the enemies of Spain."

Within 150 years, after extravagant expenditures of time and money, San Juan's walls were almost impregnable. Military sophistication was added during the 1760s, when two Irishmen, Tomas O'Daly and Alejandro O'Reilly, surrounded the city with some of Europe's most up-to-date defenses. Despite the thick walls, however, the island's defenses remained precarious because of the frequent tropical epidemics that devastated the ranks of the soldiers; the chronically late pay, which weakened the soldiers' morale; and the belated and often wrong-minded priorities of the Spanish monarchy.

A Catholic Crusade

From the earliest days of Spanish colonization, an army of priests and missionaries embarked on a vigorous crusade to convert Puerto Rico's Taínos to Roman Catholicism. King Ferdinand himself paid for the construction of a Franciscan monastery and a series of chapels, and he required specific support of the church from the aristocrats who had been awarded land grants in the new territories. They were required to build churches, provide Christian burials, and grant religious instruction to both Taíno and African slaves.

Among the church's most important activities were the Franciscan monks' efforts to teach the island's children how to read, write, and count. In 1688, Bishop Francisco Padilla, who is now included among the legends of Puerto Rico, established one of the island's most famous schools. When it became clear that local parents were too poor to provide their children with appropriate clothing, he succeeded in persuading the king of Spain to pay for their clothes.

Puerto Rico was declared by the pope as the first *see* (ecclesiastical headquarters) in the New World. In 1519, it became the general headquarters of the Inquisition in the New World. (About 70 years later, the Inquisition's headquarters were transferred to the well-defended city of Cartagena, Colombia.)

From Smuggling to Sugar

The island's early development was shackled by Spain's insistence on a centrist economy. All goods exported from or imported to Puerto Rico had to pass through Spain itself, usually through Seville. In effect, this policy prohibited any official trade between Puerto Rico and its island neighbors.

In response, a flourishing black market developed. Cities such as Ponce became smuggling centers. This black market was especially prevalent after the Spanish colonization of Mexico and Peru, when many Spanish goods, which once would have been sent to Puerto Rico, ended up in those more immediately lucrative colonies instead. Although smugglers were punished if caught, nothing could curb this illegal (and untaxed) trade. Some historians estimate that almost everyone on the island—including priests, citizens, and military and civic authorities—was actively involved in smuggling.

By the mid-1500s, the several hundred settlers who had immigrated to Puerto Rico from Spain heard and sometimes believed rumors of the fortunes to be made in the gold mines of Peru. When the island's population declined because of the ensuing mass exodus, the king enticed 500 families from the Canary Islands to settle on Puerto Rico between 1683 and 1691. Meanwhile, an active trade in slaves—imported as labor for fields that were increasingly used for sugar-cane and tobacco production—swelled the island's ranks. This happened despite the Crown's imposition of strict controls on the number of slaves that could be brought in. Sugar cane earned profits for many islanders, but Spanish mismanagement, fraud within the government bureaucracy, and a lack of both labor and ships to transport the finished product to market discouraged the fledgling industry. Later, fortunes were made and lost in the production of ginger, an industry that died as soon as the Spanish government raised taxes on ginger imports to exorbitant levels. Despite the arrival of immigrants to Puerto Rico from many countries, diseases such as spotted fever, yellow fever, malaria, smallpox, and measles wiped out the population almost as fast as it grew.

More Smuggling

As the philosophical and political movement known as the Enlightenment swept both Europe and North America during the late 1700s and the 1800s, Spain moved to improve Puerto Rico's economy through its local government. The island's defenses were beefed up, roads and bridges were built, and a public education program was launched. The island remained a major Spanish naval stronghold in the New World. Immigration from Europe and other places more than tripled the population. It was during this era that Puerto Rico began to develop a unique identity of its own, a native pride, and a consciousness of its importance within the Caribbean.

The heavily fortified city of San Juan, the island's civic centerpiece, remained under Spain's rigid control. Although it was the victim of an occasional pirate raid, or an attack by English or French forces, the outlying countryside was generally left alone to develop its own local power centers. The city of Ponce, for example, flourished under the Spanish Crown's lax supervision and grew wealthy from the tons of contraband and the high-quality sugar that passed through its port. This trend was also encouraged by the unrealistic law that declared San Juan the island's only legal port. Contemporary sources, in fact, cite the fledgling United States as among the most active of Ponce's early contraband trading partners.

Rising Power

During the 18th century, the number of towns on the island grew rapidly. There were five settlements in Puerto Rico in 1700; 100 years later, there were almost 40 settlements, and the island's population had grown to more than 150,000.

Meanwhile, the waters of the Caribbean increasingly reflected the diplomatic wars unfolding in Europe. In 1797, after easily capturing Trinidad (which was poorly defended by the Spanish), the British failed in a spectacular effort to conquer Puerto Rico. The *criollos,* or native Puerto Ricans, played a major role in the island's defense and later retained a growing sense of their cultural identity.

The islanders were becoming aware that Spain could not enforce the hundreds of laws it had previously imposed to support its centrist trade policies. Thousands of merchants, farmers, and civil authorities traded profitably with privateers from various nations, thereby deepening the tendency to evade or ignore the laws imposed by Spain and its colonial governors. The attacks by privateers on British shipping were especially severe because pirates based in Puerto Rico ranged as far south as Trinidad, bringing dozens of captured British ships into Puerto Rican harbors. (Several decades earlier, British privateers operating out of Jamaica had endlessly harassed Spanish shipping; the tradition of government-sanctioned piracy was well established.)

It was during this period that coffee—which would later play an essential role in the island's economy—was introduced to the Puerto Rican highlands from the nearby Dominican Republic.

Despite the power of San Juan and its Spanish institutions, 18th-century Puerto Rico was predominantly rural. The report of a special emissary of the Spanish king, Marshal Alejandro O'Reilly, remains a remarkably complete analysis of 18th-century Puerto Rican society. It helped promote a more progressive series of fiscal and administrative policies that reflected the Enlightenment ideals found in many European countries.

Puerto Rico began to be viewed as a potential source of income for the Spanish Empire rather than a drain on income. One of O'Reilly's most visible legacies was his recommendation that people live in towns rather than be scattered about the countryside. Shortly after this, seven new towns were established.

As the island prospered and its bourgeoisie became more numerous and affluent, life became more refined. New public buildings were erected; concerts were introduced; and everyday aspects of life—such as furniture and social ritual—grew more ornate. Insights into Puerto Rico's changing life can be seen in the works of its most famous 18th-century painter, José Campeche.

The Last Bastion

Much of the politics of 19th-century Latin America cannot be understood without a review of Spain's problems at that time. Up until 1850, there was political and military turmoil in Spain, a combination that eventually led to the collapse of its empire. Since 1796, Spain had been a military satellite of postrevolutionary France, an alliance that brought it into conflict with England. In 1804, Admiral Horatio Lord Nelson's definitive victory for England over French and Spanish ships during the Battle of Trafalgar left England in supreme control of the international sea lanes and interrupted trade and communications between Spain and its colonies in the New World.

These events led to changes for Spanish-speaking America. The revolutionary fervor of Simón Bolívar and his South American compatriots spilled over to the entire continent, embroiling Spain in a desperate attempt to hold on to the tattered remains of its empire. Recognizing that Puerto Rico and Cuba were probably the last bastions of Spanish Royalist sympathy in the Americas, Spain liberalized its trade policies, decreeing that goods no longer had to pass through Seville.

The sheer weight and volume of illegal Puerto Rican trade with such countries as Denmark, France, and—most importantly—the United States, forced Spain's hand in establishing a realistic set of trade reforms. A bloody revolution in Haiti, which had produced more sugar cane than almost any other West Indies island, spurred sugar-cane and coffee production in Puerto Rico. Also important was the introduction of a new and more prolific species of sugar cane, the Otahiti, which helped increase production even more.

By the 1820s, the United States was providing ample supplies of such staples as lumber, salt, butter, fish, grain, and foodstuffs, and huge amounts of Puerto Rican sugar, molasses, coffee, and rum were consumed in the United States. Meanwhile, the United States was increasingly viewed as the keeper of the peace in the Caribbean, suppressing the piracy that flourished while Spain's Navy was preoccupied with its European wars.

During Venezuela's separation from Spain, Venezuelans loyal to the Spanish Crown fled en masse to the remaining Royalist bastions in the Americas—Puerto Rico and, to a lesser extent, Cuba. Although many arrived penniless, having forfeited their properties in South America in exchange for their lives, their excellent understanding of agriculture and commerce probably catalyzed much of the era's economic development in Puerto Rico. Simultaneously, many historians argue, their unflinching loyalty to the Spanish Crown contributed to one of the most conservative and reactionary social structures anywhere in the Spanish-speaking Caribbean. In any event, dozens of Spanish naval expeditions that were intended to suppress the revolutions in Venezuela were outfitted in Puerto Rican harbors during this period.

A Revolt Suppressed & Slavery Abolished

During the latter half of the 19th century, political divisions were drawn in Puerto Rico, reflecting both the political instability in Spain and the increasing demands of Puerto Ricans for some form of self-rule. As governments and regimes in Spain rose and fell, Spanish policies toward its colonies in the New World changed, too.

In 1865, representatives from Puerto Rico, Cuba, and the Philippines were invited to Madrid to air their grievances as part of a process of liberalizing Spanish colonial policy. Reforms, however, did not follow as promised, and a much-publicized and very visible minirevolt (during which the mountain city of Lares was occupied) was suppressed by the Spanish governors in 1868. Some of the funds and much of the publicity for this revolt came from expatriate Puerto Ricans living in Chile, St. Thomas, and New York.

Slavery was abolished in March 1873, about 40 years after it had been abolished throughout the British Empire. About 32,000 slaves were freed following years of liberal agitation. Abolition was viewed as a major victory for liberal forces throughout Puerto Rico, although cynics claim that slavery was much less entrenched in Puerto Rico than in neighboring Cuba, where the sugar economy was far more dependent on slave labor.

The 1895 revolution in Cuba increased the Puerto Rican demand for greater self-rule; during the ensuing intellectual ferment, many political parties emerged. The Cuban revolution provided part of the spark that led to the Spanish-American War, Cuban independence, and U.S. control of Puerto Rico, the Philippines, and the Pacific island of Guam.

The Yanks Are Coming! The Yanks Are Coming!

In 1897, faced with intense pressure from sources within Puerto Rico, a weakened Spain granted its colony a measure of autonomy, but it came too late. Other events were taking place between Spain and the United States that would forever change the future of Puerto Rico.

On February 15, 1898, the U.S. battleship *Maine* was blown up in the harbor of Havana, killing 266 men. The so-called yellow press in the United States, especially the papers owned by the tycoon William Randolph Hearst, aroused Americans' emotions into a fever pitch for war, with the rallying cry "Remember the *Maine*."

On April 20 of that year, President William McKinley signed a resolution demanding Spanish withdrawal from Cuba. The president ordered a blockade of Cuba's ports, and on April 24, Spain, in retaliation, declared a state of war with the United States. On April 25, the U.S. Congress declared war on Spain. In Cuba, the naval battle of Santiago was won by American forces, and in another part of the world, the Spanish colony of the Philippines was also captured by U.S. troops.

On July 25, after their victory at Santiago, U.S. troops landed at Guánica, Puerto Rico, and several days later they took over Ponce. U.S. Navy Capt. Alfred T. Mahan later wrote that the United States viewed Puerto Rico, Spain's remaining colonial outpost in the Caribbean, as vital to American interests in the area. Puerto Rico could be used as a military base to help the United States maintain control of the Isthmus of Panama and to keep communications and traffic flowing between the Atlantic and the Pacific.

Spain offered to trade other territory for Puerto Rico, but the United States refused and demanded Spain's ouster from the island. Left with little choice against superior U.S. forces, Spain capitulated. The Spanish-American War ended on August 31, 1898, with the surrender of Spain and the virtual collapse of the once-powerful Spanish Empire. Puerto Rico, in the words of McKinley, was to "become a territory of the United States."

Although the entire war lasted just over 4 months, the invasion of Puerto Rico took only 2 weeks. "It wasn't much of a war," remarked Theodore Roosevelt, who had led the Rough Riders cavalry outfit in their charge up San Juan Hill, "but it was all the war there was." The United States had suffered only four casualties while acquiring Puerto Rico, the Philippines, and the island of Guam. The Treaty of Paris, signed on December 10, 1898, settled the terms of Spain's surrender.

A Dubious Prize

Some Americans looked on Puerto Rico as a "dubious prize." One-third of the population consisted of mulattoes and blacks, descended from slaves, who had no money or land. Only about 12% of the population could read or write. About 8% were enrolled in school. It is estimated that a powerful landed gentry—only about 2% of the population—owned more than two-thirds of the land.

Washington set up a military government in Puerto Rico, headed by the War Department. A series of governors-general were appointed to rule the island, with almost the authority of dictators. Although ruling over a rather unhappy populace, these governors-general brought about much-needed change, including tax and public health reforms. But most Puerto Ricans wanted autonomy, and many leaders, including Luís Muñoz Rivera, tried to persuade Washington to compromise. However, their protests generally fell on deaf ears.

Tensions mounted between Puerto Ricans and their new American governors. In 1900, U.S. Secretary of War Elihu Root decided that military rule of the island was inadequate; he advocated a program of autonomy that won the endorsement of President McKinley.

The island's beleaguered economy was further devastated by an 1899 hurricane that caused millions of dollars' worth of property damage, killed 3,000 people, and left one out of four people homeless. Belatedly, Congress allocated the sum of $200,000, but this did little to relieve the suffering.

Thus began a nearly 50-year colonial protectorate relationship, as Puerto Rico was recognized as an unincorporated territory with its governor named by the president of the United States. Only the president had the right to override the veto of the island's governors. The legislative branch was composed of an 11-member executive committee appointed by the president, plus a 35-member chamber of delegates elected by popular vote. A resident commissioner, it was agreed, would represent Puerto Rico in Congress, "with voice but no vote."

As the United States prepared to enter World War I in 1917, Puerto Ricans were granted U.S. citizenship and, thus, were subject to military service. The people of Puerto Rico were allowed to elect their legislature, which had been reorganized into a Senate and a House of Representatives. The president of the United States continued to appoint the governor of the island and retained the power to veto any of the governor's actions.

From Harvard to Revolution

Many Puerto Ricans continued (at times rather violently) to agitate for independence. Requests for a plebiscite were constantly turned down. Meanwhile, economic conditions improved as the island's population began to grow dramatically. Government revenues increased as large corporations from the U.S. mainland found Puerto Rico a profitable place in which to do business. There was much labor unrest, and by 1909, a labor movement demanding better working conditions and higher wages was gaining momentum.

The emerging labor movement showed its strength by organizing a cigar workers' strike in 1914 and a sugar-cane workers' strike the following year. The 1930s proved to be disastrous for Puerto Rico, which suffered greatly from the worldwide depression. To make matters worse, two devastating hurricanes—one in 1928 and another in 1932—destroyed millions of dollars' worth of crops and property. There was also an outbreak of disease that demoralized the population. Some relief came in the form of food shipments authorized by Congress.

As tension between Puerto Rico and the United States intensified, there emerged Pedro Albizu Campos, a graduate of Harvard Law School and a former U.S. Army officer. Leading a group of militant anti-American revolutionaries, he held that America's claim to Puerto Rico was illegal, since the island had already been granted autonomy by Spain. Terrorist acts by his followers, including assassinations, led to Albizu's imprisonment, but terrorist activities continued.

In 1935, President Franklin D. Roosevelt launched the Puerto Rican Reconstruction Administration, which provided for agricultural development, public works, and electrification. The following year, Sen. Millard E. Tidings of Maryland introduced a measure to grant independence to the island. His efforts were cheered by a local leader, Luís Muñoz Marín, son of the statesman Luís Muñoz Rivera. In 1938, the young Muñoz founded the Popular Democratic Party, which adopted the slogan "Bread, Land, and Liberty." By 1940, this party had gained control of more than 50% of the seats of both the upper and lower houses of government, and the young Muñoz was elected leader of the Senate.

Roosevelt appointed Rexford Guy Tugwell governor of Puerto Rico; Tugwell spoke Spanish and seemed to have genuine concern for the plight of the islanders. Muñoz met with Tugwell and convinced him that Puerto Rico was capable of electing its own governor. As a step in that direction, Roosevelt appointed Jesús Piñero as the first resident commissioner of the island. In 1944, the U.S. Congress approved a bill granting Puerto Rico the right to elect its own governor. This was the beginning of the famed Operation Bootstrap, a pump-priming fiscal and economic aid package designed to improve the island's standard of living.

Shooting at Harry

In 1946, President Harry S. Truman appointed native-born Jesús Piñero as governor of Puerto Rico, and the following year the U.S. Congress recognized the right of Puerto Ricans to elect their own governor. In 1948, Luís Muñoz Marín became the first elected governor and immediately recommended that Puerto Rico be transformed into an "associated free state." Endorsement of his plan was delayed by Washington, but President Truman approved the Puerto Rican Commonwealth Bill in 1950, providing for a plebiscite in which voters would decide whether they would remain a colony or become a U.S. commonwealth. In June 1951, Puerto Ricans voted three to one for commonwealth status, and on July 25, 1952, the Commonwealth of Puerto Rico was born.

This event was marred when a group of nationalists marched on the Governor's Mansion in San Juan, resulting in 27 deaths and hundreds of casualties. A month later, two Puerto Rican nationalists made an unsuccessful attempt on Truman's life in Washington, killing a police officer in the process. And in March 1954, four Puerto Rican nationalists wounded five U.S. Congressmen when they fired down into the House of Representatives from the visitors' gallery.

Despite this violence, during the 1950s Puerto Rico began to take pride in its culture and traditions. In 1955, the Institute of Puerto Rican Culture was established, and 1957 saw the inauguration of the Pablo Casals Festival, which launched a renaissance of classical music and a celebration of the arts. In 1959, a wealthy industrialist, Luís A. Ferré, donated his personal art collection toward the establishment of the Museo de Arte de Ponce.

Give Me Liberty or Give Me Statehood

Luís Muñoz Marín resigned from office in 1964, but his party continued to win subsequent elections. The Independent Party, which demanded complete autonomy, gradually lost power. An election on July 23, 1967, reconfirmed the desire of most Puerto Ricans to maintain commonwealth status. In 1968, Luís A. Ferré won a close race for governor, spearheading a pro-statehood party, the Partido Nuevo Progresista, or New Progressive Party. It staunchly advocated statehood as an alternative to the island's commonwealth status, but in 1972, the Partido Popular Democrático, or Popular Democratic Party, returned to power; by then, the island's economy was based largely on tourism, rum, and industry. Operation Bootstrap had been successful in creating thousands of new jobs, although more than 100,000 Puerto Ricans moved to the U.S. mainland during the 1950s, seeking a better life. The island's economy continued to improve, although perhaps not as quickly as anticipated by Operation Bootstrap.

Puerto Rico grabbed the world's attention in 1979 with the launching of the Pan-American Games. The island's culture received a boost in 1981 with the opening of the Center of the Performing Arts in San Juan, which attracted world-famous performers and virtuosos. The international spotlight again focused on Puerto Rico at the time of the first papal visit there in 1986. John Paul II (or Juan Pablo II, as he was called locally) kindled a renewed interest in religion, especially among the Catholic youth of the island.

In 1996, Puerto Rico lost its special tax-break status, which had originally lured U.S. industry to the island.

A flare-up between the U.S. Navy and Puerto Ricans, especially the islanders of Vieques, burst into the headlines in 1999. Islanders vehemently protested the Navy's use of Vieques for ordnance testing, which they'd done since 1947.

In 2001, Sila M. Calderón was inaugurated as Puerto Rico's first female governor. The daughter of a rich entrepreneur whose holdings include ice-cream factories and hotels, she was raised to a life of privilege. As head of the Popular Democratic Party, she took office and immediately angered Washington by advocating that the U.S. Navy halt bombing on Vieques. She also opposes statehood for Puerto Rico. "When I was a little girl everybody who had power were men," the new governor told the press. "Now girls know that it is very normal for power to be shared by men and women."

In 2003, the U.S. Navy closed its Roosevelt Roads Naval Station on the island of Vieques in the wake of massive protests. With the closing, more than 6,000 people lost their jobs and the island itself suffered a falloff of $300 million a year in income. Puerto Rican leaders are hoping to fill the economic gap with tourism.

The former naval base has been turned over to the U.S. Fish and Wildlife Service for use as a nature refuge, as the landmass is the home to several endangered species, both plant and animal.

In December 2005, the Bush administration asked Congress to set another vote to allow the citizens of the overpopulated island to decide on their future: to opt for statehood or else full independence. Statehood would bring the right to vote in U.S. elections, and full independence would require some islanders to relinquish their American citizenship.

Because of the possible disastrous economic consequences of full independence, only a small number of Puerto Ricans back full independence. As a state, Puerto Rico might alter the balance of power between Democrats and Republicans.

Of course, one option still remains on the table and that is for Puerto Rico to continue as a commonwealth of the U.S. At present, Puerto Rico has no voting representation in Congress. On the other hand, islanders pay no federal income taxes and, yet they benefit from billions in federal social programs.

In 2008, Gov. Aníbal Acevedo Vilá was indicted by federal authorities for crimes related to an alleged illegal campaign fundraising scheme. Ironically, he had squeaked into office in 2004 by around 3,500 votes, largely because of a series of corruption cases involving the political associates of his opponent, former Gov. Pedro Rosselló, who served from 1993 through 2000.

Rosselló's two terms in office were marked by the construction of huge government works projects, including the Tren Urbano and a north coast water aqueduct, as well as a series of government reforms. Corruption cases involving Cabinet secretaries and other officials tarnished the image of his administration, however.

THE POPULATION & POPULAR CULTURE

The inhabitants of Puerto Rico represent a mix of races, cultures, languages, and religions. They draw their heritage from the original native population, from Spanish royalists who sought refuge here, from African slaves imported to work the sugar plantations, and from other Caribbean islanders who have come here seeking jobs. The Spanish they speak is a mix, too, with many words borrowed from the pre-Columbian Amerindian tongue as well as English. Even the Catholicism they practice incorporates some Taíno and African traditions.

Nearly four million people live on the main island, making it one of the most densely populated islands in the world. It has an average of about 1,000 people per square mile, a ratio higher than that of any of the 50 states. There are nearly as many Puerto Ricans living stateside as there are on the island. If they were to all return home, the island would be so crowded that there would be virtually no room for them to live.

When the United States acquired the island in 1898, most Puerto Ricans worked in agriculture; today most jobs are industrial. One-third of Puerto Rico's population is concentrated in the San Juan metropolitan area.

When the Spanish forced the Taíno peoples into slavery, virtually the entire indigenous population was decimated, except for a few Amerindians who escaped into the remote mountains. Eventually they intermarried with the poor Spanish farmers and became known as *jíbaros*. Because of industrialization and migration to the cities, few *jíbaros* remain.

Besides the slaves imported from Africa to work on the plantations, other ethnic groups joined the island's racial mix. Fleeing Simón Bolívar's independence movements in South America, Spanish loyalists headed to Puerto Rico—a fiercely conservative Spanish colony during the early 1800s. French families also flocked here from both Louisiana and Haiti, as changing governments or violent revolutions turned their worlds upside down. As word of the rich sugar-cane economy reached economically depressed Scotland and Ireland, many farmers from those countries also journeyed to Puerto Rico in search of a better life.

During the mid–19th century, labor was needed to build roads. Initially, Chinese workers were imported for this task, followed by workers from countries such as Italy, France, Germany, and even Lebanon. American expatriates came to the island after 1898. Long after Spain had lost control of Puerto Rico, Spanish immigrants continued to arrive on the island. The most significant new immigrant population arrived in the 1960s, when thousands of Cubans fled from Fidel Castro's communist state. The latest arrivals in Puerto Rico have come from the Dominican Republic.

Islanders are most known for their contributions to popular music, and visitors here will no doubt see why. Sometimes, the whole island seems to be dancing. It's been that way since the Taínos, with music an important aspect of their religious and cultural ceremonies.

The latest musical craze born in Puerto Rico is reggaeton, an infectious blend of rap, reggae, and island rhythms, often accompanied by x-rated hip shaking. Daddy Yankee put the music on the world map with his hit "Gasolina"; other well-known island artists in the genre are the duo Wisin y Yandel and Don Omar. Vico C is a local rapper credited with being a pioneer for today's reggaeton stars.

Puerto Rico is still dominated by salsa, a mix of African, Caribbean, and North American rhythms. Salsa bands tend to be full orchestras, with brass sections and several percussionists. The beat is infectious and nonstop, but salsa dancing is all about smooth gyrations and style.

The late Tito Puente, a Latin Jazz master, was instrumental in the development of the music along with singer Ismael Miranda. Puerto Rican salsa won world-wide fame in the late 1970s and early 1980s through groups such as the Fania All Stars, who paired Héctor Lavoe, Rubén Blades and Willie Colón, and El Gran Combo, who still performs today after 40 years together. Famous contemporary practitioners are Gilberto Santa Rosa and Marc Anthony. Actress and singer Jennifer López, Anthony's wife, is another of Puerto Rico's most famous descendants. Their pet project, the biopic "El Cantante," based on Lavoe's life, was filmed in Puerto Rico and New York in 2007.

Jennifer López is not the only *borinqueña* to make a mark on the world stage: a total of four Puerto Rican women have won the Miss Universe competition, most recently Zuleyka Rivera in 2006.

The most famous Puerto Rican singer, however, is pop star Ricky Martin, who continues to be a hometown favorite and sells out shows during his frequent island performances.

Puerto Ricans have also made their mark in professional sports, particularly baseball. The most famous, of course, was Roberto Clemente, who is still a local legend and a role model for young ball players. Current professional baseball players from Puerto Rico include Jorge Posada; Carlos Delgado; Carlos Beltrán; Iván Rodríguez; and the Molina brothers, Bengie and Yadier.

Languages

Spanish is the language of Puerto Rico, although English is widely spoken, especially in hotels, restaurants, shops, and nightclubs that attract tourists. In the hinterlands, however, Spanish prevails.

If you plan to travel extensively in Puerto Rico but don't speak Spanish, pick up a Spanish-language phrase book. The most popular is *Berlitz Spanish for Travelers,* published by Collier Macmillan. The University of Chicago's *Pocketbook Dictionary* is equally helpful. If you have a basic knowledge of Spanish and want to improve your word usage and your sentence structure, consider purchasing a copy of *Spanish Now,* published by Barron's.

Many Amerindian words from pre-Columbian times have been retained in the language. For example, the Puerto Rican national anthem, titled "La Borinqueña," refers to the Arawak name for the island Borinquén, and Mayagüez, Yauco, Caguas, Guaynabo, and Arecibo are all pre-Columbian place names.

Many Amerindian words were borrowed to describe the phenomena of the New World. The natives slept in *hamacas,* and today Puerto Ricans still lounge in hammocks. The god Juracán was feared by the Arawaks just as much as contemporaries fear autumn hurricanes. African words were also added to the linguistic mix, and Castilian Spanish was significantly modified.

With the American takeover in 1898, English became the first Germanic language to be introduced into Puerto Rico. This linguistic marriage led to what some scholars call Spanglish, a colloquial dialect blending English and Spanish into forms not considered classically correct in either linguistic tradition.

The bilingual confusion was also greatly accelerated by the mass exodus to the U.S. mainland. Thousands of Puerto Rican migrants quickly altered their speech patterns to conform to the language used in the urban Puerto Rican communities of cities such as New York.

Religions

The majority of Puerto Ricans are Roman Catholic, but religious freedom for all faiths is guaranteed by the Commonwealth Constitution. There is a Jewish Community Center in Miramar, and there's a Jewish Reformed Congregation in Santurce. There are Protestant services for Baptists, Episcopalians, Lutherans, and Presbyterians, and there are other interdenominational services.

Although it is predominantly Catholic, Puerto Rico does not follow Catholic dogma and rituals as assiduously as do the churches of Spain and Italy. Because the church supported slavery, there was a long-lasting resentment against the all-Spanish clergy of colonial days. Island-born men were excluded from the priesthood. When Puerto Ricans eventually took over the Catholic churches on the island, they followed some guidelines from Spain and Italy but modified or ignored others.

Following the U.S. acquisition of the island in 1898, Protestantism grew in influence and popularity. There were Protestants on the island before the invasion, but their numbers increased after Puerto Rico became a U.S. colony. Many islanders liked the idea of separation of church and state, as provided for in the U.S. Constitution. In recent years, Pentecostal fundamentalism has swept across the island. There are some 1,500 Evangelical churches in Puerto Rico today.

As throughout Latin America, the practice of Catholicism in Puerto Rico blends native Taíno and African traditions with mainstream tenets of the faith. It has been said that the real religion of Puerto Rico is *espiritsmo* (spiritualism), a quasi-magical belief in occult forces. Spanish colonial rulers outlawed spiritualism, but under the U.S. occupation it flourished in dozens of isolated pockets of the island.

Students of religion trace spiritualism to the Taínos, and to their belief that *jípia* (the spirits of the dead—somewhat like the legendary vampire) slumbered by day and prowled the island by night. Instead of looking for bodies, the *jípia* were seeking wild fruit to eat. Thus arose the Puerto Rican tradition of putting out fruit on the kitchen table. Even in modern homes today, you'll often find a bowl of plastic, flamboyantly colored fruit resting atop a refrigerator.

Many islanders still believe in the "evil eye," or *mal de ojo*. To look on a person or a person's possessions covetously, according to believers, can lead to that individual's sickness or perhaps death. Children are given bead charm bracelets to guard against the evil eye. Spiritualism also extends into healing, folk medicine, and food. For example, some spiritualists believe that cold food should never be eaten with hot food. Some island plants, herbs, and oils are believed to have healing properties, and spiritualist literature is available throughout the island.

COMIDA CRIOLLA: PUERTO RICAN CUISINE

Some of Puerto Rico's finest chefs—Wilo Benet and Alfredo Ayala—have based their supremely successful careers on paying gourmet homage to their mothers' and grandmothers' cooking. A whole new generation of rising culinary artists is following in their footsteps by putting Puerto Rico's *comida criolla* at the front and center of their Nuevo Latino experimentation.

Comida criolla, as Puerto Rican food is known, is flavorful but not hot. It can be traced back to the Arawaks and Taínos, the original inhabitants of the island, who thrived on a diet of corn, tropical fruit, and seafood. When Ponce de León arrived with Columbus in 1493, the Spanish added beef, pork, rice, wheat, and olive oil to the island's foodstuffs.

The Spanish soon began planting sugar cane and importing slaves from Africa, who brought with them okra and taro (known in Puerto Rico as *yautia*). The mingling of flavors and ingredients passed from generation to generation among the different ethnic groups that settled on the island, resulting in the exotic blend of today's Puerto Rican cuisine.

Its two essential ingredients are *sofrito,* a mix of garlic, sweet peppers, onion, and fresh green herbs, and *adobo,* a blend of dried spices such as peppercorns, oregano, garlic, salt, olive oil, and lime juice or vinegar, rubbed on pork or chicken before it is slowly roasted. *Achiote* (annatto seeds) is often used as well, imparting an orange color to many common Puerto Rican dishes. Other seasonings and ingredients commonly used are coriander, papaya, cacao, *níspero* (a tropical fruit that's brown, juicy, and related to the kiwi), and *apio* (a small African-derived tuber that's like a pungent turnip).

The rich and fertile fields of Puerto Rico produce a wide variety of **vegetables.** A favorite is the **chayote,** a pear-shaped vegetable called *christophine* throughout most of the English-speaking Caribbean. Its delicately flavored flesh is often compared to that of summer squash. Native root vegetables such as yucca, breadfruit and plantain, called *viandas,* either accompany main meals or are used as ingredients in them.

If you're in Old San Juan and are looking for a noshing tour of the local cuisine, we highly recommend **Flavors of San Juan** (© **787/964-2447**; www.flavorsofsanjuan.com). See p. 166.

Appetizers & Soups

Lunch and dinner generally begin with hot appetizers such as *bacalaitos,* crunchy cod fritters; *surullitos,* sweet and plump cornmeal fingers; and *empanadillas,* crescent-shaped turnovers filled with lobster, crab, conch, or beef. For starters, also look to *tostones* or *arepas,* baked flour casseroles, stuffed with seafood or meat. Fried cheeses in dipping sauces made with tropical fruit are another option.

Soups are also a popular beginning, with a traditional chicken soup *caldo gallego* being a local favorite. Imported from Spain's northwestern province of Galicia, it is prepared with salt pork, white beans, ham, and *berzas* (collard greens) or *grelos* (turnip greens), and the whole kettle is flavored with spicy *chorizos* (Spanish sausages). *Sopón de pescado* (fish soup), is prepared with the head and tail intact and relies on the catch of the day. Traditionally, it is made with garlic and spices plus onions and tomatoes with the flavor enhanced by a tiny dash of vinegar and varying amounts of sherry. Variations differ from restaurant to restaurant. Recently, thick comfort soups made with *viandas,* such as plantain or pumpkin, have been taking a flavorful stand at many *nuevo criolla* restaurants.

There are also ever present accompaniments at every Puerto Rican meal. Yucca is often steamed then served in olive oil and vinegar with sweet roasted peppers and onions. Fried plantain disks called *tostones* accompany most meals. The plantains are also smashed with garlic and other seasonings and cooked into a casserole called *mofongo.* White rice and delicious stewed pink beans, called *arroz y habichuelas,* are

STRANGE fruit

Reading of Capt. James Cook's explorations of the South Pacific in the late 1700s, West Indian planters were intrigued by his accounts of the **breadfruit tree,** which grew in abundance on Tahiti. Seeing it as a source of cheap food for their slaves, they beseeched King George III to sponsor an expedition to bring the trees to the Caribbean. In 1787, the king put Capt. William Bligh in command of HMS *Bounty* and sent him to do just that. One of Bligh's lieutenants was a former shipmate named Fletcher Christian. They became the leading actors in one of the great sea yarns when Christian overpowered Bligh, took over the *Bounty,* threw the breadfruit trees into the South Pacific Ocean, and disappeared into oblivion.

Bligh survived by sailing the ship's open longboat 3,000 miles (4,830km) to the East Indies, where he hitched a ride back to England on a Dutch vessel. Later he was given command of another ship and sent to Tahiti to get more breadfruit. Although he succeeded on this second attempt, the whole operation went for naught when the West Indies slaves refused to eat the strange fruit of the new tree, preferring instead their old, familiar rice.

Descendants of those trees still grow in the Caribbean, and the islanders prepare the head-size fruit in a number of ways. A thick green rind covers its starchy, sweet flesh whose flavor is evocative of a sweet potato. *Tostones*—fried green breadfruit slices—accompany most meat, fish, or poultry dishes served today in Puerto Rico.

also ever present side dishes to most main meals. Another is *arroz con gandules,* stewed rice with pigeon peas.

Main Courses

Stews loom large in the Puerto Rican diet, and none larger than ***asopao,*** a hearty gumbo made with either chicken or shellfish. Every Puerto Rican chef has his or her own recipe. *Asopao de pollo* (chicken stew) takes a whole chicken, which is then flavored with spices such as oregano, garlic, and paprika, along with salt pork, cured ham, green peppers, chili peppers, onions, cilantro, olives, tomatoes, *chorizo,* and pimientos. For a final touch, green peas might be added. Seafood lovers will adore versions using lobster or shrimp. The most basic version simply uses rice and pigeon peas, a healthy, more economical alternative that loses little on the flavor front. Stews are usually cooked in a *caldera* (heavy kettle). Another popular one is *carne guisada puertorriqueña* (Puerto Rican beef stew). The ingredients that flavor the chunks of beef vary according to the cook's whims or whatever happens to be in the larder. These might include green peppers, sweet chili peppers, onions, garlic, cilantro, potatoes, olives stuffed with pimientos, or capers. Seeded raisins may be added on occasion.

While *mofongo* is a dependable side dish, it also takes center stage at many meals when it is formed into a hollow casserole and stuffed with seafood (shrimp, lobster, or the catch of the day) or chicken in tomato sauce. It's called *mofongo relleno. Pastelones de carne,* or **meat pies,** are the staple of many Puerto Rican dinners. Salt pork and ham are often used for the filling and are cooked in a *caldero* (small cauldron). This medley of meats and spices is covered with a pastry top and baked.

Other typical main dishes include fried beefsteak with onions *(carne frita con cebolla),* veal *(ternera)* a la parmesana, and roast leg of pork, fresh ham, lamb, or veal *a la criolla.* These roasted meats are cooked in the Creole style, flavored with *adobo. Chicharrónes*—fried pork with the crunchy skin left on top for added flavor—is very popular, especially around Christmastime. Puerto Ricans also like such dishes as *sesos empanados* (breaded calf's brains), *riñones guisados* (calf's kidney stew), and *lengua rellena* (stuffed beef tongue). Other meats tend to be slowly grilled or sautéed until tender.

Both chicken and fish are important ingredients made dozens of different ways. Two common ways of serving them are *al ajillo,* in a garlic sauce, or *a la criolla,* in a tomato sauce with pepper, onions and Spanish olives. Puerto Ricans adore **chicken,** which they flavor with various spices and seasonings. *Arroz con pollo* (chicken with rice) is the most popular chicken dish on the island, and it was brought long ago to the U.S. mainland. Other favorite preparations include *pollo al kerez* (chicken in sherry), *pollo en agridulce* (sweet-and-sour chicken), and *pollitos asados a la parrilla* (broiled chicken).

A festive island dish is *lechón asado,* or **barbecued pig,** which is usually cooked for a party of 12 to 15. It is traditional for picnics and alfresco parties; one can sometimes catch the aroma of this dish wafting through the palm trees, a smell that must have been familiar to the Taíno peoples. The pig is often basted with *jugo de naranja agria* (sour orange juice) and *achiote* coloring and then rubbed with garlic and *adobe.* Slow roasted, *lechón* done right is juicy and just melts in the mouth. Green plantains are peeled and roasted over hot stones, then served with the barbecued pig. A sour garlic sauce called *aji-li-mojili,* made from garlic, whole black peppercorns, sweet peppers, lime, and olive oil, sometimes accompanies the pig. *Pasteles,* a kind of Puerto Rican turnover, are also popular at Christmas. A paste is formed from either plantain or yucca, which is then filled with seasoned beef or chicken. After it is shaped into a rectangle, it is wrapped in plantain leaves and tied up. They are then boiled and unwrapped, served steaming hot.

Local cuisine relies on seafood, with red snapper *(chillo)* and dolphinfish *(dorado)* most likely to be offered as fresh catches of the day. Shellfish, especially conch *(carrucho),* squid, and octopus, are also frequently used in dishes. *Mojo isleno* is a delicious oil-and-vinegar-based sauce from the south-coast town of Patillas that is poured on fresh grilled fish. The sauce is made with olives and olive oil, onions, pimientos, capers, tomato sauce, vinegar, garlic, and bay leaves. Caribbean lobster is usually the most expensive item on any menu, followed by shrimp. We find it lighter but just as sweet as the more common Maine lobster. Puerto Ricans often grill shrimp *(camarones)* and serve them in an infinite number of ways. Another popular shellfish dish is *jueyes* (crabs), which are either boiled or served inside fried turnovers.

Puerto Ricans love salted codfish, with codfish fritters being one of the more popular beach snacks, always available during festivals. A better way to experience this staple is *serenate de bacalao,* in which the cod is served in an olive oil and vinegar dressing with tomato, onion, and avocado. It's a popular Easter dish.

Many tasty **egg dishes** are served, especially *tortilla española* (Spanish omelet), cooked with finely chopped onions, cubed potatoes, and olive oil.

The Aroma of Coffee

Puerto Ricans usually end a meal with a small cup of the strong, aromatic coffee grown here, either black or with a dash of warm milk. Although the island is not as associated with coffee as Colombia or even the Dominican Republic, it has been producing some of the world's best for more than 300 years. It's been known as the "coffee of popes and kings" since it was exported to Europe's royal courts and the Vatican in the 19th century, and today Puerto Rico continues to produce some of the world's tastiest.

Coffee has several degrees of quality, of course, the lowest-ranking one being *café de primera,* which is typically served at the ordinary family table. The top category is called *café super premium.* Only a handful of three coffees in the world belong to super-premium class: With Puerto Rico's homegrown Alto Grande, coffee beans sought by coffee connoisseurs around the world, joining Blue Mountain coffee of Jamaica, and Kona coffee from Hawaii.

A wave of boutique high-quality local coffee brands have popped up more recently, including Yauco Selecto, with a new generation of farmers catering to the booming worldwide demand for gourmet coffee. Alto Grande Super Premium has been grown in Lares since 1839, in the central mountains known as one of the finest coffee growing areas in the world. Yacuo Selecto, grown in Yauco on the southern slope of the Cordillera Central, also traces its roots to this period when island coffee was courted by royalty. Other coffee-growing towns are Maricao, in the western mountains, and Adjuntas, at the island's heart.

You can ask for your brew *puya* (unsweetened), *negrito con azúcar* (black and sweetened), *cortao* (black with a drop of milk), or *con leche* (with milk).

Rum: Kill-Devil or Whiskey-Belly Vengeance

Rum is the national drink of Puerto Rico, and you can buy it in almost any shade. Because the island is the world's leading rum producer, it's little wonder that every Puerto Rican bartender worthy of the profession likes to concoct his or her own favorite rum libation. You can call for Puerto Rican rum in many mixed drinks such as rum Collins, rum sour, and rum screwdriver. The classic sangria, which is prepared in Spain with dry red wine, sugar, orange juice, and other ingredients, is often given a Puerto Rican twist with a hefty dose of rum.

Today's version of rum bears little resemblance to the raw, grainy beverage consumed by the renegades and pirates of Spain. Christopher Columbus brought sugar cane, from which rum is distilled, to the Caribbean on his second voyage to the New World, and in almost no time rum became the regional drink.

It is believed that Ponce de León introduced rum to Puerto Rico during his governorship, which began in 1508. Under his reign, landholders planted large tracts with sugar cane. From Puerto Rico and other West Indian islands, rum was shipped to colonial America, where it lent itself to such popular and hair-raising 18th-century drinks as Kill-Devil and Whiskey-Belly Vengeance. After the United States became a nation, rum was largely displaced as the drink of choice by whiskey, distilled from grain grown on the American plains.

It took almost a century before Puerto Rico's rum industry regained its former vigor. This occurred during a severe whiskey shortage in the United States at the end of World War II. By the 1950s, sales of rum had fallen off again, as more and different kinds of liquor had become available on the American market.

The local brew had been a questionable drink because of inferior distillation methods and quality. Recognizing this problem, the Puerto Rican government drew up rigid standards for producing, blending, and aging rum. Rum factories were outfitted with the most modern and sanitary equipment, and sales figures (encouraged by aggressive marketing campaigns) began to climb.

No one will ever agree on what "the best" rum is in the Caribbean. There are just too many of them to sample. Some are so esoteric as to be unavailable in your local liquor store. But if popular tastes mean anything, then Puerto Rican rums, especially Bacardi, head the list. There are 24 different rums from Puerto Rico sold in the United States under 11 brand names—not only Bacardi, but also Ron Bocoy, Ronrico, Don Q, and many others. Locals tend to like Don Q the best.

Puerto Rican rums are generally light, gold, or dark. Usually white or silver in color, the biggest seller is light in body and dry in taste. Its subtle flavor and delicate aroma make it ideal for many mixed drinks, including the mojito, daiquiri, rum Collins, rum Mary, and rum and tonic or soda. It also goes with almost any fruit juice, or on the rocks with a slice of lemon or lime. Gold or amber rum is aromatic and full-bodied in taste. Aging in charred oak casks adds color to the rum.

Gold rums are usually aged longer for a deeper and mellower flavor than light rums. They are increasingly popular on the rocks, straight up, or in certain mixed drinks in which extra flavor is desired—certainly in the famous piña colada, rum and Coke, or eggnog.

Dark rum is full-bodied with a deep, velvety, smooth taste and a complex flavor. It can be aged for as long as 15 years. You can enjoy it on the rocks, with tonic or soda, or in mixed drinks when you want the taste of rum to stand out.

RECOMMENDED READING

History

- *The Caribbean People,* by Reginald Honychurch. In three volumes, this is a well-balanced account written by one of the so-called new historians of the Caribbean.
- *Puerto Rico: A Political and Cultural History,* by Artura Morales. Carrion This is one of the best major overviews of Puerto Rican history and culture.
- *The Puerto Ricans: A Documentary History,* by Kal Wagenheim and Olga Jimenez de Wagenheim. A breezy and engrossing, yet intimate and heartfelt, history of the Puerto Rican people, the book is an essential primer.
- *Sugar and Slavery in Puerto Rico: The Plantation Economy of Ponce, 1800–1850,* by Francisco A. Scarano. Scarano produces a scholarly study of an agrarian region of Puerto Rico far removed from the Spanish-controlled capital of San Juan.

Politics

- *Puerto Rico: A Colonial Experiment,* by Ramon Carr. Carr offers one of the most insightful views of island politics, which have been called the national religion of Puerto Rico.
- *Puerto Rico: The Trials of the Oldest Colony in the World,* by Jose Trias Monge. Written by one of Puerto Rico's brightest legal minds and a former Supreme Court justice, his argument about the true nature of the U.S.–Puerto Rico relationship continues to open eyes and carry weight.
- *The United States and Puerto Rico: Breaking the Bonds of Economic Colonialism,* by Roland I. Perusse. This book traces the history of trade relations in Puerto Rico, the second-largest Western trading partner of the United States, after Canada. It is a cultural and economic survey with a strongly politicized point of view.

PLANNING YOUR TRIP TO PUERTO RICO

3

Puerto Rico's unique political situation makes it a hassle-free destination for U.S. travelers, who will basically be subject to the same strictures as interstate travel. All you need is a government-issued identification. You won't face any of the hassles of foreign government entry requirements and processes you would at many other Caribbean destinations. Also, several major airlines offer direct flights to airports in San Juan and Aguadilla from major cities throughout the United States, especially from the East Coast, and beachfront guesthouses or big scale hotels are minutes from the airports. Being part of the U.S. also means there are no currency exchange hoops to jump through and your bank card will work as easily as it will at home.

It's a 3½-hour flight from New York City, and it's quick for carry-on passengers, who can be at their destinations minutes after touchdown. (Baggage claim takes forever, and the airport is not being well maintained.)

Getting to your destination fast is so important. Puerto Rico's ease of entry makes it an alternative to not only Aruba or Cancun for that winter getaway, but a viable option to Vermont or New Hampshire for a long weekend getaway in October. This chapter discusses the where, when, and how of your trip to Puerto Rico—everything required to plan your trip and get it on the road. It's what you need to do *before* you go to make this largely hassle-free destination even more manageable.

WHEN TO GO

Climate

Puerto Rico has one of the most unvarying climates in the world. Temperatures year-round range from 75° to 85°F (24°–29°C). The island is wettest and hottest in August, averaging 81°F (27°C) and 7 inches (18cm) of rain. San Juan and the northern coast seem to be cooler and wetter than Ponce and the southern coast. The coldest weather is in the high altitudes of the Cordillera, the site of Puerto Rico's lowest recorded temperature—39°F (4°C).

THE HURRICANE SEASON

The hurricane season, the curse of Puerto Rican weather, lasts—officially, at least—from June 1 to November 30. But there's no cause for panic. In general, satellite forecasts give adequate warnings so that precautions can be taken. The peaks of the season, when historically the most damaging storms are formed and hit the island, occur in August and December.

If you're heading to Puerto Rico during the hurricane season, you can call your local branch of the **National Weather Service** (listed in your phone directory under the U.S. Department of Commerce) for a weather forecast.

It'll cost 95¢ per query, but you can get information about the climate conditions in any city you plan to visit by calling ✆ **800/WEATHER** (932-8437). When you're prompted, enter your Visa or MasterCard account number, and then punch in the name of any of 1,000 cities worldwide whose weather is monitored by the **Weather Channel** (www.weather.com).

Average Temperatures in Puerto Rico

	JAN	FEB	MAR	APR	MAY	JUNE	JULY	AUG	SEPT	OCT	NOV	DEC
Temp. (°F)	75	75	76	78	79	81	81	81	81	81	79	77
Temp. (°C)	24	24	25	26	26	27	27	27	27	27	26	25

The "Season"

In Puerto Rico, hotels charge their highest prices during the peak winter period from mid-December to mid-April, when visitors fleeing from cold northern climates flock to the islands. Winter is the driest season along the coasts but can be wet in mountainous areas.

If you plan to travel in the winter, make reservations 2 to 3 months in advance. At certain hotels it's almost impossible to book accommodations for Christmas and the month of February.

A second tourism high season, especially for hotels and destinations outside San Juan, does take place in July, when most islanders take vacation.

SAVING MONEY IN THE OFF SEASON

While winter rates are still higher than summer rates at most properties, Puerto Rico is slowly becoming a year-round destination. Many hotel properties are moving towards a pricing scheme of charging a weekday and a weekend rate.

However, there still is an off season, which runs from late spring to late fall, when temperatures in the mid-80s Fahrenheit (about 29°C) prevail throughout most of the region. Trade winds ensure comfortable days and nights, even in accommodations without air-conditioning. Although the noonday sun may raise the temperature to around 90°F (32°C), cool breezes usually make the morning, late afternoon, and evening more comfortable here than in many parts of the U.S. mainland.

Dollar for dollar, you'll spend less money by renting a summer house or fully equipped unit in Puerto Rico than you would on Cape Cod, Fire Island, Laguna Beach, or the coast of Maine.

The off season in Puerto Rico—roughly from May through November (rate schedules vary from hotel to hotel)—is still a summer sale, with many hotel rates slashed from 20% to 40%. It's a bonanza for cost-conscious travelers, especially families who like to go on vacations together. In the chapters ahead, we'll spell out in dollars the specific amounts hotels charge during the off season.

But the off season has been shrinking of late. Many hotels, particularly outside of San Juan, will charge full price during the month of July and summer holiday weekends. Some properties, particularly guesthouses and small hotels in vacation towns such as Vieques and Rincón, have dispensed with off-season pricing altogether.

In San Juan, a trend among smaller properties is to charge higher rates on weekends and holidays than during the week, rather than seasonal fluctuations in price.

OTHER OFF-SEASON ADVANTAGES

Although Puerto Rico may appear inviting in the winter to those who live in northern climates, there are many reasons your trip may be much more enjoyable if you go in the off season:

- After the winter hordes have left, a less-hurried way of life prevails. You'll have a better chance to appreciate the food, culture, and local customs.
- Swimming pools and beaches are less crowded—perhaps not crowded at all. Again, some areas will be extremely crowded in July and on summer holiday weekends.
- Year-round resort facilities are offered, often at reduced rates, which may include snorkeling, boating, and scuba diving.
- To survive, resort boutiques often feature summer sales, hoping to clear the merchandise they didn't sell in February to accommodate stock they've ordered for the coming winter.
- You can often appear without a reservation at a top restaurant and get a table for dinner, a table that in winter would have required a reservation far in advance. Also, when waiters are less hurried, you get better service.
- The endless waiting game is over: no waiting for a rental car (only to be told none is available), no long wait for a golf course tee time, and quicker access to tennis courts and watersports.
- Some package-tour fares are as much as 20% lower, and individual excursion fares are also reduced between 5% and 10%.
- All accommodations and flights are much easier to book.
- Summer is an excellent time for family travel, not usually possible during the winter season.
- The very best of Puerto Rican attractions remain undiminished in the off season—sea, sand, and surf, with lots of sunshine.

OFF-SEASON DISADVANTAGES

Let's not paint too rosy a picture. Although the advantages of off-season travel far outweigh the disadvantages, there are nevertheless drawbacks to traveling in summer:

- You might be staying at a construction site. Hoteliers save their serious repairs and their major renovations until the off season, when they have fewer clients. That means you might wake up early in the morning to the sound of a hammer.

- Single tourists find the cruising better in winter, when there are more clients, especially the unattached. Families predominate in summer, and there are fewer chances to meet fellow singles than in the winter months.
- Services are often reduced. In the peak of winter, everything is fully operational. But in summer, many of the programs, such as watersports rentals, might be curtailed. Also, not all restaurants and bars are fully operational at all resorts. For example, for lack of business, certain gourmet or specialty dining rooms might be shut down until house count merits reopening them. In all, the general atmosphere is more laid-back when a hotel or resort might also be operating with a reduced staff. The summer staff will still be adequate to provide service for what's up and running.

Holidays

Puerto Rico has many public holidays when stores, offices, and schools are closed: New Year's Day, January 6 (Three Kings Day), Washington's Birthday, Good Friday, Memorial Day, July 4th, Labor Day, Thanksgiving, Veterans Day, and Christmas, plus such local holidays as Constitution Day (July 25) and Discovery Day (Nov 19). Remember, U.S. federal holidays are holidays in Puerto Rico, too.

If you are bothered by crowds, avoid visiting beach towns outside San Juan, including Vieques and Culebra, during Easter week and late July, when they are filled with local vacationers.

Puerto Rico Calendar of Events

JANUARY

Three Kings Day, islandwide. On this traditional gift-giving day in Puerto Rico, there are festivals with lively music, dancing, parades, puppet shows, caroling troubadours, and traditional feasts. January 6.

San Sebastián Street Festival, Calle San Sebastián, in Old San Juan. Nightly celebrations with music, processions, crafts, and typical foods, as well as graphic arts and handicraft exhibitions. For more information, call ✆ **787/721-2400.** Mid-January.

FEBRUARY

San Blas de Illescas Half Marathon, Coamo. International and local runners compete in a challenging 13-mile (21km) half-marathon in the hilly south-central town of Coamo. Call **Delta Phi Delta Fraternity** (✆ **787/825-4077**). Early February.

Coffee Harvest Festival, Maricao. Folk music, a parade of floats, typical foods, crafts, and demonstrations of coffee preparation in Maricao, a 1-hour drive east of Mayagüez. For more information, call ✆ **787/838-2290** or 787/267-5536. Second week of February.

Carnival Ponceño, Ponce. The island's Carnival celebrations feature float parades, dancing, and street parties. One of the most vibrant festivities is held in Ponce, known for its masqueraders wearing brightly painted horned masks. For more information, call ✆ **787/284-4141.** Mid-February.

Casals Festival, Performing Arts Center in San Juan. *Sanjuaneros* and visitors alike eagerly look forward to the annual Casals Festival, the Caribbean's most celebrated cultural event. When renowned cellist Casals died in Puerto Rico in 1973 at the age of 97, the Casals Festival was 16 years old and attracting the same class of performers who appeared at the Pablo Casals Festival in France, founded by Casals after World War II. When he moved to Puerto Rico in 1957 with his wife, Marta Casals Istomin (former artistic director of the John F. Kennedy Center for the Performing Arts), he founded not only this festival but also the Puerto Rico Symphony Orchestra to foster musical development on the island.

Ticket prices for the Casals Festival range from $30 to $40. A 50% discount is offered to students, people 60 and older, and persons with disabilities. Tickets are available through the **Puerto Rico Symphonic Orchestra** in San Juan (✆ **787/721-7727**), the **Luis A. Ferré Performing Arts Center** (✆ **787/620-4444**), or **Ticket Center** (✆ **787/792-5000**).

Information is also available from the **Casals Festival** (✆ **787/721-8370;** www.festcasalspr.gobierno.pr). The festivities take place from late February to early March.

MARCH

Emancipation Day, islandwide. Commemoration of the emancipation of Puerto Rico's slaves in 1873, held at various venues. March 22.

APRIL

Saborea, El Escambrón Beach, San Juan. A weekend culinary extravaganza every April sponsored by the Puerto Rico tourism board, Saborea brings together island flavors and chefs and draws global culinary stars. Call ✆ **787/751-8001** or visit www.saboreapuertorico.com. April 1 to 3, 2011.

Good Friday and Easter, islandwide. Celebrated with colorful ceremonies and processions. April 8 to April 10, 2011.

José de Diego Day, islandwide. Commemoration of the birthday of José de Diego, the patriot, lawyer, writer, orator, and political leader who was the first president of the Puerto Rico House of Representatives under U.S. rule. April 17.

Sugar Harvest Festival, San Germán. This festival marks the end of the island's sugar harvest, with live music, crafts, and typical foods, as well as exhibitions of sugar-cane plants and past and present harvesting techniques. Late April.

MAY

Puerto Rican Danza Week *(Semana de la "Danza" Puertorriqueña),* Convento de los Dominicos, Old San Juan. This week commemorates what is, perhaps, the most expressive art form in the Puerto Rican culture: *danza* music and dance. Throughout Danza Week, live performances and conferences are held at Convento de los Dominicos's indoor patio. The building is located on Old San Juan's Cristo Street. For information, call ✆ **800/866-7827** or 787/721-2400. Second week of May.

Heineken JazzFest, San Juan. The annual jazz celebration is staged at Parque Sixto Escobar. Each year a different jazz theme is featured. The open-air pavilion is in a scenic oceanfront location in the Puerta de Tierra section of San Juan, near the Caribe Hilton. For more information, check out the website www.prheinekenjazz.com, which has schedules and links to buy tickets and package information. End of May through the beginning of June.

JUNE

San Juan Bautista Day, islandwide. Puerto Rico's capital and other cities celebrate the island's patron saint with weeklong festivities. At midnight, *sanjuaneros* and others walk backward into the sea (or nearest body of water) three times to renew good luck for the coming year. San Juan hosts several events, from music fests to sports events, for several days before and after the holiday. June 24.

SoFo Culinary Festival, Old San Juan. Held twice a year, in the summer and autumn, during which restaurants on La Fortaleza Street open their doors to offer food and live music. Visit www.tastecuisine.net. Mid-June and mid-September.

Aibonito Flower Festival, at Road 721 next to the City Hall Coliseum, in the central mountain town of Aibonito. This annual flower-competition festival features acres of lilies, anthuriums, carnations, roses, gardenias, and begonias. For more information, call ✆ **787/735-3871.** Last week in June and first week in July.

JULY

Luis Muñoz Rivera's Birthday, islandwide. A birthday celebration commemorating

Luis Muñoz Rivera (1829–1916), statesman, journalist, poet, and resident commissioner in Washington, D.C. July 20.

El Gigante Marathon, Adjuntas. This 9¼-mile (15km) race starts at Puerta Bernasal and finishes at Plaza Pública. For more information call ✆ **787/829-3310.** Sunday before July 25. It will take place July 24, 2011.

Loíza Carnival. This annual folk and religious ceremony honors Loíza's patron saint, John *(Santiago)* the Apostle. Colorful processions take place, with costumes, masks, and *bomba* dancers (the *bomba* has a lively Afro-Caribbean dance rhythm). This jubilant celebration reflects the African and Spanish heritage of the region. For more information, call ✆ **787/876-1040.** Late July through early August.

AUGUST

Cuadragésimo Cuarto Torneo de Pesca Interclub del Caribe, Cangrejos Yacht Club. This international blue-marlin fishing tournament features crafts, music, local delicacies, and other activities. For more information, call ✆ **787/791-1015.** Mid-August.

International Billfish Tournament, at Club Náutico, San Juan. This is one of the premier game-fishing tournaments and the longest consecutively held billfish tournament in the world. Fishermen from many countries angle for blue marlin that can weigh up to 900 pounds (408kg). For specific dates and information, call ✆ **787/722-0177.** Late August to early September.

OCTOBER

La Raza Day (Columbus Day), islandwide. This day commemorates Columbus's landing in the New World. October 10.

National Plantain Festival, Corozal. This annual festivity involves crafts, paintings, agricultural products, exhibition, and sale of plantain dishes; *neuva trova* music and folk ballet are performed. For more information, call ✆ **787/859-3060.** Mid-October.

NOVEMBER

Start of Baseball Season, throughout the island. Six Puerto Rican professional clubs compete from November to January. Professionals from North America also play here. The city's Hiram Bithorn Stadium is also a frequent host for Major League Baseball series; in 2010 it was host to several New York Mets–Florida Marlins games.

Festival of Puerto Rican Music, San Juan. An annual classical and folk music festival, one of its highlights is a *cuatro*-playing contest. (A *cuatro* is a guitarlike instrument with 10 strings.) For more information, call ✆ **787/721-5274.** First week in November.

Jayuya Indian Festival, Jayuya. This fiesta features the culture and tradition of the island's original inhabitants, the Taíno Indians, and their music, food, and games. More than 100 artisans exhibit and sell their works. There is also a Miss Taíno Indian Pageant. For more information, call ✆ **787/828-2020.** Second week of November.

Puerto Rico Discovery Day, islandwide. This day commemorates the "discovery" by Columbus in 1493 of the already inhabited island of Puerto Rico. Columbus is thought to have come ashore at the northwestern municipality of Aguadilla, although the exact location is unknown. November 19.

DECEMBER

Old San Juan's White Christmas Festival, Old San Juan. Special musical and artistic presentations take place in stores, with window displays. December 1 through January 12.

Puerto Rico Heritage Artisans Fair, San Juan. The best and largest artisans fair on the island features more than 100 artisans who turn out to exhibit and sell their wares. The fair includes shows for adults and children, and typical food and drink. It's held at the beautiful Luis Muñoz Rivera Park in Puerta de Tierra and is sponsored by the government. It used to be held on the grounds of the Bacardi rum plant. December 12 through 13.

Las Mañanitas, Ponce. A religious procession that starts out from Lolita Tizol Street and moves toward the city's Catholic church, led by mariachis singing songs to honor Our Lady of Guadalupe, the city's patron saint. The lead song is the traditional Mexican birthday song, *Las Mañanitas.* There's a 6am Mass. For more information, contact **Ponce City Hall** (✆ **787/284-4141**). December 12.

Lighting of the Town of Bethlehem, between San Cristóbal Fort and Plaza San Juan Bautista in Old San Juan. This is the time that the most dazzling Christmas lights go on, and many islanders themselves drive into San Juan to see this dramatic lighting, the finest display of lights in the Caribbean at Christmas. During the Christmas season. (See www.sanjuan.pr for information on days and times.)

Hatillo Masks Festival, Hatillo. This tradition, celebrated since 1823, represents the biblical story of King Herod's ordering the death of all infant boys in an attempt to kill the baby Jesus. Men with colorful masks and costumes represent the soldiers, who run or ride through the town from early morning, looking for the children. There are food, music, and crafts exhibits in the town square. For more information, call ✆ **787/898-4040.** December 28.

Year-Round Festivals

In addition to the individual events described above, Puerto Rico has two yearlong series of special events.

Many of Puerto Rico's most popular events are during the **Patron Saint Festivals** *(fiestas patronales)* in honor of the patron saint of each municipality. The festivities, held in each town's central plaza, include religious and costumed processions, games, local food, music, and dance.

At **Festival La Casita,** prominent Puerto Rican musicians, dance troupes, and orchestras perform; puppet shows are staged; and painters and sculptors display their works. It happens every Saturday at Puerto Rico Tourism's La "Casita" Tourism Information Center, Plaza Darsenas, across from Pier 1, Old San Juan.

For more information about all these events, contact the **Puerto Rico Tourism Company** (✆ **800/866-7827** or 787/721-2400), La Princesa Building, Paseo La Princesa 2, Old San Juan, PR 00902.

For an exhaustive list of events beyond those listed here, check http://events.frommers.com, where you'll find a searchable, up-to-the-minute roster of what's happening in cities all over the world.

Entry Requirements

PASSPORTS

Because Puerto Rico is a commonwealth, **U.S. citizens** coming from mainland destinations do not need passports to enter Puerto Rico. However, because of new airport security measures, it is necessary to produce a government-issued photo ID (federal, state, or local) to board a plane; this is most often a driver's license or birth certificate.

It's best to carry plenty of documentation. Be sure that your ID is *up-to-date:* An expired driver's license or passport, for example, might keep you from boarding a plane.

Visitors from other countries, including Canada, need a valid passport to land in Puerto Rico. For those from countries requiring a visa to enter the U.S., the same visa is necessary to enter Puerto Rico.

Virtually every air traveler entering the U.S. is required to show a passport. All persons, including U.S. citizens, traveling by air between the United States and Canada, Mexico, and Central and South America are required to present a valid passport. This includes most of the Caribbean except Puerto Rico. ***Note:*** U.S. and Canadian citizens entering the U. S. at land and sea ports of entry from within the western hemisphere must now also present a passport or other documents compliant with the Western Hemisphere Travel Initiative (WHTI; see www.getyouhome.gov for details). Children 15 and under may continue entering with only a U.S. birth certificate, or other proof of U.S. citizenship.

It is advised to always have at least one or two consecutive blank pages in your passport to allow space for visas and stamps that need to appear together. It is also important to note when your passport expires. Many countries require your passport to have at least 6 months left before its expiration in order to allow you into the destination.

VISAS

For information on obtaining a Visa, please visit "Fast Facts," on p. 298.

The U.S. Department of State has a **Visa Waiver Program (VWP)** allowing citizens of the following countries to enter the United States without a visa for stays of up to 90 days: Andorra, Australia, Austria, Belgium, Brunei, Czech Republic, Denmark, Estonia, Finland, France, Germany, Hungary, Iceland, Ireland, Italy, Japan, Latvia, Liechtenstein, Lithuania, Luxembourg, Malta, Monaco, the Netherlands, New Zealand, Norway, Portugal, San Marino, Singapore, Slovakia, Slovenia, South Korea, Spain, Sweden, Switzerland, and the United Kingdom. (***Note:*** This list was accurate at press time; for the most up-to-date list of countries in the VWP, consult http://travel.state.gov/visa.) Even though a visa isn't necessary, in an effort to help U.S. officials check travelers against terror watch lists before they arrive at U.S. borders, visitors from VWP countries must register online through the Electronic System for Travel Authorization (ESTA) before boarding a plane or a boat to the U.S. Travelers must complete an electronic application providing basic personal and travel eligibility information. The Department of Homeland Security recommends filling out the form at least 3 days before traveling. Authorizations will be valid for up to 2 years or until the traveler's passport expires, whichever comes first. Currently, there is no fee for the online application. ***Note:*** Any passport issued on or after October 26, 2006, by a VWP country must be an **e-Passport** for VWP travelers to be eligible to enter the U.S. without a visa. Citizens of these nations also need to present a round-trip air or cruise ticket upon arrival. E-Passports contain computer chips capable of storing biometric information, such as the required digital photograph of the holder. If your passport doesn't have this feature, you can still travel without a visa if the valid passport was issued before October 26, 2005, and includes a machine-readable zone; or if the valid passport was issued between October 26, 2005, and October 25, 2006, and includes a digital photograph. For more information, go to **http://travel.state.gov/visa**. Canadian citizens may enter the United States without visas, but will need to show passports and proof of residence.

Citizens of all other countries must have (1) a valid passport that expires at least 6 months later than the scheduled end of their visit to the U.S.; and (2) a tourist visa.

Customs

WHAT YOU CAN BRING INTO THE U.S.

U.S. citizens do not need to clear Puerto Rican Customs upon arrival by plane or ship from the U.S. mainland. Every visitor 21 years of age or older may bring in, free of duty, the following: (1) 1 U.S. quart of alcohol; (2) 200 cigarettes, 50 cigars (but not from Cuba), or 3 pounds of smoking tobacco; and (3) $100 worth of gifts. These exemptions are offered to travelers who spend at least 72 hours in the United States and who have not claimed them within the preceding 6 months. It is forbidden to bring into the country almost any meat products (including canned, fresh, and dried meat products such as bouillon, soup mixes, and so on). Generally, condiments including vinegars, oils, pickled goods, spices, coffee, tea, and some cheeses and baked goods are permitted. Avoid rice products, as rice can often harbor insects. Bringing fruits and vegetables is prohibited, since they may harbor pests or disease. International visitors may carry in or out up to $10,000 in U.S. or foreign currency with no formalities; larger sums must be declared to U.S. Customs on entering or leaving, which includes filing form CM 4790. For details regarding U.S. Customs and Border Protection, consult your nearest U.S. embassy or consulate, or **U.S. Customs** (www.customs.gov).

WHAT YOU CAN TAKE HOME FROM PUERTO RICO

U.S. CUSTOMS On departure, U.S.-bound travelers must have their luggage inspected by the U.S. Department of Agriculture, because laws prohibit bringing fruits and plants to the U.S. mainland. Fruits and vegetables are not allowed, but otherwise, you can bring back as many purchased goods as you want without paying duty.

For information on what you're allowed to bring home, contact one of the following agencies:

U.S. Citizens: **U.S. Customs & Border Protection (CBP),** 1300 Pennsylvania Ave., NW, Washington, DC 20229 (✆ **877/287-8667;** www.cbp.gov).

Canadian Citizens: Canada Border Services Agency, Ottawa, Ontario, K1A 0L8 (✆ **800/461-9999** in Canada, or 204/983-3500; www.cbsa-asfc.gc.ca).

U.K. Citizens: HM Customs & Excise, Crownhill Court, Tailyour Road, Plymouth, PL6 5BZ (✆ **0845/010-9000;** from outside the U.K., 020/8929-0152; www.hmce.gov.uk). For information on importation of plants or animals, see the Department for Food, Environment and Rural Affairs (DEFRA) website (www.defra.gov.uk/foodfarm/food/personal-import/topics/faq.htm).

Australian Citizens: Australian Customs Service, Customs House, 5 Constitution Ave., Canberra City, ACT 2601 (✆ **1300/363-263;** from outside Australia, 612/6275-6666; www.customs.gov.au).

New Zealand Citizens: New Zealand Customs, The Customhouse, 17–21 Whitmore St., P.O. Box 2218, Wellington, 6140 (✆ **04/473-6099** or 0800/428-786; www.customs.govt.nz).

Medical Requirements

Unless you're arriving from an area known to be suffering from an epidemic (particularly cholera or yellow fever), inoculations or vaccinations are not required for entry into the United States.

GETTING THERE & GETTING AROUND

Puerto Rico is by far the most accessible of the Caribbean islands, with frequent airline service. It's also the major airline hub of the Caribbean Basin. Because it's part of the United States, there are no hassles for U.S. travelers related to border entry, currency exchange, etc.

For airline and car rental contact information, see "Airline Websites" in chapter 12, "Fast Facts."

Getting There

BY PLANE

Airlines traveling to Puerto Rico include: **American Airlines** (✆ **800/433-7300** in the U.S. and Canada; www.aa.com); **Continental Airlines** (✆ **800/231-0856** in the U.S. and Canada; www.continental.com); **Delta** (✆ **800/221-1212** in the U.S. and Canada; www.delta.com); **JetBlue** (✆ **800/538-2583** in the U.S. and Canada; www.jetblue.com); **Spirit Air** (✆ **800/772-7117** in the U.S. and Canada; www.spiritair.com); **United Airlines** (✆ **800/538-2929** in the U.S. and Canada; www.united.com); **US Airways** (✆ **800/622-1015** in the U.S. and Canada; www.usairways.com); **Air Canada** (✆ **888/247-2262;** www.aircanada.com); **British Airways** (✆ **800/AIRWAYS** [247-9297] in the U.S. and Canada; www.britishairways.com); **Iberia** (✆ **800/772-4642** in the U.S. and Canada, or 902/400-500 in Spain; www.iberia.com); and **Seaborne Airlines** (✆ **888/359-8687**; www.seaborneairlines.com).

Getting Around

BY PLANE

Cape Air (✆ **866/FLY-CAPEAIR** [359-2273247]; www.flycapeair.com) flies from Luis Muñoz Marín International Airport to Mayagüez, Ponce, and Vieques several times a day. They also offer many flights daily to St. Thomas, St. Croix, and Tortola. Seaborne offers service to several Caribbean islands and Vieques. A handful of small airlines service Vieques and Culebra with small planes that seat about a dozen passengers.

American Eagle (✆ **800/433-7300;** www.aa.com) is one of the leading regional air carriers in the world and a local leader with 37 destinations in the Caribbean and the Bahamas. It's your ticket from San Juan to the greater Caribbean.

BY RENTAL CAR

There is good news and bad news about driving in Puerto Rico. First, the good news: Puerto Rico offers some of the most scenic drives in all the Caribbean.

Of course, if you want to stay only in San Juan, having a car is not necessary. You can get around San Juan on foot or by bus, taxi, and in some cases, hotel minivan.

Now the bad news: Renting a car and driving in Puerto Rico, depending on the routes you take, can lead to a number of frustrating experiences, as our readers relate to us year after year. These readers point out that local drivers are often reckless, as evidenced by the number of fenders with bashed-in sides. The older coastal highways provide the most scenic routes but are often congested. Some of the roads, especially in the mountainous interior, are just too narrow for automobiles. If you do rent a car, proceed with caution along these poorly paved and maintained roads, which most often follow circuitous routes. Cliffslides or landslides are not uncommon.

Some local agencies may tempt you with special reduced prices. But if you're planning to tour the island by car, you won't find any local branches that will help you if you experience trouble. And some of the agencies widely advertising low-cost deals won't take credit cards and want cash in advance. Also, watch out for hidden extra costs, which sometimes proliferate among the smaller and not very well-known firms, and difficulties connected with resolving insurance claims.

If you do rent a vehicle, it's best to stick with the old reliables: **Avis, Budget,** or **Hertz.** Each of these companies offers minivan transport to its office and car depot. Be alert to the minimum-age requirements for car rentals in Puerto Rico. Both Avis and Hertz require that renters be 25 or older; at Budget, renters must be 21 or older, but those between the ages of 21 and 24 pay a $10 to $25 daily surcharge to the agreed-upon rental fee.

Added security comes from an antitheft double-locking mechanism that has been installed in most of the rental cars available in Puerto Rico. Car theft is common in Puerto Rico, so extra precautions are always needed.

Distances are often posted in kilometers rather than miles (1km = 0.62 mile), but speed limits are displayed in miles per hour.

International visitors should note that insurance and taxes are almost never included in quoted rental car rates in the U.S. Be sure to ask your rental agency about additional fees for these. They can add a significant cost to your car rental. ***Note:*** In Puerto Rico, gasoline is sold by the liter, not by the gallon. The cost of gasoline is often somewhat cheaper than in the United States. Current prices are hovering around 75¢ a liter (3.78 of which make up a gallon).

BY PUBLIC TRANSPORTATION

Cars and minibuses known as *públicos* provide low-cost transportation around the island. Their license plates have the letters "P" or "PD" following the numbers. They serve all the main towns of Puerto Rico; passengers are let off and picked up along the way, both at designated stops and when someone flags them down. Rates are set by the Public Service Commission. *Públicos* usually operate during daylight hours, departing from the main plaza (central square) of a town.

Information about *público* routes between San Juan and Mayagüez is available at **Lineas Sultana,** Calle Esteban González 898, Urbanización Santa Rita, Río Piedras (✆ **787/765-9377**). Information about *público* routes between San Juan and Ponce is available from **Choferes Unidos de Ponce,** Terminal de Carros Públicos, Calle Vive in Ponce (✆ **787/764-0540**). There are several operators listed under Lineas de Carros in the local Yellow Pages.

Fares vary according to whether the *público* will make a detour to pick up or drop off a passenger at a specific locale. (If you want to deviate from the predetermined routes, you'll pay more than if you wait for a *público* beside the main highway.) Fares from San Juan to Mayagüez range from $20 to $40; from San Juan to Ponce, from $20 to $40. Be warned that although prices of *públicos* are low, the routes are slow, with frequent stops, often erratic routing, and lots of inconvenience.

Getting around San Juan is getting easier all the time. You have two local bus lines, a *publíco* system that covers the entire metro area, the Tren Urbano, a light urban rail system connecting Santurce with the Hato Rey financial district, the university and medical center districts, and important suburban locations in Bayamón and Guaynabo. Tren Urbano riders can transfer free to city buses and vice versa.

So if you are staying in San Juan, having a car is not necessary. You can get around San Juan on foot or by bus, taxi, and in some cases, hotel minivan. The Tren Urban, a light rail system connecting Santurce to the financial, university and medical districts, and important suburban destinations in Bayamón and Guaynabo, is a great ride. Prices were slashed in half to put it at par with public buses, and riders can transfer into the bus system free of charge. The integration is aimed at increasing ridership throughout the system.

The train and accompanying buses cover virtually all of San Juan. They keep special expanded schedules during big events, such as a festival in Old San Juan, and also for when big acts play at the Puerto Rico Coliseum, or the Tourism Company throws a New Year's Eve party at the Convention Center. For more information, call ✆ **866/900-1284,** or log onto www.ati.gobierno.pr.

Taxis are also reasonably priced and work late into the evening in the city's major districts. So they are your go-to option for a night of clubbing or to get home after a late night.

MONEY & COSTS

THE U.S. DOLLAR VS. OTHER POPULAR CURRENCIES

US$	C$	UK£	Euro (€)	A$	NZ$
1.00	1.05	0.69	0.81	1.18	1.47

Frommer's lists exact prices in the local currency. The currency conversions quoted above were correct at press time. However, rates fluctuate, so before departing consult a currency exchange website, such as **www.oanda.com/convert/classic**, to check up-to-the-minute rates.

CURRENCY The U.S. dollar is the coin of the realm. Keep in mind that once you leave Ponce or San Juan, you might have difficulty finding a place to exchange foreign money (unless you're staying at a large resort), so it's wise to handle your exchange needs before you head off into rural parts of Puerto Rico.

ATMS ATMs are linked to a network that most likely includes your bank at home. Cirrus (✆ **800/424-7787;** www.mastercard.com) and PLUS (✆ **800/843-7587;** www.visa.com) are the two most popular networks in the U.S.; call or check online for ATM locations at your destination. Be sure you know your four-digit PIN before you leave home, and be sure to find out your daily withdrawal limit before you depart. You can also get cash advances on your credit card at an ATM. Keep in mind that credit card companies try to protect themselves from theft by limiting the funds someone can withdraw away from home; it's therefore best to call your credit card company before you leave and let them know where you're going and how much you plan to spend. You'll get the best exchange rate if you withdraw money from an ATM, but keep in mind that many banks impose a fee every time a card is used at an ATM in a different city or bank. On top of this, the bank from which you withdraw cash may charge its own fee.

WHAT THINGS COST IN PUERTO RICO	US$	UK£	EURO€
Taxi from airport to Condado	15.00	7.50	9.68
Average taxi fare within San Juan	15.00	7.50	9.68
Typical bus fare within San Juan	0.75	0.38	0.49
Local telephone call	0.50	0.25	0.32
Double room at the Condado Plaza (very expensive)	259.00	179.00	211.00
Double room at Numero Uno Guesthouse (moderate)	175.00	87.50	113.00
Double room at El Canario Inn (inexpensive)	107.00	69.51	78.76
Lunch for one at Parrot Club (moderate)	25.00	11.50	14.84
Lunch for one at Bebo's Cafe (inexpensive)	12.00	6.00	7.74
Dinner for one at Pikayo's (very expensive)	50.00	32.48	36.80
Dinner for one at Bodega Chic (moderate)	30.00	19.49	22.08
Dinner for one at La Bombonera (inexpensive)	20.00	12.99	14.72
Bottle of beer in a bar	4.00	2.60	2.94
Glass of wine in a restaurant	6.00	2.50	3.26
Roll of ASA 100 color film (36 exp.)	8.50	4.25	5.48
Movie ticket	6.50	3.25	4.19
Theater ticket	15.00–125.00	7.50–62.50	9.68–80.65

CURRENCY EXCHANGE There is a currency exchange at Luis Muñoz Marín International Airport and at large bank branches such as Banco Popular.

TRAVELER'S CHECKS Traveler's checks are something of an anachronism from the days before the ATM made cash accessible at any time. Even given the fees you'll pay for ATM use at banks other than your own, it is still probably a better bet than traveler's checks.

You can get traveler's checks at almost any bank. **American Express** offers denominations of $20, $50, $100, $500, and (for cardholders only) $1,000. You'll pay a service charge ranging from 1% to 4%. You can also get American Express traveler's checks over the phone by calling ✆ **800/221-7282;** Amex gold and platinum cardholders who use this number are exempt from the 1% fee.

Visa offers traveler's checks at Citibank locations nationwide, as well as at several other banks. The service charge ranges between 1% and 2%; checks come in denominations of $20, $50, $100, $500, and $1,000. Call ✆ **800/732-1322** for information. AAA members can obtain Visa checks for a $9.95 fee (for checks, minimum of $300 up to $1,500) at most AAA offices or by calling ✆ **866/339-3378. MasterCard** also offers traveler's checks. Call ✆ **800/223-9920** for a location near you.

CREDIT CARDS Credit cards are invaluable when you're traveling. They are a safe way to carry money and provide a convenient record of all your expenses. You can also withdraw cash advances from your credit cards at any bank (though you'll start paying hefty interest on the advance the moment you receive the cash). At most banks, you don't even need to go to a teller; you can get a cash advance at the ATM if you know your PIN. If you've forgotten yours, or didn't even know you had one, call the number on the back of your credit card and ask the card issuer to send it to you. It usually takes 5 to 7 business days, though some banks will provide the number over the phone if you tell them your mother's maiden name or pass some other security clearance test.

In San Juan and at all the big resorts on the island, even some of the smaller inns, credit cards are commonly accepted. Moreover, an incredible array of establishments accept payment with ATM cards. However, as you tour through rural areas and if you intend to patronize small, out-of-the-way establishments, it's still wise to carry sufficient greenbacks for emergencies. Visa and MasterCard are accepted most widely throughout Puerto Rico.

For tips and telephone numbers to call if your wallet is stolen or lost, go to "Lost & Found," in chapter 12, "Fast Facts."

STAYING HEALTHY

Puerto Rico poses no major health problem for most travelers. If you have a chronic condition, however, you should check with your doctor before visiting the islands. For conditions such as epilepsy, diabetes, or heart problems, wear a **MedicAlert Identification Tag** (✆ **800/825-3785;** www.medicalert.org), which will immediately alert doctors to your condition and give them access to your records through MedicAlert's 24-hour hot line.

Finding a good doctor in Puerto Rico is easy, and most speak English. See "Fast Facts," chapter 12, for the locations of hospitals.

If you worry about getting sick away from home, consider purchasing **medical travel insurance** and carry your ID card in your purse or wallet. In most cases, your existing health plan will provide the coverage you need. See "Fast Facts," chapter 12, for more information.

Pack **prescription medications** in your carry-on luggage, and carry prescription medications in their original containers. Also bring along copies of your prescriptions, in case you lose your medication or run out. Carry the generic name of prescription medicines, in case a local pharmacist is unfamiliar with the brand name.

And don't forget **sunglasses** and an extra pair of **contact lenses** or **prescription glasses.**

Contact the **International Association for Medical Assistance to Travelers (IAMAT;** ✆ **716/754-4883** or, in Canada, 416/652-0137; www.iamat.org) for tips on travel and health concerns in the countries you're visiting, and for lists of local, English-speaking doctors. The United States **Centers for Disease Control and**

Prevention (✆ **800/311-3435;** www.cdc.gov) provides up-to-date information on health hazards by region or country and offers tips on food safety. The website **www.tripprep.com**, sponsored by a consortium of travel medicine practitioners, may also offer helpful advice on traveling abroad. You can find listings of reliable clinics overseas at the **International Society of Travel Medicine** (www.istm.org).

It's best to stick to **bottled mineral water** here. Although tap water is said to be safe to drink, many visitors experience diarrhea, even if they follow the usual precautions. The illness usually passes quickly without medication, if you eat simply prepared food and drink only mineral water until you recover. If symptoms persist, consult a doctor.

The **sun** can be brutal, especially if you haven't been exposed to it in some time. Experts advise that you limit your time on the beach the first day. If you do overexpose yourself, stay out of the sun until you recover. If your exposure is followed by fever or chills, a headache, or a feeling of nausea or dizziness, see a doctor.

Sandflies (or "no-see-ums") can still be a problem in Puerto Rico but are not the menace they are in other Caribbean destinations. They appear mainly in the early evening, and even if you can't see these tiny bugs, you sure can "feel-um."

Your favorite insect repellent will protect you from them, should they become a problem.

Although **mosquitoes** are a nuisance, they do not carry malaria in Puerto Rico. However, after a long absence, the dreaded dengue fever has returned to Puerto Rico. The disease is transmitted by the Aede mosquito, and its symptoms include fever, headaches, pain in the muscles and joints, skin blisters, and hemorrhaging. It usually is gone after a week but the strongest cases are fatal.

Hookworm and other **intestinal parasites** are relatively common in the Caribbean, though you are less likely to be affected in Puerto Rico than on other islands. Hookworm can be contracted by just walking barefoot on an infected beach. *Schistosomiasis* (also called *bilharzia*), caused by a parasitic fluke, can be contracted by submerging your feet in rivers and lakes infested with a certain species of snail.

Like major urban areas along the East Coast, Puerto Rico has been hard hit by **AIDS** and other sexually transmitted diseases. Exercise *at least* the same caution in choosing your sexual partners and practicing safe sex as you would at home.

Most health insurance policies cover you if you get sick away from home, but they are not likely to provide for medical evacuation in case of life-threatening injury or illness. It's a good idea to buy a travel insurance policy that provides for **emergency medical evacuation.** If you have to buy a one-way same-day ticket home and forfeit your nonrefundable round-trip ticket, you might be out big bucks. And the cost of a flying ambulance could wipe out your life's savings.

Check with your insurer, particularly if you're insured by an HMO, about the extent of its coverage while you're overseas. With the exception of certain HMOs and Medicare/Medicaid, your medical insurance should cover medical treatment—even hospital care—overseas. However, most out-of-country hospitals make you pay your bills upfront, and they send you a refund after you've returned home and filed the necessary paperwork.

If you require additional insurance, try one of the following companies:

- MEDEX **International** (✆ **888/MEDEX-00** [633-3900] or 410/453-6300; fax 410/453-6301; www.medexassist.com)

- **Travel Assistance International** (✆ **800/821-2828;** www.travelassistance.com); for general information on services, call the company's Worldwide Assistance Services, Inc. at ✆ **800/777-8710.**
- **The Divers Alert Network** (**DAN;** ✆ **800/446-2671** or 919/684-2948; www.diversalertnetwork.org)

LOST-LUGGAGE INSURANCE

On domestic flights, checked baggage is covered up to $2,500 per ticketed passenger. On international flights (including U.S. portions of international trips), baggage coverage is limited to approximately $9.07 per pound, up to approximately $635 per checked bag. If you plan to check items more valuable than what's covered by the standard liability, see if your homeowner's policy covers your valuables, or get baggage insurance as part of your comprehensive travel-insurance package. Don't buy insurance at the airport, where it's usually overpriced. Be sure to take any valuables or irreplaceable items with you in your carry-on luggage, because many valuables (including books, money, and electronics) aren't covered by airline policies.

If your luggage is lost, immediately file a lost-luggage claim at the airport, detailing the luggage contents. Most airlines require that you report delayed, damaged, or lost baggage within 4 hours of arrival. The airlines are required to deliver luggage, once found, directly to your house or destination free of charge.

CRIME & SAFETY

The U.S. Department of State issues no special travel advisories for the Commonwealth of Puerto Rico, the way it might for, say, the more troubled island of Jamaica. However, there are crime problems in Puerto Rico, but they rarely surface along San Juan's Condado and Isla Verde beaches and Old San Juan. Still caution should be exercised at night, since muggings do happen, and isolated areas should be avoided.

Burglary, including vandalizing of automobiles, is another problem, so don't leave valuables in cars, even when the doors are locked.

Take precautions about leaving valuables on the beach, and exercise extreme care if you're searching for a remote beach where there's no one in sight. The only person lurking nearby might be someone not interested in surf and sand but a robber waiting to make off with your possessions.

Avoid wandering around the darkened and relatively deserted alleys and small streets of San Juan's Old City at night, especially those off the oceanside Norzagaray Boulevard, which is relatively deserted at night.

If you are traveling out on the island, plan to do your driving during the daylight hours, both for road-safety and crime-precaution reasons. A wrong turn at midnight could lead to a whole lot of trouble of all stripes.

So in short, crime exists here as it does everywhere. Use common sense and take precautions. Theft and occasional muggings do occur on the Condado and Isla Verde beaches at night, so you might want to confine your moonlit beach nights to the fenced-in and guarded areas around some of the major hotels. The countryside of Puerto Rico is safer than San Juan, but caution is always in order. Avoid narrow country roads and isolated beaches at night and exercise caution on them during the day.

Specialized Travel Resources

In addition to the destination-specific resources listed below, please visit Frommers.com for other specialized travel resources.

LGBT TRAVELERS

Puerto Rico is the most gay-friendly destination in the Caribbean, with lots of accommodations, restaurants, clubs, and bars that actively cater to a gay clientele.

A good source is www.orgulloboricua.net, which is a Web portal for the island's gay and lesbian community; it has an introduction for visitors in English. In Spanish is radio show/Web blog www.saliendodelcloset.org, which involves leading figures in the gay community and has links to several points of interest.

The **International Gay & Lesbian Travel Association (IGLTA; ✆ 800/448-8550** or 954/776-2626; www.iglta.org) links travelers up with gay-friendly hoteliers, tour operators, and airline and cruise-line representatives. It offers monthly newsletters, marketing mailings, and a membership directory that's updated once a year. Membership is $225 yearly, plus a $100 administration fee for new members.

Above and Beyond Tours (✆ 800/397-2681; www.abovebeyondtours.com) offers gay and lesbian tours worldwide and is the exclusive gay and lesbian tour operator for United Airlines.

Now, Voyager (✆ 800/255-6951; www.nowvoyager.com) is a San Francisco–based gay-owned and -operated travel service.

Olivia Cruises & Resorts (✆ 800/631-6277; www.olivia.com) charters entire resorts and ships for exclusive lesbian vacations and offers smaller group experiences for both gay and lesbian travelers. (In 2005, tennis great Martina Navratilova was named Olivia's official spokesperson.)

Gay.com Travel (✆ 800/929-2268 or 415/644-8044; www.gay.com/travel or www.outandabout.com) is an excellent online successor to the popular ***Out & About*** print magazine.

The following travel guides are available at many bookstores, or you can order them from any online bookseller: ***Spartacus International Gay Guide*** (Bruno Gmünder Verlag; www.spartacusworld.com/gayguide) and ***Odysseus: The International Gay Travel Planner*** (Odysseus Enterprises Ltd.), both good, annual, English-language guidebooks focused on gay men; and the ***Damron*** guides (www.damron.com), with separate, annual books for gay men and lesbians.

TRAVELERS WITH DISABILITIES

Most disabilities shouldn't stop anyone from traveling. There are more options and resources out there today than ever before.

The Americans with Disabilities Act is enforced as strictly in Puerto Rico as it is on the U.S. mainland—in fact, a telling example of the act's enforcement can be found in Ponce, where the sightseeing trolleys are equipped with ramps and extra balustrades to accommodate travelers with disabilities. Unfortunately, hotels rarely give much publicity to the facilities they offer persons with disabilities, so it's always wise to contact the hotel directly, in advance, if you need special facilities. Tourist offices usually have little data about such matters.

You can obtain a free copy of ***Air Transportation of Handicapped Persons,*** published by the U.S. Department of Transportation. Write for *Free Advisory Circular No. AC12032,* Distribution Unit, U.S. Department of Transportation, Publications

Division, 3341Q 75 Ave., Landover, MD 20785. No phone requests are accepted, but you can write for a copy of the publication or download it for free at http://isddc.dot.gov.

The U.S. National Park Service offers a Golden Access Passport that gives free lifetime entrance to U.S. national parks, including those in Puerto Rico, for persons who are blind or have permanent disabilities, regardless of age. You can pick up a Golden Access Passport at any NPS entrance-fee area by showing proof of medically determined disability and eligibility for receiving benefits under federal law. Besides free entry, the Golden Access Passport also offers a 50% discount on federal-use fees charged for such facilities as camping, swimming, parking, boat launching, and tours. For more information, go to www.nps.gov/fees_passes.htm, or call © **888/467-2757.**

Many travel agencies offer customized tours and itineraries for travelers with disabilities. **Flying Wheels Travel** (© **507/451-5005;** www.flyingwheelstravel.com) offers escorted tours and cruises that emphasize sports and private tours in minivans with lifts. **Access-Able Travel Source** (© **303/232-2979;** www.access-able.com) offers extensive access information and advice for traveling around the world with disabilities. **Accessible Journeys** (© **800/846-4537** or 610/521-0339; www.disabilitytravel.com) caters specifically to slow walkers and wheelchair travelers and their families and friends.

Organizations that offer assistance to travelers with disabilities include **MossRehab** (**800/CALL-MOSS** [800/225-5667]; www.mossresourcenet.org), which provides a library of accessible-travel resources online; the **American Foundation for the Blind** (**AFB;** © **800/232-5463** or 212/502-7600; www.afb.org), a referral resource for the blind or visually impaired that includes information on traveling with Seeing Eye dogs; and **SATH** (Society for Accessible Travel & Hospitality; © **212/447-7284;** www.sath.org; annual membership fees: $45 adults, $30 seniors and students), which offers a wealth of travel resources for all types of disabilities and informed recommendations on destinations, access guides, travel agents, tour operators, vehicle rentals, and companion services. **AirAmbulanceCard.com** is now partnered with SATH and allows you to preselect top-notch hospitals, in case of an emergency, for $195 a year ($295 per family), among other benefits.

For more information specifically targeted to travelers with disabilities, the community website **iCan** (www.icanonline.net) has destination guides and several regular columns on accessible travel. Also check out the quarterly magazine ***Emerging Horizons*** (www.emerginghorizons.com; $14.95 per year, $19.95 outside the U.S.); and ***Open World*** magazine, published by SATH (see above; subscription: $13 per year, $21 outside the U.S.).

A tip for British travelers: The **Royal Association for Disability and Rehabilitation (RADAR),** Unit 12, City Forum, 250 City Rd., London, EC1V 8AF (© **020/7250-3222;** fax 020/7250-0212; www.radar.org.uk), publishes information for travelers with disabilities.

FAMILY TRAVEL

Puerto Rico is an extremely family-friendly travel destination. Nearly all resorts court parents traveling with children as guests. In only a few cases did my own family find that not true of restaurants and lodgings, and I've pointed those out. To locate accommodations, restaurants, and attractions that are particularly kid-friendly, look for the "Kids" icon throughout this guide.

SENIOR TRAVEL

Mention the fact that you're a senior when you first make your travel reservations. All major airlines and many Puerto Rican hotels offer discounts for seniors.

Though much of the island's sporting and nightlife activity is geared toward youthful travelers, Puerto Rico also has much to offer the senior. The best source of information for seniors is the Puerto Rico Tourism Company (see "Year-Round Festivals," earlier), or, if you're staying in a large resort hotel, talk to the activities director or the concierge.

Members of **AARP,** 601 E St. NW, Washington, DC 20049 (✆ **888/687-2277** or 202/434-2277; www.aarp.org), get discounts on hotels, airfares, and car rentals. AARP offers members a wide range of benefits, including *AARP The Magazine* and a monthly newsletter. Anyone 50 or older can join.

The **U.S. National Park Service** offers a **Golden Age Passport** that gives seniors 62 years or older lifetime entrance to U.S. national parks for a one-time processing fee of $10. The pass must be purchased in person at any NPS facility that charges an entrance fee. Besides free entry, a Golden Age Passport also offers a 50% discount on federal-use fees charged for such facilities as camping, swimming, parking, boat launching, and tours. For more information, click onto www.nps.gov, or call ✆ **888/467-2757.**

Grand Circle Travel (✆ **800/221-2610** or 617/350-7500; fax 617/346-6700; www.gct.com) offers package deals for the 50-plus market, mostly of the tour-bus variety, with free trips thrown in for those who organize groups of 10 or more.

SAGA Holidays (✆ **800/343-0273;** http://travel.saga.co.uk/holidays.aspx) offers tours and cruises for those 50 and older. SAGA also offers a number of single-traveler tours.

Recommended publications offering travel resources and discounts for seniors include: the quarterly magazine ***Travel 50 & Beyond*** (www.travel50andbeyond.com); ***Travel Unlimited: Uncommon Adventures for the Mature Traveler*** (Avalon); ***101 Tips for Mature Travelers,*** available from Grand Circle Travel (✆ **800/221-2610** or 800/959-0405; www.gct.com); and ***Unbelievably Good Deals and Great Adventures That You Absolutely Can't Get Unless You're Over 50*** (McGraw-Hill), by Joan Rattner Heilman.

SPECIAL-INTEREST & ESCORTED TRIPS

The Active Vacation Planner

There are watersports opportunities throughout Puerto Rico, from San Juan's waterfront hotels to eastern resorts and the offshore islands of Vieques and Culebra all the way to the Rincón on the west coast and Cabo Rojo in the south.

Boating & Sailing

The waters off Puerto Rico provide excellent boating in all seasons. Winds average 10 to 15 knots virtually year-round. Marinas provide facilities and services on par with any others in the Caribbean, and many have powerboats or sailboats for rent, either crewed or bareboat charter.

Beach Warning

In San Juan, don't go walking along the beaches at night, even as tempting as it may be to do with your lover. On unguarded beaches, you will have no way to protect yourself or your valuables should you be approached by a robber or mugger, which can happen. The exceptions may be the beaches in front of Barbosa Park in Ocean Park and Parque del Indio in Condado, which are lit up at night and draw many evening visitors. Beaches on the island, especially in vacation towns such as Vieques and Culebra, Boquerón and Isabela, are genuinely safer, but it's still a good idea not to stray too far off the beaten path.

Puerto Rico is ringed by marinas. In San Juan alone, there are three large ones. The upscale **Club Nautico de San Juan** (✆ **787/722-0177**) and neighboring **San Juan Bay Marina** (✆ **787/721-8062**) are adjacent to the Condado bridge and the Convention Center district in Miramar. The other marina, the **Cangrejos Yacht Club** (Rte. 187, Piñones; ✆ **787/791-1015**), is near the airport, outside Isla Verde at the entrance to Piñones.

All three have several sailing charters and dive and fishing operators.

Fajardo, on Puerto Rico's northeast corner, boasts seven marinas, including the Caribbean's largest, the **Puerto del Rey Marina** (Rte. 3 Km 51.4; ✆ **787/860-1000** or 787/801-3010), and the popular **Villa Marina Yacht Harbour** (Rte. 987 Km 1.3; ✆ **787/863-5131** or 787/863-5011), offering the shortest ride to the best snorkeling grounds and offshore beaches. Other town marinas include **Puerto Chico** (Rte. 987 Km 2.4; ✆ **787/863-0834**) and **Puerto Real** (Playa Puerto Real; ✆ **787/863-2188**).

Along the south coast, one of the most established and charming marinas is the **Ponce Yacht & Fishing Club** (La Guancha, Ponce; ✆ **787/842-9003**).

But marinas, both small and large, can be found throughout island coasts. Check local listings for a "Club Nautico." Those with pleasure crafts, sailing, and water-sports offerings catering to tourists include **Club Nautico de Boquerón** (✆ **787/851-1336**) and **Club Nautico de La Parguera** (✆ **787/899-5590**), which are each located just outside their respective village centers.

Several sailing and ocean racing regattas are held in Puerto Rico annually. The east of Puerto Rico and the southwest are particularly attractive for sailors. Fajardo is the start of a series of ports, extending from Puerto Rico's own offshore islands through the U.S. and British Virgin Islands to the east, which is probably the Caribbean's top sailing destination.

The easiest way to experience the joys of sailing is to go out on a day trip leaving from one of the Fajardo marinas (with transportation from San Juan hotels often included). The trips usually take place on large luxury catamarans or sailing yachts, with a bar serving drinks and refreshments, a sound system, and other creature comforts. Typically, after a nice sail, the vessel weighs anchor at a good snorkeling spot, then makes a stop on one of the beautiful sand beaches on the small islands off the Fajardo coast. Operators include **Traveler Sailing Catamaran** (✆ 787/853-2821), **East Island Excursions** (✆ 787/860-3434), **Catamaran Spread Eagle** (✆ 787/887-8821), and **Erin Go Bragh Charters** (✆ 787/860-4401).

Also on the east coast is **Karolette Charter,** Palmas del Mar, AB-12 St., Rte. 3, Km 86.4, Humacao (✆ **787/850-7442**), which offers snorkeling trips for $107 per person, or charters for $640 for 4½ hours or $840 for 6 hours.

Out west, **Katarina Sail Charters** (✆ **787/823-SAIL** [7245]) in Rincón gives daily sailing trips aboard a 32-foot (9.8m) catamaran; there are both a day sail and a sunset sail.

For the typical visitor interested in watersports—not the serious yachter—our favorite place for fun in the surf is the aptly named **San Juan Water Fun** on Isla Verde Beach in back of the Wyndham El San Juan Hotel & Casino, Avenida Isla Verde in Isla Verde, San Juan (✆ **787/644-2585** or 787/643-4510). Here you can rent everything from a two-seater kayak for $30 per hour to a banana boat that holds eight passengers and costs $15 per person for a 20-minute ride.

If you're staying in eastern Puerto Rico, the best place for watersports rentals is the **water sports center** at Rio Mar Beach Resort, 6000 Rio Mar Blvd., Rio Grande (✆ **787/888-6000**), which scuba and snorkeling trips, and a great selection of small boats. WaveRunners cost about $100 per hour, and two-seat kayaks go for $35 per hour.

In the southwest, **Pino's Boat & Water Fun** (✆ **787/821-6864** or 787/484-8083) at Guánica's Playa Santa has everything from paddle boats or kayaks to water scooters for rent.

Camping

Puerto Rico abounds in remote sandy beaches, lush tropical forests, and mountain lakesides that make for fine camping.

Although it has been technically illegal to camp on beaches (except in designated areas) for the last decade, it is commonly done in off-the-beaten path coastal areas, especially in Guánica, Isabela, Fajardo, and the offshore islands of Vieques and Culebra.

Also, there are more than enough campgrounds available in coastal areas, as well as in the mountains and local state forests and nature reserves.

Some of the nicest campgrounds, as well as the best equipped and safest, are those run by the government **Compañia de Parques Nacionales** (www.parquesnacionalespr.com, Av. Fernández Juncos 1611, Santurce; ✆ **787/622-5200**).

Six of the eight campsites it operates are located on the coast—at Luquillo, Fajardo, Vieques, Arroyo, Añasco, and Vega Baja. It also runs two fine campgrounds in the mountain town of Maricao and in Camuy's Cave Park.

Some of these are simple places where you erect your own tent, although they are outfitted with electricity and running water; some are simple cabins, sometimes with fireplaces. Showers and bathrooms are communal. To stay at a campsite costs between $15 and $25 per night per tent.

Many sites offer very basic cabins for rent. Each cabin is equipped with a full bathroom, a stove, a refrigerator, two beds, and a table and chairs. However, most of your cooking will probably be tastier if you do it outside at one of the on-site barbecues. In nearly all cases, you must provide your own sheets and towels.

The agency, the National Parks Company, in English, also operates more upscale "vacation centers," which feature rustic cabins and more tourist-ready "villas," on par with many island inns.

State forests run by the **Departamento de Recursos Naturales y Ambientales** also allow camping with permits. Except for cabins at Monte Guilarte State Forest, which cost $20 per night, camping sites are available at $5 per person. For further information about permits, contact the DRNA at (Rte. 8838, Km 6.3, Sector El Cinco, Río Piedras; © **787/999-2200**).

There are seven major on-island camping sites in the following state forests: **Cambalache State Forest,** near Barceloneta; **Carite State Forest,** near Patillas; **Guajataca State Forest,** near Quebradillas; **Monte Guilarte State Forest,** near Adjuntas; **Susua State Forest,** near Yauco; **Río Abajo State Forest,** near Arecibo; and our favorite, **Toro Negro Forest Reserve,** near Villaba, where you can camp in the shadow of Puerto Rico's highest peaks.

It's also possible to camp at either of two wildlife refuges, **Isla de Mona Wildlife Refuge,** lying some 50 miles (80km) off the west coast of Puerto Rico surrounded by the rough seas of Mona Passage, and at **Lago Lucchetti Wildlife Refuge,** a beautiful mountain reservoir between Yauco and Ponce.

Meanwhile, visitors can also camp at **El Yunque National Forest** (© **787/888-1810**), which is under the jurisdiction of the U.S. Forest Service. There is no cost, but permits are required. They can be obtained in person at the Catalina Service Center (Rte. 191, Km 4.3) daily from 8am to 4:30pm, and weekends at the Palo Colorado Visitor Center (Rte. 191, Km 11.9) from 9:30am to 4pm. It's primitive camping within the rainforest.

Deep-Sea Fishing

While fishing is good year round, the winter season from October to early March is among the best. Blue marlin can be caught all summer and into the fall, and renowned big game fish tournaments take place in August and September.

Charters are available at marinas in major cities and tourism areas. Most boats range between 32 and 50 feet; fit six passengers; can be chartered for half- or full-day; and usually include bait, crew, and equipment.

Big game fish are found close to shore across Puerto Rico, so you won't waste time traveling to fishing spots. A mile off the San Juan coast, the ocean floor drops 600 feet (183m), and the awesome Puerto Rico Trench, a 500-mile-long (805km) fault that plunges to a depth of 28,000 feet (8354m), lies about 75 miles (121km) directly north. It's a 20-minute ride to where the big game fish are biting, so it's possible to leave in the morning, make the catch of the day, and be back at the marina in the early afternoon.

Deep-sea fishing is top-notch throughout the island. Allison tuna, white and blue marlin, sailfish, wahoo, dolphinfish (mahimahi), mackerel, and tarpon are some of the fish that can be caught in Puerto Rican waters, where 30 world records have been broken. Charter arrangements can be made through most major hotels and resorts and at most marinas. The big game fishing grounds are very close offshore from San Juan, making the capital an excellent place to hire a charter. A half-day of deep-sea fishing (4 hours) starts at around $550, while full-day charters begin at around $900. Most charters hold six passengers in addition to the crew.

In San Juan, experienced operators include Capt. Mike Benítez at **Benítez Fishing Charters** (© **787/723-2292**), as well as **Castillo Fishing Charters** (© **787/726-5752**), which has been running charters out of **Caribbean Outfitters** (© **787/396-8346**).

Rincón also has a number of deep-sea fishing charters, such as **Makaira Fishing Charters** (✆ **787/823-4391** or 787/299-7374) and **Moondog Charters** (✆ **787/823-3059**).

In Palmas del Mar, which has some of the best year-round fishing in the Caribbean, you'll find **Capt. Bill Burleson** (see "Palmas del Mar," in chapter 10).

Golf

With nearly 30 golf courses, including several championship links, Puerto Rico is rightly called the "Scotland," or the "golf capital," of the Caribbean, especially because they have been designed by the likes of Robert Trent Jones, his son Rees Jones, Greg Norman, George and Tom Fazio, Jack Nicklaus, Arthur Hills, and Puerto Rico's own Chi Chi Rodriguez.

Many of the courses are jewels of landscape architecture, running through verdant tropical forest and former coconut groves, or winding in dramatic switchbacks aside a breathtaking stretch of coast. Year-round summer weather and mostly gentle breezes add to the joy of playing here.

The bad news is it's often quite expensive to tee off in Puerto Rico, with prices starting at $120 and ranging up to nearly $200.

There are some bargains, however, particularly the **Berwind Country Club** (✆ **787/876-5380**) in **Loiza** (the closet course to San Juan) and the **Punta Borinquén Golf Club,** Rte. 107 (✆ **787/890-2987**), 2 miles (3.2km) north of Aquadilla's center. Berwind is the closest to San Juan, in a breathtaking setting on a former coconut plantation, while the Aguadilla course struts across a beautiful patch of coast.

The legendary Dorado courses are 35 minutes west of San Juan at the **Dorado Beach Resort & Club** (✆ **787/796-8961**), the scene of world championships and legendarily difficult holes, making it among the most challenging in the Caribbean still. Jack Nicklaus rates the challenging 13th hole at the Dorado as one of the top 10 in the world. See chapter 7 for more details.

Río Grande, however, is becoming as important a center for golf as Dorado. The **Wyndham Río Mar Beach Resort** golf offerings (✆ **787/888-7060**) have world-class rainforest and coastal courses, designed, respectively, by Greg Norman and Tom and George Fazio. **The Trump International Golf Club** (✆ **787/657-2000**) is actually four different 9-hole courses sprawled out across 1,200 acres (486 hectares) of coast. Each course is named after its surrounding environment: the Ocean, the Palms, the Mountains, and the Lakes. Also in town is the **Bahia Beach** course (✆ **787/957-5800**), recently renovated as part of a new St. Regis resort development.

Also, on the east coast, crack golfers consider holes 11 through 15 at the **Golf Club at Palmas del Mar** (p. 271) to be the toughest 5 successive holes in the Caribbean. At **El Conquistador Resort & Golden Door Spa** (p. 267), the spectacular $250-million resort at Las Croabas, east of San Juan, you play along 200-foot (61m) changes in elevation that provide panoramic vistas.

There are now golf courses along the south coast, in Coamo and Ponce, as well as the southwest in Cabo Rojo. These are a needed complement to the north-coast courses. The **Costa Caribe Golf & Country Club** (✆ **787/848-1000** or 787/812-2650), on the site of the Hilton Ponce Golf & Casino (see chapter 8), commands views of the ocean and mountains, while the **Club Deportivo del Oeste,** Hwy. 102, Km 15.4, Barrio Jogudas, Cabo Rojo (© **787/851-8880** or 787/254-3748), is more no-frills.

Hiking

The mountainous interior of Puerto Rico provides ample opportunities for hill climbing and nature treks. These are especially appealing because panoramas open at the least-expected moments, often revealing spectacular views of the distant sea.

The most popular, most beautiful, and most spectacular trekking spot is **El Yunque,** the sprawling "jungle" maintained by the U.S. Forest Service and the only rainforest on U.S. soil.

El Yunque is part of the **Caribbean National Forest,** which lies a 45-minute drive east of San Juan. More than 250 species of trees and some 200 types of ferns have been identified here. Some 60 species of birds inhabit El Yunque, including the increasingly rare Puerto Rican parrot. Such rare birds as the elfin woods warbler, the green mango hummingbird, and the Puerto Rican lizard-cuckoo live here.

Park rangers have clearly marked the trails that are ideal for walking. See "El Yunque," in chapter 7, for more details.

A lesser forest, but one that is still intriguing to visit, is the **Maricao State Forest,** near the coffee town of Maricao. This forest is in western Puerto Rico, east of the town of Mayagüez. For more details, see "Mayagüez," in chapter 9.

Ponce is the best center for exploring some of the greatest forest reserves in the Caribbean Basin, notably **Toro Negro Forest Reserve** with its **Lake Guineo** (the lake at the highest elevation on the island); the **Guánica State Forest,** ideal for hiking and bird-watching; and the **Carite Forest Reserve,** a 6,000-acre (2,428-hectare) park known for its dwarf forest. For more details, see "Ponce," in chapter 8.

Equally suitable for hiking are the protected lands (especially the **Río Camuy Cave Park**), whose topography is characterized as "karst"—that is, limestone riddled with caves, underground rivers, and natural crevasses and fissures. Although these regions pose additional risks and technical problems for trekkers, some people prefer the opportunities they provide for exploring the territory both above and below its surface. See "Arecibo & Camuy," in chapter 7, for details about the Río Camuy Caves.

Outdoor Adventure

If you'd like to experience Puerto Rico on horseback, **Hacienda Caribalí** (© **787/889-5829** or 787/690-3781; www.haciendacaribalipuertorico.com) offers 2-hour tours on majestic Paso Fino horses that take riders along the Mamayes River in the shadow of El Yunque rainforest for $60. The 600-acre ranch also offers four-track and mountain bike tours, and has a go-kart track. **Tropical Trail Rides** (© **787/872-9256;** www.tropicaltrailrides.com) gives beach tours on Paso Fino horses at a beautiful locale in Isabela, which also has cavernous cliffs and tropical forests, as well as at the 2,200 acre Hacienda Campo Rico in Carolina, in the San Juan metropolitan area. There are a number of tours, including a sunset ride, but most last 2 hours. Prices start at $40.

Several other tour operators cater to special tastes, including **Castillo Tours & Travel Service,** 2413 Laurel St., Punta Las Marias, Santurce (© **787/791-6195;** www.castillotours.com), which is known for some of the best deep-sea fishing, rainforest, and catamaran tours.

AdvenTours, Luquillo (✆ **787/530-8311;** www.adventourspr.com), features customized private tours that include such activities as bird-watching, hiking, camping, visits to coffee plantations, and kayaking.

Eco Xcursion Aquatica, Rte. 191, Km 1.7, Rio Grande, Fajardo (✆ **787/888-2887**), offers some of the best rainforest hikes and mountain-bike tours, both for individuals and groups. They also offer kayak tours to one of several **Bioluminescent Bays ★★** in Fajardo, where you enter the water at dusk and paddle through calm water teeming with small marine organisms that respond to the slightest touch by glowing an eerie greenish yellow. **Las Tortugas Adventures,** P.O. Box 1637, Canóvanas (✆ **787/809-0253** or 787/637-8356; www.kayak-pr.com), also runs tours to Fajardo's biobay, as well as river tours of the rainforest and Piñones wetlands, and kayaking/snorkeling trips to deserted beaches, rimmed with reefs and teeming schools of tropical fish. **Aventuras Tierra Adentro** (✆ **787/766-0470;** www.aventuraspr.com) offers the best island adventure tours, focusing on hiking through virgin forests, rock climbing, or cliff jumping. Four different adventures are offered, costing $150 to $170 per person, which includes transportation from San Juan. Most of the jaunts take place on weekends.

Scuba Diving & Snorkeling

SCUBA DIVING The continental shelf, which surrounds Puerto Rico on three sides, is responsible for an abundance of coral reefs, caves, sea walls, and trenches for scuba diving and snorkeling.

Open-water reefs off the southeastern coast near **Humacao** are visited by migrating whales and manatees. Many caves are located near Isabela on the west coast. A large canyon off the island's south coast is ideal for experienced open-water divers. Caves and the sea wall at **La Parguera** are also favorites. **Vieques** and **Culebra islands** have coral formations. **Mona Island** offers unspoiled reefs at depths averaging 80 feet (24m), with an amazing array of sea life. Uninhabited islands, such as **Icacos,** off the northeastern coast near Fajardo, are also popular with snorkelers and divers alike.

These sites are now within reach, because many of Puerto Rico's dive operators and resorts offer packages that include daily or twice-daily dives, scuba equipment, instruction, and excursions to Puerto Rico's popular attractions.

Introductory courses for beginners start at $125, and two-tank dives for experienced divers begin at around $85, but most cost at least $125.

In San Juan, try **Caribe Aquatic Adventures,** Normandie Hotel San Juan, Calle 19 1062, Villa Nevarez (✆ **787/281-8858**), or **Ocean Sports** (Av. Isla Verde 77; ✆ **787/268-2329**).

Diving off the east, southwest, or northwest coasts is more rewarding, however.

In Rincón, there's **Taíno Divers,** Black Eagle Marina at Rincón (✆ **787/823-6429**), which offers trips to the waters surrounding Desecheo Island natural reserve.

The ocean wall in the southwest is famous, with visibility ranging from 100 to 120 feet (30–37m) and reefs filled with abundant sea life. **Paradise Scuba Center,** Hotel Casa Blanca Building, at La Parguera (✆ **787/899-7611**), and **Mona Aquatics,** Calle José de Diego, Boquerón (✆ **787/851-2185**), are two good operators in the area.

In Guánica, there's **Sea Venture Dive Copamarina** (✆ **787/821-0505,** ext. 729), part of the Copamarina Beach Resort.

The **Dive Center** at the Wyndham Rio Mar Beach Resort (✆ **787/888-6000**) is one of the largest in Puerto Rico.

(See "Diving, Fishing, Tennis & Other Outdoor Pursuits," in chapter 6, for more details.)

Elsewhere on the island, several other companies offer scuba and snorkeling instruction. We provide details in each chapter.

SNORKELING Because of its overpopulation, the waters around San Juan aren't the most ideal for snorkeling. In fact, the entire north shore of Puerto Rico fronts the Atlantic, where the waters are often turbulent.

Yet there are some protected areas along the north coast that make for fine snorkeling, even in surf capitals such as Rincón and Aguadilla. Many of the best surfing beaches in winter turn into a snorkeler's paradise in summer when the waves calm down.

The most ideal conditions for snorkeling in Puerto Rico are along the shores of the remote islands of **Vieques** and **Culebra** (see chapter 11).

The best snorkeling on the main island is found near the town of **Fajardo,** to the east of San Juan and along the tranquil eastern coast (see chapter 10).

The calm, glasslike quality of the clear Caribbean along the south shore is also ideal for snorkeling. The most developed tourist mecca here is the city of Ponce. Few rivers empty their muddy waters into the sea along the south coast, resulting in gin-clear waters offshore. You can snorkel off the coast without having to go on a boat trip. One good place is at **Playa La Parguera,** where you can rent snorkeling equipment from kiosks along the beach. This beach lies east of the town of Guánica, to the east of Ponce. Here tropical fish add to the brightness of the water, which is generally turquoise. The addition of mangrove cays in the area also makes La Parguera more alluring for snorkelers. Another good spot for snorkelers is **Caja de Muertos** off the coast of Ponce. Here a lagoon coral reef boasts a large number of fish species (see chapter 8).

Even if you are staying in San Juan and want to go snorkeling, you are better off taking a day trip to Fajardo, where you'll get a real Caribbean snorkeling experience, with tranquil, clear water and stunning reefs teaming with tropical fish. Several operators offer day trips (10am–3:30pm) leaving from Fajardo marinas, but transportation to and from your San Juan hotel can also be arranged. Prices start at around $99 (see "Boating & Sailing," earlier in this chapter).

Surfing

Puerto Rico's northwest beaches attract surfers from around the world. Called the "Hawaii of the East," Puerto Rico has hosted a number of international competitions. October through February are the best surfing months, but the sport is enjoyed in Puerto Rico from August through April. The most popular areas are from Isabela to Rincón—at beaches such as Wilderness, Middles, Jobos, Crashboat, Las Marías, and the Spanish Wall.

There are surf spots across the entire north coast from San Juan to the northwest, including Los Tubos in Vega Baja.

San Juan itself has great surfing spots, including La 8, just outside of Old San Juan in Puerta de Tierra, near Escambrón Beach, which has some of the largest waves. Pine Grove in Isla Verde is a great spot to learn, because of the small, steady, well-formed waves there.

International competitions held in Puerto Rico have included the 1968 and 1988 World Amateur Surfing Championships and the annual Caribbean Cup Surfing Championship. Currently, Corona sponsors an annual competition circuit taking place in Isabela and Rincón.

If you want to learn to surf, or perfect your technique while in Puerto Rico, it's quite easy.

Operating right near the Ritz-Carlton and Courtyard Marriott hotels in Isla Verde, the best surf lessons are given by professional surfer William Sue-A-Quan at his **Walking on Water Surfing School** (✆ **787/955-6059;** www.gosurfpr.com). He and a few associates work right on the beach at Pine Grove and also offer lessons through the Ritz-Carlton. He's a great teacher, and takes on students as young as 5 and as old as 75.

Rincón also has many surf schools, some of which book packages including lodgings.

The Rincón Surf School (P.O. Box 1333, Rincón; ✆ **787/823-0610**) offers beginners lessons and weeklong packages. **Puntas Surf School** (P.O. Box 4319, HC-01 Calle Vista del Mar; ✆ **787/823-3618** or 207/251-1154) is another good option, run by Melissa Taylor and Bill Woodward.

Group lessons (for four) start at $35 per hour; private $45.

Board rentals are available at many island surf shops, with prices starting at $25 a day. We list them in subsequent chapters.

Windsurfing

The best windsurfing is found at Punta Las Marias in the Greater San Juan metropolitan area. Other spots on the island for windsurfing include Santa Isabel, Guánica, and La Parguera in the south; Jobos and Shacks in the northwest; and the island of Culebra off the eastern coast.

Kite-boarding is becoming increasingly popular as well. Watch them fly through the choppy waters off Ocean Park in San Juan.

Lessons, advice, and equipment rental is available at **Velauno,** Calle Loíza 2430, Punta Las Marias in San Juan (✆ **787/728-8716**).

Package Deals for the Independent Traveler

Before you start your search for the lowest airfare, you might want to consider booking your flight as part of a travel package such as an escorted tour or a package tour. What you lose in adventure, you'll gain in time and money saved when you book accommodations, and maybe even food and entertainment, along with your flight.

One good source of package deals is the airlines themselves. Also consult **Vacation Together** (✆ **877/444-4547;** www.vacationtogether.com), which allows you to search for and book packages offered by a number of tour operators and airlines. The **United States Tour Operators Association**'s website (www.ustoa.com) has a search engine that allows you to look for operators that offer packages to a specific destination.

Travel packages are also listed on major Internet travel sites and in the travel section of the local Sunday newspaper. **Liberty Travel** (✆ **888/271-1584;** www.libertytravel.com), one of the biggest packagers in the Northeast, is a bigger advertiser in print and other media, but it's website typically has at least a half dozen deals to the island at any given time.

TourScan Caribbean Vacations (✆ **800/962-2080;** www.tourscan.com) finds the best deals from the 10,000 vacation offers its Caribbean travel experts analyze. You can see some results online.

Food & Wine Trips

There is no organized culinary trip per se, but you could choose to visit during one of the annual food festivals such as **Old San Juan SoFo Culinary Fest** (in June; visit www.tastecuisine.net), when restaurants on and near South Fortaleza Street open up their doors for sampling; or **Saborea** (in early April; visit www.saborea puertorico.com), a culinary party of restaurant booths and Food Network chef demos set up along Escambrón Beach.

Also see p. 166 for our listing of the **Flavors of San Juan** noshing tour in Old San Juan (✆ **787/964-2447**; www.flavorsofsanjuan.com).

Escorted General-Interest Tours

An escorted tour is a structured group tour with a group leader. The price usually includes everything from airfare to hotel, meals, tours, admission costs, and local transportation.

Puerto Rico Tours, Condo Inter-Suite, Ste. 5M, on Isla Verde in San Juan (✆ **787/306-1540** or 787/791-5479; www.puertorico-tours.com), offers specially conducted private sightseeing tours of Puerto Rico, including trips to the rainforest, Luquillo Beach, the caves of Camuy, and other attractions, such as a restored Taíno Indian village.

Backstage Partners (✆ **787/791-0099;** www.backstagepartners.com) offers customized tours that take in a wide range of island attractions, including eco-tours, deep-sea fishing, scuba diving and snorkeling, safaris, and golf packages.

Other leading escorted tour operators include **Atlantic San Juan Tours** (✆ **787/644-9841;** www.puertoricoexcursions.com), which helps you take in all the major sights of the island from Ponce to El Yunque; and **Sunshine Tours** (✆ **866/785-3636;** www.puerto-rico-sunshinetours.com), which covers much the same ground as the others. **Legends of Puerto Rico** (✆ **787/605-9060;** www.legendsofpr.com) hosts personalized tours, specializing in entertaining cultural and nature adventure tours.

STAYING CONNECTED

Mobile Phones

Major carriers with a presence in the U.S, market, such as AT&T, Sprint, and T-Mobile, also battle it out in the island's competitive wireless market. Prices are low, and coverage is very good, even out at sea. Each carrier maintains a network and all are investing in network upgrades, with AT&T out front in the race for a 4-G network, and all are GSM networks.

Check with your carrier to see if Puerto Rico is included in national calling plans, which usually offer unlimited calling and roaming. Puerto Rico subscribers of all major carriers have the option of enrolling in a national calling plan that includes calls and free roaming to the United States mainland.

Calls can also be placed through Skype and other VoIP services via the Internet.

If your company screws you, cellular telephones can be purchased at RadioShack, Walgreens, and other stores listed throughout the guide. They come loaded with minutes and can be used on the spot and cost as little as $35. Refill cards are sold everywhere, from major grocery stores to gas stations.

Internet & E-Mail

Free Wi-Fi connections are widely available, from Old San Juan's Plaza de Armas, to Starbucks to local Burger King and McDonald's outlets throughout the island.

Many hotels and guesthouses also have public computers for use by guests, and there are Internet cafes throughout the city (such as the Cybernet Café, www.cybernetcafepr.com, with locations at Av. Isla Verde 5980, Isla Verde, and Av. Ashford 1128, Condado). Public libraries also have Internet areas.

If you have a laptop, free Wi-Fi spots abound at shopping centers, hotels, and restaurants.

Newspapers & Magazines

Caribbean Business (www.caribbeanbusinesspr.com) is a weekly business newspaper that has the most up-to-date news on Puerto Rico in English.

The *San Juan Star,* a daily English-language newspaper, closed abruptly in the summer of 2008, just over its 50th birthday. A worker's collective of former *Star* employees puts out the ***Puerto Rico Daily Sun*** (www.prdailysun.net).

USA Today sells a local edition of its newspaper, with two pages of local and tourism news. If you read Spanish, you might enjoy ***El Nuevo Día,*** the most popular local tabloid. There is also ***El Vocero*** and ***Primera Hora.*** Few significant magazines are published on Puerto Rico, but ***Time*** and ***Newsweek*** are available at most newsstands.

Telephones

Many convenience, grocery, and retail postal service stores sell **prepaid calling cards** in denominations up to $50. Many public pay phones at airports now accept American Express, MasterCard, and Visa. **Local calls** made from most pay phones cost either 25¢ or 35¢. Most long-distance and international calls can be dialed directly from any phone. **To make calls within the United States and to Canada,** dial 1 followed by the area code and the seven-digit number. **For other international calls,** dial 011 followed by the country code, city code, and the number you are calling.

Calls to area codes **800, 888, 877,** and **866** are toll-free. However, calls to area codes **700** and **900** (chat lines, bulletin boards, "dating" services, and so on) can be expensive—charges of 95¢ to $3 or more per minute. Some numbers have minimum charges that can run $15 or more.

For **reversed-charge or collect calls,** and for person-to-person calls, dial the number 0 then the area code and number; an operator will come on the line, and you should specify whether you are calling collect, person-to-person, or both. If your operator-assisted call is international, ask for the overseas operator.

For **directory assistance** (Information), dial 411 for local numbers and national numbers in the U.S. and Canada. For dedicated long-distance information, dial 1, then the appropriate area code plus 555-1212.

TIPS ON ACCOMMODATIONS

Hotels & Resorts

There is no rigid classification of Puerto Rican hotels. The word "deluxe" is often used—or misused—when "first class" might be a more appropriate term. We've presented fairly detailed descriptions of the hotels in this book, so you'll get an idea of what to expect once you're there.

Puerto Rico has had a bum rap for bad service, but our experience is that service in hotels and restaurants has been on a dramatic upswing over the last decade. There is still the slow tropical pace, what folks mean when they talk about "island time," however.

Ask detailed questions when booking a room. Entertainment in Puerto Rico is often alfresco, so light sleepers obviously won't want a room directly over a band. In general, back rooms cost less than oceanfront rooms, and lower rooms cost less than upper-floor units. Always ascertain whether transfers (which can be expensive) are included. And make sure that you know exactly what is free and what costs money. Some resorts seem to charge every time you breathe and might end up costing more than a deluxe hotel that includes most everything in the price.

Also factor in transportation costs, which can mount quickly if you stay 5 days to a week. If you want to go to the beach every day, it might be wise to book a hotel on the Condado and not stay in romantic Old San Juan, from which you'll spend a lot of time and money transferring back and forth between your hotel and the beach.

Most hotels in Puerto Rico are on the windward side of the island, with lots of waves, undertow, and surf. If a glasslike smooth sea is imperative for your stay, you can book on the leeward (eastern shore) or Caribbean (southeast coast) sides, which are better for snorkeling. The major centers in these areas are the resort complex of Palmas del Mar and the "second city" of Ponce.

MAP VS. AP, OR DO YOU WANT CP OR EP?

All resorts offer a **European Plan (EP)** rate, which means you pay for the price of a room. That leaves you free to dine around at night at various other resorts or restaurants without restriction. Another plan preferred by many is the **Continental Plan (CP),** which means you get your room and a continental breakfast of juice, coffee, bread, jam, and so on, included in a set price. This plan is preferred by many because most guests don't like to "dine around" at breakfast time.

Another major option is the **Modified American Plan (MAP),** which includes breakfast and one main meal of the day, either lunch or dinner. The final choice is the **American Plan (AP),** which includes breakfast, lunch, and dinner.

At certain resorts you will save money by booking either the MAP or AP because discounts are granted. If you dine a la carte for lunch and dinner at various restaurants, your final dining bill will no doubt be much higher than if you stayed on the MAP or AP.

These plans might save you money, but if, as part of your holiday, you like to eat in various places, you might be disappointed. You face the same dining room every night, unless the resort you're staying at has many different restaurants on the dining plan. Often they don't. Many resorts have a lot of specialty restaurants, serving, say, Japanese cuisine, but these more expensive restaurants are not included in MAP or

AP; rather, they charge a la carte prices. One option is to ask if your hotel has a dine-around plan.

Puerto Rican Guesthouses

A unique type of accommodation is the guesthouse, where Puerto Ricans themselves usually stay when they travel. Ranging in size from 7 to 25 rooms, they offer a familial atmosphere. Many are on or near the beach; some have pools or sun decks, and a number serve meals.

In Puerto Rico, however, the term "guesthouse" has many meanings. Some guesthouses are like simple motels built around pools. Others have small individual cottages with their own kitchenettes, constructed around a main building in which you'll often find a bar and a restaurant serving local food. Some are surprisingly comfortable, often with private bathrooms and swimming pools. You may or may not have air-conditioning. The rooms are sometimes cooled by ceiling fans or by the trade winds blowing through open windows at night.

For value, the guesthouse can't be topped. If you stay at a guesthouse, you can journey over to a big beach resort and use its seaside facilities for only a small fee. Although bereft of frills, the guesthouses we've recommended are clean and safe for families or single women. However, the cheapest ones are not places where you'd want to spend a lot of time because of their modest furnishings.

For further information on guesthouses, contact the **Puerto Rico Tourism Company** (✆ **800/866-7827** or 787/721-2400), La Princesa Building, Paseo La Princesa 2, Old San Juan, PR 00902.

Paradores

In an effort to lure travelers beyond the hotels and casinos of San Juan's historic district to the tranquil natural beauty of the island's countryside, the Puerto Rico Tourism Company offers ***paradores puertorriqueños*** (charming country inns), which are comfortable bases for exploring the island's varied attractions. Vacationers seeking a peaceful idyll can also choose from several privately owned and operated guesthouses.

Using Spain's parador system as a model, the Puerto Rico Tourism Company established the paradores in 1973 to encourage tourism across the island. Each of the paradores is situated in a historic place or site of unusual scenic beauty and must meet high standards of service and cleanliness. Some of the paradores are located in the mountains and others by the sea. Most have pools, and all offer excellent Puerto Rican cuisine. Many are within easy driving distance of San Juan.

Properties must meet certain benchmark standards of quality to be admitted to the program, so tourists feel comfortable staying at the property. One complaint about the program is that variances in quality still range widely from one property to the next. For more information, call ✆ **800/866-7827** or check out www.goto paradores.com.

Some of the best paradores are in western Puerto Rico (see chapter 9). The Tourism Company also operates a similar program which promotes worthy local restaurants called **Mesones Gastronómicos** (✆ **800/981-7575**).

Villas & Vacation Homes

There are also excellent vacation homes in resort communities such as Rincón and Vieques. For luxurious Old San Juan apartment rentals, check **Vida Urbana,** Calle Cruz 255, Old San Juan, PR 00901 (✆ **787/587-3031;** www.vidaurbanapr.com). Two short-term specialists in Condado and Isla Verde are **San Juan Vacations,** Cond. Marbella del Caribe, Ste. S-5, Isla Verde 00979 (✆ **800/266-3639** or 787/727-1591; www.sanjuanvacations.com), and **Ronnie's Properties,** Calle Marseilles 14, Ritz Condominium, Ste. 11-F, San Juan, PR 00907 (www.ronniesproperties.com).

Private apartments are rented either with or without maid service. This is more of a no-frills option than the villas and condos. An apartment might not be in a building with a swimming pool, and it might not have a front desk to help you. Among the major categories of vacation homes, cottages offer the most freewheeling way to live. Most cottages are fairly simple, many opening in an ideal fashion onto a beach, whereas others may be clustered around a communal pool. Many contain no more than a simple bedroom together with a small kitchen and bathroom. For the peak winter season, reservations should be made at least 5 or 6 months in advance.

Travel experts agree that savings, especially for a family of three to six people, or two or three couples, can range from 50% to 60% over what a hotel would cost. If there are only two in your party, these savings probably don't apply.

Rental Agencies

Agencies specializing in renting properties in Puerto Rico include:

- **VHR, Worldwide,** 235 Kensington Ave., Norwood, NJ 07648 (✆ **800/633-3284** or 201/767-9393; www.vhrww.com), offers the most comprehensive portfolio of luxury villas, condominiums, resort suites, and apartments for rent in the Caribbean, including complete packages for airfare and car rentals.
- **Hideaways Aficionado,** 767 Islington St., Portsmouth, NH 03801 (✆ **800/843-4433** or 603/430-4433; www.hideaways.com), provides a 144-page guide with illustrations of its accommodations, so that you can get an idea of what you're renting. Most villas come with maid service. You can also ask this travel club about discounts on plane fares and car rentals.

SUGGESTED PUERTO RICO ITINERARIES

4

Puerto Rico may be a small island but with its diverse geography and abundance of natural and cultural attractions, visitors rarely see all it has to offer, which takes some doing. You won't find a more vibrant city, with cutting edge culinary and clubbing scenes, than San Juan, and its beaches (and year-round temperatures) put those of Miami and South Florida to shame. Puerto Rico is always hot, and it has those postcard perfect white sand beaches lined with palm trees and sparkling blue sea that are the real draw for any visit to the Caribbean.

You can explore Old San Juan, discover that unspoiled beach town or remote mountain village, or go big wave surfing, spelunking, or deep sea fishing. There are world-class performances and a thriving locals arts and music scene, as well as the most varied dining of any Caribbean destination. With all that going on, it will take some planning to get the most out of your stay, no matter how long that is.

We list a "Puerto Rico in 1 Week" tour and a "Puerto Rico in 2 Weeks" tour, for those with more time. Of course these itineraries can also be customized for shorter stays and special interests. If you've been to Puerto Rico before and have already visited San Juan and El Yunque, you'll find a number of new ideas, such as the pastoral Panoramic Route, the lure of the Spanish Virgin Islands, and the beaches of the west coast, from Guánica in the southwest through Isabela in the northwest.

Puerto Rico has an advanced highway system, but if you go the least bit off the beaten path (and sometimes you won't have much choice, if you want to see anything other than urban centers), you will venture on to some narrow, swooping rural highways offering difficult driving conditions. Take along a detailed road map, and remember to blow your horn as you turn dangerous curves in the mountains.

The itineraries that follow take you to some major attractions with some surprise discoveries. The pace may be a bit breathless, so skip a town or sight occasionally for some chill-out time—after all, you're on vacation.

One thing to keep in mind, you can base yourself out of San Juan for longer time periods, seeing much of the island in separate day trips from the capital. See chapter 1, "The Best of Puerto Rico," for some ideas.

Puerto Rico is a natural travel hub to the Caribbean, and too many visitors skip it altogether en route to other sun-bleached spots. There are, however, Caribbean connoisseurs who have combined their vacations with a few day layover in San Juan for decades, and now love the city like an old friend, having come to know it a bit better over time. This is also another great way to experience Puerto Rico.

So remember, use any of these itineraries as jumping-off points for your own custom-made trip that more closely matches your interests or schedule.

THE REGIONS IN BRIEF

For a small island, Puerto Rico is a big place, with astounding geographic diversity squeezed into its 110×35-mile (177×56km) landmass. Beautiful beaches encircle its coastline, which fronts both the rough Atlantic, making for among the biggest waves in the region, and the tranquil waters of the Caribbean Sea, a sailor's and diver's paradise.

Puerto Ricans are great hosts, eager to entertain and intensely proud of their island's natural beauty, their culture, and their achievements as a people.

San Juan

The largest and best-preserved complex of Spanish colonial architecture in the Caribbean, Old San Juan (founded in 1521) is the oldest capital city under the U.S. flag. Once a lynchpin of Spanish dominance in the Caribbean, it has three major fortresses, miles of solidly built stone ramparts, a charming collection of antique buildings, and a modern business center. The city's economy is the most stable and solid in all of Latin America.

San Juan is the site of the official home and office of the governor of Puerto Rico (La Fortaleza), the 16th-century residence of Ponce de León's family, and several of the oldest places of Christian worship in the Western Hemisphere. Its bars, restaurants, shops, and nightclubs attract an animated group of fans. In recent years, the old city has become surrounded by densely populated modern buildings, including an ultramodern airport, which makes San Juan one of the most dynamic cities in the West Indies.

The Northwest: Arecibo, Rio Camuy, & More

A fertile area with many rivers bringing valuable water for irrigation from the high mountains of the Cordillera, the northwest also offers abundant opportunities for sightseeing. The region's districts include the following:

AGUADILLA Christopher Columbus landed near Aguadilla during his second voyage to the New World in 1493. Today the town has a busy airport, fine beaches, and a growing tourism-based infrastructure. It is also the center of Puerto Rico's

Puerto Rico

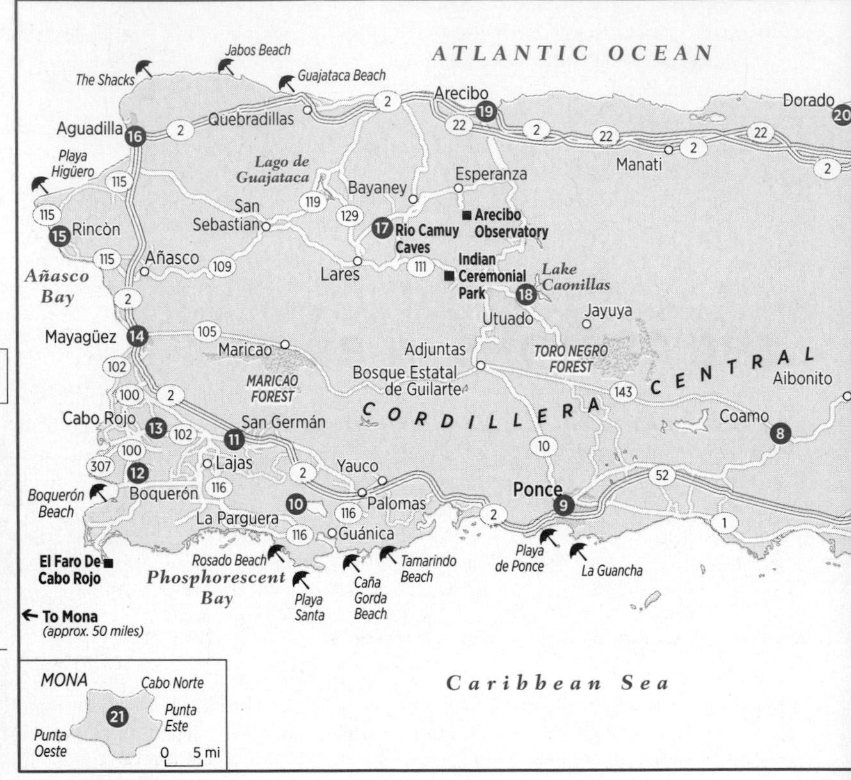

lace-making industry, a craft imported here many centuries ago by immigrants from Spain, Holland, and Belgium.

ARICEBO Located on the northern coastline a 2-hour drive west of San Juan, Arecibo was originally founded in 1556. Although little remains of its original architecture, the town is well known to physicists and astronomers around the world because of the radar/radio-telescope that fills a concave depression between six of the region's hills. Equal in size to 13 football fields and operated jointly by the National Science Foundation and Cornell University, it studies the shape and formation of the galaxies by deciphering radio waves from space.

RINCON Named after the 16th-century landowner Don Gonzalo Rincón, who donated its site to the poor of his district, the tiny town of Rincón is famous throughout Puerto Rico for its world-class surfing and beautiful beaches. The lighthouse that warns ships and boats away from dangerous offshore reefs is one of the most powerful on Puerto Rico.

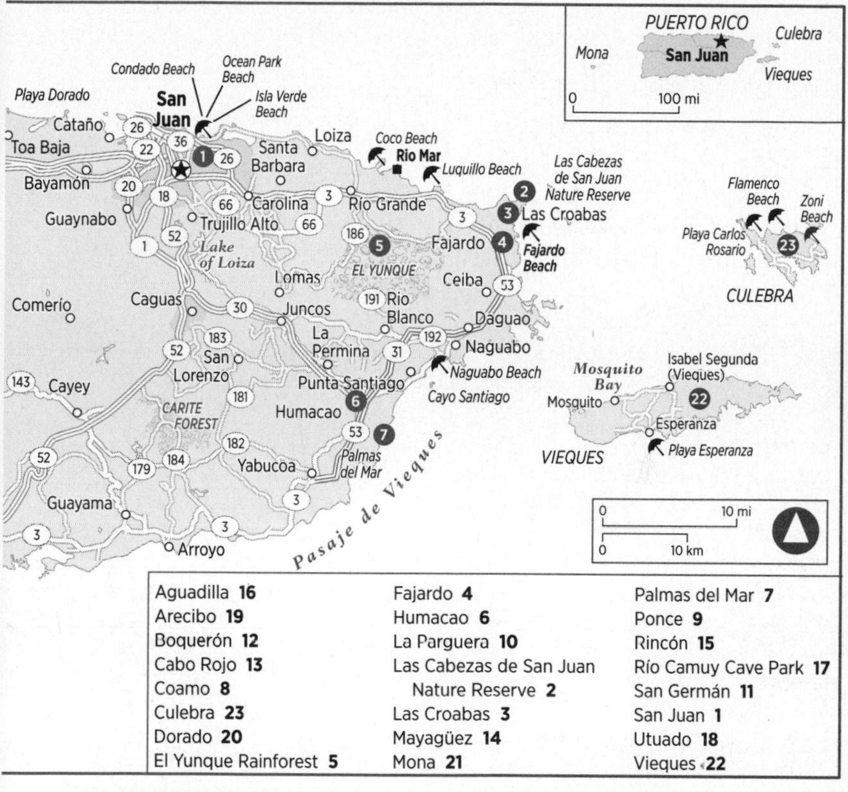

RIO CAMUY CAVE PARK Located near Arecibo, this park's greatest attraction is underground, where a network of rivers and caves provides some of the most enjoyable spelunking in the world. At its heart lies one of the largest known underground rivers. Aboveground, the park covers 300 acres (121 hectares).

UTUADO Small and nestled amid the hills of the interior, Utuado is famous as the center of the hillbilly culture of Puerto Rico. Some of Puerto Rico's finest mountain musicians have come from Utuado and mention the town in many of their ballads. The surrounding landscape is sculpted with caves and lushly covered with a variety of tropical plants and trees.

Dorado & the North Coast

Dorado, directly east of San Juan, is actually a term for a total of six white-sand beaches along the northern coast, reached by a series of winding roads. Dorado is the island's oldest resort town, the center of golf, casinos, and a once-major Hyatt resort that has closed (but on whose grounds two new luxury properties are being developed; see p. 205). Luckily, the Hyatt's golf courses remain open: 72 holes of golf, the greatest concentration in the Caribbean—all designed by Robert Trent Jones, Sr.

Meanwhile, the Embassy Suites Dorado is another jewel in this town, with its own Chi Chi Rodríguez–designed oceanfront golf course, and a beautiful beachfront location.

Several large hotel resorts have opened along the northwest of San Juan all the way down through Mayagüez. Rincón, Aguada, Aguadilla, and Isabella all have large hotels. The area offers beautiful beaches, natural wonders, and interesting attractions such as the Arecibo Observatory and the Río Camuy Cave Park.

The Northeast: El Yunque, a Nature Reserve & Fajardo

East of San Juan (see above) is a beautiful world of rain forest, stunning coastal waters, nature reserves and posh resorts. Several world-class golf courses are located here, and there is ample sailing and watersports activities. It's home to both a rainforest and a bioluminescent bay, not to mention one of the largest leatherback turtle nesting areas on U.S. soil.

EL YUNQUE The rainforest in the Luquillo Mountains, 25 miles (40km) east of San Juan, El Yunque is a favorite escape from the capital. Teeming with plant and animal life, it is a sprawling tropical forest (actually a national forest) whose ecosystems are strictly protected. Some 100 billion gallons of rainwater fall here each year, allowing about 250 species of trees and flowers to flourish.

FAJARDO There are still small and sleepy areas of this town, founded as a supply depot for the many pirates who plied the nearby waters, but it has also grown up, home to world-class resorts and attractions. There are several marinas in town, and the waters off its coast are a sailor's paradise, with beautiful offshore cayes and coral reef.

LAS CABEZAS NATURE RESERVE About an hour's drive from San Juan, this is an important and beautiful coastal natural reserve. Established in 1991 on 316 acres (128 hectares) of forest, it has mangrove swamp, offshore cays, coral reefs, freshwater lagoons and a rare, bioluminescent bay—a representative sampling of virtually every ecosystem on Puerto Rico. There are a visitor center, a 19th-century lighthouse (El Faro) that still works, and ample opportunity to forget the pressures of urban life.

El Conquistador Resort & Golden Door Spa in Fajardo near Las Croabas, a fishing village on the northeastern tip of Puerto Rico's north coast, has a commanding perch overlooking the place where the Atlantic and Caribbean meet.

It has a water park and private island paradise with sandy beaches and recreational facilities. Challenging El Conquistador are the Rio Mar and Gran Melía properties in Río Grande, which are also top-of-the-line resorts.

The Southwest: Ponce, Mayagüez, San German & More

One of Puerto Rico's most beautiful regions, the southwest is rich in local lore, civic pride, and natural wonders.

BOQUERON Famous for the beauty of its beach and the abundant birds and wildlife in a nearby forest reserve, this sleepy village is now ripe for large-scale tourism-related development. During the early 19th century, the island's most-feared pirate, Roberto Cofresi, imperiled the residents' lives along the Puerto Rican coastline from a secret lair in a cave nearby.

CABO ROJO Established in 1772, Cabo Rojo reached the peak of its prosperity during the 19th century, when immigrants from around the Mediterranean, fleeing revolutions in their own countries, arrived to establish sugar-cane plantations. Today, cattle graze peacefully on land originally devoted almost exclusively to sugar cane, and the area's many varieties of exotic birds draw bird-watchers from throughout North America. Even the offshore waters are fertile; it's estimated that nearly half of all the fish consumed on Puerto Rico are caught in waters near Cabo Rojo.

LA PARAGUERA Named after a breed of snapper *(pargos)* that abounds in the waters nearby, La Parguera is a quiet coastal town best known for the phosphorescent waters of *La Bahía Fosforescente* (Phosphorescent Bay). Here, sheltered from the waves of the sea, billions of plankton (luminescent dinoflagellates) glow dimly when they are disturbed by movements of the water. The town comes alive on weekends, when crowds of young people from San Juan arrive to party the nights away. Filling modest rooming houses, they temporarily change the texture of the town as bands produce loud sessions of salsa music.

MAYAGÜEZ The third-largest city on Puerto Rico, Mayagüez lies on the middle of the west coast, with beautiful beach areas to its north and south. While the city lacks its own beach, it is home to a few top quality hotels and has numerous attractions, including a zoo and botanical garden, so it's a good place to explore the west coast. Its history of disaster—including a great fire in 1847 and a 1918 tsunami—has allowed the city to forge a unique architectural identity, a blending of the distinct styles in vogue during the different eras of rebuilding the city has undergone throughout its history. Mayagüez has just undergone another facelift, this time in preparation of the 2010 Central American & Caribbean Games taking place in the summer of 2010, which included new sports facilities, a sprucing up of public areas, and a new waterfront park. The city has a renovated historic district surrounding Plaza Colón, its main square that has a monument to Christopher Columbus. The town is known as the commercial and industrial capital of Puerto Rico's western sector and has a large University of Puerto Rico campus, which also helps spark the local cultural and entertainment scene.

PONCE Puerto Rico's second-largest city, Ponce has always prided itself on its independence from the Spanish-derived laws and taxes that governed San Juan and the rest of the island. Long-ago home of some of the island's shrewdest traders, merchants, and smugglers, it is enjoying a renaissance as citizens and visitors rediscover its unique cultural and architectural charms. Located on Puerto Rico's southern coast, about 90 minutes by car from the capital, Ponce contains a handful of superb museums, one of the most charming main squares in the Caribbean, an ancient cathedral, dozens of authentically restored Colonial-era buildings, and a number of outlying mansions and villas that, at the time of their construction, were among the most opulent on the island.

SAN GERMÁN Located on the island's southwestern corner, small, sleepy, and historic San Germán was named after the second wife of Ferdinand of Spain, Germaine de Foix, whom he married in 1503. San Germán's central church, Iglesia Porta Coeli, was built in 1606. At one time, much of the populace was engaged in piracy, pillaging the ships that sailed off the nearby coastline. The central area of this village is still sought out for its many reminders of the island's Spanish heritage and colonial charm. With a large university and historic district, and its ideal location, the town is beginning to wake up to its tourism potential after a long sleep. Several fine restaurants have opened recently, and the pace of renovation in the old district is on the rise.

The Southeast: Palmas del Mar & More

Southeastern Puerto Rico has large-scale tourism developments but is also home to the island's wildest and least developed coastline, which runs from Guayama, which has one of the most picturesque town centers on the island, to the steep cliff sides of Yabucoa.

COAMO Although today Coamo is a bedroom community for San Juan, originally it was the site of two different Taíno communities. Founded in 1579, it now has a main square draped with bougainvillea and one of the best-known Catholic churches on Puerto Rico. Even more famous, however, are the mineral springs whose therapeutic warm waters helped President Franklin D. Roosevelt during his recovery from polio. The springs were also said to inspire the legend of the Fountain of Youth, which in turn set Ponce de León off on his vain search for them, which led him north to Florida.

HUMACAO Because of its easy access to San Juan, this small, verdant inland town has increasingly become one of the capital's residential suburbs.

PALMAS DEL MAR This sprawling vacation and residential resort community outside Humacao has great golf, tennis, and other amenities. The Equestrian Center at Palmas is the finest riding headquarters in Puerto Rico, with trails cutting through an old plantation and jungle along the beach.

Called the "New American Riviera," Palmas del Mar has 3 miles (4.8km) of white-sand beaches and sprawls across 2,800 acres (1,133 hectares) of a former coconut plantation—now devoted to luxury living and the sporting life. There are several different communities within Palmas, with both luxury homes and townhouses, as well as hotels and time share and vacation club rentals. The resort is ideal for families and has a supervised summer activities program for children ages 5 to 12.

The Offshore Islands: Culebra, Vieques & More

Few *norteamericanos* realize that Puerto Rico is host to two offshore island towns, which are among the most beautiful and, until recently, undiscovered locations in the Caribbean. Neither Vieques nor Culebra has a traffic light or fast food restaurant, and neither is likely to get either soon, despite the world-class lodging and tourist facilities beginning to appear on both islands, which have become known as the Spanish Virgin Islands.

Puerto Rico also has several islands within its jurisdiction that are intriguing nature reserves.

CULEBRA & VIEQUES Located off the eastern coast, these two islands are among the most unsullied and untrammeled areas in the West Indies, even though Vieques is being belatedly discovered. Come here for sun, almost no scheduled activities, fresh seafood, clear waters, sandy beaches, and teeming coral reefs. Vieques is especially proud of its phosphorescent bay, Mosquito Bay, among the world's best. Each island town has miles of coastline and sailing and snorkeling offshore. Although the sister Spanish Virgin Islands remain laid back, they have become increasingly sophisticated in lodging and dining options, which today are top-notch.

MONA Remote, uninhabited, and teeming with bird life, this barren island off the western coast is ringed by soaring cliffs and finely textured white-sand beaches. The island has almost no facilities, so visitors seldom stay for more than a day of swimming and picnicking. The surrounding waters are legendary for their dangerous eddies, undertows, and sharks.

Much closer to the coast, just off Rincón, is **Desecheo,** another nature reserve with great beaches and great diving offshore.

CAYO SANTIAGO Lying off the southeastern coast is the small island of Cayo Santiago. Home to a group of about two dozen scientists and a community of rhesus monkeys originally imported from India, the island is a medical experimentation center run by the U.S. Public Health Service. Monkeys are studied in a "wild" but controlled environment. They provide scientific researchers both insight into their behavior, as well as a source of experimental animals for medical research into such maladies as diabetes and arthritis. Visitors are barred from Cayo Santiago, but you can often glimpse the resident primates if you're boating offshore.

PUERTO RICO IN 1 WEEK

If you budget your time carefully, you can see some of the major highlights of Puerto Rico in just 1 week. Naturally, most of your time will be spent in **San Juan,** the capital, but you'll also have time to visit **El Yunque** (a rainforest) and a beautiful beach, probably **Luquillo** right to the east. There also will be time for days spent in **Ponce,** Puerto Rico's second city, the beautiful beaches of the southwest, the historic town of **San Germán,** and a side trip to an offshore island or the northwest coast. ***Start:*** *San Juan.*

Days 1 & 2: San Juan ★★★

Take a flight that arrives in San Juan as early as possible on **Day 1.** Check into your hotel and, if it's sunny, head for the pool or beach directly, stopping only for maybe a pick-me-up coffee and a pastry to go. As surely as there will be hours of sunshine every day on your trip here, at certain times of the year, it can also cloud up for a few hours, so we always recommend enjoying the sun while it's shining (even if it's for an hour or so).

After a quick swim and some sunshine, you can still spend the afternoon in Old San Juan, enjoying some sightseeing and shopping. A 2-hour walking tour covers the important churches, forts, and other highlights. Add another hour or so because you'll want to shop while you explore, and probably stop for refreshment, a rum

Suggested Puerto Rico Itineraries

The Best of Puerto Rico in 1 Week

Day 1
San Juan **1**

Day 2
Condado Beach **2**
Isla Verde Beach **3**
Ocean Park **4**

Day 3
El Yunque **5**
Luquillo Beach **6**

Day 4
Ponce **7**
Guánica **8**

Day 5
Boquerón **9**
San Germán **10**

Days 6
Toro Negro Forest Reserve **11**
Maricao **12**

Day 7
Rincon **13**
Aguadilla **14**

ATLANTIC OCEAN
Caribbean Sea
Pasaje de Viequs
CORDILLERA CENTRAL
San Juan
Ponce
The Shacks
Jabos Beach
Guajataca Beach
Aguadilla
Playa Higüero
Quebradillas
Arecibo
Rincòn
Añasco
Añasco Bay
Mayagüez
Cabo Rojo
Boquerón Beach
El Faro De Cabo Rojo
To Mona (approx. 50 miles)
Lago de Guajataca
San Sebastian
Lares
Bayaney
Esperanza
Rio Camuy Caves
Arecibo Observatory
Indian Ceremonial Park
Lake Caonillas
Utuado
Jayuya
Adjuntas
Bosque Estatal de Guilarte
Maricao
MARICAO FOREST
San Germán
Lajas
Boquerón
La Parguera
Phosphorescent Bay
Rosado Beach
Playa Santa
Caña Gorda Beach
Tamarindo Beach
Guánica
Yauco
Palomas
Playa de Ponce
La Guancha
TORO NEGRO FOREST
Manati
Dorado
Playa Dorado
Toa Baja
Cataño
Bayamón
Guaynabo
Condado Beach
Ocean Park Beach
Isla Verde Beach
Comerío
Aibonito
Coamo
Cayey
Caguas
Guayama
Arroyo
Trujillo Alto
Lake of Loiza
Carolina
Santa Barbara
Loiza
Coco Beach
Rio Mar
Rio Grande
Luquillo Beach
Las Cabezas de San Juan Nature Reserve
Las Croabas
Fajardo
Fajardo Beach
EL YUNQUE
Ceiba
Rio Blanco
Daguao
Naguabo
Naguabo Beach
Cayo Santiago
Lomas
Juncos
La Permina
Punta Santiago
San Lorenzo
CARITE FOREST
Humacao
Yabucoa
Palmas del Mar
PUERTO RICO
Mona
San Juan
Culebra
Vieques
0 100 mi
0 10 mi
0 10 km
MONA
Cabo Norte
Punta Este
Punta Oeste
0 5 mi
CULEBRA
Flamenco Beach
Zoni Beach
Playa Carlos Rosario
VIEQUES
Mosquito Bay
Mosquito
Isabel Segunda (Vieques)
Esperanza
Playa Esperanza

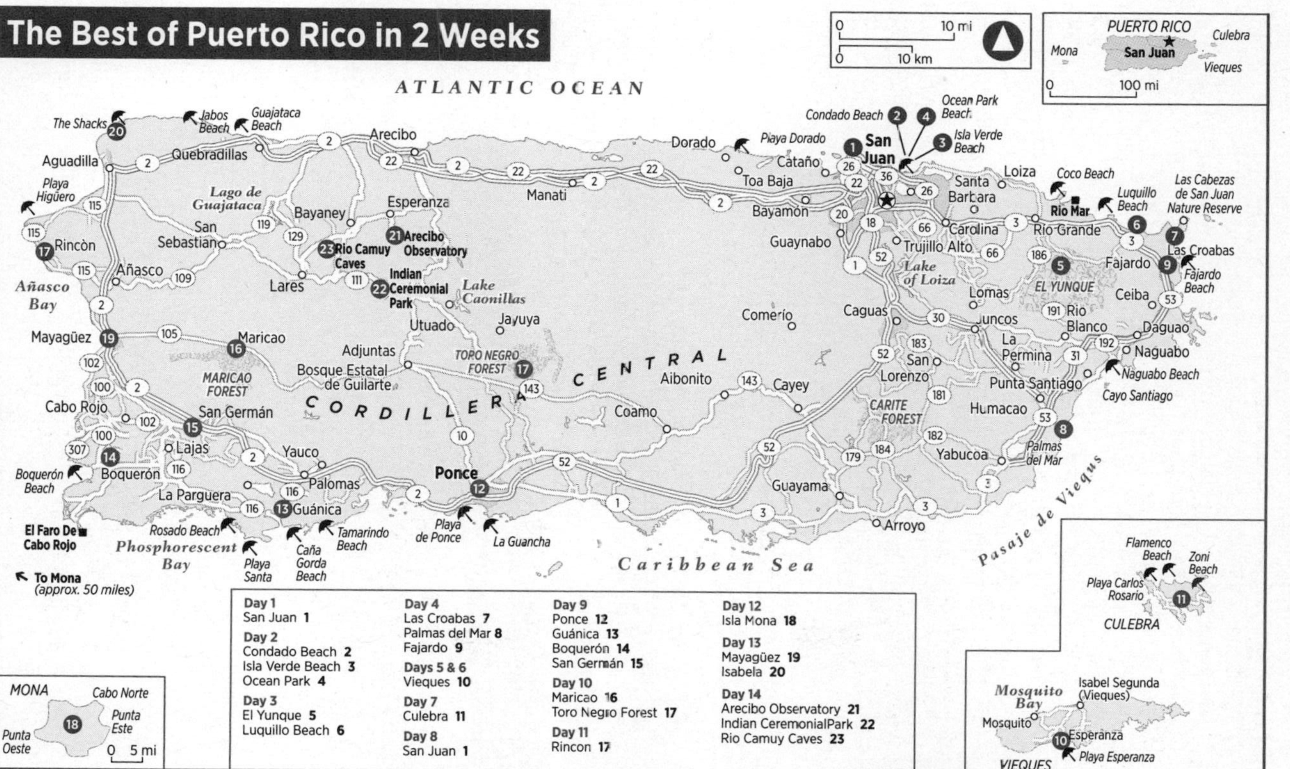
The Best of Puerto Rico in 2 Weeks
ATLANTIC OCEAN
Caribbean Sea
Pasaje de Vieques
Day 1
San Juan 1
Day 2
Condado Beach 2
Isla Verde Beach 3
Ocean Park 4
Day 3
El Yunque 5
Luquillo Beach 6
Day 4
Las Croabas 7
Palmas del Mar 8
Fajardo 9
Days 5 & 6
Vieques 10
Day 7
Culebra 11
Day 8
San Juan 1
Day 9
Ponce 12
Guánica 13
Boquerón 14
San Germán 15
Day 10
Maricao 16
Toro Negro Forest 17
Day 11
Rincon 17
Day 12
Isla Mona 18
Day 13
Mayagüez 19
Isabela 20
Day 14
Arecibo Observatory 21
Indian CeremonialPark 22
Rio Camuy Caves 23
PUERTO RICO
San Juan
Mona
Culebra
Vieques
0 100 mi
0 10 mi
0 10 km
MONA
Cabo Norte
Punta Este
Punta Oeste
0 5 mi
CULEBRA
VIEQUES
To Mona (approx. 50 miles)

drink or fresh fruit frappe, at one of the Old City's famous watering holes. The city is also one of the shopping meccas of the Caribbean, with bargains galore, lots of local arts and crafts, and high-profile retail shops.

Visit one of the area's many fine cafes and restaurants for an early dinner. Then return to your hotel for an early evening and a well-deserved rest.

On **Day 2,** with shopping and sightseeing behind you, prepare for a full day in the sun. Most hotel and resort pools are great, and the beaches in San Juan are glorious white-sand, turquoise-water affairs. For many visitors, that's why they came to San Juan in the first place. Depending on the location of your hotel, the finest beaches are **Condado Beach** (p. 169), **Isla Verde Beach** (p. 169), and **Ocean Park Beach** (p. 169). Enjoy the watersports activities along the beaches of the Greater San Juan area. See the "Diving, Fishing, Tennis & Other Pursuits" section beginning on p. 168. Of course, there's nothing wrong with spending a day at the beach.

Make it a point tonight to enjoy some of the nightlife of the capital, either bar-hopping, taking in the club or music scene, or going casino gambling. San Juan is one of the nightlife capitals of the Caribbean. There's likely a lot going on right around your hotel; Old San Juan, Condado, and Isla Verde are centers of activity. See the "San Juan After Dark" section, beginning on p. 186.

Day 3: El Yunque ★★★ & Luquillo Beach ★★★

While still based in San Juan, drive east for 25 miles (40km) to **El Yunque** for a morning visit. This 28,000-acre (11,331-hectare) attraction is the only tropical rainforest in the U.S. National Forest Service system. Stop first at **El Portal Tropical Forest Center** (p. 197) for maps and guidance. You're faced with a choice of hiking trails or else driving through. Unless you engage in extensive hiking, you can see some of the forest's greatest beauty in time for lunch.

After a visit to the rainforest, head north toward the town of Rio Grande and follow the signs to **Luquillo Beach** in the east. There are many roadside signs and kiosks where you can enjoy a tasty but inexpensive lunch. Shaded by tall coconut palms, the beach is crowded on weekends. Surfing, kayaking, diving, and snorkeling are just some of the activities you can enjoy here, along with the golden sands of the beach itself. There are also refreshment stands and a bathhouse as well as toilets. Return west to San Juan for a final night.

Days 4 & 5: Ponce & the Southwest Coast ★★

Leave San Juan on the morning of **Day 4** and drive 75 miles (121km) southwest to the city of **Ponce,** the island's "second city." Take Rte. 1 south to Hwy. 52, then continue south and west to Ponce, following the road signs. Allow at least 1½ hours for the drive. Once in Ponce, check into a hotel for 2 nights.

In Ponce, start at the **Parque de Bombas** (p. 219), the famous firehouse, on the city's gorgeous central Plaza Las **Delicias.** You can spend another few hours strolling near the plaza, visiting museums and cathedrals (see the Ponce map on p. 215).

After some shopping and a local lunch in the old town, continue on one of the beach towns to the west, along Rte. 116: **Guánica, La Parguera** or

Boquerón. Heading to the coast today will mean more time for fun in the sun the next day because Ponce has no real beach. The only reason to stay in Ponce is to go out for a great meal and enjoy the entertainment at the **Ponce Hilton,** maybe squeezing in a round of golf or some pool time in the afternoon before dinner. (If it's a weekend, there could be a concert at the nearby **La Guancha,** a public marina and boardwalk where harborfront restaurants serve up local treats and drinks.)

Guánica's three lodging options—**Copamarina Beach Resort, Mary Lee's By the Sea** and **Hotel 1812**—are among the best in their class for the region, and the town has seven spectacular beaches. La Parguera and Boquerón are considered the "Cape Cod of Puerto Rico," with ample simple, clean lodging options, from small hotels to guesthouses.

If you head out of Ponce on Day 4, you will also be able to spend 2 hours in the afternoon exploring the **Guánica State Forest,** the best-preserved subtropical ecosystem on the planet. There are 750 plants and rare tree species that grow here, and many trails descend to the beautiful coastline. Grab a fresh seafood meal at a local restaurant by your hotel. Hopefully, there's live music.

On **Day 5,** you'll want to head to the beach because among the finest on the island are all around you. In Guánica, go to **Caña Gorda** or **Playa Santa;** your best bet in La Parguera is to take a boat to **Mata La Gata** islet offshore, while the public beach at Boquerón has tranquil waters, white sand, and a healthy grove of palm trees running behind the beach.

In the afternoon, take a drive to the historic city of San Germán or farther on to Mayagüez. Make sure to drive by **El Faro de Cabo Rojo,** a lighthouse at Puerto Rico's southernmost corner, for a look. It's on a dramatic, blissfully isolated coastal perch.

In San Germán, the town's major attractions, including **Iglesia Porta Coeli** and **San Germán de Auxerre,** are in its historic downtown, a beautiful array of Spanish colonial and turn-of-the-20th-century buildings. If you go to Mayagüez, visit its beautiful downtown plaza, and then either its zoo or botanical gardens. Have dinner before heading back to your hotel.

Day 6: Mountain Retreat ★★

It's time to head up to the mountains, because you can't spend a week in Puerto Rico without spending a night at one of its country mountain retreats.

You can visit the **Toro Negro Forest Reserve** (p. 236), a 7,200-acre (2,914-hectare) park straddling the highest peak of the Cordillera Central, north of Ponce. Visit Lake Guineo or take a hike to the beautiful Juanita waterfalls. You should also have time to visit the other area forest reserve, **Monte Estado State Forest** in Maricao. There are fine country inns near both reserves. Most also offer traditional Puerto Rican fare. Have a restful night in the clean mountain air.

Day 7: Rincón & the Northwest ★★★

Get up early and begin driving up the west coast north of Mayagüez to **Rincón.** After checking in at a hotel, hit one of the town's famous beaches. If you surf or windsurf, today's the day for it because you are in the surfing capital of the Caribbean. If it's summer, and the surf is down, then the snorkeling is great. Most hotels and guesthouses have fine pools as well.

If it's winter, consider spending some time whale-watching, as it's the season they breach right offshore. It's also possible to rent a boat to take you to **Desecheo Island** (just offshore) or the much longer trek to **Mona Island,** some 40 miles off the coast. Called "the Galápagos of Caribbean," the island is inhabited by giant iguanas and three species of endangered sea turtles, among other rare plant, animal, and marine life. (If you want to squeeze this in on a 1-week trip, it would be best to eliminate the mountain retreat or the second day in the southwest.)

Rincón has a number of fine bars and restaurants, with great food and live entertainment. So make sure you have a great meal and some fun on your final night. And you'll want to be sure to watch the sun go down, which is a beautiful thing on the west coast of Puerto Rico.

The following morning, you'll find that it's only a 98-mile (158km) drive northeast back to San Juan, the hub of all the island's major transportation. The nearby Aguadilla airport, however, also has international flight service, so you could squeeze in some more beach time or another attraction (say the **Camuy Caves** or the **Arecibo Observatory**) if you do not have to return to San Juan before flying out.

PUERTO RICO IN 2 WEEKS

This tour, the longest in this chapter, is also the most recommended. It encapsulates the very essence of the island—it's "Puerto Rico in a Nutshell." Because of the island's small size, you can visit not only its three major cities (**San Juan, Ponce,** and **Mayagüez**) but also its greatest attraction, the **El Yunque** rainforest; its finest beach **(Luquillo);** its offshore islands (**Vieques** and **Culebra**); and even its most intriguing man-made attractions, such as the alien-hunting **Arecibo Observatory.** To start, follow the first 3 days of the "Puerto Rico in 1 Week" itinerary above (San Juan on Days 1 and 2, El Yunque and Luquillo Beach on Day 3), then head to Las Croabas to begin Day 4. ***Start:*** *San Juan.*

Days 1, 2 & 3: San Juan, El Yunque ★★★ and Luquillo Beach ★★★

Follow the first 3 days of the "Puerto Rico in 1 Week" itinerary above.

Day 4: Las Croabas & Palmas del Mar

The northeast corner of Puerto Rico is a water and sports enthusiast's dream, with sailing, golf, and all sorts of outdoor pursuits. It's not cheap but worth every cent to check into **El Conquistador Resort & Golden Door Spa** (p. 267) for the day, taking advantage of its vast array of facilities and restaurants, as well as its water park, health club, spa, children's programs, and watersports equipment.

Using the resort as a base, you can explore **Las Cabezas de San Juan Nature Reserve** (p. 266), with its famous lighthouse, "El Faro" and untrammeled tropical forest and beaches. There's a marina on site and several more in town, including the **Puerto del Rey** (the Caribbean's largest and most modern marina). There a beautiful white-sand, public beach, **Playa Seven Seas,** and a short hike from here is **Playa Escondido (Hidden Beach)** and **Playa El Convento,** the start of a 7-mile undeveloped strip of land. See p. 264 for more coverage of these sandy strips.

The resort has several fine restaurants, and the village of Los Croabas, a quaint fishing port, has several simple but high-quality seafood restaurants.

Another option would be to continue driving south along the east coast to **Humacao** and the nearby resort of **Palmas del Mar,** where you can participate in the best-organized sporting activities in eastern Puerto Rico, ranging from vast tennis courts to scuba diving and golf, along with deep-sea fishing (see coverage beginning on p. 80). Palmas also has 3 miles (4.8km) of exceptional white-sand beaches, all open to the public. There are also a large number of places for lunch and dinner at the resort and a good, affordable seafood restaurant serving freshly caught fish.

If you can't afford the prices of these large resorts, there are several smaller inns throughout this area, from Luquillo to Naguabo. See "Paradores," toward the end of chapter 3.

Days 5 & 6: Vieques ★

Regardless of where you are based for the night, arrive early at the port of Fajardo on Puerto Rico's eastern coast for a 1-hour ferryboat ride to the island of **Vieques,** the largest of the so-called Spanish Virgin Islands (it is, in fact, a U.S. territory). Check into a hotel here for 2 nights. Resorts and small inns come in all price ranges (coverage of hotels begins on p. 284).

A stopover in Vieques might be the most idyllic spot in your vacation, as the island offers 40 beautiful, white, sandy beaches, all open to the public. See **"The Best Beaches,"** with coverage beginning on p. 2. Lazy days in the sun aren't the only activities on the island. You can tour the luminous waters of **Phosphorescent Bay,** join mountain-bike excursions, go fishing from a kayak, take snorkeling trips, or go scuba diving. **Fort Conde de Mirasol Museum** (p. 284) is an interesting museum housed in an historic fort, and federal authorities operate two wildlife refuges on former military lands. At night Vieques offers a wide range of bars and good restaurants, the best available on any of Puerto Rico's offshore islands.

Day 7: Culebra ★

From Vieques, you can also ferry over to close by Culebra, which is far more offbeat and undiscovered than Vieques. Though still undeveloped, Culebra facilities have seen substantial upgrades in recent years, and there are many more rooms available and many more quality rooms over the last few years.

Like Vieques, Culebra is chock-full of white-sand beaches, and you can explore the **Culebra Wildlife Refuge** (p. 293). Also snorkel here, or kayak, fish, sail, or hike. The best way to explore the island is to rent and drive a jeep—although most visitors prefer to hang out for the day on one of Culebra's beaches. The main beach is the mile-long (1.6km) **Flamenco Beach,** an arcing cove with vibrant water and clean sand. The next morning return by ferry to the port of Fajardo for a continuation of the tour.

Day 8: San Juan ★★★

On the morning of **Day 8,** leave Culebra by taking a ferryboat back to the port of Fajardo. From here, drive west to San Juan for an overnight stopover. Because the city is so vast and so filled with amusements, try to use the time to mop up all the shopping, attractions, and nightlife options you missed on your first visit. See chapter 6 for all the possible options, including outdoor pursuits, awaiting you.

Day 9: Ponce and the Southwest ★★

On the morning of **Day 9,** leave San Juan and drive south to Ponce, the chief city on the southern coast. Follow the suggestions as outlined in Day 4 and Day 5 of "Puerto Rico in 1 Week" (see above).

Day 10: Mountain Retreat ★★

Follow the suggestions for Day 6 of "Puerto Rico in 1 Week," above.

Day 11: Rincón and the Northwest ★

For suggestions, refer to Day 7 in "Puerto Rico in 1 Week," above. However, save a separate day for Isla Mona (see below), which richly deserves it.

Day 12: Isla Mona ★★★

Boat excursions over to this island are not as organized as they should be, but it's worth the trouble to get to Mona, even enduring a difficult sea crossing across Pasaje de la Mona. Coverage begins on p. 244. Most visitors use Mayagüez (covered earlier) as their base for exploring Mona Island, returning to the mainland for the night. Other, more adventurous travelers camp out on the island. Lying some 50 miles (80km) off the Puerto Rican mainland, Mona has been called the Jurassic Park of the Caribbean.

A nature reserve since 1919, Mona has been uninhabited for the past half-century except for day-trippers. Every species from fish-eating bats to wild goats and pigs live here. And of course, the giant iguanas. The environment is beautiful, but potentially hostile because of its wildness. Department of Natural and Environmental Resources rangers are on hand to offer advice and guidance. There are toilets and saltwater showers at Playa Sardinera, but visitors need to bring fresh water. You can go camping, but the itinerary assumes you'd rather return to the comfort of a hotel room in Mayagüez.

Day 13: Mayagüez & the Northwest

Squeeze in some chill time by the pool in this west-coast suburban city. Go explore the beautifully restored downtown area. Highlights include the elegant central **Plaza Colón,** dominated by a monument of Christopher Columbus, surrounded by 16 bronze statues of courtly ladies, and the historic **Yaguez Theater, City Hall,** and **Post Office.** Two huge fires and an earthquake at the turn of the 20th century destroyed much of the city three different times, but there's much fine architecture from the 1920s and later.

You'll also want to visit the city's zoo, **Puerto Rico National Parks Zoo,** or its **Tropical Agriculture Research Station** (p. 240), next to the Mayagüez Campus of the University of Puerto Rico. Anyone can walk through this site for botanical research, whose grounds feature towering bamboo, wild fruit trees, and the various plant species grown here.

After lunch, as you head north out of the city, drive by its historic harbor and warehouse district with a restored Customs House from the 1920s.

You'll be going to the beautiful towns of the northwest coast, most probably **Isabela** (p. 255) with abundant affordable lodging options right near the coast, about 30 miles (48km) north. It's so close, you'll have time for a quick swim at whatever beach is right outside your hotel or at its pool. There is no bad beach here.

A kind of alternative-lifestyle vibe accompanies the town's surf culture, so the young and young at heart will find great entertainment and live music at area bars.

Day 14: Arecibo ★, Indian Ceremonial Park & Rio Camuy Caves ★★★

As you head east for your return to San Juan, you can take in three wonders of Puerto Rico. The **Observatorio de Arecibo** (p. 207), the world's largest and most sensitive radar/radio-telescope, searches the night sky for extraterrestrial life in the universe beyond. In Karst Country, the **Caguaña Indian Ceremonial Park** in Utuado (p. 211) was built by the Taíno Indians a thousand years ago. The grandest attraction of all, the **Rio Camuy Caves** (p. 208), contains the third-largest underground river in the world. With proper timing, all three of these attractions can be explored in 1 day, with time still left for the final drive back into San Juan. Arm yourself with a good map and explore the coverage of these attractions in chapter 7 before heading here.

Following your visits, continue to San Juan, at a distance of some 68 miles (109km) to the west. But remember, it's probably also possible to book a flight into San Juan and out of Aguadilla, especially during the winter high tourism season. Again, this would buy you another afternoon on the beach at Isabela.

PUERTO RICO FOR FAMILIES

Puerto Ricans love their **niños,** and places all over the island are kid-friendly. The nature of the island itself, with its parks, beach-studded seaside resorts, and amusement centers, virtually invites you for a family outing. Because of islanders' welcoming attitude toward children, you will meet a lot more Puerto Ricans on your trip if you are traveling with children. And remember, don't forget that picnic lunch. ***Start:*** *San Juan.*

Days 1 & 2: San Juan ★★★

Old San Juan has more to offer children than any other Caribbean capital. The massive wall of the square-mile Spanish colonial enclave joins the two historic fortresses that were built at the land and sea entrances to the city. Children will enjoy exploring the tunnels, vaults, look-out points, dungeons, and ramps of **Castillo de San Felipe del Morro** (the must-visit of the two) and **Fort San Cristóbal** (p. 155). And the grassy fields surrounding El Morro are a favorite spot for kite-flying. You can buy a kite at the street-side refreshment carts outside the park's entrance. You'll also want to visit **Museo del Niño (Children's Museum,** p. 167), with interactive exhibits, a rooftop nature center, play areas, and a theater. It's right in the middle of major sites, next to **Hotel El Convento** (p. 108) and **Catedral de San Juan** (p. 156). The historic city's plazas are also a playground for kids, who love feeding the pigeons in **Plaza de Las Armas** (p. 163) and running through the shooting fountains at **Plaza Quinto Centenario** (p. 162). Skateboarding is also popular at some of the plazas.

There's a free trolley to ride, a dirt-cheap ferry that goes across the bay and back in about a half-hour, and even horse and buggies to rent. Abundant high-quality Puerto Rican, Mediterranean, Asian, and European cuisines are available at Old City restaurants, so a nice lunch is in order. For recommendations on flavorful food at good prices, see chapter 5. Make sure to take a break at **Ben & Jerry's,** with free Internet, DJ music, books, magazines, big tables and chairs, and, oh yes, those baked goods and that ice cream (p. 139).

Afterwards, walk off lunch by doing some shopping and maybe taking in a few more sights. Another option is to take a cab back to the hotel for some sunshine and a swim before sunset.

The next day, you'll want to take your kids to the beach. Depending on where you are staying, that will likely be Condado, Ocean Park, or Isla Verde. And of course, kids prefer some of the resort pools, many of which cater to them with slides, tunnels, and spray and play areas.

If you don't want the little ones in the sun too long, take a cab to **Plaza las Américas** (p. 186), the largest mall in the Caribbean. There's **Time Out** (p. 167), which has top-of-the-line video games, a multiplex cinema, several restaurants, a food court and lots of great shops for kids (Discovery, a Border's with a reading room, Game Stop, and so on).

Day 3: El Yunque ★★★ & Luquillo Beach ★★★

While still based in San Juan, journey east for a day or two of the island's biggest attractions: **El Yunque** rainforest and the island's most famous and best beach, **Luquillo.** For suggestions, refer to Day 3 of "Puerto Rico in 1 Week," earlier in this chapter.

Days 4 & 5: Ponce & the Southwest Coast ★★

On the morning of **Day 4,** leave San Juan early in the morning for a scenic drive southwest to the second city of Ponce, a distance of 75 miles (121km). Stop at the historic downtown area, concentrating on the ring of sites surrounding Plaza las Delicias, the central plaza dominated by a huge lion statue. Kids will enjoy the 1883 **Parque de Bombas,** a strangely shaped, black and red, wooden firehouse. (See p. 219s.) After stretching the legs, it's time for lunch.

If your kids are just as happy at a hotel pool as a beach, then you can stay the night in Ponce, which lacks a good swimming beach. After some fun in the sun and dinner, you can take a stroll on the boardwalk along a public harbor called **La Guancha** (p. 220). This is like a more wholesome version of New York's Coney Island and is often mobbed with families. Food stands sell local delicacies and snacks, and there are often free concerts and other events with family appeal. It's particularly lively on weekends and holidays.

But unless there is some event or other compelling reason to stay in Ponce, I'd recommend heading out straight after lunch to **Guánica,** the first of a string of beach towns 21 miles (34km) west of Ponce that makes a good base to explore the southwest regardless of your budget.

En route, you can drive the family through parts of the **Guánica Dry Forest,** an internationally protected biosphere that's home to 100 rare bird species and unique vegetation that gives it its distinctive stunted forest look. There's still plenty of time for the beach after checking in. You might consider taking a 15-minute boat ride to **Gilligan's Island** (yes, the same name as that old TV sitcom). Part of the forest reserve, the island is one of a series of mangrove and sandy cays off the Caña Gorda peninsula. Kids have a blast in the shallow water surrounding it and the saltwater canals that cut through the island.

Have dinner at your hotel or head down to the main harbor in downtown Guánica. The **Blue Marlin** and several other simple seafood restaurants front the water, serving up freshly caught fish *criollo* style.

The next day, take a scenic drive west along the green Lajas Valley, with the towering Cordillera Center looming dramatically over it in the distance. Your destination is the palm-fringed public beach at **Boquerón** (p. 231), whose calm, warm waters are perfect for families. A big, wide beach, Boquerón offers plenty of room for all sorts of beach play as well as picnic tables, barbecue pits, and roofed shelters. The facilities also include showers and changing rooms, as well as restrooms. There are numerous hotel rooms for all budgets here, or you could stay a second night in Guánica.

After showering up and changing from the beach, take a short drive to the nearby fishing village of La Parguera. Restaurants in town cater to families with freshly caught seafood and local Puerto Rican food. There are also food stands selling everything from pizza and fried chicken to fresh seafood salads and turnovers made with lobster and conch. There are video game arcades and other activities for kids. After dinner and a stroll, take a 90-minute boat trip through the glowing waters of the bioluminescent bay. Boats leave frequently from the docks in town.

Day 6: Aguadilla

On the morning of **Day 6,** head to the northwest coastal town of **Aguadilla** (p. 258), which has an enormous number of reasonably priced hotels perfect for families. You'll have time to visit picture-perfect **Crash Boat Beach** (p. 255). The town is also popular with kids, since it has **Las Cascadas Water Park** (p. 258) and **Aguadilla Ice Skating Rink** (p. 258), undoubtedly the only rink of its kind in Aguadilla.

Day 7: Arecibo ★, Indian Ceremonial Park & Rio Camuy Caves ★★★

For your final day, you can take in three major island attractions before your drive east back to San Juan and its transportation hub. If you choose to fly directly out of Aguadilla, you will buy an extra afternoon in the region.

For details, refer to Day 14 under "Puerto Rico in 2 Weeks."

DRIVING TOUR: LA RUTA PANORAMICA IN 2 DAYS

"The Panoramic Route"—called *La Ruta Panorámica* by Puerto Ricans—winds its way through the Central Mountains in the heart of the island for some 100 miles (161km). This is the most scenic drive in the Caribbean. The mountains are the home of the *jíbaro,* the country farmer whose way of life is fast disappearing in modern Puerto Rico. The agricultural life and ways of the *jíbaro,* which have inspired some of the most important works of literature and a whole genre of country music, still live on in the central mountain towns, however, and this route is the most comprehensive way of seeing them. Expect winding, twisting roads, and don't forget to blow your horn as you turn blind curves. After rainstorms, there are frequent washouts. Although locals speed by you as if in a race car, it's advisable for newcomers to go no more than 25 mph (40kmph). In spite of some difficulties, it's worth the effort to cross through the Cordillera Central's dramatic peaks and valleys. The Cordillera mountains rise more than 4,000 feet (1,219m) in some places. You'll pass by **Cerro de Punta,** which at 4,389 feet (1,338m) is the highest in Puerto Rico. These mountains have helped define Puerto Rico. ***Start:*** *Drive from San Juan.*

Day 1: From Carite Forest ★ to Jayuya

Leave San Juan early in the morning for the drive south, taking Highway 52 to exit 32, which will take you to Rte. 184, also heading south. Stay on 184 as it cuts right through the most scenic parts of the **Carite Forest Reserve.** Roadside grills tempt with the succulent *lechón* (roasted pig) sold at the area's famous *lechoneras. Sanjuaneros* flock here on weekends to enjoy the cool mountain breezes, the grills, and even dance halls that line 184. There are also cool swimming holes throughout the forest and recreation areas. For more information, refer to Carite Forest Reserve (p. 213).

Highway 184 leads into Rte. 179, which you can follow out of the forest reserve (signposts lead to **Lago Carite,** the largest lake in the forest). To continue west along the route, follow the signs northwest to the town of Cayey, one of the larger towns in Puerto Rico's central mountains.

Once at Cayey, follow Rte. 1 south to Rte. 7722. On Rte. 7722, turn right onto Rte. 722 which leads directly into **Aibonito,** at 2,500 feet the highest town in Puerto Rico, and one of the prettiest.

Before town is the **Mirador Piedra Degetau,** an observation tower with a picnic area from which you can see both the Atlantic Ocean to the north and the Caribbean Sea to the south, not to mention the vast expanses of Puerto Rico visible to the west and east.

You'll feel you've wandered back in time upon arriving in Aibonito, a former vacation retreat for the wealthy, which is still marked by their majestic homes, as well as coffee plantations. The town is known as a flower growing center of the island, and has an annual flower festival that is always worth a visit, since there is plenty of local food, live music, and other entertainment.

Beyond Aibonito, the Panoramic Route traverses the spine of the Cordillera Central for the next 30 miles, offering awe-inspiring vistas along the way. You'll pass the **Cañon de San Cristóbal,** a canyon that cuts 700 feet (213m) through the mountain chain, offering waterfalls and steep cliffs. Three rivers surge through its ravines. The Conservation Trust of Puerto Rico has purchased surrounding lands to protect this natural wonder and is working on establishing interpretive trails and an observation center. At its present level of development, we recommend it only for experienced hikers.

Beyond the canyon, the route continues towards **Toro Negro Forest Reserve,** a lush cloud forest, and **Lake Guineo,** the highest lake in Puerto Rico (p. 236). The forest is also home to Cerro de Punta, at 4,390 feet high, Puerto Rico's highest peak. Stop inside the forest at the Recreativa Doña Juana, a picnic area beside a swimming pool fed by mountain streams. The restaurant here serves good Puerto Rican barbecue. The nearby **Visitor Center,** at Rte. 143, Km 32.4 (✆ **787/867-3040**), offers you a trail map; it's open daily from 8am to 4pm. There are no supplies in the park, so bring mosquito repellent and bottled water.

At the eastern side of the forest is the famous **Doña Juana Waterfall** (Rte. 149, Km 41.5), cascading 120 feet (37m) over a rock-strewn cliff.

Head for the remote mountain town of **Jayuya,** surrounded by big green mountains, to the country inn **Parador Hacienda Gripiñas** (p. 237). From Rte. 143 cut north along Rte. 149, and then turn west at the junction of Rte. 144 signposted into Jayuya. The inn is a wonderful place to relax and cool off from the Caribbean heat. The town is also a great place to explore the island's Taíno past. Make sure to visit **La Piedra Escrita** (the Written Rock), a huge boulder beside a stream with Taíno petroglyphs carved into it, and the **Cemi Museum** (Rte. 149, Km 9.3), which has a nice collection of Taíno jewelry and artifacts.

Day 2: Utuado, Adjuntas & Maricao

Leave Jayuya in the morning, cutting south on Rte. 44, then northwest along Rte. 140 (which becomes Rte. 111), following the signs into the town of **Utuado,** site of another well-known parador, **Casa Grande Mountain Retreat** (p. 210), which is another option for a stopover. For more details on the town, see p. 236.

With its Spanish-styled central plaza, Utuado still reflects its colonial roots, but it is also one of the spots in Puerto Rico that most embraces its Taíno past. Most visitors arrive here to explore the **Indian Ceremonial Park** at Caguaña (p. 210), a 1,000 year old Taíno site that was used for recreation and worship. There are ancient *bateyes* (ball courts) and stoned monoliths covered with petroglyphs. This is the largest site of Taíno ruins in Puerto Rico.

You can easily wander around for an hour or two before heading on towards **Adjuntas,** the heart of coffee country, which you get to by taking Rte. 10 south. Adjuntas is known as "the town of the sleeping giant" because of its silhouette created by the enveloping mountains. In addition to coffee, it is also an important producer of oranges.

Also worth a visit is Lago Dos Bocas, a beautiful lake surrounded by forest. Free ferries ply the lake and you can take a ride to one of the rustic cafes along the shore. The lake is stocked, so it's a nice spot to fish as well.

There is a tangle of roads leading here through the mountains to **Maricao,** a beautiful mountain town of huge coffee plantations, and the last stop along the route. Travel along Rte. 129 to Rte. 111, then continue along Rte. 128 until Rte. 431. From there, it's on to Rte. 4431, Rte. 124, and finally Rte. 120 into town. This winding road changes its number so many times, you'll lose track; follow the signposts to Maricao and not the route numbers, and you won't go wrong.

Maricao's **Monte del Estado Forest,** (see p. 260) is the largest state forest on the island, and you can spend all day exploring it. The coffee-producing town is the smallest municipality in Puerto Rico. It lies at the far western end of Ruta Panorámica, and is an idyllic retreat for exploring, as it's surrounded by mountain gorges, old bridges, terraced houses, rushing streams of cold water, and enough switchback roads to challenge the most skilled of alpine drivers.

The forest has swimming pools fed by mountain streams, a picnic area and campground with cabins for rent. It's a perfect spot to have lunch here surrounded by mountain peaks. On hot days, the forest pools, fed by mountain streams, are particularly refreshing. Locals will do their own cooking on site, but you can also bring food from any restaurant in town, such as **El Buen Café** (**✆ 787/838-4198**), right on the main plaza, which serves up cheap and flavorful sandwiches and plates of *comida criolla,* local island dishes.

There is a **Visitor Center** at Rte. 120, Km 16.2 (**✆ 787/873-5632**), which will provide maps of the forest and even hook you up with a private guide if you want to do more extensive exploring. Hours are Daily 8am to 4pm. If you climb **Torre de Piedra,** a stone observation tower, you can take in a panoramic sweep of the entire western half of Puerto Rico. It is open daily from 8am to 4pm (free admission).

The best place for overnighting in the area is **Parador Hacienda Juanita** (p. 261), a converted, 160-year-old former coffee plantation lodge in a beautiful setting. There's a wonderful restaurant on site, and meals are served in a dining room and on a back porch overlooking a lush forest. Another option is to barrel on west down to Mayagüez, and then go on to the beach towns to the northwest or to the southwest. It's a 2-hour drive from Mayagüez to San Juan, a distance of 98 miles (158km) up the west coast and across the north coast.

WHERE TO STAY & DINE IN SAN JUAN

All but a handful of visitors arrive in San Juan, the capital city. It is the political base, economic powerhouse, and cultural center of the island, home to about one-third of all Puerto Rico residents.

The second-oldest city in the Americas (behind Santo Domingo in the Dominican Republic), this metropolis presents two different faces. On the one hand, the charming historic district, Old San Juan, has some of the best examples of Spanish colonial architecture in the hemisphere, as well as stunning Art Deco and other buildings from the early part of the 20th century. From La Fortaleza (the governor's mansion) to the two old Spanish forts to the Catedral de San Juan, the wonders of the city are a short walk from each other.

5

New San Juan has its charms as well, particularly evident in its more storied residential architecture in Santurce, Miramar, and Río Piedras. The coastal areas are more modern, where parts of Condado and Isla Verde feel like a more intimate Miami Beach, with rows of luxury hotels and condominiums and fat golden beaches. The two main beach districts have their more low-key corners, however, and the residential Ocean Park community separates them. A few guesthouses are scattered amidst the luxury homes fronting San Juan's best beach.

Much of San Juan, however, is a planning disaster, with urban sprawl eliminating or stressing green areas and ugly condo towers blotting out the view and access to the coast.

Improvements are ongoing all the time, however. San Juan has quietly been transforming over the past decade, with a light-rail train system, a new coliseum, and a state-of-the-art convention center now on line.

Visitors can pretty easily live off the bus and Urban Train system and get where they want to go throughout the tourism districts of Isla Verde, Condado, and Old San Juan, as well in the other main San Juan districts: Miramar, Santurce, Hato Rey, and Río Piedras.

Old San Juan is a 7-square-block area that was once completely enclosed by a wall erected by the Spanish centuries ago. The most powerful fortress in the Caribbean, this fortified city repeatedly held off would-be attackers. By the 19th century, however, it had become one of the Caribbean's most charming residential and commercial districts. Today, it's a setting for restaurants and shops, a large concentration of art galleries and museums. Most of the major resort hotels are located nearby, along the Condado beachfront and at Isla Verde (see "Where to Stay," later). But the Old City has several first rate hotels and inns, as well.

ORIENTATION

Arriving by Plane

Visitors from overseas arrive at **Luis Muñoz Marín International Airport,** the major transportation center of the Caribbean. The airport is on the easternmost side of the city, conveniently located near the Isla Verde, Condado, and Old San Juan tourist districts.

The airport offers services such as a tourist-information center, restaurants, hair stylists, coin lockers for storing luggage, bookstores, banks, currency-exchange kiosks, and bars. There are also a number of shops selling souvenirs and local rums and coffees for last-minute shopping for gifts for folks back home.

GETTING FROM THE AIRPORT TO THE CITY

BY TAXI Some of the larger hotels outside San Juan send vans to pick up airport passengers and transport them back to the property, but they charge separately for this service. In San Juan, you'll probably opt to take a taxi to your hotel (buses at 75¢ are cheap but not very timely or practical). Dozens of taxis line up outside the airport to meet arriving flights, so you never have to wait. There are set fares for destinations within San Juan; for other destinations, the cost of the trip should be determined by the taxi meter. The island's **Puerto Rico Tourism Company** (**Transportation Division; ✆ 787/999-2100** or 787/253-0418) establishes the flat rates between the Luis Muñoz Marín International Airport and major tourist zones: From the airport to any hotel in Isla Verde, the fee is $10; to any hotel in the Condado district, the charge is $15; and to any hotel in Old San Juan, the cost is $19. Taxi service from the airport is quite well regulated, with a dispatcher handing you a ticket detailing your costs. These also include baggage costs (50¢ for each of the first three bags, then $1 per bag) and a 10% to 15% tip is expected.

Travel time can vary widely, depending on traffic conditions, with late-afternoon and early morning traffic jams common during commuting hours Monday through Friday. With no traffic delays, Condado is only a 12-minute drive from the airport, but if you get stuck in one of the island's legendary *tapones,* as traffic jams are called here, it could take up to an hour. Old San Juan, the farthest destination, is about a 20-minute ride without traffic.

BY LIMOUSINE There are more than enough reputable limousine rental companies to choose from, but arrangements must be made beforehand. Limousines don't sit at the airport like taxis. You must arrange pickup in advance or call once you get in. A simple pickup from the airport to your hotel ranges in cost from $100 to $125. Most vehicles fit six passengers comfortably. Your driver will meet you outside the baggage-claim area.

BY PUBLIC CAR Public cars, called *públicos,* are either vans or large sedans that are shared by passengers. The ride can sometimes be crowded and take longer, the more passengers there are. They are a bargain for budget travelers who have to travel a distance from the airport and do not want to rent a car. It will cost you $20 to get to Ponce and $10 to Caguas, plus baggage fee. You'll probably have to take a public bus to pick up the publico line, however.

BY CAR All the major car-rental companies have kiosks at the airport. Although it's possible to rent a car once you arrive, your best bet is to reserve one before you leave home. They provide transportation to your car. See the "Getting Around" section of chapter 3 for details.

To drive into the city, head west along Rte. 26, or the Baldorioty de Castro Expressway, which cuts just south of San Juan's Atlantic coastline. Immediately to your right, you will see an Isla Verde exit, and soon the towering oceanfront condominiums of Isla Verde are visible to the right. The road cuts through the Santurce section at the heart of San Juan. You'll see exits for Condado. All hotels have parking lots open to the public, and several lots are visible from the main roads in the area—Ashford Avenue in the Condado and Isla Verde Avenue in Condado. The road then passes by the Condado Lagoon and crosses into Puerta de Tierra near the Caribe Hilton. The road at this point becomes Avenida Muñoz Rivera, as it passes a beautifully landscaped park of the same name on one side, followed by the El Escambrón public beach. The Third Millennium Park is on the opposite side. The road then climbs a bluff overlooking the Atlantic coastline, offering a dramatic view of waves crashing against the rocky shoals.

Here, you will pass the capitol building on your left, and then the historic Spanish fortress Fort San Cristóbal at the entrance of Old San Juan. If you continue straight down into the city along Calle San Sebastián, the northern border of Plaza Colón, you will find parking at **La Cochera** near Plaza de Armas, which is the closest to the center of the historic district. Another option is to turn right and take the northern coastal road to **Ballaja,** where there is parking. If you plan on visiting the San Sebastian Street area or El Convento hotel, these two options work best.

If you plan on hanging around the jumping SoFo section near La Fortaleza, you may want to head straight at the stop sign in front of Plaza Colón, taking the street that passes beside the Tapia Theater. Right behind the theater, where the road intersects with Calle Recinto Sur, is the large **Paseo Portuario** parking garage (**© 787/722-2233**). Bear right for the entrance. Farther down the one-way street is the city-run **Doña Fela** parking garage (no phone). Another option at Plaza Colón is to turn left at Plaza Colón as if exiting the city. Take your first two rights, which will turn you around again past the Treasury Building, and park your car in another **Covadonga Parking Garage** (**© 787/721-6911**) on the left. Operating hours vary, but they are open at least until midnight during weekdays and 3am weekends. Prices vary, with municipal-run lots cheaper than private lots, but figure on paying $1 per hour.

BY BUS Those with little luggage can take a bus at a cost of 75¢. You need to hop on the B40 or the C45, taking it one stop to Isla Verde. From there, you can take the A5, which runs through Isla Verde, swings towards Condado near Avenida de Diego, and then heads into Old San Juan. To go farther into the Condado, you should switch to B21 at the Parada 18, or Stop 18, bus transfer station, or get off at the Calle Loiza and Avenida De Diego stop and transfer there.

San Juan Orientation

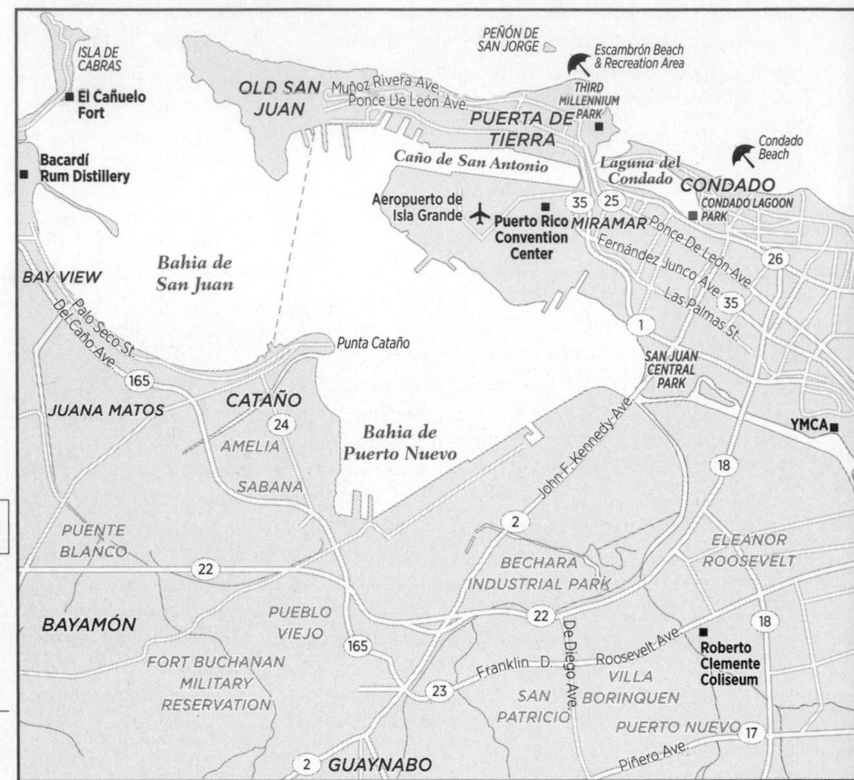

Visitor Information

The Puerto Rico Tourism Company office at **Luís Muñoz Marín Airport** (✆ **787/791-1014**), is open December to April daily from 9am to 10pm, and May to November daily 9am to 8pm. In Old San Juan, the Tourism Company operates an information center at **La Casita,** at Plaza de la Darsena, Old San Juan, near Pier 1, where the cruise ships come in (✆ **787/722-1709**). This office is open Saturday through Wednesday from 8:30am to 8pm, Thursday and Friday 8:30 am to 5pm.

City Layout

Metropolitan San Juan includes the walled Old San Juan at the end of a long peninsula, Puerta de Tierra, the narrow bridge of land between San Juan Bay and the Atlantic Ocean that connects the Old City with the rest of San Juan. You can take a bridge into Condado, a narrow strip of land between the ocean and a lagoon, or continue on to the beautiful residential Miramar neighborhood, where the once seedy waterfront section is being revamped into the world-class Convention Center District and related leisure development. The city also includes Santurce, its

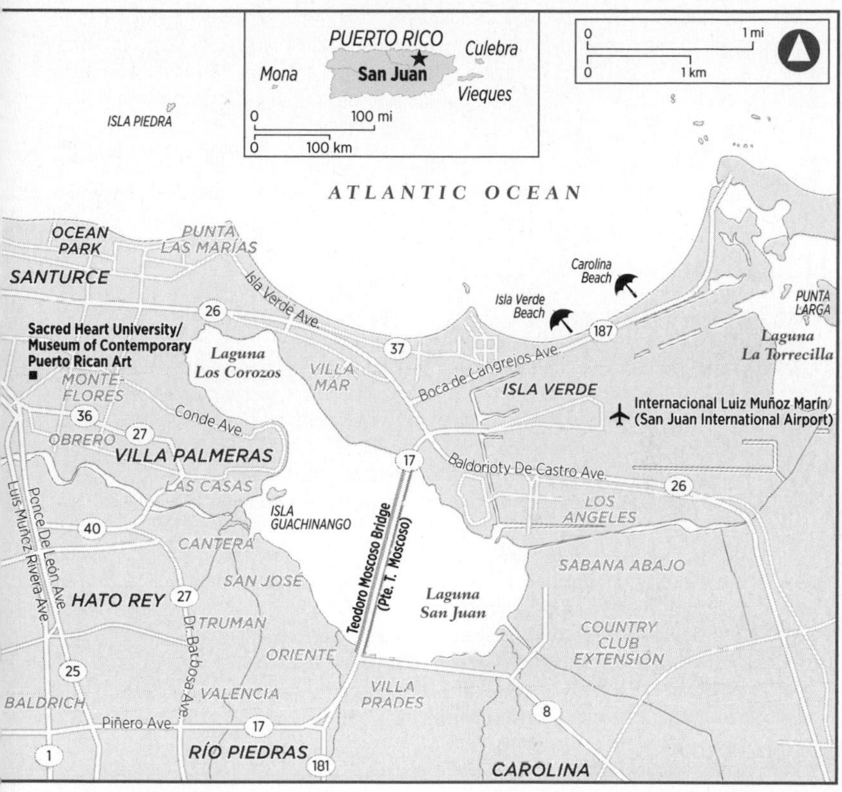

traditional downtown area, which has also been experiencing a revitalization in recent years, with large theaters and old apartment buildings being polished up so that the sector is starting to shine again like it did in its 1940s heyday. The Hato Rey financial district has taken on an almost futuristic look with its elevated Tren Urbano and distinctive Puerto Rico Coliseum, which has something exciting going on just about every week. Río Piedras is both the site of the University of Puerto Rico and one of the best street markets in the Caribbean.

The Condado strip of beachfront hotels, restaurants, casinos, and nightclubs is separated from Miramar by a lagoon. Isla Verde, another resort area, is near the airport, which is separated from the rest of San Juan by an isthmus. Ocean Park is a charming residential neighborhood between the two that has a great beach.

FINDING AN ADDRESS Finding an address in San Juan isn't always easy. You'll have to contend not only with missing street signs and numbers but also with street addresses that appear sometimes in English and at other times in Spanish. The most common Spanish terms for thoroughfares are *calle* (street) and *avenida* (avenue). When it is used, the street number follows the street name; for example, the El Convento hotel is located at Calle del Cristo 100, in Old San Juan. Locating a building in Old San Juan is relatively easy. The area is only 7 square blocks, so by walking around, it's possible to locate most addresses. Also, *sanjuaneros,* for reasons I've yet to determine, still use the stop numbers, or *paradas,* from a trolley that stopped running back in the 1950s as a reference point for directions. For example, *parada* 18 is at the heart of Santurce. In general, the higher the stop number, the farther its distance from Old San Juan.

STREET MAPS *¡Qué Pasa!,* the monthly tourist magazine distributed free by the tourist office, contains accurate, easy-to-read maps of San Juan and the Condado that pinpoint the major attractions.

Neighborhoods in Brief

Old San Juan Home to among the hemisphere's finest restorations of Spanish colonial fortresses and buildings, the Old City is all the more beautiful for its dramatic location sprawled across a headland on the western end of an isleta, or peninsula that splits the roaring Atlantic Ocean from San Juan Bay. It's encircled by water; on the north is the Atlantic Ocean and on the south and west is the tranquil San Juan Bay. The historic Spanish wall built to hold off attacks still circles the city, which is filled with beautiful churches, shady plazas, majestic promenades, and wonderful residences and gardens. It's a robust cultural and commercial district with theaters, galleries, clubs, bars and restaurants, and some of the most interesting shops in the region. There are fine lodgings with sundecks and pools, so you can work on your tan and stay in the city if that's your thing.

Puerta de Tierra Translated as "land gateway," Puerta de Tierra lies just east of the old city walls of San Juan. It is split by Avenida Ponce de León and interconnects Old San Juan with the Puerto Rican "mainland." Founded by freed black slaves, the settlement today functions as the island's administrative center and is the site of military and government buildings, including the capitol and various U.S. naval reserves. It is dominated by the green **Luis Muñoz Rivera Park** and the oceanfront **Third Millennium Park** and adjacent **El Escambrón public beach.** Its southern end is home to a rough and tumble neighborhood with a few interesting eateries.

Miramar Miramar is an upscale residential neighborhood, with a small business district and a large port across San Juan Bay. It has two marinas where fishing boats and yachts lie at anchor. The whole harbor-side area is being redeveloped, spearheaded by the state-of-the-art Puerto Rico Convention Center. A new hotel has just opened, and adjacent luxury retail, office, and residential units are being planned, as is a huge bayside promenade to connect the area to Old San Juan. It's also the site of Isla Grande Airport, where you can board flights to the islands of Vieques and Culebra.

Condado Linked to Puerta de Tierra and Old San Juan by a bridge built in 1910, the Condado was once known as the "Riviera of the Caribbean," enjoying a voguish reputation in the 1920s, which was renewed by revivals in the 1960s and again today, with several restored hotels and other properties opening after dazzling renovations along this district wedged between the Atlantic Ocean and the Condado Lagoon. It's one of the most coveted neighborhoods in Puerto Rico, and offers resorts and guesthouses right on the beach for tourists.

The beautiful oceanfront **Window of the Sea Park** is at the center of the area; it opens onto the Atlantic Ocean and is fronted by gleaming townhouses and luxury towers, home to glamorous residences, restaurants, and designer fashion stores. These include Gucci and Salvatore Ferragamo, luxury condos, and Budatai, one of the island's best restaurants. The former La

Concha has opened next door after a 10-year renovation, and luxury condos are being built in the former Vanderbilt hotel nearby. Luxury hotels and more modest guesthouses fill the sector, as do wonderful restaurants of all types.

One central road, **Avenida Ashford,** runs through Condado, which, at night especially, still evokes something of Miami Beach, with its restored Art Deco properties and modern luxury condos and hotels. The area is popular with locals, the gay community, and visitors.

Ocean Park Dividing the competitive beach resort areas of the Condado and Isla Verde, Ocean Park is a beachfront residential neighborhood with probably the prettiest and most low-key beach in San Juan. The beaches are wide here, and the sun beats down on the beach longer because there are few large condominiums. It's great for windsurfing and kite-sailing, games of paddle ball and body surfing. The tree-covered streets are filled with beautiful suburban homes, a charming mix of Malibu, Spanish, and Caribbean influences.

The white, arching **Ultimate Trolley Beach** delineates the border between Ocean Park and Punta Las Marias. Adjacent to that, the neighborhood of **Santa Teresita,** with its share of equally stunning residences, has an equally nice park, **Barbosa Park.**

The park is usually filled with soccer and basketball players. There are tennis courts, a baseball field, and a track, which are always a beehive of activity.

The beach disappears into a rock formation at **Punta Las Marías,** which is a gated community open to pedestrian visitors during the day. But unless you're a windsurfer using one of the neighborhood's famed launching points, your experience of the area will likely be confined to the **string of fine restaurants along Calle Loíza,** right before it turns into Avenida Isla Verde. The neighborhood is also popular with the gay and lesbian community, both residents and visitors.

Isla Verde East of the Condado, en route to the airport, Isla Verde—technically a part of the municipality of Carolina but in spirit more a part of San Juan—is both larger than the Condado and probably has more hotels. Here there is also an oceanfront row of luxury condos and hotels along a main oceanfront boulevard. But where Condado may score higher with its restaurants and shops, and its older and more artful architecture, Isla Verde wins hands down in the beach department—you'll find a wide, clean, white-sand beach running the full length of the neighborhood just off its main strip. The main road here is called **Isla Verde Avenue. Pine Grove Beach,** a favorite with sailors and surfers, is located east of where the main beach ends. After Isla Verde is a municipal public beach and then the undeveloped area of **Piñones,** with its rural coastal charms.

Don't come here for history or romance. Two features put Isla Verde on the tourist map: some of San Juan's best beaches and its most deluxe hotels. This district appeals to travelers who like a hotel to offer everything under one roof: entertainment, vast selections of dining, convenient shopping, pools, and an array of planned activities.

Hato Rey The city's financial district, the Wall Street of the West Indies, occupies several streets. There are high-rises, a large federal complex, and many business and banking offices.

The sector has been transformed by the **Puerto Rico Coliseum** and the **Tren Urbano,** which snakes through the towers of capitalism on elevated tracks. The new arena gets top acts (it's had the Rolling Stones and Paul McCartney). There's also the **Fine Arts Cinema,** with art and foreign films, luxury seats, gourmet food, and yes, beer and wine.

The sector also contains the huge **Luis Muñoz Marín Park,** with miles of bicycle and jogging paths, picnic areas and fields, interrupted by scores of small ponds and islands of tropical vegetation. The park also features a top-notch amphitheater and a cable car ride.

Rio Piedras South of Hato Rey and Santurce, this is the site of the **University of Puerto Rico,** whose buildings look like an Ivy League school except for the tropical vegetation. It's dominated by the landmark **Roosevelt Bell Tower,** named for Theodore Roosevelt, who donated the money for its construction. It's a top-notch institution than can boast beautiful grounds as an added attraction.

There's also a large shopping area surrounding the **Río Piedras Marketplace** (selling fresh fruit and vegetables) and the pedestrian walkway Paseo de Diego, lined with shops, eateries and bargains galore. The shops attract travelers from across the Caribbean.

The **UPR Botanical Gardens** are located here as well, with a beautifully arranged array of tropical trees and plants.

Suburban San Juan The San Juan sprawl has enveloped surrounding towns, reaching all the way down south into Caguas. Neighboring Bayamón, Guaynabo, and Carolina are practically considered part of the city, however. Guaynabo and Caguas have fine arts centers with top-name acts and full cultural performances, while Bayamón has such family activities as a bicycle linear park and the **Luis A. Ferré Science Technology Park.** Visitors will also likely go to Cataño to visit the **Bacardi Rum Plant.** It's a modest community built right across the bay from Old San Juan.

GETTING AROUND

BY TAXI There is a flat-rate system for most destinations within San Juan, which is effective, and if you're caught in impenetrable traffic, it might actually work to your advantage. The island's **Puerto Rico Tourism Company** (**Transportation Division; ✆ 787/999-2100** or 787/253-0418) establishes flat rates between well-traveled areas within San Juan. From Luis Muñoz Marín International Airport to Isla Verde, $10; to Condado, $15; and to Old San Juan, $19.

There are also set fees from the cruise-ship piers outside of Old San Juan to set destinations: Isla Verde, $19; Condado, $12; and Old San Juan, $7. You will also be charged 50¢ per bag for your first three bags and $1 per bag thereafter. Metered fares start off with an initial charge of $1.75, plus $1.90 per mile, and a 10¢ charge for each 25 seconds of waiting time. Tolls are not included in either fare. Normal tipping supplements of between 10% and 15% of these fares are appreciated.

But while meters are supposed to be used, on most trips outside the zoned rates, drivers will probably offer you a flat rate of their own devising. San Juan cabbies are loath to use the meter, more to do with ripping off the house or the taxman than the customer because more often than not, the quoted price is fair. But feel free to refer to the established flat rate (if it applies) or ask him to turn on the meter. Drivers normally comply immediately. If they refuse, you can get out and refer the driver to the Tourism Company Transportation Division numbers cited above. But if the quoted price seems fair (use the $19 flat rate for the airport to Old San Juan as a guide), it's probably easier to go ahead and pay it.

Taxis are invariably lined up outside the entrance to most of the island's hotels, but if they're not, a staff member can almost always call one for you. If you want to arrange a taxi on your own, some reliable operators in San Juan are **Metro Taxis** (**✆ 787/725-2870** or 725-3280), the **Rochdale Cab Company** (**✆ 787/721-1900**), and the **Major Cab Company** (**✆ 787/723-2460** or 723-1300).

ART ON WHEELS: painted TAXIS

Take a picture of yourself riding smooth inside one of **San Juan's fleet of painted taxis,** ranging in style from classic figurative to graffiti-inspired to abstract expressionistic works. Dozens of artists painted 40 taxis as part of the "Taxi Galería" project, which started in 2005. Local artists, including Alexander Rosado, Wichie Torres, Roberto Pérez, Celso González, and Eric French, used the entire taxi body as their canvas, completing fully realized paintings on the vehicles. The artists clearly loved the project, and participating taxi drivers say driving in a work of art instead of an ordinary taxi has increased demand for services. You'll see these painted taxis darting around the city. All you have to do is hail one.

On one of my rides in a painted taxi (it could have been one of Joan Miró's vibrant and fun pieces), the driver enthused about how his painted car had improved his existence. "People standing in the street just stare at my taxi," he said. "Most cars go down in value with age, but this one is going up."

You no longer have to negotiate a fare with the driver, usually at a flat rate, for trips to far-flung destinations within Puerto Rico. There are also now established fees for taxi rides from San Juan to island destinations. Some examples, from San Juan: Fajardo, $80; Ponce, $125; and Mayagüez, $160. The complete list is available at the Puerto Rico Tourism Company website (www.gotopuertorico.com/puerto-rico-taxis.php).

BY BUS The **Metropolitan Bus Authority** (✆ **787/767-7979** for route information) operates buses in the greater San Juan area. Bus stops are marked by upright metal signs or yellow posts that say PARADA. The bus terminal is the dock area in the same building as the Covadanga parking lot next to the Treasury Department. Fares are 75¢. Three routes are particularly useful for tourists, those that carry San Juan passengers from Old San Juan to other San Juan tourism districts: The **A5** goes to downtown Santurce, Ocean Park and Isla Verde; the **B21** down Condado's Ashford Avenue and then on to downtown San Juan, the city's financial district Hato Rey and the Plaza Las Americas mall; and the **C53,** which heads to the Convention Center District, then down Condado's oceanfront drive and on into Isla Verde. Call for more information about routes and schedules. The private **MetroBus** operates a few key express routes from Old San Juan to Río Piedras for 50¢.

One useful route is the A5, which hits downtown Santurce, Avenida de Diego near Condado, then goes along Loíza Street and down Isla Verde's oceanfront drive where all the hotels are located. You can switch to the B21 at De Diego Street, if you want to go down Condado's main drive, Avenida Ashford.

The B21 runs from Old San Juan to Condado, while also servicing Plaza Las Americas. The privately run MetroBus runs express buses between Old San Juan and Río Piedras, with stops in Hato Rey and Santurce.

Any bus marked ATI hooks up with the Tren Urbano, probably at its Sagrado Corazón Station, which is its last stop into the city. The ticket has been slashed in half to 75¢ to encourage ridership and put it on par with bus rates.

ON FOOT This is the only way to explore Old San Juan. All the major attractions can easily be covered in a day. If you're going from Old San Juan to Isla Verde, however, you'll need to rely on public transportation.

BY TROLLEY When you tire of walking around Old San Juan, you can board one of the free trolleys that run through the historic area. Departure points include the Covadonga, La Puntilla, Plaza de Armas, and the two forts, but you can board along the route by flagging the trolley down (wave at it and signal for it to stop) or by waiting at any of the clearly designated stopping points. Relax and enjoy the sights as the trolleys rumble through the old and narrow streets. The city has also begun operating a trolley along Loiza Street near Ocean Park, in Río Piedras and other areas.

BY LIMOUSINE San Juan has nearly two dozen limousine rental companies, so there are more than enough reputable companies to choose from. There is a wide range of luxury vehicle rentals, called *limosinas* (their Spanish name), available, from Lincoln Town Car limousines to deluxe stretch Hummers. A simple pickup from the airport to your hotel ranges in cost from $100 to $125. Rentals for other standard trips range from about $70 to $125 per hour, with most cars seating six passengers comfortably. Many firms use drivers who hold tour-guide permits, and limousine operators often give tours of Old San Juan, El Yunque, or other sites to small groups or families. If the driver or another guide leaves the vehicle to tour a specific place by foot, it will cost another $15 to $25 hourly.

BY RENTAL CAR See "Getting Around," in chapter 3, for details—including some reasons you should avoid driving in Puerto Rico.

BY FERRY The **Acua Expreso** (✆ **787/729-8714**) connects Old San Juan with the industrial and residential community of Cataño, across the bay. Ferries depart daily every 30 minutes from 6am to 9pm. The one-way fare to Cataño is $1.

San Juan Mass-Transit: Tren Urbano

Tren Urbano, the first mass-transit project in the history of Puerto Rico, opened in 2005, linking San Juan to suburbs such as Santurce, Bayamón, and Guaynabo. Costing about $2 billion, the system provides an easy mode of transportation to the most congested areas of metropolitan San Juan. During rush hour (5–9am and 3–6pm), the train operates every 8 minutes; otherwise, it runs every 12 minutes. There is no service daily from 11:20pm to 5:30am. The fare is 75¢ one-way and includes a transfer to buses. It's a beautiful ride and gives tourists a different experience of the city; the train passes on an elevated track through the modern, Hato Rey financial district, plunges underground in Río Piedras, and then snakes through upscale suburban neighborhoods, with tropical foliage and pools in many backyards. The fare includes a transfer because a special class of buses has been created to link up with particular Tren Urbano routes. The train and accompanying buses keep special expanded schedules during big events, such as festivals in Old San Juan. They also extend schedules when big acts play at the Puerto Rico Coliseum, or the Tourism Company throws a New Year's Eve party at the Convention Center. For more information, call ✆ **866/900-1284,** or log onto www.ati.gobierno.pr.

Departures are from the San Juan Terminal at pier number 2 in Old San Juan. However, it's best to avoid rush hours because hundreds of locals who work in town use this ferry. The ride lasts 6 minutes.

BY PUBLIC CAR Public cars, called *públicos,* are either vans or large sedans that are shared by passengers. Though they can be crowded and uncomfortable, more often than not they are quite comfortable and spacious. And they are a bargain for budget travelers who have to travel a distance from the airport and do not want to rent a car. Most public cars travel set routes at prices far below what taxis would charge. You should consider taking one from the airport if traveling on a budget to areas outside of San Juan.

In San Juan, *público* departure and arrival points include the airport, right outside Old San Juan near Plaza Colón, and by the Río Piedras public marketplace. Every town on the island has at least one area where *públicos* congregate.

If you are traveling out on the island, you also can look them up in the telephone book and Yellow Pages under *la linea,* which are public cars that will pick you up where you are staying and bring you to a specific destination at an agreed-upon price. A 2-hour drive from San Juan to Guánica costs $25 one-way. Because you travel with other passengers, you may have to wait until the driver takes them to their destinations first. He will pick up and drop off passengers according to what is best for his route and schedule.

BY BIKE **Rent the Bicycle,** Calle Del Muelle, Capitolio Plaza 205, San Juan (✆ **787/602-9696**) is at the entrance of the Old San Juan bayside waterfront. They rent bikes for $27 per day ($17 for half a day) and also conduct several tours throughout San Juan (the Piñones boardwalk tour is probably the best bet). Rentals are available at **Hot Dog Cycling,** Av. Isla Verde 5916, La Plazoleta Shopping Center (✆ **787/721-0776**), open Monday to Saturday 9am to 6pm. Charges for rentals are $15 per half-day, $25 for a full day.

[Fast FACTS] SAN JUAN

Airport See "Arriving by Plane" and "Getting from the Airport to the City," earlier in this chapter.

American Express Call the company's local toll-free customer service line: ✆ **800/327-1267.**

Banks Local banks have branches with ATMs in San Juan that function on U.S. networks. Branches are open Monday to Friday 8:30am to 4pm. Bank branches in malls are open Saturday 8:30am to 6pm and Sunday 9am to 3pm.

Bus Information See "Getting Around," above. For information about bus routes in San Juan, call ✆ **787/767-7979.**

Camera & Film **Walgreens** (✆ **787/722-6290;** Calle Cruz 201 at corner with Calle San Francisco at Plaza Colón) develops prints from film and digital cameras and also sells camera supplies. **RadioShack** (✆ **787/977-2440 Calle Fortaleza 250**) has a wide selection of digital cameras, recorders, and related equipment and supplies.

Car Rentals See "Getting Around," in chapter 3. If you want to reserve after you've arrived in Puerto Rico, try **Avis, Budget,** or **Hertz,** or the local agencies **Charlie Car Rental** or **Target Car Rental.**

Consulates Many countries maintain honorary consulates here, mostly to try to drum up mutually beneficial trade on the island, but they can be of assistance to travelers. **Britain** has a consulate at Av. Chardón 350 (© **787/758-9828**) at Hato Rey, open Monday to Friday 9am to 1pm and 2 to 5pm. The consulate for **Canada** is at Av. Ponce de León 268 (© **787/759-6629**), also at Hato Rey, and open only by appointment.

Currency Exchange The unit of currency is the U.S. dollar. Many large banks provide currency exchange at some branches, and you can also exchange money at the **Luis Muñoz Marín International Airport.** See "Money & Costs" in chapter 3.

Drugstores One of the most centrally located pharmacies is **Puerto Rican Drug Co.,** Calle San Francisco 157 (© **787/725-2202**), in Old San Juan. It's open Monday to Friday from 7:30am to 9:30pm, Saturday 8am to 9:30pm, and Sunday 8:30am to 7:30pm. **Walgreens,** Av. Ashford 1130, Condado (© **787/725-1510**), is open 24 hours. There are also other Walgreens throughout the city, one in practically every neighborhood. There are other locations in Old San Juan, Miramar, Isla Verde, and on Calle Loiza near Ocean Park.

Emergencies In an emergency, dial © **911.** Or call the local police (© **787/343-2020**), fire department (© **787/343-2020**), ambulance (© **787/766-2222**), or medical assistance (© **787/754-2550**).

Eyeglasses Services are available at **Pearle Vision Express,** Plaza Las Americas Shopping Mall (© **787/753-1033**). Hours are Monday to Saturday from 9am to 9pm and Sunday from 11am to 5pm. **Tropical Vision,** La Fortaleza St. 308, (© **787/723-5488**) is located in Old San Juan.

Hospitals **Ashford Presbyterian Community Hospital,** Av. Ashford 1451 (© **787/721-2160**), maintains a 24-hour emergency room.

Internet Access Try **CyberNet Café,** Av. Ashford 1128 (© **787/724-4033**) on the Condado; it charges $3 for 20 minutes, $5 for 35 minutes, or $7 for 50 minutes. Open Monday to Saturday 9am to 11pm, Sunday 10am to 11pm. There is another branch in Isla Verde (Av. Isla Verde 5980, Isla Verde, © **787/728-4195**). If you have a laptop or other wireless device, there are Internet hotspots throughout the city at food courts in malls, Starbucks, Burger King, McDonalds, and historic plazas in Old San Juan.

Police Call © **787/726-7020** for the local police.

Post Office In San Juan, the **General Post Office** is at Av. Franklin Delano Roosevelt 585 (© **787/622-1758**). If you don't know your address in San Juan, you can ask that your mail be sent here "c/o General Delivery." This main branch is open Monday to Friday from 5:30am to 6pm, Saturday from 6am to 2pm. A letter from Puerto Rico to the U.S. mainland will arrive in about 4 days. See chapter 12, "Fast Facts," for more information.

Restrooms Restrooms are not public facilities accessible from the street. It's necessary to enter a hotel lobby, cafe, or restaurant to gain access to a toilet. Fortunately, large-scale hotels are familiar with this situation, and someone looking for a restroom usually isn't challenged during his or her pursuit.

Safety At night, exercise caution when walking along the back streets of San Juan, and don't venture onto the unguarded public stretches of the Condado and Isla Verde beaches at night. Few muggings take place in tourist areas, but all these areas are favorite targets for muggers.

Salons Most of San Juan's large resort hotels, including the Condado Plaza, the Marriott, and the Sheraton Old San Juan Hotel, maintain hair salons. **Los Muchachos** in Old San Juan has an army of stylists cutting and sprucing walk-in traffic as well as appointments.

Taxis See "Getting Around," earlier.

Telephone, Computer & Fax There are international call, Internet, and fax and mail services available at stores near the cruise-ship docks (catering mostly to crew). Long distance calling cards are widely available in drugstores and variety shops. For more information, see "Staying Connected," in chapter 3.

Whatever your preferences in accommodations—a beachfront resort or a place in historic Old San Juan, sumptuous luxury or an inexpensive base from which to see the sights—you can find a perfect fit in San Juan.

In addition to checking the recommendations listed here, you might want to contact a travel agent; there are package deals galore, which can save you money and match you with an establishment that meets your requirements. See "Package Deals for the Independent Traveler," in chapter 3.

Before talking to a travel agent, however, you should refer to our comments about how to select a room in Puerto Rico.

Not all hotels here have air-conditioned rooms. We've pointed them out in the recommendations below. If air-conditioning is important to you, make sure "A/C" appears after *"In room"* at the end of the listing.

If you prefer shopping and historic sights to the beach, then Old San Juan might be your preferred nest. The high-rise resort hotels lie primarily along the Condado beach strip and the equally good sands of Isla Verde. The hotels along Condado and Isla Verde attract the cruise-ship and casino crowds. The hotels away from the beach in San Juan, in such sections as Santurce, are primarily for business clients.

The guesthouses of Ocean Park, free from the high rises elsewhere but with an equally beautiful beach, attract a young urban crowd and those looking for a more low-key ambience.

WHERE TO STAY

Old San Juan

Old San Juan is 1½ miles (2.4km) from the beach. You should choose a hotel here if you're more interested in shopping and attractions than you are in watersports. The closest beach is Escambrón public beach in Puerta de Tierra, about a half-hour walk from the center of Old San Juan. For most visitors, a cab ride (15 min.) or bus ride (45 min.) to Condado, Ocean Park, or Isla Verde is a better option. For the locations of hotels in Old San Juan, see the map on p. 109.

EXPENSIVE

Chateau Cervantes ★★ This 12-unit boutique hotel seamlessly blends the colonial charm of its 16th-century quarters with ultramodern interiors by local designer Nono Maldonado. The Old World charm of Hotel El Convento (see below) is still the Old City's most impressive lodging option; this is an impressive upscale alternative. The hotel's high ceilings, arched doorways, windows, and wrought-iron balcony railings are quintessential Old San Juan, but Maldonado, working from a gold and muted gemstone palette, has remade the guest rooms into a plush world of velvet and silk. Paintings by island artist Carlos Dávila add to the decor, and the

Taxes & Service Charges

All hotel rooms in Puerto Rico are subject to a tax that is not included in the rates given in this book. At casino hotels, the tax is 12%; at noncasino hotels, it's 9%. At government-sponsored country inns, called *paradores puertorriqueños,* you pay a 7% tax. San Juan also began charging a head tax on hotel guests ranging from $3 to $5 nightly. Some hotels add a 10% service charge; if not, you're expected to tip for services rendered. Many large hotels also charge resort fees, ostensibly to offset the costs of facilities such as a pool or health club, which can add substantially to your bill. Fees range from 12% to 22% of the cost of your room per night. When you're booking a room, it's a good idea to ask about these charges.

small bathrooms are lined with marble. Despite the comfort of the beds and furnishings, a 200-square-foot (19-sq.-m) room (standard) is too small for most travelers, so budget for a junior suite. Only the presidential suite has a full bathtub. The hotel is located on one of Old City's busiest streets in the midst of many bars and restaurants, so weekend noise levels bothers some guests. Rates include continental breakfast at Panza restaurant on its ground floor, which serves creative international cuisine in a chic setting.

Calle Recinto Sur 307, Old San Juan, PR 00901. ✆ **787/724-7722.** Fax 787/289-8909. www.cervantespr.com. 12 units. $225 double; $285 junior suites; $425 Cervantes suites; $925 penthouse for 4. Rates include continental breakfast. AE, MC, V. Bus: Old Town Trolley. **Amenities:** Restaurant; smoke-free rooms. *In room:* A/C, TV/CD/DVD, hair dryer, Wi-Fi.

Hotel El Convento Puerto Rico's most famous hotel came back to life after a 1997 restoration, and it remains one of the most charming historic hotels in the Caribbean and a quintessential Old San Juan experience. The core of the building was constructed in 1651 as the New World's first Carmelite convent, but over the years it played many roles, from a dance hall to a flophouse, to a parking lot for garbage trucks. It first opened as a hotel in 1962. The restoration has returned the property to its past glory, while injecting it with an urban, up-to-date feel, very much like Old San Juan itself. Its fourth-floor rooftop has a small pool, adjacent Jacuzzi, and a big sun terrace with blessed views of the nearby Catedral de San Juan, as well as views of the bay and the Atlantic. The lower two floors feature a collection of shops, bars, and restaurants, all worth staying for a while. A late-afternoon wine-and-cheese offering is served on a beautiful midfloor dining area spilling onto an outdoor terrace overlooking Calle Cristo. The midsize accommodations include Spanish-style furnishings, throw rugs, beamed ceilings, paneling, and Andalusian terra-cotta floor tiles. Each unit contains king-size, queen-size, or two double or twin beds, fitted with fine linens. The small bathrooms, with tub/shower combinations, contain scales and second phones. For the ultimate in luxury, there is the Gloria Vanderbilt restored suite, which runs for $1,490 in the high season to $1,200 in the summer season, or the Pablo Casals suite, which runs around $665 in the summer and $865 in the winter. Room no. 508 is a corner room with panoramic views.

Calle del Cristo 100, San Juan, PR 00901. ✆ **800/468-2779** or 787/723-9020. Fax 787/721-2877. www.elconvento.com. 68 units. Winter $240–$370 double, from $650 suite; off-season $175–$265 double,

Old San Juan Accommodations & Dining

Information (i) City Walls

0 1/10 mile
0 100 meters

N

area of detail

ATLANTIC OCEAN

SAN JUAN

Castillo de San Felipe del Morro

Cemeterio de San Juan

Murallas de San Juan

El Campo del Morro

Calle del Morro

Fuerte San Cristobal

Norzagaray

de Valle

Plaza San José

Calle San Sebastian

Calle Sol

C. J. J. Acosta

C. Tamarindo

Calle O'Donell

Plaza de Colon

Calle Luna

Calle San Jose

Calle Cruz

Calle San Justo

Calle Tanca

C. Capilla

Del Cristo

Calle San Francisco

Plaza de Armas

Calle Fortaleza

Calle Tetuan

Calle Recinto

Calle Braumbaugh

Paseo de la Princesa

Calle Presidio

El Arsenal

Calle Puntillo

Ave. Munoz Rivera

Ave. Ponce de Leon

Paseo de Covadonga

Ave. Fernandez Juncos

Calle Contreras

C. de Muelle

Calle Allen

Calle Marina

DINING ◆

Al Dente **22**
Amadeus **13**
Aquaviva **34**
Barú **14**
Ben & Jerry's **7**
Bodega Chic **11**
Burén **10**
Café Berlin **33**
Café Puerto Rico **31**
Caficultura **32**
Caña **6**
Carli Café Concierto **17**
Dragonfly **35**
El Hamburger **40**
El Jibarito **19**
El Patio de Sam **12**
El Picoteo **2**
Il Perugino **9**
J Taste **23**
La Bombonera **18**
La Mallorquina **21**
Makarios **38**
Old Harbor Brewery Steak and Lobster House **16**
Ostra Cosa **5**
Parrot Club **30**
Patio del Nispero **4**
Raíces **24**
Sofia **27**
Tantra **37**
Toro Salao **36**
Trois Cent Onze **25**

ACCOMMODATIONS ■

Casablanca Hotel **28**
Chateau Cervantes **29**
Da House **26**
Gallery Inn at Galería San Juan **15**
Hotel El Convento **1**
Hotel Milano **20**
Howard Johnson Old San Juan Hotel **8**
Sheraton Old San Juan Hotel & Casino **39**
The Caleta Guesthouse **3**

from $539 suite. Rates include afternoon wine and cheese reception. AE, DC, DISC, MC, V. Parking $20. Bus: Old City Trolley. **Amenities:** 4 restaurants; 3 bars; fitness center; Jacuzzi; small rooftop plunge pool; Wi-Fi; rooms for those w/limited mobility. *In room:* A/C, TV, hair dryer.

Sheraton Old San Juan Hotel & Casino ★ This may be convenient for cruise-ship passengers wanting to spend a few nights in San Juan before or after a cruise, but don't expect Old City charm. Opened in 1997, this dignified, nine-story, waterfront hotel was part of a $100-million renovation of San Juan's cruise-port facilities. Backed by buildings erected by the Spanish monarchs in the 19th century, the hotel sits on the bay coast, where it hosts the city's busiest and most modern cruise-ship terminals. It remains a good option for cruise travelers wanting to extend their trip with a stay in San Juan. Most of the major cruise ships dock nearby. On days when cruise ships pull into port, the hotel's lobby and bars are likely to be jammed with passengers stretching their legs after a few days at sea. Most of the lobby level here is devoted to a mammoth casino. Take a pass on the hotel restaurants; you are steps from SoFo (S. Fortaleza St., near Plaza Colón), which has some of the finest eateries in the city.

Calle Brumbaugh 100, San Juan, PR 00902. © **800/325-3535** or 787/721-5100. Fax 787/721-1111. www.sheraton.com. 240 units. Winter $169–$219 double, $229–$249 suite; off-season $159–$189 double, $209 suite. AE, DC, DISC, MC, V. Valet parking $21. Bus: Old City Trolley. **Amenities:** 2 restaurants; 3 bars; casino; fitness center; Jacuzzi; outdoor pool; room service; smoke-free rooms; rooms for those w/limited mobility. *In room:* A/C, TV, hair dryer, minibar.

MODERATE

Casablanca Hotel This is a funky beautiful inn, with a North African air, that makes perfect sense in the Old City's bustling retail area, with passengers and merchandise arriving in ships docking in the nearby bay. The lobby and public areas have beautiful mosaic tile, a mix of restored antiques, contemporary furnishings, bold artwork and wrought-iron lanterns. Deluxe rooms have satellite TV and step-out balconies, and superior rooms also carry sofas and reading areas. The guests are as eclectic as the interiors, and both make for a great experience. You are in the middle of SoFo, with great places to eat from dawn to past midnight just steps from your front door, along with all the area night clubs, bars, museums, and other attractions. There's a lot of space to hang out and meet other guests. The rooftop is a pleasant enough place to work on a tan. You'll leave feeling as though you've gotten a lot for your money here. If you don't need a beach, and you can't afford El Convento, this is another option.

Calle Fortaleza 316, San Juan, PR 00901. © **787/725-3436.** Fax 787/725-3435. www.hotelcasablancapr.com. 35 units. Year-round $95–$195 double. $5 continental breakfast. AE, MC, V. Bus: Old City Trolley. **Amenities:** Reading lounge, free pass to nearby gym; rooftop terrace and stone plunge pools; Wi-Fi. *In room:* A/C, TV, iPod dock and sound system.

Gallery Inn at Galería San Juan ★ This unique hotel's location and ambience are unbeatable. The inn rambles through a 300-year-old building overlooking Old San Juan's northern sea wall. There are sweeping sea views, as well as the vista across the colonial city rooftops, extending all the way down to San Juan Bay. Verdant courtyards, interior gardens, and patios and terraces appear around every bend one takes in the inn. The chatter of tropical birds and the murmur of fountains complete the atmosphere in the Caribbean's most whimsically bohemian hotel. In the 1700s, it was the home of an aristocratic Spanish family, but today Jan D'Esopo and Manuco Gandia created this inn out of their home and Jan's art studio. The entire inn is covered with clay and bronze figures, as well as other original art by Jan, and each guest room also functions as gallery space, with Jan's original silk screens, paintings, and prints on display. The least expensive doubles are fairly roomy and attractively furnished, with good beds. The rooftop Wine Deck has the best view in Old San Juan. Classical music concerts are often held in the Music Room and are free for guests. A small pool has also been added to the property. ***Note to lovers:*** The honeymoon suite has a Jacuzzi on a private balcony with a panoramic view of El Morro. From the rooftop terrace, there is a 360-degree view of the historic Old Town and the port. This is the highest point in San Juan and the most idyllic place to enjoy a breeze at twilight and a glass of wine.

Calle Norzagaray 204–206, San Juan, PR 00901. ✆ **866/572-ARTE** (2783) or 787/722-1808. Fax 787/977-3929. www.thegalleryinn.com. 22 units (some with shower only). Year-round $140–$265 double; $280 to $350 suite. Off-season specials available. Rates include continental breakfast and 6pm wine and cheese reception. AE, DC, MC, V. 6 free parking spaces, plus parking on the street. Bus: Old City Trolley. **Amenities:** Breakfast room. *In room:* A/C, hair dryer.

Hotel Milano There's not much remarkable about this hotel built from a 1920s warehouse, except clean, modern facilities at a good price in a great location, right near all the restaurants and bars along South Fortaleza Street. You enter a wood-sheathed lobby at end of Calle Fortaleza before ascending to one of the clean, well-lit bedrooms. The simple, modern rooms have cruise-ship-style decor and unremarkable views, and there's excellent Wi-Fi Internet access. The rooftop terrace has outstanding views, and is a great spot to relax or enjoy the $5 continental breakfast. The best rooms are on the upper floors overlooking the street. You're in SoFo, home to some of Puerto Rico's best restaurants.

Calle Fortaleza 307, San Juan, PR 00901. ✆ **877/729-9050** or 787/729-9050. Fax 787/722-3379. www.hotelmilanopr.com. 30 units. Winter $95–$185 double; off-season $85–$145 double. $5 continental breakfast. AE, MC, V. Bus: Old City Trolley. **Amenities:** Rooftop terrace cafe; Wi-Fi; smoke-free rooms; rooms for those w/limited mobility. *In room:* A/C, TV, fridge, hair dryer.

INEXPENSIVE

Da House This has the feel of a European hostel, with bright, sunny, affordable rooms and a young and creative clientele, all on top of the legendary Nuyorican Café. The rooftop sun deck is a great place to chill out with lounge chairs and a hot tub. The downstairs cafe is a great venue for theater and music (it can be quite loud, so if you don't want to be in the middle of a nightlife scene, this is not your place). The Wi-Fi Internet cafe in the lobby is a good spot to pick up insider tourist tips. Great art adorns the guesthouse, and the staff is friendly and helpful. Rooms are clean and comfortable.

Calle San Francisco 312, entrance down Callejon de la Capilla, San Juan, PR 00901. ✆ **787/366-5074** or 787/977-1180. Fax 787/722-3379. www.dahousehotelpr.com. 30 units. Year-round $80–$120 double. AE, MC, V. Bus: Old City Trolley. **Amenities:** Pizza restaurant; bar; music and theater nightclub. *In room:* A/C, Wi-Fi.

Howard Johnson Old San Juan Hotel Plaza de Armas This renovated apartment building at the center of Old San Juan gives you a sense of how *sanjuaneros* live in the historic quarter, with rooms wrapped around a prominent interior courtyard. It's right on Old San Juan's central Plaza de Armas, also home to San Juan City Hall and the Puerto Rico State Department. Like those at Hotel Milano (see

ROOM WITH A LOCAL'S VIEW: apartment RENTALS

Despite the explosion of Old City hotel and guesthouse rooms over the past few years, one of the best ways to experience the city remains getting a furnished apartment for a short-term rental. Many are restored, historic quarters with beautiful rooftop terraces or verdant interior courtyards, or both. You'll get a great sense during your vacation of what it feels like to live in this enchanted city, and you'll normally save money (especially if you're a large group).

Prices range from $500 weekly for a basic studio to $2,500 weekly for a three-bedroom, restored colonial beauty with rooftop terrace and ocean views. Short-term rentals are assessed a 7% tax, and many require a minimum 3-day or 4-day stay. Cleaning fees are also assessed, which can range from $50 to $75.

The expert in Old City short-term rentals is **Vida Urbana,** Calle Cruz 255, Old San Juan, PR 00901 (✆ **787/587-3031;** www.vidaurbanapr.com), a spinoff of Caleta Realty, a veteran in this field. Years ago, I found a three-bedroom apartment through Caleta, a place near Catedral de San Juan with huge adjoining living and dining rooms and a rooftop terrace running the length of the apartment. We loved it. We had a reception there, and a group of about eight friends stayed there for the week. A comparable apartment would cost around $1,500 for the week today. There are two lovely apartments for rent above the gallery and gift shop **Bóveda,** Calle Cristo 209, Old San Juan, PR 00901 (✆ **787/725-0263;** www.boveda.info), with artful, bright decor in a restored colonial building, complete with interior garden courtyard and balconies with double-door entrances. A cool tropical vibe flows through the duplex ($1,000 weekly) and studio suite ($500 weekly). **The Caleta Guesthouse,** Caleta de las Monjas 11, Old San Juan, PR 00901 (✆ **787/725-5347;** www.thecaleta.com), has affordable studios and one-bedroom furnished apartments. It's located on one of Old San Juan's most charming streets, across from a lookout over San Juan Bay, but the accommodations are fairly basic.

In **Condado** and **Isla Verde** rates range from $525 a week for a studio to $2,250 a week for a deluxe, modern, three-bedroom condo. **San Juan Vacations,** Cond. Marbella del Caribe, Ste. S-5, Isla Verde 00979 (✆ **800/266-3639** or 787/727-1591; www.sanjuanvacations.com), is the biggest name in the business. We've also worked through **Ronnie's Properties,** Calle Marseilles 14, Ritz Condominium, Ste. 11-F, San Juan, PR 00907 (www.ronniesproperties.com).

above), these are clean, comfortable rooms in the heart of the city. Visitors here know what to expect, and they leave satisfied. There are several spots for a meal, including an open-air cafe on the plaza serving tasty local coffee, as well as two drugstores, a supermarket, and Marshall's Department store—plus this is conveniently near all Old San Juan attractions. The entire plaza has Wi-Fi Internet access. Free continental breakfast is served in the lobby. The downside: there's no pool or sundeck here.

Calle San José 202, San Juan, PR 00901. ✆ **877/722-9191.** Fax 787/725-3091. www.hojo.com. 30 units. Winter $116–$199 double; off-season $100–$185 double. AE, MC, V. Bus: Old Town Trolley. **Amenities:** On-site bistro, smoke-free rooms; rooms for those w/limited mobility. *In room:* A/C, TV, Wi-Fi, hair dryer.

Puerta De Tierra

Stay in Puerta de Tierra only if you have a desire to be at the Caribe Hilton. When you stay in Puerta de Tierra, you're sandwiched halfway between Old San Juan and the Condado, but you're not getting the advantages of staying right in the heart of either. At night, you must travel by taxi or stay in your hotel. The area is not safe to walk around at night, largely because there is nowhere to walk to except the mammoth Luis Muñoz Rivera Park and the Third Millennium Park, which are beautiful places during the day but mostly deserted at night. For the location of hotels in Puerta de Tierra, see the map on p. 115.

Caribe Hilton ★ The hotel that first put Puerto Rico on the world tourism map when it opened in 1949 is still one of the most up-to-date spa and convention hotels in San Juan. This deluxe beauty, which was kept new with several dazzling renovations over the years, has a private beach and huge tropical garden and sits on a choice piece of Atlantic coastline outside Old San Juan.

Rooms have been substantially upgraded, with larger-than-expected bathrooms with tub/shower combinations, as well as comfortable, tropical-inspired furniture. In the Caribe Terrace Bar, you can order the bartender's celebrated piña colada, which was once enjoyed by movie legends Joan Crawford and Errol Flynn. An oceanfront spa and fitness center, **Las Olas,** features such tantalizing delights as couples massages, body wraps, hydrotherapy tub treatments, and soothing cucumber sun therapies.

Calle Los Rosales, San Juan, PR 00901. ✆ **800/445-8667** or 787/721-0303. Fax 787/725-8849. www.caribe.hilton.com. 812 units. Winter $244–$329 double; off-season $275–$369 double; year-round $429–$2,029 suite. Children 16 and under stay free in parent's room (maximum 4 people per room). AE, DC, DISC, MC, V. Valet parking $20; self-parking $15. Bus: B21. **Amenities:** 5 restaurants; 2 bars; babysitting; children's activities and playground; health club; room service; smoke-free rooms; rooms for those w/limited mobility. *In room:* A/C, TV, hair dryer, minibar, Wi-Fi.

Condado

The Condado has undergone a revitalization in recent years. Right at its heart, the Windows to the Sea Park has risen from the ashes of an old convention center, and La Concha, a landmark of the island's Tropical Modernism movement, has been beautifully redeveloped. Designer boutiques and trendy restaurants have been mounted on the ruins of tacky souvenir shops and cheap eateries. From one end of Ashford Avenue to the other, there are great dining options for every budget, all sorts of stores from book shops to upscale jewelers, plus spas, watersports outfitters, and anything else you might think of. The area around Magdalena Avenue has an extraordinary number of boutiques. There are good bus connections into Old San Juan, and taxis are plentiful. For the locations of hotels in Condado, see the map on p. 115.

VERY EXPENSIVE

Conrad Condado Plaza Hotel & Casino ★ This is one of the busiest hotels on Puerto Rico, with enough facilities and restaurants to keep visitors occupied. It's a favorite of business travelers, tour groups, and conventions, but it also attracts independent travelers. Spacious guest rooms and multiple lobbies recently benefited from a $65-million make-over; the rooms have private terraces and are bright and airy with deluxe beds and large, modern bathrooms. The property sprawls across Ashford Avenue, so overlooks both the Condado Lagoon and the sector's Atlantic coastline. It has one of the city's most popular casinos, and some of its finest dining spots. Right outside the casino is the Eight Noodle Bar, a favorite late-night snacking spot for San Juan's party set, with its kitchen open from noon to 4am daily. One of the island's most renowned chefs, Wilo Benet, has brought two of his signature restaurants here: Pikayo and Varita.

Av. Ashford 999, San Juan, PR 00907. ✆ **888/722-1274** or 787/721-1000. Fax 787/721-1968. www.condadoplaza.com. 570 units. Winter $199–$259 double, $259–$729 suite; off-season $159–$209 double, $219–$619 suite. AE, DC, DISC, MC, V. Valet parking $15; self-parking $10. Bus: C53, B21. **Amenities:** 5 restaurants; 3 bars; casino; children's activities; health club; 3 Jacuzzis; 3 outdoor pools; room service; spa; 2 tennis courts; watersports equipment; smoke-free rooms; rooms for those w/limited mobility. *In room:* A/C, TV, hair dryer, minibar.

La Concha: A Renaissance Resort ★★ The reopening of this hotel—50 years to the day from when it first opened to rave reviews in December 1958—took 7 years and carried a $220-million price tag, but it was well worth it. Thank former San Juan mayor and governor Sila Calderón and the Puerto Rico Architects Association for stopping the wrecking ball on this one. This renovation completes the comeback of Condado, with oceanfront rooms that feel as if they are part of the horizon, and multilevel infinity pool area and adjoining beaches that form a dreamscape in which guests willfully lose themselves. The water motif extends to the cascading fountain at its entrance, the fountains surrounding an open-air deck, and views of the sea from every vantage point. The lobby's Italian marble, white furniture, and huge window to the sea also pull the resort's exteriors and interiors together. The signature shell structure, which sits on the beach surrounded by water, is home to Perla Restaurant, a seafood restaurant run by prominent local chef Dayn Smith. The hotel's lobby bar is a great spot for tapas and wine, and the casino sits just off it. Surrounded by designer boutiques and trendy restaurants, La Concha has been a local hot spot since it reopened, and its lobby area always has the sound of Latin rhythms.

Guest rooms have the latest high-tech gadgets; understated natural wood and beige interiors form a canvas for the beautiful views and tropical prints on the walls. The hotel was set to open an additional 253-unit luxury suite tower by summer 2010.

Av. Ashford 1077, San Juan, PR 00907. ✆ **877/524-7778** or 787/721-7500. Fax 787/724-7929. www.laconcharesort.com. 248 units. Winter $309–$359 double, $399–$522 suite; off-season $199–$249 double, $289–$442 suite. AE, DC, DISC, MC, V. Valet parking $25; self-parking $18. Bus: C53, B21. **Amenities:** 6 restaurants; 2 bars; pools; room service; Wi-Fi; rooms for those w/limited mobility. *In room:* A/C, flatscreen TV, music players for any format, hair dryer.

San Juan Marriott Resort & Stellaris Casino ★ This centrally located hotel is on one of the Condado's nicest beaches and within walking distance of two parks and the best restaurants in the sector. The tallest building on the Condado, this 21-story landmark packs lots of postmodern style and has an open, comfortable lobby area. A hit with families and kids, it has extensive children's activities and a pool with two water slides. It also has a jumping casino and lobby area, the scene of big band and Latin jazz performances. Even the sports bar by the pool is active with

Puerta de Tierra, Miramar, Condado & Ocean Park Accommodations & Dining

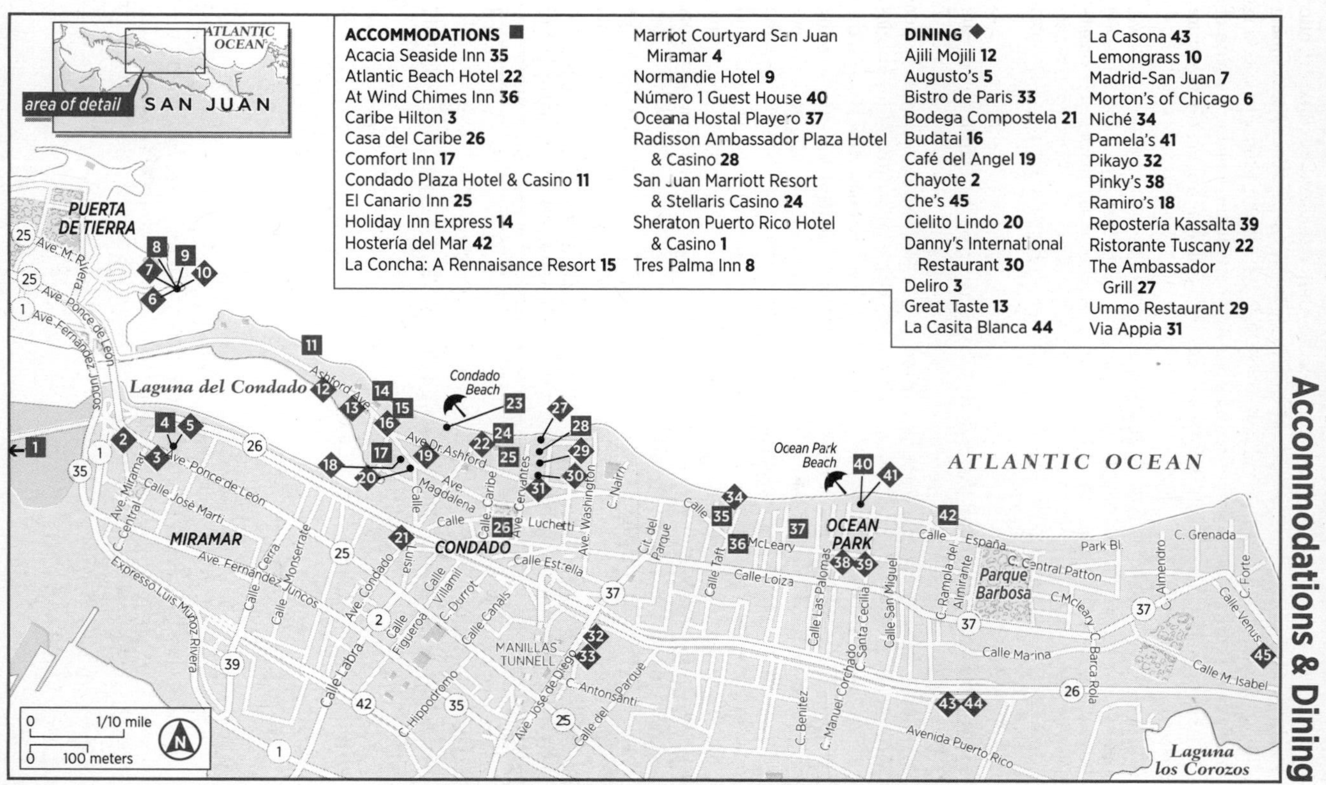

sports fans from up and down the East Coast. The guest rooms are generally spacious, with good views of the water, and each comes with a tiled bathroom with a tub/shower combination. The pastel tones of the comfortable bedrooms are a bit too washed out for our taste, but that's the only legitimate gripe about this property. Junior suites have a living area with a sofa bed. We can't say enough about its great location in the best part of Condado, which is not immediately apparent to visitors. It's an easy walk to anywhere you want to go. And the staff is among the friendliest in town.

Av. Ashford 1309, San Juan, PR 00907. ✆ **800/228-9290** or 787/722-7000. Fax 787/722-6800. www.marriott.com. 525 units. Winter $295–$390 double, $420–$745 suite; summer $189–$284 double, $314–$639 suite. Suite rate includes breakfast. AE, DC, DISC, MC, V. Valet parking $20; self-parking $16. Bus: B21, A5. **Amenities:** 3 restaurants; 3 bars; babysitting; casino; health club; Jacuzzi; 2 pools; room service; sauna; 2 tennis courts; rooms for those w/limited mobility. *In room:* A/C, TV, hair dryer, minibar, Wi-Fi.

EXPENSIVE

Doubletree by Hilton San Juan ★ Long known as the "Lucky Pierre," this ideally located property has long been one of San Juan's major bargains. After a stylish makeover, which pumped up the comfort of guestrooms and made the public areas (including the pool area) into oases for lingering, it feels twice as fine—but is no longer as much of a bargain. It's 3 blocks from the city's best beach and within walking distance of the best clubs and restaurants in Condado (so what if you take a cab back to the room at night). It also sits on a major bus line, so getting to most major San Juan attractions is a snap even if you don't rent a car. There's two good on-site restaurants, and the adjacent Gallery Plaza also hosts a few fine restaurants. The area in general is chockfull of reasonably priced restaurants. It's 2 blocks from the Puerto Rico Museum of Art. It may not feel like you are in the middle of everything, but you'll soon discover otherwise while staying here, especially if you venture into the city as much as the beach. But at these prices, you may wish to stay right on the beach.

Av. José De Diego 105, Condado, San Juan, PR 00914. ✆ **787/721-1200** Fax 787/721-3118 (reservations). www.doubletree1.hilton.com. 184 units. Year-round $199–$279 double. Rates include continental breakfast. AE, DC, DISC, MC, V. Valet parking $20; self parking $5. Bus: A5 or B21. **Amenities:** Restaurant; bar; babysitting; small health club; Jacuzzi; room service; outdoor pool; rooms for those w/limited mobility. *In room:* A/C, TV, hair dryer.

Radisson Ambassador Plaza Hotel & Casino This property is not a big enough bargain to get you to stay here. There are better bargains to be had, or you could pay a bit more and get a whole lot more. It lacks the resort amenities associated with the Hilton, the Condado Plaza, the Ritz-Carlton, and the Hotel El San Juan, as well as a sense of whimsy and fun. Accommodations are in a pair of towers, one of which is devoted to suites. Each unit has a balcony with outdoor furniture. The beds are fitted with fine linens, and each bathroom has generous shelf space and a tub/shower combination.

Av. Ashford 1369, San Juan, PR 00907. ✆ **800/333-3333** or 787/721-7300. Fax 787/723-6151. www.radisson.com. 233 units. Winter $138–$206 double, $245–$305 suite; off-season $111–$169 double, $159–$225 suite. AE, DISC, MC, V. Self-parking $8. Bus: B21 or C10. **Amenities:** 2 restaurants; 2 bars; babysitting; casino; health club; rooftop pool; room service; rooms for those w/limited mobility. *In room:* A/C, TV, hair dryer.

MODERATE

Comfort Inn ☺ This family-oriented hotel rises seven stories above a residential neighborhood across the street from Condado Beach. The accommodations are small and not particularly imaginative in their decor. Each room has either one or two queen-size beds, and each has a tub-and-shower bathroom. Some rooms have sofas that convert into beds for children. There's a small swimming pool on the premises. The bars, restaurants, and facilities of the Condado neighborhood are within walking distance. Computers with Internet access are available for guests. It's near the area's best beach right behind the newly renovated La Concha hotel, as well as a newly renovated oceanfront plaza with open-air restaurants and lots of nice spots to hang out on one of the benches. The rules (no bicycles, no ball games, no pets, no fun) will likely freak out your kids if you have them. Don't worry; they should. The beach beside it, however, is wide and partially shaded by a palm grove. The waters are partially protected by a set of breakers. A good spot for families with vendors selling ice cream, cold drinks and snacks is right here on the spot.

Calle Clemenceau 6, Condado, San Juan, PR 00907. ✆ **800/858-7407** or 787/721-0170. www.comfortinn.com. 50 units. Winter $110 double, $200 suite; summer $99 double, $200 suite. AE, DC, DISC, MC, V. Parking $11. Bus: B21 or C10. **Amenities:** Outdoor pool; rooms for those w/limited mobility, high-speed Internet. *In room:* A/C, TV, hair dryer.

INEXPENSIVE

Acacia Boutique Hotel This inn, originally built as a private home in 1943 and transformed into a simple hotel in 1948, didn't become well known until the late 1960s, when its reasonable rates began to attract families with children and college students traveling in groups. It's a stucco-covered building with vaguely Spanish-colonial detailing on a residential street lined with similar structures. For the past 4 years, it has been a sister property of the At Wind Chimes Inn, and the inn has been steadily being made over since then. The lobby and the fabulous restaurant Niché have granite walls, tiled floors with mood lighting, and are connected by an interior tropical garden. The guest rooms are bright and cheery, and there are great areas to hang out, including a rooftop terrace. The beach, among the city's finest, is at the end of the block, and guests can hang out at the Wind Chimes pool and cafe bar. Each unit has simple furniture and a small shower-only bathroom. There's a whirlpool and sun deck. You are literally steps from the beach here.

Calle Taft 8, Condado, San Juan, PR 00911. ✆ **787/725-0668.** Fax 787/728-0671. www.acaciaseasideinn.com. 15 units (shower only). Winter $105–$210 double; summer $85–$165 double. AE, DISC, MC, V. Bus: A5 or B21. Parking $10. *In room:* A/C, TV, fridge (in some).

Aleli by the Sea This is a lone budget holdout in a sea of expensive hotel options. Right on the Condado, it's a weathered guesthouse that opens onto the beach 1 block off Ashford Avenue. Most of the bedrooms, which are small to mid-size, overlook the ocean. It's a Spartan spot, with rattan furnishings and cramped shower-only bathrooms. The second-floor Sun Deck overlooks the ocean, the perfect spot to watch the sunsets, but there are no great comforts. This is near the Atlantic Beach, in the heart of gay Condado.

Calle Seaview 1125, Condado, San Juan, PR 00907. ✆ **787/725-5313.** Fax 787/721-4744. 9 units (shower only). Winter (including taxes) $76–$119 double; off-season (including taxes) $69–$108 double. AE, DISC, MC, V. Bus: B21 or C10. **Amenities:** Communal kitchen. *In room:* A/C, TV, ceiling fan, no phone.

Atlantic Beach Hotel With the pink piano in the lobby long gone, Puerto Rico's most famous gay hotel has been being quietly transformed over the last year, with a sweeping renovation of guest rooms and a change in attitude that aims to take advantage of its distinction as the only small hotel on the beach in Condado. The five-story hotel still welcomes its core gay clientele, but is also reaching out to "open-minded" straight couples and business travelers looking for clean, comfortable, attractive rooms right on the beach at a good price. Renovations throughout 2010 will target the bar and restaurant with completion expected by December. The beds and furnishings are super comfortable, and both the guest rooms and common areas have been redone in a handsome, subdued style, much like the new direction the property has taken. Some of the rooms are smaller than others, so paying a little more will get you more space plus a beach view. The bar and restaurant on the back deck, which sits about 20 feet above the beach, are still a great place to have a drink, but the flamboyant shows and weekend afternoon happy hours of debauchery are now a thing of the past. The spacious apartments are a good alternative for business travelers or small groups, and one of the best bargains in the Condado.

Calle Vendig 1, Condado, San Juan, PR 00907. ✆ **787/721-6900.** Fax 787/721-6917. www.atlanticbeachhotel.net. 36 units (all with shower only), 6 apartments. Winter $79–$109 double; off-season $69–$99 double. Apartments year-round $750–$1,250 weekly. Parking $10 per day. AE, DISC, MC, V. Bus: B21. **Amenities:** Restaurant; bar; beach chairs and umbrellas; Wi-Fi; rooms for those w/limited mobility. *In room:* A/C, TV.

At Wind Chimes Inn ★ ☺ This restored and renovated Spanish manor, 1 short block from the beach and 3½ miles (5.6km) from the airport, is one of the best guesthouses on the Condado. Upon entering a tropical patio, you'll find tiled tables surrounded by palm trees and bougainvillea. There's plenty of space on the deck and a covered lounge for relaxing, socializing, and eating breakfast. Dozens of decorative wind chimes add melody to the daily breezes. The good-size rooms offer a choice of size, beds, and kitchens; all contain ceiling fans and air-conditioning. Beds are comfortable and come in four sizes, ranging from twin to king-size. The shower-only bathrooms, though small, are efficiently laid out. Families like this place not only because of the accommodations and the affordable prices but because they can also prepare light meals here, cutting down on food costs.

Av. McLeary 1750, Condado, San Juan, PR 00911. ✆ **800/946-3244** or 787/727-4153. Fax 787/728-0671. www.atwindchimesinn.com. 22 units (all with shower only). Winter $95–$150 double, $155 suite; off-season $65–$130 double, $130 suite; major holiday weekends $105–$175 double, $185 suite. AE, DISC, MC, V. Parking $10. Bus: B21 or A5. **Amenities:** Bar; outdoor pool; room service; rooms for those w/ limited mobility. *In room:* A/C, ceiling fan, TV, kitchen (in some).

Casa del Caribe Don't expect the Ritz, but if you're looking for a bargain on the Condado, this is it. This renovated guesthouse was built in the 1940s, later expanded, and then totally refurbished with tropical decor. A very Puerto Rican ambience has been created, with emphasis on Latin hospitality and comfort. On a shady side street just off Ashford Avenue, behind a wall and garden, you'll discover Casa del Caribe's wraparound veranda. The small but cozy guest rooms have ceiling fans and air conditioners, and most feature original Puerto Rican art. The bedrooms are inviting, with comfortable furnishings and efficiently organized bathrooms. The front porch is a social center for guests, and you can also cook out at a barbecue area.

The beach is a 2-minute walk away, and the hotel is also within walking distance of some megaresorts, with their glittering casinos.

Calle Caribe 57, El Condado, San Juan, PR 00907. ✆ **787/722-7139.** Fax 787/723-2575. www.casadelcaribe.net. 13 units. Winter $85–$125 double; off-season $65–$99 double. Rates include continental breakfast. AE, DISC, MC, V. Parking $5. Bus: B21. **Amenities:** Smoke-free rooms; 1 room for those w/ limited mobility. *In room:* A/C, ceiling fan, TV, kitchen (in some).

El Canario Inn This little bed-and-breakfast, originally built as a private home, is one of the best values along the high-priced Condado strip. The location is just 1 block from the beach (you can walk there in your bathing suit). This well-established hotel lies directly on the landmark Ashford Avenue, center of Condado action, and is close to casinos, nightclubs, and many restaurants in all price ranges. Although surrounded by megaresorts, it is a simple inn, with rather small but comfortable rooms and good maintenance by a helpful staff. All units are smoke-free and have small, tiled, shower-only bathrooms. You can relax on the hotel's patios or in the whirlpool area, which is surrounded by tropical foliage. There is no elevator. Affiliated with the nearby El Canario by the Lagoon and El Canario by the Beach, which are also recommended, this is the most charming of the three El Canario properties. El Canario by the Sea is right around the block.

Av. Ashford 1317, Condado, San Juan, PR 00907. ✆ **800/533-2649** or 787/722-3861. Fax 787/722-0391. www.canariohotels.com. 25 units (all with shower only). Winter $105–$149 double; off-season $80–$110 double. $3 energy fee, $10 weekend surcharge Fri–Sat nights. Rates include continental breakfast and morning paper. AE, DC, MC, V. Bus: B21 or A5. **Amenities:** Patio, whirlpool. *In room:* A/C, ceiling fan, TV.

Holiday Inn Express This seven-story, white-painted structure, expanded in 2003, offers a desirable Condado location but without the towering prices of the grand resorts along the beach. The hotel is about a 2-minute walk from Condado Beach and is convenient to Old San Juan (a 15-min. drive) and the airport (a 20-min. drive). Most accommodations have two double beds (ideal for families) and ceiling fans, and each has a small bathroom with tub and shower. Many open onto balconies with water views. There's a small pool with a nice shaded area as well. It's close to the renovated La Concha and the Window of the Sea Park beside it. For years, we avoided this area beside the Condado Lagoon that suffered from the closure of La Concha and neighboring hotels. Compounding problems were the severe sewage backups that would occur in area streets after heavy rains. This problem has abated, and with the new hotel now opened, this area of Avenida Ashford is now home to top-name designer boutiques and great restaurants of all price ranges. So we're hot on this 'hood again, making this one of your better budget options.

Calle Marinao Ramirez Bages 1, Condado, San Juan, PR 00907. ✆ **888/465-4329** or 787/724-4160. Fax 787/721-2436. www.ichotels.com. 115 units. Winter $126–$159 double; off-season $108–$139, with weekend surcharges. Rates include continental breakfast. AE, DC, DISC, MC, V. Parking $10. Bus: B21. **Amenities:** Health club; pool; whirlpool; Wi-Fi. *In room:* A/C, TV, hair dryer.

Miramar

Miramar, a residential neighborhood, is very much a part of metropolitan San Juan, and a brisk 30-minute walk will take you where the action is. Regrettably, the beach is at least half a mile (.8km) away. The new Convention Center District and a part of the city's waterfront, and a commuter airport are also located in Miramar. For the location of hotels in Miramar, see the map on p. 115.

Sheraton Puerto Rico Hotel & Casino ★ This new property is an integral part of the Puerto Rico Convention District, and it seems as if you can see the imposing yet graceful Convention Center arch out any window you look. The two properties both embrace big, glass spaces, open to the amazing sky and the futuristic yet tropical landscape surrounding it, and even a bit of the Atlantic ocean crashing in the distance. The hotel facilities—which include the island's largest casino and a fabulous health club and spa—are first-rate, but this is still primarily a convention hotel, appropriate for those who plan on spending a lot of time at the adjacent Convention Center. The good news is the property will probably surpass most guests' expectations. The public interiors are subdued and stylish, and the good taste extends to the guest rooms, which are more comfortable and spacious than the average hotel room, especially the hotel beds. It's within a mile of most good city beaches, as well as Old San Juan and Plaza Las Americas, but that mile feels a lot longer when you are on vacation. You are better off at one of the resorts right on the Condado or Isla Verde beaches than staying here, unless you are spending your mornings at the Convention Center. They will be your destination.

200 Convention Blvd. San Juan, Puerto Rico 00907. ✆ **866/932-7269** or 787/993-3500. Fax 787/993-3505. www.sheratonpuertoricohotelcasino.com. 503 units. Winter $199–$326 double, $329–$499 suites; off-season $139–$226 double, $289–$479 suite. Children 16 and under stay free in parent's room (max. 4 people per room). AE, DC, DISC, MC, V. Valet parking $20; self-parking $15. Bus: C53. **Amenities:** 3 restaurants; 2 bars; babysitting; casino; health club; room service; complete spa; smoke-free rooms; rooms for those w/limited mobility. *In room:* A/C, TV, hair dryer, minibar, Wi-Fi.

Marriot Courtyard San Juan Miramar This handsome, budget-friendly, family-owned hotel only makes sense if you plan to rent a car and drive to a different destination everyday—or if you're tied to the nearby Convention Center, this is a viable budget alternative. Otherwise, if your main priority is the beach, this hotel is probably too far. Because the Condado Lagoon and the Baldorioty De Castro Expressway are between the hotel and the beach, you'll walk about an hour to many of favorite spots. The hotel is in upscale Miramar, with great restaurants, fun shops, and an art-film movie house. The two excellent restaurants here attract area doctors, lawyers, and politicians for lunch, and a broader cross section of *sanjuaneros* for dinner. The pool area is small but sunny, and the public areas have wireless Internet access. The guest rooms are of good quality, if uninspired. Both the Bar Association and the Justice Department are nearby.

Av. Ponce de León 801, San Juan, PR 00907. ✆ **800/289-4274** or 787/721-7400. Fax 787/722-1787. excelsior@caribe.net. 140 units. Winter $189–$249 double, $254 suite; off-season $103–$149 double, $174 suite. Top rate includes children 12 and under. Valet parking $15 daily. AE, DC, DISC, MC, V. Bus: 1, 2, A3, or A5. **Amenities:** 2 restaurants; babysitting; health club; room service; outdoor pool; rooms for those w/limited mobility. *In room:* A/C, TV/DVD, hair dryer, movie rentals.

Santurce & Ocean Park

Santurce is the traditional downtown area of San Juan, and Ocean Park is a beautiful oceanfront neighborhood wedged in between the Condado and Isla Verde tourism districts. Santurce has been undergoing a revival, with Art Deco theaters and beautiful apartments being renovated; it's now the home to the city's best museums, performing arts center and increasingly, among its best clubs and pubs. Ocean Park is a beautiful neighborhood, filled with palm trees and gorgeous homes.

MODERATE

Hosteria del Mar ★ This guesthouse offers medium-size, oceanview rooms on one of the city's best beaches. Those on the second floor have balconies; those on the first floor open onto patios. The hotel was recently renovated yet remains true to its basic, close-to-nature tropical roots. The public areas, including beachfront dining area, are now more inviting than ever. Suites and efficiencies are available. Room 201 has a king-size bed, private balcony, kitchenette, and a view of the beach; it's a private getaway. There's no pool, but you are right on the beach. Uvva is one of the hardest working restaurants in town, open from 8am to 10pm, and it doesn't just serve food. It upscales basic breakfast and lunch choices, and also throws in some cutting-edge, creative world cuisine. On a beachfront street completely enveloped by a canopy of trees, this is one of San Juan's most charming spots. Given the setting, the place is simple, but puts out its own elegance and warm hospitality.

Calle Tapía 1, Ocean Park, San Juan, PR 00911. ✆ **877/727-3302** or 787/727-3302. Fax 787/268-3302. hosteria@caribe.net. 27 units. High season $89–$239 double, $244–$264 apt; off-season $69–$179 double, $199–$209 apt. Children 11 and under stay free in parent's room. AE, DC, DISC, MC, V. Bus: A5. **Amenities:** Restaurant; room service. *In room:* A/C, TV, kitchenette (in 3 units), Wi-Fi.

Número 1 Guest House ★★ 🎁 The best of the small-scale, low-rise guesthouses in Ocean Park. A massive renovation of this 1950s private beach house transformed the place into the closest thing in Ocean Park to the kind of stylish boutique hotel you might find in an upscale California neighborhood. Much of this is thanks to the hardworking owner, Esther Feliciano, who cultivates within her walled compound a verdant garden replete with splashing fountains, a small swimming pool, and manicured shrubbery and palms. Stylish-looking bedrooms (all of which are smoke-free) contain tile floors, wicker or rattan furniture, comfortable beds, and tiled, shower-only bathrooms. The restaurant, bar and outdoor cafe attract an interesting crowd, as does the guest house. This is more low-key than Condado and Isla Verde, but the beach and the crowd are prettier, and the chatter over sunset drinks much more interesting.

Calle Santa Ana 1, Ocean Park, San Juan, PR 00911. ✆ **866/726-5010** or 787/726-5010. Fax 787/727-5482. www.numero1guesthouse.com. 13 units (shower only), including economy, oceanview, junior suites, and apts. High season (Dec 15–Apr 30) $139–$279; low season (Aug 1–Oct 31) $89–$179; midseason (May 1–July 31, Nov 1–Dec 14) $99–$209; weekend surcharge Fri–Sun $20. Extra person $20. Rates include continental breakfast. AE, MC, V. Bus: C53, A5. **Amenities:** Restaurant; bar; outdoor pool; limited room service; rooms for those w/limited mobility. *In room:* A/C, ceiling fan, TV, hair dryer, minibar, Wi-Fi.

INEXPENSIVE

Oceana Hostal Playero 🎁 Yeah, it's a block from the beach, but it's the best beach in the city—so you might say that's better than beachfront at another beach. In any case, this B&B deserves to be better known. With the recent closing of the nearby L'Habitation (still up for sale), Oceana is the best bargain in Ocean Park. It's a comfortable, snug nest with helpful, friendly staff and clean, newly renovated rooms. All units have small refrigerators and a tiled bathroom with either a tub or a shower. The entire property is a Wi-Fi Internet zone, and there's complimentary breakfast on the outdoor patio. There are small pool and sundeck areas. The Pura-Vida restaurant lounge serves good local and vegetarian cuisine. The most recent renovations have greatly improved this guesthouse since the days of the Beach Buoy Inn, and the price can still be nice.

Av. McLeary 1853, Ocean Park, San Juan, PR 00911. ✆ **787/728-8119.** Fax 787/727-5748. 17 units (some shower only, some tub only). Winter $109–$129 double, $149–$159 suites; off season $89–$109 double, $119–$129 suites. Rates include continental breakfast. MC, V. Free parking. Bus: A5 or A7. **Amenities:** Restaurant; 1 room for those w/limited mobility, Wi-Fi. *In room:* A/C, TV, fridge, no phone.

Tres Palmas Inn Across the street from the ocean, this apartment-style guesthouse overlooks a windswept stretch of beach at the eastern end of Ocean Park, right before it disappears into the rocky coastline along Punta Las Marías. The beautiful beach at Ultimo Trolley is a block west, and the hotel's pool is located in a secluded courtyard. You can also relax on the rooftop sun deck while soaking in the whirlpool. The medium-size bedrooms are simply but comfortably furnished, with rather standard motel items. Each guest room has a private entrance and a ceiling fan, and most have small refrigerators. Larger rooms also have small kitchens, and each unit has a small, tiled bathroom with either a tub or a shower. We have friends who love this place and stay here for annual visits to the island.

Ocean Park Blvd. 2212, San Juan, PR 00913. ✆ **888/290-2076** or 787/727-4617. Fax 787/727-5434. www.trespalmasinn.com. 18 units (some with shower only, some with tub only). Winter $87–$175 double; off season $73–$138 double. Rates include continental breakfast. AE, MC, V. Bus: A5 or A7. **Amenities:** Internet access; pool; sun deck; 2 whirlpools; 1 room for those w/limited mobility. *In room:* A/C, TV, fridge (in some), kitchen (in some), hair dryer.

Isla Verde

Beach-bordered Isla Verde is closer to the airport than the Condado and Old San Juan. The hotels here are farther from Old San Juan than those in Miramar, Condado, and Ocean Park. The fat golden beach is mighty fine, and El San Juan and Co. make the area a nightlife spot in its own right, plus the numerous stand-alone restaurants, pubs, and clubs of top quality. For the location of hotels in Isla Verde, see the map "Isla Verde Accommodations & Dining," on p. 123.

VERY EXPENSIVE

El San Juan Hotel & Casino: The Waldorf Astoria Collection ★ ☺ Despite formidable competition by the Ritz-Carlton for elite and sophisticated travelers, this posh resort still has the power to dazzle. The beachfront hotel is surrounded by 350 palms, century-old banyans, and gardens. It lies on a 3.2km-long (2-mile) golden sandy beach with aquamarine water that is the finest in San Juan. Lined with luxury hotels and condominiums, the beach is always full of activity and has great watersports activities.

The lobby is the most opulent and memorable in the Caribbean. Entirely sheathed in red marble and hand-carved mahogany paneling, the public rooms stretch on almost endlessly. No other hotel in the Caribbean offers such a rich diversity of dining options and such high-quality food. And with live music and DJs playing at nightclubs nearly every night, and a beautiful casino, El San Juan is still the place to be seen in the city.

The large, well-decorated rooms are outfitted with the latest in high tech. The Vista guest rooms are bright and tropical, while the Lanai rooms are imbued with honey-hued woods and rattans, with darker wooden doors, windows, and other furnishing. Bathrooms have all the amenities and tub/shower combinations; a few feature Jacuzzis. The oceanfront Lanai rooms overlook the fern-lined paths of the resort's tropical garden.

Isla Verde Accommodations & Dining

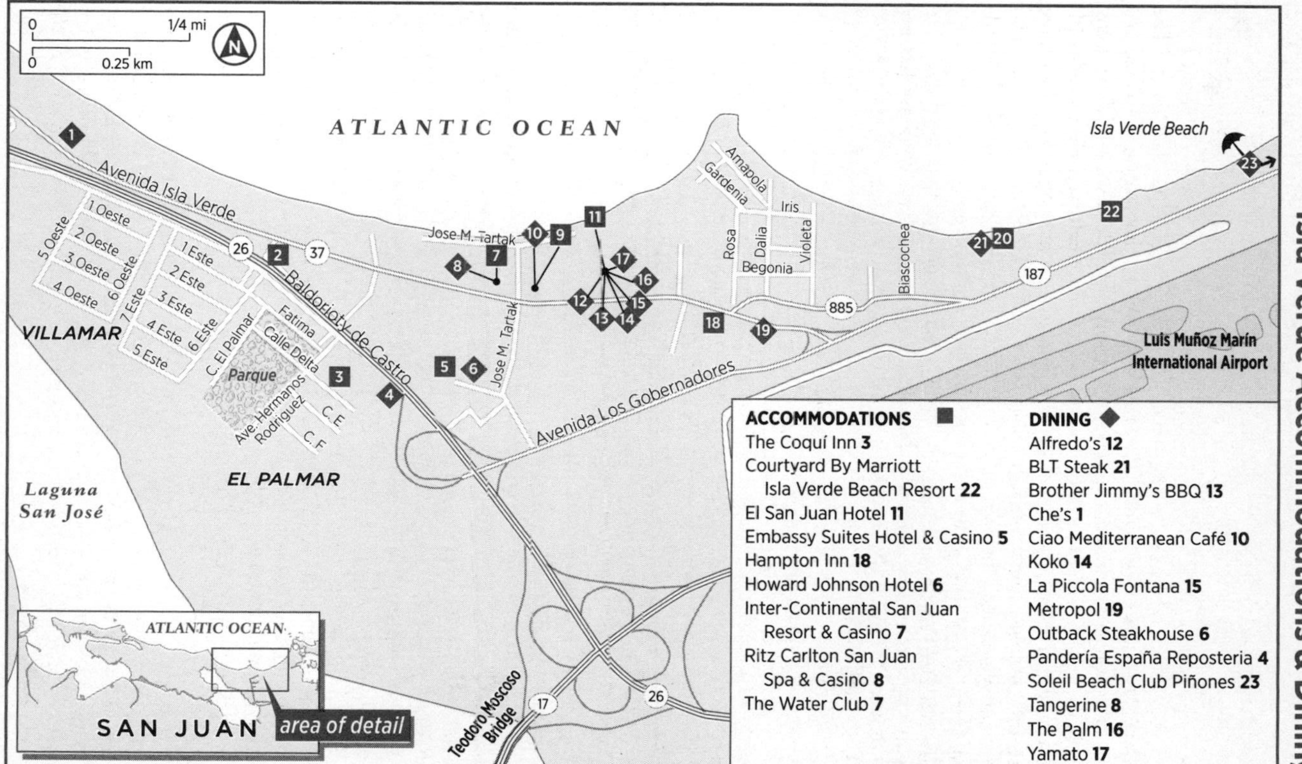

Av. Isla Verde 6063, San Juan, PR 00979. ✆ **787/791-1000** or 888/579-2632. Fax 787/791-0390. www.luxuryresorts.com. 382 units. Winter $319–$669 double, $899–$2,300 suite; off season $169–$549 double, from $769–$2,069 suite. AE, DC, DISC, MC, V. Valet parking $15; self-parking $10. Bus: A5, C53. **Amenities:** 7 restaurants; 4 bars; babysitting; casino; children's programs; health club; 2 outdoor pools; room service; sauna and steam room; spa; tennis courts; watersports equipment/rentals; rooms for those w/limited mobility. *In room:* A/C, TV w/in-house movies, hair dryer, iPod docking station, minibar, Wi-Fi.

Inter-Continental San Juan Resort & Casino We love the pool area and the cafe overlooking the beach. Along with a recent facelift, which made over guest rooms and public areas, the hotel's staff has also dramatically improved service. The comfortable, medium-size rooms have balconies and terraces and tastefully conservative furnishings. Executive Club–level rooms carry additional features, such as complimentary meals and drinks. The pool area is one of the finest in San Juan, and it fronts one of the city's prettiest and most active beaches. The oceanside Ciao Mediterranean Café is one of the best spots in the city for an afternoon drink, lunch or snack. Sit on a table along the boardwalk overlooking the beach in the shade of towering palm trees. Guests will want to venture elsewhere for nightlife, however, which is all nearby.

Av. Isla Verde 5961, Isla Verde, PR 00979. ✆ **800/468-9076** or 787/791-6100. Fax 787/253-2510. www.ichotelsgroup.com. 402 units. Winter $279–$428 double, $699–$1,043 suite; off-season $170–$348 double, $425–$743 suite. Children 15 and under stay free in parent's room. AE, DC, DISC, MC, V. Valet parking $22; self-parking $16. Bus: A5, C53. **Amenities:** 3 restaurants; lounge; babysitting; health club; pool; the Caribbean's largest free-form room service; sauna; scuba diving; whirlpool; Wi-Fi; rooms for those w/limited mobility. *In room:* A/C, TV, hair dryer, minibar.

Ritz-Carlton San Juan Spa & Casino ★★★ The Ritz-Carlton is one of the most spectacular deluxe hotels in the Caribbean. Set on 3.2 hectares (8 acres) of prime beachfront, within a 5-minute drive from the airport, it appeals to both business travelers and vacationers. The hotel decor reflects Caribbean flavor and the Hispanic culture of the island, with artwork by prominent local artists. More visible, however, is an emphasis on Continental elegance. Some of the most opulent public areas feature wrought-iron balustrades and crystal chandeliers.

Beautifully furnished guest rooms open onto ocean views or the gardens of nearby condos. Rooms are very large, with excellent furnishings and fine linens. The marble bathrooms are exceptionally plush, with tub/shower combinations, scales, bathrobes, and deluxe toiletries. Preferred accommodations are in the ninth-floor Ritz-Carlton Club, which has a private lounge and personal concierge staff.

The scope and diversity of dining here is second only to that at the El San Juan Hotel & Casino (see above), and as for top-shelf dining venues, the Ritz-Carlton has no equal. Renowned gourmet chains BLT Steak and Il Mulino of New York are both located here. The hotel also houses one of Puerto Rico's largest casinos, and it's most stylishly elegant. This is a great spot for families, with a full range of children's activities and a great beach for kids, with lots of watersports options for active families.

Av. de los Gobernadores (State Rd.) 6961, no. 187, Isla Verde, PR 00979. ✆ **800/241-3333** or 787/253-1700. Fax 787/253-1777. www.ritzcarlton.com. 416 units. Winter $439–$659 double; off season $229–$509 double; year-round from $1,109–$1,529 suite. AE, DC, DISC, MC, V. Valet parking $22; self-parking $17. Bus: A5. **Amenities:** 5 restaurants; 3 bars; nightclub; babysitting; Caribbean's largest casino; children's

family-FRIENDLY ACCOMMODATIONS

At Wind Chimes Inn (p. 118) Families like this hotel not only because of the accommodations and the affordable prices, but also because they can prepare meals here, cutting down on food costs.

Caribe Hilton (p. 113) This hotel is known for its children's programs. Its supervised Kids' Klub provides daily activities—ranging from face painting to swimming lessons—for children 5 to 12 years of age.

Hampton Inn (p. 126) For families seeking the kind of lodging values found on the mainland, this new hotel is highly desirable, as many of its rooms have two double beds. There's also a beautiful swimming pool in a tropical setting. Suites have microwaves and refrigerators.

Inter-Continental San Juan Resort & Casino (see above) This hotel began a children's program last year that leaped into the lead of San Juan hotels. The Planet Trekkers Kids Club is environmentally friendly, leading children through activities such as watching the migration of an adopted sea turtle Naya on its migratory path from Panama to Puerto Rico. The program is just plain fun, with outdoor sport and pool activities, indoor game competitions, and movie and disco nights. It lets parents enjoy their stay, too.

Ritz-Carlton (p. 124) For the family seeking an upmarket resort with lots of facilities, this is among the top choices. There's a full range of children's activities: arts and crafts, bowling, sand castle sculpting, sports, board games, and Spanish lessons. It's also a great place for active families, with plenty of watersports opportunities. Lessons and rentals are available for surfing, windsurfing, kite surfing, and sailing.

program; health club; large pool; room service; spa; 2 tennis courts; rooms for those w/limited mobility; Wi-Fi. *In room:* A/C, TV, hair dryer, minibar.

The Water Club ★★ A refreshing change from the megachain resorts of San Juan, this ultrachic hotel is hip and contemporary. Although avant-garde, the design is never off-putting. The illuminated lobby might recall *2001: A Space Odyssey,* but it's still warm and friendly. Behind glass are "waterfalls," even on the elevators, and inventive theatrical-style lighting is used to bring the outdoors inside. The one-of-a-kind glass art doors are from Murano, the famed center of glassmaking outside Venice. A drawback is that rooms are smaller than most, and so is the closet and dresser space. The hotel overlooks Isla Verde's best beach area. Unique features are the open-air 11th-floor exotic bar with the Caribbean's only rooftop fireplace. There's a rooftop pool and sundeck; it's like swimming in an ocean in the sky. This hotel is super pet friendly; it offers four-legged friends complimentary doggie bags and their owners welcome drinks. Grooming, walking, and massage services are available.

Calle José M. Tartak 2, Isla Verde, Puerto Rico 00979. ✆ **888/265-6699** or 787/253-3666. Fax 787/728-3610. www.waterclubsanjuan.com. 84 units. Winter $229–$305 double, $349–$404 suite; off season $135–$255 double, $288–$355 suite. AE, DC, DISC, MC, V. Bus: A5, B21. **Amenities:** Restaurant; 2 bars; fitness center; Jacuzzi; outdoor rooftop pool; room service; smoke-free rooms; rooms for those w/limited mobility. *In room:* A/C, TV, hair dryer, high-speed Internet, minibar.

EXPENSIVE

Courtyard by Marriott Isla Verde Beach Resort ★ ☺ This property's big drawback is its location near the airport, and its price tag, which has risen recently. It's on a beautiful beach at the end of Isla Verde, with the public beach just to the east and Pine Grove beach, popular with surfers and sailors, just to the west. Meals and drinks are served on a wraparound veranda, and there are comfortable hammocks and beach chairs beside the pool and the beach in front. Updated comfort makes it suitable for business travelers, families, or the random vacationer. The 12-floor hotel rises on the site of the old Crowne Plaza. It's a big, bustling place with many amenities and midsize and well-furnished bedrooms. Art Deco furnishings dominate, and there is plenty of comfort. The casino and lobby restaurants are filled with the sounds of Latin rhythms at night. The pool and beach are great for kids. They can get surf lessons down the beach on foam boards designed for beginners.

Boca de Cangrejos Avenida 7012, Isla Verde, PR 00979. ✆ **800/791-2553** or 787/791-0404. Fax 787/791-1460. www.sjcourtyard.com. 293 units. Winter $229–$334 double, $383–$485 suite; off season $165–$260 double, $310–$360 suite. AE, DC, DISC, MC, V. Bus: M7. **Amenities:** 3 restaurants; ice-cream parlor; bar; casino; kids' club; fitness center; pool; room service; high-speed Internet. *In room:* A/C, TV, minibar, hair dryer.

Embassy Suites Hotel & Casino ★ The location is 2 blocks from the beach, and the hotel has its own water world, with waterfalls and reflecting ponds set against a backdrop of palms. As you enter, you're greeted with an aquarium, giving a tropical-resort aura to the place. The excellent accommodations are all suites, and they're comfortably furnished and roomy, with bedrooms separated from the living rooms. Each has a wet bar, a tub/shower combination bathroom, two phones, a safe, and a dining table. The most spacious suites are those with two double beds; each of the smaller suites is furnished with a king-size bed. The best view of the water is from units above the third floor. Two restaurants are on the premises, including the Embassy Grill, a low-key indoor/outdoor affair, and an independently managed Outback Steakhouse branch. There's also a small-scale casino on the property.

Calle José M. Tartak 8000, Isla Verde, San Juan, PR 00979. ✆ **800/362-2779** or 787/791-0505. Fax 787/991-7776. www.embassysuites.com. 299 suites. Winter $210–$220 one-bedroom suite, $310 2-bedroom suite; off season $160–$170 one-bedroom suite, $260 2-bedroom suite. Rates include breakfast and free drinks 5:30–7:30pm. AE, DC, DISC, MC, V. Valet parking $16; self-parking $10. Bus: A5 or B21. **Amenities:** 2 restaurants; 3 bars; small casino; health club; pool; room service; rooms for those w/limited mobility; Wi-Fi. *In room:* A/C, TV, wet bar (in suites), fridge, hair dryer, microwave.

MODERATE

Hampton Inn ☺ Opened in 1997, this chain hotel is set across the busy avenue from Isla Verde's sandy beachfront, far enough away to keep costs down but within a leisurely 10-minute walk of the casinos and nightlife. Two towers, with four and five floors, hold the well-maintained, well-furnished, and comfortable bedrooms. There's no restaurant on the premises and no real garden; other than a whirlpool and a swimming pool with a swim-up bar, there are very few facilities or amenities. Because of its reasonable prices and location, however, this Isla Verde newcomer could be a good choice. Families are especially fond of staying here, despite the fact that there are no special children's programs; many of the rooms have two double beds, and suites have microwaves and refrigerators.

Av. Isla Verde 6530, Isla Verde, PR 00979. ✆ **800/HAMPTON** (426-7866) or 787/791-8777. Fax 787/791-8757. 201 units. Winter $169 double, $189–209 suite; off season $129 double, $139–$159 suite. Rates include breakfast bar. AE, DC, DISC, MC, V. Parking $5. Bus: A5 or C45. **Amenities:** Bar; babysitting; health club; high-speed Internet, pool; whirlpool; rooms for those w/limited mobility. *In room:* A/C, TV, fridge (in suites), hair dryer, microwave (in suites).

Howard Johnson Hotel Rising eight stories above the busy traffic of Isla Verde, this chain hotel offers comfortable but small bedrooms, furnished simply with bland, modern furniture. They're done in typical motel style, with small but serviceable tub-and-shower bathrooms. Many guests carry a tote bag to the beach across the street, and then hit the bars and restaurants of the expensive hotels nearby. There's a restaurant and a pool. Though it's simple and not very personal, this is a good choice for the money. The Fontana di Roma Italian restaurant is excellent.

Av. Isla Verde 4820, Isla Verde, PR 00979. ✆ **787/728-1300.** Fax 787/727-7150. www.hojo.com. 115 units. Year round $165–$185 double; $210 suite. AE, MC, V. Parking $6.50. Bus: A5. **Amenities:** 2 restaurants; health club; pool; rooms for those w/limited mobility. *In room:* A/C, TV, fridge, hair dryer.

INEXPENSIVE

The Coquí Inn This property incorporates three former guesthouses in the area (the Mango Inn, Green Isle Inn, and Casa Mathiesen). The beach is about a 10-minute walk, and you have to cross Baldorioty de Castro Expressway to get to Isla Verde's main drag and the beach (via pedestrian bridge)—but the inn is a real deal, and just over the bridge is the nicest part of Isla Verde. Guests get access to three pools, each with terraces with lounge chairs and umbrellas and an Asian restaurant and American–Puerto Rico cafe. You'll find free Wi-Fi Internet, public computers a video-game room, and movie rentals. The rooms are summery, simple, and comfortable, with tiled tub-and-shower bathrooms.

Calle Mar Mediterraneo 36, Villamar, Isla Verde, PR 00979. ✆ **787/726-4330** or 787/726-8662. Fax 787/268-2415. www.coqui-inn.com. 54 units. Year-round $59–$69 double; weekends $69–$79 double. AE, DISC, MC, V. Free parking. Bus: A5. **Amenities:** Restaurants; bar; shared areas w/microwaves and fridges; 3 pools; rooms for those w/limited mobility; Wi-Fi. *In room:* A/C, TV, kitchenette (in some).

WHERE TO DINE

San Juan's fine dining scene is the most varied and developed in the Caribbean. City restaurants serve up excellent Spanish, French, American, Italian, Chinese, Mexican, and Asian cuisines. For more on Puerto Rican food, see "*Comida Criolla*: Puerto Rican Cuisine" in Chapter 2.

While tasty Puerto Rican food has always been widely available on the island, in recent years, it has moved front and center at many of the city's finer restaurants. Several of the island's most talented chefs are striving to bring their hometown cuisine to new heights at some of its trendier eating establishments.

A big part of the island's culinary appeal is its diversity. San Juan literally has some of the best steakhouses in the world (BLT Steak, the Palm, Morton's of Chicago, plus a number of superb local Latino steakhouses specializing in grilled meats). And the island has long delivered expert renditions of Spanish cuisine, as well as traditional French and other Continental cookery. Of special note are the Italian restaurants (and local pizzerias), which take their inspiration directly from the New York City area and are competitive with the best in the genre stateside. Many others are Argentinean kitchens, which serve up a lighter Italian fair and delectable grilled skirt steak.

SAN JUAN'S BEST dining BETS

- **Best Classic Dining:** Out in Miramar, **Augusto's Cuisine,** in the Marriott Courtyard San Juan Miramar Hotel, Av. Ponce de León 801 (✆ **787/725-7700**), combines impeccable service and an elegant dining room while delivering one of the best French and international cuisines in the Caribbean, backed up by an extensive wine list.
- **Best Steakhouse:** In the swanky Ritz-Carlton San Juan Hotel, **BLT Steak,** De los Gobernadores 6961 (✆ **787/253-1700**), serves the most delicious steaks in Puerto Rico. French chef Laurent Tourondel reinvents the American steakhouse with the classic cooking techniques of his homeland, serving up aged beef, other meat, and fresh seafood. Sauces, sides, and desserts are all heavenly remakes of your father's favorite food, and it still tastes good today.
- **Best Food Value: Bebo's Café,** Calle Loiza 1600 (✆ **787/726-1008**), has good *comida criolla,* plus steaks, sandwiches, and fruit frappes at incredibly low prices. That's why it draws crowds despite its rather slow, if well intentioned, service. It's open all the time, nearly.
- **Best Italian Restaurant:** Across the street from Hotel El Covento, **Il Perugino,** Cristo St. 105 (✆ **787/722-5481**), takes you on a culinary tour of sunny Italy. Plate after plate of delectable northern Italian food is presented nightly—everything from grilled filets of fresh fish to succulent pastas. Service is first-rate, and the welcome warm.
- **Best French Restaurant:** Housed in a beautifully renovated building across the street from the Museo de Arte de Puerto Rico, **Bistro de Paris,** Plaza de Diego, Av. De Diego 310 (✆ **787/998-8929**), takes elements of a classic Parisian bistro and kicks up the comfort level several notches. This is classic French cuisine with innovative flourishes, prepared and served with love and precision by talented chefs and a near perfect waitstaff.
- **Best for a Romantic Dinner: Perla Restaurant,** at Hotel La Concha, Av. Ashford 1077 (✆ **787/721-7500,** ext. 6800), is a luminous, seashell-shaped restaurant, a delicate world of hand-blown glass lanterns and exotic furnishings—the perfect canvas for seafood and dancing. The flavors also largely come from the sea, which themselves are a force of nature.
- **Best Nuevo Latino Cuisine: Parrot Club,** Calle Fortaleza 363 (✆ **787/725-7370**), wows taste buds with its modern interpretation of Puerto Rican specialties. Even San Juan's mayor and the governor have made it their favorite. Borrowing from a repertoire of Puerto Rican and Spanish recipes, husband-and-wife team Emilio Figueroa and Gigi Zafero incorporate Taíno and African influences in their cuisine. The seared tuna is the best in town, and their Creole-style flank steak is worth the trek from Condado Beach.
- **Best *Asopao:*** Soul food to Puerto Ricans, *asopao* is the regional gumbo, made in as many different ways as there are chefs on the island. Most versions are too thick to be called soup; stew is more fitting. Try the seafood variety at **La Mallorquina,** Calle San Justo 207

(✆ **787/722-3261**), a delicious mix of shellfish and red snapper, in a delicious rice and tomato stew.

- **Best Spanish Cuisine:** There are authentic Spanish tapas at **El Picoteo,** at Hotel El Convento, Calle Cristo 100 (✆ **787/723-9202**), which spills along beautiful terraces and the interior courtyard of Old San Juan's most stunning historic property. The locale boasts a choice of 80 kinds of tapas (the 35 we've tried did not disappoint, and we intend to work our way through the rest) set against a background of Spanish colonial facades and blooming tropical flowers. There's often live music, including flamenco dancing.
- **Best Local Cuisine:** Devoted to *comida criolla,* **Ajili Mójili,** Av. Ashford 1006 (✆ **787/725-9195**), features food that islanders might have enjoyed in their mamas' kitchens. Try such specialties as *mofongos* (green plantains stuffed with veal, chicken, shrimp, or pork) or the most classic *arroz con pollo* (juicy chicken baked right in the middle of the pot of saffron rice).
- **Best Late-Night Dining:** With an after-hours menu that's available until dawn, **Tantra,** Calle Fortaleza 356 in Old San Juan (✆ **787/977-8141**), is the place to go when midnight munchies strike. This is where your waitress and bartender go when they get off of work. Try some tandoori chicken kebabs, coconut sesame shrimp in a mango peach salsa, or fried calamari in tomato masala sauce. Although the kitchen officially closes at 2am, it stays open until the crowd stops asking for more. It's a good place to find out what's going on around town as well.
- **Best Family Meals:** In the InterContinental San Juan Resort & Casino, Av. Isla Verde 5961 (✆ **787/791-6100**), **Ciao Mediterranean Café** offers an excellent and reasonably priced menu. Many tables are placed on a private boardwalk adjacent to the beach. Pizza and pasta are favorite dishes, and you can also choose from a large selection of other Mediterranean fare.
- **Best Nuevo Latino:** The Parrot Club, Calle Fortaleza 363 (✆ **787/725-7370**), blazed the frontier of the '90s' push to bring local fare to new creative and flavorful heights, and they are still on top of the game 15 years later. Cutting edge *nuevo cocina,* fun and tropical interiors, and warm and efficient service are still the biggest triple threat in town.
- **Best Aphrodisiac Cuisine:** Take someone special to **Ostra Cosa,** Calle del Cristo 154 (✆ **787/722-2672**), for a night of romance. Even if you aren't in the mood, the owner promises that you will be after consuming his dishes, which are "chock-full of aphrodisiacs." It's the romantic setting in a Spanish colonial courtyard that is sure to do the trick though.
- **Best Drinks:** We get thirsty just thinking about the **San Juan Water & Beach Club,** Tartek St. 2 (✆ **787/728-3666**), the ultrachic Isla Verde boutique hotel, where water gushes through the translucent walls of the lobby and elevator, which you take to **Wet.** (See the "Wet Bar" listing, in chapter 6.)

Seafood plays a big role in many local restaurants. Many of the finer San Juan restaurants use local catches or import fresh seafood from off island, especially for nonnative species such as Maine lobster and salmon. Red snapper and dolphinfish (known as *chillo* and dorado, respectively) are two local favorites, with fresh catch of each being widely available.

What may surprise the visitor is the quality and variety of Asian restaurants in the city, which include several gourmet eateries specializing in regional cuisines of China and top-notch Japanese steakhouses and sushi emporiums. There are about a dozen Lebanese and Arabian restaurants offering great food at modest prices. Many transport diners to the Middle East with Arabian music, belly-dancing, and a sheik's tent decor.

San Juan also has unexpected surprises: gourmet Indian, German baked goods, a Peruvian ceviche house, and an Irish bar and grill plucked out of midtown Manhattan.

The resort hotels along Condado and Isla Verde house excellent restaurants, among them, some of the island's finest. But you will miss out on some of the more unique and memorable dining experiences if you don't search beyond the hotel establishments.

Of course, the pleasures of eating in San Juan go beyond formal dining in restaurants. A fixture in the city is the presence of Spanish *panaderías,* or bakeries, an excellent choice for breakfast or lunch but an option for dinner as well. They have fresh baked goods, fat deli sandwiches, and traditional Spanish entrees such as *caldo gallego* and *arroz con pollo.* You get strong and tasty Puerto Rican coffee, fresh juices, and frappes as well.

Also be on the lookout for *fondas,* which are basic restaurants, often with just a counter or a few tables, that serve tasty local food at rock-bottom prices. There are a number of these around Avenida Ponce de León in downtown Santurce, which cater to office workers and students. Look to a *fonda* for an authentic island meal and a chance to brush up on your Spanish and rub elbows with Puerto Rican workers.

The city is one of the fast food capitals of the world, with all the familiar American brands, but also more obscure regional favorites such as **Pollo Tropical.** U.S. casual, chain-style restaurants also have a big presence on the island, with everything from **Chili's** to **Marcano's Macaroni Grill.**

Street-food aficionados will also find solace in San Juan. There are many stand-up only cafes throughout the city serving barbecued kebabs, fried codfish fritters, and turnovers stuffed with fish, spiced chicken, or beef. The **Piñones** area, east of Isla Verde, has oceanfront wooden stands where the *frituras,* or fried beach snacks, and kebabs are cooked over open fires.

The restaurants listed in this chapter are classified first by area and then by price, using the following categories: **Very Expensive,** dinner from $50 per person; **Expensive,** dinner from $35 per person; **Moderate,** dinner from $25 per person; and **Inexpensive,** dinner under $25 per person. These categories reflect prices for an appetizer, a main course, a dessert, and a glass of wine.

For much more on Puerto Rico's food scene, see chapter 2.

Old San Juan

For the locations of Old San Juan restaurants, see the "Old San Juan Accommodations & Dining" map, on p. 109.

VERY EXPENSIVE

Aquaviva ★★ LATINO/SEAFOOD Located on Calle Fortaleza near Plaza Colón, at the entrance of Old San Juan, the stunning foyer of this cool, turquoise-colored restaurant features stained-glass replicas of three *aquaviva* (jellyfish), each painstakingly manufactured specifically for this site. Bioluminescent drinks are served at the bar, and the hip raw bar here features sushi and a host of ceviches, including one made with dorado and mango and lemon juices, and another with marlin and garlic. The hot and cold appetizer towers are great for small groups (fried oysters, coco-flavored shrimp, fried octopus, and calamari). The best main courses include fresh swordfish served "steak frite style," sautéed in a wild mushroom sauce and served with French fries; the butter poached halibut with a spinach fondue; and the nueva paella, stuffed with shellfish and chorizo on a bed of couscous.

Calle Fortaleza 364. ✆ **787/722-0665.** Reservations not accepted. Main courses $17–$49. AE, MC, V. Lunch daily 11am–4pm; dinner Mon–Wed 6–11pm, Thurs–Sat 6pm–midnight, Sun 4–11pm. Bus: Old City Trolley.

Il Perugino ★★ ITALIAN Located across from Hotel El Convento, this is Puerto Rico's finest Italian restaurant, serving the cuisine inspired by chef and owner Franco Seccarelli's homeland of Umbria. The homemade pastas deliver the Italian classics to perfection: thin pasta with pancetta, tomatoes, and onions, and the spinach and ricotta gnocchi with fresh tomatoes. For a starter, opt for the warm goat cheese with pesto or the calamari stuffed with shrimp and fresh white fish. Seccarelli shines with his pheasant breast alla Cacciatora, baby veal chops in white wine and rosemary and the rack of lamb with fresh herbs and a rich red-wine sauce. Homemade desserts are also delicious, and wine comes from a cellar in a converted dry well in the center of the restaurant. Service is impeccable and friendly.

Cristo St. 105. ✆ **787/722-5481.** Reservations recommended. Main courses $25–$41. AE, DISC, MC, V. Thurs–Sat 11:30am–2:30pm; Tues–Sun 6:30–11pm. Bus: Old City Trolley.

Marmalade Restaurant and Wine Bar ★★ INTERNATIONAL Chef-owner Peter Schintler is a culinary globetrotter that picks up flavors from China to France to blend into his distinct culinary brand. The ultracontemporary restaurant, wine bar, and lounge, suits the menu, which its creator calls "California-French" or "Cuisine de Terre." The restaurant is a labor of love he shares with Henriet, his wife, and it's evident in the flavors and attention to detail. The spicy chorizo and smoked chicken paella bites and the red snapper citrus avocado ceviche are great starters. Follow up with stunners such as grilled, macadamia nut tuna and beef tenderloin with a roasted mushroom and cheese gratin, for one of the best meals you'll have on your trip. There's a popular tasting menu with wine pairings. The kitchen is as consistent as it is inventive.

Calle Fortaleza 317. ✆ **787/724-3969.** Mon–Thurs 6pm–midnight; Fri–Sat 6pm–2am; Sun 6–10pm. Main courses $25–$36.

EXPENSIVE

Barú ★ CARIBBEAN/MEDITERRANEAN One of the original trailblazers of a 1990s Old City restaurant revival, this ever fashionable spot remains popular, attracting beautiful crowds that appear to have just strolled in from one of those Hispanic soap operas. Named after an unspoiled island off the north coast of Colombia, it occupies a stately looking, high-ceilinged space capped with massive timbers, fronted with a hyper-convivial mahogany bar, and lush paintings. Many dishes are midway between an appetizer and a main-course, but your waitperson can help guide you in ordering the right amount of food. There are five different kinds of carpaccio (tuna, halibut, salmon, beef, or Serrano ham). Ceviche of mahimahi is appropriately tart, appealingly permeated with citrus; and the marinated lamb chops with a paprika-and-pineapple mojo sauce are flavorful. Other culinary creations include almond-encrusted goat cheese with Jamaican jerk mango dip and yucca chips, and sliced filet mignon. The house specialty is the risotto, so make sure to order at least one type. While the place is not cheap, it surpasses expectations, and service has improved, even if it means the youthful staff has to maneuvers through the packed-in crowd.

Calle San Sebastián 150. ✆ **787/977-7107.** Reservations recommended. Main courses $15–$28. AE, MC, V. Mon–Sat 6pm–3am; Sun 6pm–midnight. Bus: Old City Trolley.

Carli Café Concierto ★ INTERNATIONAL This stylish restaurant is owned by Carli Muñoz. The gold disc hanging on the wall attests to Carli's success in his previous role as a pianist for the Beach Boys. Nowadays, he entertains his dinner guests nightly with a combination of standards, romantic jazz, and original material on his grand piano, or along with a small jazz combo. Diners can sit outside on the Plazoleta, where they can enjoy a panoramic view of the bay, or they can eat inside against a backdrop of a tasteful decor of terra-cotta walls and black marble tables. There is a wide selection of tapas and appetizers, including a plantain-crusted calamari in a dark sesame sauce. Entrees include a salmon and shrimp linguini in a creamy brandy sauce, rosemary jus lamb chops and blackened ahi tuna with Cajun spices. The bar, with its mahogany and brass fittings, is an ideal spot to chill out. The concert starts every night at 8pm.

Edificio Banco Popular, Calle Tetuán 206, off Plazoleta Rafael Carrión. ✆ **787/725-4927.** Reservations recommended. Main courses $14–$36. AE, V. Mon–Fri 3:30–11pm; Sat 4–11:30pm. Bus: M2 or M3.

J Taste JAPANESE Delicious sushi, teppanyaki, teriyaki and tempura dishes, and absolutely charming service. This place is smartly minimalist. Different meats, such as breaded pork, BBQ eel, or beef, are served with rice in hot ceramic pots with different seasonings, and there are adventurous noodle dishes, from shrimp tempura soup to pan fried noodles with chicken. There are great soups and salads, edamame, grilled pepper tuna, and beef skewers to start. A specialty is the beef and seafood meals cooked on an antique stone right at your table, and the teppanyaki chefs are first rate showmen and chefs. With really wonderful service and a great ambience, this place delivers on all levels. Top rate taste.

Calle Recinto Sur 307. ✆ **787/724-4003.** Reservations not necessary. Main courses $12–$32. AE, MC, Mon–Thurs noon–11pm; Fri–Sat noon–midnight; Sun noon–10pm. Bus: Old City Trolley.

Parrot Club ★ NUEVO LATINO/CARIBBEAN This bistro and bar, owned by husband-and-wife team Emilio Figueroa and Gigi Zafero, is bright and colorful, as inventive as its Nuevo Latino cuisine, which, like the setting, delivers a new take on Puerto Rican and Cuban traditions. Latin cookery, a delicious blend of Spanish, Taíno and African influence, reach lofty heights here, but the genuinely friendly and (usually) efficient service really sets it apart from the competition. Start out with coriander crab fritters accompanied by Caribbean tartar sauce or the stewed beef and root vegetable nachos. Ceviche lovers might opt for the excellent tuna, salmon, and mahimahi ceviche, with lime and charred tomato. Main-course standouts include grilled churrasco with yellow tomato chimichurri and sautéed potatoes, and the plantain crusted mahimahi with sweet yellow pepper beurre blanc sauce and Peruvian potatoes. You have to try the "Parrot Passion" drink, made from lemon-flavored rum, triple sec, oranges, and passion fruit.

Calle Fortaleza 363. © **787/725-7370.** Reservations not accepted. Main courses $10–$23 lunch, $18–$36 dinner. AE, DC, MC, V. Daily 11am–4pm and 6–11pm. Closed 2 weeks in Sept. Bus: Old City Trolley.

Sofia Italian Kitchen & Wine Bar ITALIAN This tratorria takes you to Rome with its courtyard, arched doorways, exposed red brick, and mahogany bar. Service is first-rate, as are the market-fresh ingredients. The specialties represent the best of quintessential Italian cuisine. Photographs and pop-art paintings of the gorgeous Sophia Lauren surround the bar, an homage to the famed actress's voluptuous beauty, and to the delights on offer among the delicacies served here. There are lush, delicate designer pizzas, lusty pastas, such as the seafood linguini in a light tomato sauce, and such entrees as pork tenderloin in gorgonzola and pear-walnut sauce, and several excellent steak and seafood dishes.

Calle San Francisco 355. © **787/721-0396.** Reservations recommended at night. Main courses $18–$27, pastas $17–$24, pizzas $14–$16. AE, DC, MC, V. Mon 4–10:30pm; Tues–Thurs and Sun noon–10:30pm; Fri–Sat noon–11pm.

Toro Salao ★ SPANISH TAPAS With dark wood interior and a Spanish colonial facade, bullfighting posters and splashes of red, this is the kind of place Ernest Hemingway would have written home about. Toro Salao, "the salty bull" in Spanish, is another restaurant by Emilio Figueroa and Gigi Zaferos (owners/creators of the Parrot Club, Dragonfly and Aguaviva, among others) that seamlessly matches the cuisine with the restaurant ambience. There's something for everyone, so I always take family here; we gorge on flatbread pizza with artichokes and Mediterranean olives; a papas bravas (spicy potatoes) redux that isn't overly spicy; and seared octopus with sundried tomato vinaigrette. There's nothing better than the crisp and clean mussels in a chunky green salsa and the sweet veal meatballs with romesco sauce and plantains. Full meals include paella seafood with chicken and sausage, seared pork with coriander *mojo,* and classic *churrasco.* Order a pitcher of sangria, among San Juan's finest. There are several inventive varieties, including a tropical fruit version, which add flavor without ever losing the essence of this Spanish tavern standard.

Calle Tetuan 367. © **787/722-3330.** Reservations not accepted. Tapas $12–$25; main courses $22–$35. AE, MC, V. Mon–Sat 6pm–midnight. Bus: Old City Trolley.

Trois Cent Onze (311) ★ FRENCH Occupied for years by the photography studio that developed many of Puerto Rico's earliest movies, the building that now houses the premier French restaurant in Old San Juan revealed its hidden treasures in 1999, when the French and Puerto Rican owners of this place began to renovate for the restaurant. Buried beneath layers of bad architecture and tastelessly-executed interior design, they discovered some of the most beautiful Moorish–Andalusian tilework in San Juan's Old City. Because of those tiles, and because of the delicate Andalusian-style iron rosette above the door, they wisely decided to retain the area's Moorish embellishments during the reconfiguration of their restaurant's decor. What you'll get today is Casbah-style atmosphere, complete with a zinc bar near the entrance, a soaring and richly beamed ceiling, and decor

The Intoxicating Aroma of Local Coffee

A coffee break in Old San Juan might last an afternoon. *Taza* (cup) after *taza* of Puerto Rico's rich brew will make you desert Jamaican Blue Mountain coffee or Hawaiian Kona forever. The rich local coffees are from beans grown in Puerto Rico's lush, mountainous heartland, in towns such as Adjuntas and Jayuya, Maricao, and Las Marías. There are a growing number of fashionable cafes that offer fine local coffees, as well as gourmet brands from around the world. However, just about anywhere you go that serves coffee, will serve a rich local brew (including Starbucks, McDonald's, and Burger King!).

Try Caficultura (✆ 787/723-7731), a gorgeous new spot on a shady corner of Plaza Colón; Cuatro Estaciones (Plaza de las Armas; no phone), the outdoor cafe on the western end of Old San Juan's central plaza, adjacent to the State Department; Hacienda San Pedro (Av. De Diego 318, Santurce; ✆ 787/993-1871; www.cafehsp.com) right in the heart of the Santurce Arts District. When ordering, ask for *café con leche* (with milk), *puya* (unsweetened), *negrito con azúcar* (black and sweetened), or *cortao* (black with a dash of milk).

reminiscent of old Tangiers. Colors, textures, and flavors combine here to produce an irresistible array of dishes. The extensive menu has many hits. We were taken by appetizers such as the mouthwatering mini rack of lamb with thyme and bacon or the refreshing crab and mango salad. The Bouillabaise 311 did not let this fan of the classic French fish stew down, and steak does not get much better than the beef filet mignon in the cognac green peppercorn sauce served here. Complete your meal with a Grand Marnier soufflé or the chocolate mousse with Puerto Rican rum sauce.

Calle Fortaleza 311. ✆ **787/725-7959.** Reservations recommended. Main courses $19–$35. AE, MC, V. Tues–Thurs noon–2:30pm and 6:30–10pm; Fri–Sat noon–2:30pm and 6–11pm; Sun noon–10pm. Bus: Old City Trolley, T2, or 2.

MODERATE

Al Dente SICILIAN/ITALIAN There's a friendly and accommodating bar area near the entrance, a warm-toned color scheme of scarlets and blues, and interesting art work, including works by Margie Alcaraz Amenta, who, with Sicily-born Giancarlo Amenta owns this Old City fixture. The *osso buco* is great, so is the homemade ravioli, calamari with polenta, and *arancini di spinachi fritti* (an old Sicilian specialty and one of the restaurant's bestsellers—spinach balls with rice, ricotta cheese, and pink sauce). The chicken contandina is also a great dish. The kitchen can hit an occasional sour note in its execution, but most diners leave happy.

Calle Recinto Sur 309. ✆ **787/723-7303.** Reservations recommended. Main courses $16–$23. AE, MC, V. Mon–Fri noon–10:30pm; Sat noon–11pm. Bus: Old Town Trolley.

Bodega Chic ★ 🎁 FRENCH BISTRO This small French/Algerian bistro blends delicious Mediterranean and Caribbean herbs and flavors, reasonable prices, and unpretentious friendly service. Chef and partner Christophe Gourdain trained with chef Jean-Georges Vonegerichten, and he learned well, apparently. Start out with the baked goat cheese croustillant with eggplant caviar and the grilled calamari. The hangar steak with sautéed potatoes and string beans is as close to perfection as the fresh mussels Provençal. The braised lamb shank is also worth a try, and the roasted chicken breast in curry banana sauce is much better than it sounds. The high-ceilinged dining room and small adjacent bar room open out onto Calle Cristo just around the corner from the popular Calle San Sebastián. There's homey local memorabilia plastered on the walls. Desserts include a fantastic crème brûlée and warm chocolate cake.

Calle Cristo 51. ✆ **787/722-0124.** Reservations recommended. Main courses $15–$26. AE, MC, V. Tues-Fri 6pm-midnight; Sun 11:30am-4pm. Bus: Old City Trolley.

Burén ★ INTERNATIONAL This friendly, funky little place serves up unique, flavorful pizza, plus pastas and Latino grilled steaks—and inventive entrees are surprisingly sophisticated as well. The main bar and adjoining lounge area are brightly colored, while the back courtyard is all about earth tones. The *plátano* soup and *tostones* stuffed with shrimp in tomato sauce are excellent starters, as are the classic Greek salad and the spinach salad served with mozzarella cheese and passion fruit dressing. Pizza lovers will be happy with the usual ingredients, or some creative combinations: the Tamarindo combines proscuitto, sundried tomatoes, and manchego cheese, while the Las Monjas has feta cheese, black olives, tomatoes, and peppers. If you can resist the pizza, try the veal *osso buco* in a basil-rosemary emulsion served with fettuccini. Juicy pork medallions are served in a peppercorn pineapple sauce.

Calle Cristo 103. ✆ **787/977-5023.** Reservations recommended Main courses $16–$26. AE, DC, DISC, MC, V. Daily 6–11pm. Bus: Old City Trolley.

Café Berlin INTERNATIONAL This central European-style cafe is housed in a comfortable room with huge glass windows overlooking the charming Plaza Colón, and there's also a sidewalk cafe in front. If feels like a bit of Vienna, with the tiny marble top tables, transplanted to the tropics. There are big breakfasts and tasty entrees and sandwiches, with an emphasis on healthy and fresh ingredients, including several vegetarian choices. The stewed eggplant in *criollo* sauce and the salmon tropical (mango and balsamic vinegar sauce) are excellent, and the grilled tofu kebabs with guava barbecue sauce and the grilled vegetable parrillada are as scrumptious as the real thing. There are also delicious salads and fresh fruit frappes, as well as a beautiful bar with a nice collection of Bavarian beer. Breakfasts offer from fresh fruits and healthy cereals to full platters of fried eggs, potatoes and sausages, and for dessert how about hazelnut soy ice cream.

Plaza de Colón 407. ✆ **787/722-5205.** Main courses $11–$30; breakfast $3.50–$12. AE, MC, V. Mon–Fri 11am–10pm; Sat–Sun 8am–10pm. Bus: Old City Trolley.

Café Puerto Rico CREOLE/PUERTO RICAN This small and friendly restaurant offers flavorful bargains and outdoor seating right on Plaza de Colón. Inside, there's ceiling fans, beamed ceilings, and tile floors, and the constant whir of a blender mixing up tropical fruit drinks. The menu features hearty regional fare. Tasty options include fried fish filet, paella, and lobster cooked as you like it. Eggplant parmigiana is an excellent vegetarian option, and you might also order the excellent eye round stuffed with ham in Creole sauce or conch salad. Of course, if you're getting hungry during a day of strolling Old San Juan's windy streets, don't wait for dinner—you'll enjoy a lunch break here, too.

Calle O'Donnell 208. ✆ **787/724-2281.** Main courses $9–$24. AE, MC, V. Mon–Sat noon–3pm; Sun noon–midnight. Bus: Old City Trolley.

Caficultura ★ CAFE/BISTRO Any time's a good time to indulge yourself at this beautiful "espresso bar and marketplace kitchen" on Plaza Colón, a fitting temple to the richness of Puerto Rican coffee that delivers fresh, flavorful and inventive *comida criolla*. It opens early, offers a great respite from the heat of the day for lunch or a snack, and can be counted on most evenings for a delicious tapas menu and nightly specials. A "less is more" approach is evident in everything from its stone-washed walls and tiled floors, wooden doors and furnishings, to its select and satisfying menu of Puerto Rican coffee, beer, wine, and alcoholic beverages. You can always get a *cortadito* (espresso topped with steamed milk) or some guayaba cake, but there are smoked ham and eggs, coconut French toast and fruit salads for breakfast, and gourmet sandwiches, such as roasted beef loin with baked tomato and caramelized onion or turkey breast with manchego cheese and bacon and spring salad for lunch. Recent nightly specials include a juicy churrasco with sautéed vegetables and a pasta as tasty as unusual, and a penne with chicken and broccoli in manchego cheese and root vegetable cream sauce. Tapas are knockouts: assorted fried vegetables, shrimp ceviche with cassava fritters, and Spanish sausage in wine sauce. The baristas and waitstaff are as charming as the ornate lanterns, high ceilings, and expertly hewn prints. Like the best of Old San Juan, Caficultura pays homage to Puerto Rican tradition while staying very current.

Calle San Francisco 401, Plaza Colón Old San Juan. ✆ **787/723-7731.** Reservations not necessary. Evening tapas $3.50–$18, lunch $6.25–$12, breakfast $2.75–$8.50. AE, MC, V. Daily 7am–4pm; Thurs-Sat 6–11pm. Bus: Old San Juan Trolley.

Dragonfly ★★ LATIN/ASIAN FUSION One of San Juan's hottest restaurants, the place has been compared to both an Old San Francisco bordello and a Shanghai opium den, descriptions that evoke as much the lusty appeal and addictive power of its cuisine as the red-walled interior, a world of fringed lamps and gilded mirrors behind beaded curtains. It's good for a late meal, as the portion sizes, called *platos*, or plates, are somewhere between appetizers and entrees. The Asian marinated churrasco with wasabi fries and the Amarillo dumplings in citrus dipping sauce are must haves. Other standouts: seared tuna in green peppercorn sauce, tempura rock shrimp tacos, and Chino Latino lo mein, with Puerto Rican fried chicken chunks. This is the island's first Latin–Asian menu, and it remains one of the best anywhere. An expansion has added a lounge and full sushi bar to the original dining room, but the crowds keep filling the place, one of the city's trendiest places for a night out since 2000.

Calle Fortaleza 364. ✆ **787/977-3886.** Reservations not accepted. Main courses $12–$25. AE, MC, V. Mon–Wed 6–11pm; Thurs–Sat 6pm–midnight. Bus: Old City Trolley.

El Jibarito PUERTO RICAN This is a bustling local restaurant beloved by many *sanjuaneros* for making food like their mother's used to make. Its walls hold scenes of Old San Juan streets and the Puerto Rican countryside, which along with the rich flavors of the food served here, pay tribute to the backgrounds of owners Pedro and Aida Ruiz. This is a pleasant Old City dining room with reasonable prices, friendly service, and a tasty cube steak with onions, conch salad, oven-baked grouper, fried red snapper in garlic, as well as stuffed *mofongo* and other local specialties. Side orders could include rice and beans, fried plantains, and island staples such as rice and *gandules* or a whopping portion of *mofongo* (chopped plantains with oil and seasonings). There is no better way to end a meal here than a slice of coconut flan. Unpretentious, with polite and helpful service.

Old San Juan, Calle del Sol 280. ✆ **787/725-8375.** Reservations not necessary. Main courses $7.95-$25. Sandwiches, snacks available. Daily 10 am–9 pm. Bus: Old City Trolley.

El Patio de Sam AMERICAN/PUERTO RICAN Established in 1953, this legendary establishment often misses on its main dishes, but its burgers and finger food are the perfect complement for this legendary hangout, which lives off its live music, intriguing conversation and great local art. The juicy burgers are the mainstay. It's not that the *arroz con pollo* (chicken with rice Puerto Rican style), Latino style steaks, and paella are bad, just uninspired. Hipsters from Hunter S. Thompson to Allan Ginsburg have all hoisted a few back here. Their renowned auras influence the atmosphere of the place, as does the great music (anything from Latin jazz to ballads) and the brilliant artwork by some of the island's best artists of the last 50 years. Right across the street from Plaza San José, there's always a party going on. The front bar area is a bit cramped, but the main dining room is in the huge, airy covered courtyard in the back.

Calle San Sebastián 102 (across from the Iglesia de San José). ✆ **787/723-1149.** Sandwiches, burgers, and salads $9–$11; platters $13–$35. AE, DISC, MC, V. Daily noon–1am. Bus: Old City Trolley.

El Picoteo ★★ 📷 SPANISH Spilling across a front and interior terrace overlooking the courtyard of the historic El Convento Hotel, this is the best place in the Old City to savor some drinks and tapas while watching the action near Calle San Sebastián. On most nights, there's a parade of people walking up and down Calle Cristo in front of the restaurant as they go back and forth to the bars and restaurants just up the hill. We love the spicy potatoes *(papas bravas)*, shrimp in garlic sauce, and the brick oven pizza, but there are also full meals, such as seafood paella. With 80 tapas to choose from, there's also real Spanish flavor here, in such dishes as garbanzo salad, sausages, various ceviches, fresh octopus, and the best selection of cheese in the city. The setting amid Spanish colonial facades and wildly blooming bougainvillea is one of the Old City's most charming. It's equally inviting for a weekend lunch. Try the champagne-laced sangria. Dinner is festive, especially Thursday evenings, when there is a live flamenco show.

In El Convento Hotel, Calle del Cristo 100. ✆ **787/723-9202.** Reservations recommended. Main courses $6–$32; paella $20–$35. AE, MC, V. Tues–Sun noon–midnight. Bus: Old City Trolley.

La Mallorquina PUERTO RICAN Founded in 1848 and run by the Rojos family since 1900, this spot positively oozes Old World charm and serves up expert renditions of Puerto Rican classics such as *arroz con pollo* (chicken and rice), *asopao de mariscos* (seafood rice stew), and beef tenderloin Puerto Rican style. Start with garlic soup or gazpacho, end with flan, and you'll have eaten a meal that's authentically Puerto Rican. Neither the atmosphere nor the food has changed much over years. You can feel the decades peel away during a leisurely lunch in the dining room, with a white tiled floor and hypnotic whirring ceiling fans. The uniformed waiters move as if in dream bringing every thing one asks. Still, one of the Old City's finest dining experiences after all these years.

Calle San Justo 207. ✆ **787/722-3261.** Reservations not accepted at lunch, recommended at dinner. Dinner main courses $15–$36 (lobster is priciest); lunch from $7.95. AE, MC, V. Mon–Sat 12:30–10pm. Closed Sept. Bus: Old City Trolley.

Melao CARIBBEAN This bayside spot on the outskirts of the Old City has created its own brand of local fusion cuisine that is super flavorful and mellow on the wallet at the same time. The menu offers gourmet-upped pub fare and entrees on par with the much more pretentious and expensive restaurants in the Old City. The married couple behind this local bistro—Marelsic Colon and Nain Nun Bueiz (who is also chef)—deliver a great product at a great price and don't close till their customers say it's okay. There are changing variations on red snapper and pork loin, lamb chops and classic pastas, starters such as lobster ravioli and codfish kisses, and absolutely delicious desserts, such as crème brûlée, pistachio cheesecake, chocolate fondue, and fresh strawberries with cake. The pizza, burgers, and finger foods are also two cuts above the ordinary. Beverages include wonderful mojitos, fresh fruit frappes and blender drinks. It's great to see so much being done in a small space, which has a breezy outdoor bayside terrace for dining. There is often live music on Saturday nights.

Cond. Capitolio Plaza Ste. 201, Calle del Muelle, Viejo San Juan. ✆ **787/721-7160.** Reservations not necessary. Main courses $7.95–$25. Mon–Tues 11am–3pm; Wed–Fri 11 am–10pm; Fri 11am–11pm; Sat 3–11pm.

Old Harbor Brewery Steak and Lobster House AMERICAN San Juan's only microbrewery also has top-drawer tavern fare in an upscale mariner setting. Brewmaster Brad Mortensen handcrafts five distinct house beers, as well as seven seasonal beers, on the premises in state-of-the-art brewing facilities. The restaurant specializes in top-quality steaks and fresh Puerto Rican spiny lobster. The cuts are served steakhouse style with a choice of sauces (the mushroom and chimichurri recommended) and a la carte sides (favorites are the Lyonnais potatoes and asparagus with béarnaise). The hanging tender steak was as promised, and the New York Strip was flavorful and cooked to perfection. Caribbean lobster is lighter than Maine lobster, and the version served here is among the best on the island. Go with the citrus beurre blanc sauce rather than the coconut, almond-spiced rum. The rich French onion and lobster bisque soup are rich and hearty, and rather a rarity in the Caribbean. The Santo Viejo pilsner and Old Harbor pale ale are first rate. The restaurant dates to the 1920s, when it housed the New York Federal Bank, and it was beautifully restored before opening in 2005. A classic tavern setup surrounds the elegant brew vats, but the place is formal, with fully dressed tables, classic black and white tiles, and metal and wooden finishings.

Calle Tizol 202 (near Recinto Sur). ✆ **787/721-2100.** Reservations recommended. Platters and main courses $14–$38. AE, MC, V. Daily 8am–7pm. Bus: Old City Trolley.

Ostra Cosa 🎁 ECLECTIC/SEAFOOD This is still one of the most romantic settings for a meal in Old San Juan, amidst the branches of the quenepe tree and blooming flowers, tropical birds and singing tree frogs in the courtyard of a restored 16th century residence. By itself, meeting the owner, lifestyle guru Alberto Nazario, makes a trip here worth it, while the whimsical menu offerings get your mojo working. The large grilled (still-shelled) prawns are tasty but difficult and messy, not conducive to the kind of romantic dinner you came here for in the first place, so stick to the delicious ceviches and more standard continental fare. Also makes a good lunch stop while shopping in the Old City. The bar never misses, just like Alberto's witty musings.

Calle del Cristo 154. ✆ **787/722-2672.** Reservations recommended. Main courses $18–$29. AE, MC, V. Sun–Wed noon–10pm; Fri–Sat noon–11pm. Bus: Old City Trolley.

Patio del Nispero INTERNATIONAL Surrounded by the soaring atrium of Old San Juan's most historic hotel, this restaurant sits in a charming oasis of calm and quiet of the beautiful courtyard. It gets its name from a towering century-old fruit tree, in the patio, which is filled with verdant plants thriving under the direct sunlight of the open sky, and big canvas umbrellas shielding diners from the rain. No one will mind if you order just a drink (the daiquiris are excellent) or a cup of coffee while resting after a tour of the Old Town or the cathedral next door. It's breakfast and lunch only, and offerings include everything from Eggs Benedict to Banana Nut Pancakes to gazpacho soup, American burgers and daily specials of Puerto Rican and Italian comfort food. Also a nice spot to take a break after a day of shopping. The bar does great blender drinks and coffees as well. Formal events and parties are held here in evenings.

In the El Convento hotel, Calle del Cristo 100. ✆ **787/723-9020.** Reservations not necessary. Sandwiches $7.50–$24. AE, DC, MC, V. Daily 9am–3:30pm. Bus: Old City Trolley.

Tantra INDO-LATINO So sway to the world beat music, enjoy the culinary cultural clash and forget what country you are in. Set in the heart of "restaurant row" on Calle Fortaleza, this restaurant on the first floor and courtyard of a Spanish colonial mansion is decorated in Asian colors and handicrafts with Hindu and Buddhist imagery. The ethnic setting fits the sophisticated fusion of Latino with South Indian cuisine, a blend of slow-cooked tandoori with Puerto Rico–derived flavors, from chef and owner, India-born Ramesh Pillai. The sesame masala-crusted sushi tuna with peanut sauce is as good as it sounds; other raves include fried coconut sesame jumbo shrimp with Indian noodles, chicken tikka masala with naan (flatbread), and rice and chicken rolls with passion-fruit sauce. The house tandoori chicken sticks to tradition but then throws in manchego and mozzarella cheese, guayaba fruit, guava-flavored dip, and naan. There are also belly-dancing shows on many nights. Because the kitchen stays open until the wee hours, it's also a place for drinks and late-night snacks for local hipsters and tourists on the prowl; the bar is often packed till dawn. An appropriate way to begin a meal here is to order one of the best martinis we've ever had—a concoction flavored with cinnamon and cloves.

Calle Fortaleza 356. ✆ **787/977-8141.** Reservations only for groups. Main courses $13–$25. AE, MC, V. Mon 3pm–3am; Tues–Sat noon–3am; Sun noon–midnight. Bus: Old City Trolley.

INEXPENSIVE

Ben & Jerry's ICE CREAM/CAFE This is a great place, not just for the young, but the young at heart. Decorated in early college dorm room style, it's the perfect place to put some Cherry Garcia, Chunky Monkey, and Imagine Whirled Peace in your mouth. You can also have meals, stuff like sandwiches and wraps and salads. There are also great baked breads, cakes, cookies, and other stuff, local coffee and fruit drinks. And then there's the free Wi-Fi, a house computer, and cool music and magazines. Check for special events, such as story readings for children.

Calle del Cristo 61. ✆ **787/977-6882.** Reservations not necessary. Ice cream and meals $3.95–$9.95. Daily 11am–11pm. Bus: Old City Trolley.

La Bombonera PUERTO RICAN This place offers exceptional value in its homemade pastries, well-stuffed sandwiches, and endless cups of coffee—and it has done so since 1902. The atmosphere is turn-of-the-20th-century Castille transplanted to the New World with authentically homemade, and inexpensive, Puerto

Rican and regional dishes such as rice with squid, roast leg of pork, and seafood *asopao* (a thick rice soup). For breakfasts, the specialty is the mallorca, a sugar-coated bun stuffed with ham and cheese. For dessert, you can choose from great flan and local cakes. The bakery is up front with the cafeteria in the back. Service is polite, if a bit rushed, and the place fills up quickly at lunchtime and during the breakfast hour.

Calle San Francisco 259. ✆ **787/722-0658.** Reservations recommended. American breakfast $4.50–$6.45; main courses $6–$18. AE, MC, V. Daily 7:30am–8pm. Bus: Old City Trolley.

Raíces PUERTO RICAN Don't let the apparent touristy trappings fool you; it's not the cheapest meal in town, but it's among the tastiest and most authentic, and we recommend it for a big taste of Puerto Rican cuisine. These are Caguas boys in the kitchen, so enjoy the rustic Puerto Rican setting—beautifully outfitted with local arts and crafts—and the waitresses and waiters decked out in the beautiful folkloric dress. It's a perfect fit for its location near the cruise-ship docks, but the first location was in Caguas, which is decidedly untouristy. The "typical festival" combines a number of classic island treats, such as meat turnovers, stuffed fried plantain fritters, codfish fritters, and mashed cassava, but you'll also want to try the delicious plantain soup. The stuffed *mofongo* entrees are the real specialty here; along with the typical stuffed chicken or shrimp, the options range to breaded pork, skirt steak, and Creole-style mahimahi. If you want hearty fare, the chicken or shrimp *asopao* is another option. The coconut flan and guava cheesecake do not disappoint. Traditional Puerto Rican music, with occasional live salsa on Thursday nights, further complements the experience.

Calle Recinto Sur 315. ✆ **787/289-2121.** Reservations not necessary. Main courses $10–$26. AE, MC, V. Mon–Fri 11am–4pm and 6–11pm; Sat 11am–11pm; Sun noon–10pm. Bus: Old City Trolley.

Puerta de Tierra

For the locations of restaurants in Puerta de Tierra, see the map "Puerta de Tierra, Miramar, Condado & Ocean Park Accommodations & Dining" on p. 115.

EXPENSIVE

Lemongrass Restaurant PAN ASIAN Ensconced in a modern Zen-inspired structure, overlooking the lush grounds and ponds of a remote section of Puerto Rico's oldest resort, this restaurant is the perfect setting for local culinary star Mario Pagan's Asian Latino musings. You can watch the graceful swans from the main lounge or outside garden terrace while devouring the delicate arrangement of flavors in entrees such as the sea scallop and lamb cakes with caramelized sesame mustard sauce, the churrasco and cilanpesto with wonton chips or the shrimp lo-mein in green mango sauce. There's also a sushi bar, with incredible combinations such as truffled crab and green papaya or Tempura lobster and avocado, as well as a champagne lounge and standard bar. The setting is impressive, and the restaurant has a modern yet natural minimalism that puts the surroundings on full display. Be prepared to linger; this is a very good place for a romantic meal.

Puerta de Tierra. Caribe Hilton, Calle Los Rosales. ✆ **787/724-5888.** Reservations recommended. Main courses $25–$32. Sun–Thurs 5:30–10:30 pm; Sat 5:30–11pm. AE, MC, V. Bus: B21.

Morton's of Chicago ★ STEAKHOUSE The same great Morton's steaks in a dazzling room overlooking the oceans, and service that matches the settings. The chain of gourmet steakhouses was founded in 1978 by Arnie Morton, former executive vice president of the *Playboy* empire. Beef lovers, from Al Gore to Liza Minnelli, know they'll get quality meats perfectly cooked at Morton's. Carts laden with everything from prime Midwestern beefsteaks to succulent lamb or veal chops are wheeled around for your selection, but prime rib lovers will want to try it here; a 24-ounce porterhouse is another specialty worthy of the hype. Fresh and delicious seafood and vegetable dishes, shellfish and chicken, round out the menu. Nothing beats the house shrimp cocktail or smoked Pacific salmon for starters. For dessert, gravitate to one of the soufflés, such as raspberry or Grand Marnier. There are frequent specials and a beautiful bar known for its stiff drinks and smart conversation.

In the Caribe Hilton, Calle Los Rosales. ✆ **787/977-6262.** Reservations recommended. Main courses $20–$40. AE, DC, DISC, MC, V. Daily 5–11pm. Bus: B21.

INEXPENSIVE

El Hamburger ★ LIGHT FARE This no-frills burger stand offers tasty grilled burgers and hot dogs, cold beer, and perfectly golden french fries and onion rings. From its perch overlooking the Atlantic on the oceanfront drive into San Juan, the grill has become a late-night local favorite for those leaving the bars of Old San Juan, and is also popular for a bite during work or after the beach. A really good, cheap opportunity to soak up some real local atmosphere, the ramshackle wooden establishment is the kind of burger joint that has disappeared throughout much of the United States with the advent of the modern fast-food restaurant. One of its joys lives on here with a selection of condiments—from onions to relish, to thick tomatoes, to pickles—which is brought to your table with your burger. There's a patch of palm trees on the undeveloped coastal bluff across the street, and the ocean breeze flows all through the white wooden building. It's always packed, but service is still super fast and the conversation animated.

Muñoz Rivera 402. ✆ **787/721-4269.** Reservations not accepted. Burgers from $3.50. Cash only. Sun–Thurs 11am–11pm; Fri–Sat 11am–1am. Bus: A5, M1.

Condado

For the locations of Condado restaurants, see the map "Puerta de Tierra, Miramar, Condado & Ocean Park Accommodations & Dining" on p. 115.

VERY EXPENSIVE

Budatai ★★★ LATIN/ASIAN The new home of Puerto Rico's "Iron Chef" mixes local flavors with Asian ingredients to deliver one of San Juan's finest dining experiences. Scrumptiously situated in an Art Deco town house overlooking an oceanfront park at the heart of Condado's redevelopment revival, Budatai's muted brown interior is as stylish as the designer boutiques surrounding it. With wall-sized windows inside and a rooftop terrace, diners have great views and are pampered with oversized tables and leather chairs. Chef Roberto Trevino, who fell just short against Mario Batali on the Food Network's Iron Chef America (the secret ingredient was catfish), reworks the Nuevo Latino and Asian fusion concepts he developed at Old San Juan's Parrot Club, Dragonfly, and Aguaviva restaurants and kicks up the portion sizes. Get started with the sesame-crusted pork-wrapped asparagus with a soy mayonnaise, an explosion of flavor and texture, or if sushi's your thing, the geisha roll—lobster, cream cheese, jicama, and meringue kisses. The soy-glazed salmon with coconut hash main course artfully balances the salty and sweet, while the veal sirloin with lobster mashed Asian potatoes is as rich as it sounds. Skip the lo mein with *chicharon de pollo* and the karate pork chop, which are not bad, just ordinary. The waitstaff is friendly, efficient, and knowledgeable about the menu and extensive wine list. The second-floor bar and lounge is a hot spot for the city's young and beautiful, especially on weekends.

Av. Ashford 1056, Condado. ✆ **787/725-6919.** Main courses $24-$35. AE MC, V. Mon-Wed 11:30am-11pm; Thurs-Sat 11:30am-midnight; Sun 11:30am-10pm. Bus: A5, C53.

Pikayo ★★★ PUERTO RICAN FUSION This is an ideal place to go for the next generation of Puerto Rican fusion cuisine. Pikayo not only keeps up with the latest culinary trends, but it also often sets them, thanks to the inspired guidance of owner and celebrity chef Wilo Benet. Formal but not stuffy, and winner of more culinary awards than virtually any other restaurant in Puerto Rico, Benet makes Pikayo all about bringing his hometown cuisine to new glories. I've never been disappointed by an appetizer I've tried, which have included escargot in a wild mushroom fricassee, tuna "pegao" in a chipotle chili sauce and cheese empanadillas with truffle mojito. The adventure continues through the main courses, with blackened salmon with tomato onion compote and mustard beurre blanc, and the veal scaloppine with sweet pea risotto and julienne prosciutto. The Caribbean lobster tail is served with chorizo sausage, and a gaunabana beurre blanc sauce is pricey but delicious.

At the Conrad Condado Plaza, Ashford 999. ✆ **787/721-6194.** Reservations recommended. Main courses $29-$65. AE, DC, MC, V. Daily 6-11pm. Bus: B21, C53.

EXPENSIVE

Ajili Mójili ★ PUERTO RICAN/CREOLE This restaurant serves *comida criolla,* the starchy, down-home cuisine that developed on the island a century ago. It's housed in a huge two-story building on the Condado Lagoon. Locals come here for a taste of the food they enjoyed at their mother's knee, such as *mofongo* (green plantain casserole stuffed with veal, chicken, shrimp, or pork), *arroz con pollo* (chicken and rice), *medallones de cerdo encebollado* (pork loin sautéed with onions), *carne mechada* (beef rib-eye stuffed with ham), and *lechon asado con maposteado* (roast pork with rice and beans). Wash it all down with an ice-cold bottle of local beer. The staff will eagerly describe menu items in colloquial English.

Av. Ashford 1006. ✆ **787/725-9195.** Reservations recommended. Main courses $16-$30; lunch $13-$26. AE, DISC, MC, V. Mon-Thurs 11:45am-3pm and 6-10pm; Fri noon-3pm and 6-11pm; Sat 11:45am-3:30pm and 6-11pm; Sun 12:30-4pm and 6-10pm. Bus: B21, C53.

Bodega Compostela ★★ TAPAS/WINE CELLAR This established Galician restaurant, which for years has served the finest Spanish food in the capital, was reborn recently as a chic wine and tapas bar without losing anything in the transition. Diners walk through an accompanying wine cellar, with a translucent floor over corks, to a long bar area, or retreat back to the dining room. There are over 50 tapas, or appetizers, served here, ranging from crispy goat cheese–mesclun salad to lentil stew with chorizo and pancetta to octopus carpaccio with sundried tomatoes. Seafood selections are plentiful, but we also gorged on the red pepper stuffed with barbecued Spanish sausage and potato stuffed with lamb shank confit. For those wanting more traditional meals, Compostela still offers the outstanding dishes grounded in Spanish traditions that garnered it such a strong reputation over the years, such as seared tuna with apple julienne and couscous, or a large platter of rice with veal, pork, sausage, rabbit, and chicken for two. There's a daily dessert special. The wine cellar, comprising some 10,000 bottles, is one of the most impressive in San Juan. Av. Condado 106. ✆ **787/724-6099.** Reservations required. Tapas $3–$26; main courses $34–$45. AE, DC, MC, V. Mon–Fri noon–3pm; Mon–Sat 6:30–10:30pm. Bus: M2.

Niché 🎁 LATIN FUSION The menu's been toned down substantially to a basic international palette with local flourishes, but the flavor is still there and the small spot inside an Asian garden still makes a big impression. The single-room restaurant is outfitted with a small bar and tables with seating for 20 or so diners. Its spare design, employing natural wood, glass, and metal, makes it feel much bigger than it is. You stroll through the lobby of the quiet guesthouse on a residential block steps from the choicest beach in Condado to get here, leaving the impression you've stumbled onto a fabulous party. The roast lobster tail and salted filet mignon in red wine sauce may be familiar territory, but the chef nailed it each time I've eaten here. The poached snapper and stuffed calamari are also interesting.
At the Acacia Boutique Hotel, Calle Taft 8. ✆ **787/727-2023 ext 129.** Reservations recommended. Main courses $22–$34. AE, MC, V. Sun–Sat 6–11pm. Bus: A5.

Ristorante Tuscany ★ NORTHERN ITALIAN A consistently delicious Northern Italian restaurant known for its delicious menu, and more recently, its value-packed early bird special. While critics say the menu and decor is dated, this stuff does not go out of style: classic *osso buco* with saffron pasta, roasted chicken stuffed with spinach and ricotta cheese, grilled filet mignon with barolo sauce and thyme and fennel crusted rack of lamb with vegetables in zinfandel sauce. The risottos prepared al dente in the traditional northern Italian style are among the island's finest, and the cold and hot appetizers are meals unto themselves.
In the San Juan Marriott Resort, Av. Ashford 1309. ✆ **787/722-7000.** Reservations recommended. Main courses $18–$29. AE, DC, DISC, MC, V. Daily 6–11pm. Bus: B21.

Ummo Restaurant ★ ARGENTINE GRILL The dark wood and stone interior perfectly suits this sizzling Argentine restaurant specializing in *parrilladas,* grill platters, of steak, chicken, blood sausage and pork cutlets. There's also tasty Italian food, grilled fish and vegetable platters and a good wine collection. For starters, the house specialties are antipasto platters for couples or groups, with assorted meat, cheese and seafood combinations. There's often a singer/piano player performing inside, as well as the soccer game of the moment on the slick flat screen televisions by the bar. The front terrace is a pleasant place for a meal, if it's not too sultry, and you can watch the crowd saunter down Ashford Avenue. If it's really what you are after, a grilled steak or chicken platter might be more satisfying than a mixed grill platter, which tend to be heavy on the grilled sausage and pork cuts. Everyone can find something they like here, and the restaurant strikes a really great balance between the formal and relaxed in its ambience.
Av Ashford 1351, Condado. ✆ **787/722-1700.** Reservations recommended. Main courses $17–$32; mixed grill platters (parrilladas) $36–$44 (for 2), $72–$88 (for 4). AE, MC, V. Daily 11am–1 am. Bus: B21.

MODERATE

Most main courses in the restaurants below are at the low end of the price scale. These restaurants each have only two or three dishes that are expensive, almost invariably involving shellfish.

Great Taste ★★ CHINESE This is the place where the island's Chinese community goes to eat dim sum, and with good reason, as this restaurant has been serving up among the best Chinese food on the island for decades. It also has a sushi bar. Set in a 1970s glass and aluminum condominium, the dining room is spacious, comfortable, and bright, with Japanese prints, huge lobster tanks, and an enviable view over the Condado lagoon. Come here for the Chinese; everything you try, from the cashew chicken to the Peking duck, to the shrimp in lobster sauce, to the sizzling black pepper steak is excellent. If dim sum's your thing, this is the best on the island: sticky rice in lotus leaf, skewered beef, and steamed vegetable dumplings. Sunday specials attract droves of diners from the local Chinese community and elsewhere with a refined sense of what good dim sum is all about.

Av. Ashford 1018. ✆ **787/721-8111.** Reservations recommended. Main courses $8–$45. AE, MC, V. Daily 11am–midnight. Bus: B21, C53.

The Greenhouse INTERNATIONAL Its endless menu has this a Condado institution since opening in 1973. You can truly have it all here: from juicy burgers to succulent lobster tail, from French onion soup to western omelets, baked salmon to linguini and clam sauce. Don't expect to be wowed by the service or the decor, but the deft kitchen manages to his its marks despite the variety. And the crowd is always interesting, regardless of the hour. The place is usually packed, and it's a favorite late-night haven to satisfy the most varied of hunger pangs.

Av. Ashford 1200. ✆ **787/725-4036.** Main courses $8–$39. AE, MC, V. Sun–Thurs 11:30–2am; Fri–Sat 11:30–4am. Bus: B21.

INEXPENSIVE

Bebo's Café PUERTO RICAN/AMERICAN Tasty *comida criolla* at low prices make this a favorite with locals, so the crowd more than makes up for the otherwise sterile environment. Everybody comes here. The daily specials are heavy on comfort foods (roast pork, baked turkey, stewed chicken) and are the real bargains, but if you have not tried stuffed *mofongo,* this is a great place to do so. There's a full bar, excellent fresh fruit frappes and local coffees, as well as standard American fare such as club sandwiches and burgers. CNN en Español or the sports event of the moment is broadcast from a huge flatscreen TV in one of its dining areas. The local deserts, tropical flans, *tres leches,* and cheesecakes are wonderful. Service is often off the market, but who cares when it's always well intentioned? The vibe's as good as the value.

Calle Loiza 1600, Santurce. ✆ **787/726-1008.** Reservations not accepted. Main courses $6.95–$25. AE, MC, V. Daily 7:30 am–12:30am.

Café del Angel CREOLE/PUERTO RICAN The place looks transported from Miami's Flagler Street in 1950, and the terrace furniture won't compel you to get *Architectural Digest* on the phone. If indeed there is an "angel," as the cafe's name suggests, it is in the kitchen. Serving remarkably good food at affordable prices, this he place has been in operation for about 2 decades. Service is efficient in a relaxed atmosphere that can seat 100, with paintings and figures of its namesake angels all around. Get real island flavor here: traditional *mofongo relleno,* which is a casserole of sautéed, mashed plantain, stuffed with shrimp, chicken, beefsteak, or lobster. The fresh garlic bread is a nice touch.

Av. Ashford 1106. ✆ **787/643-7594.** Reservations not necessary. Main courses $7–$20. AE, DC, MC, V. Wed–Mon 11am–10pm. Bus: B21.

Cielito Lindo MEXICAN One of the most likable things about this restaurant is the way it retains low prices and an utter lack of pretension, despite the expensive Condado real estate that surrounds it. Even though it recently moved into larger digs next door, it still retains the feeling of a low-slung house in Puebla, Mexico, hometown of owner Jaime Pandal, who maintains a vigilant position from a perch at the cash register. The walls are still outfitted with an intriguing mix of Mexican arts and crafts and ads for popular tequilas and beer. None of the selections has changed since the restaurant was founded, a policy that long-term clients find reassuring. The place is mobbed, especially on weekends, with those looking for heaping portions of well-prepared, Mexican standards: steak or chicken fajitas, Mexican style strip steak sautéed with green peppers and onions, covered with tomatoes and spicy gravy, chicken enchiladas, covered with cheese and sour cream, and several kinds of tacos.

Av. Magdalena 1108. ✆ **787/723-5597.** Reservations not necessary. Main courses $5–$20. AE, MC, V. Mon–Fri 11am–11pm; Sat–Sun 5–11pm. Bus: B21 or C10.

Danny's International Restaurant PIZZA CAFE Don't expect atmosphere, but you can sit at the tables out on the front terrace and watch the street parade down Condado's main drag. The pizzas are thick and tasty, and there's an extensive selection, including the "mariscos," which has mussels, calamari, shrimp, octopus and a special sauce, and the *bomba,* with local sausage, olives, hot peppers, and blue cheese. There's also a complete menu of hot Italian subs and cold subs, a variety of cheese steaks, and burgers and club sandwiches. Skip the few Italian entree selections, which don't compare to the offerings right across the street. The pizza is thick and tasty, however. The place is also one of the better restaurants serving American-style breakfasts near major area lodgings, such as the Marriott and the Ambassador, and guesthouses such as El Canario. Tables are spread throughout a single dining room, and there's a round bar filled with newspapers and outfitted with televisions you can eat at from morning to night.

Av. Ashford 1351. ✆ **787/724-0501** or 724-2734. Reservations not accepted. Main courses $8.50–$15. AE, MC, V. Daily 7am–1am. Bus: B21, C10.

Via Appia ★ PIZZA/ITALIAN A favorite of *sanjuaneros* with a craving for Italian, Via Appia offers praiseworthy food at affordable prices. Its pizzas are among the best on the island, and basic pasta dishes such as baked ziti, lasagna, and spaghetti taste like somebody's Italian grandmother prepared them. However, the restaurant really shows its stuff with such dishes as clams *posillipo,* veal and peppers, broiled sirloin with red-wine mushroom sauce, and the delectable chicken Français. The house sangria is tasty and packs a punch, and the house wine is tasty and helps keep a meal here in the budget category. A wine bar and more formal dining room have been added to the original deli-like main building, but the place to sit is on one of the two terraces fronting the establishment.

Av. Ashford 1350. ✆ **787/725-8711.** Pizza and main courses $9–$30. AE, MC, V. Mon–Fri 11am–11pm; Sat–Sun 11am–midnight. Bus: A5, C53, B21.

Miramar

For the locations of restaurants in Miramar, see the map "Puerta de Tierra, Miramar, Condado & Ocean Park Accommodations & Dining," on p. 115.

EXPENSIVE

Augusto's Cuisine ★★★ FRENCH/INTERNATIONAL With its European flair, this is one of the most elegant and glamorous restaurants in Puerto Rico. It is set on the lobby level of a 15-story hotel in Miramar. Menu items use fresh, top quality ingredients. Recent samplings have included lobster risotto; rack of lamb with aromatic herbs and fresh garlic; an oft-changing cream-based soup of the day (one of the best is corn and fresh oyster soup); and a medallions of veal Rossini style, prepared with foie gras and Madeira sauce. The wine list is one of the most extensive on the island.

In the Hotel Excelsior, Av. Ponce de León 801. ✆ **787/725-7700.** Reservations recommended. Main courses $31–$50. AE, MC, V. Tues–Fri noon–3pm; Tues–Sat 7–9:30pm. Bus: A5.

Deliro ★★★ NUEVO LATINO The latest venture by the godfather of Nuevo Latino cuisine is his boldest and tastiest yet—and one of the prettiest restaurants in San Juan. The restaurant rambles through three rooms of a wooden, century-old manor house made modern with boudoir red and flat gray interiors, steel bead curtains and other metallic decor—yet, like Ayala's cuisine, the design manages to remain true to the building's traditional, classic roots. Ayala calls his food Puerto Rican cuisine influenced by flavors of the world and inspired by his life experiences in South America, Africa, Asia, and Europe. The menu changes seasonally to enable the use of the freshest ingredients. Recent selections we've sampled include grouper ceviche salad with New World sweet potatoes and corn and avocado in a pomegranate honey dressing, plus duck meatballs in a Moroccan sauce with balsamic and passion fruit extract with Spanish almonds. There has also been roasted cod filet was served in a Puerto Rican celeriac puree, with leeks and sweet pea cream; beef tenderloin bathed in a mushroom Provençal sauce; and a signature dish, pan-seared tuna with bacon crust, served with lime risotto in a Parmesan broth. Ayala is a serious mixologist as well; two recent creations are the Delirium Tremens (beet-infused white rum, yuzu lime, and rosemary) and the Caribbean Breeze (white rum, ginger juice, cream of tartar, and lime juice). Deliro occasionally hosts cooking workshops and other special events.

Av. Ponce de León 762. ✆ **787/722-0444** or 722-6042. Reservations recommended. Main courses $26–$40. AE, MC, V. Tues–Fri noon–3:30pm; Tues–Thurs 6–10:30pm; Fri–Sat 6–11:30pm; closed Sun–Mon. Bus: M1, A5.

Santurce & Ocean Park

For the locations of restaurants in Santurce and Ocean Park, see the map "Puerta de Tierra, Miramar, Condado & Ocean Park Accommodations & Dining," on p. 115.

VERY EXPENSIVE

Bistro de Paris ★★ FRENCH This elegant version of a classic Paris bistro sits across from Puerto Rico's beautiful art museum, and the growing legend of its classic French cuisine attracts a huge local following. The restrained beige-and-green bistro has a front terrace under shaded awnings and a dining room with huge glass windows and doors all around. Roomy and comfortable chairs and tables are the only things not authentic about the place. Basic genre dishes, such as French onion soup, Niçoise salad, and mussels Provençal are executed with perfection. The boneless whole trout in "Meuniere" sauce was the best fish one member of our party ever tried, and the shrimp blazed with Pastis liquor, ratatouille, and sun-dried tomatoes also knocked some socks off. A big question each night is whether to go for the strip loin with tomatoes Provençal or the steak au poivre. The crème brûlée is fantastic, but the warm apple tart also reigns supreme.

Plaza de Diego, Av. José de Diego 310. © **787/998-8929.** Reservations recommended. Main courses $25–$37; weekend brunch $17. AE, MC, V. Tues–Thurs noon–10pm; Fri–Sat noon–midnight; closed Sun. Bus: A5.

La Casona ★ SPANISH/INTERNATIONAL Housed in a turn-of-the-20th-century mansion, La Casona is all Old World Spanish charm, with a tiled courtyard, blooming gardens, tropical birds and strolling guitarists. You can't go wrong with the classics: paella marinara or *zarzuela de mariscos* (seafood medley), but there are other temptations: grilled, rosemary lamb chops with Lyonnais potatoes and asparagus, or grilled prawns with a cognac risotto. Grilled red snapper is a specialty, and you can order it with almost any sauce you want, although the chef recommends one made from olive oil, herbs, lemon, and toasted garlic. The cuisine here has both flair and flavor.

Calle San Jorge 609 (at the corner of Av. Fernández Juncos). © **787/727-2717.** Reservations required. Main courses $25–$39. AE, DC, MC, V. Mon–Fri noon–3pm; Mon–Sat 6–11:30pm. Bus: M1, A5.

EXPENSIVE

Pamela's ★ CARIBBEAN FUSION The food here matches its impressive setting on a white-sand beach free of the high-rises that dominate much of the city's coast. It's simply the best place to eat on the beach in San Juan, with a menu that takes flavors from distinct Caribbean cuisines and wraps them around classic continental fare. The result is appetizers such as guava toasted sesame chicken satay, smoked chicken sour apple spring rolls, and spicy Jamaican jerked calamari. Main courses include sundried tomato escabeche codfish, the blackened dorado with mango relish, and the massive N.Y. steak, crusted with a plantain and manchego coating. Diners can eat in a courtyard, marked by hand-painted tiles and stone fountains, or take a table under a palm tree outside and listen to the rumble of the ocean. Tasty snacks, sandwiches, and salads and a full-service bar make this a great spot for a beach break, too. You can get a table right on the beach, beneath some palm trees right outside the guesthouse.

In the Número 1 Guest House, Calle Santa Ana 1, Ocean Park. © **787/726-5010.** Reservations recommended. Lunch $8–$24; main course $25–$29. AE, MC, V. Daily noon–3pm and 7–10:30pm. Tapas daily 3–7pm. Bus: A5, C53.

INEXPENSIVE

Boulangerie Tradición Francaise & Bistro FRENCH This French country cafe is on the edge of a pretty, but cramped residential Santurce neighborhood, a few blocks from Condado beach. The heavenly bread and baked goods (fruit tarts and Napoleons, Tiramisu tarts, almond stuffed croissants and cakes) draw crowds. The French roast coffee is another dream, as are the tasty and hearty breakfasts and weekend brunches, which draw crowds out the door on Saturdays and Sundays. There are equally compelling gourmet sandwiches and pasta dishes for lunch and the dinner entrees are top drawer French executions of excellence: bouillabaisse, steak au poivre, and fresh dorado (mahimahi) in a Dijon mustard sauce. There's a nice little wine selection and Orangina, the taste of European summer. You have to get dessert, even if you get it to go.

Calle Taft 174. © **787/721-6272.** Main courses $15–29, sandwiches $6.25–$11, breakfast $3.50–$13. AE, MC, V. Tue–Sun 7am–10pm. Bus: A5.

Pinky's CAFE/DELI This tiny spot didn't lose its groove when it moved inside a funky restored bar near Santurce's Plaza de Mercado from its hole-in-the-wall former digs near Ocean Park's best beach. Ocean Park is worse off, however. There are still the same delicious wraps, fruit frappes and gourmet sub that made Pinky's famous overnight. The toughest thing is deciding between the likes of the Surfer (turkey, mozzarella, basil, tomato, onion and pesto mayo), the Pink Sub (turkey, salami, mozzarella, basil, olive, tomato, and onion), the pork and sweet plantain wrap, or the upscale sashimi-grade tuna with wasabi mayo and salad combo. The filet mignon and grilled onion sandwich tastes even better with a cold beer. The stream-of-consciousness menu ramblings live on, as do the great breakfasts.

María Moczo 51 (off Av. McLeary). ✆ **787/727-3347.** Wraps and specialty sandwiches $5.50–$13. MC, V. Mon–Sat 7am–8:30pm; Sun 7am–8pm. Bus: A5, M1.

Repostería Kasalta SPANISH/PUERTO RICAN This is the most widely known of San Juan's cafeterias/bakeries/delicatessens. You'll enter a cavernous room flanked with sun-flooded windows and a long row of display cases filled with seasonal pastries, then cold cuts and cheeses, and finally rows of ceviche and chicken salad, roasted peppers, and other delicacies. You order at the counter then bring the food back to one of the many tables. The spot is packed from early morning through the afternoon, which testifies to its quality breakfasts, sandwiches, and other meals. Patrons line up to place their orders at a cash register, and then carry their selections to one of the many tables. Knowledge of Spanish is helpful but not essential. Among the selections are steaming bowls of Puerto Rico's best *caldo gallego,* a hearty soup laden with collard greens, potatoes, and sausage slices, served in thick earthenware bowls with hunks of bread. Also popular are Cuban sandwiches (sliced pork, cheese, and fried bread), steak sandwiches, a savory octopus salad, and an assortment of perfectly cooked omelets. Paella Valenciano is a Sunday favorite.

Av. McLeary 1966. ✆ **787/727-7340.** Reservations not accepted. Full American breakfast $3.50–$8.50, soups $3–$6, sandwiches $4.50–$12, entrees $5–$22. AE, DC, MC, V. Daily 6am–10pm. Bus: A5, C53.

Near Ocean Park

For the locations of these restaurants, see the map "Puerta de Tierra, Miramar, Condado & Ocean Park Accommodations & Dining," on p. 115.

EXPENSIVE

Che's ARGENTINE This established Argentine steakhouse is in a low-key, airy spot that could be southern California. It has among the best *churassacos,* grilled flank steak, and other cuts in the city. If you're not in the mood for beef, there are really good pasta, seafood, and chicken dishes as well. These, along with the standard sides and desserts, are perfectly prepared. There's nothing fancy here, but the quality is top drawer, and its unpretentiousness is refreshing. The meats here are very tender and well flavored, and the chimichurri sauce is the city's best.

Calle Caoba 35. ✆ **787/726-7202.** Reservations recommended for dinner. Main courses $15–$30. AE, DC, DISC, MC, V. Sun–Thurs 11:30am–10:45pm; Fri–Sat noon–midnight. Bus: A5.

MODERATE

La Casita Blanca ★ CREOLE/PUERTO RICAN It's a worthwhile trip off the beaten path to get to this restaurant, which service up traditional comida criolla with a traditional Puerto Rican countryside experience. Dig into *carne guisado y arroz* *con gandule* (stewed beef and rice with pigeon peas) or *serenata del bacalao* (salted codfish in a ceviche sauce). There's everything from pigs' trotters in a Creole sauce to stewed rabbit and veal with sautéed onions. Eating here is like having a meal on the back porch of a country home. The staff is amazingly friendly and genuinely welcoming of guests, so it's a great experience for visitors to the island, and locals will feel transported back to an idyllic past. Plan on taking a taxi both to and from here, as Villa Palmeras is not a neighborhood you want to walk through.

Calle Tapía 351. ✆ **787/726-5501.** Main courses $9–$23; Sun buffet $12–$15. MC, V. Mon–Thurs 11:30am–6:45pm; Fri–Sat 11:30am–9:30pm; Sun noon–4:30pm. Bus: C10 or C11.

Isla Verde

For the locations of restaurants in Isla Verde, see the map "Isla Verde Accommodations & Dining," on p. 123.

VERY EXPENSIVE

Alfredo's ITALIAN/STEAKHOUSE There's certainly nothing unusual about a restaurant in classic quarters serving up a refined Italian and steakhouse menu, and, in this case, even the name is to be expected. This restaurant actually delivers, however. The food is just incredibly good and unique. It really grabs you too because everything up to that first bite appeared so predictable. There's a full line of steaks and chops in Creole, guava, BBQ or chimichurri sauce. This place is defined by its pastas, however, with dreamy concoctions such as lobster ravioli in a garlic rosemary veal au jus, or taglioni and shellfish in a spicy tomato sauce, or the incredible penne with spicy Italian sausage, onions, tomatoes and roasted peppers. There are basic soups and salads and a small appetizer menu with eggplant alla parmigiana, tuna carpaccio, fried shrimp, and a mixed antipasto platter, with roasted vegetables cheeses and prosciutto. The young chef behind this place is also on target with the desserts, which are luxurious.

In the Inter-Continental San Juan Resort & Casino, Av. Isla Verde 187. ✆ **787/253-1717.** Reservations recommended. Main courses $15–$30. AE, DC, MC, V. Sun–Thurs 6–10pm; Fri–Sat 6–11pm. Bus: A5.

BLT Steak ★★ STEAKHOUSE French chef Laurent Tourondel takes the American steakhouse to new highs with an awesome selection of Black Angus, Prime and Kobe beef, as well as chicken, lamb, veal, and fresh fish. There's nothing fancy here–just the best steakhouse fare you can imagine prepared by a chef with the talent to match the quality of the ingredients. We started with some littleneck clams from the raw bar and the crab cakes. The signature steak is a bone-in sirloin for two, which was among the finest cuts we've had on the island. The sautéed Dover sole is an old-school classic that hits its mark. We loved the potato gratin and Parmesan gnocchi, as well as the roasted tomatoes and poached green beans. Steaks are served with a selection of sauces including chimichurri, béarnaise, peppercorn, and horseradish. The blueberry-lemon pie makes for a refreshing finale. There's also peanut butter chocolate mousse with banana ice cream, and warm coconut-bread pudding with rum ice cream if you dare.

In the Ritz-Carlton San Juan Hotel, Spa & Casino, Av. de los Gobernadores (State Rd.) 6961, no. 187, Isla Verde. ✆ **787/253-1700.** Reservations required. Main courses $22–$88; fixed-price menus $45–$75. AE, DC, DISC, MC, V. Sun–Thurs 6–10:30pm; Fri–Sat 6–11pm. Bus: A5.

DINING WITH kids

Puerto Ricans love children and are more likely to bring them out to dinner than in many other countries. As a result, most restaurants are used to dealing with children and are most often prepared to handle them. Likewise, large family groups going out to restaurants are very common. The **Ciao Mediterranean Café** (p. 152), right on the beach in Isla Verde, is a great place for lunch, especially if you are enjoying the beach. Pizzas, pastas, salads, and sandwiches are offered at reasonable prices. The buffets on offer at the **La Vista Restaurant and Ocean Terrace** (Marriot Hotel Stellaris Casino; ✆ **787/723-7000**) are good for a family splurge, with enough variety to meet everyone's taste. The buffets change nightly, and there are breakfast and lunch buffets as well. It's hard to do better than **Bebo's Café** (p. 144) for a family outing. There's great local food, and basic American fare to satisfy all wishes. There's a full bar and range of fruit frappes, great desserts, and the price is right. In Old San Juan, both El Jibarito and Raíces are family friendly and local, but the **Parrot Club** (p. 132) has the tastiest kid's menu in town.

La Piccola Fontana ★ NORTHERN ITALIAN Just off a luxurious wing of El San Juan Hotel, this restaurant delivers plate after plate of delectable food nightly. From its white linens to its classically formal service, it enjoys a fine reputation. The food is straightforward, generous, and extremely well prepared. You'll dine in one of two neo-Palladian rooms whose wall frescoes depict Italy's ruins and landscapes. Menu items range from the appealingly simple (grilled filets of fish or grilled veal chops) to more elaborate dishes such as *tortellini San Daniele,* made with veal, prosciutto, cream, and sage; or *linguine scogliere,* with shrimp, clams, and seafood. Grilled medallions of filet mignon are served with braised arugula, Parmesan cheese, and balsamic vinegar.

In El San Juan Hotel & Casino, Av. Isla Verde 6063. ✆ **787/791-0966.** Reservations required. Main courses $29–$75. AE, MC, V. Daily 6–11pm. Bus: A5, C53.

The Palm ★★ STEAK/SEAFOOD The Palm, a legendary New York steakhouse, fits right in to this elegant hotel with a stylish dining room with artfully simple linen-covered tables and caricatures of local personalities. The drinks are stiff and the conversation scintillating at the bar. Diners enjoy the same Palm favorites here as elsewhere, such as the famous and famously pricey lobster, and gargantuan portions of crabmeat cocktail, Caesar salad, lamb chops with mint sauce, grilled halibut steak, prime porterhouse steak, and steak "a la stone," which finishes cooking on a sizzling platter directly atop your table. One thing is certain—you'll never go hungry here.

In El San Juan Hotel & Casino, Av. Isla Verde 6063. ✆ **787/791-1000.** Reservations recommended. Main courses $25–$52 (lobster priced by the lb. and can easily exceed $22/lb.). AE, DC, MC, V. Daily 5–11pm. Bus: A5.

EXPENSIVE

Koko CARIBBEAN The menu boldly charts a modern Caribbean cuisine, forged from down island, Puerto Rican, and other Pan Caribbean influences. The matted natural interiors, which mesh the look and feel of lush vegetation and flowing water, coconut shells and palm fronds, aims to be the perfect setting for that. The seared halibut with coconut risotto, the guava-braised short ribs and the passion-fruit-glazed duck are all delicious. There's a great seafood bar, and dazzling apps such as crab fritters and ginger pork croquettes. There's also a lounge and rum bar here, and it draws a crowd well into the evening.

At El San Juan Hotel & Casino, Av. Isla Verde 1660. ✆ **787/791-7078.** Reservations not accepted. Main courses $23–$46. AE, MC, V. Daily 4pm–midnight. Bus: A5.

Yamato ★ JAPANESE The artfully simple decor at Yamato shows the kind of modern urban minimalism that you might expect in an upscale California restaurant. Separate sections offer conventional seating at tables; at a countertop within view of a sushi display; or at seats around a hot grill where chefs shake, rattle, and sizzle their way through a fast but elaborate cooking ritual. Many visitors include at least some sushi with an entree such as beef sashimi with tataki sauce, shrimp tempura with noodle soup, filet mignon or chicken with shrimp or scallops, or several kinds of rice and noodle dishes. Genre aficionados rave about the sushi cuts and quality, and the chefs at the grill put on quite a show.

In Wyndham El San Juan Hotel & Casino, Av. Isla Verde 6063. ✆ **787/791-1000.** Reservations recommended. Sushi $2.50–$3 per piece; sushi and teppanyaki dinners $25–$43. AE, MC, V. Daily 6pm–midnight. Bus: A5.

MODERATE

Brother Jimmy's BBQ ☺ AMERICAN/STEAK El San Juan Hotel sure showed it was secure enough in its poshness to open up its 8,000 square foot roof to this fun, relaxed establishment, drawing both a sports crowd and family dining for weekend lunches and early evening dinners. This southern barbecue joint/sports bar, decorated like a frat house, features the Swamp Water Cocktail Bar, specializing in specialty drinks, and a few dozen flatscreen TVs and a massive 25×25-ft. television, where big games (and movies at certain times) are shown. The place to "put some south in your mouth," there's St. Louis–style ribs of all types, cider glazed pork chops, country fried steak, and all sorts of chicken and burgers. Sides include corn fritters, fried green tomatoes, and biscuits and gravy, and you can always start off with some stuffed jalapeños, fried okra or pickles, hot wings, or spinach and artichoke dip. The food's great, even if the mechanical bull does not thrill you.

In El San Juan Hotel & Casino, Av. Isla Verde 6063. ✆ **787/791-1000.** Reservations not necessary. Mon–Fri 5pm–midnight, Sat–Sun noon–midnight. Main courses $13–$24. AE, DC, DISC, MC, V. Mon–Fri 5pm–midnight; Sat–Sun noon–midnight. Bus: A5.

Outback Steakhouse STEAK This Puerto Rican branch of the two-fisted, Australian-themed restaurant chain occupies a dark-paneled room with booths positioned around a prominent bar area. Here you can study memorabilia devoted to the Land Down Under while ordering such drinks as a genuinely delicious Wallabee Darn. There's a simple steak-and-potato-with-salad special, priced at $14, a cost-conscious meal in itself. But more appealing are some of the chain's signature dishes, such as a Bloomin' Onion (a batter-dipped deep-fried onion that fans out from its platter like a demented lotus and tastes delicious with beer); at least four kinds of steaks, including filet mignon; fish, including mahimahi and salmon; and our favorite of the lot, Alice Springs chicken, a breast of chicken layered with bacon, mushrooms, and cheese, and served with honey-mustard sauce and french fries.

In the Embassy Suites Hotel & Casino, Calle José M. Tartak 8000. ✆ **787/791-4679.** Reservations not accepted. Main courses $14–$23. AE, MC, V. Mon–Thurs 5:30–10:30pm; Fri–Sat 5:30pm–midnight; Sun 3–10pm. Bus: A5, M7.

INEXPENSIVE

Ciao Mediterranean Café ★★ ☺ MEDITERRANEAN This is one of the most charming restaurants in Isla Verde, with a roofed bar and dining area beside the hotel's gorgeous pool area, and tables running along a boardwalk fronting Isla Verde's best beach. It's draped with bougainvillea and shaded by towering palm trees, and the prices are not bad given the astounding setting. Pizzas and pastas are popular here, and there is also grilled shrimp and an excellent calamari dish. Compared to most of the restaurants around here, this cafe serves lighter fare that kids go for, especially in its selection of pizzas and pastas. The desserts are also luscious. It's a great spot for lunch if you're out on the beach, even if you are not staying here.

In the Inter-Continental San Juan Resort & Casino, Av. Isla Verde 5961. ✆ **787/791-6100.** Reservations recommended for dinner. Pizzas and salads $8–$20; main courses $12–$20. AE, MC, V. Daily 11:30am–11pm. Bus: A5.

Metropol CUBAN/PUERTO RICAN/INTERNATIONAL This local restaurant (with multiple locations) serves the best Cuban food, although there is plenty of Puerto Rican and Dominican fare as well. The classic, Havana black-bean soup is expertly prepared, and there is plenty of garlic bread. My family loves the Cornish game hen stuffed with Cuban rice and beans, and the marinated flank steak. Rice and beans, fried rice, and yucca and plantains in varying forms accompany most meals, and there's no other way to finish but with a flan. Big, tasty portions and low prices keep this place a hit after all these years.

Club Gallistico, Av. Isla Verde. ✆ **787/791-4046.** Main courses $10–$30. AE, MC, V. Daily 11:30am–11:30pm. Bus: C53, A5.

Panadería España Repostería LIGHT FARE The Panadería España makes San Juan's definitive Cuban sandwich—a cheap meal all on its own. The biggest sandwich weighs 3 pounds, 1.5 kilos. Drinks and coffee are dispensed from behind a much-used bar. You can purchase an assortment of gourmet items from Spain, arranged as punctuation marks on shelves set against an otherwise all-white decor. The place has been serving simple breakfasts, drinks, coffee, and Cuban sandwiches virtually every day since it opened around 1970.

Centro Comercial Villamar, Marginal Baldorioty de Castro. ✆ **787/727-3860.** Reservations not necessary. Soups and tapas $4–$6; sandwiches $5–$8. AE, DISC, MC, V. Daily 6am–10pm. Bus: A5.

Near Isla Verde

For the location of this restaurant, see the map "Isla Verde Accommodations & Dining," on p. 123.

Soleil Beach Club Piñones ★★ 🎁 CARIBBEAN When it opened in 1997, Soleil was a pioneer in operating a fine-dining establishment among the barbecues, wooden shacks, and open-air bars of the Piñones dining scene. More than a decade later, Soleil still rules from its roost amidst the sand dunes and palm trees of the undeveloped beach it fronts. Soak in that breeze and listen to those waves from a table or the bar on the oceanfront terrace, and have a pre-dinner drink as the sun goes down. The food here's as good as its rustic beachfront surroundings. For starters, we like the fish skewers with mango sauce and the coconut breaded shrimp in aioli sauce. The surf and turf pairs Argentinean style skirt steak with shrimp, baby octopus, mahimahi, and scallops. The halibut is served in an oriental beurre blanc sauce and cassava *mofongo,* while the tuna is grilled, topped with a tropical fruit salsa, and served with cilantro jasmine rice. This is the best oceanfront dining in San Juan, and one of the best in Puerto Rico. Today, the restaurant hosts corporate dinners and special events, with facilities for concerts and live shows, a dance floor, and DJ area. There's also Wi-Fi Internet service.

Soleil Beach Club, Carretera 187, Km 4.6, Piñones. ✆ **787/253-1033.** Reservations recommended. Dinner main courses $13–$39; lunch specials $7–$10. AE, DISC, MC, V. Sun–Thurs 11am–11pm; Fri–Sat 11am–2am. Call ahead to arrange free transportation to and from your hotel in the Soleil Beach Club van.

Hato Rey

El Cairo Restaurant MIDDLE EASTERN This is one of the best of the many fine Middle Eastern and Lebanese restaurants found in San Juan. The service here is among the friendliest in the city, and I've always been a sucker for the hand-carved wooden chairs with pharaoh heads, Persian rugs, and colorful Arabian veils hanging from the ceiling. With the fine food and sizzling belly-dancing shows, it adds up to the seductive world of a harem. The appetizers—baba ghanouj, falafels, hummus, and tabbouleh among others—are all really tasty, and the kebabs—chicken, beef, lamb, shrimp and combos—are perfectly grilled and perfectly seasoned. The grilled lamb shank, stuffed grape leaves, curry dishes, and keiba (ground beef) dishes are equally tasty. A real surprise is the wonderful grilled salmon. Entrees come with a tasty cucumber and tomato salad and Arabian rice pilaf with almonds. Don't leave without trying the baklava; there's a reason it's the oldest dessert in the world. On Thursday, Friday, and Saturday nights, a belly-dancing show starts at 8pm. It's a great show.

Calle Ensenada 352 (corner Av. Franklin Delano Roosevelt). ✆ **787/273-7140.** Reservations recommended on Fri–Sun evenings. Main courses $12–$30. AE, MC V. Tues–Thurs and Sun noon–10pm; Fri–Sat noon–11pm. Bus: B21.

Cataño

Don Tello ★ PUERTO RICAN This authentic, family-run restaurant lost nothing when it moved from Santurce to Cataño, the town across the bay from Old San Juan. The traditional *comida criolla* is inspired, and you'll find such gems as grilled mahimahi in a plantain sauce and the house chicken stuffed with meat, cheese, and vegetables. There's a variety of stuffed *mofongo, asopao,* and other Puerto Rican classics such as grilled red snapper, local paella, grilled *churrasco,* and *chuletas kan kan* (breaded and fried pork chops). The restaurant overlooks San Juan Bay and the view to Old San Juan across it. A good stop after taking the Bacardi tour, before returning on the ferry. There are excellent tropical fruit frappes.

Av. Las Nereidas 36, Cataño. ✆ **787/724-5752.** Reservations suggested. Main courses $7.95–$40. AE, V, MC. Tues–Sat 11am–10pm (sometimes later); Sun noon–8pm. Old San Juan Ferry.

6 WHAT TO SEE & DO IN SAN JUAN

The Spanish began to settle in the area now known as Old San Juan around 1521. At the outset, the city was called Puerto Rico ("Rich Port"), and the whole island was known as San Juan.

The streets are narrow and teeming with traffic, but a walk through Old San Juan—in Spanish, *El Viejo San Juan*—makes for a good stroll. Some visitors have likened it to a "Disney park with an Old World theme." Even fast food restaurants and junk stores are housed in historic buildings. It's the biggest and best collection of historic buildings, stretching back 5 centuries, in all the Caribbean. You can do it in less than a day. In this historic 7-square-block area of the western side of the city, you can see many of Puerto Rico's chief sightseeing attractions and do some shopping along the way.

On the other hand, you might want to plop down on the sand with a drink or get outside and play. "Diving, Fishing, Tennis & Other Outdoor Pursuits," later in this chapter, describes the beaches and sports in the San Juan area.

SEEING THE SIGHTS

Forts

Castillo de San Felipe del Morro ★ ☺ Called "El Morro," this fort stands on a rocky promontory dominating the entrance to San Juan Bay. Constructed in 1540, the original fort was a round tower, which can still be seen deep inside the lower levels of the castle. More walls and cannon-firing positions were added, and by 1787, the fortification attained the complex design you see today. This fortress was attacked repeatedly by both the English and the Dutch.

The U.S. National Park Service protects the fortifications of Old San Juan, which, together, have been declared a World Heritage Site by the United Nations. With some of the most dramatic views in the Caribbean, you'll find El Morro an intriguing labyrinth of dungeons, barracks, vaults, lookouts, and ramps. Historical and background information is provided in a video in English and Spanish. The nearest parking is the underground facility beneath the Quincentennial Plaza at the Ballajá barracks (Cuartel de Ballajá) on Calle Norzagaray. Park rangers will lead hour-long tours for free, although you can also visit on your own.

The park, along with Fort San Cristóbal (see below), form the **San Juan National Historic Site.** The forts are connected by ancient underground tunnels, but today two modern trolleys ferry visitors back and forth. The walk, however, is beautiful along the oceanfront Calle Norzagary. A museum at El Morro provides a history of the fort through exhibits of historic photographs and artifacts, written orientations, and a video presentation. A guided tour is offered hourly, but informational brochures allow you to walk around on your own while learning the story. There's also a gift shop. Make sure to walk out on the northernmost point, a narrow wedge overlooking the waves crashing into the rocky coast. The promenade circling the base of the fort is also worth exploring. The grounds of El Morro are a great spot to fly a kite, and families and children are out every weekend doing so. An annual festival is in March. You can buy a kite at stands right in front of the fort, or at Puerto Rico Drug or Walgreens on Plaza Colón.

At the end of Calle Norzagaray. ✆ **787/729-6960.** Admission $3 adults (16 and older) for one fort, $5 for both, $2 for seniors, free for children 15 and under. Daily 9am–5pm. Bus: A5, B21, or B40.

Fort San Cristóbal ★ Construction on this huge fortress began in 1634. The structure was reengineered in the 1770s, and is one of the largest ever built in the Americas by Spain. Its walls rise more than 150 feet (46m) above the sea—a marvel of military engineering. San Cristóbal protected San Juan against attackers coming by land as a partner to El Morro, to which it is linked by a half-mile (.8km) of monumental walls and bastions filled with cannon-firing positions. A complex system of tunnels and dry moats connects the center of San Cristóbal to its "outworks," defensive elements arranged layer after layer over a 27-acre (11-hectare) site. You'll get the idea if you look at the scale model on display. Like El Morro, the fort is administered and maintained by the U.S. National Park Service. Be sure to see the Garita del Diablo (the Devil's Sentry Box), one of the oldest parts of San Cristóbal's defenses, and famous in Puerto Rican legend. The devil himself, it is said, would snatch away sentinels at this lonely post at the edge of the sea. In 1898, the first shots of the Spanish-American War in Puerto Rico were fired by cannons on top of San Cristóbal during an artillery duel with a U.S. Navy fleet. Park rangers lead hour-long tours for free here, too, but wandering on your own is fun.

In the northeast corner of Old San Juan (uphill from Plaza de Colón on Calle Norzagaray). ✆ **787/729-6960.** Admission $3 adults (16 and older) one fort, $5 both forts, free for children 15 and under. Daily 9am–5pm. Bus: A5, B21, or B40; then the free trolley from Covadonga station to the top of the hill.

Churches

Capilla de Cristo Cristo Chapel was built to commemorate what legend says was a miracle. In 1753, a young rider lost control of his horse in a race down this very street during the fiesta of St. John's Day and plunged over the precipice. Moved by the accident, the secretary of the city, Don Mateo Pratts, invoked Christ to save the youth, and he had the chapel built when his prayers were answered. Today it's a landmark in the old city and one of its best-known historical monuments. The chapel's gold and silver altar can be seen through its glass doors. Because the chapel is open only 1 day a week, most visitors have to settle for a view of its exterior.

Joggers' Trail or Romantic Walk

El Morro Trail, a jogger's paradise, provides the Old City's most scenic views along San Juan Bay. The first part of the trail extends to the San Juan Gate. The walk then goes by El Morro and eventually reaches a scenic area known as Bastion de Santa Barbara. The walk passes El Morro's well-preserved walls, and the trail ends at the entrance to the fortress. The walkway is designed to follow the undulating movement of the ocean, and sea grapes and tropical vegetation surround benches. The trail is romantic at night, when the walls of the fortress are illuminated. Stop at the tourist office for a map, and then set off on the adventure.

Calle del Cristo (directly west of Paseo de la Princesa). ✆ **787/722-0861.** Free admission. Tues 8am–5pm. Bus: Old City Trolley.

Catedral de San Juan ★★ The spiritual and architectural centerpiece of Old San Juan began construction in 1540 as a replacement for a thatch-roofed chapel that was blown apart by a hurricane in 1529. Chronically hampered by a lack of funds and a recurring series of military and weather-derived disasters, it slowly evolved into the gracefully vaulted, Gothic-inspired structure you see today. Among the many disasters to hit this cathedral are the following: In 1598, the Earl of Cumberland led the British navy in a looting spree; in 1615, a hurricane blew away its roof; in 1908, the body of Ponce de León was disinterred from the nearby Iglesia de San José and placed in a marble tomb near the transept, where it remains today (see the box "Ponce de León: Man of Myth & Legend," in chapter 2 for more about Ponce de León). The cathedral also contains the wax-covered mummy of St. Pio, a Roman martyr persecuted and killed for his Christian faith. The mummy has been encased in a glass box ever since it was placed here in 1862. To the right of the mummy is a bizarre wooden replica of Mary with four swords stuck in her bosom. After all the looting and destruction over the centuries, the cathedral's great treasures, including gold and silver, are long gone, although many beautiful stained-glass windows remain. The cathedral faces Plaza de las Monjas (the Nuns' Square), a shady spot where you can rest in front of Hotel El Convento.

Calle del Cristo 153 (at Caleta San Juan). ✆ **787/722-0861.** Free admission. Mon–Sat 8am–4pm; Sun 8am–2pm. Bus: Old City Trolley.

Museums

Many of the museums in Old San Juan close for lunch between 11:45am and 2pm, so schedule your activities accordingly if you intend to museum-hop.

Felisa Rincón Museum de Gautier The most heralded woman of modern Puerto Rico served as the mayor of San Juan for 22 consecutive years, between 1946 and 1968. The museum that commemorates her memory is in a 300-year-old building a few blocks downhill from San Juan's cathedral, near one of the medieval gates (La Puerta San Juan) that pierces the walls of the Old City. The interior is devoted to the life and accomplishments of Felisa Rincón de Gautier, and proudly displays some of her personal furniture and artifacts, as well as 212 plaques, 308 certificates of merit, 11 honorary doctorates, and 113 symbolic keys to other cities, such as Gary,

Old San Juan Attractions

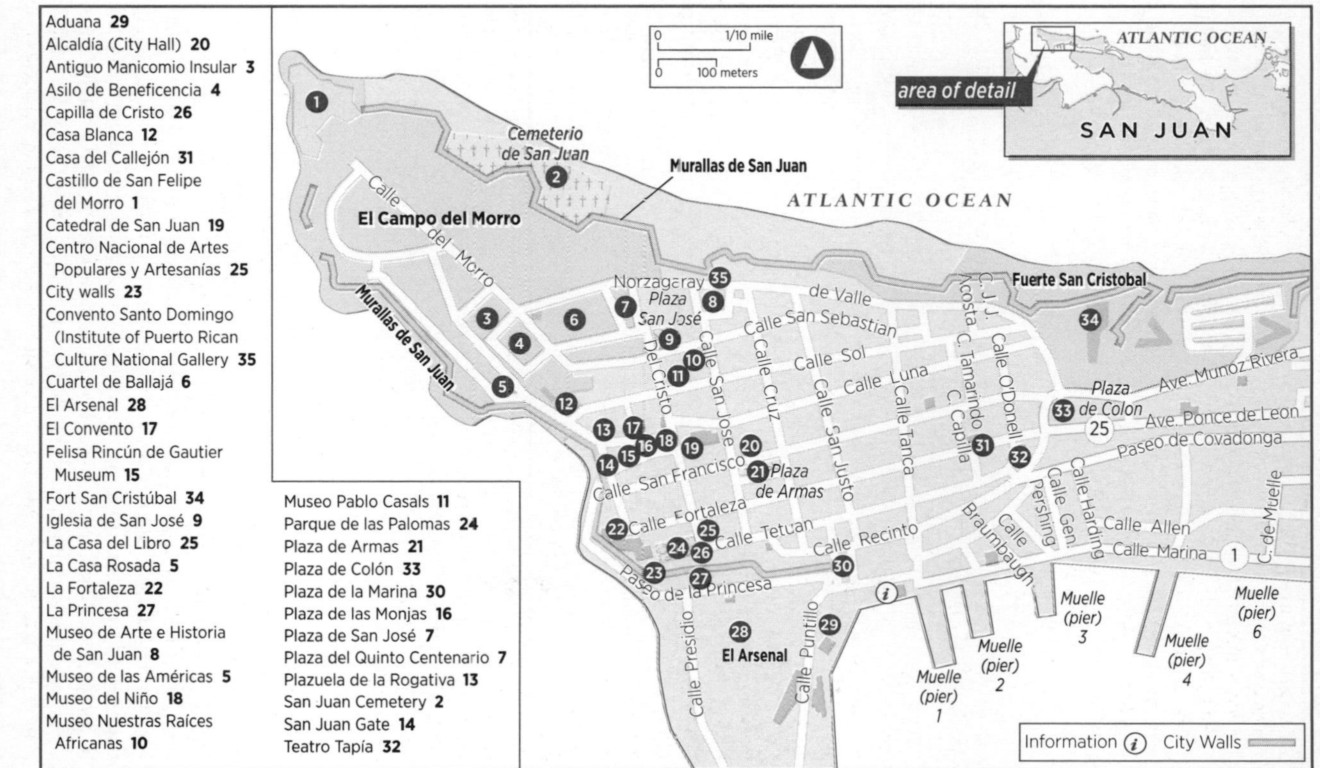

San Juan Attractions

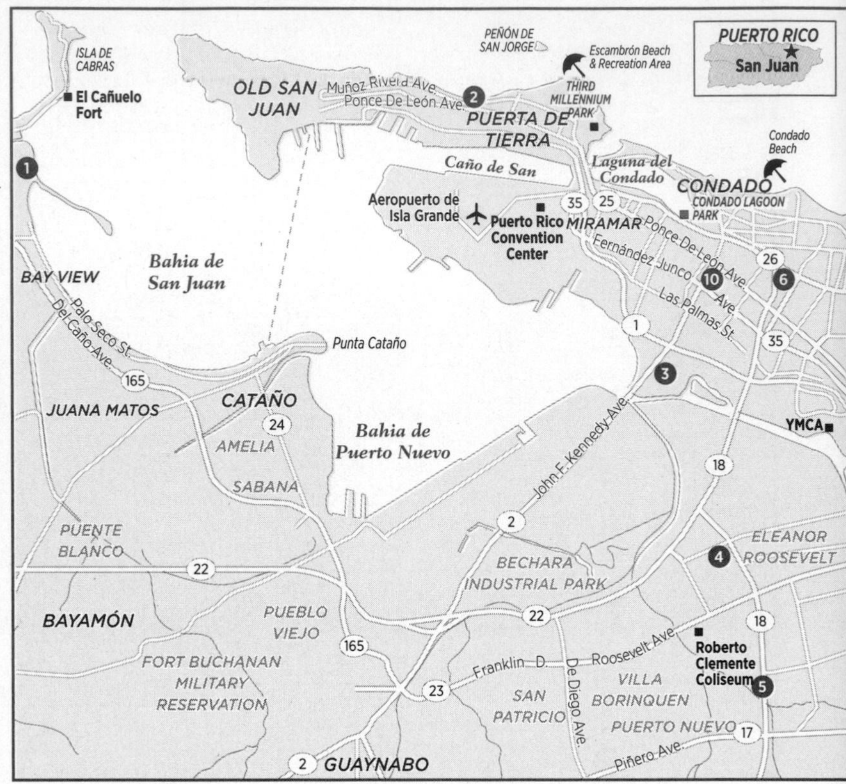

Indiana, and Perth Amboy, New Jersey. Her particular areas of influence included child welfare and elementary education. Photographs show her with luminaries ranging from Eleanor Roosevelt to the pope. The oldest of nine children, and the daughter of a local lawyer and a schoolteacher, she shouldered the responsibilities of rearing her younger siblings after the death of her mother when she was 12. Today the museum illuminates Doña Felisa's life as well as the reverence in which Puerto Ricans hold their most celebrated political matriarch. As such, it's a quirky, intensely personalized monument that combines a strong sense of feminism with Puerto Rican national pride.

Caleta de San Juan 51, at Recinto Oeste. ✆ **787/723-1897.** Free admission. Mon–Fri 9am–4pm. Bus: Old City Trolley.

Luis Muñoz Marín Foundation A 30-minute drive south of San Juan, this museum offers a chance to visit the former home of the island's most famous governor, Luis Muñoz Marín. As the first elected governor of Puerto Rico, Muñoz Marín enjoys somewhat the same position in Puerto Rican history that George Washington does for the mainland United States. A documentary acquaints you with the governor's

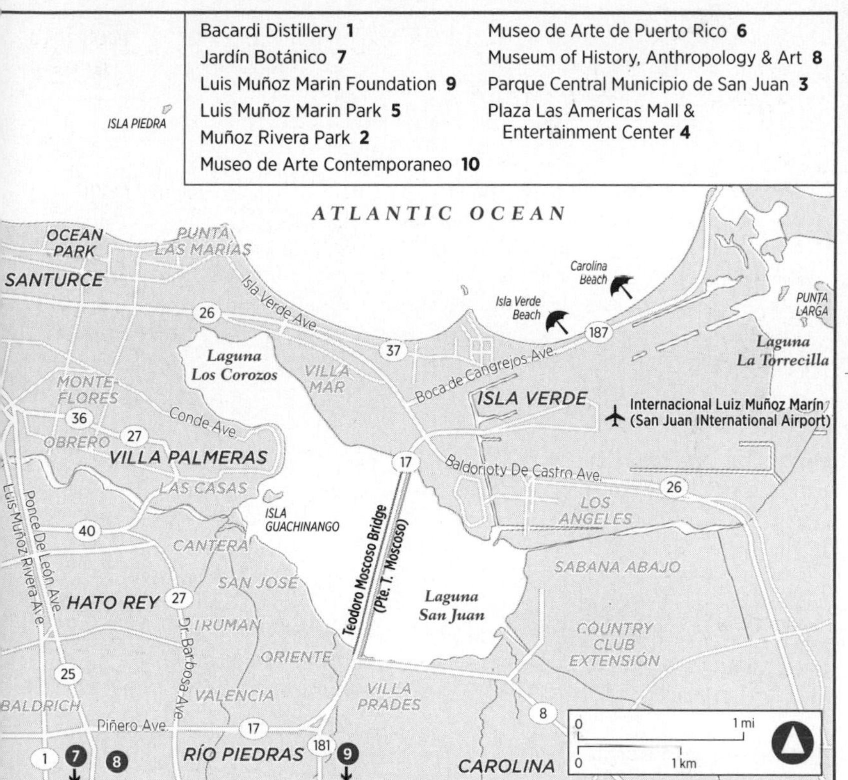

life and achievements. You can walk through Marín's study and library and view his extensive art collection, and later you can relax in his tropical garden and gazebo. There's an historic archive; the shop and the grounds surrounding the foundation have been restored recently.

Marginal Rd. 877, Km 0.4, Trujillo Alto Expwy. ✆ **787/755-7979.** Admission $2 adults, $1 children. Tours Mon–Fri (reservations required) 10am and 2pm. Bus: C31 or public car from Plaza Colón (easier).

Museo de Arte de Puerto Rico ★★ Puerto Rico's most important art museum since opening in 2000, it was constructed at a cost of $55 million and is a state-of-the-art showcase for the island nation's rich cultural heritage, as reflected mainly through its painters. Housed in a former city hospital in Santurce, the museum features both a permanent collection and temporary exhibitions. Prominent local artists are the stars—for example, Francisco Oller (1833–1917), who brought a touch of Cézanne or Camille Pissarro to Puerto Rico (Oller actually studied in France with both of these impressionists). Another leading star of the permanent collection is José Campeche, a late-18th-century classical painter. The museum is like a living textbook of Puerto Rico, beginning with its early development and going on to showcase camp aspects, such as the poster art created here in the mid–20th century. All the important modern island artists are also presented, including the late Rafael Tufiño and Angel Botello, Arnaldo Roche Rabelle, and Antonio Martorell. The building itself is a gem, and you have to stroll through the relaxing botanical gardens behind. On Wednesdays, admission is free between 2 and 8pm.

Av. José de Diego 299, Santurce. ✆ **787/977-6277.** www.mapr.org. Admission $6 adults; $3 students, seniors, and children; free for children 4 and under and seniors over 75. Tues and Thurs–Sat 10am–5pm; Wed 10am–8pm; Sun 11am–6pm. Bus: A5 or B21.

Museo de Arte e Historia de San Juan Located in a Spanish colonial building at the corner of Calle MacArthur, this cultural center was the city's main marketplace in the mid–19th century. Local art is displayed in the east and west galleries, and audiovisual materials reveal the history of the city. Sometimes major cultural events are staged in the museum's large courtyard. English- and Spanish-language audiovisual shows are presented Tuesday to Friday every hour on the hour from 9am to 4pm. Some of the city's finest young artists show here.

Calle Norzagaray 150. ✆ **787/724-1875.** Free admission, but donations accepted. Tues–Fri 9am–4pm; Sat–Sun 10am–4pm. Bus: To Old San Juan terminal; then the Old City Trolley.

Museo de las Américas ★ This museum showcases the artisans of North, South, and Central America, featuring everything from carved figureheads from New England whaling ships to dugout canoes carved by Carib Indians in Dominica. It is unique in Puerto Rico and well worth a visit. Also on display is a changing collection of paintings by artists from throughout the Spanish-speaking world, and a permanent collection called "Puerto Rican *Santos,*" donated by Dr. Ricardo Alegría. Make sure to see the Indigenous Peoples of the Americas exhibit.

Sala Cuartel de Ballajá, at Calle Norzagaray and Calle del Morro. ✆ **787/724-5052.** Admission $3 students with ID, $2 children 12 and under and seniors 65 and up. Tues–Wed and Sun 10am–4pm; Thurs–Fri 9am–4pm. Bus: Old City Trolley.

Museo de Pablo Casals This museum is devoted to the memorabilia left to the people of Puerto Rico by the musician Pablo Casals. The maestro's cello is here, along with a library of videotapes (which can be played upon request) of some of his festival concerts. This small 18th-century house also contains manuscripts and photographs of Casals. The annual Casals Festival draws worldwide interest and internationally known performing artists; it's held from the end of February through early March.

Plaza San José, Calle San Sebastián 101. ✆ **787/723-9185.** Admission $1 adults, 50¢ students and children. Tues–Sat 9:30am–4pm. Bus: Old City Trolley.

Historic Sights

In addition to the forts and churches listed earlier, you might want to see the sites described below.

San Juan Gate, Calle San Francisco and Calle Recinto Oeste, built around 1635, just north of La Fortaleza, several blocks downhill from the cathedral, was the main point of entry into San Juan, if you arrived by ship in the 17th and 18th centuries. The gate is the only one remaining of the several that once pierced the fortifications of the old walled city. For centuries it was closed at sundown to cut off access to the historic Old Town. (Bus: Old City Trolley.)

Plazuela de la Rogativa, Caleta de las Monjas, is a little plaza with a statue of a bishop and three women, commemorating one of Puerto Rico's most famous legends. In 1797, from across San Juan Bay at Santurce, the British held Old Town under siege. That same year they mysteriously sailed away. Later, the commander claimed he feared that the enemy was well prepared behind those walls; he apparently saw many lights and believed them to be reinforcements. Some people believe that those lights were torches carried by women in a *rogativa,* or religious procession, as they followed their bishop. (Bus: Old City Trolley.)

The **city walls** around San Juan were built in 1630 to protect the town against both European invaders and Caribbean pirates. The city walls that remain today were once part of one of the most impregnable fortresses in the New World and even today are an engineering marvel. Their thickness averages 20 feet (6m) at the base and 12 feet (3.7m) at the top, with an average height of 40 feet (12m). At their top, notice the balconied buildings that served for centuries as hospitals and also residences of the island's various governors. Between Fort San Cristóbal and El Morro, bastions were erected at frequent intervals. The walls come into view as you approach from San Cristóbal on your way to El Morro. (Bus: Old Town Trolley.)

San Juan Cemetery, on Calle Norzagaray, officially opened in 1814 and has since been the final resting place for many prominent Puerto Rican families. The circular chapel, dedicated to Saint Magdalene of Pazzis, was built in the 1860s. Aficionados of old graveyards can wander among marble monuments, mausoleums, and statues, marvelous examples of Victorian funereal statuary. Because there are no trees, or any other form of shade here, it would be best not to go exploring in the noonday sun. In any case, be careful—the cemetery is often a venue for illegal drug deals and can be dangerous. (Bus: Old City Trolley.)

Alcaldía (City Hall) The City Hall, with its double arcade flanked by two towers resembling Madrid's City Hall, was constructed in stages from 1604 to 1789. Still in use, this building today contains a tourist-information center downstairs plus a small art gallery on the first floor.

Calle San Francisco. ✆ **787/724-7171.** Free admission. Mon–Fri 8am–5pm. Closed holidays. Bus: Old City Trolley.

Casa Blanca Ponce de León never lived here, although construction of the house—built in 1521, 2 years after his death—is sometimes attributed to him. The work was ordered by his son-in-law, Juan García Troche. The parcel of land was given to Ponce de León as a reward for services rendered to the Crown. Descendants of the explorer lived in the house for about 2½ centuries, until the Spanish government took it over in 1779 for use as a residence for military commanders. The U.S. government also used it as a home for army commanders. On the first floor, the **Juan Ponce de León Museum** is furnished with antiques, paintings, and artifacts from the 16th through the 18th centuries. In back is a garden with spraying fountains, offering an intimate and verdant respite.

Calle San Sebastián 1. ✆ **787/725-1454.** Admission $3. Weds–Sun 8am–4:30pm. Bus: Old City Trolley.

El Arsenal The Spaniards used a shallow craft to patrol the lagoons and mangroves in and around San Juan. Needing a base for these vessels, they constructed El Arsenal in the 19th century. It was at this base that they staged their last stand, flying the Spanish colors until the final Spaniard was removed in 1898, at the end of the Spanish-American War. Changing art exhibitions are held in the building's three galleries.

La Puntilla. ✆ **787/723-3068.** Free admission. Wed–Sun 8:30am–4:30pm. Bus: Old City Trolley.

La Casa del Libro This restored 19th-century house shelters a library and museum devoted to the arts of printing and bookmaking, with examples of fine printing, which date back 5 centuries, and some illuminated medieval manuscripts.

Calle del Cristo 255. ✆ **787/723-0354.** Free admission. Tues–Sat 11am–4:30pm. Bus: Old City Trolley.

La Fortaleza The office and residence of the governor of Puerto Rico is the oldest executive mansion in continuous use in the Western Hemisphere, and it has served as the island's seat of government for more than 3 centuries. Its history goes back even further than that to 1533, when construction began on a fortress to protect San Juan's Spanish settlers during raids by Carib tribesmen and pirates. The original medieval towers remain, but as the edifice was subsequently enlarged into a palace, other modes of architecture and ornamentation were also incorporated, including baroque, Gothic, neoclassical, and Arabian. La Fortaleza has been designated a national historic site by the U.S. government. Proper attire is required (informal okay).

Calle Fortaleza, overlooking San Juan Harbor. ✆ **787/721-7000,** ext. 2211. Free admission. 30-min. tours of the gardens and building (conducted in English and Spanish) given every half-hour. Mon–Fri 9am–3:30pm. Bus: Old City Trolley.

Museo Nuestras Raíces Africanas Set within the Casa del Contrefueras, this museum documents the African contribution to the sociology of Puerto Rico. You'll find a series of tastefully arranged art objects, including musical instruments, intricately carved African masks, drums, graphics, and maps that show the migratory patterns, usually through the slave trade, from Africa into Puerto Rico. There are graphic depictions of the horrendous disruptions to families and individuals caused by the slave trade during the plantation era.

Plaza San José, Calle San Sebastián. ✆ **787/724-4294.** Admission $2 adults; $1 seniors, children, and students; free for ages 12 and under. Wed–Sun 8am–4:30pm. Bus: Old City Trolley.

Teatro Tapía Standing across from the Plaza de Colón, this is one of the oldest theaters in the Western Hemisphere, built about 1832. In 1976, a restoration returned the theater to its original appearance. Much of Puerto Rican theater history is connected with the Tapía, named after the island's first prominent playwright, Alejandro Tapía y Rivera (1826–82). Various productions—some musical—are staged here throughout the year, representing a repertoire of drama, dance, and cultural events.

Av. Ponce de León. ✆ **787/721-0180.** Prices vary. Access limited to ticket holders at performances (see "San Juan After Dark," later in this chapter). Bus: A5, B21, any other to Old San Juan Station.

Historic Squares

In Old San Juan, **Plaza del Quinto Centenario (Quincentennial Plaza)** overlooks the Atlantic from atop the highest point in the city. A striking and symbolic feature of the plaza, which was constructed as part of the 1992–93 celebration of the 500th anniversary of the discovery of the New World, is a sculpture that rises 40 feet (12m) from the plaza's top level. The monumental sculpture in black granite and ceramics symbolizes the earthen and clay roots of American history and is the work of Jaime Suarez, one of Puerto Rico's foremost artists. From its southern end, two needle-shaped columns point skyward to the North Star, the guiding light of explorers. Placed around the plaza are fountains, other columns, and sculpted steps that represent various historic periods in Puerto Rico's 500-year heritage.

Sweeping views extend from the plaza to El Morro Fortress at the headland of San Juan Bay and to the Dominican Convent and San José Church, a rare New World example of Gothic architecture. Asilo de Beneficencia, a former indigents' hospital dating from 1832, occupies a corner of El Morro's entrance and is now the home of the Institute of Puerto Rican Culture. Adjacent to the plaza is the Cuartel de Ballajá, built in the mid–19th century as the Spanish army headquarters and still the largest edifice in the Americas constructed by Spanish engineers; it houses the Museum of the Americas.

Centrally located, Quincentennial Plaza is one of modern Puerto Rico's respectful gestures to its colorful and lively history. It is a perfect introduction for visitors seeking to discover the many rich links with the past in Old San Juan.

Once named St. James Square, or Plaza Santiago, **Plaza de Colón** at the main entrance to Old San Juan is at times bustling and busy, but also has a shady, tranquil section. Right off Calle Fortaleza, the square was renamed Plaza de Colón to honor the 400th anniversary of Christopher Columbus' so-called discovery of Puerto Rico, which occurred during his second voyage. Of course, it is more politically correct today to say that Columbus explored or came upon an already inhabited island. He certainly didn't discover it. But when a statue here, perhaps the most famous on the island, was erected atop a high pedestal, it was clearly to honor Columbus, not to decry his legacy. There are some benches beside a newspaper stand in a shady part of the plaza that make a great place to sit. You can grab something cool to drink from a corner store.

Plaza de Las Armas is located at the heart of Old San Juan. The main square is home to San Juan City Hall, built in 1789 as a replica of the Madrid City Hall, and the Puerto Rico State Department, in a beautiful colonial building from the 18th century. The plaza also has a fountain (which unfortunately is usually not working) with four statues representing the four seasons and some gazebos and a cafe. The Cuatro Estaciones, or Four Seasons, cafe is a nice spot for a strong cup of coffee or a cold drink. In a recent renovation, large trees were planted in the plaza, which provides blissful shade in several spots.

The **Paseo de la Princesa** is a wide bayside promenade with outstanding views. The walkway runs along the bay beneath the imposing Spanish colonial wall that surrounds the Old City. It takes its name from a prominent building along it, La Princesa, a former prison in the 1800s that has been blissfully restored and now houses the Puerto Rico Tourism Company Headquarters. The sexy fountain at its center, "Raíces," or "Races," shoots powerful streams of water over the bronze naked Adonises and Amazon warrior goddesses riding huge horses and fish, so you'll get wet if you get too close. Spanish artist Luis Sanguino undertook the work as part of the 500th anniversary of San Juan's founding. The statue is meant to show the Taíno, African, and Spanish roots of Puerto Rico and its people. Farther along, the promenade bends around the bay and passes a shaded area before heading down to San Juan Gate. The new El Morro trail, which goes around the base of the fortress, is actually an extension of this promenade. There are food and drink vendors and often artisans selling their crafts, especially at the start of the route near the cruise ship docks.

Enter near the cruise ship docks at the corner of Recinto Sur and Calle La Puntilla or via the San Juan Gate (Calle San Francisco and Calle Recinto Oeste).

Parks & Gardens

Jardín Botánico Administered by the University of Puerto Rico, Jardín Botánico is a lush tropical garden with some 200 species of vegetation. You can pack a picnic lunch and bring it here if you choose. The orchid garden is exceptional, and the palm garden is said to contain some 125 species. Footpaths blaze a trail through heavy forests opening onto a lotus lagoon.

Barrio Venezuela (at the intersection of routes 1 and 847), Río Piedras. ✆ **787/765-1845.** Free admission. Daily 6am–6pm. Bus: 19.

Luis Muñoz Marín Park ★ ☺ This 140-acre (57-hectare) park is the best-known, most frequently visited children's playground in Puerto Rico—although it has equal appeal to adults. Conceived as a verdant oasis in an otherwise crowded urban neighborhood, it's a fenced-in repository of swings, jungle gyms, and slides set amid several small lakes and rolling green fields. Here you'll also find an incomparable view of San Juan. A small-scale cable car carries passengers aloft at 10-minute intervals for panoramic views of the surrounding landscape ($2 per person).

Av. Piñero, at Hato Rey. ✆ **787/763-0787.** Free admission for pedestrians; parking $2 or $3. Wed–Sun 8am–6pm. Bus: B-17.

Luis Muñoz Rivera Park This 27-acre (11-hectare) park, frequently confused with Luis Muñoz Marín Park (see above), is a green rectangle in the middle of Puerta de Tierra. You'll drive by the seaward-facing park on your way to San Juan. It was built 50 years ago to honor Luis Muñoz Rivera, the Puerto Rican statesman, journalist, and poet. It's filled with picnic areas, wide walks, shady trees, landscaped grounds, and recreational areas. There's a new children's playground that's filled with fun on weekends. Its centerpiece, El Pabellon de la Paz, is sometimes used for cultural events and expositions of handicrafts. A new pedestrian and bicycle path connects the park with the oceanfront Tercer Milenio, or Third Millennium Park, across Avenida Muñoz Rivera. The Commonwealth Supreme Court is located at the eastern side of the park.

Btw. aves. Muñoz Rivera and Ponce de León. ✆ **787/721-6133.** Free admission; parking $3.20. Daily 24 hrs. Bus: A5.

Parque Central Municipio de San Juan This mangrove-bordered park was inaugurated in 1979 for the Pan-American Games. It covers 35 acres (14 hectares) and lies southeast of Miramar. Joggers appreciate its labyrinth of trails, and a long boardwalk runs along mangrove canals. Recently renovated, it boasts 20 tennis courts, four racquetball courts, a full track-and-field area with stadium bleachers, a cafe, and children's play area (just look for the huge jacks sculpture). A golf course is being developed on an adjacent former landfill and a brand-new Olympic standard diving and swimming arena was completed in 2006. Fat, huge iguanas slither from the mangrove-choked channels and into the park's pathways.

Calle Cerra. ✆ **787/722-1646.** Free admission for pedestrians; parking $1. Mon–Thurs 6am–10pm; Fri 6am–9pm; Sat–Sun 6am–7pm. Bus: A1.

THE BEST PLACES TO SEE puerto rican art

With its dozen or so museums and even more art galleries, Old San Juan is the greatest repository of Puerto Rican arts and crafts. Galleries sell everything from pre-Columbian artifacts to paintings by well-known artists such as Angel Botello, who died in 1986, and Rafael Tufiño, who died in 2008. There's also contemporary traditional crafts, such as *santos,* the hand-carved wooden saints the island is known for. Galleries also show a large cast of talented established and up-and-coming contemporary artists.

Art openings at galleries are usually big affairs, with wine and cheese receptions, and occasionally live music or theatrical performances. Bars and restaurants get into the act and hold art shows or performances. **CIRCO,** an international art fair held at the new Puerto Rico Convention Center annually in April, is growing in stature and quality each year, and many local art venues plan special shows for the occasion.

A cluster of galleries is spread along Calle Cristo and Calle San José, which is 1 block east. For specific galleries, see "Art," later in this chapter. The **Galería Nacional,** or National Gallery, located inside Old San Juan's Antiguo Convento de los Dominicos, a restored former convent, has exhibits from the Institute of Puerto Rican Culture's vast holdings. It displays many of the most important works by Puerto Rican painters, from José Campeche and Francisco Oller to Rafael Tufiño and the generation of painters from the 1950s (✆ **787/977-2700**). Another good place to see Puerto Rican art is the **Museum of History, Anthropology & Art** (✆ **787/763-3939**). Because of space limitations, the museum's galleries can exhibit only a fifth of their vast collection at one time, but the work is always top-notch. The collection ranges from pre-Columbian artifacts to works by today's major painters.

Santurce, however, is equally important as the Old City, now that it has some of the island's top museums. The grandest repository of art in San Juan is at the **Museo de Arte de Puerto Rico** (p. 159), which is a virtual textbook on all the big names in the art world who rose from Puerto Rico, often to international acclaim. The gorgeously restored building is also part of the appeal, as are the adjoining botanical gardens. The **Museo de Arte Contemporáneo** (✆ **787/977-4030;** avs. Ponce de León and Robert H. Todd) is also an exceptional museum in a restored brick schoolhouse, showing contemporary art from Puerto Rico, but also throughout Latin America and the Caribbean.

Outside San Juan, the greatest art on the island can usually be seen at the **Museo de Arte de Ponce** (p. 218). In addition to such European masters as Reubens, Van Dyck, and Murillo, the museum features works by Latin American artists, including Diego Rivera. Puerto Rican artists who are represented include José Campeche and Francisco Oller. The museum was slated to reopen in 2010 following a major renovation. During the repairs, the museum lent some of its permanent collection out to traveling shows. However, the MAP continued to be a force in the island's art scene through an exhibition space and store at the San Juan's **Plaza Las Américas,** the largest mall in the Caribbean, called **MAP at Plaza** (Av. Franklin Delano Roosevelt 525, 3rd floor, Plaza Las Américas; ✆ **787/200-7090** or 787/848-0505; admission $5 for adults, $2.50 for students, children, and seniors; Mon–Fri 11am–7pm, Sat 11am–8pm, and Sun 11am–5pm).

Sightseeing Tours

If you want to see more of the island but you don't want to rent a car or manage the inconveniences of public transportation, perhaps an organized tour is for you.

Castillo Sightseeing Tours & Travel Services, 2413 Calle Laurel, Punta La Marias, Santurce (✆ **787/791-6195**), maintains offices at some of the capital's best-known hotels, including the Caribe Hilton and San Juan Marriott Resort. Using six of their own air-conditioned buses, with access to others if demand warrants it, the company's tours include pickups and drop-offs at hotels as an added convenience. Other reputable operators include **Sunshine Tours** (✆ **787/647-4545**), **Rico Suntours** (✆ **800/844-2080**), and **AAA Island Tours** (✆ **787/793-3678**).

All their offerings are pretty similar. One of the most popular half-day tours departs most days of the week between 8:30 and 9am, lasts 4 to 5 hours, and costs about $50 per person, $68 if you take one of the more extensive hiking tours. Leaving from San Juan, it tours along the northeastern part of the island to El Yunque. Another favorite is a city tour of San Juan that departs daily around 1pm. The 4-hour trip costs around $50 per person and includes a stop at the Bacardi Rum Factory. Other trips include the Arecibo Observatory and the Camuy Caves, as well as snorkeling and offshore beach excursions on plush catamarans.

Few cities of the Caribbean lend themselves so gracefully to walking tours. You can embark on these on your own, stopping and shopping en route. The best of course is a walking tour of Old San Juan. There are several suggested routes from which to choose, or you could go and get lost and cover the entire mile-square historic sector. (See the Old San Juan Attractions map on page 157.) There are also guided tours available. One of the most informative is by **Legends of Puerto Rico** (✆ **787/605-9060;** www.legendsofpr.com), which hosts personalized tours, specializing in entertaining cultural and nature adventure tours. **Sunshine Tours** also has experienced, knowledgeable guides. **San Juan Oculto,** or Hidden San Juan (✆ **787/748-7248;** www.fusamp.org; $20 suggested donation), is a monthly walking tour through Old San Juan to visit important, and largely unknown, architectural and historic buildings and other works. The project is undertaken in coordination with the University of Puerto Rico School of Architecture.

For a fantastic overview of authentic Puerto Rican cuisine, we highly recommend the walking/noshing tour, **Flavors of San Juan** (✆ **787/964-2447**; www.flavorsofsanjuan.com; $75; no children under 18; daily 2-hour tours at 5pm). Itineraries vary, but samples may include *tostones, mofongo*, tapas at a Spanish restaurant (where the owner serenaded us a cappella), rum or beer samples, and possibly a mojito and French fries at tour guide Leslie Padró's favorite French bistro. Padró is a former CNN staffer from Atlanta, and she kept this tour informative and relaxed, as if sharing her local finds with friends. Very pregnant during our tour, she nonetheless got behind the bistro bar to help make the mojitos. Book in advance.

Especially for Kids

Puerto Rico is one of the most family-friendly islands in the Caribbean, and many hotels offer family discounts. Programs for children are also offered at a number of hotels, including day and night camp activities and babysitting services. Trained counselors at these camps supervise children as young as 3 in activities ranging from nature hikes to tennis lessons, coconut carving, and sand-sculpture contests.

Teenagers can learn to hip-hop dance Latino-style with special salsa and merengue lessons, learn conversational Spanish, indulge in watersports, take jeep excursions, or scuba-dive in some of the best diving locations in the world. All the major hotels have full children's programs, so it might depend on what you are looking for. Top city hotels such as **Inter-Continental San Juan Hotel & Casino** (p. 124), the **Ritz-Carlton San Juan** (p. 124), the **San Juan Marriott & Stellaris Casino** (p. 114), and the **Caribe Hilton** (p. 113) have great pool facilities for kids, day camp activities, watersports and other sports equipment, play areas for little kids, and video arcades for older ones.

Children love **El Morro Fortress** (see "Forts," earlier in this chapter) because it looks just like the castles they have seen on TV and at the movies. On a rocky promontory, El Morro is filled with dungeons and dank places and also has lofty lookout points for viewing San Juan Harbor. The grounds make for great kite flying. The city's historic plazas offer their own possibilities, such as running through the gushing fountains of Quincentennial Plaza or feeding the pigeons at Plaza de Armas.

Luis Muñoz Marín Park (see "Parks & Gardens," above) has the most popular children's playground in Puerto Rico. It's filled with landscaped grounds and recreational areas—lots of room for fun in the sun. And kids love the short cable-car ride.

Ben & Jerry's Café Galería Puerto Rico ☺ You can't go to Old San Juan with a kid without stopping here. It's the perfect ending to an afternoon of exploring the ancient oceanfront forts and flying kites afterwards, something a kid will always remember. The full 32 flavors—10 of them low-fat—taste particularly good on hot, steamy days. We still love Cherry Garcia, the Chocolate Fudge Brownie, and the Chunky Monkey. But the place also has homemade goodies, pita pizzas, sandwiches, burgers, salads, and snacks. They also have DJ music, art exhibits, Internet access, books, magazines, and more. A great place.

Calle del Cristo 61. ✆ **787/977-6882.** Daily 11am–11pm. Bus: Old City Trolley.

Museo del Niño (Children's Museum) ☺ In the late 1990s, the city of San Juan turned over one of the most desirable buildings in the colonial zone—a 300-year-old villa directly across from the city's cathedral—to a group of sociologists and student volunteers. Jointly, they created the only children's museum in Puerto Rico. Through interactive exhibits, children learn simple lessons, such as the benefits of brushing teeth or recycling aluminum cans, or the value of caring properly for pets. Staff members include lots of student volunteers who play either one-on-one or with small groups of children. Nothing here is terribly cerebral, and nothing will necessarily compel you to return. But it does provide a play experience that some children will remember for several weeks.

Calle del Cristo 150. ✆ **787/722-3791.** Admission $5 adults, $4 children 14 and younger. Tues–Thurs 9am–3:30pm; Fri 9am–5pm; Sat–Sun 12:30–5pm. Bus: Old City Trolley.

Time Out Family Amusement Center ☺ All the latest games are at this video game arcade right off the sprawling food court of the Caribbean's largest mall. Packed all weekend, it draws kids of all ages and grown-ups who want to get their kid out.

Plaza de las Américas, Las Américas Expwy. at Av. Franklin Delano Roosevelt, Hato Rey. ✆ **787/753-0606.** Free admission (prices of activities vary). Mon–Thurs 9:30am–10pm; Fri–Sun 9am–11pm. Bus: B21 from Old San Juan.

THE CATHEDRAL OF rum

Called "the Cathedral of Rum," the **Bacardi Distillery** at Rte. 888, Km 2.6, at Cataño (✆ **787/788-1500**), is the largest of its kind in the world. Reached by taking a 20-minute ferry ride across San Juan Bay ($1 each way), the distillery produces 100,000 gallons of rum daily. At the site, you can go to the **Casa Bacardi Visitor Center,** Carretera 165, Cataño (✆ **787/788-8400**), for free 90-minute tours Monday to Saturday from 9am to 4:30pm, Sunday 10am to 3:30pm. You are taken on a visit of seven historical displays, including the Bat Theatre, and the Golden Age of the Cocktail Art Deco bar.

Upon entering the first floor, you'll get a glimpse of what rum production was like a century ago, including oak barrels used in the aging process and an old sugar-cane wagon. On the fifth floor, you'll enter the Hall of Rum, with a collection of beverages made by the corporation over a period of years. You'll then witness "the birth of rum"—the fermentation processes of molasses (it takes 100 gal. of molasses to produce one barrel of rum).

You'll visit the Bacardi Family Museum, and you can watch a short video about the bottling process. At the end of the tour you can sample the produce. Try Morir Soñado ("To Die While Dreaming), which mixes orange and pineapple juices, coconut milk, and Bacardi Orange.

DIVING, FISHING, TENNIS & OTHER OUTDOOR PURSUITS

Active vacationers have a wide choice of things to do in San Juan, from sunning on the beach to kite sailing to surfing. There are numerous land sports to do under the sun, such tennis and bicycle touring. Most beachside hotels, of course, offer on-site watersports activities, which are also available for nonguests (see chapter 5).

The Beaches

Some San Juan beaches can get crowded, especially during summer and holiday weekends, but for most of the week, they are deliciously roomy. It's rare to find yourself alone on a beach in San Juan, but if you do, be careful. Petty crime is a reality you need to keep in mind. The city beaches are actually very safe, friendly and well protected places. They are also surprisingly pretty; Ocean Park and Pine Grove are among the most charming beaches in all of Puerto Rico, for example.

All beaches on Puerto Rico, even those fronting the top hotels, are open to the public. Public bathing beaches, with lifeguards and facilities, are called ***balnearios*** and charge for parking and for use of lockers and showers. Beach hours in general are 9am to 5pm in winter, to 6pm off-season. Most ***balnearios*** are operated by the Puerto Rico National Parks Company, with others operated by island municipalities. For all *balnearios,* entrance is free but the parking carries a fee. So even when the beaches are closed, you can still enjoy them. There just won't be facilities open, lifeguards, or, in some cases, available parking.

There are two public beaches in the San Juan area with lifeguards, bathing and changing rooms, and showers. **El Escambrón public beach** (Ave. Muñoz Rivera,

Pda. 8—that is, *parada,* or stop 8—Puerta de Tierra; © **787/721-6133;** Wed–Sun and holidays 8:30am–5pm; parking $3.20) is right next to the Caribe Hilton and surrounded by two sprawling parks. There's a great swimming beach protected by reefs and rock formations jutting out of the water. The famed El 8 surf spot is just to the west, however. There's good snorkeling around the rocks with lots of fish. There's a snack bar and a full-scale restaurant located here. The other public beach is **Isla Verde public beach** (Av. Los Gobernadores, Carolina; © **787/791-8084;** Tues–Sun 8:30am–5pm; parking $4), a huge expanse of white sand and tranquil waters between Isla Verde and Piñones. There are lifeguards; changing rooms, bathrooms and showers; and picnic areas and barbecue grills, as well as an on-site restaurant.

Famous with beach buffs since the 1920s, **Condado Beach ★★** put San Juan on the map as a tourist resort. Backed up against high-rise hotels, it seems more like Miami Beach than any other beach in the Caribbean. All sorts of watersports can be booked at the activities desk of the hotels. A small beach near the Condado Plaza hotel is the only one with lifeguards, which are on duty from 8:30am to 5pm. There are also outdoor showers. The beaches in the rest of the Condado are much nicer, but because there are no lifeguards and the surf can get rough, particularly by the San Juan Marriott, swimmers should exercise caution. There are powerful rip tides here that have been responsible for past drownings. There are no public toilets here. People-watching is a favorite sport along these golden strands, which stretch from the Ventana del Mar park to beyond the Marriott. The best stretch of beach in the Condado runs from the Ashford Presbyterian hospital to Ocean Park. The area behind the Atlantic Beach Hotel is popular with the gay crowd; the beach farther along, with Marriott guests and surfers, is also pretty but has extremely rough waters at times.

One of the most attractive beaches in the Greater San Juan area is **Ocean Park Beach ★★**, a mile (1.6km) of fine, gold sand in a neighborhood east of Condado. This beach attracts young people, travelers looking for a guesthouse rather than the large hotel experience, and those looking for a big gay crowd. The beach runs from Parque del Indio in Condado all the way to the Barbosa Park in the area known as El Ultimo Trolley and offers paddle tennis, kite-boarding, and beach volleyball. You can grab lunch and refreshments from several area guesthouses, and vendors walk up and down the beach, selling cold beer, water and soft drinks, and even snacks such as fried seafood turnovers. Farther east, there's no real beach at **Punta Las Marías,** but it's one of the favorite launch points for windsurfers.

Isla Verde Beach ★★ is the longest and widest in San Juan. It is ideal for swimming, and it, too, is lined with high-rise resorts a la Miami Beach. Many luxury condos are on this beachfront. Isla Verde is good for watersports, including parasailing and snorkeling, because of its calm, clear waters, and many kiosks will rent you equipment, especially by the El San Juan. There are also cafes and restaurants at hotels and more reasonably priced individual restaurants nearby.

Isla Verde Beach extends from the end of Ocean Park to the beginning of a section called Boca Cangrejos. The most popular beach is probably behind the Hotel El San Juan and the Inter-Continental San Juan hotels. But Pine Grove beach, behind the Ritz-Carlton, is a great swimming beach and very popular as well, particularly with surfers and sailors.

Sports & Other Outdoor Pursuits

ADVENTURE Two adventure areas in the San Juan suburbs are worth a visit. Go flying through the trees on a zip-line at **La Marquesa Original Canopy Tour Park,** La Marquesa Forest Reserve, Guaynabo (**© 787/789-1598** or 444-0110). Costs vary depending on group size but run around $99 per person. You'll get a bird's view of a tropical forest as you soar along suspended cables, from10 to 70 feet or 3 to 21.33 meters high, traversing across 14 different platforms during the thrilling 2-hour tour. Speed demons, here's your shot at an adrenalin rush; but if you'd rather take it easy, you can control your speed with a grip. Being 50 feet, or 15.24 meters up and leaping through the air is a rush, even with the harness strapped to the cable and the redundant safety features. Skateboarders can get their ya-yas out at **Moisty Skate & Family Park,** Rd. 196, Caguas, (**© 787/903-0504** or 903-6064) but there is so much more at this 40-acre (16-hectare) park in the suburb south of San Juan. Take Luis A Ferré Expressway 52 S., and get off at exit 18 for Aguas Buenas and turn right at Rte. 196. Founded by an island skateboard champion, the ramps and skate areas are challenging. There is also a wave pool, adventure rope course, go-karts, gotcha paint-ball course, and an inflatable park for the young children. You pay for parking and then for each activity. Equipment rental and skate-park entrance is $15, while the wave pool is $8 for adults and $5 for children. Go-kart rides are $6 a shot.

BIKE RENTALS The best places to bicycle are in city parks such as Luis Muñoz Marín (Hato Rey) and Luis Muñoz Rivera (Puerta de Tierra). You can make it from Condado to Old San Juan driving mostly through the latter park. There are also bicycle trails; I recommend the coastal boardwalk running along Piñones, which is beautiful and safe, especially on the weekends, if a little beat up. There are bike rentals available in the area during weekends, although most San Juan streets are too crowded for bicycle riding. **Rent the Bicycle,** Calle Del Muelle, Capitolio Plaza 205, San Juan (**© 787/602-9696**) is at the entrance of the Old San Juan bayside waterfront. It rents bikes for $27 per day ($17 for a half day) and also conducts several tours throughout San Juan (the Piñones boardwalk tour is probably the best bet). Rentals are available at **Hot Dog Cycling,** Av. Isla Verde 5916, La Plazoleta Shopping Center (**© 787/721-0776**), open Monday to Saturday 9am to 6pm. Charges for rentals are $15 per half-day, $25 for a full day.

CRUISES For the best cruises of San Juan Bay, go to **Caribe Aquatic Adventures** (see "Scuba Diving," below). Bay cruises start at $25 per person.

DEEP-SEA FISHING ★ Deep-sea fishing is top-notch here. Allison tuna, white and blue marlin, sailfish, wahoo, dolphin (mahimahi), mackerel, and tarpon are some of the fish that can be caught in Puerto Rican waters, where 30 world records have been broken. Charter arrangements can be made through most major hotels and resorts. The big game-fishing grounds are very close offshore from San Juan, making the capital an excellent place to hire a charter. A half-day of deep-sea fishing (4 hours) starts at around $550, while full-day charters begin at around $900. Most charters hold six passengers in addition to the crew.

There are three marinas in the San Juan metropolitan area, with fishing charters and boat rentals available at all three. The **Cangrejos Yacht Club** (Rte. 187, Piñones; **© 787/791-1015**) is right near the airport on Rte. 187, the road from Isla

Verde to Piñones, while the two other marinas are next to each other near the Condado bridge and the Convention Center in Miramar: **San Juan Bay Marina** (✆ **787/721-8062**) and **Club Nautico de San Juan** (✆ **787/722-0177**).

Benitez Fishing Charters can be contacted directly at P.O. Box 9066541, Puerto de Tierra, San Juan, PR 00906 (✆ **787/723-2292,** until 9pm). The captain offers a 14m (45-ft.) air-conditioned deluxe Hatteras called the *Sea Born.* Capt. Mike Benítez is the most experienced operator in San Juan sailing out of Club Nautico. His crew is knowledgeable and informative, and the *Sea Born* is plush and comfortable. Fishing tours for parties of up to six cost $642 for a half-day excursion, $1,017 for a full day, with bottled water and all equipment included. (See "Scuba Diving," below, for another deep-sea fishing option.) Another veteran outfit is **Castillo Fishing Charters** (✆ **787/726-5752**), that has been running charters out of the San Juan Bay Marina since 1975. Capt. Joe Castillo runs the company with his son José Iván and daughter Vanessa and they all know their stuff. The Legend, a 48-foot Hatteras, is also an excellent vessel built for fishing and comfort. Rates are $700 half day (8am–noon or 1–5pm) and $1,100 full day (8am–4pm).

GOLF The city of San Juan has opened the **San Juan Golf Academy and Driving Range** (Marginal Av. Kennedy, entrance to San Juan Obras Publicas department; ✆ **787/771-8962** or 480-4580; $5 for 50 balls, $10 for 100 balls, clubs are also available; Tues–Sat 7am–9pm, Sun and holidays 11am–6pm). Besides the driving range, there are putting greens and chipping ranges.

In the San Juan suburb of Bayamón is the 9-hole **Río Bayamón Golf Course** (✆ **787/740-1419**), a municipal course in the San Juan suburb Bayamón. Greens fees are $30 and rentals just $15.

The **Berwind Country Club** (✆ **787/876-5380**) in Loiza is the nearest full-size course to the city. Built on a former coconut plantation, it's a beautiful place, with ocean views, towering palms, and frenzied tropical foliage. Experts say the course is quite challenging, with plenty of water hazards and three of the toughest holes to finish on the island. The regular green fees start at $50, and special rates, during twilight and certain weekday hours, can drop it to $35. On Saturdays until 2pm, the course is reserved for members.

The island's best golf courses are within a short drive of San Juan, including those clustered around Dorado to the west and Río Grande to the east (see chapter 7).

HORSE RACING Great thoroughbreds and outstanding jockeys compete year-round at **Camarero Racetrack,** Calle 65 de Infantería, Rte. 3, Km 15.3, at Canovanas (✆ **787/641-6060**), Puerto Rico's only racetrack, a 20-minute drive east of the center of San Juan. Races begin at 2:45pm Monday, Wednesday, Friday, Saturday, Sunday, and holidays. There are from seven to nine races daily, and bets include Win, Place, the "Exacta," Daily Double, Trifecta, Superfecta, Pick Six, and Pick Three. The clubhouse has a fine-dining restaurant, the Terrace Room, that serves good local food, and there's Winner's Sports Bar with pub fare. The grandstand has free admission.

RUNNING The cool, quiet, morning hours before 8am are a good time to jog through the streets of Old San Juan. Head for the wide thoroughfares adjacent to El Morro and then San Cristóbal, whose walls jut upward from the flat ground. The seafront Paseo de la Princesa, at the base of the governor's mansion La Fortaleza, is another fine site. **San Juan Central Park** (Calle Cerra; exit from Av. Muñoz Rivera

PUERTO RICO chic

Those comparisons to South Beach don't really make it, but San Juan—and much of Puerto Rico, really—has its own sense of style that is just as vibrant and a whole lot more soulful. Sure Puerto Rican royalty (from Benicio del Toro to Marc Anthony and J-Lo to Ricky Martin) are regularly jetting in, but it's the local talent that will more likely wow visitors. The city has been transformed by the opening of the **Puerto Rico Miguel José Miguel Agrelot Coliseum** (500 Arterial B St., Hato Rey; ✆ **877/265-4736;** box office Mon–Fri 10am–5pm) and the **Puerto Rico Convention Center** (100 Convention Blvd., San Juan; ✆ **800/214-0420**). Since the opening of "the Coliseo," as the coliseum is known locally, performers such as Paul McCartney, the Rolling Stones, Elton John, the Police, and Billy Joel have played there, and it regularly gets top-name Latino acts, such as Shakira and Juanes. The Convention Center is attracting all sorts of national groups as well as other entertainment events. CIRCO, an annual art fair, is getting serious attention, and the center is also the host of an annual fashion week with shows by local and international designers. The Puerto Rico Tourism Company has held an annual New Year's Eve party here that is broadcast live on Spanish-language television and features some of the top names in Latino music. Even when there are no stars, both venues have cafe-bars that have become hangouts for young urban professionals to let loose after work, especially on Thursday and Friday nights.

There is no trendier place in San Juan today than the new temple of island art, **Museo de Arte** (p. 159). It took $55 million to turn this 1920s city hospital in Santurce, an eyesore for decades, into this new home for art. The new museum has become a way of life for some Puerto Ricans, many of whom go here at least once a week—perhaps to see a production in the 400-seat theater, named for Raúl Juliá, the late Puerto Rican actor, or perhaps to go for a romantic stroll through the museum's 5-acre (2-hectare) garden.

San Juan even has **SoFo,** a once abandoned sector of La Fortaleza Street that is now buzzing with activity, home to some of Old San Juan's best restaurants, bars, and clubs. A play on the name of New York City's SoHo, SoFo purportedly refers to South Fortaleza Street. The name has stuck, even though it's geographically inaccurate, as the area is actually East Fortaleza Street. The **Parrot Club** (p. 132) is the original hot spot of the neighborhood, opening more than a decade ago with its brash and flavorful Nuevo Latino cuisine in a land of crusty Chinese restaurants and delis, run-down tourist shops, and dusty fabric stores. Today, these run-down businesses have been renovated. The

or Rte. 2; ✆ **787/722-1646**) has an excellent professional track in an outdoor track-and-field stadium with bleachers. There is a similar setup at **Parque Barbosa** right off the beach in Ocean Park. A renovation of the park was recently completed in 2009.

Condado's Avenida Ashford and the hard-packed sands of Isla Verde are busy sites for morning runners as well.

SCUBA DIVING In San Juan, the best outfitter is **Caribe Aquatic Adventures,** 1062 Calle 19, Villa Nevarez (✆ **787/281-8858;** www.diveguide.com/p2046.htm).

area is a center for world cuisine, where you can find everything from French **Trois Cent Onze** (p. 133) to Indian **Tantra** (p. 139) to Asian Fusion **Dragonfly** (p. 136).

We would put the beach at Ocean Park against that at South Beach. It's just naturally far more beautiful, and its guesthouses and restaurants attract an eclectic set of trendsetters: students, surfers, gay people, and urban creatives from the East Coast who prefer its low-lying skyline and laid-back ambience over the big resorts and condos of Condado and Isla Verde.

The Condado, however, has undergone its own revival, with the renovation of **La Concha** hotel, the opening of some of the city's best restaurants (such as **Budatai** and the relocated **Pikayo**), the establishment of an ocean front park, and a string of boutiques of the world's top names in fashion and jewelry.

And there's perhaps no place as timelessly chic as the **Plaza de Mercado de Santurce** (near Calle Canals and Av. Ponce de León). The traditional food market is a great place to buy tropical fruits and vegetables, and there's a bunch more oddities, such as old Puerto Rican music recordings, herbs, and religious artifacts involving *santería.* There are several good restaurants in the surrounding neighborhood (**José Enrique's** and **La Tasca del Pescador**) and several bars. The neighborhood is a swirl of activity from early in the day through late evening. On Thursday and Friday nights, large crowds gather as the streets are blocked off from traffic. Several spots have live music. It's a favorite after-work spot for locals and a lot of fun. Just join the crowd and meander from one spot to the next. Seafood fritters, chicken kebabs, and meat turnovers are sold from street vendors, and there is music everywhere.

The city also has several beautiful green parks with loads of activities during weekends. A plan to connect them via bicycle and pedestrian pathways is underway. It will build on the **Parque Lineal Marti Coli,** which stretches for nearly 2 miles (3.2km) along Caño de Martín Peña, from Hato Rey to Parque Central. Eventually this boardwalk will reach a distance of nearly 12 miles (19km), linking the Old City with Río Piedras. Biking, hiking, and jogging pathways are planned; one day bikers will be able to go along the breadth of San Juan without having to encounter traffic. In the meantime, enough trails have been completed for a memorable stroll.

Later you can head to Old San Juan for some island music, either to **Rumba** (p. 188) or the **Nuyorican Café** (p. 188) to dance the night away to the sounds of salsa and Latin rhythms with an African beat.

Its dive shop is open daily from 9am to 9pm. This outfitter will take you to the best local dive sites in the Greater San Juan area. A local dive in Puerta de Tierra costs $60. Other dives cost $125 per person, and a resort course for first-time divers costs $150. Escorted dive jaunts to the eastern shore are also offered. Snorkeling lessons or tours lasting 1 hour and including basic equipment go for $50.

Another good outfitter is **Ocean Sports.** Its main office is Av. Isla Verde 77 (**© 787/268-2329**), but it also has other offices. It offers diving courses and scuba diving and snorkeling trips in San Juan, off the east coast, even out to Mona Island.

Swimmers, Beware

You have to pick your spots carefully if you want to swim along many San Juan beaches, especially Condado Beach. The waters at the beach beside the Condado Plaza Hotel are calmer than in other areas because of a coral breakwater. The beach near the Marriott is not good for swimming because of rocks, a strong undertow, and occasional rip tides. There are no lifeguards except at public beaches. Ocean Park is better for swimming, but can still be hazardous when the tides kick up. Isla Verde beach is generally much calmer, especially at its eastern end. The surf off Piñones, farther east, may be the most treacherous of all.

A two-tank dive off the east coast will run from $95 to $150. There are kayak and snorkeling trips around San Juan.

SNORKELING Snorkeling is better in the outlying portions of the island than in overcrowded San Juan. But if you don't have time to explore greater Puerto Rico, you'll find that most of the popular beaches, such as Luquillo and Isla Verde, have pretty good visibility and kiosks that rent equipment. Snorkeling equipment generally rents for $15. If you're on your own in the San Juan area, one of the best places is the San Juan Bay marina near the Caribe Hilton.

Watersports desks at the big San Juan hotels at Isla Verde and Condado can generally make arrangements for instruction and equipment rental and can also lead you to the best places for snorkeling, depending on where you are in the sprawling metropolis. If your hotel doesn't offer such services, you can contact **Caribe Aquatic Adventures** (see "Scuba Diving," above), which caters to both snorkelers and scuba divers.

Still, even if you are staying in San Juan and want to go snorkeling, you are better off taking a day trip to Fajardo, where you'll get a real Caribbean snorkeling experience, with tranquil, clear water, and stunning reefs teaming with tropical fish. Several operators offer day trips (from 10am–3:30pm) leaving from Fajardo marinas (most likely Villa Marina or Puerto del Rey), but transportation to and from your San Juan hotel can also be arranged. Prices start at around $69 per person, or $99 including transportation to and from San Juan. Even if you don't particularly want to snorkel, the trips are still worth it for a day of fun in the sun. The trips usually take place on large luxury catamarans, holding about 20 passengers or more. Most have a cash bar serving drinks and refreshments, a sound system, and other creature comforts. Typically, after a nice sail, the cat will weigh anchor at different snorkeling spots and then in sheltered waters near one of the scores of small islands lying off Fajardo's coast, the perfect spot for a swim or sunbathing. Most trips include lunch, which usually is served on a beach. The boats know the best reefs and hot spots for bigger fish, and will plan the trip according to weather conditions and other variables. A huge reef extending east to Culebra protects the ocean off Fajardo's coast, which makes for calm seas with great visibility.

Inquire at your hotel desk about operators providing service there. There are many reputable companies. Myself or friends have all been satisfied with **Fajardo Tours Traveler** (✆ **787/863-2821**), **East Island Excursions** (✆ **787/860-3434**), and

Catamaran Spread Eagle (✆ **787/887-8821**). **Erin Go Bragh Charters** (✆ **787/860-4401**) offers similar day trips aboard a 50-foot sailing ketch, which is an equally pleasurable experience.

SPAS & FITNESS CENTERS **The Ritz-Carlton San Juan Hotel, Spa & Casino** ★, Avenida de los Gobernadores 6961, no. 187, Isla Verde (✆ **787/253-1700**), set a new standard of luxury in San Juan hotels. That special treatment is no more evident that at its spa, with state-of-the-art massages, body wraps and scrubs, facials, manicures, pedicures, and a salon guaranteed to make you look like a movie star. In an elegant marble-and-stone setting, there are 11 rooms for pampering, including hydrotherapy and treatments custom-tailored for individual needs. The 12,000 square foot spa features a 7,200-square-foot outdoor swimming pool, male and female steam baths, a co-ed sauna and a whirlpool. There's also a complete fitness center with free weights and weight machines, cardiovascular equipment and aerobics, and personal trainer services. Treatment specialties include the latest in skin, touch and soak therapies, and wellness salon services. Caribbean fruits and flowers, and botanical treatments culled from El Yunque rainforest are employed in the treatments. Two house specialties are the detoxifying coffee body scrub and coconut milk moisturizing session, or a rainforest stone massage with passion fruit oil. Specialty sessions range in price from $130 to $275, depending on length and technique.

The 12,000-foot Olas Spa at the **Carib Hilton,** Calle Los Rosales (✆ **787/721-0303**) offers everything from traditional massages to more exotic body and water therapies, using such products as honey, cucumber, sea salts, seaweed, or mud baths. You can choose your delight among the massages, including one called "Rising Sun," a traditional Japanese form of massage called shiatsu that uses pressure applied with hands, elbows, and knees on specific body points. Among body wraps is one known as Firm Away, a super-firming, brown and green algae body cocoon therapy for a soft, toned, and smooth skin. Other services include manicures and pedicures, a full service hair salon, and many day-spa packages. There's also an adjacent gleaming and modern health club with machines, weights, all sorts of classes, and everything else you might need, with in-house personal trainers. The spa is in a really beautiful setting. There are lengthy and pricey specialty treatments, such as the 4-hour Agua ($350), which includes a sea detox and elixir, a facial, hydrotherapy, seaweed body wrap, aromatherapy, deep cleansing, and more.

The Inter-Continental San Juan Resort & Casino, 5961 Av. Isla Verde, (✆ **787/791-6100**) also recently got into the spa game, with a nice facility adjacent to its beautiful pool area that has breathtaking ocean views. The masseuses, trained locally and throughout the world, are among the best in San Juan, with the spare tropical setting as mellow as the house Swedish massage. The Caribbean Wrap aims to improve skin condition over the long haul, while the After Sun Pampering Massage looks to improve its elasticity and smoothness. There's also a 24-hour health club and gym with the usual top notch equipment and services, plus those beautiful ocean views.

El San Juan Hotel & Casino, Av. Isla Verde 6063 (✆ **787/791-1000**), offers a stunning panoramic view of San Juan and a relaxing environment offering fitness evaluations, supervised weight-loss programs, aerobics classes, a sauna, a steam room, and luxury massages. A daily fee for individual services is assessed if you want special treatment or care.

Another option is **Zen Spa,** Av. Ashford 1054, Condado (© **787/722-8433**), which has a full range of massages, facial treatments, body wraps and therapeutic services. It's open 8am to 7pm weekdays, 9am to 6pm weekends. Specialty massages, which start at $55 for 25 minutes, include a detoxifying massage and a combo Swedish and Shiatsu.

Most hotels have quality gyms. If your hotel doesn't have a gym or health club of its own, consider working the kinks out of your muscles at **International Fitness ★**, Av. Ashford 1131, Condado (© **787/721-0717**). It's air-conditioned, well equipped, and popular with residents of the surrounding high-rent district. Entrance costs $15 per visit, $50 for 5 days, or $55 for a week. Hours are Monday to Thursday 5am to 10pm, Friday 5am to 9pm, Saturday 9am to 7pm, and Sunday 10am to 3pm.

TENNIS Most of the big resorts have their own tennis courts for their guests. There are 20 public courts, lit at night, at **San Juan Central Park,** at Calle Cerra (exit F on Rte. 2; © **787/722-1646**), open daily. Fees are $3 per hour from 6am to 5pm, and $4 per hour from 6 to 10pm. There are also four racquetball courts here. The **Isla Verde Tennis Club** (© **787/727-6490**) is open all week, weekdays from 8am to 10pm, Saturdays from 8am to 7pm, and Sundays from 8am to 6pm. Courts cost from $15 to $20 hourly.

WINDSURFING & SAILING Great windsurfing and kite-sailing advice and lessons are available at **Velauno,** Calle Loíza 2430, Punta Las Marías in San Juan (© **787/728-8716;** www.velauno.com). Their instructors will also rent equipment, with prices starting at about $75 daily. A 1-hour beginner lesson costs $70, and other courses on offer range from 1 to 10 hours. The staff here will guide you to the best windsurfing, which is likely to be the Punta Las Marías in the greater San Juan metropolitan area. Office hours are Monday to Friday 10am to 7pm, Saturday 11am to 7pm. Other spots on the island for windsurfing include Santa Isabel, Guánica, and La Parguera in the south; Jobos and Shacks in the northwest; and the island of Culebra off the eastern coast.

SHOPPING

Because Puerto Rico is a U.S. commonwealth, U.S. citizens don't pay duty on items brought back to the mainland. And you can still find great bargains on Puerto Rico, where the competition among shopkeepers is fierce. Even though the U.S. Virgin Islands are duty-free, you can often find far lower prices on many items in San Juan than on St. Thomas. Since November 2006, a local 7% sales and use tax has been instituted on most goods and services.

The streets of the Old City, such as Calle Fortaleza, Calle San Francisco, and Calle del Cristo, are the major venues for shopping. After years of trying, local restrictions on operating hours of stores, aimed at protecting small businesses and the religious nature of Sundays in Roman Catholic Puerto Rico, were finally overturned in 2010. Shops and stores are now free to open anytime except between 6am and 11am Sunday mornings. In general, malls in San Juan are open Monday to Saturday 9am to 9pm and Sunday from 10am to 7pm. In such tourism districts as Old San Juan and Condado, most stores still close by 7pm, but Old City shops remain open late whenever cruise ships are at harbor. There are now more 24-hour grocery stores and pharmacies, and Walmart has instituted the concept at a few stores in suburban San Juan.

Know When the Price Is Right

The only way to determine if you're paying less for an item in San Juan than you would at home is to find out what the going rate is in your hometown. Obviously, if you can find items in San Juan cheaper than back home, go for it. But know the prices before you go. Otherwise, you could end up lugging merchandise back on an airplane when the same item was available at about the same price, or less, where you live.

Native handicrafts can be good buys, including needlework, straw work, ceramics, hammocks, and papier-mâché fruits and vegetables, as well as paintings and sculptures by Puerto Rican artists. Among these, the carved wooden religious idols known as *santos* (saints) have been called Puerto Rico's greatest contribution to the plastic arts and are sought by collectors. For the best selection of *santos,* head for Galería Botello (see "Art," below), Olé, or Puerto Rican Arts & Crafts (see "Gifts & Handicrafts," later in this chapter).

Condado also has a lot of interesting shops, most of which line Avenida Ashford, along with the restaurants, hotels and luxury condominiums.

Puerto Rico's biggest and most up-to-date shopping mall is **Plaza Las Américas,** in the financial district of Hato Rey, right off the Las Américas Expressway. This complex, with its fountains and modern architecture, has more than 200 mostly upscale shops. The variety of goods and prices is roughly comparable to that of large stateside malls. There are also several top-notch restaurants, a full Cineplex, plus art galleries and food stores. If you want a break from the sun (or if it's raining), there are entertainment options here for all.

Unless otherwise specified, the following stores can be reached via the Old City Trolley. Likewise, store hours are noted only when they stray from those mentioned above.

Antiques

El Alcazar 🎁 Established in 1986 by retired career officers with the U.S. Army and the U.S. Department of State, this is the largest emporium of antique furniture, silver, and art objects in the Caribbean. There is a massive inventory at the main location, on Calle San José between Calle Luna and Calle Sol, but the collection of art and antiques of owners Sharon and Robert Bartos takes up other nearby locales as well. You'll find antique silver, crystal, delicate porcelain, glittering chandeliers, Russian icons, and objects of religious devotion such as *santos.* Some of the objects, especially the 1930s-era dining-room sets, whose chair backs are composed of wood medallions held in place by woven canes or wicker, derive from Puerto Rico. The majority of the objects, however, are culled from estates and galleries throughout Europe. Calle San José 103. ✆ **787/723-1229.**

Art

Butterfly People Butterfly People is a gallery in a handsomely restored building in Old San Juan. Butterflies, sold here in artfully arranged boxes, range from $35 for a single mounting to thousands of dollars for whole-wall murals. The butterflies are preserved and will last forever. The dimensional artwork is sold in limited editions and can be shipped worldwide. Most of these butterflies come from farms around the world, some of the most beautiful hailing from Indonesia, Malaysia, and New Guinea. It's open Saturday and Sunday from 10am to 6pm. Calle Cruz 257. © **787/723-2432.**

Galería Botello ★ A contemporary Latin American art gallery, Galería Botello is a living tribute to the late Angel Botello, one of Puerto Rico's most outstanding artists. Born after the Spanish Civil War in a small village in Galicia, Spain, he fled to the Caribbean and spent 12 years in Haiti. His paintings and bronze sculptures, evocative of his colorful background, are done in a style uniquely his own. This galería is his former colonial mansion home, which he restored himself. Today it displays his paintings and sculptures, showcases the works of many outstanding local artists, and offers a large collection of Puerto Rican antique *santos,* hand-carved wooden statues of the saints. Calle del Cristo 208. © **787/723-9987.**

Galería Exodo This exciting gallery shows work from young contemporary island and regional artists, many of whom are not afraid to engage in bold experimentation. The work ranges from Radamés Rivera's limestone and coral art pieces that could have existed at the time of the dinosaurs to Yolanda Velasquez's vibrant abstract paintings. Over 40 artists, from Cuba to Mexico, showcase work here. Calle Cristo 200B. © **787/725-4252.**

Galería Sánchez ★ This gallery represents a collection of talented international artists with different styles, including: Heriberto Nieves, a sculptor; Moisés Castillo, expressionist; and Erick Sánchez, neo-impressionist. Open Monday through Wednesday from 1 to 6pm, Thursday through Saturday from 1 to 9pm. In SoFo, Calle Fortaleza 320. © **787/829-4663** or 466-5494.

Galería San Juan This shop, located at the Gallery Inn, specializes in the sculpture and paintings of Jan D'Esopo, a Connecticut-born artist who has spent decades living in Puerto Rico, most of the time in this beautiful rambling home overlooking the Old San Juan oceanfront. Many of her fine pieces are in bronze. In the Gallery Inn, Calle Norzagaray 204. © **787/722-1808.**

Haitian Gallery This is the best store, now with two locations, in San Juan for Haitian art and artifacts. Its walls are covered with framed versions of primitive Haitian landscapes, portraits, crowd scenes, and whimsical visions of jungles where lions, tigers, parrots, and herons take on quasi-human personalities and forms. Most paintings range from $20 to $350, although you can usually bargain them down a bit. Look for the brightly painted wall hangings crafted from sheets of metal. Also look for satirical metal wall hangings, brightly painted, representing the *tap-taps* (battered public minivans and buses) of Port-au-Prince. They make amusing and whimsical souvenirs of a trip to the Caribbean. Open daily from 10am to 6pm. Calle Fortaleza 206. © **787/721-4362.** The other location is at Calle Fortaleza 367. © **787/725-0986.**

Obra Galería Alegría 🎁 A bit off the well worn gallery route along Calle Cristo and Calle San José, this gallery is worth searching out for its representation of such important masters as Lorenzo Homar; Domingo García; Julio Rosado del Valle; and younger, accomplished, contemporary artists such as Nick Quijano, Jorge Zeno, and Magda Santiago. The gallery was started by José Alegría, with the assistance of his uncle Ricardo Alegría, the founder of the Institute of Puerto Rican Culture. It's open

Tuesday through Saturday from 11am to 6pm. Calle Cruz 301 (corner Recinto Sur). ✆ **787/723-3206.**

Books

Border's This huge book, music, and DVD store has a thriving cafe and magazine rack, and a huge children's area. From chess tournaments to children's-book readings, from musical performances to book-release parties, something always seems to be going on at the mega retailer's main store on the island. In addition to English-language best sellers, it has a huge collection of Puerto Rican literature and other books, as well as a large, more general Spanish-language collection. Plaza Las Americas, Av. Franklin Delano Roosevelt, Hato Rey. ✆ **787/767-5202.** Bus: B21.

La Tertulia A bookstore with a wide selection of books and music in a large, beautiful setting, La Tertulia carries the latest hits in Spanish and English, plus nonfiction, fiction, and classics in both Spanish and English. It's open Monday through Saturday from 9am to 10pm and Sunday from 10am to 8pm. Recinto Sur 305, Old San Juan. ✆ **787/724-8200.**

Carnival Masks

La Calle ★ Every Puerto Rican knows that the best, and cheapest, place to buy brightly painted carnival masks *(caretas)* is in Ponce, where the tradition of making them from papier-mâché originated. But if you can't spare the time for a side excursion to Ponce, this store in Old San Juan stocks one of the most varied inventories of *vegigantes* in the Puerto Rican capital. Depending on their size and composition (some include coconut shells, gourds, and flashy metal trim), they range in price from $10 to $2,500 each. Side-by-side with the pagan-inspired masks, you'll find a well-chosen selection of paintings by talented local artists, priced from $25 to $2,800 each. Calle Fortaleza 105. ✆ **787/725-1306.**

Cigars

The Cigar House This is retail outlet has a great selection of cigars, including Puerto Rican–based *jibarito* cigars, but it sells quality Dominican brands as well. It's a no-frills cigar shop with a nice selection. At the Doll House (which sells souvenirs now; "No dolls!" the owner will shriek at you). Calle Fortaleza 255. ✆ **787/723-7797** or 725-0652.

Don Collin's Cigars This is the main store of this locally produced brand of cigars, hand rolled on the island from locally grown tobacco and wraps, and sometimes mixed with fine tobacco from the Dominican Republic and elsewhere. There are nine varieties, and five-count and nine-count variety packs are available. Open daily from 9am to 8pm. Calle Cristo 59. ✆ **787/977-2983.**

Clothing & Beachwear

Costazul This surf shop stocks major brands of beachwear, surf wear, sunglasses, and bathing suits for men, women, and children. The prices are not bad, and the merchandise is top rate. Worth a stop if you really need something for the beach. Calle San Francisco 264. ✆ **787/722-0991.**

Hecho a Mano ★ Beautiful ethnic clothing for women, using island fabric but also that from Guatemala, Indonesia, India, and Africa. Styles range from willowy

GROTESQUE masks

The most popular of all Puerto Rican crafts are the frightening ***caretas***—papier-mâché masks worn at island carnivals. Tangles of menacing horns, fang-toothed leering expressions, and bulging eyes of these half-demon/half-animal creations send children running and screaming to their parents. At carnival time, they are worn by costumed revelers called *vegigantes. Vegigantes* often wear bat-winged jumpsuits and roam the streets either individually or in groups.

The origins of these masks and carnivals may go back to medieval Spain and/or tribal Africa. A processional tradition in Spain, dating from the early 17th century, was intended to terrify sinners with marching devils, in the hope that they would return to church. Cervantes described it briefly in *Don Quixote.* Puerto Rico blended this Spanish procession with the masked tradition brought by slaves from Africa. Some historians believe that the Taínos were also accomplished mask makers, which would make this a very ancient tradition indeed.

The predominant traditional mask colors were black, red, and yellow, all symbols of hellfire and damnation. Today, pastels are more likely to be used. Each *vegigante* sports at least two or three horns, although some masks have hundreds of horns, in all shapes and sizes. Mask-making in Ponce, the major center for this craft, and in Loíza Aldea, a palm-fringed town on the island's northeastern coast, has since led to a renaissance of Puerto Rican folk art.

The premier store selling these masks is **La Calle** (p. 179). Masks can be seen in action at the three big masquerade carnivals on the island: the Ponce Festival in February, the Festival of Loíza Aldea in July, and the Día de las Máscaras at Hatillo in December.

dresses and wraps in tribal patterns, to more modern, tropical-fashion party dresses. It has gorgeous clothes, plus handmade jewelry and other interesting finds. The ambience in the store is wonderful, complete with incense, world music, and the beautiful sales staff outfitted in the store's fashions. Founded in 1993, the company prides itself on its dealings with its artisans and its efforts to undertake practices and designs in harmony with nature. Now with 12 locations, including Condado and Plaza Las Américas. Main location open Monday through Saturday from 10am to 7pm, Sunday from 11am to 5pm. Calle San Francisco 260, Viejo San Juan. ✆ **787/722-5322.**

Lost Surf Shop The friendliest, trendiest surf shop in town. It's got everything you need, from boards to surf wax, to hit the waves; but if you are just interested in looking good on the beach, this is your place too. The store features top of the line surf wear and beach fashion, but there are frequent specials on quality goods and some real bargains can be had. Come here for great sunglasses and other accessories. Av. Ashford 1129, Condado. ✆ **787/723-4750.**

Mrs. and Miss Boutique The home of the "the magic dress," which is crafted in Morocco of a silky-looking blend of rayon and cotton, in 10 different colors or patterns, each of which can be worn 11 different ways. There are much better deals on the sarongs and long dresses, sometimes from Indonesia. Calle Fortaleza 154. ✆ **787/724-8571.**

Nono Maldonado Named after its owner, a Puerto Rico–born designer who worked for many years as the fashion editor of *Esquire* magazine, this is one of the most fashionable and upscale haberdashers in the Caribbean. Selling both men's and women's clothing, it contains everything from socks to dinner jackets, as well as ready-to-wear versions of Maldonado's twice-a-year collections. Both ready-to-wear and couture are available here. Av. Ashford 1051. ✆ **787/721-0456.** Bus: A7.

Polo Ralph Lauren Factory Store It's as stylish and carefully orchestrated as anything you'd expect from one of North America's leading clothiers. Even better, its prices are often 35% to 40% less than in retail stores on the U.S. mainland. You can find even greater discounts on irregular or slightly damaged garments, but inspect them carefully before buying. The store occupies two floors of a pair of colonial buildings. Calle del Cristo 201. ✆ **787/722-2136.**

Wet Boutique The ever-chic Erika has been selling the sexiest swimsuits in town for decades. There's a wide selection of the top-name bikini and one-piece designs, plus upscale beach accessories. Calle Cruz 150, Old San Juan. ✆ **787/722-2052.**

Coffee & Spices

Corné Port-Royal Chocolatier A purveyor of the finest chocolate in the world: Belgian chocolates, pralines, and truffles. The smell of warm chocolate hits you as soon as you enter. There's also sell gourmet coffee, cookies, and jellies. With a multilingual owner, and visitors from around the world popping in, you are as likely to hear French or German, as English or Spanish. Open Monday through Saturday 10am to 6pm. Calle San Justo 204, Old San Juan. ✆ **787/725-7744.**

Spicy Caribbee This shop has the best selection of Puerto Rican coffee, which is gaining an increasingly good reputation among aficionados. We love the jerk rub, banana ketchup, mango chutney and all the fiery sauces, such as mango pepper or

The Coffee of Kings & Popes

Of all the coffees of Puerto Rico, the best is Alto Grande, which has been a tradition in Puerto Rican households since 1839. Over the years, this super-premium coffee has earned a reputation for being the "coffee of popes and kings," and is hailed as one of the top three coffees in the world. A magnificently balanced coffee, Alto Grande is a rare and exotic coffee with a sweet, pointed aroma and a bright sparkling flavor. The bean is grown in the highest mountains of the Lares range. This coffee is served at leading hotels and restaurants in Puerto Rico. Should you develop a taste for it, it is also available at most groceries in Puerto Rico and through various specialty stores throughout the United States.

Besides Alto Grane, there are other well-known specialty brands, such as **Yauco Selecto,** and an avalanche of boutique coffee blends have popped up recently. My favorite is **Finca Cialitos** (www.finacialitos.com), which has rich, complex flavor that becomes familiar fast. It is grown by Joaquin Pastor in Ciales, Puerto Rico. Coffee lovers might want to try Joaquin's gourmet coffee and a few more of the new small labels, which manually roast their coffee to maximize flavor. The regular Puerto Rican coffee—Café Crema or Yaucono, for instance—is also quite good.

green fire. There are also such delicacies as rum balls, great colorful recipe books, wonderful music, and handicrafts. The flavors of the Caribbean flow through this shop in many ways. Calle Cristo 154. ✆ **787/725-4690.**

Department Stores

Marshalls This store, part of the U.S. discount chain, is one of the best in the whole Caribbean. Thousands of *sanjuaneros* flock here for the cut-rate prices on designer clothes, housewares, home furnishings, and shoes, plus a variety of other merchandise. There's also an incredible amount of quality stuff at good prices for the traveler: from bathing suits to shorts to sandals to luggage to sunglasses. In fact, this is probably your best bet for an affordable bathing suit. In Plaza de Armas, across from the City Hall, at Calle Rafael Cordero 154, Old San Juan. ✆ **787/722-3020.**

Gifts & Handicrafts

Art-Furniture-Art Located at La Cochera parking garage in the heart of the historic zone, this gallery of fine-art furniture and furnishings is a cool respite and well worth a look. Designer Diana M. Ramos began making reproductions and originals of classic Caribbean plantation furniture and more traditional Spanish colonial work, but has now moved on to creating spare, modern pieces. Both are still on display and for sale, in what are essentially limited editions. Their common traits are the artistic standards brought to them through their organic form and creativity. Calle Luna 204, Old San Juan. ✆ **787/722-4181.**

Barrachina The birthplace, in 1963, of the piña colada (an honor co-claimed by the staff at the Caribe Hilton), Barrachina's is a favorite of cruise-ship passengers. It offers one of the largest selections of jewelry, perfume, cigars, and gifts in San Juan. There's a patio for drinks where you can order (what else?) a piña colada. There is also a Bacardi rum outlet (bottles cost less than stateside but cost the same as at the Bacardi distillery), a costume jewelry department, a gift shop, and a section for authentic silver jewelry, plus a restaurant with nightly flamenco shows. The city's most famous tourist trap but worth at least a look and a piña colada, even though I'm in the Hilton camp. Calle Fortaleza 104 (btw. Calle del Cristo and Calle San José). ✆ **787/725-7912.**

Bóveda ★ This long, narrow space is crammed with exotic jewelry, clothing, greeting cards with images of life in Puerto Rico, some 100 handmade lamps, antiques, Mexican punched tin and glass, and Art Nouveau reproductions, among other items. Calle del Cristo 209. ✆ **787/725-0263.**

Ecléctica Two spacious locations in the Old City offer teak furniture, artisan jewelry, textiles, hammocks lamps and other home furnishings and handicrafts. There's a nice mix of Spanish colonial and Asian-Caribbean style running through most items. With "style and harmony" as its motto, this shop has beautiful stuff for home and gourmet items. From soap and candles to kitchen utensils, there's some beautiful stuff here for homebodies, or those who want to get a gift for one. Calle O'Donnell 204, Plaza Colón. ✆ **787/721-7236.** Also at Calle Cruz 205, Plaza de Armas. ✆ **787/725-3163.**

Mundo Taíno Get a taste of the beauty of Puerto Rican culture, in this appropriately bright and friendly shop with local jewelry, statues, prints, fabrics and other handicrafts, plus music and literature. You can also get a CD with rainforest sounds,

shopping FOR *SANTOS*

The most impressive of the island's crafts are the *santos,* carved religious figures that have been produced since the 1500s. Craftspeople who make these are called *santeros;* using clay, gold, stone, or cedar wood, they carve figurines representing saints, usually from 8 to 20 inches (20–51 cm) tall. Before the Spanish colonization, small statues, called *zemi,* stood in native tribal villages and camps as objects of veneration, and Puerto Rico's *santos* may derive from that pre-Columbian tradition. Every town has its patron saint, and every home has its *santos* to protect the family. For some families, worshipping the *santos* replaces a traditional Mass.

Art historians view the carving of *santos* as Puerto Rico's greatest contribution to the plastic arts. The earliest figures were richly baroque, indicating a strong Spanish influence, but as the islanders began to assert their own identity, the carved figures often became simpler.

In carving *santos,* craftspeople often used handmade tools. Sometimes such natural materials as vegetable dyes and even human hair were used. The saints represented by most *santos* can be identified by their accompanying symbols; for example, Saint Anthony is usually depicted with the infant Jesus and a book. The most popular group of *santos* is the Three Kings. The Trinity and the Nativity are also depicted frequently.

Art experts claim that *santos*-making approached its zenith at the turn of the 20th century, although hundreds of *santeros* still practice their craft throughout the island. Serious *santos* collectors view the former craftsmen of old as the true artists in the field. The best collection of *santos* is found at Puerto Rican Arts & Crafts (p. 183).

Some of the best *santos* on the island can be seen at the Capilla de Cristo in Old San Juan. Perhaps at some future date, a museum devoted entirely to *santos* will open in Puerto Rico.

gourmet coffee, local sweets, rum, and other delicacies. A young, helpful, and friendly staff who know their stuff work here. Calle San José 151, Old San Juan. © **787/723-2214.** Bus: Old City Trolley.

Olé ★ Browsing this store is a learning experience. Even the standard Panama hat takes on new dimensions. Woven from fine-textured *paja* grass and priced from $20 to $1,000, depending on the density of the weave, the hats are all created the same size, and then blocked—by an employee on-site—to fit the shape of your head. Dig into this store's diverse inventory to discover a wealth of treasures—hand-beaten Chilean silver, Peruvian Christmas ornaments, Puerto Rican *santos*—almost all from Puerto Rico or Latin America. Calle Fortaleza 105. © **787/724-2445.**

Puerto Rican Arts & Crafts ★ Set in a 200-year-old colonial building, this unique store is one of the premier outlets on the island for authentic artifacts. Of particular interest are papier-mâché carnival masks from Ponce, whose grotesque and colorful features were originally conceived to chase away evil spirits. Taíno designs inspired by ancient petroglyphs are incorporated into most of the sterling-silver jewelry sold here. There's an art gallery in back, with silk-screened serigraphs by local artists. The outlet has a gourmet Puerto Rican–food section with such items as coffee, rum, and hot sauces for sale. A related specialty of this well-respected store involves the exhibition and sale of modern replicas of the Spanish colonial tradition of *santos,* which are carved and sometimes polychromed representations of the Catholic saints and the infant Jesus. Priced from $50 to $1,100 each, and laboriously carved by artisans in private studios around the island, they're easy to pack in a suitcase because the largest one measures only 12 inches (31cm) from halo to toe. Closes at 6pm Monday through Saturday and 5pm Sunday. Calle Fortaleza 204. ✆ **787/725-5596.**

Vaughn's Gifts & Crafts This store offers crafts from Puerto Rico and elsewhere, but specializes in straw and Panamanian hats. It's quite a large collection for the tropical hat collector, plus other colorful crafts from the island and elsewhere in the region. Calle Fortaleza 262. ✆ **787/721-8221.**

Jewelry

Bared & Sons Now in its 4th decade, is the main outlet of a chain of at least 20 upscale jewelry stores on Puerto Rico. On the ground floor are gemstones, gold, diamonds, and watches. One floor up, there's a monumental collection of porcelain and crystal. It's a great source for hard-to-get and discontinued patterns from Christofle, Royal Doulton, Wedgwood, Limoges, Royal Copenhagen, Lalique, Lladró, Herend, Baccarat, and Daum. San Justo 206 (at the corner of Calle Fortaleza). ✆ **787/724-4811.**

Emerald Isles This jewelry boutique in the Old Town is smaller than other entities that specialize in colored gemstones, but because of its much lower overhead, its prices can sometimes be more reasonable. It specializes in Colombian emeralds, set into silver or gold settings already, or waiting for you to select one. But as long as you're in the shop, look also at the unusual inventories of contemporary reproductions of pre-Columbian jewelry, some of it gold-plated and richly enameled. Many of these pieces sell for around $50 each, and some of them are genuinely intriguing. Calle Fortaleza 105. ✆ **787/977-3769.**

Joyería Riviera This is an emporium of 18-karat gold and diamonds, and the island's leading jeweler. Adjacent to Plaza de Armas, the shop has an impeccable reputation. It carries Patek Philippe, Bedat & Co., and Carl F. Bucherer watches. Calle Fortaleza 257. ✆ **787/725-4000.**

Reinhold Jewelers ★ This is one of Puerto Rico's top shops featuring work by local and world-renowned jewelry designers. Its main location, and the adjacent David Yurman design boutique, spread across two locations at the ground floor of Plaza Las América inside one of its main entrances. Gaze through the beautiful windows at the dazzling creations inside. There's also a location at El San Juan Hotel Gallery. With two prime retail locations in San Juan, this store offers creations by internationally renowned jewelry designers and is probably both the most respected and dazzling shop in town. It's also known for its top service and its annual holiday catalog for clients. Home to Tiffany & Co., David Yurman, Robert Lee Morris, Vera Wang, Mikimoto, John Hardy, and Lisa Jenks. Plaza Las Américas 24A, 24B, Hato Rey. ✆ **787/554-0528.** Other location at El San Juan Hotel Gallery, Isla Verde. ✆ **787/796-2521.**

Venetian Jewelers This thriving jewelry store in the Old City has a beautiful collection and carries such items as Sophia Fiori's award-winning diamond rings,

A Dying Art: Old Lace

Another Puerto Rican craft has undergone a big revival just as it seemed that it would disappear forever: lace. Originating in Spain, *mundillos* (tatted fabrics) are the product of a type of bobbin lace-making. This 5-centuries-old craft exists today only in Puerto Rico and Spain.

The first lace made in Puerto Rico was called *torchon* (beggar's lace). Early examples of beggar's lace were considered of inferior quality, but artisans today have transformed this fabric into a delicate art form, eagerly sought by collectors. Lace bands called *entrados* have two straight borders, whereas the other traditional style, *puntilla,* has both a straight and a scalloped border.

The best outlet in San Juan for lace is **Linen House** (p. 185).

including blue diamonds, Phillip Stein watches, Kabana's mother of pearl, and House of Taylor. Calle Fortaleza 259. ✆ **787/722-6960.** A second location is at Calle Tanca 252. ✆ **787/724-1211.**

Lace & Linens

Linen House This unpretentious store specializes in table linens, bed linens, and lace and has the island's best selection. Some of the most delicate pieces are expensive, but most are moderate in price. Inventories include embroidered shower curtains, lace doilies, bun warmers, place mats, and tablecloths that seamstresses took weeks to complete. Some astonishingly lovely items are available for as little as $30. The aluminum/pewter serving dishes have beautiful Spanish-colonial designs. Prices here are sometimes 40% lower than those on the North American mainland. Calle Fortaleza 250, 104. ✆ **787/721-4219** or 787/725-6233.

Leather & Equestrian Accessories

Coach Here you can find fine leather goods, from belts to bags to purses. This outlet sells discontinued products, so you can find some real bargains. Calle Cristo 150. ✆ **787/722-6830.**

Dooney & Bourke Factory Store Leather lovers will also want to pass through here, especially for the buttery smooth women's handbags. You can find bargains on its complete line of high-quality leatherwear, which also includes briefcases, wallets, and belts. Real bargains on first-rate products. Calle Cristo 200, Old San Juan. ✆ **787/289-0075.**

Lalin Leather Shop Although it lies in an out-of-the-way suburb (Puerto Nuevo), about 2 miles (3.2km) south of San Juan, this is the best and most comprehensive cowboy and equestrian outfitter in Puerto Rico, probably in the entire Caribbean. Here you'll find all manner of boots, cowboy hats, and accessories. More important, however, is the wide array of saddles and bridles, some from Colombia, some from Puerto Rico, with both cost-conscious and extravagant prices. Even the highest-priced items cost a lot less than their U.S. mainland equivalents, so if you happen to have a horse or pony on the U.S. mainland, a visit here might be worth your while. If you decide to make the rather inconvenient pilgrimage, you won't be alone. Regular clients come from as far away as Iceland, the Bahamas, and New

York. Everything can be shipped. Av. Piñero 1617, Puerto Nuevo. ✆ **787/781-5305** or 749-4815. No bus.

Malls

Belz Factory Outlet World The largest mall of its kind in Puerto Rico, and the Caribbean as well, opened in 2001 in Canóvanas, east of San Juan en route to El Yunque. Totally enclosed and air-conditioned, it re-creates the experience of strolling through the streets of Old San Juan, sans the traffic and heat. Five interconnected buildings comprise the mall, with dozens of stores from Nike to Gap, from Dockers to Levi's to Maidenform, from Samsonite to Guess, and from Papaya to Geoffrey Beene. The factory-outlet pricing is on everything, including the movies. Hwy. 3 18400, Barrio Pueblo, Canóvanas. ✆ **787/256-7040.** No bus.

Plaza Las Américas ★ The island's first big mall and still the largest in the Caribbean, Plaza, as it is known by locals, is a world unto itself. Even by U.S. standards, it's a remarkable place with top-name retailers, full-service restaurants, a Cineplex, two food courts, a spa, and hair stylists. Retail outlets include Macy's, Armani Exchange, Banana Republic, and Guess, as well as high-quality designer boutiques, with over 300 stores in all. There is also a U.S. post office, branches of all major island banks, and a full medical and office center. There are often shows and special events—from boat and racecar exhibits to fashion shows and concerts—taking place along its hallways. There's action from morning to night, and it's a quick trip from any San Juan hotel. Av. Franklin Delano Roosevelt 525, Hato Rey. ✆ **787/767-5202.** Bus: B21.

Markets

Plaza del Mercado de Santurce ★ Puerto Rico shows its Latin American side with this traditional marketplace, rescued in a recent renovation from an offbeat curiosity to a rich and integral part of the life of San Juan. There are all sorts of local fruits and vegetables; "botanicas" hawking everything from medicinal herbs to Puerto Rican bay rum; small fondas serving up typical Puerto Rican dishes, including roast pork; and you can also order the best mango, papaya, or banana frappes on the island. The surrounding seafood and *comida criolla* restaurants are some of the best in the city, at affordable prices, and the streets are closed to traffic weekend evenings; it is often the hottest spot to go in town. Calle Dos Hermanos at Calle Capitol, Santurce. ✆ **787/723-8022.** Bus: B5.

SAN JUAN AFTER DARK

San Juan nightlife comes in all varieties. From the vibrant performing-arts scene to street-level salsa, and with the casinos, discos, and bars, there's plenty of entertainment available almost any evening.

Island nightlife begins very late, especially on Friday and Saturday nights. Hang out until the late, late afternoon on the beach, have dinner around 8pm (9 would be even better), and then the night is yours. The true party animal will rock until the broad daylight. Many bars and nightclubs are open until 2am during the week, and 4am on weekends. Many clubs and some bars are closed on Mondays and Tuesdays.

¡Qué Pasa!, the official visitor's guide to Puerto Rico, lists cultural events, including music, dance, theater, film, and art exhibits. It's distributed free by the tourist

office. Local newspapers, such as the English-language weekly *Caribbean Business* (which carries a daily website at www.caribbeanbusinesspr.com), often have entertainment information and concert and cultural listings, as do the English-language *Puerto Rico Daily Sun* and the Spanish-language *El Vocero, El Nuevo Día,* and *Primera Hora* daily newspapers. Also check the Ticketpop website (www.ticketpop.com), which lists upcoming major acts.

The Performing Arts

Centro de Bellas Artes In the heart of Santurce, the Performing Arts Center is a 6-minute taxi ride from most of the Condado hotels. It contains the Festival Hall, Drama Hall, and the Experimental Theater. Some of the events here will be of interest only to Spanish speakers; others attract an international audience. Av. Ponce de León 22. © **787/724-4747** or 725-7334 for the ticket agent. Tickets $40–$200; 50% discounts for seniors. Bus: A-5, M1.

Teatro Tapía Standing across from Plaza de Colón and built about 1832, this is one of the oldest theaters in the Western Hemisphere (see "Historic Sights," earlier in this chapter). Productions, some musical, are staged throughout the year and include drama, dances, and cultural events. You'll have to call the box office (Mon–Fri 9am–6pm) for specific information. Av. Fortaleza at Plaza Colón. © **787/721-0180.** Tickets $20–$30, depending on the show. Bus: Old San Juan bus station, trolley.

The Club & Music Scene

Club Brava and Ultra Lounge ★ This club is part of the reason the El San Juan has a reputation as the city hotel with the best nightlife. The young and privileged, local celebs, and urbane visitors mix it up on the club's dance floor to a soulful mix of house, reggaeton, and Latin music styles. The nightclub is designed in the form of a circle, with a central dance floor and a wraparound balcony. There's also a laid back lounge area for conversation and table service. One of the best sound systems in the Caribbean, its stage is often the scene of memorable performances. Right off the hotel's lively lobby and casino. Open Thursday through Saturday from 10pm until 5am. In El San Juan Hotel & Casino, Av. Isla Verde 6063, Isla Verde. © **787/791-2781.** Cover hovers around $15, depending on event; free for guests of El San Juan Hotel (just show room key). Bus: A5.

Music While You Munch

Several restaurants in Old San Juan, and elsewhere throughout the city, have live music on certain days of the week. Knowing the schedule could help you decide on where to eat dinner. **The Parrot Club** has live Latin jazz and salsa a few nights weekly. **Carli Café Concierto** (© **787/725-4927;** www.carlicafeconcierto.com) has live jazz nightly at 9pm, while **Barrachina Restaurant** (p. 182) has a live flamenco music and dance show nightly. **La Playita** in Isla Verde hosts weekend troubadours, while Condado's **Yerba Buena,** Av. Ashford 1350, Condado (© **787/721-7500**) has Latin Jazz on Monday nights and Cuban salsa Fridays.

Club Lazer This Old San Juan Club has been hopping for nearly 2 decades through various transformations. A huge cavernous place in the middle of town, there's salsa and other tropical music Friday nights and reggaeton Saturdays. Sundays, ladies night, are particularly jamming. The club opens at 10pm Wednesday and Friday through Sunday and attracts a large local crowd as well as regular customers who work on the cruise-ship lines, and young people from throughout the world. Calle Cruz 251, Old San Juan. ✆ **787/722-7581.** Cover charges range from $10–$15.

The Latin Roots ★ This mammoth lounge and dinner club is the spot to hear salsa and other Latin rhythms. You can take salsa dance lessons, eat fine Puerto Rican cooking and listen to Latin big bands performing that brash tropical sound every night. The establishment is decorated with photographs and memorabilia from the golden days of salsa and pays tribute to some of the greats of tropical music. This is the place that San Juan needed, as it guarantees an opportunity to listen to and dance salsa. An impressive spot with its own store. Edificio Galeria Portuario, Recino Sur y Calle Comercio, Old San Juan. ✆ **787/977-1887.**

Lupi's Mexican Grill & Sports Cantina The rock *en Español* is as hot as the salsa at this Mexican pub and restaurant. Yankees fans will want to know that former ace Ed Figueroa owns the spot. Familiar dishes, such as fajitas, nachos, tacos, and burritos, are served, as well as seafood and local platters. Caribbean and rock music are played on weekend nights and there are plenty of televisions to see the game. There are both Isla Verde and Old San Juan locations. Isla Verde: Av. Isla Verde, Km. 187. ✆ **787/253-1664.** Old San Juan: Recinto Sur 313. ✆ **787/722-1874.**

Nuyorican Café ★★ When the Rolling Stones played the new Coliseum during their last world tour, Mick Jagger and Keith Richards came straight here to listen to the salsa. The house band, the Comborican, burns down the house whenever it takes the stage. There's also Latin jazz and reggae, theatrical performances, art exhibits, and a damn good kitchen (the pizza is one of the island's best). Recent performers have included the top names in Puerto Rican music, including Pedro Guerra, Roy Brown, Alfredo Naranjo, Cultura Profética, and salsa greats Bobbie Valentín, Ray Santiago, Polito Huerta, Luis Marín, Jerry Medina, and Tito Allen. The cafe also hosts special weeklong musical festivals and has put on long-running performance art and theatrical programs, usually earlier in the evening before the bands get going. Also some very fine rock *en Español*. The bar is open until at least 3am. Calle San Francisco 312 (entrance down the alley), Old San Juan. ✆ **787/977-1276** or 366-5074.

Rumba This club has a full bar up front, a huge back room with a stage for live bands, and a big dance floor. It's so photogenically hip that it was selected as the site for the filming of many of the crowd scenes within *Dirty Dancing: Havana Nights*.

Romantic Sunsets

There is no better place on a Sunday night from 5:30 to 7pm to watch the sun set over Old San Juan than at Paseo de la Princesa. In this evocative colonial setting, you can hear local trios serenade you as the sun goes down. Or walk around and follow it along around the base of El Morro. A great place to share the moment with your lover.

Set immediately adjacent to the also-recommended restaurant, Barú, with which it's not associated, it's known as another great venue for live music, with excellent salsa, Latin jazz, and other tropical music. There's a great crowd here, of different styles ranging from college kids to well-dressed gray beards who remember the music back in its heyday. The common denominator is the love of the music and dance. Open Tuesday to Sunday 9pm to 4am. Calle San Sebastián 152, Old San Juan. ✆ **787/725-4407.**

The Bar Scene

Unless otherwise stated, there is no cover charge at the bars recommended below.

Amadeus Bistro Bar There's great food and frequent live music nightly along with the inventive Puerto Rican nouvelle cuisine. You can hear Latin jazz and Spanish ballads most nights from the early evening. Near the financial district, federal court, and other important office buildings, the place caters to the local professional crowd. Av. Chardón 350, Hato Rey. ✆ **787/294-5011.** Bus: B21.

The Brick Haus A pub open to the wee hours serving good old "gringo Rican" cuisine. There's a big-screen television for sports events (even if it's poker) and great grub, such as steaks, fish, Mexican, burgers, and sandwiches. A favorite with Coast Guard personnel and their local girlfriends. Calle O'Donnell 359, Old San Juan. ✆ **787/723-1947.** Bus: Old City Trolley.

Eight Noodle Bar Chinese Right outside the entrance to San Juan's liveliest casino, this Asian bar serves up classic Chinese that tastes straight from New York City's Chinatown: sticky rice, dumplings, all kinds of noodle dishes, scallion pancakes, pork pot stickers, delicious shrimp tempura, and walnut chicken. The small spot draws partiers from across Condado into the wee hours of the morning, as well as the casino refugees. It is a great spot, open daily from 4pm to 4am. Av. Ashford 999, Condado Plaza Hotel, Condado. ✆ **787/723-8881.**

El Batey 🎁 Graffiti and business cards cover the walls of this dive bar with a great jukebox and a view of the procession up and down Calle Cristo during weekend nights. Drawings of the legends of this storied watering hole are hung in its main room. There's always somebody to talk to at the bar, which draws an eccentric local crowd and independent-minded visitors. Patrons play chess and backgammon as well. The jukebox has great classic and psychedelic rock, some great Sinatra, and some priceless jazz standards by the likes of Duke Ellington and Charlie Parker. A haven for hipsters living in or strolling into town for decades. Calle Cristo 101. ✆ **787/725-1787.** No bus.

El Patio de Sam Come here for a drink and a snack on your bar crawl through Old San Juan. A guitar player entertains most nights, and there are always interesting folks hanging out. One of the city's most popular late-night joints with a good selection of beers. Open daily noon to 1am. Calle San Sebastián 102. ✆ **787/723-1149.** Bus: Old Town Trolley.

El San Juan Hotel & Casino Lobby Bar This beautiful bar, one of the nicest in the entire Caribbean, lures hotel guests and well-heeled locals who vie to look as fabulous as the setting; they make up at least a quarter of the business at this fashionable rendezvous. Set in an oval wrapped around a sunken bar area, amid marble and burnished mahogany, it offers a view of one of the world's largest chandeliers. After 7pm on Monday through Saturday, live music, often salsa and merengue, emanates

THE birth OF THE PIÑA COLADA

When actress Joan Crawford tasted the piña colada at what was then the Beachcombers Bar in the **Caribe Hilton,** Calle Los Rosales (✆ **787/721-0303**), she claimed it was "better than slapping Bette Davis in the face."

One story has it that the famous drink is the creation of bartender Ramon "Monchito" Marrero, now long gone, who was hired by the Hilton in 1954. He spent 3 months mixing, tasting, and discarding hundreds of combinations until he felt he had the right blend. Thus, the frothy piña colada was born. It's been estimated that some 100 million of them have been sipped around the world since that fateful time.

Monchito never patented his formula and didn't mind sharing it with the world. Still served at the Hilton, here is his not-so-secret recipe:

2 ounces light rum
1 ounce coconut cream
1 ounce heavy cream
6 ounces fresh pineapple
½ cup crushed ice
Pineapple wedge and maraschino cherry for garnish

Pour rum, coconut cream, cream, and pineapple juice in blender. Add ice. Blend for 15 seconds. Pour into a 12-ounce glass. Add garnishes.

The folks at Barrachina, meanwhile, insist a bartender employed with the restaurant, Ramón Portas Mingot, developed the drink that put the island on the world cocktail map.

from an adjoining room. Watch the models strut by, the honeymoon couple, or the table of high rollers from New York having a drink before trying their luck again. This is still the place to be seen in the city. Open daily 6pm to 3am. In El San Juan Hotel & Casino, Av. Isla Verde 6063, Isla Verde. ✆ **787/791-1000.** Bus: A5.

Ficus Café This modern, open-air cafe has quickly become a favorite with *sanjuaneros*. It's a fabulous spot, with the illuminated Convention Center looming behind it and a huge fountain in front performing an unending dance of liquid and light, as if this were the better future to which Puerto Rico is headed. There are great drinks and haute tropical bar food: shark bites, Caribbean hummus, seared churrasco strips. The cafe is open Friday and Saturday nights, with live entertainment and DJs. It's also open for Sunday brunch from 9am to 6pm. At the Puerto Rico Convention Bureau, 100 Convention Blvd. ✆ **787/641-7722.**

La Sombrilla Rosa A nice neighborhood bar with daily happy hours, a relaxed atmosphere with friendly staff and patrons, and good music. Weekdays, until 3pm, it serves great *comida criolla* at prices ranging from $5.50 to $8. Basic stuff such as steak and onions and grilled chicken, everything with rice and pink beans and *tostones*. At night, there are often beer and drink specials, great music, sometimes live performances, and always interesting people in this great neighborhood bar. Open from 9:30am to 3pm for lunch, then from 7pm to at least 3am nightly. Calle San Sebastián 154. ✆ **787/725-5656.** Bus: Old Town Trolley.

Maria's Forget the tacky decorations. This is the town's most enduring bar, a favorite local hangout and a prime target for Old City visitors seeking frozen tropical drinks. The atmosphere is fun, and the tropical drinks include piña coladas and frosties made of banana, orange, and strawberry, as well as the Puerto Rican beer Medalla. Open daily 10:30am to 3am (closes at 4am Fri–Sat). Calle del Cristo 204. ✆ **787/721-1678.** Bus: Old Town Trolley.

Pa'l Cielo This "chinchorro glorificado," a kind of glorified greasy spoon, serves tasty food in a bright, tropical, funky setting and plays host to some great bands. The result is its one of the most popular spots in town for the young, creative crowd. There's tasty Latin and regional flair, with some Asian and Middle Eastern influences mixed in, plus tasty pizzas and salads. The music often impresses, as does the crowd. There's everything from Latin jazz standard singers to Spanish punk bands. A great place to mix with locals. Open Wednesday to Saturday 5pm to 2am, and Sunday 4pm to 1am. The kitchen closes at 11pm Wednesday and Sunday and midnight Thursday to Saturday. Calle Loiza 2056. ✆ **787/727-6798.** Bus: A5.

Solera ★★ Having some drinks and tapas off the lobby of this renovated beauty of a hotel is a great way to taste the essence of San Juan nightlife. The sophisticated but comfortable setting spills from the lobby to a multilevel pool area, and you can sit on beautiful, tropical furnishings under the stars and amid lush vegetation, or within the marble cool of indoors. The sangria here is delicious; and there are also pitchers of mojitos and other drinks to go down with such delicacies as coconut calamari sticks, juicy Asian churrasco, paella, and sushi rolls. The lobby bar is the spot for the young and beautiful, and the adjacent casino never closes. Av. Ashford 1077, San Juan. ✆ **787/721-7500.** Bus: C53, B21.

Surf Shack This tiny sidewalk grill has a great beer selection and a limited menu of tasty burgers, shark chicarrones, baked chicken, and stewed beef *empanadas.* Prices are right—the chicken wings selection at $6.75 is the most expensive thing on the menu—but the quality is there. Chef Roberto Trevino, of Iron Chef and Budatai fame, shows us here what he likes to eat at home. Vegetarians will find their satisfaction in the falafel burger, which, like all burgers, are served in a homemade bun with fries. Open Tuesday to Sunday 11:30am to 2am. Av Ashford 1106. ✆ **787/723-2517.** Bus: B21, C53.

Wet Bar This chic drinking spot operates out of San Juan's finest boutique hotel, the Water Club. This is the best bar for watching the sun set over San Juan. Located on the 11th floor, it features jazz music and the Caribbean's only rooftop fireplace, for those nippy nights in winter when you want to drink outside. The sensuous decor here includes striped zebra-wood stools, futons, pillowy sofas, and hand-carved side tables. The walls feature Indonesian carved teak panels. It overlooks the brilliant Isla Verde coastline and its palm-fringed beachfront below. Latin rhythms mix with R&B standards and world rhythms. You can order sushi under the stars or some other delicacies from a limited menu. It's a beautiful place, with trendy martinis and plush comforts. Thursday through Saturday, the Wet Bar is open 7pm to 1am. In the San Juan Water & Beach Club, Calle José M. Tartak 2. ✆ **787/728-3666.** Bus: A5.

Hot Nights in Gay San Juan

San Juan has probably the largest and most influential gay community in the Caribbean, and Puerto Rico is largely accepting and supportive of it. That was evident when Ricky Martin officially came out of the closet in 2010, and he was embraced with waves of support from his island fans. So visitors seeking gay and lesbian friendly

La Rumba Party Cruise

The trouble with most nightlife venues in San Juan is that the real parties in conventional nightclubs begin at hours so impossibly late that the average visitor will tend to be deep asleep by the time the dance floors at city clubs begin getting filled up. So if you love to salsa and merengue, but if you maintain relatively conservative ideas about your bedtime, consider the **La Rumba Party Cruise** as a viable option. It all takes place aboard a neon-lit two-level minicruiser that's moored most of the time to a point near Old San Juan's cruise pier no. 1 (Plaza Darsenas). Schedules vary according to business, but cruises tend to last 120 minutes each, and depart every Friday and Saturday at 10:30pm, 12:30am, and 2:30am; and every Sunday at 7:30, 9:30, and 11:30pm. You can get onboard about an hour before departure, shaking your booty to Latino music as the boat sits in port, music blaring, waiting for other clients. Cruises cost $14 per person (tax included), with children's rates $7 and seniors $10. There's a cash bar on board selling beer for between $4 and $6 each, depending on the brand. There's a sightseeing benefit to the experience as well: En route, as it chugs out to sea, participants garner sea-fronting views of both of San Juan's 18th-century forts and the coastline of Isla Verde. For reservations and more information, call 787/375-5211, 263-2962, or 525-1288.

establishments will find ample choices and have lots of opportunities to interact with both locals and visitors. Some discos, known for the hot music and dancing, also draw straight couples as well. Many mainstream restaurants and nightclubs have core gay clientele as well, especially in the Condado, Santurce, and Old San Juan areas.

Circo Bar A stylish spot that is probably the number-one gay bar for men in San Juan. The DJs pump up the house while the crowd gets loose on the dance floor. There are also dance and video bars, a lounge to kick back in and an outdoor atrium with intimate seating areas. The crowd does not begin forming until after midnight, when the boys behind the bar rip off their shirts and the party really gets going. A few blocks from Condado's main tourism drag, it's a quick cab ride away and there is private, secure parking. No cover charge. There are also shows and karaoke depending on the night. Open daily 9pm to 5am, even holidays. Calle Condado 650, Condado. © **787/725-9676.** Bus: B21.

Krash Klub This two-level nightclub is still the city's biggest gay club, with cutting-edge music and bathrooms with creative decor. The festive dance club draws a party crowd, and you might think for a moment you're inside one of those converted warehouse clubs in downtown New York or L.A. Gorgeous people and a smart-looking spot. Don't bother coming before midnight. Open Wednesday to Sunday 10pm to 3am or 5am. Av. Ponce de León 1257, Santurce. © **787/722-1131.** Cover $5–$10, more for special events. Bus: 1.

Tia Maria's Liquor Store This is not a liquor store, but a bar that caters to both locals and visitors. The place has a very welcoming and unpretentious attitude,

barhopping THROUGH THE OLD CITY

A good place to start your night is the bright and enchanting **El Picoteo** in the El Convento Hotel, Calle del Cristo 100 (✆ **787/723-9020**). Get warmed up with some tapas and a fine sangria as you sit at one of the tables on a terrace overlooking Cristo Street and the hotel's interior courtyard. It's a good hangout for late-night dialogues. At the bar inside, you can often hear live jazz. Older locals mingle with hotel guests, the patronage mainly in the post-35 age group.

Afterwards, head for a pair of holes in the wall across the street from the El Convento Hotel. **El Batey,** Calle del Cristo 101 (no phone), and **Don Pablo,** Calle del Cristo 103 (no phone), are battered, side-by-side hangouts with a clientele of locals, expatriates, and occasional visitors. Whereas El Batey's music remains firmly grounded in the rock-'n'-roll classics of the 1970s, with a scattering of Elvis Presley and Frank Sinatra hits, Don Pablo prides itself on cutting-edge music that's continually analyzed by the counterculture aficionados who hang out here. El Batey is open daily from 2pm to 6am; Don Pablo, daily from 8pm to 4am.

You'll next want to head up the hill to **San Sebastián Street,** a place where Puerto Ricans have been partying for years. There is a line of restaurants and bars, running from Calle Cristo along this street down to Calle Cruz. On weekend evenings, the area is packed with fashionable crowds out for fun. **Nono's** (Calle San Sebastián 100, at the corner of Cristo; ✆ **787/579-5851**), is a great spot to watch the action out on Plaza San José. **El Patio de Sam** (p. 137) has been a favorite watering hole for locals and tourists since the 1950s. **Candela** (100 Calle San Sebastián; ✆ **787/977-4305**) is a late-night avant-garde club that plays eclectic lounge music until the earlier morning hours. There are often festivals of experimental music and art held here. Any of the bars along this strip is worth a look; many have pool tables and jukeboxes with great selections of classic salsa. A must-stop, however, is **Rumba** (San Sebastián 152; ✆ **787/977-4305**), where you will find live salsa and other tropical music. Your final stop will likely be **Aqui Se Puede** (corner of San Justo, 50 Calle San Justo; ✆ **787/579-5851**), which has great music, either live or on the jukebox, plus frequent special events such as performances and art shows.

If you need sustenance after all that drinking, head to Tantra, Calle Fortaleza 356 (✆ **787/977-8141**), which has the best late-night menu in town, as well as a creative martini menu, including versions with mango, passion fruit, and, a personal favorite, a version with cinnamon and clove. Live belly dancers amuse the crowd on Friday and Saturday nights, and any night of the week you can rent, for $20, a Mogul-style hookah pipe for every member of your dining table, if the idea of playing pasha for a night appeals to you.

attracting both men and women. Don't come here for entertainment, but to hang out with the locals. It's best to come here during early evening happy hours, which attract an after-work professional crowd. Near many other gay discos. Open Monday to Thursday and Sunday 11am to midnight; Friday to Saturday 10am to 2am. Av. José de Diego 326 (near the corner of Av. Ponce de León), Santurce. ✆ **787/724-4011.** Bus: B1.

Casinos

Many visitors come to Puerto Rico on package deals and stay at one of the posh hotels at the Condado or Isla Verde just to gamble.

Nearly all the large hotels in San Juan/Condado/Isla Verde offer casinos, and there are other large casinos at some of the bigger resorts outside the metropolitan area. The atmosphere in the casinos is casual, but still you shouldn't show up in bathing suits or shorts. Most of the casinos open around noon and close at 2, 3, or 4am. Guest patrons must be at least 18 years old to enter.

The casino generating all the excitement today is the 18,503-square-foot (1,719-sq.-m) **Ritz-Carlton Casino,** Avenue of Governors, Isla Verde (✆ **787/253-1700**), the largest casino in Puerto Rico. It combines the elegant decor of the 1940s with tropical fabrics and patterns. This is one of the plushest and most exclusive entertainment complexes in the Caribbean. It features traditional games such as blackjack, roulette, baccarat, craps, and slot machines. In Old San Juan, you'll have to try your luck at the **Old San Juan Hotel & Casino,** Calle Brumbaugh 100 (✆ **787/721-5100**), where five-card stud competes with some 240 slot machines and roulette tables. There's a stately gaming parlor just off the lobby at the **El San Juan Hotel & Casino** (one of the most grand), Av. Isla Verde 6063 (✆ **787/791-1000**); and the **Condado Plaza Hotel & Casino,** Av. Ashford 999 (✆ **787/721-1000**), remains one of the city's busiest and most exciting casinos.

Cockfights

A brutal sport not to everyone's taste, cockfights are legal in Puerto Rico. The most authentic are in Salinas, a town on the southern coast with a southwestern ethos, which has *galleras,* or rings, for cockfighting. But you don't have to go all the way there to see a match. About three fights per week take place at the **Coliseo Gallistico,** Av. Isla Verde 6600, Av. Isla Verde, Esquina Los Gobernadores. Call ✆ **787/791-6005** for the schedule and to order tickets, which cost $10, $12, $20, or $35, depending on the seat. The best time to attend cockfights is from January to May, as more fights are scheduled at that time. Hours are Tuesday or Thursday 4 to 10pm and Saturday 2 to 9pm.

NEAR SAN JUAN

7

Within easy reach of San Juan's cosmopolitan bustle are superb attractions and natural wonders. With San Juan as your base, you can explore the island by day and return in time for a final dip before dinner and an evening on the town.

In fact, travelers looking to have an extended vacation in Puerto Rico may consider cutting back on hotel expenses by renting a furnished condo on one of San Juan's beaches or a high-ceilinged historic rooftop apartment in the Old City. San Juan, with its historic sites, gorgeous beaches, and vibrant cultural activities and nightlife can easily keep you occupied for 2 weeks or more. But the lure of a long-term rental in the city increases exponentially when you realize how many beautiful places there are to see and how many great things there are to do within a leisurely day trip from the city.

Conversely, travelers looking for the ultimate Caribbean vacation experience, but who also appreciate San Juan's cosmopolitan charms, will find some of Puerto Rico's best resorts within an hour's drive of San Juan. In Río Grande, there's the Río Mar Beach Resort and Spa, a Wyndham Grand Resort, and the Gran Mélia Golf Resort & Villas.

To the west, there are two vacation and golf clubs operating out of the grand old facilities of the former Hyatt resorts on a breathtaking oceanfront coconut plantation. Plans are underway to develop two new ultraluxury resorts on the property. Dorado has many other lodging options, such as the Embassy Suites Dorado Del Mar Beach & Golf Resort. Its stunning setting and facilities (including a Chi Chi Rodríguez Golf Course) live up to its resort billing.

Also, road improvements have cut the travel time from San Juan to other destinations and resorts covered in subsequent chapters. For example, you can get from San Juan to Fajardo and its mammoth El Conquistador Resort & Golden Door Spa in 45 minutes. Even the sprawling Palmas del Mar vacation community, with hotels, luxury villas, and vacation homes, approaches the 1-hour day trip test. While it's halfway down Puerto Rico's East Coast, it's accessible through two major highways. And Ponce is now a 90-minute drive, making it possible to visit the city in the morning, hit the beach in Guánica for 3 hours, and return to San Juan in the early evening.

Many of Puerto Rico's must-see sites lie much closer to San Juan, however. A bit more than an hour west of San Juan is the world's largest radar/radio-telescope, **Arecibo Observatory.** After touring this awesome facility, you can travel west to nearby **Río Camuy Cave Park,** for a good look at marvels below ground. Here you can plunge deep into the subterranean beauty of a spectacular cave system carved over eons by one of the world's largest underground rivers. The caves are part of a wider natural wonderland known as Karst Country, which you can also further explore, as well as an adjacent section of the central mountains laced with beautiful lakes.

Just 35 miles (56km) east of San Juan is El Yunque National Forest, the only tropical rainforest in the U.S. National Park System. Named by the Spanish for its anvil-shaped peak, **El Yunque** receives more than 100 billion gallons of rainfall annually. If you have time for only one side trip, this is the one to take. Waterfalls, wild orchids, giant ferns, towering tabonuco trees, and sierra palms make El Yunque a photographer's and hiker's paradise. Pick up a map and choose from dozens of trails graded by difficulty, including El Yunque's most challenging—the 6-mile (9.7km) El Toro Trail to the peak. The best one is probably the hike to La Mina Falls, a 45-minute walk through plush jungle, with interpretative nature signs explaining the foliage along the way. The trail ends at a beautiful spot where waterfalls crash into a wondrous natural pool in the mountain stream below. At El Yunque is El Portal Tropical Center, with 10,000 square feet (929 sq. m) of exhibit space, plazas, and patios. This facility greatly expands the recreational and educational programs available to visitors. La Coca Falls and an observation tower are just off Rte. 191.

Visitors can combine a morning trip to El Yunque with an afternoon of swimming and sunning on tranquil **Luquillo Beach.** Soft white sand, shaded by coconut palms and the blue sea, makes this Puerto Rico's best and best-known beach. Plan on having lunch, sampling local delicacies at a group of food kiosks right beside the public beach.

Fajardo, and its beautiful Caribbean coast, is about 15 minutes farther east. As noted previously, sailing and snorkeling trips off Fajardo are an easy day trip from San Juan through one of the luxury catamaran outfits that include transportation to and from San Juan area hotels (see chapter 6). Or you could visit undeveloped stretches of Fajardo beachfront, around **Las Cabezas de San Juan** nature reserve and **Seven Seas public beach** on your own (see chapter 10).

Many visitors overlook trips to San Juan suburbs in the capital's backyard. Bayamón has a great science park and zoo, while Guyanabo has an interesting sports museum and Caguas a sprawling skate park and entertainment complex, and a botanical and cultural garden.

Central mountain towns, such as Cayey and Aibonito, are also accessible by day trips from the capital. Having a lunch of roast pork and other Puerto Rican delicacies and breathing in the clean mountain air is reason enough for a drive from the capital. A favorite spot is **Guavate,** a 45-minute drive south, where open-air barbecue restaurants are lined along a country road with a mountain stream of the Carite Forest as a backdrop.

EL YUNQUE ★★★

25 miles (40km) E of San Juan

The El Yunque rainforest, a 45-minute drive east of San Juan, is a major attraction in Puerto Rico. The El Yunque National Forest is the only tropical forest in the U.S.

National Forest Service system. The 28,000-acre (11,331-hectare) preserve was given its status by President Theodore Roosevelt. Today the virgin forest remains much as it was in 1493, when Columbus first sighted Puerto Rico.

Getting There

From San Juan, take Rte. 26 or the Baldorioty de Castro Expressway east to Carolina, where you will pick up Rte. 66 or the Roberto Sánchez Vilella Expressway. The $1.50 toll road will take you farther along Rte. 3, putting you in Canóvanas. Go right, east, on Rte. 3, which you follow east to the intersection of Rte. 191, a two-lane highway that heads south into the forest. Take 191 for 3 miles (4.8km), going through the village of Palmer. As the road rises, you will have entered the Caribbean National Forest. You can stop in at the El Portal Tropical Forest Center to pick up information (see below).

Visitor Information

El Portal Tropical Forest Center, Rte. 191, Río Grande (© **787/888-1880**), an $18-million exhibition and information center, has 10,000 square feet (929 sq. m) of exhibition space. Three pavilions offer exhibits and bilingual displays. The actor Jimmy Smits narrates a documentary called "Understanding the Forest." The center is open daily from 9am to 5pm; it charges an admission of $3 for adults and $1.50 for children under 12.

El Yunque is the most popular spot in Puerto Rico for hiking; for a description of our favorite trails, see "Hiking Trails" below. Hikers will find useful information at any of the park's visitor information centers or at the **El Yunque Catalina Field Office,** near the village of Palmer, beside the main highway at the forest's northern edge (© **787/888-1880**). The staff can provide material about hiking routes, and, with 10 days' notice, help you plan overnight tours in the forest. If you reserve in advance, the staff will also arrange for you to take part in 2-hour group tours. These tours are conducted Saturday to Monday every hour on the hour from 10:30am to 3:30pm; they cost $5 for adults and $3 for children 12 and under.

Exploring El Yunque

Encompassing four distinct forest types, El Yunque is home to 240 species of tropical trees, flowers, and wildlife. More than 20 kinds of orchids and 50 varieties of ferns share this diverse habitat with millions of tiny tree frogs, whose distinctive cry of *coquí* (pronounced "ko-*kee*") has given them their name. Tropical birds include the lively, greenish blue, red-fronted Puerto Rican parrot, once nearly extinct and now making a comeback. Other rare animals include the Puerto Rican boa, which grows to 7 feet (2.1m). (It is highly unlikely that you will encounter a boa. The few people who have are still shouting about it.)

El Yunque is the best of Puerto Rico's 20 forest preserves. The forest is situated high above sea level, with El Toro its highest peak. You can be fairly sure you'll be showered upon during your visit, as more than 100 billion gallons of rain fall here annually. However, the showers are brief, and there are many shelters. On a quickie tour, many visitors reserve only a half-day for El Yunque. But we think it's unique and deserves at least a daylong outing.

HIKING TRAILS The best hiking trails in El Yunque have been carefully marked by the forest rangers. Our favorite, which takes 2 hours for the round-trip jaunt, is called **La Mina & Big Tree Trail,** and it is actually two trails combined. The La Mina Trail is paved and signposted. It begins at the picnic center adjacent to the visitor center and runs parallel to La Mina River. It is named for gold once discovered on the site. At La Mina Falls, there is a great waterfall and natural pool where you should take a dip. The mountain stream seems freezing at first, but becomes absolutely refreshing nearly instantaneously. Beyond the falls, the Big Tree Trail begins (also signposted). It winds a route through the towering trees of Tabonuco Forest until it approaches Rte. 191. Along the trail you might spot such native birds as the Puerto Rican woodpecker, the tanager, the screech owl, and the bullfinch.

Those with more time might opt for the **El Yunque Trail,** which takes 4 hours round-trip to traverse. This trail—signposted from El Caimitillo Picnic Grounds—takes you on a steep, winding path. Along the way you pass natural forests of sierra palm and *palo colorado* before descending into the dwarf forest of Mount Britton, which is often shrouded in clouds. Your major goal, at least for panoramic views, will be the lookout peaks of Roca Marcas, Yunque Rock, and Los Picachos. On a bright, clear day, you can see all the way to the eastern shores of the Atlantic.

DRIVING THROUGH EL YUNQUE If you're not a hiker but you appreciate rainforests, you can still enjoy El Yunque. You can drive through the forest on Rte. 191, which is a tarmac road. This trail goes from the main highway of Rte. 3, penetrating deep into El Yunque. You can see ferns that grow some 120 feet (37m) tall, and, at any minute, you might expect a hungry dinosaur to peek between the fronds, looking for a snack. You're also treated to lookout towers offering panoramic views, waterfalls, picnic areas, and even a restaurant.

Where to Stay

Ceiba Country Inn If you're looking for an escape from the hustle and bustle of everyday life, this is the place for you. This small, well-maintained bed-and-breakfast is located on the easternmost part of Puerto Rico (you must rent a car to reach this little haven in the mountains). El Yunque is only 15 miles (24km) away, and San Juan is 40 miles (64km) to the west. The rooms are on the bottom floor of a large, old family home, and each has a private shower-only bathroom. They are decorated in a tropical motif. There's a bar with a television, free Wi-Fi in the lounge and in the Spanish patio and a library.

Rd. no. 977, Km 1.2 (P.O. Box 1067), Ceiba, PR 00735. ✆ **888/560-2816** or 787/885-0471. Fax 787/885-0471. 9 units (all shower only). $85–$125 double. Rate includes breakfast. AE, DISC, MC, V. Free parking. **Amenities:** Bar (guests only); patio for outdoor entertainment. *In room:* A/C, fridge, ceiling fan.

El Yunque Rainforest Inn 🎁 The Inn serves healthy breakfasts, has a great library with books and movies, a Wi-Fi connection and house computer. You'll breath in fresh air, and really relax. The Lost Machete Trail is a challenging hike through the Inn's 5-acre rainforest plot, descending down along a jungle stream to a beautiful waterfall. This is private property in the midst of the federal rainforest reserve, so you will likely encounter very few people, if anyone at all. There are also massage and other spa services. El Yunque Caribbean National Forest surrounds the property, so you are at a perfect vantage point to explore. There are only three lodging options. The Chalet is a two-bedroom suite, $135; the Villa has an elegant lodge feel (complete with a fireplace) and is the nicer of the offerings for couples at $165. The management also offers a $425 villa that sleeps four and up and has a pool. Upon reserving,

Attractions Near San Juan

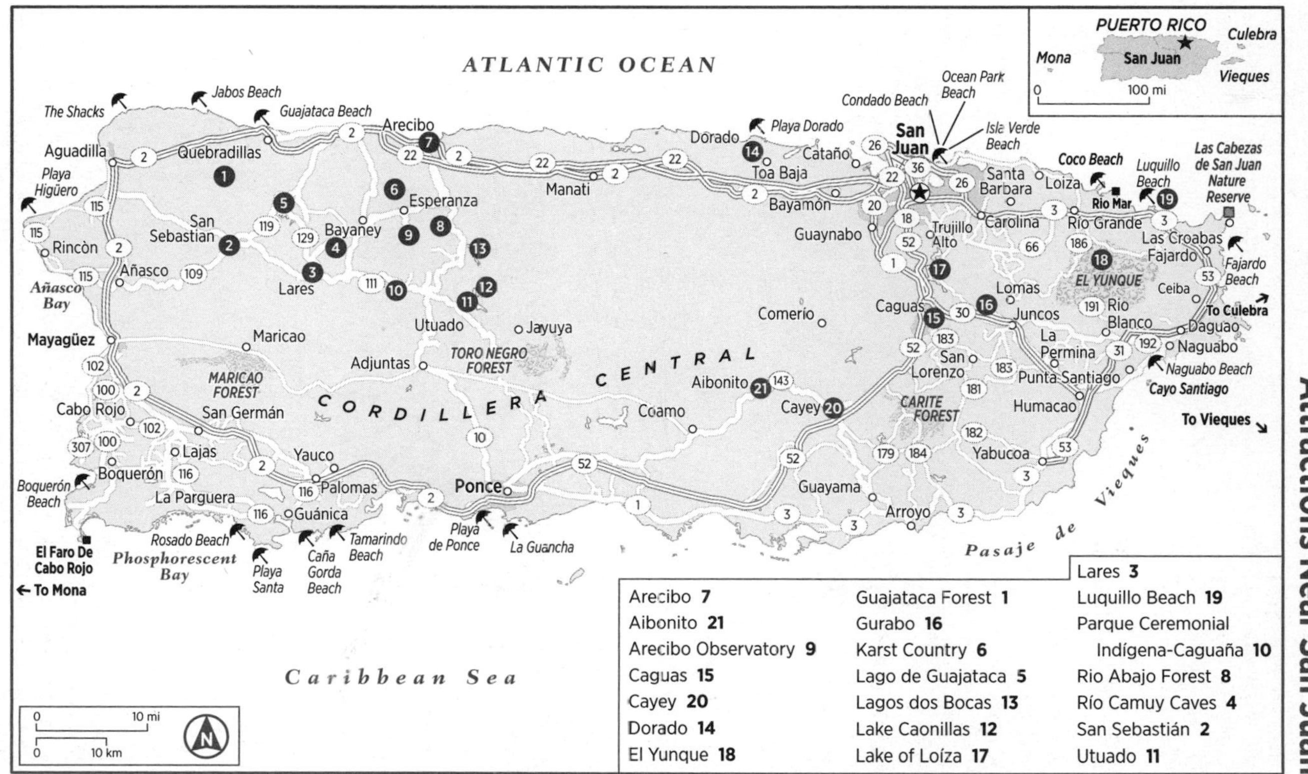

you'll get explicit directions e-mailed to you, but from Hwy. 3, take the exit for Rte. 956, which is before the Palmer exit that you take for the forest reserve. Follow signs for Galateo. Turn right on Rd. 186. The inn is on your right.

Rd. no. 186 (P.O. Box 2087), Río Grande, PR 00745. ✆ **888/560-2816** or 787/809-8426 or 800/672-4992. Fax 787/885-0471. www.rainforestinn.com 3 villas. $135–$425 depending on villa. Rate includes breakfast. AE, DISC, MC, V. Free parking. **Amenities:** Bar (guests only); patio for outdoor entertainment. *In room:* A/C, fridge, ceiling fan.

LUQUILLO BEACH ★★★

31 miles (50km) E of San Juan

Luquillo Beach is the island's best and most popular public stretch of sand. From here, you can easily explore El Yunque rainforest (see above). "Luquillo" is a Spanish adaptation of *Yukiyu,* the god believed by the Taínos to inhabit El Yunque.

Getting There

If you are driving, from San Juan, take Rte. 26 or the Baldorioty de Castro Expressway east to Carolina, where you will pick up Rte. 66 or the Roberto Sánchez Vilella Expressway. The $1.50 toll road will take you farther along Rte. 3, putting you in Canóvanas. Go right, east, on Rte. 3 into Río Grande. The entrance to El Yunque is on the right, and just beyond is the left turn to the Wyndham. The Gran Melía Puerto Rico is also off Hwy. 3.

A hotel limousine (✆ **787/888-6000**) from the San Juan airport costs $225 per carload to the Wyndham Río Mar Beach Resort and Spa. A taxi costs approximately $70. Hotel buses make trips to and from the San Juan airport, based on the arrival times of incoming flights; the cost is $28 per person, each way, for transport to El Conquistador; $25 per person, each way, to the Wyndham.

Hitting the Beach

Luquillo Beach ★★, Puerto Rico's finest beach, is palm-dotted and crescent-shaped, opening onto a lagoon with calm waters and a wide, sandy bank. It's very crowded on weekends but much better during the week. There are lockers, tent sites, showers, picnic tables, and food stands that sell a sampling of the island's *frituras* (fried fare), especially cod fritters and tacos. The beach is open from 8:30am to 5pm, Wednesday through Sunday, plus holidays.

You can also snorkel and scuba dive (see below) among the living reefs with lots of tropical fish. Offshore are coral formations and spectacular sea life—eels, octopuses, stingrays, tarpon, big puffer fish, turtles, nurse sharks, and squid, among other sea creatures.

Great Golf

The Río Grande–Fajardo area is quickly becoming the golf hot spot in Puerto Rico, which itself is known as the Ireland of the Caribbean because of the number and quality of its greens. Tom Kite and Bruce Besse designed two 18-hole courses for the **Trump International Golf Club Puerto Rico,** 100 Clubhouse Dr., Río Grande 00745 (✆ **787/657-2000**), adjacent to the well-recommended Gran Melia Puerto Rico (see below). You face a spectacular vista of fairways, lakes, and the Atlantic beyond, with two courses with their own character, which fan out from the Caribbean's largest clubhouse, which has been redone in the regal style of the Trump name. Luxury vacation villas, condominiums, and a beach club are being developed by Trump and his local partner Arturo Díaz.

The **Bahia Beach Plantation Resort and Golf Club,** Rte. 187, Km 4.2 (© **787/857-5800**), with greens fees weekdays at $225 and weekends at $275, has just undergone a renovation by Robert Trent Jones, Jr. The breathtaking 7,014-yard (6,414m) course, sprawling across some 480 acres (194 hectares) of lush beachfront, running from the tip of Loiza River to the mouth of the Espíritu Santo River, overlooks a verdant green valley of El Yunque rainforest. A new luxury St. Regis resort is being developed on the beautiful site with a planned opening in winter 2010. Jones' father, Trent Jones, Sr., designed the legendary Dorado Beach East golf course, and brother Rees Jones undertook the Palmas del Mar's Flamboyán course in 1999.

The **Wyndham's Río Mar Beach Resort** (see below) has two world-class courses that stretch out in the shadow of El Yunque rainforest along a dazzling stretch of coast. The entire 6,782 yards (6,201m) of Tom and George Fazio's Ocean Course has seaside panoramas and breezes, and fat iguanas scampering through the lush grounds. The other course, a 6,945-yard (6,351m) design by golf pro Greg Norman, follows the flow of the Mameyes River through mountain and coastal vistas. Greens fees are $165 for guests, $200 for nonresident walk-ons. **El Conquistador's** golf offerings in nearby Fajardo are also well regarded (see chapter 10).

Scuba Diving & Snorkeling

The best people to take you diving are at the **Dive Center** at the Wyndham Rio Mar Beach Resort (© **787/888-6000**). This is one of the largest dive centers in Puerto Rico, a PADI five-star facility with two custom-designed boats that usually take no more than 6 to 10 divers. Snorkeling and skin diving costs $75 for a half-day. The center also offers a full-day snorkeling trip, including lunch and drinks, for $95 per person. Boat tours are available daily from 9am to 4pm. For scuba divers, a two-tank dive costs $135 to $185. **Atlantica Diving Tours** at Gran Melia Puerto Rico (© **787/420-3483**) has a full diving and snorkeling program, with trips and lessons for all ages and skill levels. A full day diving trip to Culebra is $185; there are also courses for children.

Sports & Adventure

Hacienda Carabalí, Road 992, Km 4, Luquillo, (© **787/889-5820** or 889-4954) is a 600 acre ranch that gives horseback riding tours, mountain bike, and all terrain vehicle tours on trails running through the rainforest, along river banks and ocean coast. There's also a go-kart track and restaurant with entertainment. Soar through the rainforest with the folks from **Yunque Zipline Adventure** (© **787/242-3368**), a fabulous, fun 3-hour tour costing $99 per person. The course is beautiful and includes the island's longest zip-line at 850 feet or 259 meters. The tour also involves rappelling, so a moderate degree of physical fitness is required.

Where to Stay

Gran Melía Puerto Rico ★★★ ☺ Checking into this pocket of posh on the Miquillo de Río Grande peninsula is the best reason for heading east of San Juan. An all-suite luxury resort, it has set new standards for comfort, convenience, and amenities along the Atlantic northeastern shoreline. Set amid gardens of 40 acres (16 hectares), it opens onto the white sands of the mile-long (1.6km) shoreline of Coco Beach. From watersports to two 18-hole golf courses, the resort has everything on-site, including whirlpool baths and massage tables. Spa treatments revitalize and rejuvenate.

You can also wander the globe in the widely varied restaurants, ranging from Italian to Southeast Asian. Naturally, the chefs also prepare locally caught seafood imbued with Creole flavor. One restaurant serves only Caribbean and Puerto Rican cuisine, whereas another offers its take on contemporary California. Yet another serves teppanyaki dinners with an adjoining sushi bar.

Melía ditched the original all-inclusive concept and reopened emphasizing the resort's luxury, golf, spa, and other top-flight amenities. Royal Service entitles guests to continental breakfast, evening drinks and hors d'oeuvres, use of a private lounge, and other benefits. Bedrooms and suites are spacious and furnished luxuriously. The signature suites are divided among 20 elegant two-story bungalows. Rich mahogany pieces and elegant fabrics are used throughout. If you can afford it, opt for a Royal Service Suite; some even have a private Jacuzzi facing the Atlantic. The marble bathrooms are sumptuous.

There's a lot to do here. The world-class golf courses are adjacent to the property at the **Trump International Golf Club Puerto Rico,** there's a full-service spa, a slew of watersports possibilities, and a Kids Club that will keep your young ones happy and busy. The staff is great at organizing water polo and beach volleyball games, and you can take salsa and merengue dancing lessons by the pool. It's a big reason why this resort is a cut above some competitors, and why you will have so much fun here. We're still talking about our stunning, come-from-behind beach volleyball victory nearly a year later.

Coco Beach Blvd. 1000, Río Grande, PR 00745. ✆ **866/436-3542** or 787/809-1770. Fax 787/809-1785. www.grand-melia-puerto-rico.com. 582 units. Winter suites for 2 $180–$350, off-season suite for 2 $143–$265. AE, DISC, MC, V. **Amenities:** 6 restaurants; 3 bars; babysitting; fitness center; 2 golf courses; gym; kids' clubs; 2 outdoor pools; room service; spa; sauna; 3 lit tennis courts; smoke-free rooms; rooms for those w/limited mobility. *In room:* A/C, TV, kitchenette, minibar, hair dryer.

The Río Mar Beach Resort & Spa, a Wyndham Grand Resort ★ This is a great spot to have fun in the sun and relax, but if you're expecting roaring nightlife or a cultural experience, stay elsewhere. The resort lies between the El Yunque rainforest and the Atlantic coastline. One of its championship golf courses, designed by George and Tom Fazio, crisscrosses the dramatic coastline, while the other, by Greg Norman, winds through lush tropical forest. Watersports offerings include sailing, snorkeling, scuba, parasailing, windsurfing, kite boarding, and others. There are also other sports activities, such as volleyball and water polo, and lots for children to do, including the Iguana Club for kids and a game room. There's a kids' pool next to the adult pool, which are both right near the beach. And you can actually fulfill a Caribbean dream and go horseback riding through the rainforest and along the beach. (We highly recommend this.)

Landscaping includes several artificial lakes situated amid tropical gardens. Guest rooms either overlook the palm-lined Atlantic or the green mountains of the rainforest. The style is Spanish hacienda with nods to the surrounding jungle; unusual art and sculpture alternate with dark woods, deep colors, rounded archways, big windows, and tile floors. In the bedrooms, muted earth tones and natural woods add to the ambience. Bedrooms are spacious, with balconies or terraces, and good mattresses, plus tub/shower combinations in the large bathrooms.

The resort has ample meeting space, and the number of conventions held here is cause for complaint for some visitors. There's not much going on at night except the lobby bar and the hotel's 6,500-square-foot (604-sq.-m) casino. The restaurants include Italian, Latin American, Oriental, steak and seafood for fine-dining choices, and three different cafes. We like especially Palío, but it's on the expensive side, which is the case with most of the resort restaurants.

Río Mar Blvd. 6000, Río Grande, PR 00745. ✆ **877/636-0636** or 787/888-6000. Fax 787/888-6600. www.wyndhamriomar.com. 600 units. Winter $175–$499 double; off-season $131–$444 double; year-round from $260–$700 suite, $1,682s governor's suite. Children ages 5–17 staying in parent's room $85, including meals and activities; free for 4 and under. AE, DC, DISC, MC, V. 19 miles east of Luís Muñoz Marín International Airport, with entrance off Puerto Rico Hwy. 3. **Amenities:** 8 restaurants; 4 bars; casino; children's programs; deep-sea fishing; health club and spa; horseback riding nearby; outdoor pool; room service; sailing; 13 tennis courts; smoke-free rooms; rooms for those w/limited mobility. *In room:* A/C, TV, fridge, hair dryer, high-speed Internet access.

Where to Dine

Brass Cactus 🎁 AMERICAN/REGIONAL On a service road adjacent to Rte. 3 at the western edge of Luquillo, within a boxy-looking concrete building that's in need of repair, is one of the town's most popular bar/restaurants. Permeated with a raunchy, no-holds-barred spirit, this amiable spot has thrived since the early 1990s, when it was established by an Illinois-born bartender who outfitted the interior with gringo memorabilia. It's a great American-style pub, where you can hear rock 'n' roll or catch a game on television. Menu items include king crab salad; tricolor tortellini laced with chicken and shrimp; several kinds of sandwiches, burgers, and wraps; and platters of churrasco, T-bone steaks, chicken with tequila sauce, barbecued pork, and fried mahimahi. A second location has opened in Canóvanas along Hwy. 3 that has a children's area where they can play video games or do other activities, leaving you to eat in peace. We love the barbecue here, especially the ribs in the Jack Daniels sauce. Portions are large.

In the Condominio Complejo Turistico, Rte. 3, Marginal. ✆ **787/889-5735.** Reservations not necessary. Sandwiches $6.95–$8.95; main courses $14–$20. MC, V. Sun–Thurs 11am–11pm; Fri–Sat 11am–midnight.

Palio ★ ITALIAN This intimate, elegant, richly decorated restaurant is the perfect setting for its classic northern Italian fare, and the kitchen here cuts close to culinary tradition. Everything I've had has been satisfying: the butternut squash sage ravioli, the grilled lemon swordfish with capers, and the lamb loin, crusted with pesto and goat cheese and topped with roasted artichoke, zucchini, and tomatoes. Get a good bottle of wine and start off slow with the house antipasto. It's not over until the terrific tiramisu.

In the Wyndham Rio Mar Beach Resort and Golf Club. ✆ **787/888-6000.** Reservations recommended. Main courses $22–$52. AE, DC, MC, V. Daily 6am–11pm.

Sandy's Seafood Restaurant & Steak House ★ 🏷 SEAFOOD/STEAKS/PUERTO RICAN Huge platters of fresh, tasty seafood have made this nondescript, concrete and glass restaurant near the town square famous. Set about a block from the main square of the seaside resort of Luquillo, it was founded in 1984 by

Miguel Angel, aka Sandy. Most platters, especially the daily specials, are huge. They include fresh shellfish served on the half-shell, *asopaos,* four kinds of steak, five different preparations of chicken (including a tasty version with garlic sauce), four kinds of gumbos, paellas, a dozen preparations of lobster, and even jalapeño peppers stuffed with shrimp or lobster.

Calle Fernandez García 276. ✆ **787/889-5765.** Reservations not necessary. Main courses $8–$25; lunch special Mon–Fri 11am–2:30pm $5. AE, MC, V. Wed–Mon 11am to btw. 9:30 and 11pm, depending on business.

DORADO ★

18 miles (29km) W of San Juan

Dorado—the name itself evokes a kind of magic—is a small town with some big resorts, a world of storied luxury hotels and villas unfolding along Puerto Rico's north shore west of San Juan. For decades, the Hyatt Cerromar and Dorado Beach formed the epicenter of this stunning coastal stretch of rolling palm groves and white-sand beaches. Currently, vacation and golf clubs are operated on the former site, and there are plans to renovate the old resort buildings and reopen as a luxury resort.

The site was originally purchased in 1905 by Dr. Alfred T. Livingston, a Jamestown, New York, physician, who developed it as a 1,000-acre (405-hectare) grapefruit-and-coconut plantation. Dr. Livingston's daughter, Clara, widely known in aviation circles as a friend of Amelia Earhart, owned and operated the plantation after her father's death. It was she who built the airstrip here. In 1955, Clara Livingston sold her father's 1,700-acre (688-hectare) Hacienda Sardinera to the Rockefeller family. Her former house, now called Su Casa, which served as a golf clubhouse in the '70s and restaurant from 1982 to 2006, remains on the property. On May 31, 2006, 48 years after Laurence Rockefeller officially opened the hotel, the resorts that had made Dorado synonymous with upscale tourism closed their doors. It brought an end to a legendary resort—with a list of clients including former presidents John F. Kennedy, Dwight Eisenhower, Gerald Ford, and George H. W. Bush, as well as athletic greats Joe Namath, Mickey Mantle, and Joe DiMaggio, and actresses Joan Crawford and Ava Gardner. The golf and tennis courses are still functioning and two upscale resorts are being developed on the beautiful site.

Getting There

If you're driving from San Juan, take Expwy 22 west. Take exit 22-A to get on Rte. 165 north to Dorado. Alternately, you can take the meandering coastal route along Hwy. 2 west to Rte. 693 north to Dorado (trip time: 40 min.). You'll pass a couple interesting beaches and coastal lookouts, as well as a fine spots to eat.

Hitting the Beaches

If you take this later route, you'll want to detour down Rte. 870 in the Palo Seco area of Toa Alta. This narrow road runs through the middle of a narrow peninsula famous for the restaurants serving seafood and Puerto Rican cuisine running along it. At the end of the road is the **Parque Nacional Isla de Cabra** (Rte. 870, Toa Baja; ✆ **787/384-0542;** Wed–Sun and holidays 8:30am–5pm; parking $3), a fascinating spit of land at the mouth of San Juan Bay that has an incredible view of the Old City.

WORLD-CLASS golf AT THE FORMER HYATT DORADO

The Hyatt Dorado Beach and Cerromar closed their doors in May 2006, but luckily their world-class golf courses and country club are still open and a limited number of vacation rentals are available (see below). The former **Dorado Beach resort's professional golf courses ★★**, designed by Robert Trent Jones, Sr., match the finest anywhere. They are now operated by the **Dorado Beach Resort & Club.** The two original courses, known as East and West, were carved out of a jungle and offer tight fairways bordered by trees and forests, with lots of ocean holes. His son, Robert Trent Jones, Jr., will oversee a renovation of the East course in 2010, followed by the West course. The somewhat newer and less noted Sugarcane and Pineapple courses, now called the Plantation Club, feature wide fairways with well-bunkered greens and an assortment of water traps and tricky wind factors. Each is a par-72 course (call ✆ **787/796-8961** or 626-1006, the Dorado Beach Pro Shop, for tee times). The longest is 7,047 yards (6,444m). On the Pineapple and Sugarcane courses, regular green fees are $135 and on the East and West courses they rise to $195. Both are open daily from 7am until dusk. Golf carts are included for all courses, and the two pro shops have both a bar and snack-style restaurant. There are plenty of opportunities for a post-game meal in Dorado afterwards, including the restaurant right on site Zafra (call ✆ **787/796-8999** for either). ***Tip:*** Ask about rates for game play that starts after 1:30pm, which is sometimes marked down significantly. Two resorts under development on the property will open under the Ritz and Fairmont flags.

The water here is not great for swimming, but there are play areas and green picnic areas with great views. There are also small restaurants and bars, everywhere a great coastal view and the whole area with great breezes. The area was a former leper colony built by the Spanish and then was a shooting range and training area for many decades for the police. There is a small fort within the park called **El Cañuelo** that was built to protect the entrance of the Bayamón River and back up the much larger El Morro across the bay, by providing crossfire to invading ships. This is a favorite picnic area for Sundays and a good spot to ride a bike or fly a kite.

There are also a few fine bathing beaches along this route before getting to Dorado. The best is probably **Cerro Gordo** public beach (Rte. 690, Vega Alta; ✆ **787/883-2730**), along with the **Manuel "Nolo" Morales** public beach along Dorado's "Costa del Oro," or "Gold Coast" (✆ **787/796-2830**). Both charge $3 per car parking fee and keep the same hours as other public beaches and parks, Wednesday through Sunday and holidays, 8:30am to 5pm.

Where to Stay

Dorado's lodging options were severely limited when the two Hyatt properties shut their doors, but staying at the former Hyatt resort is still possible, and the Embassy Suites property is a unique, all-suites resort with great facilities.

Embassy Suites Dorado del Mar Beach & Golf Resort ★ This beachfront property in Dorado lies less than 2 miles (3.2km) from the center of Dorado and within easy access from the San Juan airport. It is the only all-suite resort in Puerto Rico, and it has been a success since its opening in 2001. The property offers two-room suites with balconies and 38 two-bedroom condos.

The suites are spread over seven floors, each spacious and furnished in a Caribbean tropical motif, with artwork and one king-size bed or two double beds. Most of them have ocean views of the water. Each condo has a living room, kitchen, whirlpool, and balcony.

Although the accommodations are suites or condos, one bedroom in a condo can be rented as a double room (the rest of the condo is shut off). Likewise, it's also possible for two people to rent one bedroom in a condo, with the living room and kitchen facilities available (the other bedroom is closed off). Because condos contain two bedrooms, most of them are rented to parties of four.

The hotel attracts many families because of its very spacious accommodations. It also attracts golfers because of its Chi Chi Rodriguez signature par-72, 18-hole golf course set against a panoramic backdrop of mountains and ocean.

Dorado del Mar Blvd. 210, Dorado, PR 00646. ✆ **787/796-6125.** Fax 787/796-6145. www.embassysuitesdorado.com. 212 units. Year-round $160–$250 suite; $260–$485 1-bedroom villa; $360–$560 2-bedroom villa. AE, DC, DISC, MC, V. **Amenities:** 2 restaurants; bar and grill; golf; pool; room service; massage; tennis court; rooms for those w/limited mobility. *In room:* A/C, TV, hair dryer, kitchenette, wet bar.

Where to Dine

El Vigia 🎁 PUERTO RICAN En route to Dorado from San Juan, stop by this down-to-earth restaurant with a great ocean view. It's the first restaurant on the main road into Isla de Cabras, which is lined with similar establishments, so you can try your luck further on as well. This unpretentious place serves great seafood and Puerto Rican cuisine. On nice days you can eat on a wooden deck with the waves crashing against the rocks below. There are about 50 different items—plenty of seafood, steaks, and Puerto Rican food—on the menu. You can't go wrong with the *mofongo* stuffed with stewed conch or shrimp, or the mixed seafood Puerto Rican stew, *asopao*. There's also a delicious surf and turf, with a filet mignon and lobster tail. I love the red snapper Creole style, which is in a light, sweet tomato sauce. There are plenty of nonseafood dishes, a mix of Puerto Rican and American fare. The house sangria is tasty and has a kick.

Calle Principal, Entrance Isla de Cabras. ✆ **787/788-5000.** Main courses $11–$40. AE, MC, V. Daily 11am–10pm.

Zafra Restaurant NEW WORLD CUISINE The main dining room and veranda overlook the lush valley surrounding the Plantation Clubhouse and the mountains looming in the distance over its surrounding greens. From the cassava-crusted salmon over tomato pepper salsa to the classic Paella Valenciana to the beef and lobster in béarnaise, I love this menu. It's a great spot for lunch on a drive out west, or a good meal after a round of golf.

Dorado Beach Resort & Club, 100 Dorado Beach Drive, Ste. 1, Dorado. ✆ **787/626-1025.** Main courses $24–$39. AE, MC, V. Daily 11:30am–4pm; Fri–Sat 6:30–9:30pm; bar menu available from 11am–11pm Sun–Thurs.

ARECIBO & CAMUY ★

68 to 77 miles (109–124km) W of San Juan

Getting There

Arecibo Observatory lies a 1¼-hour drive west of San Juan, outside the town of Arecibo. From San Juan head west along four-lane Rte. 22 until you reach the town of Arecibo. At Arecibo, head south on Rte. 10; the 20-mile (32km) drive south on this four-lane highway is almost as interesting as the observatory itself. From Rte. 10, take exit 75-B and follow the signposts along a roller-coaster journey on narrow two-lane roads. First you will go right on Rte. 652 and take a left on Rte. 651. Proceed straight through the intersection of Rte. 651 and Rte. 635, and then turn left at the cemetery onto Rte. 625, which will lead you to the entrance of the observatory.

On the same day you visit the Arecibo Observatory, you can also visit the Río Camuy Cave Park. The caves also lie south of the town of Arecibo. Follow Rte. 129 southwest from Arecibo to the entrance of the caves, which are at Km 18.9 along the route, north of the town of Lares. Like the observatory, the caves lie approximately 1½ hours west of San Juan.

Exploring the Area

To get to the **Observatorio de Arecibo,** take Expwy PR 22 heading east. Take Rte. 129 south toward Utuado. Go left on Calle 1 and take a right on Rte. 651. At Rte. 635, take a left, and then go left on Rte. 625, which you will follow to the entrance of the observatory.

Dubbed "an ear to heaven," **Observatorio de Arecibo ★★** (**© 787/878-2612;** www.naic.edu) contains the world's largest and most sensitive radar/radio-telescope. The telescope features a 20-acre (8-hectare) dish, or radio mirror, set in an ancient sinkhole. It's 1,000 feet (305m) in diameter and 167 feet (51m) deep, and it allows scientists to monitor natural radio emissions from distant galaxies, pulsars, and quasars, and to examine the ionosphere, the planets, and the moon using powerful radar signals. Used by scientists as part of the Search for Extraterrestrial Intelligence (SETI), this is the same site featured in the movie *Contact* with Jodie Foster. This research effort speculates that advanced civilizations elsewhere in the universe might also communicate via radio waves. The 10-year, $100-million search for life in space was launched on October 12, 1992, the 500-year anniversary of Columbus's arrival on the shores of the New World.

Unusually lush vegetation flourishes under the giant dish, including ferns, wild orchids, and begonias. Assorted creatures, such as mongooses, lizards, and dragonflies, have also taken refuge there. Suspended in an outlandish fashion above the dish is a 600-ton (544,311kg) platform that resembles a space station. This is not a site where you'll be launched into a Star Wars journey through the universe. You are allowed to walk around the platform, taking in views of this gigantic dish. At the Angel Ramos Foundation Visitor Center, you are treated to interactive exhibitions on the various planetary systems and introduced to the mystery of meteors and educated about intriguing weather phenomena. Tours are available at the observatory Wednesday through Friday from noon to 4pm, Saturday and Sunday from 9am to 4pm. There's a souvenir shop on the grounds. Plan to spend about 1½ hours at the observatory (Rte. 625 final, Arecibo; ✆ **787/878-2612;** www.naic.edu; Wed–Sun 9am–4pm; admission $5 adults, $3 seniors and children).

Parque de las Cavernas del Río Camuy (Río Camuy Caves) ★★ (✆ **787/898-3100**) contains the third-largest underground river in the world. It runs through a network of caves, canyons, and sinkholes that have been cut through the island's limestone base over the course of millions of years. Known to the pre-Columbian Taíno peoples, the caves came to the attention of speleologists in the 1950s; they were led to the site by local boys already familiar with some of the entrances to the system. The caves were opened to the public in 1986. You need at least 2 hours for an adequate experience, but the more adventurous can take full-day tours exploring a part of the mysterious world with private tour operators.

Today, visitors explore most sites via the park trolley: a 200-foot-deep (61m) sinkhole, a chasm containing a tropical forest, complete with birds and butterflies and a huge water fall, and the entrance of Cueva Clare, the park's premiere cave, a 45-minute odyssey through a fascinating underworld of stalactites and sculpted cavern walls. Tres Pueblos Sinkhole is 65 feet (20m) wide and 400 feet (122 m) deep; it's named for its location at the border of the towns of Camuy, Hatillo, and Lares (north at Km 2 on Rte. 129, from Rte. 111; ✆ **787/898-3100;** Wed–Sun and holidays 8:30am–5pm; admission $12 adults, $7 children 4–12, $5 seniors; parking $3).

Back down in Arecibo, a fun and interesting stop, especially if you are traveling with children, is the **Arecibo Lighthouse & Historic Park** (Hwy. 655, El Muelle, Barrio Islote, Arecibo; ✆ **787/880-7540;** www.arecibolighthouse.com). Housed in a lighthouse built by the Spanish in 1898, this "cultural theme park" takes visitors on a history tour of Puerto Rico. But it's a very tactile tour, where you can actually walk through many of the exhibits. It really hits kids; it hit the kid in us. The slave quarters were riveting, the mammoth pirate ship was thrilling, and then there was the pirate's cave, with its alligators and sharks. Bring sun block, hats, and comfortable shoes and clothes. Tickets are $10 adults, and $8 children and seniors. The park is open 9am to 6pm weekdays and holidays and 10am to 7pm weekends. Parking costs $2.

Where to Dine

If you want to eat before heading back to the city, Arecibo is a good place, with several fine restaurants. The hands-down best, however, is the nearby **Salitre Mesón Costero** (Rte. 681, Km 3.8, Barrio Islote, Arecibo; ✆ **787/816-2020**). You can taste the salt of the sea in the breeze blowing through this charming oceanfront restaurant's terrace dining area and in the smacking fresh seafood served here. The dining room has big windows overlooking the coast and there's also a comfortable bar. This is a great place to watch the sunset. The house specialty, a kind of *criolla* version of the classic Spanish seafood paella, called *mamposteado de mariscos,* has mussels; shrimp; and freshly caught fish, octopus, or calamari. Its seafood-stuffed *mofongo* platters and the whole red snapper with *tostones* are hard to beat, but the mahimahi in parcha sauce came close.

KARST COUNTRY ★★

One of the most interesting areas of Puerto Rico is the large **Karst Country,** south of Arecibo. This other-worldly group of rock formations were created by the process of water sinking into limestone. As time goes by, larger and larger basins are eroded, forming sinkholes. *Mogotes* (karstic hillocks) are peaks of earth where the land didn't sink into the erosion pits. The Karst Country lies along the island's north coast, directly northeast of Mayagüez in the foothills between Quebradillas and Manatí. The region is filled with an extensive network of caves. The world's largest radio/radar telescope dish, the 20-acre (8-hectare) Arecibo Observatory (see above), rests within one of these sinkholes.

South of the Karst Country looms the massive central mountain region and Utuado at the heart of the massive Cordillera Central mountain range, which rides the island's back from east to west like an elevated spine.

The Karst Country area was deforested in the late 1940s; alluvial valleys and sinkholes were then used for pastures, shifting cultivation, and coffee plantations. In this region, most of the coffee sites were abandoned in the 1960s, and today most of these sites are covered with secondary forests. The recovery of these forests has been very rapid because of a close seed source—trees left on the steep slopes—and the presence of large populations of dispersers, mainly bats.

Getting There

The only way to explore the Karst Country, which is easy to reach from San Juan, is by car. Leave San Juan on the four-lane highway, Rte. 22, until you come to the town of Arecibo, a 1½-hour drive, depending on traffic. Once at Arecibo, take Rte. 10 south, in the direction of Utuado.

If you'd like a specific goal for exploring in the Karst Country, visit the Arecibo Observatory and the Río Camuy Caves, previewed above. However, you can also spend a day driving at random, exploring lakes and forests at your leisure. If you decide to go this route, make the commercial town of **Arecibo** your base. Although not of tourist interest itself, it is the capital of the Karst Country and the starting point from which you can drive south along many interesting and winding roads.

From Arecibo, you can take Rte. 10 south in the direction of Utuado (see "Central Mountains," below), which serves as the southern border to Karst Country. Along the way, you'll pass **Lagos dos Bocas ★**, one of the most beautiful lakes of the Karst Country, and this is a reservoir adjacent to the Río Abajo Forest. Lagos dos Bocas, which lies 12 miles (19km) south of Arecibo, is in the mountains of Cordillera Central. Along with a nearby lake, **Lake Caonillas,** it is the main source of water for the North Coast Superaqueduct, which provides water for north coast towns stretching from Arecibo to San Juan.

Take time out at Lagos dos Bocas to ride one of the free government-operated **launches ★** that traverse the lake. Established as a taxi service for residents of the area, these launches can be used by sightseers as well. The launches leave from a dock along Rte. 123 on the west side of the lake, with departures scheduled every

Get a Good Map

Arm yourself with the most detailed map you can find at one of the bookstores in San Juan. The free maps dispensed by the tourist office are not sufficiently detailed and do not show the tiny secondary roads you'll need to traverse for a motor tour of the Karst Country.

hour unless the weather is bad. It's a 30-minute ride across the lake to the other main dock. On weekends, modest wooden restaurants around the lake open to serve visitors, and the launch makes stops at them. Most have tasty snacks, fried turnovers and the like, and cold drinks. Rancho Marina is good for a typical Puerto Rican country lunch. The launch will take you back to your car, and then you can continue your journey.

You can head back down to Arecibo, and then take the expressway back to San Juan.

CENTRAL MOUNTAINS ★

Utuado marks the southern border of Karst Country. It's a municipality at the dead center of the island that sprawls across the spine of the Cordillera Central mountain range. To experience the island's central mountains, continue driving up into the mountains above Lago Dos Bocas. After about 20 minutes you'll reach the **Casa Grande Mountain Retreat** (p. 210), which is open from 5 to 8:30pm weekdays and 3 to 8:30pm on weekends. This establishment, a guesthouse and restaurant, serves upscale *comida criolla*–inspired dishes with vegetarian options. Café Casa Grande spills from a dining room and patio to a veranda overlooking a lush mountain valley. But you may want to spend the night if you dine too late. The property is reached via curving country roads, which can be tough to handle at night.

This is Utuado, a good base in the Cordillera Central massif overlooking the heartland of karst. Utuado is a stronghold of *jíbaro* (country folk) culture, reflecting the mountain life of the island as few other settlements do.

Just south of here you'll hook up again with Rte. 111 going west to Lares. You'll almost immediately come to **Parque Ceremonial Indígena Caguaña (Indian Ceremonial Park at Caguaña).** The site is signposted and need not take up more than 30 minutes of your time. Built by the Taíno Indians some 1,000 years ago, the site was used for both recreation and worship, and it is encircled by mountains near the Tanama River. You can still see the outlines of the ancient *bateyes* (ball courts), which are bordered by carved stone monoliths decorated with petroglyphs (see "Life After Death: Taíno Burial & Ceremonial Sites," below). The best-known petroglyph is the much-photographed *Mujer de Caguaña,* a figure squatting in the position of an earth-mother fertility symbol. There is a small and very minor museum of Indian artifacts and skeletons on-site. The site is open daily from 8am to 4pm. Admission free. For more information, call ✆ **787/894-7300** (Rte. 111, Km 12.3).

From Lares, take Rte. 129 south to return to Arecibo, a good spot for a meal before taking the expressway back to San Juan (p. 95).

Where to Stay

Casa Grande Mountain Retreat This parador, situated on 107 lush and steeply inclined acres (43 hectares) of a former coffee plantation in the Caonillas Barrios district, about 1½ hours from San Juan, originated in the 19th century as a hacienda. Thanks to Steve Weingarten, a retired lawyer from New York City, the isolated compound functions today as a simple, eco-sensitive hotel. The cement-sided core of the original hacienda is on view in the lobby and in the likable eatery, which serves an array of well-prepared international and Puerto Rican Creole-style dishes. Eat in the inside dining, patio, and on the veranda. Open for breakfast, lunch, and dinner. Nonguests can eat here daily from 7:30am to 9:30pm.

LIFE AFTER DEATH: TAÍNO BURIAL & CEREMONIAL sites

The **Taíno Indians** who lived in Puerto Rico before Europeans came here were ruled by *caciques,* or chiefs, who controlled their own villages and several others nearby. The Taínos believed in life after death, which led them to take extreme care in burying their dead. Personal belongings of the deceased were placed in the tomb with the newly dead, and bodies were carefully arranged in a squatting position. Near Ponce, visitors can see the oldest known Indian burial ground in the Antilles, the **Tibes Indian Ceremonial Center** (p. 220).

Even at the time of the arrival of Columbus and the conquistadores who followed, the Taínos were threatened by the warlike and cannibalistic Carib Indians coming up from the south. But though they feared the Caribs, they learned to fear the conquistadores even more. Within 50 years of the Spanish colonization, the Taíno culture had virtually disappeared, the Indians annihilated through either massacres or European diseases.

But Taíno blood and remnants of their culture live on. The Indians married with Spaniards and Africans, and their physical characteristics—straight hair, copper-colored skin, and prominent cheekbones—can still be seen in some Puerto Ricans today. Many Taíno words became part of the Spanish language that's spoken on the island even today. Hammocks, the weaving of baskets, and the use of gourds as eating receptacles are part of the heritage left by these ill-fated tribes.

Still standing near Utuado, a small mountain town, **Parque Ceremonial Indígena-Caguaña (Indian Ceremonial Park at Caguaña),** Rte. 111, Km 12.3 (✆ **787/894-7325**), was built by the Taínos for recreation and worship some 800 years ago. Stone monoliths, some etched with petroglyphs, rim several of the 10 *bateyes* (playing fields) used for a ceremonial game that some historians believe was a forerunner to soccer. The monoliths and petroglyphs, as well as the *dujos* (ceremonial chairs), are extant examples of the Taínos' skill in carving wood and stone.

Archaeologists have dated this site to approximately 2 centuries before Europe's discovery of the New World. It is believed that the Taíno chief Guarionex gathered his subjects on this site to celebrate rituals and practice sports. Set on a 13-acre (5.3-hectare) field surrounded by trees, some 14 vertical monoliths with colorful petroglyphs are arranged around a central sacrificial stone monument. The ball complex also includes a museum, which is open daily from 8:30am to 4pm; admission is $2, free for children under 2.

There is also a gallery called Herencia Indígena, where you can purchase Taíno relics at reasonable prices, including the sought-after *Cemis* (Taíno idols) and figures of the famous little frog, the *coquí.* The Taínos are long gone, and much that was here is gone, too. This site is of special interest to those with academic pursuits, but of only passing interest to the lay visitor.

Accommodations lie within five wood-sided cottages (four units to a cottage, some of them duplex) scattered throughout the surrounding acreage. Each unit has deliberately simple, spartan-looking decor with exposed wood, airy verandas, a balcony, hammock, view of the mountains, and a small bathroom with shower. None has TV, phone, or air-conditioning—as such, they're popular with urbanites who want to get back to nature, and some come here to brush up on yoga and meditation skills. A nature trail is carved out of the surrounding forest. Under separate management, a riding stable offers horseback riding a short distance away.

P.O. Box 1499, Utuado, PR 00641. ✆ **888/343-2272** or 787/894-3900. Fax 787/894-3900. www.hotelcasagrande.com. 20 units. Year-round $95–$115 double. AE, DISC, MC, V. From Arecibo, take Rte. 10 south to Utuado, then head east on Rte. 111 to Rte. 140; head north on Rte. 140 to Rte. 612 for ¼ mile (.4km). **Amenities:** Restaurant; bar; pool. *In room:* Ceiling fan, no phone.

The Southern Route to the Mountains

A much easier way to the central mountains from San Juan is to head south along the Luis A. Ferré Expressway, Hwy. 52, to **Cayey** and even farther up to **Aibonito.** You can take an afternoon drive and have dinner as the sun sets in the mountains; from some vantage points, the view goes all the way to the coast.

In fact, this path is well worn by *sanjuaneros* heading south with mountain air and food on their minds. Their first stop is usually **Guavate.** Take the exit for Rte. 184, which winds through rolling farmland and farther up along a mountain stream flowing through the lush **Carite State Forest.** In addition to the eateries, the sector is famous for local arts and crafts and plants and flowers that are sold from stands along the roadway. While the area began gaining fame years ago for a cluster of restaurants outside the natural reserve's main entrance, the string of *lechoneras* has now extended along the entire route from the expressway. Indeed, **Los Amigos,** at the Expressway exit, is for those who want to dive in to the genuine experience, and make a quick escape. (On Sun afternoons, especially around Christmas season, traffic is often clogged along the country road.) It has among the best food we've had here, and though utterly drab (like a restaurant converted from a gas station), it draws a lively crowd from early on. A merengue band was getting the party started right when we last stopped in around 2pm on a Sunday, when patrons were already burning up the dance floor in between the cafeteria and the food stands in front of the open-air fire pits where whole pigs, chickens, and turkeys were being slowly roasted Puerto Rican style.

The best restaurants, however, have a certain rustic charm in addition to their utilitarian nature. Some look like wooden tropical chalets with blooming flowers, while others are set in front of a stream gushing through a lush mountainside. Our favorites include **La Casa del Guanime** (Rte. 184, Km 27.8; ✆ **787/744-3921**), **El Rancho Original** (Rte. 184, Km 27.5; ✆ **787/747-7296**), **Los Pinos** (Rte. 184, Km 27.7; ✆ **787/286-1917**), and **El Mojito** (Rte. 184, Km 32.9; ✆ **787/738-8888**). The truth, however, is that we rarely have been disappointed in any of the restaurants we visited.

Most have live music on weekend afternoons, so whether your taste runs from salsa to merengue to local *jíbaro* country music or to something more contemporary may play a big role in your choice. Also, the road carves through a lush forest and a string of restaurants along its right-hand side is set in front of the mountain stream; several have dining rooms overlooking the stream and in the quieter ones its gurgling is the only music you'll hear.

The atmosphere is important, but the main thing about Guavate is the food: roast pork and chicken, fried rice and pigeon peas, boiled root vegetables soaked in oil and spices, blood sausage. This is traditional Puerto Rican mountain food, but the level of the cooking keeps getting better every time we return. The roast turkey (yes, they keep it juicy) is a healthy alternative to the pig; it has recently been showing up *escabeche* style, drenched in olive oil, garlic and onions, roasted peppers and herbs—absolutely delicious.

Just south of Guavaté is the northern entrance to the **Carite Forest Reserve ★**, a 6,000-acre (2,428-hectare) reserve that spreads from Cayey to neighboring Caguas and San Lorenzo, and all the way down to Patillas and Guayama on the south coast. The forest ranges from heights of 820 to 2,963 feet (250–903m) above sea level, and, from several peaks, you can see clear down to the south coast and Ponce. The forest, with frequent rain and high humidity, is covered with Caribbean pine and has several ponds and streams. Some of the forest's most interesting sites are near the northern entrance by Guavate. On one peak is Nuestra Madre, a Catholic spiritual meditation center that permits visitors to stroll the grounds. The large natural pond, called Charco Azul, is a favorite spot for a swim. It is surrounded by a picnic area and campground. There are over 50 species of birds in the forest.

Guavate is just the start of Cayey, which is a beautiful town through which to take a drive. Another mountain road with fine restaurants is found in its **Jájome** sector. All of these are open Thursday through Sunday for lunch and dinner. This is probably a better choice for visitors wanting a more refined dining experience than the raucous pig roasts in Guavaté. To get here, take the main exit to Cayey, turn left on Rte. 1, and then exit on to Rte. 15 on the left and follow signs to the community. From some spots you can see all the way down to the south coast. Two of these are the **Jájome Terrace** (Rte. 15, Km 18.6, Cayey; ✆ **787/738-4016**) and the **Sand and the Sea Inn** (Rte. 715, Cayey; ✆ **787/738-9086**). The Jájome Terrace offers solid food and fine views, while the Sand and the Sea Inn has been serving great meals in the countryside for decades. From seafood to steak, from French to Puerto Rican, the food is always good and the view even better.

Farther up into the mountains is **Aibonito,** a pretty town overlooking the island's gorgeous green valleys. From Rte. 15, take the exit to Rte. 14 and follow signs for Aibonito. A good time to visit is during the annual Fiesta de las Flores at the end of June and beginning of July, a festival stretching across 2 weeks where local growers present some of the most beautiful flowers grown on the island, including locally grown orchids. This mountain town, with its cool, crisp air, is worth a trip any time of the year, however.

PONCE & THE SOUTHWEST

8

For those who want to see a less urban side of Puerto Rico, head south to Ponce and the breathtaking southwest, for great beaches, dramatic coastal bluffs, and green flatlands unfolding across the horizon to the foothills of the Cordillera Central mountain range.

Ponce is a great center for sightseeing, and you can take a side trip to the bonsai-like Guánica State Forest; visit Puerto Rico's second-oldest city and site of the oldest church in the New World, San Germán; and venture north through the island's central mountains to the lush Toro Negro rainforest. Both nature reserves are hits with hikers and bird-watchers.

Founded in 1692, Ponce is Puerto Rico's second-largest city, and its historic sectors have been beautifully restored. San Germán and Ponce are home to some of the finest historic architecture in the hemisphere.

Ponce also attracts beach lovers. No, there's no real beach in town, but to the west are the coastal towns of Guánica, La Parguera, and Boquerón, where the best swimming beaches on the island are located. The southwest is where Puerto Ricans go for holidays by the sea. This is the real Puerto Rico; it hasn't been taken over by high-rise resorts and posh restaurants.

Puerto Rico's west coast mimics the U.S. southwest; cacti pop up from sun-baked rock crevices, while cattle graze in the rolling Lajas Valley in the shadow of the majestic central mountains. Comparisons have also been made between the peninsula of Cabo Rojo here and Baja, California. All across the region, a beautiful western sunset settles over its charming beach towns, with their white sands and aquamarine waters, bringing very much to mind the best of the California coastline.

PONCE ★★

75 miles (121km) SW of San Juan

"The Pearl of the South," Ponce was named after Loíza Ponce de León, great-grandson of Juan Ponce de León. Founded in 1692, Ponce is today Puerto Rico's principal shipping port on the Caribbean. The city is well kept and attractive, with an air of being stuck in the past, like a provincial Mediterranean town. On weekday afternoons, men dressed in starched *guayaberas* and hats play dominoes while uniformed school girls run along the large walkways.

Ponce

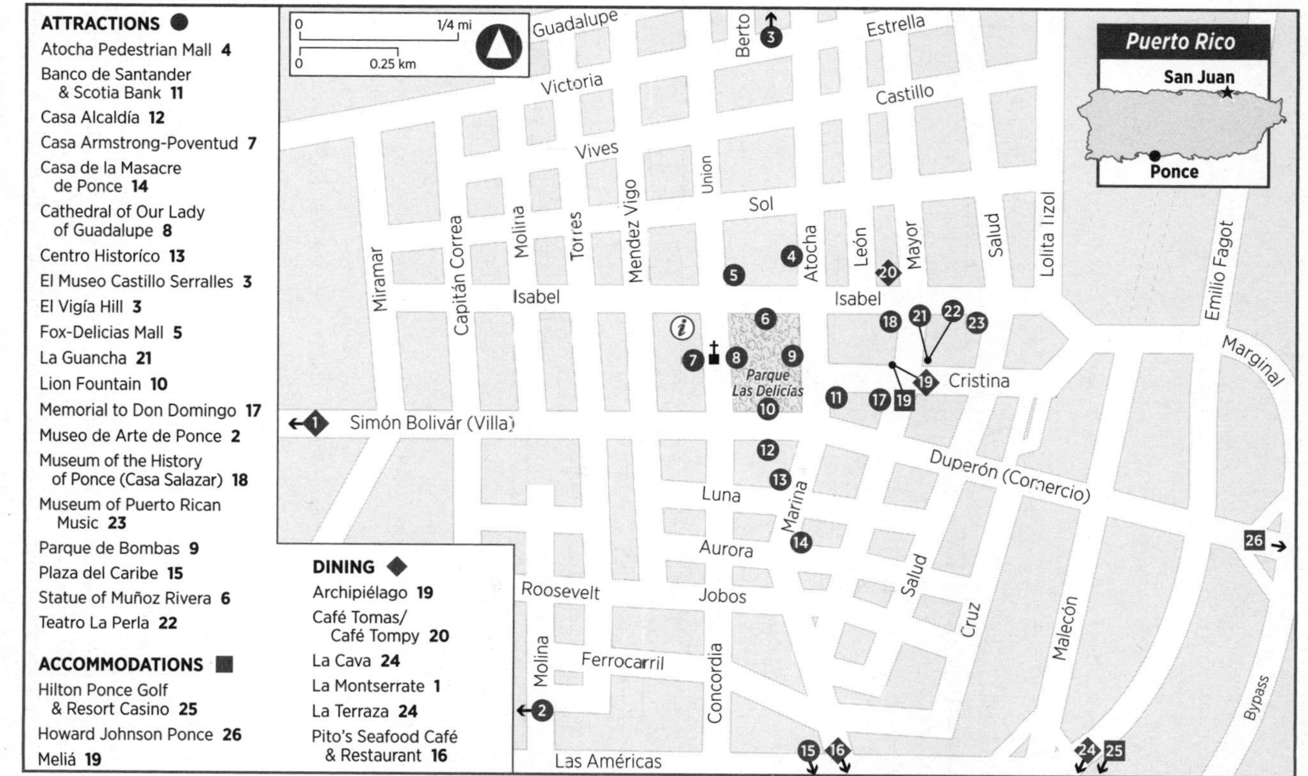
ATTRACTIONS
Atocha Pedestrian Mall 4
Banco de Santander & Scotia Bank 11
Casa Alcaldía 12
Casa Armstrong-Poventud 7
Casa de la Masacre de Ponce 14
Cathedral of Our Lady of Guadalupe 8
Centro Historíco 13
El Museo Castillo Serralles 3
El Vigía Hill 3
Fox-Delicias Mall 5
La Guancha 21
Lion Fountain 10
Memorial to Don Domingo 17
Museo de Arte de Ponce 2
Museum of the History of Ponce (Casa Salazar) 18
Museum of Puerto Rican Music 23
Parque de Bombas 9
Plaza del Caribe 15
Statue of Muñoz Rivera 6
Teatro La Perla 22
ACCOMMODATIONS
Hilton Ponce Golf & Resort Casino 25
Howard Johnson Ponce 26
Meliá 19
DINING
Archipiélago 19
Café Tomas/ Café Tompy 20
La Cava 24
La Montserrate 1
La Terraza 24
Pito's Seafood Café & Restaurant 16
0 1/4 mi
0 0.25 km
Puerto Rico
San Juan
Ponce
Guadalupe
Victoria
Vives
Berto
Estrella
Castillo
Union
Sol
Miramar
Capitán Correa
Molina
Torres
Mendez Vigo
Isabel
Atocha
León
Mayor
Salud
Lolita Tizol
Emilio Fagot
Marginal
Parque Las Delicias
Cristina
Simón Bolivár (Villa)
Duperón (Comercio)
Luna
Marina
Aurora
Roosevelt
Jobos
Cruz
Malecón
Ferrocarril
Concordia
Bypass
Las Américas

Its historic district underwent a $440-million restoration for 1992's 500th anniversary celebration of Christopher Columbus's voyage to the New World, and improvements have continued. The streets are lit with gas lamps and lined with neoclassical buildings, just as they were a century ago. Horse-drawn carriages roll by, and strollers walk along sidewalks edged with pink marble. Contemporary Ponce has been restored to its former splendor, the city as it was at the turn of the 20th century, when it rivaled San Juan as a wealthy business and cultural center.

Sitting in its sun-bleached plaza on a sunny afternoon, visitors may be struck by Ponce's heat, and the nearly always-dry weather conditions. Threats of rain are most often held at bay by the central mountains; you can see the potential humidity condensing into a violet haze over them in the distance as the late afternoon finally begins to fade.

Essentials

GETTING THERE Flying from San Juan to Ponce five times a day, **Cape Air** (© **800/352-0714;** www.flycapeair.com), a small regional carrier, offers flights for $154 round-trip. Flight time is 25 minutes.

If you're driving, take Las Américas Expressway south to the Luis A. Ferré Expressway Hwy. 52, then continue south. Once you pass over the central mountain range and reach the south coast, you will continue west until Ponce. The trip takes about 1½ hours.

GETTING AROUND The town's inner core is small enough that everything can be visited on foot. Taxis provide the second-best alternative.

VISITOR INFORMATION Maps and information can be found at the **tourist office,** Paseo del Sur Plaza, Ste. 3 (© **787/841-8044**). It's open daily 8am to 4:30pm.

Seeing the Sights

ATTRACTIONS IN PONCE

Most visitors go to Ponce to see the city's rebuilt historic section. The renovations beautifully restored much of the city's whimsical architectural style. While the city dates back to 1692, its unique "Ponce Creole" architecture, mixing Spanish colonial, Caribbean, and contemporary influences, was mostly created from the 1850s through the 1930s. The style is marked by the use of wide balconies, distinctive masonry work, and neoclassical touches: plaster garlands, punched tin ceilings, and stained glass panels. Other architectural motifs such as metal grill work are present within specific geographic areas of the city. The style takes European concepts, but adapts them to the city's tropical climate by using pastel colors on building facades and adding high ceilings that help keep houses cool.

The city's unique architecture was created during the years of Ponce's heyday, in the 19th century, when it trumped San Juan as the island's most important city and rose as a regional trading power. Cut off from San Juan because of geographic barriers, Ponce's trade brought foreign influences and style, which shows in its architecture, as well as its wider culture, including music and cuisine.

In addition to the attractions listed below, the **weekday marketplace,** open Monday through Friday from 8am to 5pm, at calles Atocha and Castillo, is colorful. Perhaps you'll want to simply sit in the plaza, watching the Ponceños at one of their favorite pastimes—strolling about town.

Casa de la Masacre de Ponce ★ This small museum is a memorial to one of the bloodiest chapters of political violence in Puerto Rican history—the Ponce Massacre. Police killed 19 people and wounded 100 during a Nationalist Party march in the city on Palm Sunday, March 21, 1937, after shots rang out. Party members had planned a march to protest the imprisonment of their leader Pedro Albizu Campos, but authorities cancelled their permit under pressure from American colonial governor Blanton Winship. The shooting occurred when protesters met up with a police blockade. Both protesters and bystanders were among the dead, which included a woman and a 7-year-old girl. The remnants of the Nationalist Party still mark the occasion with a ceremony here each year, and it is an important date for independence supporters. The museum is located at the site of the tragedy in a restored shoemaker's shop that used to be a meeting place for Nationalist Party members. The museum also documents other episodes of the political persecution of island *independentistas,* including the infamous *carpetas,* the secret dossiers that a police intelligence unit, with the backing of U.S. government officials, kept on independence supporters over the course of decades. The museum is a concise review of the political repression of independence supporters and will prove illuminating for many visitors.

At calles Aurora and Marina, Plaza Las Delicias. ✆ **787/844-9722.** Free admission. Tues–Sun 8:30am–4pm.

Cathedral of Our Lady of Guadalupe ★ In 1660 a rustic chapel was built on this spot on the western edge of the Plaza Las Delicias, and since then fires and earthquakes have razed the church repeatedly. In 1919 a team of priests collected funds from local parishioners to construct the Doric- and Gothic-inspired building that stands here today. Designed by architects Francisco Porrato Doría and Francisco Trublard in 1931, and featuring a pipe organ installed in 1934, it remains an important place for prayer for many. The cathedral, named after a famous holy shrine in Mexico, is the best-known church in southern Puerto Rico.

At calles Concordia and Union. ✆ **787/842-0134.** Free admission. Mon–Fri 6am–12:30pm; Sat–Sun 6am–noon and 3–8pm.

El Museo Castillo Serralles ★ Two miles (3.2km) north of the center of town is the largest and most imposing building in Ponce, constructed high on El Vigía Hill (see below) during the 1930s by the Serrallés family, owners of a local rum distillery. One of the architectural gems of Puerto Rico, it is the best evidence of the wealth produced by the turn-of-the-20th-century sugar boom. Guides will escort you through the Spanish Revival house with Moorish and Andalusian details. Highlights include panoramic courtyards, a baronial dining room, a small cafe and souvenir shop, and a series of photographs showing the tons of earth that were brought in for the construction of the terraced gardens, a beautiful place to sit outside the castle that overlooks the city. You'll need to take a taxi if you don't have a car.

El Vigía 17. ✆ **787/259-1774.** Admission $9 adults, $4.50 seniors, $4 children and students. (Admission includes all attractions on El Vigía Hill.) Tues–Sun 9:30am–5pm.

El Vigía Hill The city's tallest geologic feature, El Vigía Hill (300 ft./91m) dominates Ponce's northern skyline. Its base and steep slopes are covered with a maze of 19th- and early-20th-century development. In addition to the castle, as soon as you reach the summit, you'll see the soaring Cruz del Vigía (Virgin's Cross). Built in 1984 of reinforced concrete to replace a 19th-century wooden cross in poor repair, this modern 100-foot (30m) structure bears lateral arms measuring 70 feet (21m) long and an observation tower (accessible by elevator), from which you can see all of the natural beauty surrounding Ponce. The cross commemorates Vigía Hill's colonial role as a deterrent to contraband smuggling. In 1801, on orders from Spain, a garrison was established atop the hill to detect any ships that might try to unload their cargoes tax-free along Puerto Rico's southern coastline. Make sure to take a break in the beautifully tranquil Japanese garden, with bonsai plantings and dry areas, and elevated bridges running between ponds and streams; it's a perfect spot for a break.

At the north end of Ponce.

Museo de Arte de Ponce ★★★ The museum is closed while undergoing extensive renovations but is set to reopen better than ever in late 2010. In the meantime, the museum is holding exhibitions at an annex it opened in San Juan's Plaza Las Américas, and it is lending some of its best pieces out to traveling shows at fine arts institutions throughout the world.

Donated to the people of Puerto Rico by the late Luís A. Ferré, the former governor who founded the pro-statehood New Progressive Party, this museum has the finest collection of European and Latin American art in the Caribbean. The building itself was designed by Edward Durell Stone (who also designed the John F. Kennedy Center for the Performing Arts in Washington, D.C.) and has been called the "Parthenon of the Caribbean." Its collection represents the principal schools of American and European art of the past 5 centuries. Among the nearly 400 works on display are exceptional pre-Raphaelite and Italian baroque paintings. Visitors will also see artworks by other European masters, as well as Puerto Rican and Latin American paintings, graphics, and sculptures. On display are some of the best works of the two "old masters" of Puerto Rico, Francisco Oller and José Campéche. The museum also contains a representative collection of the works of the old masters of Europe, including Gainsborough, Velázquez, Rubens, and Van Dyck. The museum is best known for its pre-Raphaelite and baroque paintings and sculpture—not only from Spain, but from Italy and France as well.

Av. de Las Américas 23–25. ✆ **787/848-0505.** www.museoarteponce.org. Follow Calle Concordia from Plaza Las Delicias 1½ miles (2.4km) south to Av. de Las Américas.

Museum of the History of Ponce (Casa Salazar) Opened in the Casa Salazar in 1992, this museum traces the history of the city from the time of the Taíno peoples to the present. Interactive displays help visitors orient themselves and locate other attractions. The museum has a conservation laboratory, library, souvenir-and-gift shop, cafeteria, and conference facilities.

Casa Salazar ranks close to the top of Ponce's architectural treasures. Built in 1911, it combines neoclassical and Moorish details, while displaying much that is typical of the Ponce decorative style: stained-glass windows, mosaics, pressed-tin ceilings, fixed jalousies, wood or iron columns, porch balconies, interior patios, and the use of doors as windows.

Calle Reina Isabel 51–53 (at Calle Mayor). ✆ **787/844-7071.** Free admission. Tues–Sun 8:30am–4pm.

Museum of Puerto Rican Music This museum showcases the development of Puerto Rican music, with displays of Indian, Spanish, and African musical instruments that were played in the romantic *danza,* the favorite music of 19th-century Puerto Rican society, as well as the more African-inspired *bomba* and *plena* styles.

Also on view are memorabilia of composers and performers. It is housed in one of the city's most beautiful private residences designed by Alfredo Wiechers and dating from the turn of the 20th century.

Calle Isabel 50. ✆ **787/848-7016.** Free admission. Wed–Sun 8:30am–4pm.

Parque de Bombas ★★ Constructed in 1882 as the centerpiece of a 12-day agricultural fair intended to promote the civic charms of Ponce, this building was designated a year later as the island's first permanent headquarters for a volunteer firefighting brigade. It has an unusual appearance—it's painted black, red, green, and yellow. A tourist-information kiosk is situated inside the building (see "Visitor Information," above).

Plaza Las Delicias. ✆ **787/284-3338.** Free admission. Daily 8am–5pm.

Teatro la Perla This theater, built in the neoclassical style in 1864, remains one of the most visible symbols of the economic prosperity of Ponce during the mid–19th century. Designed by Juan Bertoli, an Italian-born resident of Puerto Rico who studied in Europe, it was destroyed by an earthquake in 1918, and rebuilt in 1940 according to the original plans; it reopened to the public in 1941. It is noted for acoustics so clear that microphones are unnecessary. The theater is the largest and most historic in the Spanish-speaking Caribbean. Everything from plays to concerts to beauty pageants takes place here.

At calles Mayor and Christina. ✆ **787/843-4322.** Prices and hours vary.

NEARBY ATTRACTIONS

Hacienda Buena Vista ★ Built in 1833, this hacienda preserves an old way of life, with its whirring water wheels and artifacts of 19th-century farm production. Once it was one of the most successful plantations on Puerto Rico, producing coffee, corn, and citrus. It was a working coffee plantation until the 1950s, and 86 of the original 500 acres (35 of 202 hectares) are still part of the estate. The rooms of the hacienda have been furnished with authentic pieces from the 1850s. Hacienda Buena Vista is located in Barrio Magüeyes along the rural mountain road to Adjuntas. From Av. de las Americas, go west until Rte. 500, which you will take to Rte. 123 (Calle La Poncena) and turn left. At km 16.8 you will find the Hacienda.

Rte. 123, Barrio Magüeyes Km 16.8. ✆ **787/722-5882** (weekdays), 787/284-7020 (weekends). Tours $7 adults, $4 children and seniors. Reservations required. 2-hr. tours Wed–Sun at 8:30am, 10:30am, 1:30pm, and 3:30pm (in English only at 1:30pm). A 30-min. drive north of Ponce, in the small town of Barrio Magüeyes, btw. Ponce and Adjuntas.

Take a Break

Stop for an ice cream or drink at **King's Ice Cream (✆ 787/843-8520)**, right across the street from the Parque de Bombas on the city's main square. This institution has been scooping up delicious ice cream for decades. The almond is wonderful, as are tropical fruit flavors parcha or tamarind. The product feels closer to Italian than U.S. ice cream. Another option is a drink or sandwich at the **Café Tomas/Café Tompy,** Calle Isabel at Calle Mayor (**✆ 787/840-1965**). Divided into less formal and more formal sections, it is open daily from 7am to midnight. For more information, see "Where to Dine," below.

Tibes Indian Ceremonial Center ★ Bordered by the Río Portuguéz and excavated in 1975, this is the oldest cemetery in the Antilles. It contains some 186 skeletons, dating from A.D. 300, as well as pre-Taíno plazas from A.D. 700. The site also includes a re-created Taíno village, seven rectangular ball courts, and two dance grounds. The arrangement of stone points on the dance grounds, in line with the solstices and equinoxes, suggests a pre-Columbian Stonehenge. Here you'll also find a museum, an exhibition hall that presents a documentary about Tibes, a cafeteria, and a souvenir shop. Go east along Av. De las Americas until Av. De Hostos, which turns immediately into Calle Salud. Take a left at Calle Trioche and a right at Calle Mayor Cantera, which leads into the Carretera Tibes. Go right on Rte. 503, then bear left to stay on road.

Rte. 503, Tibes, at Km 2.2. ✆ **787/840-2255.** Admission $3 adults, $2 children. Guided tours in English and Spanish are conducted through the grounds. Tues–Sun 9am–4pm. 2 miles (3.2km) north of Ponce.

Beaches & Outdoor Activities

Ponce is a city—not a beach resort—and should be visited mainly for its sights. There are no beaches within the city, but an offshore cay ringed with white sand and aquamarine waters filled with marine life is just a ferry ride away.

About 30 minutes to the west, however, are some of Puerto Rico's best beaches. They ring the coast from Guánica through Cabo Rojo.

Because the northern shore of Puerto Rico fronts the often-turbulent Atlantic, many snorkelers prefer the more tranquil southern coast, especially the waters off the coast of **La Parguera.** Throughout the southwest coast, water lovers can go snorkeling right off the beach, and it isn't necessary to take a boat trip. Waters here are not polluted, and visibility is usually good, unless there are heavy winds and choppy seas.

La Guancha is a sprawling boardwalk around Ponce's bayside harbor area near the Ponce Hilton. Several eateries are located here, and it is the scene of free concerts and other events at night. There's no beach, but during weekend afternoons children and their families come here to fly kites or ride bicycles. Hundreds of yachts and pleasure craft tie up here, which is also home to the Ponce Yacht Club. La Guancha is a relatively wholesome version of Coney Island, with a strong Hispanic accent and vague hints of New England. On hot weekends, the place is mobbed with families who listen to merengue and salsa. Lining the boardwalk are small establishments selling beer, party drinks, fried beach snacks, and souvenirs. There is also a lookout tower here, which is worth a climb.

A ferry runs from La Guancha to **Caja de Muertos,** or **Coffin Island,** an uninhabited cay that's covered with mangrove swamps and ringed with worthwhile beaches. It's some of the best snorkeling in the southwest. A 125-passenger ferry run by **Island Venture** (✆ **787/842-8546** or 787/866-7827) provides transportation on weekends to and from the island. Roundtrip fare is $15 for adults, and $10 for children. Other private outfits will take passengers to the island, with some providing snorkeling equipment and even lunch to guests. There are hiking trails, gazebos and basic bathrooms but no running water. The island has an old lighthouse and a nice beach.

The city owns two **tennis complexes,** one at Poly Deportivos, with nine hard courts, and another at Rambla, with six courts. Both are open from 9am to 10pm daily and are lighted for night play. You can play for free, but you must call to make a reservation. For information, including directions on how to get there, call the city

Sports and Recreation Department at © **787/840-4400.** You can also find tennis facilities at the two following country clubs, which also offer golf.

One of the south coast's finest and newest courses is the **Costa Caribe Golf & Country Club ★** (© **787/848-1000** or 787/812-2650), on the site of the Hilton Ponce & Casino (see below). This 27-hole course charges from $85 ($75 for guests) to play 18 holes. The beautifully landscaped holes—with commanding views of the ocean and mountain—are laid out in former sugar-cane fields. The no. 12 hole, one of the most dramatic, calls for a 188-yard carry over water from the back tees. Trade winds add to the challenge. The three 9's can be played in 18-hole combinations, as conceived by golf architect Bruce Besse. The greens are undulating and moderate in speed, averaging 6,000 square feet (557 sq. m). Golf carts are included in the greens fees, and both gas and electric carts are available.

Another course, **Club Deportivo del Oeste,** Hwy. 102 Km 15.4, Barrio Joyuda, Cabo Rojo (© **787/851-8880** or 787/254-3748), lies 30 miles (48km) west of Ponce. This course is an 18-holer, open daily from 7am to 5pm. Greens fees are $45 and include a golf cart.

Shopping

If you feel a yen for shopping in Ponce, there are many shops in the renovated downtown area that have local arts and crafts. **The Atochoa Pedestrian Mall** (© **787/841-8044**) runs along Calle Cristina just off the city's central **Plaza Las Delicias.** It's been one of Ponce's main shopping areas for decades. There's not a whole lot here, but it's fun to walk around, and the shops and offerings are a throwback to a simpler time.

For artisans' work, try **El Palacio del Coquí Inc.,** Calle Marina 9227 (© **787/812-0216**), whose name means "palace of the tree frog." This is the place to buy the colorful *veijantese* masks (viewed as collectors' items) that are used at carnival time. Ask the owner to explain the significance of these masks.

Utopía, Calle Isabel 78 (© **787/848-8742**), conveniently located in Plaza Las Delicias, has the most imaginative and interesting selection of gift items and handicrafts in Ponce. Prominently displayed are *vegigantes,* brightly painted carnival masks inspired by carnival rituals and crafted from papier-mâché. In Ponce, where many of these masks are made, they sell at bargain prices of between $20 and $500, depending on their size. Other items include cigars, pottery, clothing, and jewelry; gifts imported from Indonesia, the Philippines, and Mexico; and rums from throughout the Caribbean. Julio and Carmen Aguilar are the helpful and enthusiastic owners, who hail from Ecuador and Puerto Rico, respectively.

The big mall in town is **Plaza del Caribe,** Hwy. 2 (© **787/848-5566** or 787/848-1229) located right off exit 104-B from the Luis A Ferrre Expressway 52. A smaller version of Plaza las Américas, there are still 140 stores, many of them similar to the San Juan mall, in more than 7,000 square feet of shopping space. If you are looking for it, you can find it here. Plus there are lots of good places to eat and Cineplex.

Where to Stay

EXPENSIVE

Hilton Ponce Golf & Casino ★★ On a 30-hectare (74-acre) tract of land right on the coast, this is the best, full-service hotel in southern Puerto Rico. A 10-minute drive from downtown, near the La Guancha waterfront district, the hotel has a

27-hole golf course, sprawling pool area, lush grounds and spacious rooms, done up in attractive tropical style with great amenities and furnishings. Even basic rooms have private balconies and roomy, gleaming bathrooms. There's a playground and pool for the kids, great fitness and health club, a busy casino, and lively lobby area. The resort has a top rate business center and other services for business travelers. The hotel restaurants are among the city's finest. The Player's Lounge outside the casino has live music on weekends. There are often weekend live concerts and other events at the nearby La Guancha.

Av. Caribe 1150 (P.O. Box 7419), Ponce, PR 00716. ✆ **800/445-8667** or 787/259-7676. Fax 787/259-7674. www.hilton.com. 153 units. Year-round $159–$189 double; $375–$659 suite. AE, DC, DISC, MC, V. Valet parking $10; self-parking $4.50. **Amenities:** 2 restaurants; 2 bars; casino; night club; bikes; children's program; playground; 27-hole golf course; fitness center; lagoon-shaped pool ringed w/gardens; room service; 2 tennis courts; rooms for those w/limited mobility. *In room:* A/C, TV, hair dryer, minibar.

MODERATE

Howard Johnson Ponce ☺ This hotel, a 15-minute drive east of Ponce, has nice bedrooms that are comfortable and decked out with contemporary furnishings. Each unit has a small tiled bathroom with tub/shower combination. The prices appeal to families. The hotel is set on a hill overlooking the coast right near a string of popular coastal seafood restaurants. Unless you have kids, who will enjoy the pool, you are probably better off staying in town.

Turpo Industrial Park 103, Mercedita, Ponce, PR 00715. ✆ **800/465-4329** or 787/844-1200. Fax 787/841-8085. www.hojo.com. 120 units. Year-round $99–$163 double; $186–$196 suite. AE, DC, DISC, MC, V. Free parking. East of Ponce on Hwy. 52, opposite the Interamerican University. **Amenities:** Restaurant; bar/disco; gym; pool; children's wading pool; whirlpool; room service; rooms for those w/limited mobility. *In room:* A/C, TV, hair dryer.

Meliá A city hotel with southern hospitality, the Meliá, which has no connection with the international hotel chain, attracts businesspeople and visitors who want to explore the city's historic offerings. The location is a few steps away from the Cathedral of Our Lady of Guadalupe and from the Parque de Bombas (the red-and-black firehouse). Although the more expensive Hilton long ago outclassed this old and somewhat tattered hotel, many people who can afford more upscale accommodations still prefer to stay here for its old-time atmosphere. The lobby floor and all stairs are covered with Spanish tiles of Moorish design. The desk clerks speak English. The small rooms are comfortably furnished and pleasant enough, and most have a balcony facing either busy Calle Cristina or the old plaza. Bathrooms are tiny, each with a shower stall. Breakfast is served on a rooftop terrace with a good view of Ponce. You can park your car in the lot nearby.

Calle Cristina 2, Ponce, PR 00731. ✆ **800/448-8355** or 787/842-0260. Fax 787/841-3602. www.hotelmeliapr.com. 73 units (shower only). Year-round $100–$140 double. Rates include continental breakfast. AE, MC, V. Parking $3. **Amenities:** Restaurant; bar; outdoor pool; room service; rooms for those w/limited mobility. *In room:* A/C, TV, free high-speed Internet, hair dryer.

Where to Dine

EXPENSIVE

Archipiélago ★ PUERTO RICAN/SEAFOOD The new place to be in Ponce is this sixth floor restaurant that offers sweeping views of the historic district and innovative *criolla* and continental fusion cuisine. The interior dining area is as smart and modern as the menu with subdued tones and an expansive glass window that brings the view from above Plaza las Delicias right into the room. There are two outdoor terraces that will make you feel lost in Europe as you look out at the cathedral and the Victorian firehouse. If you are with a group, start out with the Archipielago platter, which has fried manchego cheese and tomato jam, fried local cheese with guava and prosciutto ham, fried plantains topped with stewed shredded meat, mushroom caps stuffed with pesto and fried calamaris. The lobster in Creole sauce and the chicken stuffed with sundried tomatoes, mushrooms and Italian cheese were both excellent. The rack of lamb, crusted with annatto and panko, also impresses. There are also simple vegetarian dishes, burgers and straight up Puerto Rican classics. So while there are some budget busters on the menu, there are bargains as well. The desserts are the chef's specialty, and it showed in the coffee crème brulée and the Puerto Rican Strudel with dark rum caramel sauce. There is also a lounge area and bar, so this is a one of the city's top nightspots as well. Occasional performances and special events are held here. It's a great place for a drink if you're not in the mood for a full meal.

Calle Cristina 76, Ponce, PR 00731. ✆ **787/812-8822.** Reservations recommended. Main courses $14–$37. AE, DC, MC, V. Dinner Wed–Sun 5pm–1am; lunch Fri and Sun noon–5pm.

La Cava ★ INTERNATIONAL The restaurant recently underwent a modern makeover, but the food is still classic continental and its still one of this southern city's best dining experiences. Start out with the duck terrine and lingonberries or the lobster empanadillas with spicy mango sauce, and move on to the crusted veal chop with Spanish sausage, provolone cheese and a rioja wine risotto, or a red snapper filet with capers and lime. The menu is filled with similar thrills. If you need a good meal in Ponce, you are guaranteed one here.

In the Ponce Hilton, Av. Caribe 1150. ✆ **787/259-7676.** Reservations recommended. Main courses $26–$45. AE, DC, DISC, MC, V. Mon–Sat 6:30–10:30pm.

Pito's Seafood Café & Restaurant ★ SEAFOOD This is the best of the string of seafood restaurants along the undeveloped waterfront west of the city center. The building has a handsome wooden structure on the water, with three different dining levels with open air views of the sea. There is a large and fine wine selection, with 25 bottles available by the glass, and a cigar menu available at a separate smoking bar. The spot offers the freshest seafood, in the finest of island and Spanish recipes. A really great spot to experience the best Puerto Rican seafood meal of your vacation. It's a great place to try grilled Caribbean lobster, which is lighter than its Maine cousin. I've also tried the Ponce style conch salad and mahimahi in mango curry coconut sauce. The halibut filet sautéed with pesto and shrimp is as tasty as it sounds, but everything looks great. If it's anything like mine have been, your meal will be as perfect as the view.

Hwy. 2, Las Cucharas, Ponce. ✆ **787/841-4977.** Reservations recommended. Main courses $12–$35. AE, MC, V. Sun–Thurs 11am–10pm, Fri–Sat 11am–midnight.

MODERATE

La Montserrate PUERTO RICAN/SEAFOOD This is one of a string of seaside restaurants specializing in Puerto Rican cuisine and seafood lined along the beautiful coastline about 4 miles (6.4km) west of the town center. This restaurant draws a loyal following, and has a large dining room overlooking the waterfront. Specialties, concocted from the catch of the day, might include octopus salad, several different kinds of *asopao,* a whole red snapper in Creole sauce, or a selection of steaks and grills. Nothing is innovative, but the cuisine is typical of the south of Puerto Rico, and it's a family favorite. The fish dishes are better than the meat selections.

Sector Las Cucharas, Rte. 2. ✆ **787/841-2740.** Main courses $12–$29. AE, DISC, MC, V. Daily 11am–10pm.

La Terraza INTERNATIONAL This big and sunny restaurant has a dramatic view. Two-story walls of windows sweep the eye out over the greenery of the hotel's garden. At nighttime, there is a different themed special and a sprawling soup-and-salad bar (access to which is included in the price of any main course). On the standard menu, there's a pepper covered flat-iron steak and the smoked chicken linguini with pesto and roasted artichokes that are both excellent. The restaurant also serves breakfast buffets and weekend brunch buffets.

In the Ponce Hilton, Av. Caribe 1150. ✆ **787/259-7676.** Dinner main courses $24–$36, breakfast buffet $19, brunch buffet $22. AE, DC, DISC, MC, V. Daily 6:30–10:30am, 6:30–10:30pm.

INEXPENSIVE

Café Tomas/Café Tompy PUERTO RICAN The more visible and busier section of this establishment functions as a simple cafe for neighbors and local merchants. At plastic tables often flooded with sunlight from the big windows, you can order coffee, sandwiches, or cold beer, perhaps while relaxing after a walking tour of the city. The family-run restaurant in back is more formal. Here, amid a decor reminiscent of a Spanish *tasca* (tapas bar), you can enjoy such simply prepared dishes as salted filet of beef, beefsteak with onions, four kinds of *asopao,* buttered eggs, octopus salads, and yucca croquettes.

Calle Isabel 56, at Calle Mayor. ✆ **787/840-1965.** Breakfast $2.50–$6, main courses lunch and dinner $5–$10. AE, MC, V. Restaurant daily 6:30am–10:30pm.

THE SOUTHWEST COAST

The southwest corner of the island is where the locals go to kick back and chill out. The area is a favored vacation spot for San Juan and Ponce residents, as well as a weekend getaway destination. In fact, for many travelers the area will be too crowded during Easter week and the month of July, the height of the Puerto Rico tourism season. Here are some of Puerto Rico's great beaches, notably the beaches of **Guánica** and **Boquerón Beach ★★**, and a lot of mom-and-pop operations that offer nightly rentals and good seafood dinners.

Southern Puerto Rico is increasingly gaining a reputation among **scuba divers,** although the outfitters are a bit lean here and not as well organized or plentiful as in the Cayman Islands. The attraction is the continental shelf that drops off a few miles off the southern coast. Within this watery range is a towering wall that is some 20 miles (32km) long and filled with one of the best assortments of marine life in the West Indies. Diving is possible from the town of La Parguera in the west all the way to Ponce in the east. The wall drops from 60 to 120 feet (18–37m) before it "vanishes" into 1,500 feet (457m) of sea. With a visibility of around 100 feet (30m), divers experience the beautiful formations of some of Puerto Rico's most dramatic coral gardens.

Bird-watchers should head to the **Guánica State Forest,** which is the sanctuary that has the greatest number of birds on the island. For beachcombers, there are many hidden places, such as Gilligan's Island off the coast of the little village of

Guánica. For snorkelers, there are miles of coral reefs, awash with tropical fish, coral, and marine life. The Cabo Rojo lighthouse, south of Boquerón, offers views of the rocky coastline and a panoramic sweep of the Caribbean.

Guánica

Guánica, on the Caribbean Sea, lies 73 miles (118km) southwest of San Juan and 21 miles (34km) west of the city of Ponce. The Guánica Dry Forest and adjacent area is a UNESCO-designated world biosphere reserve. The rare bonsai-like forest is home to more than 100 species of migratory and resident birds, the largest number in Puerto Rico. The beach at Guánica is pristine, and the crystal-clear water is ideal for swimming, snorkeling, and diving. Directly offshore is the famed Gilligan's Island, plus six of Puerto Rico's best sites for night or day dives. The area was once known for its leaping bullfrogs. The Spanish conquerors virtually wiped out this species. But the bullfrogs have come back and live in the rolling, scrub-covered hills that surround the 18-acre (7.3-hectare) site of the Copamarina Beach Resort, the area's major hotel (see below.)

Guánica is adjacent to the unique Dry Forest and experiences very little rainfall. Nearby mountains get an annual rainfall of 15 feet (4.6m), but Guánica receives only about 15 inches (38 cm). This is the world's largest dry coastal forest region. The upper hills are ideal for hiking. Guánica was once the haunt of the Taíno Indians, and it was the place where Ponce de León first explored Puerto Rico in 1508. One of his descendants later founded the nearby city of Ponce in 1692.

It is also the site of the landing of the Americans in 1898 during the Spanish-American war that began Puerto Rico's century-long relationship with the United States. You reach the harbor by taking the main exit to Guánica from Rte. 116 to Avenida 25 de Julio. A large rock monument on the town's *malecón,* or harbor, commemorates the landing. The Williams family, descendants of a doctor who arrived with the troops and settled here after marrying a local girl, still live in one of the historic wooden homes along the waterfront. The area has lots of seafood restaurants and bars, as well as snack vendors along a bayside promenade. It is festive on weekend evenings.

HIKING & BIRD-WATCHING IN GUANICA STATE FOREST ★★

Heading directly west from Ponce, along Rte. 2, you reach **Guánica State Forest ★** (**© 787/821-5706**), a setting that evokes Arizona or New Mexico. Here you will find the best-preserved subtropical ecosystem on the planet. UNESCO has named Guánica a World Biosphere Reserve. Some 750 plants and tree species grow in the area.

The Cordillera Central cuts off the rain coming in from the heavily showered northeast, making this a dry region of cacti and bedrock, a perfect film location for old-fashioned western movies. It's also ideal country for birders. Some 50% of all of the island's terrestrial bird species can be seen in this dry and dusty forest. You might even spot the Puerto Rican emerald-breasted hummingbird. A number of migratory birds often stop here. The most serious ornithologists seek out the Puerto Rican nightjar, a local bird that was believed to be extinct. Now it's estimated that there are nearly a thousand of them.

To reach the forest, take Rte. 334 northeast of Guánica, to the heart of the forest. There's a ranger station here that will give you information about hiking trails. The booklet provided by the ranger station outlines 36 miles (58km) of trails through the four forest types. The most interesting is the mile-long (1.6km) **Cueva Trail,** which gives you the most scenic look at the various types of vegetation. You might even encounter the endangered bufo lemur toad, once declared extinct but found, thankfully, still jumping in this area.

SCUBA DIVING, SNORKELING & OTHER OUTDOOR PURSUITS

The best dive operation in Guánica is **Sea Venture Dive Copamarina** (✆ **787/821-0505,** ext. 729), part of the **Copamarina Beach Resort.** Copamarina has a long pier where fishing is permitted, and a 42-foot (13m) Pro Jet dive boat. Guánica is one of the Caribbean's best areas for day and night dives. A two-tank dive costs $119, with full diving equipment. You can also rent snorkeling gear or take a ride to one of the islands nearby. It's good to reserve in advance to assure the dive master is working that day.

Whale-watching excursions can be arranged from January to March at the hotel's tour desk, which also offers ecotours, kayaking, deep-sea fishing, and sunset sails. Horseback riding and sunset biking are also available.

At one of the local beaches, **Playa Santa,** west of town, **Pino's Boat & Water Fun** (✆ **787/821-6864** or 787/484-8083) will rent you a paddle boat or kayak at prices ranging from $13 to $22 hourly. A banana-boat ride costs $7.50 per person, while water scooters cost $45 for a half-hour.

One of the most visited sites is **Gilligan's Island,** a series of mangrove and sand cays near the Caña Gorda peninsula. Part of the dry forest reserve, it is set aside for recreational use. A small ferry departs from in front of Restaurant San Jacinto, just past Copamarina Beach Resort, every hour daily from 10am to 5pm, weather permitting; round-trip costs $6. **Ballena Beach** is farther down Rte. 333, in the coastal border of the Dry Forest. This is a beautiful beach, with huge palm trees and golden sand. During winter storms, surfers flock here for rare, tubular waves.

WHERE TO STAY

Copamarina Beach Resort ★★ Charming, low key, and discreetly elegant, the Copamarina spreads out easily along a landscaped palm grove, with gentle waters and offshore cays, a large pool, and shady grounds. The attractively decorated units have tile floors, lots of exposed wood, and louvered doors with screens that open onto large verandas or terraces. Everything is airy and comfortable. Bathrooms are large and up-to-date. The fine-dining restaurant, Alexandra, serves great food, and it's less formal than most San Juan restaurants of similar quality, and staffed by a hardworking crowd of young people. The dive facilities here are the best and most varied in western Puerto Rico, attracting divers of all levels of expertise. The array of watersports and sports activities is incredible, and tours can be gotten here to anywhere on the island, including next door at the Guánica Dry Forest reserve. The hotel also offers guests all-inclusive options. We recommend renting a car and trying some of the local restaurants in Guánica and other coastal villages you will visit while staying here, and visiting beaches throughout the area.

Rte. 333 Km 6.5, Caña Gorda (P.O. Box 805), Guánica, PR 00653. ✆ **888/881-6233** or 787/821-0505. Fax 787/821-0070. www.copamarina.com. 106 units. High season $190–$240 double; low season $145–$185 double; year-round $295–$395 suite, $722–$1,000 villa. AE, DC, MC, V. From Ponce, drive west along Rte. 2 to Rte. 116 and go south to Rte. 333, then head east. **Amenities:** 2 restaurants; bar; babysitting; health club; 2 outdoor pools; room service; tennis courts; rooms for those w/limited mobility. *In room:* A/C, TV, dataport, fridge, hair dryer.

Mary Lee's by the Sea ★ Owned and operated by Michigan-born Mary Lee Alvarez, a former resident of Cuba and a self-described "compulsive decorator," this is an informal collection of cottages, seafront houses, and apartments, located 4 miles (6.4km) east of Guánica. Five California-style houses are subdivided into eight living units, each suitable for one to three couples. Rooms are whimsically decorated in an airy, somewhat bohemian way, with a sense of 1960s comfort and a sometimes soothing sense of clutter. Each unit has a small, tiled bathroom with a tub. The entire compound, which grew in an artfully erratic way, is landscaped with flowering shrubs, trees, and vines. Overall, the ambience is kind and low-key.

There aren't any formally organized activities here, but the hotel sits next to sandy beaches and a handful of uninhabited offshore cays. The management maintains rental boats with motors, two waterside sun decks, and several kayaks for the benefit of active guests. Hikers and bird-watchers can go north to the Guánica State Forest.

Don't come here looking for nighttime activities or enforced conviviality. The place is quiet, secluded, and appropriate for low-key vacationers looking for privacy. There isn't a bar or restaurant here, but each unit has a modern kitchen and an outdoor barbecue pit. The rooms are serviced weekly, although guests can arrange daily maid service for an extra fee.

Rte. 333 Km 6.7 (P.O. Box 394), Guánica, PR 00653. ✆ **787/821-3600.** Fax 787/821-0744. www.maryleesbythesea.com. 11 units. Year-round $80–$120 double; $100–$140 studio and 1-bedroom apt; $160–$200 2-bedroom apt; $250 3-bedroom house. MC, V. From Ponce, take Rte. 2. When you reach Rte. 116, head south toward Guánica. The hotel is signposted from the road. **Amenities:** Laundry service, barbeque. *In room:* A/C, kitchen, coffeemaker, iron, safe, no phone.

Parador Guánica 1929 This charming property lies on one of the island's prettiest roads, enveloped by a canopy of trees as it winds along Ensenada Bay and a line of plantation homes atop a hill overlooking it. Guánica's Ensenada sector was once the site of one of the largest sugar mills in the Caribbean, but it's been a bit of a ghost town since it shut down in the 1980s. Shadows of its former opulence can be glimpsed in the sun-baked decaying structures throughout the area, as well as the few restored buildings, such as this immaculate hotel. A classic Spanish-style plantation home, with a wide, wrap-around veranda on each of its two levels, its rooms have subdued tropical decor and are comfortable and well equipped. Breakfast is served on the downstairs side veranda overlooking the large pool area, with sun chairs on its surrounding deck. The food at the on-site restaurant is only okay. Prices at area restaurants are extremely competitive.

Rte. 3116 Km 2.5, Av. Los Veteranos, Ensenada, Guánica 00767. ✆ **787/821-0099** or 787/842-0260. Fax 787/841-3602. www.tropicalinnspr.com. 21 units. Year-round $102 double. Rates include continental breakfast. AE, MC, V. **Amenities:** Pool, gym, game room, playground and basketball court, Wi-Fi in common areas, coin laundry facility. *In room:* A/C, satellite TV, high-speed Internet, kitchen, hair dryer.

WHERE TO DINE

Alexandra ★ INTERNATIONAL This is a genuinely excellent restaurant with a kitchen team turning out delectable dishes that include sautéed shrimps in roasted garlic cream sauce, lobster tail in mustard and mango sauce with provenzal plantain fries and Cornish hen in warm bacon relish over fried risotto. The interior is air-conditioned but tropical in its feel, providing a welcome dose of relaxed glamour.

In the Copamarina Beach Resort, Rte. 333 Km 6.5, Caña Gorda (P.O. Box 805), Guánica. ✆ **787/821-0505.** Reservations recommended. Main courses $17–$36. AE, DC, DISC, MC, V. Sun–Thurs 6–10:30pm; Fri–Sat 6–11pm.

The Blue Marlin ★ SEAFOOD The most established restaurant on Guánica's famous harbor, this is still the best place for local seafood. Housed in a rambling plantation style structure overlooking the pretty bay, there is a large but relaxed quiet dining area, with some tables on balconies overlooking the harbor, serving excellent local meals, with an accent on freshly caught seafood. We love everything from the Caribbean lobster ceviche salad to the *mofongo* stuffed with mixed seafood (conch, octopus, shrimp, and red snapper) in a light tomato sauce. But culinary landlubbers can find satisfaction here with budget priced *comida criolla.* Even the pork chops are tasty. There's an adjacent bar area with a jukebox playing all sorts of local hits—from reggaeton to classic salsa—and televisions tuned to sports or music videos. The long rectangular bar not only overlooks the harbor-side drive, but also one of its sides is actually on the street. Tasty snacks like seafood turnovers and fried fish fritters are available as well as more substantial menu items. There's even a more informal outdoor terrace area with cafeteria-style booths perfect for families who want a quick snack after the beach.

55 Calle Esperanza Idrach, Malecón de Guánica (at the end of Calle 25 de Julío), Guánica. ✆ **787/821-5858.** Reservations recommended. Main courses $9.50-$23. MC, V. Thurs-Mon 11am-1am.

Bodegas Andreu Solé 🎁 ★★ WINERY/TAPAS If you think Puerto Rican wine sounds like a joke, you won't after visiting this restored plantation home on Ensenada Bay: a bodega on the grounds of what was once the largest sugar mill in the Caribbean serving homegrown wine using tempranillo, cabernet sauvignon, merlot and other grapes and an excellent Spanish tapas menu. Only open on Friday and Saturday nights (available for private functions at other times), there is excellent live music nightly: from jazz to Spanish ballads to Puerto Rican folk music. There is a bar and dining room inside, but most visitors stick to the tables outside overlooking the bay. The excellent house paella comes in seafood, meat and vegetable varieties, and there are grilled burgers and veggie burgers plus changing specials. Diners can request special meals when making reservations. Normally, there is no admission, except for special functions featuring well-known acts, but even then admission prices generally hover around $10. The house wine are grown from a vineyard in town and elaborated on premises. I can vouch for the smoothness of the house red, which at $20 a bottle is also a bargain. A wide-variety of boutique wines and hand-craft liquors are also available here. You can just stop in if you want to try the local wine, hear some music and pick on tapas, but reservations are required if you want a full meal.

Rte. 3116 Km 2.5, Av. Los Veteranos, Ensenada, Guánica 00767. ✆ **787/951-9622.** Reservations required. MC, V. Tapas $5-$10, entrees $10-$20. Fri-Sat 7pm-1am.

La Paraguera ★

This charming fishing village lies 78 miles (126km) southwest of San Juan and 26 miles (42km) west of Ponce, just south of San Germán. From San Germán, take Rte. 320 directly south and follow the signposts. Note that this route changes its name several times along the way, becoming Rte. 101, 116, 315, 305, and then 304 before reaching La Parguera—even though it's all the same highway.

The name of the village comes from *pargos,* meaning snapper. Its main attraction, other than its beaches and diving, is **Phosphorescent Bay,** which contains millions of luminescent dinoflagellates (microscopic plankton). A disturbance causes them to light up the dark waters. For dramatic effect, they are best seen on a moonless

PUERTO RICO'S SECRET beaches

Some of Puerto Rico's most beautiful and isolated beaches lie on the island's southwestern coast, on the Caribbean Sea, far from major highways. Stretching between Ponce in the east and Cabo Rojo on Puerto Rico's extreme southwestern tip, these beaches flank some of the least densely populated parts of the island. And because the boundaries between them are relatively fluid, only a local resident (or perhaps a professional geographer) could say for sure where one ends and the other begins.

If you consider yourself an aficionado of isolated beaches, it's worth renting a car and striking out for these remote locales. Drive westward from Ponce along Hwy. 2, branching south along Rte. 116 to **Guánica,** the self-anointed gateway and capital of this string of "secret beaches."

By far the most accessible and appealing beach is **Caña Gorda ★**. Set about a quarter mile (.4km) south of Guánica, at the edge of a legally protected marsh that's known for its rich bird life and thick reeds, Caña Gorda is a sprawling expanse of pale beige sand that's dotted with picnic areas and a beach refreshment stand/bar, showers, bathrooms and other facilities. Just beyond the public beach is the well-recommended hotel, the **Copamarina Beach Resort** (✆ **787/821-0505**); see p. 226. You can check in for a night or two of sun-flooded R&R. Even if you're not staying at the hotel, consider dropping in for a *cuba libre,* a margarita, or a meal.

Farther along is **Ballena Beach,** which stretches for a mile or more along a deserted beachfront, protected by rocky bluffs and a grove of towering palm trees. There are several other smaller beaches as Rte. 333 cuts farther into the dry forest and ends at an undeveloped parking area, adjacent to a foundation built right on the coast, with the sandy **Tamarindo Beach** beyond it. Hills surround the area, covered by the dwarfed pines at the outskirts of the reserve.

Another beautiful beach in town is **Playa Santa,** which also lies off Rte. 116 (the exit to Rte. 325 is signposted). The white-sand beach has incredibly tranquil salty water, and there is a string of eateries serving snacks and cold drinks around a harbor beside it. **La Jungla** and **Manglillo** are two other beautiful, undeveloped beaches bordering here, with great snorkeling because of coral reefs just offshore and interesting mangrove canals. The road to Playa Santa first cuts through a section of undeveloped dry forest before ending at the beach town. An unmarked dirt road on the left-hand side leads to another breathtakingly beautiful sand beach.

In the very southwest sector of Puerto Rico are some relatively hidden and very secluded beaches, although getting to them is a bit difficult along some potholed roads. Head west on Rte. 101, cutting south at the junction with Rte. 301, which will carry you to one of the most westerly beaches in Puerto Rico, Playa Sucia. The beach opens onto **Bahia Sucia ★**, whose name rather unappetizingly translates as "Dirty Bay." Actually it isn't dirty; it's a lovely spot. Hikers willing to walk a while will also be rewarded for their efforts from the Boquerón public beach and over the bluffs bordering it.

All these beaches might be hard to reach, but persevere and you'll be met with warm water and long, uncrowded stretches of sand, where towering king palms and salt-tolerant sea grapes provide an idyllic tropical backdrop for sun and surf. Keep in mind that most of the beaches mentioned here have virtually no services or public utilities. Pack what you'll need for the day—food, water, sunscreen, and so forth.

night. Boats leave for a troll around the bay nightly from 7:30pm to 12:30am from La Parguera pier, depending on demand. The trip costs $7.50 per person.

Offshore are some 12 to 15 reefs with a variety of depths. The Beril reef goes down to 60 feet (18m), then drops to 2,000 feet (610m). This wall is famous among divers, and visibility ranges from 100 to 120 feet (30–37m). These reefs also provide some of the best snorkeling possibilities in Puerto Rico. Marine life is both abundant and diverse, including big morays, sea turtles, barracudas, nurse sharks, and manatees. **Paradise Scuba & Snorkeling Center,** Hotel Casa Blanca Building, at La Parguera (© **787/899-7611**), offers the best diving and snorkeling. A two-tank dive costs $100; a 3-hour snorkeling jaunt goes for $40 per person, with equipment included. Lessons and a variety of trips are available.

WHERE TO STAY

Parador Villa Parguera ★ ☺ Although the water in the nearby bay is too muddy for swimming, guests can enjoy a view of the harbor and take a dip in the swimming pool. Situated on the southwestern shore of Puerto Rico, this parador is favored by *sanjuaneros* for weekend escapes. It's also known for its seafood dinners (the fish are not caught in the bay), comfortable and uncomplicated bedrooms, and location next to the bay's famous phosphorescent waters. Each unit has either a balcony or a terrace. Bathrooms are rather cramped but well maintained, and each has either a shower or a tub. This place is more gregarious and convivial, and usually more fun, than the Porlamar, a few steps away.

The spacious, air-conditioned restaurant, where the occasionally slow service might remind you of Spain in a bygone era, offers traditional favorites, such as filet of fish stuffed with lobster and shrimp. Non-guests are welcome here, and there's a play area for children. Because the inn is popular with local vacationers, there are frequent specials, such as a $395 weekend (Fri–Sun) special for two that includes welcome drinks, breakfasts, dinners, flowers, and dancing, along with a free show.

There's a dock right outside the restaurant where boats tie up, which is convenient because the thing to do here is to hire a boat and explore the beautiful shallow coast replete with reefs and tropical sea life.

Main St. 304 (P.O. Box 3400), Carretera 304 Km 303, La Parguera, Lajas, PR 00667. © **787/899-7777.** Fax 787/899-6040. www.villaparguera.net. 74 units (all with either shower or tub). Year-round $107–$165 double. 2 children 9 or under stay free in parent's room. AE, DC, DISC, MC, V. Drive west along Rte. 2 until you reach the junction with Rte. 116; then head south along Rte. 116 and Rte. 304. **Amenities:** Restaurant; bar; babysitting; pool; rooms for those w/limited mobility. *In room:* A/C, TV.

WHERE TO DINE

Besides the following recommendation, the formal dining room at **Parador Villa Parguera** (see "Where to Stay," above) also is an excellent dinner option.

La Casita ☺ SEAFOOD This is the town's most consistently reliable and popular restaurant. It has flourished here since the 1960s, in a simple wooden building. Inside, lots of varnished pine acts as a decorative foil for platters of local and imported fish and shellfish. Filets of fish can be served in any of seven different styles; lobster comes in five. Even the Puerto Rican starchy staple of *mofongo* comes in versions stuffed with crab, octopus, shrimp, lobster, and assorted shellfish. Begin with fish chowder, a dozen cheese balls, or fish croquettes. End with coconut-flavored flan. Don't expect grand service or decor, but rather a setting where food is the focus.

Calle Principal 304. ✆ **787/899-1681.** Reservations not necessary. All main courses $8. AE, MC, V. Tues–Sun 11am–10:30pm. Closed 2 weeks in Sept.

Boqueron

Lying 85 miles (137km) southwest of San Juan and 33 miles (53km) west of Ponce is the little beach town of Boquerón. It is just south of Cabo Rojo, west of the historic city of San Germán, and near the western edge of the Boquerón Forest Preserve.

What puts sleepy Boquerón on the tourist map is its lovely public beach, one of the island's finest for swimming. It is also known for the shellfish found offshore. The beach has facilities, including lockers and changing places, plus kiosks that rent watersports equipment. Parking costs $2. On weekends the resort tends to be crowded with families driving down from San Juan.

The outfitter that offers the best scuba diving and snorkeling in the area is **Mona Aquatics,** on Calle José de Diego, directly west of the heart of town (✆ **787/851-2185**) near the town marina and Hotel Boquemar. It offers several dive packages (a two-tank dive starts at $105 per person), including trips to Desecheo and Mona Island some 50 miles (81km) out to sea, a sanctuary known for its spectacular dive opportunities. The company also rents snorkeling gear and, if enough people are interested, conducts boat tours of the Bahía de Boquerón.

From Boquerón you can head directly south to **El Faro de Cabo Rojo** at the island's southernmost corner. The century-old Cabo Rojo Lighthouse lies on Rte. 301, along a spit of land between Bahía Sucia and Bahía Salinas. Looking down from the lighthouse, you'll see a 2,000-foot (610m) drop along jagged limestone cliffs. The lighthouse dates from 1881, when it was constructed under Spanish rule. The famous pirate Roberto Cofresi used to terrorize the coast along here in the 19th century and was said to have hidden out in a cave nearby.

WHERE TO STAY

Bahia Salinas Beach Resort & Spa ★★ 🎁 You live close to nature here. Nature lovers and bird-watchers are drawn to this intimate inn in Cabo Rojo in the far southwestern corner of Puerto Rico. At the tip of the western coast, the sanctuary is bordered by a mangrove reserve, bird sanctuaries, and salt flats in the undeveloped

A Wildlife Refuge for Bird Fanciers

The area around Cabo Rojo, the Refugio Nacional Cabo Rojo (Red Cape National Refuge; ✆ 787/851-7297) attracts serious bird-watchers to its government-protected sector. The refuge, run by the U.S. Fish & Wildlife Service, is on Rte. 301 at Km 5.1, 1 mile (1.6km) north of the turnoff to El Combate. At the entrance to the refuge is a visitor center. The only time you can visit the refuge is from 7:30am to 4pm Monday to Friday; admission is free. Migratory birds, especially ducks and herons as well as several species of songbirds, inhabit this refuge. Birders have reported seeing at least 130 species. Trails for bird-watchers have been cut through the reserve. The best time to observe the birds is during the winter months, when they have fled from their cold homelands in the north.

coastal region near the Cabo Rojo Lighthouse. Salt mineral waters, similar to those of the Dead Sea, supply water for the on-site Jacuzzi and for treatments at its Cuni Spa, which gives a full range of beauty and relaxation treatments. There is ample opportunity for jogging and hiking in the natural surroundings as well as all sorts of watersports. It is near many white-sand beaches, including the town's large public beach. Its **Agua al Cuello** is excellent and the **Bohemio Bar** has an enviable view of the sea and unstoppable blenders. The bedrooms are midsize to large, and are furnished in the so-called "hacienda" Puerto Rican style, which means wooden colonial-style furniture and four-poster beds. The place is well run and maintained.

Rd. 301 Km 11.5, Sector El Faro, Cabo Rojo, PR 00622. ✆ **787/254-1212.** Fax 787/254-1215. www.bahiasalina.com. 22 units. Year-round $193–$205 double. Children 11 and under stay free in parent's room. AE, MC, V. **Amenities:** Restaurant; bar; 2 outdoor pools; high-speed Internet access; room service; rooms for those w/limited mobility. *In room:* A/C, TV.

Cofresi Beach Hotel Set on the town's main road across from one of the area's best dive shops, this is a choice for clients who can live without maid service and other resort-oriented amenities—there is no full-time reception or concierge staff. The apartments here have kitchens with cutlery, plates, and cooking equipment, durable furniture, and comfortable beds; each has a small, tiled bathroom with a tub and shower. It's about as laissez-faire as they come.

Calle Muñoz Rivera 57, P.O. Box 1209, Boquerón, PR 00622. ✆ **787/254-3000.** Fax 787/254-1048. www.cofresibeach.com. 12 units. Year-round $129 1-bedroom; $165 2-bedroom; $219 3-bedroom. AE, MC, V. **Amenities:** Pool. *In room:* A/C, TV, kitchenette, hair dryer.

Parador Boquemar This family favorite lies right at the heart of town by Boquerón Beach. A recent renovation has spruced up the common areas and guest rooms, which gives them a more tropical feel, but the hotel still lacks character. Despite the small units here, Puerto Rican families like this place a lot, causing readers to complain that children sometimes run up and down the corridors. Rooms are simple but comfortable and clean. This is not the place to stay if you are going for ambience, but it is a good deal at a great location. Kids will enjoy the pool. Stay here only if you plan to spend most of your time outside the hotel. The hotel's restaurant, **Las Cascadas,** has good food, but again the atmosphere leaves much to be desired (see "Where to Dine," below).

Carretera 101, Poblado de Boquerón, Cabo Rojo, PR 00622. ✆ **787/851-2158.** Fax 787/851-7600. www.boquemar.com. 75 units (shower only). Year-round $100–$120 double; $125 junior suite. AE, DC, MC, V. **Amenities:** Restaurant; bar; babysitting; outside pool; rooms for those w/limited mobility. *In room:* A/C, TV, small fridge.

Wildflowers The rooms in this guesthouse have charming classic furnishings, which are as comfortable as they are appealing, and all the modern convenience you need. Original work by local artists hangs throughout the premises, including inside guest rooms, which also adds tremendously to the ambience. Near town and the beach, its proximity is also a plus, except during summer and holiday weekends, when the roving partygoers will keep you up until 1am. The rooms are sizeable and can sleep up to four people.

Calle Muñoz Rivera 13, Poblado de Boquerón, Cabo Rojo, PR 00622. ✆ **787/851-1793.** Fax 787/255-4096. www.wildflowersguesthouse.com. 8 units. Winter $100–$125 double; off season $75–$100. AE, MC, V. **Amenities:** A/C, TV, small fridge.

WHERE TO DINE

Boquerón has great roadside food stands. You can get everything from fresh oysters to hand-rolled burritos from vendors set up along the beach village's main drag. Open air bars and restaurants also sell turnovers stuffed with fresh fish, lobster, or conch, as well as seafood ceviche salad in plastic cups.

Galloway's ★ CREOLE/CONTINENTAL This is our favorite restaurant in Boquerón, right near the center of town but set back along the water. Sit in the back dining room that is on a dock over Boquerón Bay. It's a great spot for a fresh seafood meal as you watch one of those perfect western sunsets. This is a casual spot, but the food is first rate. Being right on the water, we can't help but take our seafood straight up—such as a whole fried red snapper and boiled Caribbean lobster. While much of the menu is typical of the area, specializing in local cuisine and seafood, you'll also find great ribs, steaks, and pub fare. The bar near the entrance is a good spot to mix with locals and ex-pats and pick up tips on area activities. On weekends, there's often live music.

12 Calle José de Diego, Poblado de Boquerón, Cabo Rojo. ✆ **787/254-3302.** Reservations not necessary. Main courses $10–$29. AE, MC, V. Thurs–Tues noon–midnight; closed Wed.

Las Cascadas CREOLE/CONTINENTAL One of the best restaurants in the area, this popular bar and restaurant is a *meson gastronómico,* a Puerto Rico Tourism Company program that sponsors local restaurants it deems of sufficient quality to cater to tourists. Among its other virtues, Parador Boquemar boasts an interior waterfall. The day begins early here. The chef's breakfast specialty is an omelet Cascada, with ham, tomatoes, onions, peppers, and cheese. At dinner many Creole recipes appear, such as *mofongo relleno* (stuffed mashed plantains); the plantains can be stuffed with lobster, shrimp, octopus, or conch.

The meats, such as filet mignon, are imported but tasty. Choose among five different sauces to be served with your lobster. Other specialties of the chef include chicken breast stuffed with lobster or shrimp. The tastiest appetizers are fish and cheese balls.

In the Parador Boquemar, Carretera 101, Poblado de Boquerón, Cabo Rojo. ✆ **787/851-2158.** Reservations not necessary. Breakfast $5–$10; main courses $12–$29. AE, MC, V. Daily 7:30–11:30am; Thurs–Tues 6–10pm.

Roberto's Fish Net/Roberto's Restauarant Villa Playera 🎁 PUERTO RICAN These two restaurants sit on the same sleepy street in the center of Boquerón and both are run by Roberto Aviles and offer fresh seafood, specialties like stuffed *mofongo* and *asopao,* whole fried snapper, and local favorites.

Calle José de Diego s/n (without number). ✆ **787/851-6009** or 787/254-3163. Reservations not necessary. Main courses $10–$25. AE, DISC, MC, V. Fish Net Wed–Sun 11am–10pm, Villa Playera Fri–Tues 11am–8pm.

SAN GERMÁN ★★

104 miles (167km) SW of San Juan, 34 miles (55km) W of Ponce

Only an hour's drive from Ponce and right near the beaches of the southwest coast, and just over 2 hours from San Juan, San Germán, Puerto Rico's second-oldest town, is a little museum piece. It was founded in 1512 and destroyed by the French in

1528. Rebuilt in 1570, it was named after Germain de Foix, the second wife of King Ferdinand of Spain. Once the rival of San Juan, San Germán harbored many pirates who pillaged the ships that sailed off the nearby coastline. Indeed, many of today's residents are descended from the smugglers, poets, priests, and politicians who once lived here.

The pirates and sugar plantations are long gone, but the city retains colorful reminders of its Spanish colonial past. Flowers brighten some of the patios here as they do in Seville. Also, as in a small Spanish town, many of the inhabitants stroll through the historic zone in the early evening. Nicknamed *Ciudad de las Lomas* (City of the Hills), San Germán boasts verdant scenery that provides a pleasant backdrop to a variety of architectural styles—Spanish colonial (1850s), *criolla* (1880s), neoclassical (1910s), Art Deco (1930s), and international (1960s)—depicted in the gracious old-world buildings lining the streets. So significant are these buildings that San Germán is included in the National Register of Historic Places.

The city's 249 historical treasures are within easy walking distance of one another. Regrettably, you must view most of them from the outside. If some of them are actually open, count yourself fortunate, as they have no phones, keep no regular hours, and are staffed by volunteers who rarely show up. Also, be aware that the signage for the historic buildings can be confusing, and many of the streets in the old town tend to run one-way. Most of the city's architectural treasures lie uphill from the congested main thoroughfare (Calle Luna). We usually try to park on the town's main street (Carretera 102, which changes its name within the borders of San Germán to Calle Luna), and then proceed on foot through the city's commercial core before reaching the architectural highlights described below.

One of the most noteworthy churches in Puerto Rico is **Iglesia Porta Coeli (Gate of Heaven)** ★ (✆ **787/892-0160**), which sits atop a knoll at the eastern end of a cobble-covered square, the Parque de Santo Domingo. Dating from 1606 and built in a style inspired by the Romanesque architecture of northern Spain, this is the oldest church in the New World. Restored by the Institute of Puerto Rican Culture, and sheathed in a layer of salmon-colored stucco, it contains a museum of religious art with a collection of ancient *santos,* the carved figures of saints that have long been a major part of Puerto Rican folk art. Look for the 17th-century portrait of St. Nicholas de Bari, the French Santa Claus. Inside, the original palm-wood ceiling and tough ausobo-wood beams draw the eye upward. Other treasures include early choral books from Santo Domingo, a primitive carving of Jesus, and 19th-century Señora de la Monserrate Black Madonna and Child statues. Admission is $3 for adults, $2 for seniors and children over 12, free for children12 and under. The church is open Wednesday through Sunday from 8:30am to noon and 1 to 4:30pm.

Less than 100 feet (30m) downhill from Iglesia Porta Coeli, at the bottom of the steps that lead from its front door down to the plaza below, is the **Casa Morales** (also known as the **Tomás Vivoni House,** after its architect), San Germán's most photographed and widely recognized house. Designed in the Edwardian style, with wraparound porches, elaborate gables, and elements that might remind you of a Swiss chalet, it was built in 1913, reflecting the region's turn-of-the-20th-century agrarian prosperity. (Note that it is a private residence and can be admired only from the outside.)

The long and narrow, gently sloping plaza that fronts Iglesia Porta Coeli is the Parque de Santo Domingo, one of San Germán's two main plazas. Street signs also identify the plaza as the Calle Ruiz Belvis. Originally a marketplace, the plaza is paved with red and black cobblestones. It is bordered with cast-iron benches and portrait busts of prominent figures in the town's history. This plaza merges gracefully with a second plaza, which street signs and maps identify as the Plaza Francisco Mariano Quiñones, the Calle José Julian Acosta, and the Plaza Principal. Separating the two plazas is the unused (and closed to the public) **Viejo Alcaldía (Old Town Hall).** Built late in the 19th century, it's awaiting a new vision, perhaps as a museum or public building.

San Germán's most impressive church—and the most monumental building in the region—is **San Germán de Auxerre** (✆ **787/892-1027**), which rises majestically above the western end of the Plaza Francisco Mariano Quiñones. Designed in the Spanish baroque style, it was built in 1573 in the form of a simple chapel with a low-slung thatch roof. Its present grandeur is the result of at least five subsequent enlargements and renovations. Much of what you see today is the result of a rebuilding in 1688 and a restoration in 1737 that followed a disastrous earthquake. Inside are three naves, 10 altars, three chapels, and a belfry that was rebuilt in 1939, following an earthquake in 1918. The central chandelier, made from rock crystal and imported from Barcelona in 1866, is the largest in the Caribbean. The pride of the church is the *trompe l'oeil* ceiling, which was elaborately restored in 1993. A series of stained-glass windows with contemporary designs was inserted during a 1999 restoration. The church can be visited daily from 8 to 11am and 1 to 3pm.

A few lesser sights are located near the town's two main squares. **Farmacia Martin,** a modern pharmacy, is incongruously set within the shell of a graceful but battered Art Deco building at the edge of the Parque Santo Domingo (Calle Ruiz Belvis 22; ✆ **787/892-1122**). A cluster of battered and dilapidated clapboard-sided houses line the southern side of the Calle Dr. Ueve, which rambles downhill from its origin at the base of the Iglesia Porta Coeli. The most important house is no. 66, the **Casa Acosta y Fores.** Also noteworthy is **Casa Juán Perichi,** a substantial-looking structure at the corner of Calle Dr. Ueve and Parque Santo Domingo, nearly adjacent to the Iglesia Porta Coeli. Both houses were built around 1917, of traditional wood construction, and are viewed as fine examples of Puerto Rican adaptations of Victorian architecture. Regrettably, both are seriously dilapidated, although that might change as San Germán continues the slow course of its historic renovations.

To the side of the Auxerre church is the modern, cement-sided **Public Library,** Calle José Julia Acosta, where you might be tempted to duck into the air-conditioned interior for a glance through the stacks and periodical collection. It's open Monday through Thursday from 8am to 8:30pm, Friday from 8am to 6pm, and Saturday from 8am to 1pm and 2 to 4:30pm. Behind the Auxerre church is at least one masonry-fronted town house whose design might remind you of southern Spain (Andalusia), especially when the flowers in the window boxes add splashes of color.

Where to Eat

Restaurante L'Auxerre ★ 🎁 This French restaurant is that rare eatery in downtown San Germán that actually lives up to its surroundings. The artfulness of the cuisine in San Germán is as surprising as the historic district itself in a region of kitschy beach towns. The menus change weekly, but chef Pierre Saussy, who has worked with such names as Roger Verger to Rocco Dispirito, keeps his fine contemporary cuisine simple and on point, taking advantage of fresh seasonal ingredients.

Recent items include filet mignon with truffle potato pureé, and roast asparagus, linguini with chicken in an almond basil pesto and roast mahimahi in a brown butter caper sauce with potato pureé. It's also a perfect spot fro Sunday brunch if you are in the area, with goat cheese and shrimp omelets and steak and eggs available. The restaurant is inside a Spanish hacienda in the heart of the historic district. Sit outside in the interior patio to soak up all its charm; the inside dining room is a bit cramped.

Calle Estrella 16, San Germán. ✆ **787/892-8844.** Reservations recommended. Entrees $14–$31. AE, MC, V. Wed–Thurs 6–10pm; Fri–Sat 6–midnight, Sun 11am–4pm.

Tapas Café ★ 🎁 This charming restaurant is a favorite spot in the historic district of San Germán, an oasis of sophistication in the provincial countryside. The interior dining room, with mosaic tiles and blue stars on the ceiling, offers a cool respite from the heat. Portions are sizeable. The seafood paella is loaded with prawns, mussels, and lobster, and the beef medallions in blue cheese did not disappoint. Other menu items range from Spanish sausage sautéed in wine sauce to the classic soup *caldo gallego* to fried fish fritters.

50 Calle Dr. Santiago Veve, San Germán. ✆ **787/264-0610.** Reservations not necessary. Tapas $2–$15. AE, MC, V. Thurs–Fri 4:30–11pm; Sat 11am–11pm; Sun 11am–9pm.

THE SOUTHERN MOUNTAINS

The mountain towns surrounding the gorgeous Toro Negro Forest Reserve straddle Puerto Rico's highest peaks that run along the center of the island. The area is included here because it is most accessible from the south, from Ponce and surrounding towns. The mountain towns include Villalba, Orocovis, Adjuntas, and Jayuya, as well as parts of Utuado, Coamo, and Juana Díaz. Even from Ponce, the best route to this region is to head east first along the coastal Hwy. 2 to neighboring Juana Díaz. Then take Rte. 149 north through town and into the lush mountains of Villalba. Continue straight until the intersection of Rte. 143 west to get to **Toro Negro Forest Reserve** (there's an entrance at Km 32.4).

TORO NEGRO FOREST RESERVE ★ & LAKE GUINEO ★

North of Ponce, **Toro Negro Forest Reserve ★** (✆ **787/867-3040**) lies along the Cordillera Central, the cloud-shrouded, lush central mountain chain that spans Puerto Rico's spine from the southeast town of Yabucoa all the way to outside Mayagüez on the west coast. This 7,000-acre (2,833-hectare) park, ideal for hikers, straddles the highest peak of the Cordillera Central at the very heart of Puerto Rico, quite near the midway point between east and west coasts. A forest of lush trees, the reserve also contains the headwaters of several main rivers and lakes, and has several crashing waterfalls. The reserve lies at the borders of four mountain towns: Villalba, Jayuya, Adjuntas and Orocovis.

The lowest temperatures recorded on the island—some 40°F (4°C)—were measured at **Lake Guineo ★**, the island's highest lake, which lies within the reserve. The best trail to take here is a short, paved, and wickedly steep path on the north side of Rte. 143, going up to the south side of **Cerro de Punta,** which at 4,390 feet (1,338m) is the highest peak on Puerto Rico. Allow about half an hour for an ascent. Once at the top, you'll be rewarded with Puerto Rico's grandest view, sweeping across the lush interior from the Atlantic to the Caribbean coasts. Other mountains in the reserve also offer hiking possibilities. The reserve spans several distinct types, including a sierra palm forest, which in places forms a complete canopy from the sun, and a mountainous cloud forest, with dwarfed, but vibrantly green plants and trees.

The main entrance to the forest is at the Doña Juana recreational area, which has a swimming pool filled with cold water from the mountain streams, a picnic area, and a rustic campground. An adjacent restaurant serves up Puerto Rican barbecued chicken and pork and other local delicacies. Many hiking trails originate from this area. One of the best is a 2-mile (3.2km) trek to an observation post and the impressive 200-foot (61m) Doña Juana Falls.

Jayuya lies north of the reserve, but to access it, you must return east along Rte. 143 to Rte. 149, and take that north, farther into the central mountains to Rte. 144, which you'll take back west to access the town. This is a beautiful area, filled with old coffee estates and lush mountain forest. The local parador is a country inn built on the grounds of an old coffee plantation (**Parador Hacienda Gripiñas;** see below), which is one of the best places to stay in Puerto Rico's interior. There's also a fine restaurant on the grounds. Built by a Spanish coffee baron more than 150 years ago, the restored plantation home is surrounded by gardens and coffee fields.

Jayuya is also known for the relics found here from Puerto Rico's Taíno past. Off Rte. 144 is La Piedra Escrita, the Written Rock, a huge boulder beside a stream, with Taíno petroglyphs carved into the stone. It's a wonderful picnic spot. Jayuya also hosts an annual Indigenous Festival in November, which combines native crafts with music and food. The **Cemi Museum,** Rte. 144 Km 9.3 (✆ **787/828-1241**), in town has a collection of Taíno pottery and *cemís,* amulets sacred to the island's indigenous peoples. The adjacent **Casa Museo Canales,** Rte. 144 Km 9.4 (✆ **787/828-1241**), is a restored 19th-century coffee plantation home with interesting exhibits. Both museums charge $1 for adults and 50¢ for children and are open from 9am to 3pm every day.

WHERE TO STAY & DINE

Hacienda Gripiñas ★ This restored plantation home is set amidst 20 acres of coffee fields and nature. It's a charming respite from the 21st century. Take a walk in the cool mountain countryside, then stake out a hammock or rocking chair on the porch or one of the many balconies and relax awhile. First built in 1853 by coffee baron and Spanish nobleman Eusebio Pérez del Castillo, the former plantation home was turned into an inn in 1975 but retains the elegance and grandeur of its past. A wide porch wraps around this restored plantation home, and there are gorgeous gardens and coffee fields surrounding it. There are also reading rooms and common areas in which to lounge. The sweet song of chanting *couquís,* ubiquitous small Puerto Rican tree frogs, fills the air. There is also an excellent restaurant on the premises and a pool. A small trail from here leads to the summit of Cerro Punta, Puerto Rico's highest peak. There are frequent specials with meals included that make sense for visitors because of the parador's isolation. If you are looking for solitude, go during the week, and you will likely have the place to yourself and a few other guests and save a few bucks on your tab.

Rte. 527 Km 2.5, Jayuya PR 00664. ✆ **787/828-1717.** Fax 787/828-1718. www.haciendagripinas.com. 48 units. Year-round Mon–Wed $90 double; Thurs–Sun $105 double. AE, MC, V. **Amenities:** Restaurant; bar; game room; library; 2 pools. *In room:* A/C, TV.

MAYAGÜEZ & THE NORTHWEST

9

Mayagüez lies in the middle of Puerto Rico's west coast, a major fun-in-the-sun zone, but it lacks its own quality beach.

Yet Puerto Rico's third largest city is close enough to several world-class beaches to make it worth a stay. And it can offer guests different visions of the Caribbean vacation.

To the north, along the northwest coast that stems from Rincón to Isabella, lie the Caribbean's best surfing beaches, which compare favorably to those of California when conditions are right. These are the beaches we'll focus on in this chapter. And to the south are equally attractive beaches with among the calmest waters in the Caribbean, offering excellent snorkeling, scuba, and sailing opportunities (see chapter 8).

The city is not as renowned for its historic sites, architecture, and attractions as San Juan or Ponce, but it has all three.

Mayagüez is also close to the western mountains, especially Maricao, perhaps the prettiest of the mountain towns in Puerto Rico. You can stay here in a renovated coffee plantation house, or just have lunch on its charming veranda. Or rent a cabin at the Monte del Estado national park, or just spend the day in its swimming pool fed by mountain streams.

Throughout the northwest beach towns, there are a few top-level properties, several modestly priced and attractive hotels and guesthouses, and a few noteworthy paradores, privately operated country inns approved by the Puerto Rico Tourism Company that choose to participate in its joint promotion program.

This western part of Puerto Rico contains the greatest concentration of paradores, along the coast and in the cool mountainous interior of the west. They're a wonderful escape from pollution and traffic on a hot day.

Mona Island can also be explored from the coast near Mayagüez. It's one of the island's biggest adventure jaunts in Puerto Rico, and shouldn't be missed.

MAYAGÜEZ ★

98 miles (158km) W of San Juan; 15 miles (24km) S of Aguadilla

Approaching from the north, where Hwy. 2 swoops down along beautiful coastal overpasses, it's easy to dismiss Mayagüez at first glimpse as a rather drab commercial port city, but the so-called "Sultan of the West" tends to win over visitors who give it a chance to show off its charms.

Despite outward appearances as a city, Mayagüez makes for a convenient stopover for those exploring the west coast.

If you want a big-wave beach with dramatic coastal cliffs, you can head north to Rincón, Aguadilla, and Isabella (see Rincón, later). And if you want white sand and palms, with tranquil aquamarine water, head south to Cabo Rojo, Lajas, and Guánica (see chapter 8).

Famed for the size and depth of its **harbor** (the second largest on the island, after San Juan's harbor), Mayagüez was built to control the **Mona Passage,** a route essential to the Spanish Empire when Puerto Rico and the nearby Dominican Republic were vital trade and defensive jewels in the Spanish crown. Today this waterway is notorious for the destructiveness of its currents, the ferocity of its sharks, and the thousands of boat people who arrive illegally from either Haiti or the Dominican Republic, both on the island of Hispaniola.

Queen Isabel II of Spain recognized Mayagüez's status as a town in 1836. Her son, Alfonso XII, granted it a city charter in 1877. Permanently isolated from the major commercial developments of San Juan, Mayagüez, like Ponce, has always retained its own distinct identity.

Today, the town has been hit by the closure of its tuna packing industry (which once packed 60% of the tuna consumed in the United States) and its manufacturing plants, victims to the exodus of jobs to countries where labor can be bought at a cheaper price.

But the town has a future in tourism and in some of the life science and high-tech manufacturing springing up around the fine University of Puerto Rico Mayagüez campus, which specializes in engineering and the sciences. The university community adds much to the city's cultural life. The city has also been abuzz with construction of a $400-million public-works project in preparation to host the 2010 Caribbean and Central American Games. New sports facilities, an athletes' village, and a pedestrian park along the city's west coast have all sprung up.

Essentials

GETTING THERE **Cape Air** (✆ **800/352-0714;** www.flycapeair.com) flies from San Juan to Mayagüez twice daily (flying time: 40 min.). Round-trip passage is $122 per person.

If you rent a car at the San Juan airport and want to drive to Mayagüez, it's fastest and most efficient to take the northern route that combines sections of the newly expanded De Diego Expressway, Rte. 22, with the older Rte. 2. Estimated driving time for a local resident is about 120 minutes, although newcomers usually take about 30 minutes longer. The southern route, which combines the modern Rte. 52 with transit across the outskirts of historic Ponce, and final access into Mayagüez via the southern section of Rte. 2, requires a total of about 3 hours and affords some worthwhile scenery across the island's mountainous interior.

GETTING AROUND **Taxis** meet arriving planes. If you take one, negotiate the fare with the driver first, because cabs are unmetered here.

There are branches of **Avis** (✆ **787/832-0406**), **Budget** (✆ **787/832-4570**), and **Hertz** (✆ **787/832-3314**) at the Mayagüez airport.

VISITOR INFORMATION The **Mayagüez Municipal Tourism Development Office** (✆ **787/832-5882**) can help orient visitors. In Aguadilla, there is also a **Puerto Rico Tourism Company** office (✆ **787/890-3315**). If you're starting out in San Juan, you can inquire there before you set out (see "Visitor Information" under "Orientation" in chapter 5).

Exploring the Area

MAYAGÜEZ ATTRACTIONS

The area surrounding the city's elegant central Plaza Colón is among the prettiest in the city, with several restored historic buildings. A bronze monument of Christopher Columbus atop a globe surrounded by 16 female statues dominates the plaza, which is also marked by mosaic tiled walkways and gurgling fountains, blooming tropical gardens, and squat leafy trees.

The neo-Corinthian **Mayagüez City Hall** and the **Nuestra Señora de la Candelaria,** which has gone through several incarnations since the first building went up in 1780, are noteworthy buildings right off the plaza.

Make sure to stroll down nearby **Calle McKinley,** home to the fabulous, recently restored **Yaguez Theater.** The neoclassical jewel served as both an opera and a silent movie house and is still in active use today. Originally inaugurated in 1909, a fire destroyed the structure in 1919, but it was rebuilt. The city's smashing Art Deco post office is also located here.

Mayagüez's historic waterfront district, with a restored 1920s Custom House and rows of neat warehouses, is also worth a look. The century-old **University of Puerto Rico Mayagüez** campus is also beautiful.

To soak in the magical sunsets of the Puerto Rican west coast, either head to the hills surrounding the city or down to the new lineal coastal park that was built as part of a host capital works projects for the city's hosting of the 2010 Caribbean and Central American Games.

Juan A. Rivero Zoo This 14-acre (5.7-hectare) zoo recently underwent a $14-million renovation. The African safari exhibit has lions, elephants, zebras, and rhinos, and jaguars are part of a Caribbean exhibit. There's also a butterfly and lizard exhibit and gorgeous grounds. The birdhouse has a fantastic elevated walkway where you look down on colorful tropical birds such as parrots. There are also eagles, hawks, and owls. You can see the entire zoo in 2 hours.

Rte. 108, Barrio Miradero, Mayagüez Union. ✆ **787/834-8110.** Admission $10 adults, $5 children and seniors, free children 4 and under and seniors 75 or older. Parking $3. Wed–Sun and holidays 8:30am–4pm.

The Tropical Agricultural Research Station This is not a botanical garden but a working research facility of the U.S. Department of Agriculture. It's located on Rte. 65, between Post Street and Rte. 108, adjacent to the University of Puerto Rico Mayagüez campus and across the street from the **Parque de los Próceres (Patriots' Park).** At the administration office, ask for a free map of the tropical gardens, which have one of the largest collections of tropical plant species intended for

Mayagüez

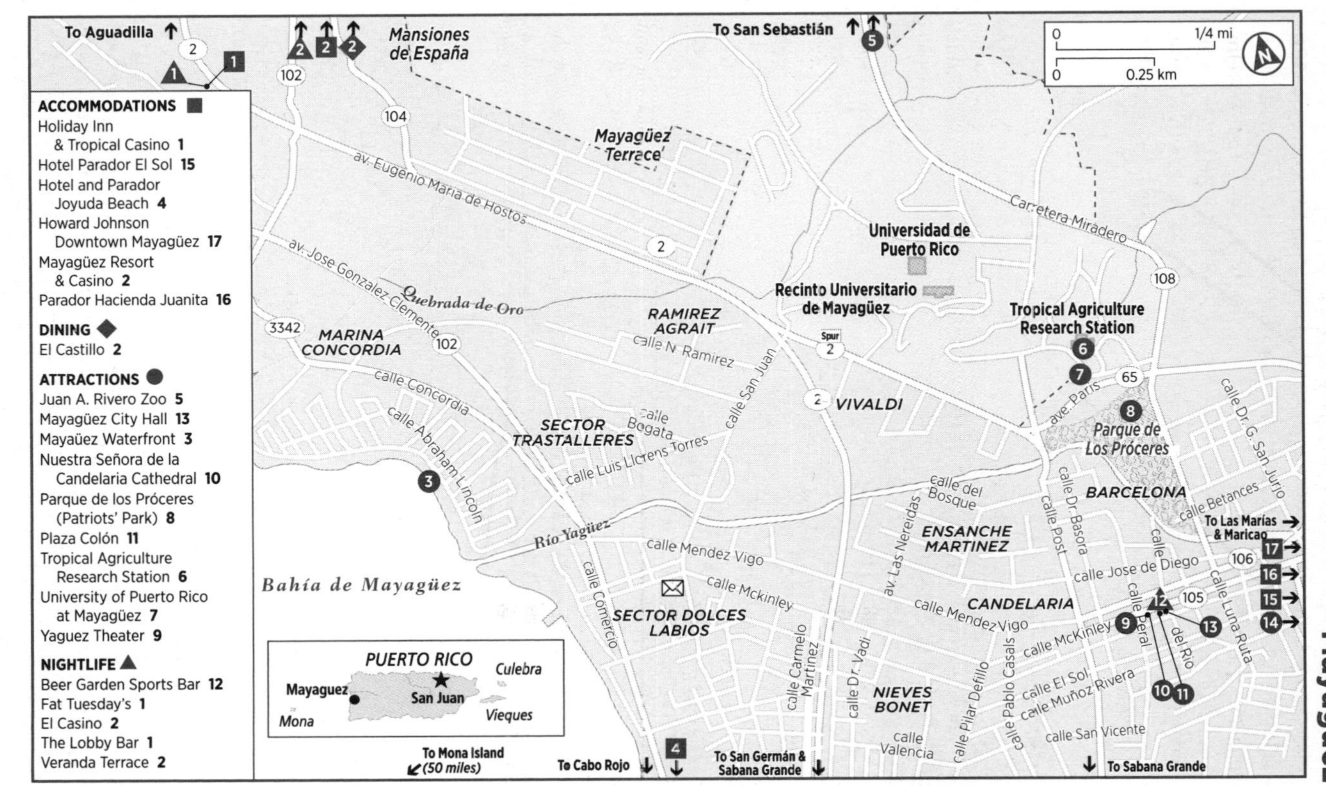

To Aguadilla
Mansiones de España
To San Sebastián
0 1/4 mi
0 0.25 km
ACCOMMODATIONS
Holiday Inn & Tropical Casino 1
Hotel Parador El Sol 15
Hotel and Parador Joyuda Beach 4
Howard Johnson Downtown Mayagüez 17
Mayagüez Resort & Casino 2
Parador Hacienda Juanita 16
DINING
El Castillo 2
ATTRACTIONS
Juan A. Rivero Zoo 5
Mayagüez City Hall 13
Mayaüez Waterfront 3
Nuestra Señora de la Candelaria Cathedral 10
Parque de los Próceres (Patriots' Park) 8
Plaza Colón 11
Tropical Agriculture Research Station 6
University of Puerto Rico at Mayagüez 7
Yaguez Theater 9
NIGHTLIFE
Beer Garden Sports Bar 12
Fat Tuesday's 1
El Casino 2
The Lobby Bar 1
Veranda Terrace 2
Mayagüez Terrace
av. Eugenio Maria de Hostos
av. Jose Gonzalez Clemente
Quebrada de Oro
Universidad de Puerto Rico
Recinto Universitario de Mayagüez
Carretera Miradero
Tropical Agriculture Research Station
RAMIREZ AGRAIT
calle N. Ramirez
MARINA CONCORDIA
calle Concordia
calle Abraham Lincoln
SECTOR TRASTALLERES
calle Bogata
calle Luis Llorens Torres
calle San Juan
Spur
VIVALDI
ave. Paris
Parque de Los Próceres
calle Dr. G. San Jurjo
BARCELONA
calle Betances
calle del Bosque
calle Post
calle Dr. Basora
To Las Marías & Maricao
Río Yagüez
calle Mendez Vigo
ENSANCHE MARTINEZ
av. Las Nereidas
calle Jose de Diego
Bahía de Mayagüez
calle Comercio
calle Mckinley
SECTOR DOLCES LABIOS
CANDELARIA
calle Peral
calle Luna
Ruta
del Rio
calle McKinley
calle Carmelo Martinez
calle Dr. Vadi
NIEVES BONET
calle Valencia
calle Pilar Defillo
calle Pablo Casals
calle El Sol
calle Muñoz Rivera
calle San Vicente
PUERTO RICO
Mayaguez
San Juan
Culebra
Vieques
Mona
To Mona Island (50 miles)
To Cabo Rojo
To San Germán & Sabana Grande
To Sabana Grande

practical use, including cacao, fruit trees, spices, timbers, and ornamentals. There are lots of trees and a wide variety of plants. A hacienda-style building houses the visitor's office. The area is divided into fruit trees, a palm plantation, a bamboo forest, and a botanical garden. There are labs, greenhouses, and other research facilities throughout the area.

2200 Av. Pedro Albizu Campos. ✆ **787/831-3435.** Free admission. Mon–Fri 9am–5pm.

BEACHES & WATERSPORTS

Nearly the entire west coast has great beaches except for Mayagüez, but beach lovers might consider staying here if they want to explore several different beaches. That's because the city perhaps alone puts visitors in such easy reach of the tranquil Caribbean waters to its south, or the rough surfing paradise to its north.

Trips to either area, which can be combined with, say, a day of sailing and snorkeling or windsurfing lessons, can be arranged through either of the large hotels. Or refer to the destination location either below (for the north) or chapter 10 for the south.

Where to Stay

Holiday Inn & Tropical Casino This six-story hotel competes with the Mayagüez Resort & Casino, though we like the latter better. The Holiday Inn is well maintained, contemporary, and comfortable. It has a marble-floored, high-ceilinged lobby, an outdoor pool with a waterside bar, and a big casino, but it's a rather nondescript property, lacking the character of the competing Mayagüez resort. Bedrooms here are comfortably but functionally outfitted in motel style; they've recently been refurbished. Each unit is equipped with a tiled bathroom with a tub/shower combination. The restaurant serves Puerto Rican and International cuisine. The lobby bar area is often fine, especially on weekends when there is live music.

2701 Rte. 2, Km 149.9, Mayagüez, PR 00680-6328. ✆ **800/465-4329** or 787/833-1100. Fax 787/833-1300. www.hidpr.com. 142 units. Year-round $100–$108 double; $147 suite. AE, DC, DISC, MC, V. **Amenities:** Restaurant; 2 bars; casino; gym; outdoor pool; room service; rooms for those w/limited mobility. *In room:* A/C, TV, hair dryer.

Howard Johnson Downtown Mayagüez This converted monastery is a charming historic hotel right near Plaza Colón. With its wide tiled walkways wrapped around an interior courtyard and Spanish colonial furnishings, this hotel is at home in the city's prettiest neighborhood. The construction allows the breeze in and affords nice vistas of historic Mayagüez. There's a pool in one courtyard and the hotel is outfitted with high-speed Internet and other modern amenities. There's no restaurant on premises but there are several nearby, including the delectable Rico-mini Café across the street, where you'll have your free continental breakfast. It can get noisy on weekends.

Calle Mendez Vigo Este 57, Mayagüez, PR 00680. ✆ **787/832-9191.** Fax 787/832-9122. www.hojo.com. 35 units. Year-round $100–$155 double. Rates include continental breakfast at neighboring bakery. AE, MC, V. $4 parking. **Amenities:** Pool; 1 room for those w/limited mobility. *In room:* A/C, TV, fridge, hair dryer, Internet access (in some rooms).

Mayagüez Resort & Casino ★ This is the largest and best general hotel resort in western Puerto Rico, appealing equally to business travelers and vacationers. Set atop a hill, it benefits from a country-club format spread of 20 acres (8 hectares) of tropical landscaping with trees and gardens. The landscaped grounds have been designated an adjunct to the nearby Tropical Agriculture Research Station. Five species of palm trees, eight kinds of bougainvillea, and numerous species of rare flora are set adjacent to the institute's collection of tropical plants, which range from a pink torch ginger to a Sri Lankan cinnamon tree. The river pool is also set among palms and boulders. There is high-speed Internet access throughout the property.

The hotel's well-designed bedrooms open onto views of the swimming pool, and many units have private balconies. Guest rooms tend to be small, but they have good beds. The restored bathrooms are well equipped with makeup mirrors, scales, and tub/shower combinations.

For details about El Castillo, the hotel's restaurant, see "Where to Dine," below. The hotel is the major entertainment center of Mayagüez. Its casino has free admission and is open 24 hours a day. You can also drink and dance at the Victoria Lounge.

Rte. 104 Km 0.3 (P.O. Box 3781), Mayagüez, PR 00680. ✆ **888/689-3030** or 787/832-3030. Fax 787/265-3020. www.mayaguezresort.com. 140 units. Year-round $189–$259 double; $335 suite. AE, DC, DISC, MC, V. Parking $4.50. **Amenities:** 2 restaurants; 3 bars; casino; babysitting; small fitness room; Jacuzzi; playground; Olympic-size pool; children's pool; room service; steam room; 3 tennis courts; rooms for those w/limited mobility. *In room:* A/C, TV, high-speed Internet, minibar.

Where to Dine

El Castillo INTERNATIONAL/PUERTO RICAN This is one of the best large-scale dining rooms in western Puerto Rico, as well as the main restaurant for the largest hotel and casino in the area. The food has real flavor and flair, unlike the typical bland hotel fare so often dished up. Known for its generous lunch buffets, El Castillo serves only a la carte items at dinner, including seafood stew served on a bed of linguine with marinara sauce, grilled salmon with a mango-flavored Grand Marnier sauce, and filets of sea bass with a cilantro, white-wine, and butter sauce. Steak and lobster are served on the same platter, if you want it.

In the Mayagüez Resort & Casino, Rte. 104, Km 0.3. ✆ **787/832-3030.** Breakfast buffet $13; Mon–Fri lunch buffet $16; Sun brunch buffet $27; main courses $14–$36. AE, MC, V. Daily 6:30am–midnight.

Mayagüez After Dark

Beer Garden Sports Pub Overlooking Plaza Colon, this bar and pool hall draws a college and young professional crowd. There is frequent live music on weekends, pool, sports on televisions and great views from the balconies. This is just one of many nightspots catering to the city's university population. Open Monday to Saturday 7pm to 2am. Calle Méndez Vigo at Plaza Colón, Mayagüez. ✆ **787/647-1967.**

El Casino At the completely remodeled casino at the Mayagüez Resort & Casino, with the adjoining Player's Bar, you can try your luck at blackjack, dice, slot machines, roulette, and minibaccarat. Open 24 hours. At the Mayagüez Resort & Casino, Rte. 104. ✆ **787/832-3030,** ext. 3301.

Fat Tuesday's It's always Mardi Gras at this chain pub that specializes in frozen daiquiris and letting the good times roll. At the Holiday Inn & Tropical Casino Mayagüez, Rte. 104. ✆ **787/833-1100.**

The Lobby Bar The spacious bar and lobby area gets busy around happy hour, especially when live music is performed on weekends. The adjoining Tropical Casino is another attraction. At the Holiday Inn & Tropical Casino Mayagüez, Rte. 104. ✆ **787/833-1100.**

MONA ISLAND: THE galápagos OF PUERTO RICO

Off Mayagüez, the unique **Isla Mona ★★★** teems with giant iguanas, three species of endangered sea turtles, red-footed boobies, and countless other seabirds. It features a tabletop plateau with mangrove forests and cacti, giving way to dramatic 200-foot-high (61m) limestone cliffs that rise above the water and encircle much of Mona.

A bean-shaped pristine island with no development at all, Mona is a destination for the hardy pilgrim who seeks the road less traveled. It lies in the middle of the Mona Passage, about halfway between Puerto Rico and the Dominican Republic. A pup tent, backpack, and hiking boots will do fine if you plan to forego the comforts of civilization and immerse yourself in nature. Snorkelers, spelunkers, biologists, and eco-tourists find much to fascinate them in Mona's wildlife, mangrove forests, coral reefs, and complex honeycomb, which is the largest marine-originated cave in the world. There are also miles of secluded white-sand beaches and palm trees.

Uninhabited today, Mona was for centuries the scene of considerable human activity. The pre-Columbian Taíno Indians were the first to establish themselves here. Later, pirates used it as a base for their raids, followed by guano miners, who removed the rich crop fertilizer from Mona's caves. Columbus landed in Mona during his 1494 voyage, and Ponce de León spent several days here en route to becoming governor of Puerto Rico in 1508. The notorious pirate Captain Kidd used Mona as a temporary hide-out.

Mona can be reached by organized tour from Mayagüez. Camping is available at $10 per night. Everything needed, including water, must be brought in, and everything, including garbage, must be taken out. For more information, call the **Puerto Rico Department of Natural and Environmental Resources** at ✆ **787/999-2200.**

The Puerto Rico government invested $1.7 million on a new visitor's center on Mona, which includes living quarters for researchers and park rangers.

To reach the island, contact **Adventures Tourmarine,** Rte. 102, Km 14.1, Playa Joyuda, Cabo Rojo (✆ **787/375-2625**). Captain Elick Hernández operates boat charters to Mona with a minimum of 10 passengers, each paying $135 for a round-trip day adventure. **Acampa Nature Adventures** (Av. Piñero 1221, San Juan; ✆ **787/706-0659**) runs a 4-day, 3-night trip to Mona, which includes all equipment, meals, and guides. The trips are run in groups with a 10-person limit. Price depends on how many people are in the group. San Juan dive shops, such as **Ocean Sports,** Av. Isla Verde 77, (✆ **787/268-2329**), will also run dive trips off Mona Island. However you plan to get there, make your reservations well in advance.

Warning: The passage over is extremely rough, and many passengers prone to seasickness take Dramamine the night before the boat ride. There is no bottled water on the island, so bring your own. Also bring food, mosquito repellent, and even toilet paper. Alcoholic drinks are forbidden. While Mona's uninhabited landscape and surrounding turquoise water are beautiful, this can also be a dangerous, unforgiving place. In 2001, a Boy Scout got lost and died from hypothermia; in 2005, a psychologist suffered the same fate.

RINCÓN

100 miles (161km) W of San Juan; 6 miles (9.7km) N of Mayagüez

North of Mayagüez lies the resort town of Rincón, the first of a string of beach destinations you'll encounter as you head north, but not the closest, as the town lies at the western end of a piece of land jutting off the coast.

I always lose my bearings driving to and around Rincón, and any Google Maps or GPS system you are relying on will surely go haywire (basically giving a different direction each time you punch in the locations). That's probably as it should be as you drive a jumble of circuitous country roads over La Cadena Hills to reach the town, the center of which eludes most visitors, who head to the guesthouses and hotels along the coast. Rincón sits on a flattened peninsula of land jutting off Puerto Rico's western coast, so there's water surrounding it on three sides, which has another confusing effect.

Rincón long ago stopped being that sleepy coastal village attracting surfers and bohemian travelers from around the world. They, of course, are still coming, but a building boom has brought a wave of new condo, hotel, and luxury vacation residence projects, which has attracted more and more visitors here over the last decade. In fact, the town is beginning to worry about the pace of development and its effect on the beautiful natural resources here.

There's still a lot of space to get lost in, though, with the surrounding hills on one side, and water on the town's other three borders. Rincón dates from the 16th century when a landowner allowed poor families to set down roots on his land. It was a sleepy agricultural town for centuries afterwards. It eventually gained fame as the Caribbean's best surfing spot, a fact reinforced by its hosting the World Surfing Championship in 1968. It remains the surfing capital of the Caribbean, a center for ex-patriot North Americans, and a tourist magnet.

With over a dozen beaches in town, great surfing, sailing, and snorkeling, and an ever better nightlife and cultural scene, it's not hard to see why. It continues evolving as a destination, reinforcing the fact it's one of the best stops to make in Puerto Rico.

There was a time when nonsurfers visited Rincón for only one reason: the Horned Dorset Primavera Hotel, not only one of the finest hotels in Puerto Rico, but one of the best in the entire Caribbean. Now there are several reasons for them to come.

Surfing & Other Outdoor Pursuits

There are 8 miles (13km) of beachfront in Rincón, and each little spot seems to have its own name: **Las Maria's, Indicator, Domes, the Point, Steps-Tres Palmas, Dog Man's.** The reasons behind the names are also varied. One stems from the hulk of an abandoned nuclear power plant just off the beach, another for an old man who lived nearby.

Part of the town's appeal is that it has both rough surfing beaches and tranquil Caribbean coastal areas. Along the north side of Rincón, the Atlantic coast gets large, powerful waves, while other beaches are tranquil, perfect for snorkeling. Yet many beaches provide both, depending on the time of year.

During winter, uninterrupted swells from the North Atlantic form perfect waves, averaging 5 to 6 feet (1.5–1.8m) in height, with rideable rollers sometimes reaching 15 to 20 feet (4.6–6.1m). In 2008, a rare winter storm created 25-foot to 30-foot

(7.6–9.1m) waves here that had local surfers musing whether it was the biggest surf ever. On the southern side of Rincón, the ocean is calm, and long, wide sand beaches unfold with swaying palm trees along them.

The best surfing beaches include **Las Maria's, Spanish Wall,** and **Domes** near the town lighthouse on the north side. **Córcega** is probably the best of the Caribbean beaches. Some beaches, meanwhile, can show different faces at different times of the year. For instance, **Steps,** which is also named **Tres Palmas,** is a great surfing beach in winter, but in summer is calm and one of the best spots for snorkeling. It was recently named a natural marine reserve.

Visitors need to proceed with caution during winter when venturing into the surf off Rincón, which can be particularly strong, with powerful riptides and undertows that routinely cause drownings. This should not stop visitors from coming here, however. The town has beaches with both tranquil and strong surf. Just proceed with caution and ask locals about surf conditions.

Windsurfing, and increasingly kite-boarding, is also extremely popular here, with **Sandy Beach** a favored site because it does not have the rocks found on the ocean floor that some of the other beaches in the area have. Also, from December to February it gets almost constant winds every day. Windsurfers wait on the terrace of Tamboo Tavern (see "Where to Dine," later in this chapter) for the right wind conditions before hitting the beach.

Excellent scuba, snorkeling, parasailing, and sailing are also available in Rincón, making it one of the most active of Caribbean destinations.

Endangered humpback whales winter here, attracting a growing number of whale-watchers from December to March. The lighthouse at El Faro Park is a great place to spot these mammoth mammals.

Rincón remains a mecca for surfing aficionados, but it's also a great place to learn the sport. **The Rincón Surf School** (P.O. Box 1333, Rincón; ✆ **787/823-0610**) offers beginners lessons or can teach surfers how to improve their performance. One lesson costs $95, and there are also 2-day ($180), 3-day ($260), and 5-day ($390) packages. A private 2-hour lesson is $150, $75 each for two people. The school also arranges surf vacation packages in conjunction with the Casa Verde Guesthouse. **Puntas Surf School** (P.O. Box 4319, HC-01 Calle Vista del Mar; ✆ **787/366-1689** or 939/697-8040) is another great option. It's run by Melissa Taylor and Bill Woodward, whose love of the sport is infectious, and they say they can teach would-be surfers of any age, from 5 to 105. Private lessons cost $45 per hour, $75 for 2 hours. Group rates and package deals are also available. Board rentals are $25 per day, $60 for 3 days, $100 for a week. A professional photographer takes photos of lessons for sale.

There are many surfing outfitters in town, and one of the most established is the **West Coast Surf Shop,** Muñoz Rivera 2E, Rincón (✆ **787/823-3935**), open daily 9am to 6pm. The shop rents surfing equipment and gives lessons. It was undergoing a renovation in early 2010 to celebrate its 25th birthday. The **Hot Wavz Surf Shop,** Maria's Beach (✆ **787/823-3942**), also rents long boards, as well as boogie boards. Prices for board rentals start at around $25 daily. Snorkeling gear can also be rented at these shops.

Good snorkeling can be found just off the beach. When conditions are right, **Tres Palmas–Steps** is a great spot. Scuba divers and snorkeling enthusiasts will also want to head out to **Desecheo Island,** the large mass of land seen offshore from Rincón looking west. A quick half-hour boat trip, the small island is a nature reserve

Western Puerto Rico & the Northwest Coast

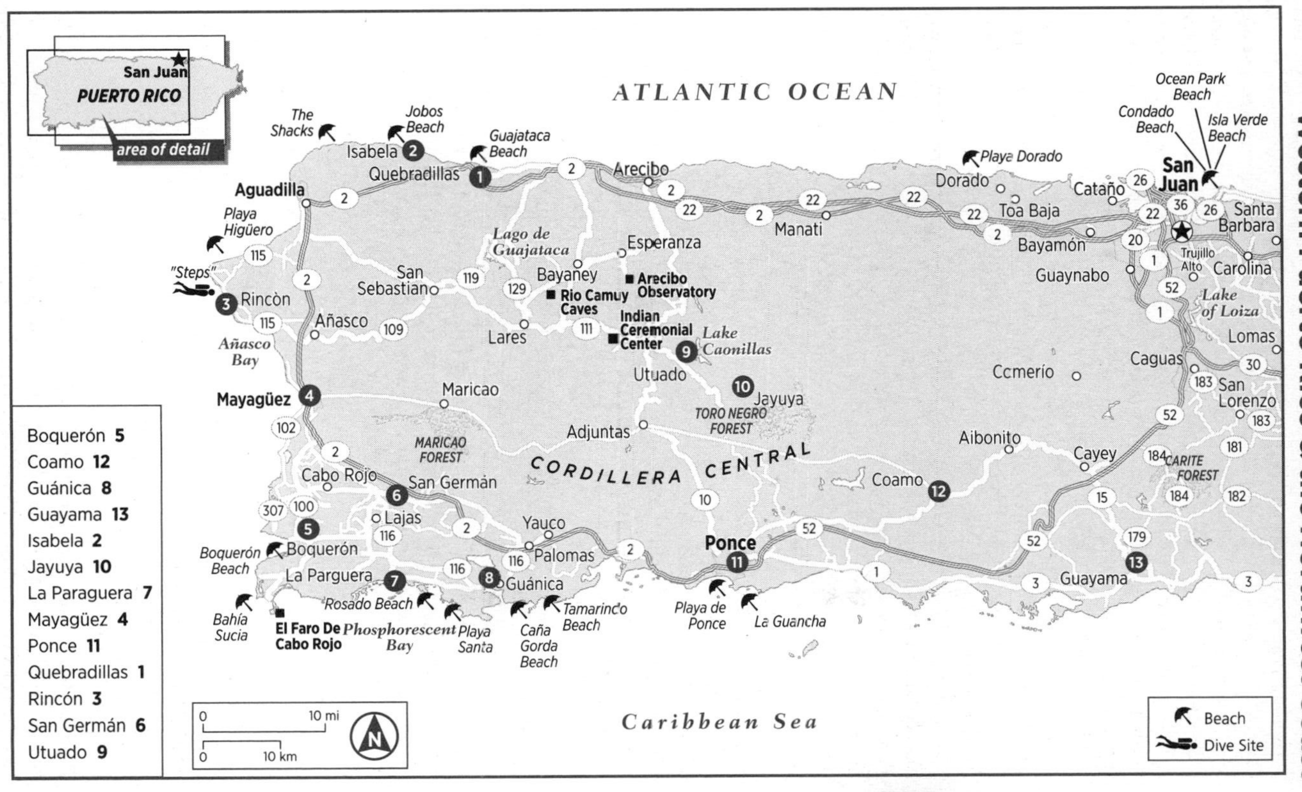

with great coral formations and large reef fish. Visibility is 100-plus feet (30m), and average water temperature is between 80° and 86°F (27°–30°C).

A good scuba outfitter is **Taíno Divers,** Black Eagle Marina at Rincón (**© 787/823-6429**), which offers local boat charters along with scuba and snorkeling trips. The Desecheo day trip departs at 8am and returns at 2pm. They offer a 6-hour snorkeling trip to Desecheo Island for $95, while a 2-tank dive is $129, plus $25 for equipment rental. A beginner scuba course to Desecheo is $170. Prices include gourmet sandwiches and drinks. The outfit also runs half-day fishing charters for $1,200 and whale-watching expeditions and sunset cruises for $50.

Makaira Fishing Charters (P.O. Box 257, Rincón; **© 787/823-4391** or 787/299-7374) offers fishing charters from a no-frills, tournament-rigged, 35-foot 2006 Contender that fits six comfortably. Half-day rates are $575 and full-day $850. **Moondog Charters** (**© 787/823-3059**) also runs fishing excursions and dive charters aboard a 32-foot Albermarle Express Sport Fisherman.

Katarina Sail Charters (**© 787/823-SAIL** [7245]) gives daily sailing trips aboard a 32-foot catamaran. The day sail (from around 10:20am–2:30pm) consists of some fine cruising, a stop for a swim and snorkel, and then lunch. It costs $70, $30 for children 12 and under. The sunset sail ($50 for adults and $25 for kids) leaves at 4:30pm and returns after sunset about 2 hours later. Watching the western sunset while sailing and listening to great music is wonderful, with rum punch, beer, and nonalcoholic drinks. The vessel is also available for private charters.

Most hotels on the beach have good watersports rentals, and **Flying Fish Parasail** (**© 787/823-2359**) runs parasailing trips out of the Black Eagle Marina. **Capital Water Sports Xtreme Rentals** (**© 787/823-2789**) at Sunset Village by the public beach also rents water sports equipment, including jet skis and small boats, and gives "banana boat" tow rides and runs water skiing trips.

The most visible and sought-after whale-watching panorama in Rincón is **Parque El Faro de Rincón (Rincón Lighthouse Park),** which lies on El Faro Point peninsula at the extreme western tip of town. Within its fenced-in perimeter are pavilions that sell souvenirs and snack items, rows of binoculars offering 25¢ views, and a stately looking lighthouse built in 1921. The park is at its most popular from December to March for whale-watching, and in January and February for surfer gazing. The park is locked every evening between midnight and 7am. Otherwise, you're free to promenade with the locals any time you like.

The park's snack bar is called **Restaurant El Faro,** Barrio Puntas, Carretera 413, Km 3.3 (no phone), which serves basic Puerto Rican fare and burgers. Best for a drink or ice cream.

Pintos "R" Us (**© 787/361-3639** or 516-7090) offers a variety of horseback riding tours and lessons every day, all of which go along the beach and through forest trails; they are really beautiful rides. The standard tour is 2 hours, but there are also half-day, full-day, and full-moon rides. Prices range from $55 to $185. Riders meet at the Black Eagle Marina for tours.

Where to Stay

VERY EXPENSIVE

Horned Dorset Primavera ★★★ This is the most sophisticated hotel on Puerto Rico and one of the most exclusive and elegant small properties anywhere in the Caribbean. The Relais & Châteaux property is set on 8 acres (3.2 hectares) and opens onto a secluded semiprivate beach. Built on the massive breakwaters and seawalls erected as part of a century-old railroad, the hacienda evokes an aristocratic Spanish villa, with wicker armchairs, hand-painted tiles, ceiling fans, seaside terraces, and cascades of flowers. The Primavera Suites (getaways that lack electronics) and the Horned Dorset Residences (which are more fully equipped and furnished) ramble amid lush gardens. The decor is tasteful, with four-poster beds and brass-footed tubs (with showers) in marble-sheathed bathrooms. Rooms are spacious and luxurious, with Persian rugs over tile floors, queen-size sofa beds in the sitting areas, and fine linens and tasteful fabrics on the elegant beds.

The Casa Escondida villa, set at the edge of the property, adjacent to the sea, is decorated with an accent on teakwood and marble. Some of the units have private plunge pools; others offer private verandas or sun decks. Each contains high-quality reproductions of colonial furniture by Baker. The hotel's two restaurants are excellent but quite pricey.

Apartado 1132, Rincón, PR 00677. ✆ **800/633-1857** or 787/823-4030. Fax 787/823-5580. www.horneddorset.com. 55 units. Winter $596–$1,070 suites, $770–$1,385 residences; holidays $696–$1,270 suites, $970–$1,585 residences; off-season $360–$770 suites, $470–$880 residences. AE, MC, V. Children 11 and under not accepted. **Amenities:** 2 restaurants; bar; 3 outdoor pools (1 infinity); fitness center; kayaking (free); room service; massage; library. *In room:* A/C, hair dryer.

EXPENSIVE

Rincón Beach Resort ★ Romantic lovebirds and families check into this secluded hideaway. At this beachfront resort, an open-air boardwalk stretches along the coastline at the end of an "infinity pool." It's perhaps the most welcoming place along the western coastline, with a sheltered beachfront. The staff can help you arrange everything from watersports to golf. Guests meet fellow guests in the lobby bar, and later enjoy a savory Caribbean cuisine in Brasas Restaurant, with its open-air terrace. You're given a choice of oceanview or poolview units, and can also rent well-furnished one- and two-bedroom apartments. The decor is tropical throughout, with vibrant colors. It is in a remote location, far from the most traveled Rincón beaches and the center of town, but with a great restaurant, poolside bar and grill, watersports, and other activities, it does not matter. Wherever you stay in this town, it's just a quick ride to surf, dive, or party. Don't expect the clock-work efficiency of bigger resorts, but you won't miss it. The staff is incredibly friendly and helpful, more than willing to fulfill any request, and you'll feel welcomed like a family member.

Rte. 115, Km 5.8, Añasco, PR 00610. ✆ **866/598-0009** or 787/589-9000. Fax 787/589-9040. www.rinconbeach.com. 118 units. Winter $260–$300 double, $355 junior suite, $459 1-bedroom suite, $650 2-bedroom suite; summer $210–$250 double, $315 junior suite, $405 1-bedroom suite, $575 2-bedroom suite. Rates include continental breakfast. AE, DISC, MC, V. **Amenities:** Restaurant; grill; 3 bars; babysitting; gym; outdoor pool; smoke-free rooms; rooms for those w/limited mobility. *In room:* A/C, TV, fridge, hair dryer, Internet access, kitchenettes in suites.

Rincón of the Seas Grand Caribbean Hotel ★ This lush beachfront property draws a wildly diverse crowd, from island reggaeton producers to families. From Connecticut suburbanites to surf bums to yuppie Wall Street investment bankers, you can meet anyone here. The amenities are not quite on par with the Rincón Beach, but it has fabulous gardens and palm trees throughout the property, as well as a great pool area, beautiful beach and central location. The place has got style, and there's always a party going on somewhere, but there's also always someplace where you can go to chill out. Its lobbies, terraces and guestrooms are a blend of classic Caribbean and Art Deco style, which keeps things a bit modern and playful. The beach and the pool area are among the finest in the area, and the staff is almost as friendly and hardworking as the folks at the Rincón Beach, where the rooms are plusher. The Art Deco Suites here are beautiful, but steeply priced. You get a lot of bang for the buck here though. The restaurant has excellent food, and the pool bar is too much fun.

Rte. 115, Km 12.2, Rincón, PR 00677. © **866/274-6266** or 787/823-7500. Fax 787/823-7500. www.rinconoftheseas.com. 112 units. Year round $180–$200 double, $445 Art Deco suite. **Amenities:** Restaurant; grill; 3 bars; babysitting; gym; outdoor pool; smoke-free rooms; rooms for those w/limited mobility. *In room:* A/C, TV, fridge, hair dryer, Internet access, kitchenettes in suites.

MODERATE

Casa Isleña Inn ★ This oceanfront hacienda-style property has bright Caribbean colors and Spanish tiles and woodwork. This is a private, tranquil world that offers large and comfortably furnished guest rooms, gorgeous terraces and patios, a great pool and adjacent beach. The Olympic-size pool is surrounded by a sundeck with lounge chairs and a row of palm trees fronting the beach. You can see humpback whales migrating offshore in the winter, and the view goes out to the Mona Passage and the Aguadilla Bay. Breakfast is served on the veranda, where a fine tapas restaurant operates from 3 to 9pm Tuesday through Sunday. If you like being left alone, this is a great spot.

Barrio Puntas Carretera Interior 413, Km 4, Rincón, PR 00677. © **888/289-7750** or 787/823-1525. Fax 787/823-1530. www.casa-islena.com. 9 units (shower only). Winter $165–$205 double, off-season $125–$165 double. Extra person $25. MC, V. **Amenities:** Tapas restaurant, bar; 1 room for those w/limited mobility. *In room:* A/C, TV, no phone.

Lemontree Waterfront Suites ★ Right on a narrow sandy beach, these spacious apartments with kitchenettes are for those who don't want to limit themselves to hotel rooms and meals. With the sound of the surf just outside your private back porch, these well-furnished seaside units can provide a home away from home, with everything from ceiling fans to air-conditioning, from paperback libraries to custom woodworking details. The suites have comfortable furnishings and tropical colors, and the property is well maintained. Families enjoy the three-bedroom, two-bathroom oceanfront suite called "Papaya;" "Mango" and "Pineapple" are ideal for two persons. Each unit contains a midsize shower-only bathroom. The least expensive units, "Banana" and "Coconut," are studio units for those who want a kitchen but don't require a living room. There are studio, one-bedroom, and two-bedroom units as well. Spa treatments are available as well as scuba-diving lessons. The cottages lie a 10-minute drive west of Rincón.

Rte. 4290 (P.O. Box 3200), Rincón, PR 00677. © **888/418-8733** or 787/823-6452. Fax 787/823-5821. www.lemontreepr.com. 6 units (shower only).Winter $145–$265; summer $125–$225; fall $115–$200. AE, MC, V. *In room:* A/C, TV, kitchenette.

Tres Sirenas Beach Inn ★ This sumptuous, regal B&B opens onto Sandy Bottom Beach, giving you a chance to live in a certain tropical elegant style. It's casual but oh, so tasteful. A boutique hotel, the complex is sometimes rented as a private oceanfront villa to a dozen or so guests (high season $870 per night; low season $800). Otherwise you have a choice of two spacious and elegantly furnished bedrooms or else two apartments, all with a certain old–Puerto Rican charm. The pool studio is ideal for families, as it accommodates two adults and two children, and features a private balcony. Apartments sleep four and come with a loft and full kitchen. Innkeepers Lisa and Harry are wonderful hosts, attentive but never intrusive, and breakfast is delicious.

Sea Beach Dr. 26, Rincón, PR 00677. ✆ **787/823-0558.** www.tressirenas.com. 4 units. Winter $180 double, $225 studio for 4, $300 apt; off-season $170 double, $205 studio for 4, $285 apt. AE, DC, MC, V. **Amenities:** Room service; outdoor pool; hot tub; Wi-Fi; smoke-free rooms. *In room:* A/C, TV, beverage maker, hair dryer, kitchenette, minibar.

INEXPENSIVE

Beside the Pointe Guesthouse This tiny guesthouse sits on a lovely spot on the beach and has a popular tavern and restaurant and shop on the grounds. With only a handful of rooms though, this is probably not for everyone. I recommend the more expensive oceanfront double and the oceanview suites on the upper deck, which are removed enough from the public areas to maintain a sense of privacy. The view is also beautiful, and there's a great sun deck.

Carretera 413, Km 4 Sandy Beach, Rincón. ✆ **888/823-8550.** Fax 787/823-8550. www.besidethepointe.com. 8 units. Winter $110–$170 double, $185–$210 apartments, off-season $85–$140 double, $165–$190 apartments. AE, MC, V. **Amenities:** Restaurant; bar; gift shop w/local crafts; Wi-Fi (in lobby). *In room:* A/C, TV, fridge, kitchenette (suites).

The Lazy Parrot Set within an unlikely inland neighborhood, this place is nonetheless one of the best spots in Rincón to stay. It's one of the only hotels on Rte. 413, the so-called "road to happiness" because it's the main road to town from the rest of Puerto Rico. It looks like a nondescript storefront from outside, but climb its stairs and you enter an oasis of tropical tranquillity. "Value" rooms are located on the first floor. They are clean, well-organized, and comfortable, if not overly large. They have no view, but each has either a deck, patio, or balcony, and attractive decor of light, natural colors. The upstairs "panoramic" rooms have a view to the pretty Cadena Hills and the coast and overlook the pool area. These are also larger and have upgraded facilities such as flatscreen TVs. Definitely pay the extra cost for an upstairs room if privacy is important to you. The other rooms are close to the interior lobby and restaurant. Behind the main building, you'll descend into an immense open, interior area overlooking the distant hills, where the sprawling pool and deck area are located. There are also a store, the main office and the Rum Shack bar-restaurant. The Lazy Parrot restaurant has a dining room overlooking the pool area and interior courtyard and is among the best eateries in Rincón. The Rum Shack, which serves light fare and drinks poolside, can be a lot of fun at night. This is one of the better-managed properties in town. Its inland location is not a drawback; you need a car rental anyway, as you will want to travel to a different beach each day. The pool area is among the best in town.

Rd. 413, Km 4.1, Barrio Puntas, Rincón, PR 00677. ✆ **800/294-1752** or 787/823-5654. Fax 787/823-0224. www.lazyparrot.com. 21 units. Year-round $125 double value rooms; $165 double panoramic rooms. The smallest room goes for $99 single or double. Rates include continental breakfast. AE, DISC, MC, V. **Amenities:** 2 restaurants; bar; babysitting; gift shop w/local crafts; pool; room service; Wi-Fi (in lobby). *In room:* A/C, TV, fridge.

Parador Villa Antonio ☺ Unless you are traveling with a bunch of children and want to save cash by cooking your own meals, there is no really good reason to stay here. Sure, it's on a nice beach, and the rooms are cheap and functional, with kitchenettes to make up for the lack of aesthetics, but you're better off spending a few bucks to stay across the street at Villa Cofresi. Villa Antonio is very crowded and very noisy during weekends and holidays, and suffers from a lack of care all the time. The guests and staff are super friendly, but show up at the wrong time; and the property will be crowded, trashed, and ear-splittingly loud. If you're visiting during the week outside of a major holiday season, and want to cook your own meals, this could be your place. The economy-level "apartments" are cramped and a bit worn, like a beach shack barracks; the suites and 2-bedroom units are better. Kids will have a blast though, because it's clear they are in charge here, especially on holiday weekends. There's a big pool, video and game room, playground with basketball court, and other activities.

Rte. 115, Km 12.3 (P.O. Box 68), Rincón, PR 00677. ✆ **787/823-2645.** Fax 787/823-3380. www.villa-antonio.com. 61 units (shower only). $115–$145 studio (up to 2 people); $155–$170 2-bedroom apt (up to 4 people); $140 junior suite; $150 suite. AE, DISC, MC, V. **Amenities:** 2 pools; babysitting; playground; 2 tennis courts; Wi-Fi, rooms for those w/limited mobility. *In room:* A/C, TV.

Villa Cofresi ☺ The staff at this clean, family-run hotel make their money the old-fashion way: making guests feel welcome. That warm hospitality will linger in the memory despite the hotel's many other attributes: clean and airy rooms, with comfortable furnishings, a beautiful beachfront location and wonderful facilities, including an outdoor pool and sun terrace, lively bar, and excellent restaurant overlooking the coast and a game room. The units have white-tile floors and small bathrooms with tubs and showers. Most rooms have two double beds; some have two twin beds. All are smoke-free. The two units that tend to be reserved out long in advance are nos. 47 and 55, which have windows opening directly onto the sea. The in-house restaurant serves hardy local cooking, such as *mofongo* stuffed with seafood, breaded scampi served either with Creole sauce or garlic, and very good steaks. This spot also fills up on holiday weekends, but it remains more low-key than its neighbor.

Rd. 115, Km 12.0, Rincón, PR 00677. ✆ **787/823-2450.** Fax 787/823-1770. www.villacofresi.com. 80 units. Winter $135–$155 double, $160 suite; off-season $115–$135 double, $160 suite. AE, DC, MC, V. **Amenities:** Restaurant; bar; outdoor pool; room service; rooms for those w/limited mobility. *In room:* A/C, TV, fridge, hair dryer.

Where to Dine

VERY EXPENSIVE

The Blue Room ★ FRENCH/CARIBBEAN This French Caribbean Bistro at the gorgeous Horned Dorset has entrees every bit as breathtaking as the property's more acclaimed Restaurant Aaron and more basic stuff of the finest quality. It's much less buttoned down, and serves both French (*coq au vin* and lamb provençal) and Latino (*mofongo* stuffed with shrimp and red snapper in green sauce) classics, plus casual fare such as delicious burgers, "four seasons" pizza, and coconut crab chowder. I love the sides (ratatouille and green beans almondine) and the tropical sorbet trio.

In the Horned Dorset Primavera Hotel, Apartado 1132. ✆ **787/823-4030.** Reservations recommended. Entrees $26–$38; fixed-price dinner $78 for 4 dishes, $110 for 9 dishes; wine pairing $42–$84. AE, MC, V. Wed–Sun 7–9:30pm.

Restaurant Aaron ★★ FRENCH/CARIBBEAN The formal Restaurant Aaron may be the finest restaurant in western Puerto Rico—so romantic it draws guests from San Juan just for an intimate dinner. A masonry staircase sweeps from the garden to the second floor, where soaring ceilings and a plush villa setting awaits you. The menu changes nightly and includes a chef's tasting menu with wine pairings. Appetizers might include sautéed sweetbreads with bacon and egg, roasted squab with confit potato and prune sauce and open lobster ravioli with peas and asparagus. Entrees on the chef's palette include seared tuna with red wine pancetta sauce, sautéed tournedo of beef with boulangère potatoes, or roasted breast of chicken with mushrooms, shallots, tomatoes and lentils. A great way to end it all is with chocolate fondue and fresh fruit.

In the Horned Dorset Primavera Hotel, Apartado 1132. ✆ **787/823-4030.** Reservations recommended. Entrees $32–$42; fixed-price dinner $110 for 5 dishes; wine pairing $42–$84. AE, MC, V. Wed–Sun 7–9:30pm.

EXPENSIVE

Brasas Restaurant ★★ The inventive Caribbean fusion cuisine served here is one of the best meals in the Rincón area, and the setting and service only add to the pleasures of dining here. So if you are staying at the Rincón Beach, you can eat here for several evenings without getting bored; and, if you are not, it is definitely worth a trip here for a great meal. The menu is subject to change, but I've eaten from two versions and have yet to be disappointed. Try tempting entrees such as rack of veal grilled and served in a guava port sauce, or chicken breast stuffed with ground *viandas* (salted codfish) in a sun dried tomato cream sauce or a delectable tomato cognac sea bass. The restaurant also serves a delicious breakfast, with everything from fresh fruit to breakfast ham and sausage to omelets and French toast. Lunch—tasty gourmet salads and sandwiches mostly—is served at the poolside Pelican Café. Brasas has an attractive Spanish-hacienda-style dining room, and outdoor dining in a flowery courtyard. They also serve meals on a back deck made of dark wood and modern metal.

Rte. 115, Km 5.8, Añasco, PR 00610. ✆ **787/589-9000.** AE, DISC, MC, V. Reservations recommended. Main courses $18–$29; breakfast buffet $14. Daily 6:30–10:30am and 5:30–11pm.

The Lazy Parrot Restaurant ★★ INTERNATIONAL With an inventive menu and beautiful laid-back setting high up in this beautiful coastal village, this is one of Rincón's finest restaurants. The menu mixes Caribbean and European flavors for optimal impact, and diners sit in an open-air terrace with panoramic views of the pool area, tropical garden, and green mountains. I could not pass up the coconut red curry crab cakes with papaya slaw or the fried calamari and roasted garlic in marinara sauce to start. If you want meat, the grilled rib-eye in bordelaise sauce won't disappoint, and seafood lovers will lap up the Caribbean bouillabaisse (a mix of shell fish and mahimahi with avocado and local vegetables). Everything I've tried here–including the penne pasta and coriander crusted tuna–has been excellent.

Rd. 413, Km 4.1, Barrio Puntas, Rincón, PR 00677. ✆ **787/823-0101.** AE, DISC, MC, V. Reservations not necessary. Main courses $20–$36. Daily 5:30–10pm.

The Spot at Black Eagle ★ INTERNATIONAL A restaurant during dinner hours, it turns into a beach bar hangout later in the evening, this seaside locale is the perfect setting for a gourmet meal, or to party hearty to some island rhythms later in the evening. Don't let the weathered, salty-dog-saloon look fool you, the beauty of this place is precisely the contrast between the refinement of its cuisine, and the unvarnished waterfront setting, which is still remarkably beautiful. Charcuterie (an Italian sausage and roast pepper delicacy) and the mahimahi tempura are unavoidable appetizers, and the stuffed pork loin and the shrimp spaghetti were exceptional main courses. The menu is full of them. Tables stretch out along the beachfront, and it becomes more beautiful in the evening in the candlelight. It's a great place to watch the sun go down, and it really hops during its weekly reggae night.

At the Black Eagle Marina, off Rte. 413, Rincón, PR 00677. ✆ **787/823-3510.** AE, MC, V. Reservations not necessary. Main courses $20–$36. Open Wed–Mon 5:30–10pm.

MODERATE

The Rum Shack ★ The pool bar and cafe at the Lazy Parrot has much better food than you'd expect, perhaps Rincón's most consistently good meal. It's also a delightful setting on a stone terrace, which draws an eclectic mix of customers into the evening. The bar is a good place to pick up travel tips and meet other visitors and resident ex-pats. The food ranges from casual but tasty wraps, burgers, and burritos to churrasco and mahimahi entrees. The appetizers really kick it, though—stuff like conch fritters in classic remoulade and grilled chicken kebabs.

Rd. 413 Km 4.1, Barrio Puntas, Rincón, PR 00677. ✆ **787/823-0101.** AE, DISC, MC, V. Reservations not necessary. Main course $18–$22, light fare $6–$12. Daily 11am–11pm.

Tamboo Tavern and Seaside Grill Restaurant AMERICAN-CARIBBEAN This tavern and restaurant at Beside the Pointe Guesthouse on Sandy Beach is the favored hangout for the young and beautiful beach crowd and surfing enthusiasts from the island and across the planet. It's a great place to eat, offering good food and a beautiful setting, no matter who you are. Beachfront dining does not get realer than this. Tables are stretched along a deck running along the beach, with tables spread out among the palm trees. It's basic steaks, ribs, and lots of seafood, but it's well prepared and tastes extra great while you're breathing in the sea and the salt. The mahimahi in caper sauce and grilled Caribbean lobster are both recommended, and you might want to start out with a platter of the mixed Puerto Rican appetizers. Burgers, wraps, and salads are also available for lunch and dinner.

Carretera 413, Km 4, Sandy Beach, Rincón. ✆ **888/823-8550** or 787/823-8550. Reservations not accepted. Main courses $16–$26 dinner; lunch items $7–$12. MC, V. Bar daily noon–2am; restaurant Thurs–Tues noon–9:30pm.

Rincón After Dark

Happy hour starts at in the late afternoon in Rincón, which is filled with great places to watch the sunset. Join the surfers for a "sundowner" at **Calypso's Tropical Bar,** Maria's Beach (✆ **787/823-1626**), which lies on the road to the lighthouse. Happy-hour specials are daily 5 to 7pm and the bar stays open until the last customer leaves (usually long after midnight).

One of the most *simpático* bars is **Rock Bottom,** adjoining Casa Verde Guest House along Sandy Beach Road (✆ **787/823-3756**). It serves burgers and other stateside food. The upstairs surfer bar is decorated with dozens of graffiti surfboards and has a tree-house feel to it. Great piña coladas and daily drink specials. The kitchen is open until 11pm and the bar 2am. Drink specials throughout the week.

A young crowd gathers at **Tamboo Tavern** (✆ **787/823-8550**), another surfer's bar in a tropical dream location right on Sandy Beach. The action percolates throughout the day, and really takes off as the sun begins to set. Watch it from the terrace or sit at the bar inside tapping your feet to rock *en Español* and progressive American music. There's live music most weekend nights. The **Rum Shack** (✆ **787/823-0101**) is a good place to rub shoulders with local ex-pats and a diverse group of travelers. Don't miss the full-moon party or reggae nights if one is occurring while you are in town. **The Spot At Black Eagle** (✆ **787/823-3510**) draws a mellow crowd at sunset and dinner, but later in the evening lets its hair down as a very funky beach bar. Thursday evenings are reggae nights, and it's the best party in town.

AGUADILLA & THE NORTHWEST

Aguadilla is the biggest town on Puerto Rico's northwest corner, which is filled with great beaches and other natural blessings for an active vacation experience. And it makes a good base from which to explore the area, with lots of hotels, restaurants, good infrastructure, a fairly large mall, and lots of attractions, such as a water park and golf course.

Several airlines now run direct flights to the town's **Rafael Hernández Airport,** especially during the high season. It's the island's second international airport after Luis Muñoz Marín in San Juan. So visitors who want to spend their whole vacation in the west don't have to go through San Juan. Puerto Rico's best surfing spots run from Rincón south of here, around the northwest corner to Isabela and points east along the north coast.

The region also is near such major attractions as the **Arecibo Observatory** and the **Río Camuy Cave Park** (see chapter 7). In addition to its coast, there are mountain forests and lakes nearby. Aguadilla has an ice-skating rink, water park, and a very reasonably priced golf course, adding to its family appeal.

Crash Boat beach is popular, and gets crowded on weekends, but during the week it's usually quiet and picturesque. There are a few beach shacks and stands selling seafood, snacks and cold drinks, and brightly colored wooden fishing boats are often parked on the beach. There's a former Navy fueling pier on the beach, where aquamarine water kisses the white sand. In winter, the northern end of the beach faces open water and is much rougher. Waves at Aguadilla's beaches are among the fiercest in the island, carrying in them the full force of the Atlantic.

Aguadilla is more than its beaches. It's coming into its own in other ways. With an international airport, several offshore companies with operations here, a large U.S. Coast Guard presence, it's one of the island's more prosperous areas. You can see this in the renovations taking place in Aguadilla's historic downtown waterfront district, and the continual growth in new hotels, restaurants, shops and services for tourists each year.

The **Isabela** coastline is also beautiful. Narrow country roads weave between cliffs and white beaches, set off by dramatic rock formations and submerged coral reefs that send surf crashing skyward. This is an area of salt-water wells and blowholes, through which dramatic eruptions of saltwater spew from submerged sea caves. Several are found in the area known as **La Princesa,** and **Jobos** beach is home to the most famous, **El Pozo de Jacinto,** which is located on a huge rock formation at the eastern end of Jobos Beach. There is a local legend surrounding the sinkhole, where the strong ocean currents blast through the huge opening, so that it has become something of a tourist attraction. Visitors should be warned, climbing out to see El Pozo can be very dangerous as the rocks are slippery. They also must respect the power of the sea, as local riptides have caused the drowning deaths of many area swimmers.

Jobos, the heart and soul of the Isabela-Aguadilla coastline, is a large beach with a famed surf break, which cuts from its eastern to western end, but swimmers can frolic along more protected areas along this mammoth shore. There are also guesthouses and restaurants here, and on summer and holiday weekends it's got a party atmosphere.

For many reasons, the eastern end of Jobos is the place to be. An area at the base of the rock formation is partially sheltered from the strong ocean currents and is the best place for casual bathing. Even if you want to surf, you can walk out to the end of the rock formation, as it's a point break here. Surfers catch waves that crash at an angle towards the coastline, so the waves stretch across Jobos beach as they make their way to shore. Finally, this is the closest spot to the **Sonia Rican Café** (**© 787/872-1818**), a beachfront dive serving the coldest beer and tastiest seafood and *comida criolla* in the area that is an institution in the northwest. Have a cold beer at the beachfront bar (forget the inside dining room where t-shirts are required) and feel the bliss that gripped Anthony Bourdain during his lost weekend here. The food is truly excellent, from the fried-fish turnovers to the seafood *mofongo,* and it's the perfect spot to find out whatever you want to learn about the area. The bar is full of amiable characters, especially on sunny weekends, and there's brash salsa on the jukebox.

Further east, **Montones Beach** has rock outcroppings and reefs that make a beguiling seascape and also protect the water from the raging surf in this area. You won't find the restaurants and bars here that you will in Jobos, but you can find your own secluded spot on the beach.

Area development, however, appears to be accelerating, and newly built condominiums and other properties have marred access to some beaches. There are still miles of open beachfront though, and most development is confined to small hotels and low-slung villas.

The good surfing, and increasingly the burgeoning northwest beach culture, extends east beyond Arecibo to Barceloneta and Manatí. East of Isabela, steep cliffs drop in flat jagged lines to the rough surf along the rugged Atlantic coastline of **Quebradillas. Guajataca Beach,** named after a powerful Taíno Indian chief, is a great spot, but think twice about swimming here. The currents are extremely powerful and dangerous, and while surfers love it, casual swimmers should proceed with caution. The white sand is as smooth as silk though, so it's a great spot for sunbathing and watching the surfers risking all and loving every minute of it. It's a great spot for seashell collecting. The beach is also called **El Tunel** because there's a large abandoned railroad tunnel carved out of a mountain at the entrance to the beach. It was once part of a railroad that ran all around the Puerto Rico coast to haul sugar cane. There is a parking area here and a no-frills, open-air restaurant and bar. It's a nice shady spot, a cool respite from the sun-bleached beach.

Essentials

GETTING THERE & GETTING AROUND Both JetBlue and Continental have nonstop flights from East Coast destinations, particularly from New York and Florida, direct to the **Rafael Hernández Airport** (Antigua Base Ramey, Hangar 405, Aguadilla; ✆ **787/891-2226**). Many other flights offer connections from San Juan onto Aguadilla.

There are branches of **Avis** (✆ **787/890-3311**), **Budget** (✆ **787/890-1110**), and **Hertz** (✆ **787/833-3170**) at the Aguadilla airport.

If you're driving from San Juan, travel west on the De Diego Expressway, Rte. 22, then Rte. 2 (trip time: 2 hr.).

VISITOR INFORMATION There is a Puerto Rico Tourism Company office in Aguadilla for the whole northwest region, from Mayagüez in the south through Isabela on the north coast (✆ **787/890-3315**).

Watersports & Other Outdoor Pursuits

While Rincón has wider name recognition, Aguadilla and Isabela have equally good surf spots. In fact, the Puerto Rican Pipeline is actually composed of beaches in the three towns. **Gas Chambers, Crash Boat, Surfer's,** and **Wilderness** rule in Aguadilla, while the preferred spots in **Isabela** include **Jobos, Middles and Shacks.** The best time to surf is from November through March, but summer storms can also kick up the surf. In the summer season, however, when the waves diminish, these northwest beaches double as perfect spots for windsurfing and snorkeling, with calm waters filled with coral reefs and marine life. The towns are quite close together, and the string of beaches through both really forms a single destination.

Shacks draws both snorkelers and scuba divers, who converge on one section of the large beach filled with reefs and coral caverns that teem with rainbow-hued fish. It's also the best spot in the area for kite-boarding and windsurfing.

The good surfing extends east from Isabela to Arecibo, and beyond out to Barceloneta and Manatí, and really all the way into San Juan.

Aquatic Dive, Bike and Surf Adventures (Rte. 110, Km 10, outside gate 5 of Rafael Hernández Airport, Aguadilla; ✆ **787/890-6071**) is a full-service dive and surf shop, but it also rents equipment and gives lessons in scuba and surfing. The outfit also runs mountain-bike excursions to the Guajataca Forest. Prices depend on season and group size, but surf lessons cost from $45 to $65 for 1½ hours, and a 2-tank scuba dive is from $75 to $125. Bicycle tours cost around $65 per person and last up to 3 hours. Surf and scuba equipment rentals run from $20 to $45 per day, while bicycles are $25 per day.

The Hang Loose Surf Shop (Rte. 4466, Km 1.2, Playa Jobos, Isabela; ✆ **787/872-2490;** Tues–Sun 10am–5pm) is well stocked with equipment. It gives surf lessons ($60 per hour private lesson) and rents boards for $25 daily. The shop is owned by Werner Vega, a great big-wave rider, who is one of Puerto Rico's premier board shapers.

Tropical Trail Rides (Rte. 4466, Km 1.9, Isabela, ✆ **787/872-9256**), gives excellent horseback riding tours along the undeveloped Isabela coast. The basic 2-hour tour ($45 per person) brings you through an almond forest, along deserted beaches and explores an area of coastal caves. This is the place to fulfill that horseback riding on the beach fantasy.

The Northwest has more going for it than its beaches, however. That's especially so with **Aguadilla,** which has converted many of the old facilities of the former Ramey Air Force Base and put them to good public use (such as developing an international airport on a portion of it). **Punta Borinquén Golf Club,** Rte. 107 (✆ **787/890-2987**), 2 miles (3.2km) north of Aquadilla's center, across the highway from the city's airport, was originally built by the U.S. government as part of Ramey Air Force Base. Today, it is a public 18-hole golf course, open daily from 7am to 7pm. Greens fees are a bargain at $20 per round; a golf cart that can carry two passengers rents for $30 for 18 holes. A set of clubs can be rented for $15. The clubhouse has a bar and a simple restaurant. It's also a nice course with coastal views. **Parque Aquatico Las Cascadas** (Hwy. 2, Km 126.5, Aguadilla; ✆ **787/819-0950** or 787/819-1030) is a water park run by the municipality that the kids will love. There are giant slides and tubes and the Río Loco rapids pool. From May through September, it's open 10am to 5pm daily. It opens again in winter on weekends from 10am to 5pm. Tickets are $20 for adults and $18 for kids ages 4–12.

You probably did not come to Puerto Rico to go ice skating, but you can do it at the **Aguadilla Ice Skating Rink** (Hwy. 442; ✆ **787/819-5555,** ext. 221). This is another city-run facility open from 10am to 6:30pm, and then from 7 to 11:30pm. It's popular with kids and is a training facility for island figure skaters. Cost is $10 per hour during the day and $13 per hour in the evening (including skates).

Isabela enjoys a reputation for horse breeding. This activity is centered on Arenales, south of the town, where a number of horse stables are located.

WHERE TO STAY & DINE

Buenas Olas Hotel 🎁 Spacious, uncluttered, white, open spaces dominate this spotless hotel, surrounded by pure blue sky and sea. You are within walking distance to great beaches, Jobos and Shacks, which offer challenges for every skill level as well as opportunities for snorkeling and kite-boarding. The staff of local surfers will point you in the right direction for just about anything you want to do, and they provide friendly, if laid-back, service at the excellent on-premises bar/restaurant **Machete Rojo Restaurante and Cantina.** Despite its unfinished look, and the feel of still being a work-in-progress, this is a great place to stay, especially considering its rates, and proximity to the beach. And the Zen-like decor, including a hammock in the lobby, is actually the perfect fit for the breathtaking setting. The bar-restaurant has been the new place to be in Playa Jobos since it opened, with cool crowds at night and DJ shows and occasional live music. There are excellent fish tacos, burgers, and ceviche, and adventurous specialty bar drinks. If you want to play hard all day, you can find it all here at your doorstep at night.

Road 4466, Km 2.5, Playa Jobos, Isabela. ✆ **787/872-1818.** www.buenasolashotel.com. 14 units. Year-round $95 Fri–Sun, $85 Mon–Thurs. AE, MC, V. **Amenities:** Restaurant; bar; Wi-Fi. In room: AC, TV, hammock, Wi-Fi.

Marriott Courtyard Aguadilla ☺ The whole family will love this hotel with pool, aquatics playground, and spacious guest rooms near some of the prettiest beaches on the island, and right around such attractions as the Camuy Caves, Arecibo Observatory, local water park, and ice-skating rink. Beautiful beaches ring the coast here from Isabela to the east and Rincón to the west. It's built on the old Ramey Air Force Base near a coastal suburb. Great location and facilities make a good base to explore the northwest. The hotel was built for the business people who visit the area's international manufacturing plants, and the related facilities are top rate. The hotel restaurants are quite good, especially the friendly local services.

West Parade/Belt Road Antigua Base Ramey, Aguadilla, PR 00603. ✆ **800/321-2211** or 787/658-8000. Fax 787/658-8020. www.marriott.com. 152 units. Year-round $169–$199 double. AE, MC, V. **Amenities:** 2 restaurants; 2 bars; babysitting; fitness center; 2 pools; room service; Wi-Fi. *In room:* A/C, TV, Internet access.

Ocean Front Hotel and Restaurant The rooms are spartan but when they front this beautiful of a beach, who cares? About half the rooms here have an ocean view, so request one. You stumble out of your room right on to the middle of Jobos. The price is also right, and there is a beautiful sundeck and terrace, a great bar, and a good restaurant too. And you've got live music on weekends. During the week, the sound of the sea and the smell of the surf guarantee you a great night's sleep. Location, location, location!

Carretera 4466, Km 0.1, Playa Jobos, Isabela, PR 00662. ✆ **787/872-0444.** Fax 787/830-2482. 25 units (shower only). Year-round $85–$100 double; $125–$150 quad. AE, MC, V. **Amenities:** Restaurant; bar; sundeck. *In room:* A/C, TV, balconies.

One-Ten Thai This evocative, unpretentious restaurant serves delicious Thai food and handcrafted beers from around the world. It also has on tap the Old Harbor brew made in Old San Juan. The menu is split between stir fry platters, noodle dishes, and curry bowls, and my family and I love them all. I literally had tears in my eyes the first time I discovered that quality Thai existed in Puerto Rico. And I have been coming here to cry in my green or red curry whenever I'm in the area ever since. The place is small and fills up on weekend evenings. Another wonderful sign that suburban Aguadilla is getting more urbane. Eat in or take out.

Carretera 110, Km 0.1, Playa Jobos, Isabela, PR 00662. ✆ **787/890-0113.** Reservations not accepted. AE, MC, V. Main course $10–$14. Wed–Sun 5–10pm.

Parador El Guajataca Sure the view is great, but that's no reason to stay here or at the **Parado Vistamar** nearby. Stop for lunch or a drink, for sure, but you are better off pushing on ahead to your ultimate destination. The food is only okay, but it's served in a glassed-in dining room where all windows face the sea, which is the real reason to be here. Both properties specialize in local weddings, and really don't offer the quality accommodations most visitors expect. But the view is a killer.

Rte. 2, Km 103.8 (P.O. Box 1558), Quebradillas, PR 00678. ✆ **800/965-3065** or 787/895-3070. Fax 787/895-3589. www.elguajataca.com. 38 units. Year-round $130–$165 double. AE, MC, V. From Quebradillas, continue northwest on Rte. 2 for 1 mile (1.6km); the Parador is signposted. Hotel advertises specials as low as $82. **Amenities:** Restaurant; bar; 2 pools; room service. *In room:* A/C, TV.

Villas del Mar Hau ★ ☺ Opening onto a long, secluded beach, this family-friendly parador complex is peppered with typical Puerto Rican country cottages in vivid Caribbean pastels with Victorian wood trim. The location is midway between the west coast cities of Arecibo in the east and Aguadilla in the west, right outside the smaller town of Isabela. Under the shelter of Casuarina pine trees, most guests spend their days lying on Playa Montones. The huge tidal "wading" pool is ideal for children. The place is unpretentious but not completely back-to-nature, as the beachfront cottages are well furnished and equipped, each with a balcony and with capacities for two to six guests. Neighboring developments have grown up around this vacation compound, which has also expanded over the years. Some rooms have ceiling fans, others have air-conditioning, and all units are equipped with small, tiled, shower-only bathrooms. Since 1960, the Hau family has run this little beach inn. The on-site restaurant is well known in the area for its seafood and meats.

Carretera 4466, Km 8.3, Playa Montones, Isabela, PR 00662. ✆ **787/830-8315.** Fax 787/830-4988. 42 units (shower only). Winter $110–$160 double, $185–$260 cottage; off-season $90–$140 double, $175–$200 cottage. AE, MC, V. From the center of Isabella, take Rte. 466 toward Aguadilla. **Amenities:** Restaurant; bar; barbecue area; babysitting; convenience store; horseback riding; pool w/snack bar; beach toy rental; tennis. *In room:* A/C, TV (in most rooms), kitchenette.

Villa Montana Beach Resort ★ This breathtaking property is set on a 35-acre (14-hectare) beachfront plot. The rooms and villas are spread across Caribbean-style plantation buildings with large verandas and balconies. The buildings have cathedral ceilings, peaked tin roofs, and interior courtyards. The facades use muted pastel colors, and rooms are beautifully decorated in a subdued tropical aesthetic using large terra-cotta tiles. There are two beautiful pools and a 3-mile (4.8km) beach, where every watersport you can imagine is possible to practice. You can also hike through tropical forests, ride horses, go biking, or use the climbing wall on the property. There's a health club, spa, and sports facilities such as basketball courts. Both restaurants, Eclipse and O, have quality food but are on the expensive side. The grounds are lush and beautiful, and there are numerous tropical birds. This is a place to kick way back.

Carretera 4466, Km 1.9, Barrio Bajuras, Isabela, PR 00662. ✆ **888/780-9195** or 787/872-9554. Fax 787/872-9553. 60 units. $200–$400 double; $400–$600 villas. AE, MC, V. **Amenities:** 2 restaurants; bar; babysitting; basketball court; climbing wall; 2 pools; spa; store; tennis court; volleyball court. *In room:* A/C, TV, ceiling fans, kitchenette (in villas).

THE WESTERN MOUNTAINS

The west is also a good area to head up into the mountains, and Maricao, west of Mayagüez, is one of the prettiest of Puerto Rico's mountain towns. You can reach Maricao from Mayagüez, but you'll have to take a number of routes heading east. First take Rte. 106 east to Rte. 119. Turn right onto Rte. 119. Take this until the community of Las Vegas, then turn left on Rte. 357 toward Maricao, which you will reach when you intersect with Rte. 105. The scenery is beautiful, but the roads are narrow and the going is slow. It's quicker to head south along Hwy. 2 to Sabana Grande, and then take Hwy. 120 directly to Maricao.

One of the nicest spots is the **Monte del Estado National Park** (Rte. 120, Km 13.2; ✆ **787/873-5632**), a picnic area and campground in the Maricao Forest, with wonderful pools fed by mountain streams. The stone observation tower, at 2,600 feet (792m) above sea level, provides a panoramic view across the green mountains up to the coastal plains, and you can see clear out to Mona Island. Nearly 50 species of birds live in this forest, including the Lesser Antillean pewee and the scaly naped pigeon. Nature watchers will delight to know that there are some 280 tree species in this reserve, 38 of which are found only here. The area has about 18 rivers and creeks running through the forest.

Marcaio is coffee country, and there are several plantations and historic plantation houses in the town. **Parador Hacienda Juanita** is a beautiful inn and restaurant in a restored former coffee plantation house that was built in 1836.

Nearby is **Lares,** which has a lovely central plaza with shady trees and scattered tropical gardens. The plaza, La Plaza de la Revolucíon, is named after one of the few nationalist uprisings in Puerto Rican history. In 1863, El Grito de Lares ("The Cry of Lares") took place when hundreds of Puerto Rican patriots seized the town from the Spanish on September 28, 1868. While a republic of Puerto Rico was declared, the Spanish quickly resumed control. Today, thousands of independence supporters come here to commemorate the event each year on its September 28 anniversary. Surrounded by mountains and green valleys, it is one of the island's prettiest towns, though it lacks hotels and attractions for tourists.

From Isabela, you can visit **Lago de Guajataca** and the **Guajataca Forest Reserve,** which are located in the mountains south of town.

Before heading into **Bosque Estatal de Guajataca (Guajataca Forest) ★★**, you can stop in at the **Dept. de Recursos Naturales Oficina,** Rte. 446, Km 9, Barrio Llanadas (✆ **787/872-1045** or 787/999-2000), which is open daily 7am to 3:30pm. The office has a stock of detailed hiking routes through the forest reserve. Guajataca Forest sprawls across nearly 2,400 acres (971 hectares) of forestland, rising and falling at various elevations, ranging from 500 to 1,000 feet (152–305m) or more. The woodland in the forest is punctuated by *mogotes* (tropical cone and tower karsts) and covered with 25 miles (40km) of hiking trails. It is also home to the endangered Puerto Rico boa (you are unlikely to encounter one) and is the habitat of nearly 50 different species of birds. The highlight of the forest is the *Cueva del Viento,* the "Cave of the Wind." The hiking trails have been well marked by park rangers.

Reaching the lake from the forest can be difficult. Take Rte. 446 south until you reach Rte. 119. The **Lago de Guajatac ★**, one of the most majestic bodies of water on Puerto Rico, is our favorite lake for some R&R on the island. It is both a 4-mile-long (6.4km) body of water and a wildlife refuge. For a scenic look at the lake, drive along its north shore which is a haven for island freshwater anglers. You can go fishing here, but you have to bring your own equipment. The most sought-after fish is *tucunare,* with which the lake is stocked. At the dam here, you can gaze upon an evocative "lost valley" of conical peaks.

WHERE TO STAY & DINE

Parador Hacienda Juanita ★ Named after one of its long-ago owners, a matriarch named Juanita, this pink stucco building dates from 1836, when it was a coffee plantation. Situated 2 miles (3.2km) west of the village of Maricao, beside Rte. 105 heading to Mayagüez, it has a long veranda and a living room furnished with a large-screen TV and decorated with antique tools and artifacts of the coffee industry. Relatively isolated, it's surrounded by only a few neighboring buildings and the jungle. Situated on 24 acres (9.7 hectares) of plantation, the parador is a beautiful spot to hike around. It has a fine restaurant, and both breakfast and dinner are included with the room. There's a swimming pool, billiards table, and ping-pong table on the premises. Its restaurant, **La Casona de Juanita,** serves tasty, hearty Puerto Rican fare. The best spot to dine is on the veranda overlooking the verdant grounds. The bedrooms are simple and rural, with ceiling fans, rocking chairs, and rustic furniture, plus small tub-and-shower bathrooms. All are smoke-free. None of the rooms has air-conditioning (ceiling fans suffice in the cool temperatures of this high-altitude place). It sits at 1,600 feet (488m) above sea level.

Rte. 105, Km 23.5 (HC01 Box 8200), Maricao, PR 00606. ✆ **787/838-2550.** Fax 787/838-2551. www.haciendajuanita.com. 21 units. $107 double. Rate includes breakfast and dinner. Children 11 and under stay free in parent's room. AE, MC, V. Free parking. **Amenities:** Restaurant; bar; pool; tennis; smoke-free rooms; 1 room for those w/limited mobility. *In room:* TV, ceiling fan, Internet access, no phone.

EASTERN PUERTO RICO

The northeast corner of the island, less than an hour from San Juan, contains the island's major attractions, El Yunque rainforest, two of the world's rare bioluminescent bays whose waters glow at night, and several great beaches, including Luquillo Beach (see chapter 7 as well). There are a variety of landscapes, ranging from miles of forest to palm groves and beachside settlements. Here you will find one of the best resorts on the island, El Conquistador Resort, which literally sits on the northeast corner of Puerto Rico, where the Atlantic Ocean and the Caribbean Sea meet.

10

At Fajardo, a preeminent sailor's haven, you can catch ferries to the nearby island municipalities of Vieques and Culebra (see chapter 11). The east coast city is actually the start of a chain of islands, moving onwards to the island towns and weaving along the neighboring U.S. and British Virgin Islands and beyond. The area forms perhaps the greatest pleasure boating area in the world.

The Navy completed its exodus from Roosevelt Roads base south of Fajardo in 2004, and the government is proposing a massive tourism development, but for the moment Ceiba and Naguabo are sleepy, quaint towns that are worth a look.

Halfway down the coast is Humacao, home to **Palmas del Mar Resort,** an ever-growing resort and upscale vacation-home community on a wildly gorgeous beachfront. There's a Sheraton Five Points hotel, and two five-star hotels are under development: a Mandarin Oriental Resort Spa and Regent Hotel Resort, both slated for opening in 2011.

Visitors can also rent private vacation homes and villas throughout the resort, which sprawls across 2,700 acres (1,093 hectares) and has a yacht club, equestrian center, the Caribbean's largest tennis center, a beach and country club, great beaches, and lush tropical grounds. Plenty of watersports activities are available. Luxury residences, used as both vacation properties and year-round homes, are divided into distinct communities. Palmas also has its own school and post office.

The Robert S. Vilella Expressway 53 heads south from Humacao and then joins Rte. 3, and turns the southeast corner of Puerto Rico towards Guayama and Puerto Rico's long Caribbean coast, which is actually at its prettiest at its eastern and western extremes.

At Yabucoa, take the coastal Rte. 901, which switches back and forth along oceanfront cliffs and sleepy coastal villages, to experience one of the most breathtaking series of views on the island. The road continues to hug the coast as it reconnects with Hwy. 3 and rounds the southeast corner of Puerto Rico to Guayama. There are several nice beaches.

This once important sugar town has long since been converted into an industrial and commercial center, but time stands still at its downtown plaza, which has beautiful Spanish colonial architecture, restored buildings, and a provincial air.

FAJARDO

35 miles (56km) E of San Juan

A huge submerged coral reef off Fajardo's coast protects its southeastern waters, which are also blessed by trade winds—a sailors' delight. The Caribbean waters here are run through with coral and marine life, from barracudas and nurse sharks to shimmering schools of tropical fish, making this area a diving and snorkeling paradise.

There are dozens of small islands off the coast of this eastern town. Fajardo itself has untrammeled beaches, surrounded by wilderness, with great snorkeling and scuba opportunities right offshore. It also has a bioluminescent bay and other natural wonders. Its unvarnished town center has atmospheric bars and *cafetíns* serving up cold drinks and tasty Creole cooking at bargain prices.

There are at least seven marinas in town, and with reason. Fajardo is the first of a string of ports extending to Vieques and Culebra, the U.S. and British Virgin Islands, and the Windward island chain, the pleasure boating capital of the Caribbean. There are also gorgeous beaches, snorkeling spots, and untamed forest.

Las Croabas, a seafront village within the municipality, is the site of the El Conquistador Resort & Golden Door Spa, a leader in luxury since its casino was used as the setting for pivotal scenes in the 1964 James Bond classic film *Goldfinger.* Today, the Mediterranean-inspired fantasy resort has its own funicular, water park, several pools in a breathtaking setting, a marina, a private ferry and private island with caverns, nature trails, horseback riding and watersports, plus classically beautiful beaches. The resort is divided into a main hotel, an upscale Andalusian village, and two modern resort communities, all tied together with lush landscaping. It also has full sports, spa, health, and beauty facilities.

The resort sprawls across a dramatic cliff and down along a harbor area, overlooking the coast with an infinite view of water stretching out from all sides. The back terraces and circular casino share the view, as do the leveled infinity pools stretching across the bluff. The buildings are wrought with Mediterranean motifs, from blooming Spanish courtyards to elegant neoclassical facades and fountains. A tramway takes guests down to sea level and the resort marina, and a ferry takes guests to the resort's beach on an offshore island.

Las Croabas is a charming fishing village, with boats tied up at harbor and open-air seafood restaurants. Many are clustered along Rte. 987 at the entrances of the Seven Seas public beach and Las Cabezas de San Juan Nature Reserve, over 300 acres (121 hectares) of dry forest, virgin coast, and mangrove swamp. It also borders the exquisite biobay, with glowing nocturnal waters. The restored 19th-century lighthouse still functions. The road ends in a circle, which wraps around a park at the village harbor. Several operators rent kayaks for daytime snorkeling trips or evening trips to the biobay at the adjacent nature reserve. You can paddle across the bay and through mangrove canals to make it to the biobay.

Getting There

El Conquistador staff members greet guests at the San Juan airport and transport them to the resort. Guests can take a taxi to the resort for $80, but that's more than the roundtrip fare aboard the plush resort shuttle from Luis Muñoz Marín Airport ($74 adults, $54 for children 12 and under—for hotel guests only). If you're driving from San Juan, head east along the new Rte. 66 Corridor Noreste highway and then Rte. 3 toward Fajardo. At the intersection, cut northeast on Rte. 195 and continue to the intersection with Rte. 987, at which point you turn north. To fully enjoy all El Conquistador's offerings, you'll probably want to stay there for several days. You might want to rent a car from Fajardo for only part of your stay, and take the shuttle to and from the airport.

Outdoor Activities

In addition to the lovely beach and the many recreational facilities that are part of the El Conquistador (p. 267), there are other notable places to play in the vicinity.

Some of the best snorkeling in Puerto Rico is in and around Fajardo. Its public beach, **Playa Seven Seas,** is an attractive and sheltered strip of sand. The beach lies on the southwestern shoreline of Las Cabezas peninsula and is crowded on weekends. For even better snorkeling, walk to the western end of this beach and along a dirt path cutting though a wooded mount. After about a half-mile (.8km), you'll come to another path heading to **Playa Escondido** (Hidden Beach), a small white-sand cover with coral reefs in aquamarine waters right off this beach. If you continue straight for another mile, you will come to the gorgeous **El Convento Beach,** stretching out along the miles-long undeveloped coastline between Fajardo and Luquillo.

The area has managed to ward off development despite the building craze taking place across much of the rest of Puerto Rico, with only a few unmarked dirt roads providing access, and paths such as the one from Seven Seas. The area is a nesting ground for endangered sea turtles, and its waters teem with reefs and fish. A small forest runs along much of the beach, and behind it stands the imposing El Yunque rainforest, looming over the white-sand beach and pristine blue waters. About a mile down the beach is the governor's official beach house, El Convento, a rustic wooden cottage. Just beyond the cottage is a great spot to snorkel. The water plunges steeply just offshore and is pocked with large reefs, which draw even large fish close to shore.

Environmentalists have pushed to protect this area from development, while developers want to build two large resorts. The administration is currently drawing up boundaries of a proposed nature reserve, which is to allow some "low-impact" tourism back from the coast.

Eastern Puerto Rico

To get here, you can hike from Fajardo's Seven Seas Public Beach, outside the resort just before Las Croabas village. It's a 2-mile (3km) hike through a trail in the shrub forest on its eastern end to El Convento Beach, a miles-long stretch of largely untouched beachfront, home to sea turtles and reef-studded waters with great snorkeling. The official vacation home of Puerto Rico's governor is the only development to speak of. The dirt road leading to it is the only road near the beach, one of the reasons it has been able to escape the stampede of development that has remade most of Puerto Rico over the last several decades.

TENNIS The seven Har-Tru courts at the **El Conquistador ★★** are among the best tennis courts in Puerto Rico, rivaling those at Palmas del Mar. The staff at the pro shop are extremely helpful to beginning players. Courts are the least crowed during the hottest part of the day, around the lunch hour. If you're a single traveler to the resort and in search of a player, the pro shop will try to match you up with a player of equal skill.

WATERSPORTS Several operators offer day sailing trips (10am–3pm) from Fajardo marinas, which include sailing, snorkeling, swimming, and a stop at one of

TO THE lighthouse: EXPLORING LAS CABEZAS DE SAN JUAN NATURE RESERVE

Las Cabezas de San Juan Nature Reserve is better known as El Faro, or "the Lighthouse." Located in the northeastern corner of the island, it is one of the most beautiful and important areas in Puerto Rico. Here you'll find seven ecological systems and a restored 19th-century Spanish colonial lighthouse. From the lighthouse observation deck, majestic views extend to islands as far off as St. Thomas in the U.S. Virgin Islands.

Surrounded on three sides by the Atlantic Ocean, the 316-acre (128-hectare) site encompasses forestland, mangroves, lagoons, beaches, cliffs, offshore cays, and coral reefs. Boardwalk trails wind through the fascinating topography. Ospreys, sea turtles, and an occasional manatee are seen from the windswept promontories and rocky beach.

The nature reserve is open Wednesday through Sunday. Reservations are required; for reservations during the week, call ✆ **787/722-5882;** during the weekend, reserve by calling ✆ **787/860-2560** (weekend reservations must be made on the day of your visit). Admission is $7 for adults, $4 for children 13 and under, and $2.50 for seniors. Guided 2½-hour tours are conducted at 9:30, 10, and 10:30am, and 2pm (in English at 2pm).

Laguna Grande, within the reserve, is one of the world's best bioluminescent bays, along with one on the neighboring island of Vieques. The presence of multitudes of tiny organisms, called dinoflagellates, in the protected bay is responsible for the nocturnal glow of its waters. They feed off the red mangroves surrounding the water. Kayaking through the bay at night should be on your bucket list. We highly recommend **Las Tortugas Adventures,** P.O. Box 1637, Canóvanas 00729 (✆ **787/636-8356** or 787/809-0253; http://kayak-pr.com). Gary Horne is one of the most experienced guides in Puerto Rico; he's a certified dive master and Coast Guard veteran. There are two nightly tours of the bay at 6 and 8pm Monday through Saturday, which cost $45 per person—or daytime kayak and snorkel adventures for $65, which we highly recommend as well. Another option is a kayak adventure through the Río Espirtu Santo, a beautiful river through El Yunque rainforest.

the island beaches, where lunch is usually served. It's the easiest way to really experience the Caribbean marine world while in Puerto Rico. Prices, including lunch and equipment, start from $69 per person. The trips are aboard luxury catamarans, with plush seating, a sound system, and other comforts, such as a bar. Captains know the best spots, where reefs attract schools of feeding fish, depending on conditions. These are among the most gin-clear and tranquil waters in Puerto Rico. They are teeming with wildlife, including several species of fish such as grouper, but also lobster, moray eels, and sea turtles. Among the local operators are **Traveler Sailing Catamaran** (✆ **787/853-2821**), **East Island Excursions** (✆ **787/860-3434**), and **Catamaran Spread Eagle** (✆ **787/887-8821**). **Erin Go Bragh Charters** (✆ **787/860-4401**) offers similar day trips aboard a 50-foot sailing ketch.

For scuba divers, **La Casa del Mar** (✆ **787/863-3483** or 863-1000, ext. 7919) is one good option operating out of El Conquistador. You can go for ocean dives on the outfitter's boats; a two-tank dive goes for $150, including equipment. A PADI snorkel program, at $65 per person, is also available. It's located at the marina. **Sea Ventures Dive Center** (Rte. 3, Km 51.4, Puerto del Rey; ✆ **787/863-3483**) has a $95 offer for a two-tank dive.

Fajardo's seven marinas are proof that it is a sailor's paradise. The most renowned is the **Puerto del Rey Marina** (Rte. 3, Km 51.4; ✆ **787/860-1000** or 801-3010). The swankiest marina in Fajardo, it's a beautiful 1,100-slip facility south of town, the largest in the Caribbean. It's like a city unto itself with restaurants, bars, and a host of other services. **Villa Marina Yacht Harbour** (Rte. 987, Km 1.3; ✆ **787/863-5131** or 863-5011) is the other main marina in town, and is the shortest ride to the offshore cays and isolated white-sand beaches on the mainland. Charters operate out of both. There's a private 35-slip marina at the lowest level of the El Conquistador (✆ **787/863-1000**).

Where to Stay

VERY EXPENSIVE

El Conquistador Resort: The Waldorf Astoria Collection ★★ ☺ El Conquistador is a destination unto itself. Its array of facilities sits on 500 acres (202 hectares) of forested hills sloping down to the sea. Accommodations are divided into five separate sections united by their Mediterranean architecture and lush landscaping. Most lie several hundred feet above the sea. At the same altitude, a bit off to the side, is a replica of an Andalusian hamlet, Las Casitas Village, which seems straight out of the south of Spain. These pricey units, each with a full kitchen, form a self-contained enclave.

A short walk down the hill takes you to a circular cluster of tastefully modern accommodations, Las Olas Village. And at sea level, adjacent to an armada of pleasure craft bobbing at anchor, is La Marina Village, whose balconies seem to hang directly over the water. The accommodations are outfitted with comfortable furniture, tropical colors, and robes. All the far-flung elements of the resort are connected by serpentine, landscaped walkways and by a railroad-style funicular that makes frequent trips up and down the hillside.

One of the most comprehensive spas in the Caribbean, the Golden Door maintains a branch in this resort. The hotel is sole owner of a "fantasy island" (Palomino Island), with caverns; nature trails; horseback riding; and watersports such as scuba diving, windsurfing, and snorkeling. Free private ferries at frequent intervals connect the island, which is about a half-mile (.8km) offshore, to the main hotel. There's also a 35-slip marina. The hotel operates an excellently run children's club with activities planned daily. The resort has opened up a water park that's a hit with the kids (and the young at heart) with water slides, a lazy river, and a large pool. It's on the harbor level, right by the water, below the pool's main deck.

Av. Conquistador 1000, Las Croabas, Fajardo, PR 00738. ✆ **888/543-1282** or 787/863-1000. Fax 787/863-6500. www.elconresort.com. 918 units. Winter $199–$369 double, $738–$1,200 suites, $489–$1,200 Las Casitas villas; off-season $149–$269 double, $538–$807 suites, $389–$789 Las Casitas villas. MAP (breakfast and dinner) packages are available. Children ages 16 and under stay free in parent's room. AE, DC, DISC, MC, V. Valet parking $21; self-parking $16 per day. **Amenities:** 12 restaurants; 8 bars; casino; nightclub; children's programs; dive shop; fishing; golf course; health club; 35-slip marina; 7 pools; room service; sailing; spa; 7 Har-Tru tennis courts; smoke-free rooms; rooms for those w/limited mobility. *In room:* A/C, TV, fridge, hair dryer, minibar.

TOP CARIBBEAN spa: THE GOLDEN DOOR

Perched atop a stunning 300-foot (91m) bluff overlooking the Caribbean Sea and the Atlantic Ocean, the **Golden Door ★★** in Las Casitas Village complex at the Wyndham El Conquistador Hotel (✆ **787/863-1000**), is the most sophisticated, well-managed, and comprehensive spa in the Caribbean, and it is one of the finest in the world. One of only three branches of a spa founded in Escondido, California, and today administered by the Wyndham group, it's devoted to the relaxation and healing of body, soul, and mind. Spa rituals are taken seriously; New Age mysticism is gracefully dispensed within a postmodern setting that's a cross between a Swiss clinic, a state-of-the-art health club, and a Buddhist monastery. Spa treatments begin at $160. The spa is open daily from 6:30am to 8:30pm. American Express, MasterCard, and Visa are accepted.

MODERATE

The Fajardo Inn ★ 🎁 A good base for those visiting El Yunque, this inn is ideal for those who are seeking a location in the east and don't want to pay the prices charged at the El Conquistador (see above). Lying on a hilltop overlooking the port of Fajardo, this parador evokes a Mediterranean villa with its balustrades and grand staircases. The midsize bedrooms, most of which open onto good views, are spotless, and each has a small shower-only bathroom. The inn and its pool are handsomely landscaped. The on-site Star Fish restaurant specializes in Creole and Continental cuisine, especially fresh fish, with indoor and outdoor dining. The Blue Iguana Mexican Grill & Bar is a casual pub with good food. Coco's Park is a new pool area with such activities as a beach pool, slide, Jacuzzi, tennis, basketball, and miniature golf. It's separated from the rest of the hotel so as not to disturb the relative tranquillity of the rest of the grounds.

Parcela Beltrán 52, Fajardo, PR 00740. ✆ **787/860-6000.** Fax 787/860-5063. www.fajardoinn.com. 105 units (shower only). Year-round $110–$175 double; $175–$300 suite. AE, DISC, MC, V. 15-min. walk east of the center of Fajardo. **Amenities:** 2 restaurants; 2 bars; pool; room service; snorkeling and diving arranged; 1 room for those w/limited mobility. *In room:* A/C, TV, hair dryer.

Where to Dine

EXPENSIVE

Blossoms ★ CHINESE/JAPANESE Blossoms boasts some of the freshest seafood in eastern Puerto Rico. Sizzling delights are prepared on teppanyaki tables, and there's a zesty selection of Hunan and Szechuan specialties. On the teppanyaki menu, you can choose dishes ranging from chicken to shrimp, from filet mignon to lobster. Sushi bar selections range from eel and squid to salmon roe and giant clams.

Rte. 987, Km 3.4, in the El Conquistador Resort. ✆ **787/863-1000.** Reservations recommended. Main courses $18–$49. AE, DC, DISC, MC, V. Daily 6–11:30pm.

La Estación 🎁 **★** BARBECUE This funky outdoor restaurant in a converted gas station is one of a myriad of beautiful results of the decades long culture clash between Puerto Rico and New York. The *nuyorican* barbecue served here is a down-to earth culinary proposition, and it's executed to smoky perfection, thanks to the natural charcoal barbecue method, fresh seafood, and fine cuts and delicious sauces. A classically trained chef, Kevin Roth worked in such hit restaurants in New York as Quilty and Compass before opening up the Fajardo grill place with his partner Idalia García. The green papaya salad and house Caesar salad (with Serrano ham and manchego cheese) are great openers, and everything I've ever tried–shrimp kebabs, grilled mahimahi, and pork medallions–has been excellent. There's a different grilled fish and selection of fresh grilled vegetables daily. You dine on terraces spreading out from the kitchen, which is in the old gas station, and there is also a bar on a huge cedar deck. Right on the road to Las Croabas.

Rte. 987, Km. 4, Las Croabas, Fajardo. ✆ **787/863-4481.** Reservations recommended. Main courses $10–$30. AE, DC, DISC, MC, V. Mon–Wed 5pm–midnight; Fri–Sun 3pm–midnight.

La Picolla Fontana ★ NORTHERN ITALIAN Dine by candlelight in a neo-Palladian ambience, and feel like Roman royalty. The menu is straight-ahead, northern Italian cuisine, but it's prepared to perfection in a romantic room that drips old-time glamour. It has the same great menu as the El San Juan location and the same sky-high prices. Start out with sautéed clams in white wine and garlic sauce, escargot in butter or a caprese salad, then move on to a shrimp fra diavolo or chicken saltimboca. The pastas (from the penne with Mediterranean vegetables to the Spinach taglioni in a porcini cream sauce) are wonderful, and so are the risottos.

Rte. 987, Km 3.4, in the El Conquistador Resort. ✆ **787/863-1000.** Reservations recommended. Main courses $26–$75. AE, DC, DISC, MC, V. Daily 6–10:30pm.

Stingray Café ★★ CARIBBEAN FUSION I love this resort's harbor-side restaurant, with a deliciously crafted seafood menu and views of the Caribbean and Palomino Island. The modern decor is inconsequential compared to the view and the Latin, down-island, and Asian-infused Continental classics. Flavors float in the air with the smell of the sea—saffron clams and *chorizo* and the cilantro conch chowder, seared tuna in a Szechuan au poivre, and the lemon sole filet lobster beurre blanc. But the filet mignon in roasted bacon shallot sauce and the pistachio-crusted veal medallions also command attention. Fruit sorbets are the dessert specialty. Really, it's all about the food and the view.

Rte. 987, Km 3.4, in the El Conquistador Resort. ✆ **787/863-1000.** Reservations recommended. Main courses $29–$50. AE, DISC, MC, V. Daily 6–10:30pm.

CEIBA & NAGUABO

South of Fajardo is Ceiba, the site of the former Roosevelt Roads Navy base, and the seaside fishing town of Naguabo. Once dominated by the Navy presence, which set sail in 2004, the two towns are now sleepy places, waiting for government plans to transform the former military base into a new "Caribbean Riviera." Today, you can come here to a nice seafood lunch at the town harbors or visit the south side of El Yunque rainforest.

The local Ports Authority has taken over the former Navy airport. Visitors can catch flights to San Juan, Vieques and Culebra and other Caribbean islands from here.

Naguabo's town harbor is fronted by modest seafood restaurants and is a great place to stop for a lunch on a sunny afternoon. I've eaten at several of the numerous casual, open-air seafood restaurants, serving tasty, economically priced seafood and other local specialties and have never been disappointed. The 1917 revival mansion Castillo Villa del Mar, now a National Historic Monument, is at the harbor's southern end.

Naguabo is also home to a charming guest house, Casa Flamboyant, nestled in the lush south side of El Yunque rainforest, about a half-hour drive along country roads from the town harbor.

Getting Around

The Ceiba International Airport (✆ **787/534-4101**) has replaced the Fajardo and Humacao airports. The Fajardo airport has closed and the Humacao airport is only used on weekends and holidays by local private pilots. It is no longer certified for scheduled passenger or commercial travel. The Ceiba airport hosts several small airlines serving Vieques and Culebra and other destinations. All the small airlines–Vieques Air Link, Isla Nena, Air Flamenco–that served the islands from Fajardo now serve them from Ceiba. To get here from Fajardo, take Expressway 53 south to exit 2 (the Puerto del Rey Marina exit) and pick up Hwy. 3 south. Follow signs to the Ceiba airport until you exit on Tarawa Drive. You'll pass a guardhouse at the entrance to the former base and proceed along the main road for the airport. Parking runs about $10 daily.

Where to Stay

Casa Flamboyant ★ 🎁 This stylish Caribbean bed and breakfast ensconced in the south side of the lush El Yunque rainforest is a stunning find in southeast Puerto Rico. Surrounded by lush jungle, just downstream from a gushing waterfall, the rooms have fantastic views of the rainforest and the Caribbean coastline. Old world glamour and sumptuous bedding and furnishings add to the appeal. Three rooms are available in the main house, all with private bathrooms. The private Rainbow Room suite is set apart. All the rooms have gorgeous, private views, either from terraces or balconies, and the pool, courtyards and other common areas are also spectacular. Hike through tropical forest right from the property, take a swim in a natural pool of a nearby river, or take a plunge in the waterfall just upstream from the B&B. The owner lives here with her dogs and serves excellent, hearty breakfast.

Off Rte. 191. Mailing address: P.O. Box 175, Naguabo, PR 00718. ✆ **787/874-6074.** Fax 787/559-9800. www.elyunque.com/flamboy.html. 4 units. Year-round $200 double; $250 private suite. AE, MC, V. 15-min. walk east of the center of Fajardo. **Amenities:** Pool, A/C, DVD, print and music library. *In room:* flatscreen TV, CD player, DVD player, and refrigerators with water.

PALMAS DEL MAR

46 miles (74km) SE of San Juan

Halfway down the east coast, south from Fajardo, lies the resort and luxury residential community of Palmas del Mar in the municipality of Humacao. Here you'll find one of the most action-packed sports programs in the Caribbean, offering golf, tennis, scuba diving, sailing, deep-sea fishing, and horseback riding. Palmas del Mar's location is one of its greatest assets. The pleasing Caribbean trade winds steadily blow across this section of the island, stabilizing the weather and making Palmas del Mar ideal for many outdoor sports.

But the quickest way to get here from San Juan is to head south to along Hwy. 52 and then east Hwy. 30 to Humacao.

Palmas del Mar sprawls across 2,700 acres (1,092 hectares) of beautifully landscaped coast, a self-contained resort and residential community with several different luxury neighborhoods, ranging from Mediterranean-style villas to modern marina town houses. On the grounds are six pools, two golf courses, 20 tennis courts, a fitness center, and a dive shop. Fishing, bike or car rentals, babysitting, and horseback riding can be arranged.

It's a town unto itself with a school, hospital and post office, several restaurants, shops, and other facilities that any town center would have. There's one existing hotel and two luxury properties under construction. Several of the residences are available for rent through a vacation club or real estate office.

Getting There

You'll want a rental car to get around anyway (unless you are content with a golf cart and staying within the resort). If you're driving from San Juan, take Hwy. 52 south to Caguas, then take Hwy. 30 east to Humacao. Follow the signs from there to Palmas del Mar.

A van ride to the San Juan international airport is $90 for the first three passengers, $25 per person for four or more. For reservations, call © **787/285-4323.** Call the resort if you want to be met at the airport.

The Ceiba International Airport north of Humacao is the closet airport. It's located at the old Roosevelt Roads Naval Base in Ceiba (see above.)

Beaches & Outdoor Activities

BEACHES Palmas del Mar Resort has 3 exceptional miles (4.8km) of white-sand beaches (all open to the public). Nonguests must park at the hotel parking ($2 per hour), and there are showers and bathrooms near the beach. The waters here can get rough in winter but are generally calm, and there's a watersports center and marina. (see "Scuba Diving & Snorkeling," below).

FISHING Some of the best year-round fishing in the Caribbean is found in the waters just off Palmas del Mar. **Capt. Bill Burleson,** based in Humacao (© **787/850-7442**), operates charters on his customized, 46-foot sport-fisherman, *Karolette,* which is electronically equipped for successful fishing. Burleson prefers to take fishing groups to Grappler Banks, 18 nautical miles (33m) away, which lie in the migratory paths of wahoo, tuna, and marlin. A maximum of six people are taken out, costing $680 for 4½ hours, $840 for 6 hours, or $1,140 for 8 hours. Burleson also offers snorkeling charter expeditions starting at $640 for up to six people for 4½ hours or $840 for 6 hours.

GOLF Few other real-estate developments in the Caribbean devote as much attention and publicity to their golf facilities as the **Palmas del Mar Country Club ★★** (© **787/285-2256**). Today, both the older course, the Gary Player–designed Palm course, and the newer course, the Reese Jones–designed Flamboyant course, have pars of 72 and layouts of around 2,250 yards (2,057m) each. Crack golfers consider holes 11 to 15 of the Palm course among the toughest 5 successive holes in the Caribbean. The pro shop that services both courses is open daily from

6:30am to 6pm. To play the course costs $85 for guests of Villas at Palmas and Four Points by Sheraton and $100 for nonguests.

HIKING Palmas del Mar's land is an attraction in its own right. Here you'll find more than 6 miles (9.7km) of Caribbean ocean frontage—3½ miles (5.6km) of sandy beach amid rocky cliffs and promontories. Large tracts of the 2,700-acre (1,093-hectare) property have harbored sugar and coconut plantations over the years, and a wet tropical forest preserve with giant ferns, orchids, and hanging vines covers about 70 acres (28 hectares) near the resort's geographic center.

SCUBA DIVING & SNORKELING Some of the best dives in Puerto Rico are right off the eastern coast. Two dozen dive sites south of Fajardo are within a 5-mile (8km) radius offshore. See "The Best Scuba Diving" section, in chapter 1.

Set adjacent to a collection of boutiques, bars, and restaurants at the edge of Palmas del Mar's harbor, **Palmas Sea Ventures Dive Center ★**, Palmas Del Mar Marina, 110 Harbor Dr. (✆ **787/863-3483**), owns a 44-foot-long dive boat with a 16-foot (4.9m) beam to make it stable in rough seas. They offer both morning and afternoon sessions of two-tank dives (for experienced and certified divers only), priced at $119 each (equipment included). Half-day snorkeling trips, priced at $60 per participant and departing for both morning and afternoon sessions, go whenever there's demand to the fauna-rich reefs that encircle Monkey Island, an offshore uninhabited cay.

TENNIS The **Tennis Center at Palmas del Mar ★★** (✆ **787/852-6000,** ext. 51), the largest in Puerto Rico, features 13 hard courts, two Omni courts, and four clay courts, open to resort guests and nonguests. Fees for guests are $20 per hour during the day and $25 per hour at night. Fees for nonguests are $25 per hour during the day and $33 per hour at night. Within the resort's tennis compound is a **fitness center,** which has the best-equipped gym in the region; it's open Monday to Friday 6am to 9pm, Saturday and Sunday 6am to 8pm.

Where to Stay

Some of the nicest lodging options are the privately owned villas and vacation homes spread throughout the several luxury communities that comprise Palmas del Mar. Prices start as low as $150 nightly, and range are the way up to $750. Weekly rates range from $1,500 to $5,000. The studios and villas at **Villas at Palmas del Mar,** 295 Palmas Inn Way, Ste. 6, Carretera no. 3, Km 86.4, Candelero, Humacao, PR 00791 (✆ **800/468-3331;** fax 787/852-0927), have long been favorites of vacationers with their resort-level accommodations. But other rentals are available at Rentals in the Marbella Club, Los Lagos, Aquabella, and several other communities can be arranged through the Palmas del Mar Resort (✆ **800/PALMAS-6;** [725-6276]; www.palmasdelmar.com).

Four Points by Sheraton Palmas del Mar Resort ★ A plethora of on-site activities may keep you from ever leaving the premises: championship golf courses, a country club, a casino and pool bar, along with an "infinity pool," are just some of the offerings. Furnishings are tasteful and exceedingly comfortable, typical of Sheraton's deluxe hotels. Available extras include private balconies, luxury bathrooms, and work desks. The hotel also offers business services for commercial travelers, plus a special pool for kids. The hotel restaurant offers a varied international menu (some dine here every night), and you'll also find a wine and cigar bar. Location

Where the Locals Go for Soul Food

To escape the confines of the resort for the evening, there are plenty of simple restaurants and seafront shacks serving up fresh and tasty seafood and *comida criolla* in atmospheric settings on the east coast. Several such restaurants can be found in the Punta Santiago sector just off Hwy. 3. **Paradise Seafood,** off Hwy. 3, on Calle Isidro Andreu, the main road in Punta Santiago Humacao (✆ **787/852-1180**) has been serving such food for 7 decades in an attractive, no-frills setting. Memorable renditions of *mofongo* stuffed with seafood and hearty seafood stews, grilled fresh fish, baked lobster, and a wide variety of fish and shellfish served in tasty garlic, Creole, and citrus sauces. **Pescao y Salsa** (✆ **787/850-6666**) on the same road is another excellent choice, for fresh seafood, with fresh lobsters and red snapper available every evening. Besides the basic seafood and local cuisine, there are more sophisticated choices here, with several specials every evening like halibut in a roasted pepper puree and saffron risotto and skirt steak with tamarind chimichurri and mashed cassava and potatoes. You can also get tasty seafood turnovers and excellent conch or octopus ceviche salad sold in plastic cups in several of Punta Santiago's modest establishments, the perfect combination with a cold beer. Another delicacy is *arepas,* a delicate island biscuit usually stuffed with sautéed seafood or ceviche salad. There are several restaurants in this sector, but these two are among the best.

is its real draw—right in the middle of Palmas del Mar, a world unto itself on the island's east coast.

Candelero Dr. 170, Humacao, PR 00791. ✆ **787/850-6000.** Fax 787/850-6001. www.starwoodhotels.com. 107 units. Year-round $155–$275 double; winter $275–$295 suite; off-season $270 suite. AE, MC, V. Valet parking $15; self-parking $12. **Amenities:** Restaurant; 2 bars; casino; fitness center; golf; kids' pool; outdoor pool; room service; scuba diving; tennis; smoke-free rooms; rooms for those w/limited mobility. *In room:* A/C, TV, beverage maker, fridge, hair dryer.

Where to Dine

Thanks to the kitchens that are built into virtually every unit in Palmas del Mar, many guests prepare at least some of their meals "at home." This is made relatively feasible thanks to the on-site supermarket at the Palmanova Plaza, which has well stocked fresh produce and meats, a wide variety of goods and an excellent wine.

Bistro Rico FRENCH Chef Daniel's take on informal bistro and cafe fare, with inventive sandwiches (smoked trout, grilled duck breast); bistro classics, such as grilled steak; and such things as an awesome house salad with artichokes and tomatoes and veal burgers. It's a good spot for a shrimp cocktail, crab salad or other delicious appetizer as well. Right by the water next door to Chez Daniel.

Anchor's Village Marina at Palmas del Mar. Harbour Drive 110, Ste. 5, Humacao 00791. ✆ **787/850-3838.** Reservations required. Main courses $28–$39 at dinner; $8.50–$20 at lunch. AE, DISC, MC, V. Mon–Sat noon–10pm; Fri–Sun noon–3pm. Closed June.

Blue Hawaii CHINESE This is the best Chinese restaurant in the region. It combines Polynesian themes (similar to a toned-down Trader Vic's) with an Americanized version of Chinese food that's flavorful and well suited to Puerto Rico's hot, steamy climate. The menu is huge, and includes grilled lobster with garlic-flavored cheese sauce; blackened salmon, and a wonderful beef teriyaki. There's a superb house version of honey chicken. It's in the courtyard of the resort's shopping center, with tables for alfresco dining. There's also a dining room inside, and a small bar/ lounge. Your host is Tommy Lo, former chef aboard the now-defunct ocean liner SS *United States*.

In the Palmanova Shopping Center. ✆ **787/285-6644.** Reservations recommended. Main courses $15–$50. AE, MC, V. Daily noon–10:30pm.

Chez Daniel ★ FRENCH Faithfully executed classic French cuisine—bouillabaisse, onion soup, lobster and chicken pies—is served at this restaurant along the Palmas del Mar Marina. Normandy-born Daniel Vasse, the owner, along with his French Catalonian wife, Lucette, maintain a dining room that is the most appealing in Palmas del Mar. There's grilled asparagus and a delicious tomato and goat cheese tart to start, and the Marseille bouillabaisse, loaded with grouper, snapper, lobster, shrimp and mussels, unless you want one of the delicious steaks. The desserts are also classics delivered with perfection. The owner also opened **The Tapas Bar** next door, an informal tapas bar, open Wednesday to Sunday noon to 11pm. There, you can pick from a raw bar with ceviche and sushi, but I started with gazpacho and went on to the grilled fish and mango and veal meatballs.

Marina de Palmas del Mar. ✆ **787/850-3838.** Reservations required. Main courses $28–$39 at dinner; $8–$19 at lunch; $42 Sun brunch (includes 1st drink). AE, DISC, MC, V. Wed–Mon 6:30–10pm; Fri–Sun noon–3pm. Closed June.

THE SOUTHEAST

More and more visitors are discovering the bewitching allure of Puerto Rico's wild and wooly southeast coast, with deep sand beaches, powerful waves, and cliffs cutting across the landscape straight down to the coast. There are still empty beaches with lighthouses, but now there are more restaurants and lodging options than just a few years ago.

In Yabucoa, you can also catch the start of the Panoramic Route, a tangle of narrow country roads crisscrossing Puerto Rico's mountainous interior from the east to west coasts (see chapter 4). The coastal Rte. 901 cuts along steep oceanfront cliffs and descends into such sleepy coastal villages as Maunabo and Patillas. Along the way is El Horizonte, where the food is as satisfying as the views. At Punta Tuna, along this road in town, there is a beautiful lighthouse built in 1892 and a wide public beach beside it with restaurants, bathroom facilities and an outdoor picnic area. A better place to go swimming is Playa Emajaguas, a rare, thick sandy beach in the area. It does not get as crowded as Playa Lucía, farther down the road, right next door to larger hotel.

Beyond Maunabo, the main coastal road merges with Hwy. 3 as it passes through the pretty town of Patillas, which has one of the nicest resorts of in the area. Arroyo has the fine Centro Vacacional Punta Guiliarte, a National Parks Company public beach and vacation center.

Off Rte. 3, Rte. 901 climbs steep oceanfront cliffs, cutting back and forth in switchbacks that afford outstanding views of the Caribbean and the islands in the distance. The road again descends into Maunabo, a sleepy coastal village that despite its charms remains off the beaten path for most visitors to Puerto Rico. At Punta Tuna, there is a beautiful lighthouse built in 1892 and a nice public beach beside it, with restaurants, bathroom facilities, and an outdoor picnic area. The wide sand beach here is among the nicest in the region. Elsewhere in town, the beaches are mostly deserted, used more by fishermen than beachgoers. The sand is heavier, darker, and deeper than elsewhere in Puerto Rico, and the currents can be strong. The beaches, protected by palm trees and bluffs, are beautiful, however.

Where to Stay & Dine

MODERATE

Caribe Playa Resort ★ This rustic beachfront resort has a bit of style and is beautifully situated among the swaying palm trees on an isolated, sandy beach that calls you to linger and relax on it. There's a free form pool and terrace area, and you can lounge on a chair along the beach or in a hammock strong from the trees. The on-sight restaurant serves pretty good local and international food from breakfast through dinner. Meals are served on a terrace overlooking the ocean. Surrounded by lush mountainsides, this is truly an isolated getaway yet just an hour from San Juan. The snorkeling is great just offshore. I've always found the accommodations clean, though some rooms are so well decorated they feel boutique-y, while others feel dated and scream for a makeover. All are beachfront with balcony or terrace view, so no room is that bad. A great property if you want to relax by the beach and not do much of anything. There is on site massage therapy ($30 for 30 min.; $50 for an hour). The resort also has plenty of beach towels, hammocks, and beach chairs.

Hwy. 3, Km 112.1, Patillas, PR 00767. ✆ **787/839-7717.** www.caribeplaya.com. 34 units (shower only). Year-round $120–$135 double. AE, MC, V. **Amenities:** Restaurant; bar; pool. *In room:* A/C, TV, refrigerator.

El Nuevo Horizonte PUERTO RICAN/SEAFOOD With the best view in southeast Puerto Rico and great food, this restaurant in the coastal hills of Yabucoa is probably our favorite of the typical Puerto Rican eateries on the island. Seafood is the star here. The house special is the paella rey, or king paella, prepared to moist perfection and loaded with lobster, clams, shrimp, and mussels. The stuffed *mofongo* with seafood is among the island's best, and the restaurant has a great stuffed lobster dish as well. While the restaurant is simple, the view is outstanding. The dining room is perched on a cliff overlooking the Caribbean, and you can see clear out to Vieques and the other islands. The restaurant has an outdoor deck that serves drinks and food in a more informal environment with the same beautiful view.

Rte. 901, Km. 8.8, Yabucoa. ✆ **787/893-5492.** Reservations not necessary. Main courses $12–$45. AE, MC, V. Thurs–Sat 11am–9pm; Sun 11am–8pm.

Hotel Parador Palmas de Lucía ★ In the southeastern corner of Puerto Rico, where accommodations are scarce, this parador is a knockout discovery. It lies at the eastern end of Ruta Panorámica, a network of scenic, winding roads along which you can take in some of the finest views in the Caribbean before coming to rest at Palmas de Luca, just steps from the pleasant sands of Playa Lucía. This is one of the newest hotels in eastern Puerto Rico, filling a vast gap in accommodations in this remote part of the island. The López family is your host, and their complex combines colonial styling with tropical decoration. Each midsize bedroom is well furnished and has a poolview balcony and an efficiently organized, tiled, shower-only bathroom. The López family, under its Tropical Inns Puerto Rico company, also runs two nearby small hotels we also recommend, **Parador Costa del Mar** in Yabucoa and **MaunaCaribe** in nearby Maunabo. All are clean, well managed, and surprisingly affordable for what you get.

Palmas de Lucía, rtes. 901 and 9911, Camino Nuevo, Yabucoa, PR 00767. ✆ **787/893-4423.** Fax 787/893-0291. www.palmasdelucia.com. 34 units (shower only). Year-round $102 double. AE, MC, V. From Humacao, take Rte. 53 south to Yabucoa, to the end of the hwy., where you connect with Rte. 901 to Maunabo. After a 2-min. drive, turn left at the signposted Carretera 9911, which leads to Playa Lucía. **Amenities:** Restaurant; bar; basketball court; pool. *In room:* A/C, TV.

VIEQUES & CULEBRA

Long the best-kept secret of local travelers and a few in-the-know visitors, largely from the East Coast, Puerto Rico's island municipalities Vieques and Culebra are finally getting their due.

The towns remain blissfully undeveloped (without a fast food restaurant or traffic light between them) and both still retain the air of Puerto Rico back in the 1950s.

You will find sandy beaches and breathtaking coastal waters, and the colorful wooden cottages and flaming flamboyant trees so typical of the Puerto Rican countryside.

The islands are still a bargain, and both remain places to kick back and relax. Increasingly, however, island accommodations and restaurants have grown upscale, with ever more sophisticated offerings, and there has been an explosion of island services and products directed at visitors on both islands.

Now known as the Spanish Virgin Islands, the two islands are creating a buzz with their unspoiled beaches and stylish inns and vacation homes. With the opening of the W Retreat & Spa Vieques Island in 2010, complete with a signature restaurant by Alain Ducasse, Vieques has finally arrived as a full-scale tourism destination.

Smaller Culebra remains more unvarnished. The improvements have been substantial (not that long ago, your option for food after 8pm was a lone Chinese restaurant), but it may not be long before some discriminating visitors, who might also crave a bit more excitement find this place. For most people, however, the spectacular quality of its beaches, and the offshore fishing and diving, more than compensates and will continue to drive Culebra's popularity.

While more and more inns have opened on both islands, a great way to stay on both Vieques and Culebra is to rent a luxury vacation home, many of which have bold architectural designs and fabulous pools and vistas.

Both towns have escaped the larger development that has taken place on less blessed Caribbean islands through their painful histories as U.S. Navy military training grounds. After years of protest, the Navy finally abandoned its Vieques firing range in 2003, after 6 decades, while it had ended its Culebra training back in the 1970s.

Vieques, which has more tourist facilities than Culebra, lies 7 miles (11km) off the eastern coast of the Puerto Rican "mainland." It is visited mainly for its 40-odd white-sand beaches.

Vieques was occupied at various times by the French and the British before Puerto Rico acquired it in 1854. The ruins of many sugar and pineapple plantations testify to its once-flourishing agricultural economy.

The U.S. military took control of two-thirds of the island's 26,000 acres (10,522 hectares) in 1941. The area was used for military training with live-fire maneuvers. After massive protests, the U.S. announced in 2003 that it was shutting down its Roosevelt Roads Naval Station, the site of the Atlantic Fleet Weapons Training Facility.

Culebra, 18 miles (29km) east of the Puerto Rican "mainland" and 14 miles (23km) west of St. Thomas in the U.S. Virgin Islands, is surrounded by coral reefs and edged with nearly deserted, powdery, white-sand beaches. Much of the island has been designated a wildlife refuge by the U.S. Fish and Wildlife Service. It's a small outpost for sailors and divers to dig into their thing, and this tiny island may have the most brilliant beaches in Puerto Rico. The growth of quality inns and gourmet restaurants will only add to its growing appeal.

Celebrity sightings are still a rarity on both islands, but more and more visitors are discovering the undeniable charm of the Spanish Virgin Islands. That will undoubtedly change the nature of both Vieques and Culebra, so see them now while they are still young and full of promise, not to mention a relative bargain in the Caribbean.

VIEQUES ★

41 miles (66km) E of San Juan, 7 miles (11km) SE of Fajardo

About 7 miles (11km) east of the big island of Puerto Rico lies Vieques (Bee-*ay*-kase), an island about twice as large as New York's Manhattan, with about 10,000 inhabitants and some 40 palm-lined white-sand beaches.

From World War II until 2004, about two-thirds of the 21-mile-long (34km) island was controlled by U.S. military forces, both its western and eastern ends. In the west, there was a base and munitions storage facility. In the east, vast swaths of the wilderness and pasture land were leased for grazing to local cattle farmers, which created a buffer zone between the civilian population and the war games and bombing range farther out to the east.

Unlike the U.S. military, the Spanish conquistadores didn't think much of Vieques. They came here in the 16th century but didn't stay long, reporting that the island and neighboring bits of land held no gold and were, therefore, *las islas inútiles* (the useless islands). The name Vieques comes from the native Amerindian word *bieques* meaning "small island."

The Spaniards later changed their minds and founded the main town, **Isabel Segunda,** on the northern shore. Construction on the last Spanish fort built in the New World began here around 1843, during the reign of Queen Isabella II, for whom the town was named. The fort, never completed, is not of any special interest. The island's fishermen and farmers conduct much of their business here. The **Punta Mula lighthouse,** north of Isabel Segunda, provides panoramic views of the land and sea.

On the south coast, **Esperanza,** once a center for the island's sugar-cane industry and now a pretty little fishing village, lies near **Sun Bay (Sombe) public beach ★**.

Vieques & Culebra

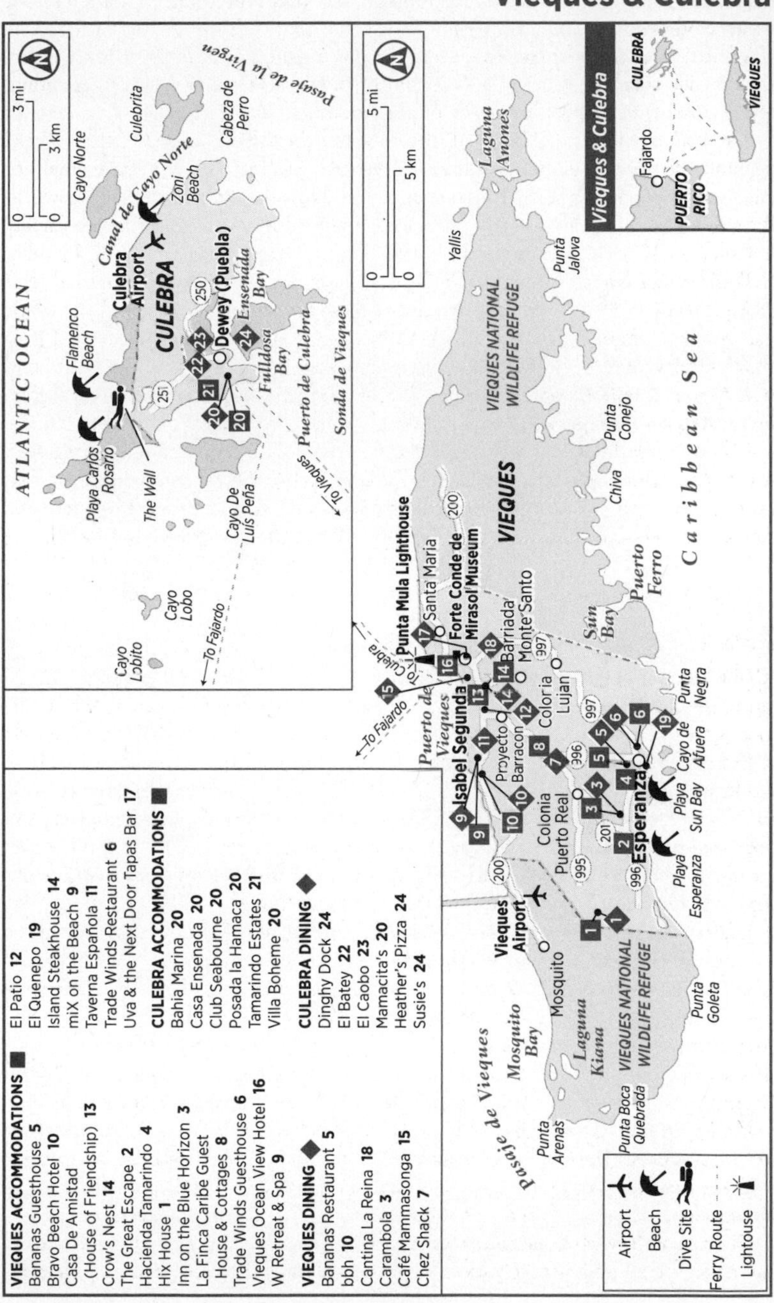

Sun Bay, a government-run, panoramic crescent of sand, is the beach to visit if you have only 1 day to spend on the island. It's a beautiful beach that tumbles endlessly along a graceful arc, blessed by palm trees and patches of scrub forest. The ruins of the Playa Grande sugar plantation, once the center of life in Vieques, lie on former Navy lands near the southwest coast. Playa Grande's former boulevard, once lined with stylish wooden mansions, continued to cut a swath through the dense dry tropical forest as a kind of civilized stronghold during the 6 decades of Navy occupation. Today you can visit the ruins, which have undergone some restoration work since the Navy left. Nearby **Playa Grande** beach is a long, palm lined, white sand beach, but the sea here can be rough and unpredictable, with killer rip tides.

With 40 beaches, all sorts of watersports adventures are possible. The island's varied terrain also offers plenty of land adventures. Kicking back continues to be the number-one pastime in Vieques, however.

Essentials

GETTING THERE Unless you're on a budget, skip the ferry and fly to Vieques, especially if your time is limited. The money you'll save will buy you another day on one of its beautiful beaches, a bargain for the $100 you'll spend on roundtrip airfare. Flights to Vieques leave from Isla Grande Airport near the heart of San Juan as well as the main Luis Muñoz Marín International Airport near Isla Verde. Your best hassle-free option is Isla Grande. **Vieques Air Link** (✆ **888/901-9247** or 787/741-8331) has the most flights and among the best prices. It operates six flights from the smaller and more convenient Isla Grande Airport and three daily flights from LMM International as well as. The VAL flight from Isla Grande, about $98 round-trip, is the most reliable and convenient travel option to Vieques. It's about half the rate from LMM International, which is $198. **Seaborne Airlines** (✆ **877/772-1005** or 787/292-6656) began service to coincide with the opening of the W Resort in March 2010. Round-trip from San Juan's Isla Grande Airport is $120. **Isla Nena** (✆ **787/741-8331**) is an on-demand airline that flies to Vieques from the Luis Muñoz Marín International Airport outside Isla Verde (round-trip around $180). **M&N Aviation** (✆ **787/791-7008**) is another option and has some of the best aircraft servicing the island.

The **Puerto Rico Port Authority** operates two **ferries** a day to Vieques from the eastern port of Fajardo; the trip takes about an hour. The round-trip fare is $4.50 for adults, $2 for children. Tickets for the morning ferry that leaves Saturday and Sunday sell out quickly, so you should be in line at the ticket window in Fajardo before 8am (it opens at 6:30am) to be certain of a seat on the 9am boat. Otherwise, you'll have to wait until the 3pm ferry, if it's a weekend, or the 1pm on weekdays. For more information about these sea links, call ✆ **800/981-2005** or 787/863-0705 (Fajardo), or 787/741-4761 (Vieques). Ferries leave Fajardo for Vieques at 9:30am and 1, 4:30, and 8pm during the week; 9am, and 3 and 6pm on weekends and holidays. They return from Vieques to Fajardo at 6:30am and 11am, 3 and 6pm weekdays; and at 6:30am and 1 and 4:30pm on weekends and holidays.

GETTING AROUND Public cabs or vans called *públicos* transport people around the island. To fully experience Vieques, however, you should rent a jeep. The mountainous interior, more than a dozen beaches, and the nature reserves on former military bases absolutely require it. *Publicos* are economical, however, and can be used to and from the airport and ferry on the days you arrive and leave Vieques if you plan to veg at the hotel pool and beach those days, and you can cut down on car expenses.

Most island rental companies offer economic Jeep Wranglers, Trackers and similar vehicles, and prices generally range from $45 to $85 daily; but you can find even better deals, if you don't mind a beat up vehicle (and if it's just a Tracker to get you to the beach, you may not) or you rent for a week or longer. **Maritza Car Rentals** (**© 787/741-0078**) is the market leader, and **Marcos Car Rental** (**© 787/741-1388**) is usually the best deal in town. I've used each dozens of times and have no complaints. Marcos is not perfect but does bend over backwards to rectify errors, such as the time he lent me his own jeep after my reservation had been misplaced. **Vieques Island Car and Jeep Rental** (**© 787/741-1037** or 435-1323) and **Martineau Car Rental** (**© 787/741-0078**) are good bets, as are **Acevedo's** (**© 787/741-4380**) and **Chepito's** (**© 787/741-8691**). Try to arrange a pick up at the airport; if the rental agency won't do it, your hotel probably will.

Beaches & Other Natural Treasures

The **Vieques National Wildlife Refuge ★★★** is comprised of 15,500 acres (6,273 hectares)—much of it awesome beachfront property—relinquished by the U.S. Navy to the U.S. Fish & Wildlife Service when the Navy abandoned its Vieques training ground in 2003. This is now the largest landmass of its kind in the Caribbean. Refuge lands lie on both the eastern and western ends of Vieques. In 2001, 3,100 acres (1,255 hectares) on the western end were already turned over to the refuge. These tracts of virgin landscape contain several ecologically distinct habitats, including the island's best white-sand beaches along with upland forests and mangrove wetlands, the latter the habitat of some endangered species such as the sea turtle, the manatee, and the brown pelican. Binocular-bearing bird-watchers also flock to the site. The coastal area of the refuge is characterized by coral reef and sea-grass beds, and there are scores of beautiful beaches. The refuge is open to the public and also contains a **Visitor Center at Vieques Office Park,** Rd. 200, Km 0.4 (**© 787/741-2138**). The refuge is open 7 days a week during daylight hours.

Aficionados of Vieques praise the island for its wide profusion of sandy beaches. Since the pullout of the U.S. Navy, some of the sites that were formerly off-limits have been made accessible to hikers, cyclists, bird-watchers, beachcombers, and other members of the public. There are 40 beaches on this small island! That's a whole lot of endless afternoons of exploring.

Along the eastern end, the best beaches are **Red Beach (Bahia Corcha), Blue Beach (Bahia de la Chiva),** and **Playa Plata.** To reach these, take the tarmac-covered road that juts eastward from a point near the southern third of Rte. 997. Entrance to this part of the island, formerly occupied by the Navy, will be identified as **Refugio Nacional de Vida Silvestre de Vieques,** with warnings near its entrance that camping and littering are not allowed. Drive for about a mile (1.6km) along this road, turning right at the sign pointing to Red Beach (Bahia Corcha). En route, you'll have one of the few opportunities in the world to gun your rented car along the battered tarmac of what used to be a landing strip (a very long one). Pretend, if you like, however briefly, that you're on a test track for the Indianapolis 500, naturally exercising all due caution. The Fish & Wildlife Service has been doing improvement work at many of the beaches within the reserve and periodically closes off public access while work is ongoing.

The crescent-shaped Red Beach, with wide-open views of the ocean, and Blue Beach, protected by mangroves and scrub trees, are two of the more beautiful east end beaches. There are signs, within the park, to minor beaches, **Playa Caracas, Caya Melones,** and even **Playuela,** but the access roads are blocked off by the Park Service.

Myriad coves, such as **Playa Chiva,** pepper the coastline between Blue Beach and the end of the line, Playa Plata, which is covered with sea grapes, scrub trees, and palmettos.

Also near the border of the former eastern Navy holdings, is **Sun Bay Beach, or *Balneario Público Sun Bay.*** Its entrance lies off the southern stretch of Rte. 997. You'll recognize it by a metal sign. Just beyond, you'll see a park dotted with trees, an absurdly large number of parking spaces (which no one uses), and a formal entryway to the park, which virtually everybody ignores. Locals, as a means of getting closer to the water and the sands, drive along the access road stretching to the left. It parallels a ¾-mile (1.2km) stretch of tree-dotted beachfront, and they park wherever they find a spot that appeals to them. If you continue to drive past the very last parking spot along Sun Bay Beach, a rutted and winding and very hilly road will lead, after a right-hand fork, to **Media Luna Beach** and **Navio Beach,** two beautiful and isolated beaches, perfect for snorkeling and evening barbecues. A left-hand fork leads to the muddy and rutted parking lot that services Mosquito Bay (or Phosphorescent Bay). Right beside Esperanza village is **Playa Esperanza,** which is a great place for snorkeling.

Take a drive to the west end of the island to visit more beaches. The former Navy base and ammunition storage post has two fine beaches: Green Beach, in the northwest corner of the island beside a nature reserve and a south coast beach beside the ruins of the Playa Grande sugar plantation; and the eerie Navy radar facility, a field of antennas. Much of the land is run through with rows and rows of cement munitions bunkers, and the military also left a huge pier, which originally was to form a bridge to the main island of Puerto Rico. (The attack on Pearl Harbor put a stop to the original plans.)

The beaches are beautiful, but the western end is more physically haunted by the island's military past. Most of the eastern end remains off limits to people, as decades of bombardment from aircraft and offshore carriers have left it littered with unexploded ordnance.

Diving & Other Outdoor Pursuits

For a small island, Vieques offers big opportunities for diving, snorkeling, sailing, and a huge array of other watersports. Natural conditions are incredible, and prices remain a bargain. More and more operators are popping up each year, which should only improve the offerings and the value for customers. **Blue Caribe Kayaks,** Calle Flamboyan 149 (El Malecón; ✆ **787/741-2522**), is one of the most experienced and comprehensive watersports outfits on Vieques, with kayaking, snorkeling, scuba-diving, fishing, or swimming in the nighttime waters of Vieques's bioluminescent bays. They've been doing it for more than a decade. **Kayak rentals** are $10 an hour, $25 for a half-day, and $45 for a full day. **Snorkeling equipment** (fins, mask, and snorkel) rent for $12 daily. **Guided snorkeling tours** by kayak transport you for $35 through gin-clear waters, with stunning coral and brilliantly colored tropical fish, en route to an offshore cay with great beaches. These jacks-of-all-watersports also run a half-day **spin-casting fishing tour from a kayak,** wherein you'll fish for barracuda, grouper, or other reef fish, using segments of squid or octopus as bait. The trip costs $50 per person. Tours last from around 3pm to sundown daily, as well as nighttime trips to the local biobay ($33 per person), one of the world's best bioluminescent bays.

If you want to go diving, the Vieques veteran is **Nan-Sea Charters,** Calle Flamboyan 149, Vieques (✆ **787/741-2390**), which brings an insider's knowledge to your dive experience.

Abe's Snorkeling & Bio-Bay Tours (✆ **787/741-2134;** www.abessnorkeling.com) also offers competitive rates, hands-on inspection of marine critters, and some amusing storytelling, at least if you're with Abe. A 2-hour "Cayo Afuera Snorkel Tour" is $35 per person, a 2-hour "Mosquito Pier Tour" is $30 per person, and a "Tres Palmitas Kayak Tour" is 3 hours and $60 per person. Ask about full-day island tours.

Black Beard Sports, Calle Muñoz Rivera 101, Isabela Segunda, Vieques ✆ **787/741-1892,** is a PADI dive center offering introductory dive trips and half-day open-water dives with equipment included for $150. If you have your gear, the open water dive is $120. They also have class programs ranging from $120 to $450, and varying in skill level and duration. Its downtown location in a restored Puerto Rican casita has a great sporting goods and sportswear shop. They rent dive equipment, snorkels and fins, mountain bikes, kayaks, fishing gear and other stuff, even tents!

A well-rehearsed outfit that's good at leading newcomers into the island's most savage landscapes is **Vieques Adventure Company** (✆ **787/692-9162;** www.bikevieques.com). Gary Lowe and members of his staff lead mountain bikers on half-day ($75 per person) and full-day ($105 per person) tours of obscure trails that are noteworthy for their panoramas and technical difficulties. Use of a mountain bike, usually an aluminum-framed, 28-speed, state-of-the-art model, is included in the price. You can rent one of these bikes, without the services of a trail guide, for $25 per day. The company also rents sea kayaks ($45 daily). Anglers will want to try a kayak fly-fishing tour at a price of $150 for a truly unique experience.

The Luminous Waters of Phosphorescent Bay ★

One of the major attractions on the island is **Mosquito Bay ★**, also called **Phosphorescent Bay,** with its glowing waters produced by tiny bioluminescent organisms. These organisms dart away from boats, leaving eerie blue-white trails of phosphorescence. The *Vieques Times* wrote: "By any name, the bay can be a magical, psychedelic experience, and few places in the world can even come close to the intensity of concentration of the dinoflagellates called pyrodiniums (whirling fire). They are tiny (1/500-in./.13cm) swimming creatures that light up like fireflies when disturbed, but nowhere are there so many fireflies. Here a gallon of bay water may contain almost three-quarters of a million." The ideal time to tour is on a cloudy, moonless night. If the moon is shining on a cloudless night, you can save your money, as you'll see almost nothing. Some boats go, full moon or not. You should wear a bathing suit because it's possible to swim in these glowing waters.

Island Adventures (✆ **787/741-0720**) operates trips in Phosphorescent Bay aboard *Luminosa*. These trips are not offered around the time of the full moon. The charge is $30, and most jaunts last about 2 hours. Similar tours are also offered on kayaks that also costs $30, offered by both **Blue Caribe Kayak** (✆ **787/741-2522**), and **Abe's Snorkeling & Bio-Bay Tours** (✆ **787/741-2134;** www.abessnorkeling.com).

Seeing the Sights

Fort Conde de Mirasol Museum, Barriada Fuerte at Magnolia 471 (© **787/741-1717**), is the major man-made attraction on the island. In the 1840s, Count Mirasol convinced the Spanish government to build a defensive fortress here. Today the carefully restored fort houses a museum of art and history celebrating the story of Vieques. There are Indian relics, displays of the Spanish conquest, and old flags of the Danes, British, and French. The French sugar-cane planters and their African slaves are depicted, and there's even a bust of the great liberator Simón Bolivar, who once visited Puerto Rico. A unique collection of maps shows how the world's cartographers envisioned Vieques. The museum and fort are open Wednesday through Friday, 9am to 5pm, Saturday and Sunday 8:30am to 4pm. Admission is $3, or free for ages 11 and younger.

Where to Stay

EXPENSIVE

Bravo Beach Hotel ★ In a secluded residential area, this boutique hotel, with its Frette linens and Philippe Starck designs, comes as a surprise—and a pleasant one. Most of the bedrooms are within only 30 feet (9.1m) of the Atlantic with a good, white sandy beach. Units open onto a private terrace facing the sea. It's the little things that count here: an honor bar poolside, those Aveda bath products in the bathroom, or the box lunch the staff will pack for you to take to the beach. Rooms are decorated in a minimalist style, effectively using lots of white, draped plantation-era beds, and wicker furnishings. On-site is a two-bedroom cottage, a vision in white, accented by bamboo and mahogany pieces. You can even check your e-mail poolside, or else enjoy Caribbean-inspired tapas served outdoors.

North Shore Rd. 1, Vieques, PR 00765. © **787/741-1128.** www.bravobeachhotel.com. 12 units. Year-round $190–$275 double; $300 suites; $550 villas. AE, DC, MC, V. **Amenities:** Restaurant; bar; 2 outdoor pools; smoke-free rooms. *In room:* A/C, TV, beverage maker, hair dryer, minibar.

Hix House ★★ Angular and avant-garde, and minimalist to the point of looking almost barren, Hix House is one of the most iconoclastic and most admired pieces of eco-sensitive architecture in the Caribbean. It is set on 12 acres (4.9 hectares) of land, formerly used for the cultivation of sugar cane, on a scrub- and tree-covered landscape on a hillside in the center of the island. The inn consists of four separate buildings, designed with triangular, circular, or rectangular floor plans. Each of them was created by the celebrated Toronto-based architect John Hix (a climate and design architect), who has won awards for his designs for low-maintenance houses in chilly Canada. The 13 rustic loft apartments have huge open windows and no air-conditioning, and each is aggressively outfitted with mosquito netting, low-wattage lighting (brighter lights attract mosquitoes), and virtually indestructible furniture that's crafted either from poured and polished concrete or pressure-treated lumber.

Other than yoga classes, conducted 3 mornings a week from 10:30am till noon, there's virtually nothing to do other than the entertainment you create yourself. The pool and surrounding area is gorgeous and refreshing. Rooms come with refrigerators that are stocked with milk, orange juice, eggs, cereal, freshly baked bread, and fruit. None has a bathtub, and showers are artfully rustic affairs set within open-air concrete alcoves.

Rte. 995, Km 1.5, Vieques, PR 14902. ✆ **787/741-2302.** Fax 787/741-2797. www.hixislandhouse.com. 13 units. Winter $265–$450 double; off-season $175–$275 double. AE, MC, V. **Amenities:** Outdoor pool. *In room:* Ceiling fans; open-air showers.

Inn on the Blue Horizon ★★ One of the finest places to stay on Vieques, it's located on a wide, flat bluff overlooking the beautiful southern coastline. The Mediterranean-style main building has huge main lobby, with an outrageously high ceiling, overlooking an infinity pool and blue horizon beyond. The soaring living area of the airy seafront house that opens onto a view of the Caribbean coastline, right at the property's edge.

Three of the bedrooms are in the main house; a half-dozen others are in a trio of bungalows, each of which contains two spacious and comfortable units, each with a private balcony and sea view. Airy and clean, they're outfitted with early-19th century North American antiques and eclectic art from a variety of artists. Two units contain tubs, and the rest are equipped with showers.

Symmetrically positioned arbors are covered with cascades of bougainvillea, with a pool and lawns that slope gracefully down to cliffs at the edge of the sea. The area is beautifully landscaped with bougainvillea and mosaic tile. The sea adjacent to the hotel has a rocky coastline. Although there's one nearby beach, you're better off visiting one of the dozens of fine local beaches. The views from the circular bar and the cliff-side bar and dining area are spectacular. The restaurant, Carambola, is one of the island's most respected. In addition to a great pool, there are two tennis courts (court charge is $25 per hour day/$35 per hour night) and a gym, which costs $10 per hour.

Rte. 996 (P.O. Box 1556), Km 4.3, Vieques, PR 00765. ✆ **787/741-3318.** Fax 787/741-0522. www.innonthebluehorizon.com. 10 units (some with shower only). Winter $160–$375 double; off-season $130–$260 double; holidays $200–$400 double. AE, MC, V. Closed Sept–Oct. **Amenities:** Restaurant, cafe/bar; gym; outdoor pool; tennis courts. *In room:* A/C, hair dryer, no phone.

W Retreat & Spa ★★★ The W has arrived on Vieques, only the second beach-front W Retreat & Spa in the world. (The first was in the Maldives.) If you want an independent, fully eco-conscious escape, stay at the Hix House, above. The W is where you stay for a more pampered experience, which begins with the decked-out welcome center at the Vieques airport. Surprisingly, the W is also somewhat eco-friendly and doesn't sacrifice tranquility for style. The property feels outfitted for a world-class party, though the pace and the volume felt toned down here on our visit, allowing us to relax and enjoy the gorgeous setting. Rooms and suites have warm, natural interiors that manage to still feel cutting edge. Outdoors: relax on colorful, high-end West-Elm-ish furniture on the outdoor decks; lounge on the small beach areas or by infinity-edge pools (which buzz underwater with tunes); play a giant version of Connect Four on the grass; or gather around a fire pit for long conversations after dusk while you sip rum cocktails. (Try the Dragon Daquiri, with spiced rum, various juices, home made syrup, Thai chili, and raspberries.) The Spa Chakra has Asian lagoons and teak boardwalks running through it.

The helpful staff and concierge will set you up with snorkeling and kayaking trips or kid-friendly excursions by taxi; you might also consider a Jeep rental. Save room for at least one meal at Alain Ducasse's **miX on the Beach** (p. 289).

Route 200, Km 3.2 Vieques, PR 00765. ✆ **787/741-4100.** Fax 954/624-1712. www.starwoodhotels.com. 157 units. Winter $589–$739 double, $1,339–$2,180 suites; off-season $329–$479 double, $1,079–$1,680 suites. AE, DC, MC, V. **Amenities:** 2 restaurants; 3 bars; free airport transfer; bicycle rental; concierge; health club; 2 infinity-edge pools; 24-hour room service; spa; tennis courts until sunset; watersport equipment; business center. *In room:* A/C, CD/DVD, iPod docking station, cable TV, minibar, hair dryer, free Wi-Fi.

MODERATE

Crow's Nest ★ Set high on 5 acres (2 hectares) of forested hillside, about 1½ miles (2.4km) west/southwest of Isabel Segunda, the grounds of this inn circle its beautiful pool area surrounded by hills. The comfortable, attractive units all have cooking facilities. It's one of my favorite places to stay. Rooms are more upscale-looking than those at either Bananas (which is very basic) or Trade Winds, but they're less elegant and charming than those at Inn on the Blue Horizon. Each unit has a neatly tiled, shower-only bathroom. Like most of the other hotels on the island, this one requires a car ride of around 10 minutes for access to the nearest worthwhile beach.

Rte. 201, Km 1.6, Barrio Florida (P.O. Box 1521), Vieques, PR 00765. © **787/741-0033.** Fax 787/741-1294. www.crowsnestvieques.com. 17 units (shower only). Year-round $135 double; $245 suite. AE, MC, V. **Amenities:** Bar; pool; Wi-Fi. *In room:* A/C, kitchen, microwave.

Hacienda Tamarindo ★ Established in the late 1990s on the site of an expanded nightclub, less than a mile (1.6km) west of Esperanza, this inn has lots of flair, style, and pizzazz. Vermont-born owners Burr and Linda Vail transformed a thick-walled, rather unimaginative-looking concrete building into a replica of a Spanish colonial hacienda, thanks to Linda's skills as a decorator. The inn was built around a massive 200-year-old tamarind tree, whose branches rise majestically through the hotel's atrium. Its production of fruit (Feb–Mar) is heralded with much excitement. Rooms are stylish, tiled, and spacious. Each contains an eclectic mish-mash of art and dark-wood antiques, some of which were brought from Vermont. Bathrooms are modern, clean, and well designed; some contain a tub, others a shower. Although the inn is set about one-eighth mile (.2km) from the sea, there's access to a beach via a footpath, and there's a pool. The restaurant and cafe at the Inn on the Blue Horizon lie within a 5-minute walk. No children 12 and under in the off-season, 16 and under in season.

Rte. 996, Km 4.5, Barrio Puerto Real (P.O. Box 1569), Vieques, PR 00765. © **787/741-0420.** Fax 787/741-3215. www.haciendatamarindo.com. 17 units (some with shower only, some with tub only). Winter $180–$255 double, $240–$375 suite; off-season $135–$185 double, $175–$275 suite. Rates include full breakfast. AE, MC, V. **Amenities:** Bar; pool; Wi-Fi. *In room:* A/C, hair dryer, no phone.

INEXPENSIVE

Bananas Guesthouse On the island's south shore, on the main tourist strip of Esperanza and best known for its bar and restaurant (see "Where to Dine," below), this guesthouse has eight simple rooms. Each has a ceiling fan; and some rooms are air-conditioned and have screened-in porches. Book one of the air-conditioned rooms rather than those without, as a means of cutting down on heat as well as the noise from the outside. Each unit has a bathroom with a tub. The units are unadorned cubicles with little architectural interest; they provide shelter and calm, and a basic level of comfort. The ambience is convivial, the staff friendly and accommodating. The best room is the $100 unit with air-conditioning and a deck.

Barrio Esperanza, 142 Calle Flamboyan (P.O. Box 1300), Vieques, PR 00765. © **787/741-8700.** Fax 787/741-0790. www.bananasguesthouse.com. 8 units. Year-round $70–$100 double. AE, MC, V. **Amenities:** Restaurant; bar. *In room:* A/C (in 4 units), ceiling fans, no phone.

Casa de Amistad (House of Friendship) Until it was radically renovated in 2002 by a likable former resident of Wisconsin and Minnesota, this boxy-looking, two-story cement building functioned as a battered and run-down boardinghouse that focused on cheap mattresses and cheap but bountiful meals for itinerant workers. Today, in far better-maintained premises, something of the same spirit still prevails, albeit in cleaner, more hip, and more convivial circumstances, thanks to the owner's friendly sense of informality. The house has a bar tucked away in one corner, a communal kitchen where residents are invited to prepare their own meals, a tiny "lending library" stocked with dog-eared paperback books, computer and television areas, free Wi-Fi, and a gift shop with the owner's artwork on sale. Bedrooms are angular, tawny-colored units that are breezy and airy enclaves with simple but comfortable furniture and a sense of well-intentioned *laissez-faire*. Although any hotel on the island genuinely welcomes gay and lesbian clients, this guesthouse is especially gay friendly. The establishment's social center is within a cement-walled courtyard, around a very small, L-shaped swimming pool sheathed in cerulean-blue tiles.

Calle Benitez Castaño 27, Vieques, PR 00765. ✆ **787/741-3758.** www.casadeamistad.com. 7 units. Year-round $75–$90 double; $90 suite. MC, V. **Amenities:** Small outdoor pool; courtyard garden/sun terrace; rooftop sun deck; communal kitchen; TV room; small gift boutique. *In room:* A/C, small unstocked fridge, fan.

The Great Escape ★ 🎁 This attractive, well-maintained bed-and-breakfast occupies a pair of blue-and-white concrete houses, set on the crest of a hill, in a rural neighborhood just north of Esperanza. Your hostess is Danuta Schwartzwald, a Polish émigré who selected Vieques as a place to live after years of self-imposed exile in Switzerland. You might feel just a wee bit isolated here, located as it is behind metal gates, at the end of a long, uphill, and rutted road from Rte. 201. But the size and solid, surprisingly upscale furnishings—including some mahogany, four-poster beds; tiled floors; upscale bathrooms; and the sense of calm that reigns over the place, might eventually persuade you that, indeed, this is a desirable, although uneventful, place to stay. No meals are served other than breakfast, but the staff and managers of this place will offer advice about nearby venues. There are also two-bedroom to four-bedroom suites that fetch between $200 and $450. Danuta now rents out her own house as well for $400 nightly.

Barrio La Llave, directly off Rte. 201, 2 miles (3.2km) northwest of Esperanza, Vieques, PR 14501. ✆ **787/741-2927.** www.enchanted-isle.com/greatescape. 11 units. Winter $125 double; off-season $115 double; year-round $200 1-bedroom apts (3-day minimum rental required for all apts). AE, DISC, MC, V. **Amenities:** Pool; bar. *In room:* Ceiling fan.

La Finca Caribe Guest House & Cottages This bare-bones, eco-sensitive establishment caters to budget-conscious travelers and youthful adventurers. *Finca,* a rustic estate, has as its centerpiece a guesthouse with a spacious porch, outfitted with hammocks and swinging chairs. An admirably maintained garden wraps itself around the scattered components of the compound. The rustic-looking outbuildings include a bathhouse, a communal kitchen, and two self-contained cottages suitable for up to three (the Casita) or four (the Cabana) occupants. There is also the Casa Nueva, perhaps the most upscale digs, built on a hill, which sleeps five. The Cabanita is a cute one-bedroom cottage, and there is a beautiful family unit as well as larger buildings for groups. Cottages have private decks and kitchens. There's a pool on the premises and a crew of entrepreneurs that takes clients on bike tours to obscure parts of Vieques (see "Beaches, Diving & Other Outdoor Pursuits," later in this chapter). La Finca is situated on a forested hillside 3 miles (5km) from Sun Bay.

Rte. 995, Km 1.2 (P.O. Box 1332), Vieques, PR 00765. ✆ **787/741-0495.** Fax 787/741-3584. www.lafinca.com. 6 units (all with shared bathroom), 2 cottages. Winter $90 double, $105–$185 cottage double, weekly cottages $735–$1,295; off-season $70 double, $85–$165 cottage double, weekly cottages $550–$1,085. MC, V. Closed Sept. **Amenities:** Communal kitchen, pool. *In room:* Kitchen (in cottages).

Trade Winds Guesthouse Along the shore on the south side of the island, in the fishing village of Esperanza, this oceanside guesthouse offers 11 units, four of which are air-conditioned and have terraces; some others have terraces and ceiling fans. Bedrooms are white-walled and durable, with absolutely no imagination in terms of decor; the units (all smoke-free) might remind you of a barracks. They're almost equivalent to the rooms at Bananas, a few buildings away, but they're just a bit better. Each unit has a small, tiled, shower-only bathroom. Because of their low rates, they're usually booked solid, often with divers from the United States or residents of the Puerto Rican mainland who want low rates. This place is well known for its hospitable ambience and its open-air restaurant overlooking the ocean (see "Where to Dine," below).

Calle Flamboyan 107, Barrio Esperanza (P.O. Box 1012), Vieques, PR 00765. ✆ **787/741-8666.** Fax 787/741-2964. www.enchanted-isle.com/tradewinds. 11 units (shower only). Winter $70–$90 double; off-season $60–$70 double. AE, MC, V. **Amenities:** Restaurant; bar. *In room:* A/C (in 4 units), fan (in some), no phone.

Vieques Ocean View Hotel Situated in the heart of Isabel Segunda, directly on the coast and a block from the wharf where the ferry lands, this three-story building on the town's harbor has a great location and is cheap, but don't expect glamour. Built in the early 1980s, it offers simple rooms with uncomplicated furniture and balconies overlooking either the sea or the town. Most of the rooms are air-conditioned, and each has a small shower-only bathroom. The hotel restaurant serves Chinese and Creole food daily from 11am to 11pm, so that's a plus. So is its location next to the ferry. Get a seafront room and leave the balcony door open and get the sleep of your life despite the drab interiors.

Calle Plinio Peterson 57, Isabel Segunda (P.O. Box 124), Vieques, PR 00765. ✆ **787/741-3696.** Fax 787/741-1793. 35 units (shower only). Year-round $90 double. AE, MC, V. **Amenities:** Restaurant; bar; pool. *In room:* A/C, TV, no phone.

Where to Dine

EXPENSIVE

Carambola ★★ INTERNATIONAL Set in the lovely premises of the Inn on the Blue Horizon (see "Where to Stay," above), this is one of the best spots to eat on Vieques. Also on-site is a bar that loyalists declare one of their favorites in the world, so consider starting your evening with a drink or two in the octagonal Blue Moon Bar. Meals are served within the inn's main building or beneath an awning on a seafront terrace lined with plants. I love the pork loin in rum chutney and the daily stuffed *mofongo* special. Expect a crowd of fashion-industry folk, temporarily absent from New York and Los Angeles, and local residents, all mixing in ways that are gregarious, stylish, and usually a lot of fun. There is also now a casual eatery on a cliffside deck run by the kitchen team.

In the Inn on the Blue Horizon, Rte. 996, Km 4.3 (1 mile/1.6km west of Esperanza). ✆ **787/741-3318.** Reservations required. Main courses $24–$33. AE, MC, V. Wed–Sun 6–10pm. Closed Sept–Oct.

El Quenepo CONTINENTAL This is the fanciest restaurant in Esperanza, and the service you'll get here is among the most attentive on the island, so it's worth a splurge one night, even if the place feels as if it were dropped here from Cape Cod. In general, the food is tasty; the seared tuna, pumpkin gnocchi, and lava rock churassco are excellent, and the conch fritters and duck appetizer are a great way to get things going. End it all with some pecan pie, vanilla cheese cake, or chocolate mousse.

Calle Flamboyan 148, Barrio Esperanza. ✆ **787/741-1215.** Reservations recommended. Dinner $15–$40. AE, MC, V. Tues–Sun 5–11pm.

Island Steak House ★ INTERNATIONAL Set in the cool and breezy highlands of Vieques, on a verdant hillside with sweeping views of the island's interior, this restaurant is perched within a gracefully proportioned open-sided building that gives the impression of something midway between a simplified gazebo and a tree house. Its bar offers great happy hour specials that draw a crowd. Menu items include up to four different kinds of steak, lamb chops, chicken breasts stuffed with goat cheese and cherry tomatoes, jumbo fried shrimp, and Vieques lobster basted with a sauce made from spiced rum and butter. Burgers are also an option.

In the Crow's Nest hotel, Rte. 201, Km 1.6, Barrio Florida. ✆ **787/741-0033.** Reservations recommended. Burgers $8–$9; main courses $17–$39. AE, MC, V. Fri–Tues 6–9:30pm; bar till midnight.

miX on the Beach ★★ FRENCH CARIBBEAN Alain Ducasse's signature restaurant at the new W Resort & Spa takes on gourmet beach food and results in a short but elegant and compelling menu that explores Latino-Caribbean flavors from a classic French perspective. The chef's famed affection for the Mediterranean is evident in dishes like the artisanal pasta appetizer (with crushed zucchini and tomato marmelade) and halibut with eggplant caviar in a lemon garlic sauce—but the pork entrée takes its inspiration from the mountain towns of Puerto Rico while the barramundi platter in a mango honeydew sauce cannot taste more Caribbean. Ducasse's signature dish—the cookpot—tenderly melds together the island's vegetables. A breakfast menu offers straightforward but satisfying plates of French toast, egg platters, bagels and lox, and more. Cocktails are top notch and usually include several types of rum.

In the W. Retreat & Spa Vieques Island, Route 200, Km 3.2 Vieques, PR 00765. ✆ **787/741-4100.** Reservations recommended. Breakfast $5–$18 Dinner $28–46. AE, MC, V. Breakfast daily 7–11am, dinner Sun–Thurs 6-9:30 pm, Fri–Sat 6–10pm.

MODERATE

Cantina La Reina ★ MEXICAN This Mexican bar-restaurant serves flavorful and inventive fish tacos and sizzling fajitas in a restored historic building on the main road into Isabela Segunda that mixes revolutionary and religious imagery. Get fresh catch of the day served in a tasty mango salsa or the grilled chicken in a red onion and avocado salsa. The second-floor bar and rooftop terrace is often the site of the biggest party in town. The bar specializes in making all sorts of margaritas and rum punches.

Calle Antonio G. Mellado 351, Isabel Segunda. ✆ **787/741-2700.** Main courses $13–$20. MC, V. Tues–Sat 5–10pm; Sun 11am–2pm.

Chez Shack ★ INTERNATIONAL Chez Shack is a funky, brightly painted, rustic, wooden spot, with a small bar, no frills dining room, and great flavor. Hugh

Duffy, who has been operating such places in the Caribbean since Mama Cass waitressed at his Love Shack in St. Thomas, is often on hand spinning a tale. The food is always good, but save your night out here for Monday barbecue nights, with great food and a live band playing reggae music. Menu items include tried-and-true favorites, many of which attract repeat diners who memorized the menu long ago. Examples include baked crab, seafood cocktail, steaks, fish filets, and barbecued ribs. The wooden shack is on the edge of a beautiful country road that runs through the island's central hills and the tropical forest.

Hwy 995, Km 1.8 (northwest of Esperanza; Airport Rd.). ✆ **787/741-2175.** Reservations recommended. Main courses $18–$22. MC, V. Mon–Fri 6–10pm. Closed Sept–Oct.

Taverna ★ MEDITERANNEAN The spirit of the Mediterranean runs through this restaurant, which has gourmet sandwiches and fresh salads for lunch, and creative Italian classics for dinner, including pasta, brick-oven pizza, and some fish specials. For lunch, there's a vegetable wrap with eggplant, hummus, tomato relish, and balsamic onion marmalade, and a killer meatloaf sandwich. At night, the chicken Athena is sautéed with tomatoes, kalamata olives, and feta cheese; and the clams linguini is served with pancetta, garlic, and crushed red peppers. The pastas and pizza are tasty. Fridays are totally different, given over to a Thai menu with such delights as yellow chicken curry or drunken noodles with crab.

Calle Carlos Lebrum 453, right off the plaza Isabel Segunda. ✆ **787/741-7760.** Reservations recommended for dinner. Main courses $10–$30. AE, MC, V. Tues–Fri 11am–3pm and 5:30–9pm; Sat 11–3pm.

Trade Winds Restaurant STEAK/SEAFOOD This restaurant beside the oceanfront esplanade in the fishing village of Esperanza serves excellent breakfasts in a great setting overlooking the sea. Dinners are notoriously inconsistent. Although the bar is a great place for an early evening drink along the harbor, you are better off having dinner elsewhere. If you do have dinner, stick to the lobster and fresh fish specials; everything else, at best, is just okay. For years, however, this has been the best place to have breakfast on the Esperanza strip. There are delicious omelets and eggs Benedict, and there's no better spot to read the morning papers, one of those dying joys of life that live on in Vieques.

In Trade Winds Guesthouse, Calle Flamboyan, Barrio Esperanza. ✆ **787/741-8666.** Reservations recommended. Breakfast $4.50–$13; main courses $13–$28. AE, MC, V. Dec–May daily 8am–2pm and 6–9:30pm; June–Nov Fri–Sun 6–9:30pm.

INEXPENSIVE

Bananas Restaurant INTERNATIONAL A reliable casual restaurant that serves tasty burgers, salads, steaks, and other entrees. The simple wood bar and dining room fill a large room is open to Esperanza's pretty harbor and rows of tropical plants. Bar food and cold drinks sums up the offerings here, but everything is quite nicely done, and the employees are friendly and informative. The menu includes Caesar salads, grilled or jerk-marinated chicken; grilled pork chops; grilled fish; steaks; baby back ribs; pizzas; and sandwiches that include BLTs, burgers, and chicken-breast sandwiches. Service is not speedy, but hey you're in Vieques, who cares?

Calle Flamboyan (El Malecón), in Esperanza. ✆ **787/741-8700.** Reservations not necessary. Salads and sandwiches $5–$11; main courses $15–$17. MC, V. Daily 11am–10pm (kitchen). Bar is open later.

El Patio ★ PUERTO RICAN This simple and completely unpretentious restaurant serves an impressive number of locals and visitors 6 days a week from breakfast

through dinner, often with lots of banter about island personalities and politics. The food is flavorful and filling, and the place intensely local and friendly; I recommend it highly. It's been run by the local Romero family since 1993. Breakfasts have such basics as oatmeal and ham and eggs, and there are several daily specials for lunch and dinner. There are such basic items as steak and chicken, and Puerto Rican classics such as breaded chicken and rice and beans (which they rightfully brag are the best in town). Steer towards the seafood, such as fresh grouper in sweet tomato sauce, the *asopao de mariscos* (seafood stew with fresh fish), marinated octopus, or conch salad.
Calle Antonio G. Mellado 340 (Rte. 200, in Isabel Segunda). ✆ **787/741-6381.** Reservations not accepted. Breakfast platters $1.50–$6; main courses $6–$25. MC, V. Mon–Sat 7am–10pm.

Shopping

Exciting new shopping opportunities on Vieques have mushroomed in recent years in the wake of the Navy exit and the ensuing tourist influx. In general, the consumer products stores, and the tourist and souvenir shops in both Isabel Segunda and Esperanza have gotten more sophisticated. For the first time in years, the clothing stores in Isabel Segunda and Esperanza are actually in fashion. Another place where the upgrade trend is also evident is in the quality of food and beverage offerings at grocery and convenience stores (which mirrors improvement in restaurant quality). Foodies might want to pick up some of the local hot sauce **Coqui Fire Sauce** (✆ **787/435-1099;** www.coquifire.com), which is available throughout the island in mango garlic, papaya lime, and Komodo dragon varieties.

Nowhere is the burst of creativity greater than in the growth of island art galleries. A number of international artists have settled in Vieques, and together with the sizeable number of fine island artists, there is a particularly vibrant arts community. Because the island is such an obvious influence on the artists, their work tends to reflect the beauty of Vieques. The Vieques pioneer Siddhia Hutchinson is still going strong. The **Siddhia Hutchinson Fine Art Studio & Gallery,** Calle 3, A15, Isabel Segunda (✆ **787/741-8780**), located between the lighthouse and the ferry dock, offers the owner's prints of local seascapes and landscapes, native flowers, fish, and birds for sale. Serbian artist Aleksandar Janjic opened **Deda Galeria de Arte,** Calle Muñoz Rivera and Calle Carlos Lebrun (✆ **787/741-1297;** Mon–Fri 10am–3pm, Sat 6–9pm), to showcase his own and island artists' work. His graphics on canvas are warm and delicate prints of local flora inspired by classic Japanese art. Ileana Jové, **Birdnestudios,** outside Isabel Segunda, Rte. 997, Km 1.5 (✆ **787/616-4214**), offers gorgeous jewelry and other mosaic works. Ileana Jové herself is now a talented metal sculptress. She rents two studios on her secluded property. It's a beautiful setting housing her studio and gallery. **Caribbean Walk Gallery,** Calle Antonio Mellado 357, Isabel Segunda (✆ **787/741-7770**), sells beautiful local crafts, paintings, and sculptures made by more than 30 local artists. It also has some of the island works of talented landscape painter Ellie Harold, which are some of the most evocative of their kind of Vieques.

Vieques After Dark

This is still a relatively quite place, but there are more places to party, and the parties are getting more festive every year. In general, there is still no place better than the Esperanza *malecón* on a Friday night, drinking cheap, cold beer and listening to some great music and conversation.

Bar Plaza 🎁 The double doors are left wide open in this dusty bar with high ceilings and slowly whirring fans, which helps the clientele cool off with the icy cold beers. You expect Hemingway to stumble out off this 1940s-era Spanish Caribbean tavern, which has thick cement walls that also help cool things down. With posters advertising defunct products, the place feels frozen in time, like it could be in colonial Havana or Madrid during the Spanish Civil War. There's a pool table in the corner, an old-fashioned cement trough that functions as the men's urinal, and a staff and stoic regular patrons that indeed show their age. No food of any kind is served—only drinks. Beer starts at $2.50. Open daily 9am to 9pm. Plaza del Recreo, in Isabel Segunda. ✆ **787/741-2176.**

Duffy's This rustic tavern on the Esperanza waterfront has good food and a lively bar scene. This spot is run by the son of the legendary Caribbean entrepreneur Hugh Duffy and draws a loyal local crowd and is a favorite with visitors, so it's a good place to mingle. This place is more classic rock and burgers—don't come here expecting Puerto Rican food or serenity—but there are surprisingly good sandwiches (the Ruben) and seafood specials. Duffy's Punch, the house dark rum punch, is worth a try as is the Parcharita, a passion fruit drink. The joint gets jumping on weekend nights. The bar is open late every night. Calle Flamboyán (El Mallecón) Esperanza, Vieques. ✆ **787/741-7000.**

Lazy Jack's ★ This bar and pizza joint has the kitchen that's often the last to close in Esperanza, serving a big selection of frozen drinks and specialty beers; chances are you will wind up here at some point. Sit on patio furniture outside or belly up to the bar. This is an amiable ex-pat spot, where it would not be surprising to hear that old Jimmy Buffett tune (even if it's just in your head). There's always something going on—holiday parties, live music, Wii bowling tournaments, karaoke nights, etc. Sit down here for a fine breeze and animated conversation, both available most of the time. Open daily at noon. Kitchen closes at 11pm except Friday and Saturday (11:30pm). Bar is open late every night. Calle Flamboyán (El Mallecón) Esperanza, Vieques. ✆ **787/741-1864.**

Mar Azul Bar This colorful waterfront bar draws ex-patriots from the states who have settled here, but it's also a hit with local *viequenses* and visitors. As such, it's a great spot for travel tips (check out the bulletin board packed with useful info). Overlooking the sound between the island and Puerto Rico's east coast, this waterfront pub is right next to the ferry, so is practically an obligatory stop. The main room has a big square bar, with surrounding tables, and an outside deck has small tables overlooking the water that are made for couples wanting a more quiet drink together. An adjoining room has pool tables and a jukebox. There's basic pub fare, sandwiches and burgers, but the brisk demand is for rum punches and frozen piña coladas. It's open Sunday through Thursday 11am to midnight, Friday and Saturday 11am to 2am. On the Waterfront, adjacent to the ferryboat piers, in Isabel Segunda. ✆ **787/741-3400.**

CULEBRA ★

52 miles (84km) E of San Juan; 18 miles (29km) E of Fajardo

Sun-bleached Culebra, 18 miles (29km) east of Puerto Rico's main island and halfway to St. Thomas in the U.S. Virgin Islands, is just 7 miles (11km) long and 3 miles

(5km) wide and has only 2,000 residents. The island is blessed by the persistent enchantment of the tropical weather, and the landscape is dotted with everything from scrub and cacti to poinciana, frangipanis, and coconut palms. It has stunning beaches and emerald waters, and some of the finest diving, snorkeling, and sailing in the region, not to mention a gorgeous countryside.

This small island is all about having fun in the surf and the sun, but after a hard day at the beach, you can kick it back several notches and relax. There are a growing number of chic vacation homes and upscale inns, and places to get a good meal. But most visitors will want to save their energy for Culebra's white-sand beaches, clear waters, and long coral reefs.

Culebra was settled as a Spanish colony in 1886. Like Puerto Rico and Vieques, it became part of the United States after the Spanish-American War in 1898. In fact, Culebra's only town, a fishing village called **Dewey,** was named for Admiral George Dewey, a U.S. hero of that war, although the locals defiantly call it **Puebla.**

From 1909 to 1975, the U.S. Navy used Culebra as a gunnery range and as a practice bomb site in World War II. Today the four tracts of the **Culebra Wildlife Refuge,** plus 23 other offshore islands, are managed by the U.S. Fish and Wildlife Service. The refuge is one of the most important turtle-nesting sites in the Caribbean, and it also houses large seabird colonies, notably terns and boobies.

Culebrita, a mile-long (1.6km) coral-isle satellite of Culebra, has a hilltop lighthouse and crescent beaches. There are nearly two dozen other cays surrounding the island in the midst of stunning Caribbean waters.

Essentials

GETTING THERE **Vieques Air-Link** (✆ **787/741-8331**) flies to Culebra twice a day from San Juan's Isla Grande Airport. Round-trip is $105. We recommend flying, as you will spend the entire day traveling to get to the island otherwise. Another option is **Air Flamenco** (✆ **787/724-1818** or 721-7332).

The **Puerto Rico Port Authority** operates one or two **ferries** per day (depending on the day of the week) from the mainland port of Fajardo to Culebra; the trip takes about an hour. The round-trip fare is $4.50 for adults, $2.25 for children 3 to 12 (free for 2 and under). For reservations, call ✆ **800/981-2005,** 787/742-3161, or 863-0705 (Fajardo).

GETTING AROUND With no public transportation, the only way to get to Culebra's beaches is by bike or rental car.

There are a number of little **car-rental** agencies on the island, mostly renting small Jeeps or similar vehicles. Prices range from $45 to $85 daily, and as low as $325 on a weekly basis. **Carlos Jeep Rental,** Parcela 2, Barriada Clark, Dewey (✆ **787/742-3514**), lies a 3-minute ride from the airport. The outfitter rents Jeeps and, with advance notice, will meet you at the airport. When you drop off your rental, the staff will also drive you back to the airport. Charging exactly the same prices is another reliable operator, **Coral Reef,** Carretera Pedro Marquez 3, Dewey (✆ **787/742-0055**). A final option for vehicles is **Willie's Jeep Rental,** Calle Escudero, Barriada Clark, Dewey (✆ **787/742-3537**), lying a 5-minute walk from the airport. Vehicles here also start at $45 per day.

Bike riding is a popular means of getting around the island's hills, dirt trails, and bad roads. You can rent mountain bikes at **Dick and Cathy** (✆ **787/742-0062**) or

Culebra Bike (✆ **787/742-2209** or 209-2543). Just call to reserve, and they will deliver to your hotel. You can also rent scooters from **JM Rentals** (✆ **787/717-7583**), **Culebra Scooter Rentals** (✆ **787/909-1069**), or **Scooter Rentals** (✆ **787/742-0195** or 367-0219), starting at $25 for 8 hours.

Beaches, Diving & Other Outdoor Pursuits

The island's most popular beach is **Flamenco Beach ★**, a mile-long (1.6km) horseshoe-shaped cove on the northwestern edge. It's a mile-long arc of the silkiest, lightest white sand you will ever see, fronting a sapphire covered sea. It's one of the most photographed beaches on the Caribbean, and with reason.

Walk over the hill beside the beach to **Playa Carlos Rosario ★**. The sands here aren't quite as good as those at Flamenco, but the snorkeling is even better in these clear waters. A barrier reef protects this beach, so you are almost guaranteed tranquil waters. Snorkelers can also walk south from Playa Carlos Rosario for a quarter-mile (.4km) to a place called **"the Wall" ★**. There are 40-foot (12m) drop-offs into the water where you are likely to see schools of fish gliding by.

The isolated **Zoni Beach** is a 1-mile (1.6km) strip of sand flanked by large boulders and scrub. Located on the island's northeastern edge, about 7 miles (11km) from Dewey (Puebla), it's one of the most beautiful beaches on the island. Snorkelers, but not scuba divers, find it particularly intriguing; there are beautiful reefs just offshore but the surf sometimes makes underwater visibility a bit murky during rough weather.

Known for its beautiful corals, unspoiled underwater vistas, and absence of other divers, Culebra is what the Caribbean used to be before crowds of divers began exploring the sea. At least 50 dive sites, all around the island, are worthwhile. **Culebra Divers,** Calle Pedro Marquez 138 (✆ **787/742-0803**), offers a resort course for novice divers, including training in a sheltered cove, and a tank dive in 15 to 20 feet (4.6–6.1m) of water ($110). Full PADI certification costs $395 and includes five open-water dives. You'll have to arrange to study the material before arrival, and you'll do the real practice once you are here. Certified divers pay $98 for a two-tank open-water dive. The outfitter rents equipment for $15 daily. It's rare that more than six divers go out in one of these boats on any day. Captain Bill Penfield gives tours on his ***Pez-Vela*** (✆ **787/215-3809**), a 33-foot sailing catamaran with room for six passengers. Go on a snorkel/picnic, deep-sea fishing or simply take a leisure sail to nearby islands, coves and deserted beaches. Bill is an excellent and professional captain who will provide you with a quintessential Caribbean experience, and customize the tour to the wants of the group. Lunch, drinks, and snacks are included in a $125 per person rate. Tours are given daily, and group rates are available. **Snorkel SVI-Culebra** (✆ **787/930-2111**) offers kayak snorkel and fishing trips for $95 full day, $65 half-day from the island that traverse waters choked with tropical fish and reefs and venture on to deserted cays. Veteran operator **Jim Petersen's Ocean Safari,** Calle Escudero 189, Dewey (✆ **787/379-1973**), has similar prices. Jim will show you the best spots to enjoy this sport and also runs full-day tours to Isla Culebrita or Cayo Luis Peña for similar rates.

Where to Stay

MODERATE

Bahia Marina ★★ These one-bedroom and two-bedroom villas are among Culebra's finest accommodations, wonderful amenities in a setting of natural wonder. The properties are built across a ridge bordered by a 100-acre nature reserve and overlooking Fulladosa Bay and a beautiful coastline. The villas are cheerful, comfortable, well maintained and well equipped, and they all have two bathrooms and balconies with killer views and constant breezes. The units are sufficiently large, all have well-equipped kitchens (not kitchenettes) for a family of four to fit comfortably in a one-bedroom. Units have cable television, DVD players, and comfortable furnishings. There are three restaurants with bars at this property's clubhouse, and you can find some of the best food on the island here, especially the Dakity Restaurant and the Shipwreck Bar & Grill. There is also a circular sundeck that provides panoramic views, and two pools on different levels. It's not the Ritz, but the service is wonderfully earnest and the friendly staff members are more than happy to share their love and knowledge of the island with you. A sailing catamaran offers a daylong sail, among the best adventures for vacationers. This property may have a higher per-night charge than many guesthouse rooms, but you are getting more for your money here. It's great for families or small groups.

Rte. 250, Km 2.5, Fulladosa Bay, Culebra, PR 00775. ✆ **787/742-3169.** Fax 787/742-0210. www.bahiamarina.net. 28 units. Winter $219 1-bedroom, $292 2-bedroom; off-season $149 1-bedroom, $219 2-bedroom. Rates include continental breakfast. AE, MC, V. From Dewey (Puebla), follow Rte. 250 (also called Fulladosa Rd.) along the south side of the bay for 1¾ miles. **Amenities:** 3 restaurant; 2 bars; DVD library; 2 pools; free Wi-Fi throughout property. *In room:* A/C, TV, full kitchen, no phone.

Club Seabourne Overlooking Fulladosa Bay, this property is set in a garden of crotons and palms, at the mouth of one of the island's best harbors, Ensenada Bay, which is reached via a winding country road from town. There are villas scattered across the hillside and some rooms inside a central structure with the restaurant, bar, and main lobby. The pool is a plus, and the restaurant remains one of the best on the island, with fresh lobster, shrimp, snapper, grouper, and conch, as well as steaks. The patio bar is a great spot. Dive packages and day sails can be arranged at the office. Rooms are big and airy, but the property is in need of a refresh.

Fulladosa Rd. (P.O. Box 357), Culebra, PR 00775. ✆ **787/742-3169.** Fax 787/742-0210. www.clubseabourne.com. 12 units (shower only). Year-round $124–$189. Rates include continental breakfast. AE, MC, V. From Dewey (Puebla), follow Rte. 250 (also called Fulladosa Rd.) along the south side of the bay. It's 1½ miles/2.4km from town. **Amenities:** Restaurant; bar; pool; 1 room for those w/limited mobility. *In room:* A/C, fridge, no phone.

Tamarindo Estates On 60 lush acres (24 hectares) beside a private bay, this is a small, intimate Puerto Rican beachfront resort of kitchen-equipped cottages. Living here is like occupying your second home. There is a simple, even pristine, aura here, but comfort nonetheless, with panoramic views from the roofed verandas. Each unit has either one or two bedrooms. The mecca of this nicely secluded place is a swimming pool with an ocean view and a roofed deck. There is easy access to shoreline snorkeling in gin-clear waters. The resort lies a 10-minute drive from town, and all cottages are screened and have ceiling fans. Each cottage has a shower-only bathroom. Housekeeping is not provided.

Tamarindo Beach Rd., Culebra, PR 00775. ✆ **787/742-3343.** Fax 787/742-3342. www.tamarindo estates.com. 12 cottages (shower only). Winter $169 double, $335 quad; off-season $140 double, $240 quad. AE, MC, V. **Amenities:** Pool; beach house. *In room:* A/C, TV, kitchen.

Villa Boheme This modest guesthouse opens onto views of Ensenada Bay, and its hosts invite you to explore their little island in kayaks or bikes. Out back is a great terrace with hammocks that invite you to lead the life of leisure. The best units are a trio of large efficiencies; they are better equipped than the other units here. Each of another three rooms has a small kitchen with a large refrigerator. Occupants of the rest of the rooms share a fully equipped modern kitchen that is located in the patio area. Beds range from twins to king-size. Rooms 2 and 12 can house up to six guests comfortably.

Calle Fulladosa 368, Dewey, Culebra, PR 00775. ✆/fax **787/742-3508.** www.villaboheme.com. 11 units. Year-round $107–$152 double. $16 per extra person. AE, MC, V. **Amenities:** Communal kitchen; cable TV. *In room:* A/C, fridge (in some), kitchen (in some), no phone.

INEXPENSIVE

Casa Ensenada Waterfront Guesthouse This is a laid-back, tropical-looking house with relatively humble but clean and comfortable bedrooms. Many guests begin their day by taking a kayak over to the Dinghy Dock restaurant (see "Where to Dine," below) for breakfast and later return to sunbathe on the patio. In the evening, guests gather again on the patio for drinks and for barbecue—the catch of the day on the grill. Each unit is midsize and has a tiled, shower-only bathroom. All are smoke-free. You can rent the Pequeño unit, which sleeps two in a double bed, or the Grande unit for four (two in a king-size bed in the master bedroom and two on a double futon in the living room). The on-site Estudio unit sleeps four, in twin beds and a double futon.

Calle Escudero 142, Dewey, Culebra, PR 00775. ✆ **866/210-0704** or 787/742-3559. Fax 787/742-0278. www.casaensenada.com. 3 units (shower only). Winter $125–$175 double; spring and summer $100–$150; fall $85–$115. MC, V. **Amenities:** Bikes; kayaking; library; scuba diving; snorkeling. *In room:* A/C, kitchenette.

Posada la Hamaca ★ This was one of Culebra's original guesthouses, lying in town next to the Dewey Bridge. Although more recent competition has opened to challenge it, this place is still going strong. Basic but bright and comfortable rooms are housed in a modest island home. Although simply furnished, each of the rooms is well maintained and tidily kept, each with a private bathroom with shower. Beach towels, coolers, and free ice are provided for beach outings. You'll also find an exterior shower to wash sand off your body before you enter. Room no. 8 is the coziest nest and is often rented by honeymooners. Some units are large enough to accommodate four guests, making them suitable for families. One apartment is spacious enough to accommodate 8 to 12 guests.

Calle Castalar 68, Culebra, PR 00775. ✆ **787/742-3516.** www.posada.com. 10 units. Winter $89–$109 double, $102–$129 studio, $169 apt; off-season $72–$85 double, $89–$99 studio, $139 apt. MC, V. **Amenities:** Wi-Fi. *In room:* A/C, TV, beverage maker (in some), kitchenette (in some).

Where to Dine

MODERATE

Dinghy Dock AMERICAN/CARIBBEAN/PUERTO RICAN For the best of laid-back tropical Culebra, head here. The hangout lies on the banks of Ensenada

Honda, just south of the Dewey drawbridge, and it has a dock where dinghies and other boats anchor. Come here for the bar or the restaurant—or perhaps both—and meet the locals along with visiting boaters from the Puerto Rican mainland. It's a great spot for a drink and to watch the sunset; there are great breakfasts, lunches, and dinner. There are tropical fruit-flavored waffles for breakfast, freshly grilled tuna for lunch, and a lobster and rice dish for dinner.

Punta del Soldado Rd., outside Dewey. ✆ **787/742-0233** or -0581. Reservations not necessary. Breakfast $5–$10; lunch $5.25–$15; main courses $14–$30. AE, MC, V. Daily 8am–11am, 11:30am–2:30pm, and 6–9pm.

Mamacita's ★ PUERTO RICAN A colorful spot right on the Dewey channel, this guesthouse/restaurant has fine food and a lively bar and dining area on its back patio. On weekends and holidays, a great breakfast buffet is served. I recommend the chicken, shrimp, and sausage carbonara, or the blackened dorado with scampi butter for dinner; the Mexican salad is a good choice for lunch. There are some nice rooms here; two suites have kitchenettes, and the one on the top floor has a great view.

Calle Castelar 64–66. ✆ **787/742-0090.** Reservations not required. Lunch $6.50–$15; main courses $12–$29. MC, V. Daily 10:30am–4pm and 6–9:30pm; weekend and holiday breakfast buffet 8am–11am.

Suzie's ★ TROPICAL FUSION This cute, homey spot serves up surprisingly creative and tasty fusion food, which relies on local herbs and produce. I was wowed by the curried yucca soup and the salmon-and-potato-patty appetizer with hot Chinese mustard. The coriander-crusted lamb chops served with saffron risotto and the sautéed shrimp with garlic and tarragon cream sauce are examples of the type of food that just was not possible to get in Culebra a short time ago. There's a comfortable dining room, or eat out back overlooking the canal. There's enough to try on the menu to warrant repeat visits.

Calle Sardinas 2 Dewey. ✆ **787/742-0574.** Reservations recommended. Main courses $7–20. V, MC. Tues–Sun 6–10pm.

INEXPENSIVE

El Batey DELI Across from the harbor and cooled by its breezes, this pub has great burgers and sandwiches and a fun bar. Fresh seafood platters are served for dinner. On Saturday nights, young folk come out to dance to salsa. There are pool tables and live music on some weekend nights.

Parque de Pelota, Rte. 250, Km 0.1. ✆ **787/742-3828.** Sandwiches $10–$13. No credit cards. Wed–Sun noon–midnight (till 2am Fri–Sat).

Heather's Pizzeria PIZZA This is the best place to go for pizza on the island. With its funky decor, it is a popular hangout for local expatriates. In addition to those piping-hot pies, the kitchen also turns out an array of freshly made salads, pastas, and well-stuffed sandwiches. The food here is quite good, and it's a fun, friendly place.

Calle Marques 14, Dewey. ✆ **787/742-3175.** Reservations not necessary. Pizzas, sandwiches, and platters $9–$25. No credit cards. Daily 6–11pm. Closed first 2 weeks of Oct.

FAST FACTS

12 FAST FACTS: PUERTO RICO

Area Codes Puerto Rico has two area codes: the more common **787** and the newer **939.** The codes are not geographic specific. For all calls on the island, the area code must be used.

Banks The U.S. banking presence has markedly diminished on the island in recent years, but island banks, led by Banco Popular, are hooked into the U.S. banking system, use the same ATM networks, and have the same fee structures. Many have a presence on the U.S. mainland. Spanish and Canadian banks also have a presence. Normal banking hours are 8am to 5pm Monday through Friday and 8:30am to noon on Saturday. Most banks have some branches with extended hours, open all day Saturday and on Sundays from 11 to 4pm, as well as extended evening hours to 7pm.

Business Hours Offices are generally open 9am to 5pm Monday through Friday, but most institutions are open Saturday for at least a half day. Stores are generally open from 9am to 6pm or 1am to 7pm Monday through Saturday, Sunday 11am through 6pm. Most malls and big box retailers are open 9am to 9pm Monday to Saturday, 11am to 7pm on Sundays.

Cellphones (Mobile Phones) See "Staying Connected," p. 69.

Currency The U.S. dollar is used throughout Puerto Rico. See "Money & Costs," in chapter 3, for more information.

Drinking Laws The legal age for purchase and consumption of alcoholic beverages is 18; proof of age is required and often requested at bars, nightclubs, and restaurants, so it's always a good idea to bring ID when you go out.

Do not carry open containers of alcohol in your car or any public area that isn't zoned for alcohol consumption. The police can fine you on the spot. Don't even think about driving while intoxicated.

Other than the lower drinking age, Puerto Rico treats drinking and driving as seriously as most other U.S. states.

Driving Rules See "Getting There & Getting Around," p. 51.

Drugs A branch of the Federal Narcotics Strike Force is permanently stationed on Puerto Rico, where illegal drugs and narcotics are a problem. Convictions for possession of marijuana can bring severe penalties, ranging from 2 to 10 years in prison for a first offense. Possession of hard drugs, such as cocaine or heroin, can lead to 15 years or more in prison.

Drugstores It's a good idea to carry enough prescription medications with you to last the duration of your stay. If you're going into the hinterlands, take along the medicines you'll need. If you need any additional medications, you'll find many drugstores in San Juan and other leading cities. One of the most centrally located **pharmacies** is **Walgreens,** 1130 Ashford Ave., Condado (✆ **787/725-1510**), open 24 hours. There is at least one 24-hour Walgreens in every tourist district (Condado, Old San Juan, and Isla Verde), and they are linked with the U.S. chain for prescriptions.

There are also locations throughout the island in major cities and shopping malls. Another option is the **Puerto Rico Drug Co.,** Calle San Francisco 157 (✆ **787/725-2202**), in Old San Juan, which is open daily from 7:30am to 9:30pm.

Electricity Like Canada, the United States uses 110 to 120 volts AC (60 cycles), compared to 220 to 240 volts AC (50 cycles) in most of Europe, Australia, and New Zealand. Downward converters that change 220 to 240 volts to 110 to 120 volts are difficult to find in the United States, so bring one with you.

Embassies & Consulates Because Puerto Rico is part of the United States, there is no U.S. embassy or consulate. Instead, there are branches of all the principal U.S. federal agencies. Foreign governments have no embassies here, as Puerto Rico is part of the United States. A number of governments, however, have honorary consulates on the island. Britain has a consulate at Av. Chardón 350 (✆ **787/758-9828**) in Hato Rey, while the Canada consulate is at Av. Ponce de León 268 (✆ **787/759-6629**).

All embassies are in the nation's capital, Washington, D.C. Some consulates are in major U.S. cities, and most nations have a mission to the United Nations in New York City. If your country isn't listed below, call for directory information in Washington, D.C. (✆ **202/555-1212**), or check **www.embassy.org/embassies**.

The embassy of **Australia** is at 1601 Massachusetts Ave. NW, Washington, DC 20036 (✆ **202/797-3000;** http://australia.visahq.com). Consulates are in New York, Honolulu, Houston, Los Angeles, and San Francisco.

The embassy of **Canada** is at 501 Pennsylvania Ave. NW, Washington, DC 20001 (✆ **202/682-1740;** www.canadainternational.gc.ca/washington). Other Canadian consulates are in Buffalo (New York), Detroit, Los Angeles, New York, and Seattle.

The embassy of **Ireland** is at 2234 Massachusetts Ave. NW, Washington, DC 20008 (✆ **202/462-3939;** www.embassyofireland.org). Irish consulates are in Boston, Chicago, New York, San Francisco, and other cities. See website for complete listing.

The embassy of **New Zealand** is at 37 Observatory Circle NW, Washington, DC 20008 (✆ **202/328-4800;** www.nzembassy.com). New Zealand consulates are in Los Angeles, Salt Lake City, San Francisco, and Seattle.

The embassy of the **United Kingdom** is at 3100 Massachusetts Ave. NW, Washington, DC 20008 (✆ **202/588-6500;** http://ukinusa.fco.gov.uk). Other British consulates are in Atlanta, Boston, Chicago, Cleveland, Houston, Los Angeles, New York, San Francisco, and Seattle.

Emergencies In an emergency, dial ✆ **911.** Or call the local police (✆ **787/726-7020**), fire department (✆ **787/725-3444**), or medical emergency line (✆ **787/754-2550**).

Gasoline (Petrol) Taxes are already included in the printed price. One U.S. gallon equals 3.8 liters or .85 imperial gallons. Gas prices on the island are listed in liters and are currently hovering around 76¢ per liter for regular.

Holidays Banks, government offices, post offices, and many stores, restaurants, and museums are closed on the following legal national holidays: January 1 (New Year's Day), the third Monday in January (Martin Luther King, Jr., Day), the third Monday in February (Presidents' Day), the last Monday in May (Memorial Day), July 4 (Independence Day), the first Monday in September (Labor Day), the second Monday in October (Columbus Day), November 11 (Veterans' Day/Armistice Day), the fourth Thursday in November (Thanksgiving Day), and December 25 (Christmas). The Tuesday after the first Monday in November is Election Day, a federal government holiday in presidential-election years (held every 4 years, and next in 2012). Puerto Rico holds its elections at the same time. In addition, the island also celebrates several important local holidays, such as July 25, the anniversary of the Puerto Rico constitution and the birth of its commonwealth political status. For more information on holidays see "Puerto Rico Calendar of Events," in chapter 3.

Hospitals In a medical emergency, call ✆ **911. Ashford Presbyterian Community Hospital,** Av. Ashford 1451, San Juan (✆ **787/721-2160**), maintains 24-hour emergency service and is the most convenient to the major tourism districts. Another option is **Pavia Hospital,** 1462 C. Asia, Santurce (✆ **787/727-6060**). Service is also provided at **Clinica Las Americas,** Franklin Delano Roosevelt Ave. 400, Hato Rey (✆ **787/765-1919**), and at **Puerto Rico Medical Center,** Av. Americo Miranda, Río Piedras (✆ **787/777-3535**).

Insurance If you are considering buying travel insurance, expect to pay between 5% and 8% of the vacation itself. You can get estimates from various providers through **InsureMyTrip.com**. Enter your trip cost and dates, your age, and other information for prices from more than a dozen companies.

Trip-cancellation insurance will help retrieve your money if you have to back out of a trip or depart early, or if your travel supplier goes bankrupt. Permissible reasons for trip cancellation can range from sickness to natural disasters. In this unstable world, trip-cancellation insurance is a good buy if you're purchasing tickets well in advance—who knows what the state of the world, or of your airline, will be in 9 months? Insurance policy details vary, so read the fine print and make sure that your airline or cruise line is on the list of carriers covered in case of bankruptcy. A good resource is "Travel Guard Alerts," a list of companies considered high-risk by Travel Guard International (see website below). Protect yourself further by paying for the insurance with a credit card—by law, consumers can get their money back on goods and services not received, if they report the loss within 60 days after the charge is listed on their credit card statement.

For more information, contact one of the following recommended insurers: **Access America** (✆ 866/807-3982; www.accessamerica.com); **Travel Guard International** (✆ 800/826-4919; www.travelguard.com); **Travel Insured International** (✆ 800/243-3174; www.travelinsured.com); and **Travelex Insurance Services** (✆ 888/457-4602; www.travelex-insurance.com).

For information on traveler's insurance, trip-cancellation insurance, and medical insurance while traveling, please visit www.frommers.com/tips.

Internet Access See "Staying Connected," p. 69.

Language English is understood at the big resorts and in most of San Juan. Out in the island, Spanish is still *numero uno.*

Legal Aid If you are "pulled over" for a minor infraction (such as speeding), never attempt to pay the fine directly to a police officer; this could be construed as attempted bribery, a much more serious crime. Pay fines by mail, or directly into the hands of the clerk of the court. If accused of a more serious offense, say and do nothing before consulting a lawyer. Here, the burden is on the state to prove a person's guilt beyond a reasonable doubt, and everyone has the right to remain silent, whether he or she is suspected of a crime or actually arrested. Once arrested, a person can make one telephone call to a party of his or her choice. The international visitor should call his or her embassy or consulate.

Mail At press time, domestic postage rates were 28¢ for a postcard and 44¢ for a letter. For international mail, a first-class letter of up to 1 ounce costs 98¢ (75¢ to Canada and 79¢ to Mexico); a first-class postcard costs the same as a letter. For more information go to **www.usps.com**.

If you aren't sure what your address will be in Puerto Rico, mail can be sent to you, in your name, c/o General Delivery at the main post office of the city or region where you expect to be. (Call ✆ **800/275-8777** for information on the nearest post office.) The addressee must pick up mail in person and must produce proof of identity (driver's license, passport, and so on). Most post offices will hold mail for up to 1 month, and are open Monday to Friday from 8am to 6pm, and Saturday from 9am to 3pm.

Always include zip codes when mailing items in the U.S. If you don't know your zip code, visit www.usps.com/zip4.

Newspapers & Magazines See "Staying Connected," p. 69.

Passports See "Embassies & Consulates," above, for whom to contact if you lose your passport while traveling in the U.S. For other information, contact the following agencies:

For Residents of Australia Contact the Australian Passport Information Service (✆ **61/131-232**), or visit www.passports.gov.au.

For Residents of Canada Contact the central **Passport Office,** Department of Foreign Affairs and International Trade, Ottawa, ON K1A 0G3 (✆ **800/567-6868;** www.ppt.gc.ca).

For Residents of Ireland Contact the **Passport Office,** Setanta Centre, Molesworth Street, Dublin 2 (✆ **01/671-1633;** www.foreignaffairs.gov.ie).

For Residents of New Zealand Contact the **Passports Office,** Department of Internal Affairs, 47 Boulcott St., Wellington, 6011 (✆ **0800/225-050** in New Zealand, or 04/474-8100; www.passports.govt.nz).

For Residents of the United Kingdom Visit your nearest passport office, major post office, or travel agency or contact the **Identity and Passport Service (IPS),** 89 Eccleston Square, London, SW1V 1PN (✆ **0300/222-0000;** www.ips.gov.uk).

For Residents of the United States To find your regional passport office, check the U.S. Department of State website (travel.state.gov/passport) or call the **National Passport Information Center** (✆ **877/487-2778**) for automated information.

Police In an emergency, dial ✆ **911.** Or call the local police (✆ **787/726-7020**), fire department (✆ **787/725-3444**), or medical emergency line (✆ **787/754-2550**).

Smoking Stringent antismoking regulations have been passed banning smoking in all public areas, including restaurants, bars, casinos, and hotel rooms. Enforcement, however, is less strict here than in other areas in the United States. Smoking is even banned at outdoor cafes that are serviced by waiters or waitresses, but this prohibition is often overlooked.

Taxes The United States has no value-added tax (VAT) or other indirect tax at the national level. Every state, county, and city may levy its own local tax on all purchases, including hotel and restaurant checks and airline tickets. These taxes will not appear on price tags. Puerto Rico levies a 7% sales and use tax on most major goods and services. All hotel rooms on Puerto Rico are subject to a 9% to 11% tax.

Telephones See "Staying Connected," p. 69.

Time Puerto Rico is in the Atlantic Time Zone, which is 1 hour ahead of Eastern Standard Time (EST), and identical to Eastern Daylight Time (EDT). When the U.S. East Coast is on daylight time, EDT, there is no time difference. The continental United States also contains Central Standard Time (CST), Mountain Standard Time (MST), and Pacific Standard Time (PST), which range from 1 to 3 hours behind EST. San Juan time is normally 4 hours ahead of Los Angeles, but only 3 hours during EDT.

Daylight saving time runs from 1am on the second Sunday in March to 1am on the first Sunday in November, except in Arizona, Hawaii, the U.S. Virgin Islands, and Puerto Rico. Daylight saving time moves the clock 1 hour ahead of standard time.

Tipping In hotels, tip **bellhops** at least $1 per bag ($2–$3 if you have a lot of luggage) and tip the **chamber staff** $1 to $2 per day (more if you've left a big mess for him or her to clean up). Tip the **doorman** or **concierge** only if he or she has provided you with some specific service (for example, calling a cab for you or obtaining difficult-to-get theater tickets). Tip the **valet-parking attendant** $1 every time you get your car.

In restaurants, bars, and nightclubs, tip **service staff** and **bartenders** 15% to 20% of the check, tip **checkroom attendants** $1 per garment, and tip **valet-parking attendants** $1 per vehicle.

As for other service personnel, tip **cab drivers** 15% of the fare; tip **skycaps** at airports at least $1 per bag ($2–$3 if you have a lot of luggage); and tip **hairdressers** and **barbers** 15% to 20%.

Toilets You won't find public toilets or "restrooms" on the streets in most Puerto Rico Cities, but they can be found in hotel lobbies, bars, restaurants, museums, department stores, railway and bus stations, and service stations. Large hotels and fast-food restaurants are often the best bet for clean facilities. Public beaches, called *balnearios,* run by the commonwealth's National Parks or by municipal governments, have restroom, shower, and changing facilities. Restaurants and bars in resorts or heavily visited areas may reserve their restrooms for patrons.

Visas For information about U.S. Visas, go to **http://travel.state.gov** and click on "Visas." Or go to one of the following websites:

Australian citizens can obtain up-to-date visa information from the **U.S. Embassy Canberra,** Moonah Place, Yarralumla, ACT 2600 (✆ **02/6214-5600**), or by checking the U.S. Diplomatic Mission's website at **http://canberra.usembassy.gov/consul**.

British subjects can obtain up-to-date visa information by calling the **U.S. Embassy Visa Information Line** (✆ **0891/200-290**), or by visiting the "Visas to the U.S." section of the American Embassy London's website at **www.usembassy.org.uk**.

Irish citizens can obtain up-to-date visa information through the **U.S. Embassy Dublin,** 42 Elgin Rd., Ballsbridge, Dublin 4 (✆ **353/1-668-8777;** http://dublin.usembassy.gov).

Citizens of **New Zealand** can obtain up-to-date visa information by contacting the **U.S. Embassy New Zealand,** 29 Fitzherbert Terrace, Thorndon, Wellington (✆ **644/472-2068;** http://newzealand.usembassy.gov).

Visitor Information For information before you leave home, visit **www.gotopuertorico.com** or contact the **Puerto Rico Tourism Company** offices at La Princesa Building, Paseo La Princesa 2, Old San Juan, PR 00902 (✆ **800/866-7827** or 787/721-2400).

Other Tourism Company offices are located at **Luís Muñoz Marín Airport** (✆ **787/791-1014**), open December to April daily from 9am to 10pm, May to November daily 9am to 8pm; and **La Casita,** at Plaza de la Darsena, Old San Juan, near Pier 1, where the cruise ships come in (✆ **787/722-1709**). This office is open Saturday through Wednesday from 8:30am to 8pm, Thursday and Friday 8:30am to 5pm.

There are several tourism-related websites on Puerto Rico. Some of the best are dedicated to specific areas: **The Tourism Association of Rincón** (www.rincon.org), **Insider's Guide to South Puerto Rico** (www.letsgotoponce.com), **Enchanted Isles** (www.enchanted-isle.com) and **Discover Culebra** (www.culebra-island.com). **Puerto Rico Travel Maps** (www.travelmaps.com) offers useful interactive and downloadable travel maps, while **EyeTour Puerto Rico** (http://places.eyetour.com) offers travel videos of sites, attractions, hotels, and restaurants. Ask for a copy of ***Qué Pasa,*** the official visitors' guide, which is distributed free at many hotels and restaurants. ***Bienvenidos,*** a publication of the Puerto Rico Hotel & Tourism Association, is also chock-full of up-to-date visitor information and is also distributed free at island hotels.

You might also want to contact the U.S. Department of State for regional background bulletins, which supply up-to-date information on crime, health concerns, import restrictions, and other travel matters. Write to the **Superintendent of Documents,** U.S. Government Printing Office, Washington, DC 20402 (✆ **866/512-1800** or 202/512-1800).

A good travel agent can be a source of information. Make sure your agent is a member of the American Society of Travel Agents (ASTA). If you get poor service from an ASTA agent, you can write to the **ASTA—The American Society of Travel Agents**—at 1101 King St., Alexandria, VA 22314 (✆ **703/739-2782;** www.astanet.com).

Water Although tap water is said to be safe to drink, many visitors experience diarrhea, even if they follow the usual precautions. It's best to stick to bottled water. The illness usually passes quickly without medication if you eat simply prepared food and drink only mineral water until you recover. If symptoms persist, consult a doctor.

Wi-Fi See "Staying Connected," p. 69.

Index

See also Accommodations and Restaurant indexes, below.

General Index

D

E

S

T

Accommodations

Restaurants